Titles in *Counseling and Pr*

CACREP Standards	Sangganjanavanich, Introduction to Professional Counseling	Watson, Counseling Assessment and Evaluation	Conyne, Group Work Leadership	Parsons, Becoming a Skilled Counselor	Parsons, Counseling Theory	Individuals Through the Life Span	Duan, Becoming a Multiculturally Competent Counselor	Wright, Research Methods for Counseling	Tang, Career Development and Counseling	Scott, Counselor as Consultant	Zhang, Field Experience
1. **PROFESSIONAL ORIENTATION AND ETHICAL PRACTICE**	1a 1b 1d 1e 1f 1g 1h 1i 1j	1j	1b 1j	1b 1d 1e 1j	1j	1j	1j	1j	1b 1j	1b 1j	1b 1c 1d 1e 1f 1g 1h 1i 1j
2. **SOCIAL AND CULTURAL DIVERSITY**	2c 2f 2g	2g	2d 2e 2g	2b 2c 2g	2c 2e 2g	2a 2b 2c 2d 2e 2g	2c 2e 2f 2g	2g	2g	2d 2g	2d
3. **HUMAN GROWTH AND DEVELOPMENT**			3f			3b	3a 3b 3c 3d 3e 3f 3g	3d 3e	3e		
4. **CAREER DEVELOPMENT**		4f							4a 4b 4c 4d 4e 4f 4g	4c	4b 4c 4e 4g
5. **HELPING RELATIONSHIPS**	5a 5b 5c 5f 5g 5h		5b 5c 5d 5e	5a 5b 5c 5d	5b 5c 5d 5e 5g	5b	5b 5e		5b 5c	5b 5c 5f 5g 5h	5c 5d 5e 5f 5g
6. **GROUP WORK**			6a 6b 6c 6d 6e								6d 6e
7. **ASSESSMENT**		7a 7b 7c 7d 7e 7f 7g	7b	7b		7f		7c 7d 7e			7g
8. **RESEARCH AND PROGRAM EVALUATION**								8a 8b 8c 8d 8e			8d 8e 8f

Counseling and Professional Identity

Series Editors: Richard D. Parsons, PhD, and Naijian Zhang, PhD

Becoming a Skilled Counselor—Richard D. Parsons and Naijian Zhang

Research Methods for Counseling: An Introduction—Robert J. Wright

Group Work Leadership: An Introduction for Helpers—Robert K. Conyne

Introduction to Professional Counseling—Varunee Faii Sangganjanavanich and Cynthia Reynolds

Counseling Theory: Guiding Reflective Practice—Richard D. Parsons and Naijian Zhang

Counselor as Consultant—David A. Scott, Chadwick W. Royal, and Daniel B. Kissinger

Counseling Assessment and Evaluation: Fundamentals of Applied Practice—Joshua C. Watson and Brandé Flamez

Counseling Individuals Through the Lifespan—Daniel W. Wong, Kimberly R. Hall, Cheryl A. Justice, and Lucy Wong Hernandez

Becoming a Multiculturally Competent Counselor—Changming Duan and Chris Brown

Ethical Decision Making for the 21st Century Counselor—Donna S. Sheperis, Michael Kocet, and Stacy Henning

Career Development and Counseling: Theory and Practice in a Multicultural World—Mei Tang and Jane Goodman

Field Experience: Transitioning From Student to Professional—Naijian Zhang and Richard D. Parsons

Becoming a Multiculturally Competent Counselor

We affectionately dedicate this text to our families for their unwavering support and to our students, clients, and colleagues who have inspired our journey to cultural competence.

SAGE was founded in 1965 by Sara Miller McCune to support the dissemination of usable knowledge by publishing innovative and high-quality research and teaching content. Today, we publish more than 850 journals, including those of more than 300 learned societies, more than 800 new books per year, and a growing range of library products including archives, data, case studies, reports, conference highlights, and video. SAGE remains majority-owned by our founder, and after Sara's lifetime will become owned by a charitable trust that secures our continued independence.

Los Angeles | London | New Delhi | Singapore | Washington DC

Becoming a Multiculturally Competent Counselor

Changming Duan
University of Kansas

Chris Brown
University of Missouri–Kansas City

Los Angeles | London | New Delhi
Singapore | Washington DC

Los Angeles | London | New Delhi
Singapore | Washington DC

FOR INFORMATION:

SAGE Publications, Inc.
2455 Teller Road
Thousand Oaks, California 91320
E-mail: order@sagepub.com

SAGE Publications Ltd.
1 Oliver's Yard
55 City Road
London EC1Y 1SP
United Kingdom

SAGE Publications India Pvt. Ltd.
B 1/I 1 Mohan Cooperative Industrial Area
Mathura Road, New Delhi 110 044
India

SAGE Publications Asia-Pacific Pte. Ltd.
3 Church Street
#10-04 Samsung Hub
Singapore 049483

Associate Director: Kassie Graves
Senior Editorial Assistant: Carrie Montoya
eLearning editor: Lucy Berbeo
Production Editor: Laura Barrett
Copy Editor: Amy Harris
Typesetter: C&M Digitals (P) Ltd.
Proofreader: Ellen Howard
Indexer: Amy Harris
Cover Designer: Candice Harman
Marketing Manager: Shari Countryman

Printed in the United States of America

Library of Congress Cataloging-in-Publication Data

Duan, Changming.
Becoming a multiculturally competent counselor / Changming Duan, Chris Brown.

pages cm
Includes bibliographical references and index.

ISBN 978-1-4522-3452-6 (pbk. : alk. paper)
1. Cross-cultural counseling. 2. Counseling psychology—Practice. I. Title.

BF636.7.C76D83 2016
158.3—dc23 2015022811

This book is printed on acid-free paper.

15 16 17 18 19 10 9 8 7 6 5 4 3 2 1

Contents

Editors' Preface xvii
Richard Parsons
Naijian Zhang

Preface xix

Acknowledgments xxvi

About the Authors xxix

Section I Professional Counseling: A Cultural Occurrence 1

Chapter 1 Monocultural Context of Counseling as a Helping Profession 3

Chapter Overview 3
Self-Assessment of Pre-Existing Awareness and Knowledge 3
Learning Objectives 4
The Cultural and Value Foundations of Counseling in the United States 6
Individualistic and Egocentric Focus 7
Ethnocentric Perspectives 8
Monocultural Approaches Toward Human Behavior Evaluation and Change 10
How Mental Health Is Viewed 10
How Counseling Goals Are Conceptualized and Defined 12
How Change Processes Are Pursued and Evaluated 14
Communication Practices 16
A Call for Multicultural Professional Identity Development in Transforming the Field of Counseling 18
Multicultural Professional Identity and the Profession's Ethical Standards 19
Summary 22
Takeaway Messages 22
Recommended Resources 23

Chapter 2 Demands for Multicultural Professional Counseling 27

Chapter Overview 27
Self-Assessment of Pre-Existing Awareness and Knowledge 28
Learning Objectives 28

The Presence and History of Cultural and Social Oppression 31
Oppression by Isms 33
Culturally Diverse Clients and Needed Counseling Services 35
Is Multicultural Competence Really Needed? 37
Demographic Changes in the United States 41
Increasing Trend of Racial and Ethnic Minorities 42
Increasing Trend of Openly Sexual Minorities 44
Increasing Religious Diversity 44
Immigration and Globalization 45
Increasing Presence of Immigrants 45
Counseling Becoming International 46
Necessary Multicultural Ethics 47
Summary 48
Takeaway Messages 49
Recommended Resources 49

Chapter 3 Multicultural Movement: The Fourth Force 52

Chapter Overview 52
Self-Assessment of Pre-Existing Awareness and Knowledge 52
Learning Objectives 53
The Context and History of the Multicultural Movement 57
Colonization and Its Psychological Effects 57
Civil Rights Movement: Race, Ethnicity, and Identity 58
Women's Movements: Sex, Sexual Orientation, and Identity 61
Gay Rights Movement: Sexual Orientation and Identity 62
Globalization: Nationality and Identity 63
Social Class, Age, Disability/Ability, and Other Dimensions of Diversity 64
The Focus and Scope of Multicultural Counseling 66
The Issue of Power and Privilege 66
Cultural Values and Worldviews 68
Complexity of Diversity 70
A Necessary Multicultural Competency: Social Advocacy 71
Summary 73
Takeaway Messages 73
Recommended Resources 73

Section 2 Counseling in the 21st Century: A Multicultural Phenomenon 77

Chapter 4 Multicultural Contexts of Professional Counseling in the 21st Century 79

Chapter Overview 79
Self-Assessment of Pre-Existing Awareness and Knowledge 80

Learning Objectives 80
Cultural Context at the Individual Level 83
Attending to the Intersection of Multicultural Identities: Working With Syria 85
Challenges of Integrating Individual Multicultural Contexts in Counseling Practice 86
Cultural Context at the Societal Level 87
Attending to the Societal Cultural Context: Working With Syria and James 89
Challenges of Integrating Societal Multicultural Context in Counseling Practice 91
Cultural Context at the International Level 93
Attending to the International Cultural Context: Working With Syria and James 95
Challenges of Integrating International Multicultural Context in Counseling Practice 95
Internationalizing Counseling and International Power Structure 95
International Counseling and Cultural Encapsulation 96
Working With Visible and Invisible International Contexts in the United States 96
Summary 97
Takeaway Messages 97
Recommended Resources 98

Chapter 5 Redefining and Renewing the Counseling Profession in the 21st Century 100

Chapter Overview 100
Self-Assessment of Pre-Existing Awareness and Knowledge 101
Learning Objectives 101
Redefining and Renewing: Now Is the Time 103
Barriers to Multicultural Counseling 104
Ethnocentric and Monocultural Values of Counseling Theories 104
Counseling Professionals' Personal Beliefs and Thinking Styles 106
Lack of Equity and Access by Some Members of Society 110
Effective Service to the Culturally Diverse 111
Why Must We Redefine Counseling Practice? 111
The Intersection of Multiple Dimensions of Cultural Identity in Counseling Practice 114
Emerging and Necessary: Developing International Competence 117
Effectively Serving the Culturally Diverse: A Process of Renewing the Profession 119
Working With Cultural Diversity: A Basic Ethical Responsibility 121

Summary 123
Takeaway Messages 123
Recommended Resources 124

Section 3 Becoming Multiculturally Competent 127

Chapter 6 Developing a Multicultural Identity 129

Chapter Overview 129
Self-Assessment of Pre-Existing Awareness and Knowledge 130
Learning Objectives 130
A Model of Multicultural Competence Development 132
Why Do We Need to Develop a Multicultural Identity? 134
A Definition of Multicultural Identity 137
Dimensions of Multicultural Identity 138
Challenges of Multicultural Identity Development: Dominant Group Identities 139
Racial and Ethnic Identities 140
Seven Phases of Development 140
Sex, Gender, and Sexual Orientation Identities 144
Becoming Aware of Sexist Privileges 144
Gender and Cisgender Identity Development 145
Heterosexual Identity Development 146
Social Class Identity Development 148
Ableism and Multicultural Identity Development 149
Other Isms and Multicultural Identity Development 150
Age and Ageism 150
Religion and Religious Prejudice 150
Nationality and Nativism 151
Self-Assessment of Multicultural Self 152
Summary 154
Takeaway Messages 154
Recommended Resources 154

Chapter 7 Understanding Social Oppression and Cultural Pluralism 157

Chapter Overview 157
Self-Assessment of Pre-Existing Awareness and Knowledge 158
Learning Objectives 158
Social Oppression: Results of Unearned Privileges by Dominant Groups 161
Agents of Social Oppression 162
White Privilege 163
Male Privilege 168

Heterosexual Privilege 169
Ability Privilege 169
Class Privilege 169
U.S. Citizen Privilege 170
Complexity of Privilege and Responsibility of the Agent 170
Social Oppression: Unjust, Unfair, and Damaging 171
The Myth of a Just-Society Perspective 171
Pervasive Oppression Due to Isms 172
Institutional Racism 172
Individual Racism 173
Cultural Racism 173
Environmental Racism 174
Microaggression 176
Understanding the Culturally Diverse 179
Impact of Social Oppression 179
Cultural Pluralism 180
Worldviews 180
Cultural Values and Traditions 181
Counselors' Social and Professional Responsibility in Eliminating Oppression 184
Summary 184
Takeaway Messages 185
Recommended Resources 185

Section 4 Exercising Multicultural Competencies: Working With the Culturally Diverse 189

Chapter 8 Working With Diversity in Racial, Ethnic, and Nationality Contexts 191

Chapter Overview 191
Self-Assessment of Pre-Existing Awareness and Knowledge 192
Learning Objectives 192
Understanding the Cultural Contexts of the Racially and Ethnically Diverse 195
Effect of Racism, Discrimination, and Microaggression 195
Racial Disparities in Economics 195
Racial Disparities in Education 196
Racial Disparities in Employment 196
Racial Disparities in Health and Health Care 197
Implication of Cultural Value Differences 198
Family Structures, Communities, and Relationship Patterns 198
Cultural Values, Traditions, and Strengths 199

Communication: Cross-Cultural Dynamics 200
Nonverbal Communication 201
Context-Driven Communication 202
Cultural Identity Development of the Racially and Ethnically Diverse 205
Black Racial Identity Development 205
Minority Racial/Cultural Identity Development 207
Biracial and Multiracial Identity Development 210
Immigrant Acculturation and Identity Development 210
Assessment, Prevention, and Intervention 212
Recognizing Cultural Strengths of Racial and Ethnic Minorities 212
Respecting Racial and Ethnic Minority Clients' Worldviews and Perspectives 213
Supporting Traditional Cultural Healing Methods 214
Advocating for Social Justice Through Psychological Prevention and Intervention 214
Summary 215
Takeaway Messages 215
Recommended Resources 216

Chapter 9 Working With Diversity in Gender and Sexual Orientation Contexts 219
Chapter Overview 219
Self-Assessment of Pre-Existing Awareness and Knowledge 220
Learning Objectives 220
Understanding Sexual Orientation and Gender Identity 224
Lesbian, Gay, and Bisexual Identity Development 224
Gender Identity Development 225
Transgender Identity Development 227
Working Ethically and Effectively With Sexual Minorities 227
Training Issues 228
Sexual Orientation 228
Sexual Orientation and Counselor Competency 230
Counseling Competencies 231
Knowledge 231
Awareness 232
Skills 233
Working With Nonbinary Gender Identity 234
Summary 239
Takeaway Messages 239
Recommended Resources 239

Chapter 10 Working With Diversity in Social Class Contexts 247
Chapter Overview 247
Self-Assessment of Pre-Existing Awareness and Knowledge 248
Learning Objectives 248
Social Class and Classism 250
Classism 251
Social Class and Privilege 251
Intersectionality of Social Class With Race and Other Dimensions of Diversity 253
White, Middle-Class Privilege 253
Social Class and Poverty 255
Understanding the Social Context of the Poor 257
Effects of Poverty 257
Effects of Classism, Discrimination, and Microaggression 259
Disparities Due to Social Class 259
Stereotypes of the Poor 260
Upward Mobility Expectations and Biases 261
Hostility of Microaggression 261
Social Class Identity, Values, and Worldviews 262
Social Class Identity 262
Social Class Values and Worldviews 264
Assessment, Prevention, and Intervention 265
Overcoming Social Class Biases 265
Eliminating Unintentional Victim Blaming 266
Respect, Validate, and Be Strength Based 268
Social Advocacy 269
Summary 270
Takeaway Messages 270
Recommended Resources 270

Chapter 11 Working With Diversity in Physical Ability 274
Chapter Overview 274
Self-Assessment of Pre-Existing Awareness and Knowledge 274
Learning Objectives 275
Including Disability Diversity: Developing Multicultural Competence 279
Disability Defined 279
Disability as a Multicultural Issue 281
Disability as a Social Construction 283
Ableism 284
Models of Disability 285
To Which Model of Disability Does Your Client Subscribe? 289
Disability and Ethical Practice 293

Summary 294
Takeaway Messages 295
Recommended Resources 295

Chapter 12 Working With Diversity in Religion and Spirituality 298

Chapter Overview 298
Self-Assessment of Pre-Existing Awareness and Knowledge 299
Learning Objectives 299
Religion and Spirituality: A Cultural Diversity Context 302
Religion and Spirituality Defined 302
My Client Is Religious or Spiritually Oriented: Shouldn't I Refer My Client to the Clergy? 303
What Do We Know About the Religious/Spiritual Orientation of Counseling Professionals? 305
Religion and Spirituality in Counseling 306
Accepting Clients as Spiritual and/or Religious Beings 307
Understanding Religion and Spirituality Development 308
Integrating Religion/Spirituality Interventions 310
Training for Religion/Spirituality Competencies 311
Religion, Spirituality, and Ethical Considerations 312
Client Welfare 314
Professional Obligations 315
Avoiding Values Imposition 315
Assessing Religion and Spirituality: The Clinical Interview 316
When Do Religion and Spirituality Become Harmful or Pathological? 318
Summary 322
Takeaway Messages 323
Recommended Resources 323

Section 5 Social Justice and Multicultural Counseling 327

Chapter 13 Role of Social Justice in Counseling 329

Chapter Overview 329
Self-Assessment of Pre-Existing Awareness and Knowledge 329
Learning Objectives 330
Social Injustice or Inequality 332
Marginalized Communities 332
Types of Social Injustice 336
Victimizing Effects of Social Inequality 338
Lack of Opportunity Toward Success 338
Being Viewed as Problems 339
Vulnerability to Victimization and Revictimization 340

Social Justice 342
Social Justice and Counseling 344
Social Justice Counseling in Schools 345
Social Justice Counseling in Career and Vocational Areas 346
Social Justice Counseling in the International Arena 347
Promoting a Socially Responsive Approach of Counseling 348
A Group Activity 350
Counseling Student Refuses to Counsel Gay Client
About Relationship Issues 350
Summary 352
Takeaway Messages 352
Recommended Resources 352

Chapter 14 Developing Social Justice Counseling and Advocacy Skills 356

Chapter Overview 356
Self-Assessment of Pre-Existing Awareness and Knowledge 357
Learning Objectives 357
Taking Personal Responsibility: Social Justice Competency Development 359
Starting a Personal Journey 360
Becoming an Ally for Social Justice 362
Taking Professional Responsibility:
A Social Justice Counseling Paradigm 366
Social Justice-Informed Counseling Strategies 367
Strength-Based Approach 367
Preventive Focus of Counseling 368
Empowerment: Validation and Education 369
Empowerment: Outreach and Community Services 370
Social Advocacy Practice 371
Training for Social Justice Competencies 372
Taking Social Responsibility: Community Advocacy for Social Justice 378
Good, Ethical Practice in a Multicultural World 379
Summary 382
Takeaway Messages 382
Recommended Resources 383

Section 6 Applying Multicultural Competencies: Case Examples 385

Chapter 15 Helping Jermaine Feel "Normal" 386

Setting 386
Meeting Jermaine 386
Mr. Scott's Reflection 387

The Brief Phone Call 388
Mr. Scott's Reflection 389
Intake and Session 1 389
Client Profile 391
Mr. Scott's Reflection 392
Session 2 392
Observations of Mr. Scott's Work With Jermaine 394
General Discussion 394
How Can We Be Most Effective in Helping Jermaine? 394

Chapter 16 Helping Darryl and Samar to "Fight Fairly" 395

Backgrounds 395
Clients 395
Counselor 396
Dialogue 1 396
Dr. Goody: Reflection 1 397
Dialogue 2 397
Dr. Goody: Reflection 2 399
Dialogue 3 399
Dr. Goody: Reflection 3 400
Dialogue 4 401
Observations of Dr. Goody's Work With Darryl and Samar 402
General Discussion 403
How Can You Be Most Effective in Helping Darryl and Samar? 403

Epilogue From the Authors' Chairs 404

Index 407

Editors' Preface

Counseling and Professional Identity in the 21st Century

Becoming a Multiculturally Competent Counselor by Changming Duan and Chris Brown is a text that will not only introduce you to the concept of multicultural counseling but will invite you . . . no, actually . . . guide you into ***becoming*** a multiculturally competent counselor.

Throughout the pages that follow, you will come to understand that ***Becoming a Multiculturally Competent Counselor*** is more than the acquisition of knowledge or the development of skills. ***Becoming a Multiculturally Competent Counselor*** is an essential part of ethical professional practice and a core component to your professional identity as a counselor.

Becoming a Multiculturally Competent Counselor is a text that is clear, cogent, and comprehensive. However, beyond the explication of the core concepts and theories of multicultural counseling, the text, with its rich use of case illustrations and guided exercises, helps you to personalize the material presented and begin to incorporate that information into the development of your own professional identity and skill set. Obviously, any one text or any one learning experience will not be sufficient for the successful formation of your professional identity and practice. Becoming and being a counselor will be a lifelong process—a process that we hope to facilitate through the presentation of this text along with the creation of our series *Counseling and Professional Identity in the 21st Century.*

Counseling and Professional Identity in the 21st Century is a fresh, pedagogically sound series of texts targeting counselors-in-training. This series is *not* simply a compilation of isolated books matching those already in the market. Rather, each book, with its targeted knowledge and skills, will be presented as part of a larger whole. The focus and content of each text serves as a single lens through which you can view your clients, engage in your practice, and articulate your own professional identity.

Counseling and Professional Identity in the 21st Century is unique not just in the fact that it "packaged" a series of traditional texts but that it provides an integrated curriculum targeting the formation of your professional identity and efficient, ethical practice. Each book within the series is structured to facilitate the ongoing professional formation of the reader. The materials found within each text are organized in order to move you to higher levels of cognitive, affective, and psychomotor functioning, resulting in your assimilation of the materials presented into both your professional identity and approach to professional practice. While each text targets a specific set of core competencies (cognates and skills) aligned with those identified by the Council for Accreditation of Counseling & Related Educational Programs (CACREP) as essential to the practice of counseling (see page i), each book in the series will emphasize each of the following:

a. The assimilation of concepts and constructs provided across the text found within the series, fostering the reader's ongoing development as a competent professional
b. The blending of contemporary theory with current research and empirical support
c. A focus on the development of procedural knowledge with each text employing case illustrations and guided practice exercises to facilitate the reader's ability to translate the theory and research discussed into professional decision making and application
d. The emphasis on the need for and means of demonstrating accountability
e. The fostering of the reader's professional identity and with it the assimilation of the ethics and standards of practice guiding the counseling profession

We are proud to have served as coeditors of this series and feel sure that each book within it will serve as a significant resource to you and your development as a professional counselor. Let your journey begin!

Richard Parsons, PhD

Naijian Zhang, PhD

Preface

Writing this book has been a tremendous learning experience. We were surprised by the extent of our personal and professional growth, which we attributed to reviewing relevant literature, learning and relearning about the progress and challenges in multicultural counseling, discerning the critical issues, and engaging in continuous self-reflection. Our experience in writing this book is indeed a testament that developing a *multicultural identity*, *multicultural consciousness*, and *multicultural competence* is a lifelong commitment—we are thrilled to have had the opportunity to refuel our commitment. For us, constructing, deconstructing, and reconstructing knowledge and learning to be multiculturally competent through teaching and research are major aspects of our professional work, yet we acknowledge that we are not exempt from biases and prejudices rooted in various isms. As such, we, too, must welcome the opportunity for professional growth and development by engaging in continuous learning and educational experiences.

This process of becoming multiculturally competent can at times be challenging, but overall it is ultimately rewarding. We invite you, our readers, to join us on this professional journey. We are traveling on the same ship in the middle of an ocean toward a land that symbolizes the bright tomorrow. No matter where each of us sits—the first, the second, the third, or the fourth class—the fate of the ship affects us all. Even the first-class travelers, the most prestigious, won't remain unaffected by damage caused by a submerged reef in the corner of the fourth-class area of the ship.

The counseling profession faces the challenge of providing effective and affordable care to the culturally diverse in the 21st century. Professional counseling as we know it today is a product of many years of research and clinical exploration by researchers, theorists, and practitioners in the United States and some European countries. The progress toward understanding human psychological health and the implementation of professional prevention strategies and interventions have contributed significantly to the health of our society. However, we must acknowledge that our counseling profession in the United States has fallen short in providing competent services to clients from culturally diverse backgrounds. By and large, our counseling profession has not adequately attended to the contextual uniqueness of diverse clients, resulting in failure to provide unbiased and culturally responsive services to those who are socially marginalized and culturally diverse. In many situations, this failure has not only hurt the culturally diverse client but has also contributed to the perpetuation of social and cultural injustice and oppression in society. Although different explanations may account for this lack of adequate service, it is quite possible that one reason is due to practicing counselors who lack sufficient multicultural competence.

Our counseling training programs must take responsibility for ensuring that *all* students receive sufficient multicultural competence training prior to receiving endorsement into the profession.

It is good news, however, that multicultural competence training has received significant attention from the counseling profession. The Council for the Accreditation of Counseling and Related Educational Programs (CACREP, 2009) has specified "social and cultural diversity" as one of the eight common core areas required of accredited programs and has mandated that training must "provide an understanding of the cultural context of relationships, issues, and trends in a multicultural society," including all of the following:

a. Multicultural and pluralistic trends, including characteristics and concerns within and among diverse groups nationally and internationally

b. Attitudes, beliefs, understandings, and acculturative experiences, including specific experiential learning activities designed to foster students' understanding of self and culturally diverse clients

c. Theories of multicultural counseling, identity development, and social justice

d. Individual, couple, family, group, and community strategies for working with and advocating for diverse populations, including multicultural competencies

e. Counselors' roles in developing cultural self-awareness, promoting cultural social justice, advocacy and conflict resolution, and other culturally supported behaviors that promote optimal wellness and growth of the human spirit, mind, or body

f. Counselors' roles in eliminating biases, prejudices, and processes of intentional and unintentional oppression and discrimination (pp. 10–11)

To ensure that these goals are met, CACREP further identified the following competencies in diversity and advocacy:

a. Understands how living in a multicultural society affects clients who are seeking clinical mental health counseling services

b. Understands the effects of racism, discrimination, sexism, power, privilege, and oppression on one's own life and career and those of the client

c. Understands current literature that outlines theories, approaches, strategies, and techniques shown to be effective when working with specific populations of clients with mental and emotional disorders

d. Understands effective strategies to support client advocacy and influence public policy and government relations on local, state, and national levels to enhance equity, increase funding, and promote programs that affect the practice of clinical mental health counseling

e. Understands the implications of concepts such as internalized oppression and institutional racism, as well as the historical and current political climate regarding immigration, poverty, and welfare

f. Knows public policies on the local, state, and national levels that affect the quality and accessibility of mental health services

g. Maintains information regarding community resources to make appropriate referrals

h. Advocates for policies, programs, and services that are equitable and responsive to the unique needs of clients

i. Demonstrates the ability to modify counseling systems, theories, techniques, and interventions to make them culturally appropriate for diverse populations (pp. 32–33)

Demonstrating competence in *all* these areas can be overwhelming for both counseling students and practicing counselors. In fact, one can argue that it is impossible to know all "characteristics and concerns within and among diverse groups nationally and internationally" or to understand "how living in a multicultural society affects clients who are seeking clinical mental health counseling services" due to the diversity and complexity of cultures and of individual experiences of cultures. While we may agree or disagree with these arguments, we can't ignore our responsibility to train accordingly. Based on our years of teaching multicultural counseling, supervising and counseling from a multicultural lens, reviewing the multicultural counseling literature, and consulting with professional colleagues and graduate students regarding multicultural training, we realize that simply emphasizing a multicultural counseling approach by teaching multicultural knowledge and skills is insufficient and potentially harmful to diverse clients. We believe that training should first focus on helping students develop a multicultural identity as the foundation of knowledge and skill acquisition. It is our conviction that the formation of a multicultural personal identity is a necessary requisite for a multicultural professional identity, and both are crucial for developing specific multicultural competencies. A person can't be a multiculturally competent counselor without being a multiculturally open-minded, sensitive, and insightful person.

To help provide readers with a clear understanding of what we hope to accomplish by emphasizing multicultural identity development in counselor training, we define *multicultural identity* as follows:

> Sense of self as a counselor who defines one's own personal and professional roles with a set of attitudes, beliefs, values, motives, experiences, skills, and practices that enable oneself to accurately understand and effectively intervene on behalf of clients and communities in our culturally pluralistic society. A necessary component of this identity is being a non- and anti-ist in all dimensions of diversity and supporting social justice for all.

The development of a multicultural identity is an ongoing, lifelong process and needs to be continuously renewed as the environment changes. A multicultural identity will allow the counselor to operate with a multicultural consciousness and become both intellectually and emotionally available in understanding and helping his or her socially oppressed and culturally diverse clients.

Our targeted readers of this book are counselors-in-training, and our focus is on counseling the culturally diverse, especially the socially oppressed. We intend to have trainees examine their developmental level, while also considering where general training experiences need to be strengthened. We are aware that some of the topics we discuss in this book (e.g., racism, heterosexism, other isms) remain sensitive for the general public. In order that our readers gain the most from our writing, we believe it beneficial to share information about our backgrounds, including our biases, and the expectations we hold for counselors in the 21st century.

Our social and professional perceptions are shaped by our own cultural, social, and professional identities. Our brief biographic information can be found on pp. xxix–xxx. In society, we both hold nondominant-group memberships in that neither of us is White or male; in addition, Dr. Duan is an immigrant. Nondominant-group membership status allows us access to the experiences of some minority groups that may not be apparent or fully understood by White males. On the other hand, we also share the privilege of being cisgender, heterosexual, well educated, employed, middle class, able-bodied, and without obvious age disadvantage at this time. We attempted to remain aware of our own cultural biases and to set them aside, but we acknowledge that our writings may be influenced by our cultural stances.

As we engage in our ongoing and lifelong commitment to developing a multicultural identity, we invite our readers to join us in the journey toward multicultural competence. In doing so, you may, at times, experience defensiveness for being made to feel you were a perpetrator of someone else's injustices and oppression, and at other times you may recognize your privileges as being salient. You are encouraged to examine your own narratives that best reflect your social and cultural positions and consciousness. Our goal is to be facilitators and encouragers of the motivation and investment needed to promote multicultural counseling competence.

Our philosophical starting point reflects our respect for humanity and is service driven, not politically focused. If readers find some of the arguments presented (e.g., social justice for sexual minorities) to be politically couched, we encourage them to redirect their focus on the people involved—which is consistent with our multicultural training. Although we do not deny that social justice issues often intertwine with politics, we have a professional responsibility to provide effective mental health services to the socially oppressed and culturally diverse. Although it may appear that our positions on some issues coincide with certain political views, it is not our intent to be political. We hope that you remain open and are able to embrace the humanity and service-driven orientation that frames our writing. For instance, the 2014 event in Ferguson, Missouri, in which an unarmed African American teenage male was shot to death by a White policeman is discussed in Chapter 13. Regardless of your political views and in preparation of becoming a professional counselor, we encourage you to exercise your multicultural consciousness in understanding the impact of this event on African Americans, their communities, and our whole nation. A professional counselor's focus should be different than that of a politician, lawyer, or bystander. Counselors demonstrate empathy and compassion, which are cornerstone in the promotion of humanity and the provision of culturally responsive services.

We believe that social justice is the core of multicultural counseling. Selma Yznaga, the current president of the Division of Counselors for Social Justice of American Counseling Association, stated the following:

> For our clients, oftentimes the victims of social inequity, the stakes are much higher. If being witness to human suffering is distressing, being the subject is many times worse. Many of our clients come to us precisely because of their experience with institutional or personal discrimination, government-sanctioned abuse, or the thick, tarry wrapper of poverty. To treat our clients' symptoms without addressing the social perpetrators is useless at best, negligent at worst. ("President's Message," 2013)

We agree with this observation and believe that a multicultural identity facilitates and prepares the counselor for seeing and validating the clients' pain as a result of social injustice and oppression. Counselors' efforts at addressing social justice issues should be reflected in their counseling sessions as well as in community advocacy.

We emphasize the importance of considering the intersectionality of cultural identities, especially for clients who possess multiple minority identities. We specifically discuss certain identities and their social contexts. For some of these identities (e.g., race, sexual identity, social class), we devoted whole chapters and have underscored why understanding the breadth and depth of these identities is crucial to multicultural identity development. Although it is true that "everyone is multicultural," we must not minimize the fact that some disadvantaged groups and their members experience more degradation and social injustice than others. A multicultural identity provides the foundation for understanding and appreciating our clients' lived experiences as seen through their multiple cultural identities. Finally, we are encouraged to address their concerns from a social justice perspective.

We promote experiential learning. There is no doubt that intellectual learning is necessary, but we believe it is far from sufficient for developing multicultural competence. In order to effectively intervene on behalf of clients who have experienced social marginalization and oppression, counselors must be both intellectually and emotionally available. From the learning activities provided throughout the chapters, our readers are given opportunities to personally reflect upon and apply the chapter information with consideration of both their personal background and experiences and those of their clients. Counselors, as the most important helping instruments, must embrace their clients' experiences and recognize the roles they play in their clients' cultural contexts, which requires experiential learning. For example, a White female counselor needs to be aware of how her cultural identity has influenced her Latino client's social experience.

We encourage our readers to take risks by immersing themselves in learning that is intended to promote their multicultural identity development, such as being open to the experience of different cultures and acknowledging the harsh reality of social oppression. We envision that to achieve a multicultural professional identity and develop multicultural competence, we will need to accomplish the following:

1. Observe multiculturally competent role models and study multiculturally sensitive behaviors
2. Understand our multicultural self, including positive and negative contributions we make to social oppression and injustice, through critical assessment and evaluation of existing cultural identity
3. Understand the societal contexts for diverse individuals and communities and recognize the role of social oppression/discrimination and variation in worldviews and cultural values and practices
4. Understand and respect individuals and communities in their social and cultural contexts, including the specific characteristics identified in Pamela Hays's (1996) ADRESSING model
5. Develop skills and practices, including advocating for necessary policies, in the provision of services for diverse individuals and communities

To conclude, we applied the CACREP standards as a guide, presented a model for multicultural professional identity development, and introduced step-by-step processes to help counseling students begin this lifelong journey.

References

Council for Accreditation of Counseling and Related Educational Programs. (2009). *2009 standards.* Retrieved from http://www.cacrep.org/wp-content/uploads/2013/12/2009-Standards.pdf

Hays, P. A. (1996). Addressing the complexities of culture and gender in counseling. *Journal of Counseling & Development, 74*, 332–338.

Yznaga, S. (2013). President's message. Retrieved from http://www.counselorsforsocialjustice.net/message.html

Organization of the Book

The book is organized into six sections that cover 16 chapters. CACREP standards and expected curricular experiences are followed in the design of these sections and chapters.

Section 1 contains three chapters that help readers examine the counseling profession's responsibility of providing culturally responsive mental health services to the culturally diverse, the concerns that exist in our current models of service delivery, and the challenges we must wrestle going forward. Specific arguments are provided to elucidate that with or without our acknowledgment, counseling has largely been a monocultural phenomenon, and this warrants our attention and commitment to change for the 21st century. A brief history of the change efforts in developing multicultural counseling is provided, including the role of multicultural competence in the future of the counseling profession.

Section 2 includes two chapters that expand our focus on the important role of multicultural counseling in the sustainment of the counseling profession in the 21st century. We discuss and clarify why our counseling methods and interventions need to be redefined and the counseling profession as a whole continuously renewed. This redefinition and renewal process will help prepare counseling professionals to work effectively with culturally diverse and socially oppressed clients.

Section 3 focuses on helping our readers to understand the critical role of a multicultural identity in multicultural competence building. Chapter 6 presents a process model of multicultural competence development that outlines the step-by-step method that counselors-in-training may follow to become multiculturally competent. The foundation of this multicultural development is introduced as Step 1 and discussed in detail. Chapter 7 provides awareness of the pervasive effect of social oppression (Step 2) and understanding that the socially privileged enjoy unearned advantages at the expenses of the oppressed.

Section 4 contains five chapters (Steps 3 and 4), each focusing on one area of diversity. We are limited by a restricted number of pages and therefore unable to discuss all dimensions of diversity. We chose five diversity topics—race, gender and sexual identity, social class status, physical ability, and religion and spirituality—because the oppression related to isms in these areas is widely observed, and the emotional valence of both the privileged and the oppressed in these areas is high and visible in the public. Although we chose to explore only these five diversity topics, we in no way mean to imply that other dimensions of diversity are not equally important.

The two chapters in Section 5 (Step 5) address the promotion of social justice in all contexts of how we intervene on behalf of our clients. As mentioned earlier, we believe that social justice is a critical element of counseling in the 21st century. As such, we encourage the promotion of social justice–oriented and responsive counseling in working with clients and social advocacy efforts that inform positive social changes in communities and society.

The final section, Section 6, presents clinical case demonstrations with verbatim counselor-client interactions. Also included are counselors' reflections as related to understanding clients in context and examples of socially responsive counseling.

Ancillaries

The companion website at **study.sagepub.com/duan** provides password-protected instructor resources including a test bank, PowerPoints and instructor's manual, as well as free student study tools including practice quizzes, multimedia links, and more.

Acknowledgments

We would like to express our sincere gratitude to our counseling and counseling psychology students, graduates, and colleagues for their willingness to share their personal narratives and illustrate the important role of culture and diversity in the counseling process. Their experiences and subsequent contributions throughout the chapters have aided us in identifying and addressing the most salient multicultural and social justice topics within the field of counseling. Throughout our writing, it has been our expectation that our readers would be touched by the practicality and real-world examples that are offered to help in the development and formulation of a multicultural professional identity. We could not have met this expectation without the thoughtful contributions of our students, graduates, and colleagues. We recognize that the journey toward developing multicultural understanding and competence is no easy task; hence, we offer a wholehearted thank you to our contributors for sharing their personal experiences and/or creating case studies that add richness and life to the material presented in our chapters. There is no doubt that your contributions have been a guiding light in helping us prepare the next decade of counseling professionals to be multiculturally competent in their provision of services. We thank you!

Taryn Acosta

Alex Barajas

LaVerne Berkel

Jackie Bhattarai

Erika Blue

Tracey Dashjian

Dagoberto Heredia

Toy Jones

Eli Kean

Bobby Kizer

Kevin Lysaught

Genevieve Maliszewski

Angela Nakoulima

Darryl Narcisse

Teresa Pan

Kristen Sager

Amber Samson

Dominick Scalise

Michael Ternes

Marcy Vandament

Devon White

E. Zhang

We would also like to extend our gratitude to our many counseling and counseling psychology students who provided us with case studies of real-life counseling scenarios, which helped to inform our thinking and writing. The inclusion of real-life examples of both multicultural counseling challenges and successes has helped us to identify the latest topics critical to the multicultural counseling field. The issues that you grappled with and learned from as related to the contextual uniqueness of your clients served as important resources in developing the experiential learning content of our writing—we sincerely appreciate your contributions!

Chris Bedwell

Marci Benigno

Neil Corriston

Amy Dvorak

Michelle Farrell

Suzanne Heflin

Julie Kohlhart

Yujia Lei

G Wei Ng

Emily Plotkin

Young Song

Mimi Steinhaus

Cynthia Taylor

In addition, we offer special appreciation to our counseling graduate students who have informed our work in ways they would not otherwise realize without our mention. Over the years as students in our classes, you have shared your experiences and received and provided feedback regarding assignments and in-class discussions—all of which have fueled our understanding and challenged us to dig deeply to uncover and explore issues pertinent to multicultural competence training. You, unknowingly, have also inspired us to continue on our own journey toward multicultural competence. Thank you for being a significant part of our learning!

Finally, we offer a very special thank you to our series editors, Drs. Richard D. Parsons and Naijian Zhang for trusting us with this very important project. We are grateful for the opportunity to participate in this unique book series and appreciate your guidance and encouragement throughout our writing process. Carrie Montoya, senior editorial assistant, Kassie Graves, associate director, and Amy Harris, copy editor, of SAGE Publications, we could not have finalized our work without your support and assistance; thank you for your invaluable help and for keeping us on track throughout the writing of this book.

About the Authors

Changming Duan, PhD, is a cisgender, female, heterosexual Chinese American psychologist and currently a professor in the Department of Psychology and Research in Education at the University of Kansas. Changming Duan grew up in China and received all her postgraduate education in North America, including a doctoral degree in counseling psychology and social psychology from the University of Maryland. She has over 20 years of experience in teaching counselor preparation programs. One of the courses that she has taught most consistently is the multicultural counseling class. She feels she is always a beginner in teaching this class. Her professional interest also includes researching counseling processes and outcomes in various cultural contexts. Dr. Duan has been invited to speak on topics related to multicultural counseling and multicultural training for counselors by various organizations both nationally and internationally. She travels back to China often to conduct training and research.

Dr. Duan has authored or coauthored over 40 refereed professional articles and book chapters, with many in the area of cross-cultural understanding of counseling and counseling processes. She is the recipient of many honors and awards, including the *Trustees' Award for Excellence in Teaching* and the *Diversifying Curriculum Award* from the University of Missouri–Kansas City and the *Travel Award* from the American Psychological Association. Dr. Duan has also been a licensed psychologist in Missouri and Kansas.

Chris Brown, PhD, is a cisgender, heterosexual, middle-aged, female African American counseling psychologist who currently serves as interim dean of the School of Education at the University of Missouri–Kansas City (UMKC) and is also a professor in the School of Education's Division of Counseling and Educational Psychology. She earned her doctorate degree in counseling psychology from UMKC, a master's degree in counseling from California State University, Long Beach, and a bachelor's degree from the University of California at Los Angeles. Prior to her interim dean role, she served as chair of the Division of Counseling and Educational Psychology at UMKC and also served as coordinator of the master's program in counseling and guidance (mental health and couples and family). She has over 22 years of teaching in counselor preparation programs and over 33 years of experience providing counseling to culturally diverse populations. She is a licensed psychologist in Missouri and Kansas and provides consultation to various organizations, including continuing education workshops on ethics and professional issues to mental health professionals.

Dr. Brown has authored/coauthored over 45 refereed journal articles, many of which have a multicultural focus. Among the several courses she has taught (ethics and professional issues in counseling, couples and family therapy, theories and methods of sex therapy, career development, assessment, and counseling practicum), she has infused the important role of multiculturalism in her training initiatives. The focus of her research includes cultural dimensions of career development, gender transitions, and ethics and professional issues in counseling. She has received various acknowledgments and awards for her work, with the most recent being UMKC's *Lavender Award for Outstanding Faculty* for her multicultural sensitivity and emphasis on training counseling students to embrace and understand the importance of individual and cultural diversity. In her varied roles as educator, researcher, practitioner, and consultant, Dr. Brown strives to generate knowledge that can be used to address social concerns and individual problems and is committed to educating and mentoring counseling students.

Section I

Professional Counseling: A Cultural Occurrence

Major CACREP Standards for the Section

CACREP Standard 2a: Social and Cultural Diversity—multicultural and pluralistic trends, including characteristics and concerns between and within diverse groups nationally and internationally

CACREP Standard 2b: attitudes, beliefs, understandings, and acculturative experiences, including specific experiential learning activities designed to foster students' understanding of self and culturally diverse clients

Specific Competencies Identified by CACREP Diversity and Advocacy Standards for Clinical Mental Health Counseling Addressed in Section I

CACREP Knowledge 1: Understands how living in a multicultural society affects clients who are seeking clinical mental health counseling services

CACREP Knowledge 2: Understands the effects of racism, discrimination, sexism, power, privilege, and oppression on one's own life and career and those of the client

After Reading Section I, Students Will Be Able to Do the Following:

a. Recognize the monocultural nature of extant counseling theories and practices (Chapter 1)

b. Understand the necessity for counselors in the 21st century to develop a multicultural professional identity (Chapter 1)

c. Understand how the counseling profession has historically failed in providing culturally just and fair services to the socially oppressed and the culturally diverse (Chapter 2)

d. Understand the negative impact of racism, discrimination, sexism, power, privilege, and oppression on many individuals in our society and on counseling practice (Chapter 2)

e. Be knowledgeable of the multicultural movements and advances in the counseling profession in recent years (Chapter 3)

f. Recognize the demand and need for the counseling profession to transform itself in order to effectively serve the socially oppressed and culturally diverse (Chapter 3)

Section Introduction

This section is devoted to helping students understand the monocultural nature of professional counseling, the demand for a multiculturally effective counseling profession in the United States and globally, and the profession's efforts concerning greater inclusivity and respect for cultural diversity. The overarching goal is to help counselors-in-training embrace a personal, social, and professional responsibility toward developing a multicultural professional identity, which will provide the foundation for practicing as a multiculturally competent counselor.

In Chapter 1, we describe the ways in which the counseling profession reflects ethnocentric views of psychological health and helping. In theories and in practice, the cultural values and worldviews of the dominant cultural groups are the bases and foundations while communication styles of the European middle class are the vehicles of counseling.

Chapter 2 provides a description of the demands for multicultural counseling from several angles. Due to the presence of social oppression, increasing demographic changes in the United States, and ongoing globalization, there is a high demand for a multiculturally efficacious counseling profession.

Chapter 3 outlines the progress of the recent multicultural movement and its future direction. It is clear that continuing to practice monocultural counseling will not only be unhelpful to the culturally diverse, but it will also perpetuate the damaging social injustices that have existed in U.S. history.

We hope that our attention to the historical and monocultural context of counseling and the recent multicultural movement will encourage counselors-in-training to develop multicultural competencies.

Monocultural Context of Counseling as a Helping Profession

Not to know is bad; not to wish to know is worse.

—West African Proverb

CHAPTER OVERVIEW

This chapter presents a detailed analysis of the monocultural context of the counseling profession by describing the values and worldviews reflected in the counseling profession with particular attention to our extant counseling theories and mode of practice. We also discuss our ethical obligations to understand client problems in a cultural context and provide understanding for the need to develop a multicultural professional identity.

SELF-ASSESSMENT OF PRE-EXISTING AWARENESS AND KNOWLEDGE

- What is my understanding of the cultural foundation of the counseling profession?
- What are the values of the counseling profession that are consistent or inconsistent with my own?

- How do I perceive people who are racially, ethically, socially, or culturally different from me?
- What thoughts do I have about the multicultural movement in the field of counseling?
- In what way am I prepared (or not prepared) to emotionally and intellectually engage in the helping relationship with clients from socially oppressed and marginalized groups (e.g., lesbian/gay/bisexual/transgender clients)?
- What challenges might I encounter in trying to develop a multicultural professional identity?
- How might I demonstrate my commitment to developing a multicultural consciousness?

LEARNING OBJECTIVES

After reading this chapter, students will be able to do the following:

1. Recognize the counseling profession as a culture-laden practice
2. Describe the cultural values and worldviews on which extant counseling theories are based
3. Understand why it is unprofessional, nontherapeutic, and unethical to practice counseling without considering clients' cultural contexts
4. Self-assess their interest and motivation for intellectual and emotional engagement in multicultural learning
5. Understand the necessity of developing a multicultural professional identity and multicultural competencies

CASE ILLUSTRATION 1.1

The Case of Xilin

Xilin is a 49-year-old Asian American female who emigrated from China when she was 14 years old. She received high school, college, and graduate education in computer science in the United States and has worked for a major telephone company since receiving her master's degree. She sought counseling from a White, middle-aged, experienced female counselor (Dr. T.) after having some "major conflicts" related to disciplining their only teenage daughter with her husband, a successful information technology professional. After six counseling sessions, Xilin separated from her husband and moved out with their daughter. She initiated termination after the seventh session, reporting, "I think I am doing fine."

About eight months later (by then she and their daughter had moved back in with her husband), Xilin ran into the first author of this book (Changming Duan, an Asian American counseling psychologist) and shared her counseling experience with Dr. T. She said that initially she felt the counseling was very helpful because Dr. T. helped her get in touch with her feelings, which included her sadness about having conflicts with her husband of 25 years and anger about him not letting her discipline their daughter in a way she saw fit. However, in retrospective, she said although it was all her own fault, she was "very mad" at Dr. T. because she led her to focus on her anger toward her husband "almost exclusively" by spending a lot of time talking about her anger in sessions. She said that she did not remember having much discussion about disciplining their daughter or helping her husband understand her thoughts and parenting style, which was the original reason that she sought counseling.

Xilin said she felt "stupid" when Dr. T. pointed out the lack of an egalitarian relationship in her marriage because she never thought about it. She said that talking about her anger toward her husband session after session led her to experience increased anger toward him, to the point which she "realized" that he never respected her as a person and his dominance compromised her independence and autonomy. She said she remembered feeling very resentful that her husband had treated her, a competent professional, as "a person without her own mind and like a docile housewife." She recalled feeling embarrassed for not being emotionally independent. To pursue her independence, she separated from her husband.

Xilin reported that moving out had started her regrettable "curved road." She said that following several weeks of being on her own, she experienced more and more sadness and noticed changes in her relationships with their daughter and her social network at her church. Their daughter became increasingly defiant toward her and would say and do hurtful things to her, especially blaming her for her dad's stroke and subsequent declining health. The unsupportive looks and comments from many fellow Asian American churchgoers (i.e., "Wow, you are independent now," or "Heard you have left your husband—are you happy now?") made her feel unwelcomed, and she no longer wanted to attend church activities.

In tears, Xilin said, "I never felt that miserable, isolated, and incomplete, but I did not want to admit that I was wrong. It was his stroke that completely woke me up and gave me an excuse to move back home. Maybe it is God who used his stroke to teach me a lesson." She concluded her story by saying, "I had wanted our daughter to be a clinical psychologist because I thought that was a noble occupation, but no longer."

GUIDED PRACTICE EXERCISE 1.1

Think Culture, Feel Culture, and Be Cultural!

Identify one iconic person in your life (hero/heroine, artist, leader, etc.) and share in a small group the reasons for your admiration, respect, and/or high regard for him or her. Then with the help of all members of the group, discuss the ways in which your choice and reasons for selecting this person reflect your culture, social positions, and cultural values. Do you think your choice is shared by others who are similar or different from you? Why?

SMALL-GROUP CLASS ACTIVITY 1.1

Is Counseling a Cultural Phenomenon?

In a small group of three to four students, discuss your reactions to Dr. T.'s counseling approach and Xilin's story.

What do you think Dr. T. should or should not have done? Why?

What recommendations would you offer to her?

With this case as a context, comment on this statement: *Good counseling is good counseling.*

This case illustrated how a well-intentioned counselor failed in helping an ethnic minority client by practicing counseling rooted in mono-Western individualistic culture values and without awareness of the client's cultural context. The failed outcome is not necessarily due to intentional harm by Dr. T. or any deliberate wrongdoing, as her intervention strategies (focusing on client emotions, especially negative emotions toward others, and client needs for autonomy and self-actualization) are supported by various traditional theories and most likely can be effective for clients whose cultural background is consistent with that in which these theories were developed. However, blind application of traditional monocultural counseling theories and practices may cause unintentional harm for ethnic minorities. In this case, Dr. T. based her intervention on the assumption of the importance of independence and autonomy for individuals' emotional health and neglected the strong value for unity and harmony of an Asian American woman and the social and cultural context in which she lives and thrives. The self-focused intervention led to a self-focused solution, which caused Xilin's self-doubt and rejection from her support system. It is clear that the sacred, dominant American values for individual rights, autonomy, and independence may not be shared by all people and may not be useful bases for psychological interventions for ethnic minorities.

The Cultural and Value Foundations of Counseling in the United States

The development of professional counseling in the United States was the result of a "convergence of many unique historical, social, political, and professional influences and developments during the first half of the 20th century" (Munley, Duncan, McDonnell, & Sauer, 2004, p. 248). According to Glosoff (2009), the counseling profession has been shaped by the following factors: (a) vocational guidance movement, (b) mental health counseling movement, (c) development of professional identity, (d) influence of federal legislation, (e) history of the American Counseling Association (ACA), and (f) credentialing and the professionalization of counseling. In addition to these important facets, the history of counseling has emphasized the importance of individual choice in a society that embraces autonomy (i.e., freedom to choose) as an ideal. Moreover, the evolution of counseling is reflective of the culture and values of its society—as society changes, so must the counseling profession.

The European American worldview has been the basis for the development of counseling as a profession, and the White, middle-class values have set the tone, the limit, the scope, and the process for counseling practices. In general, European American culture values include rugged individualism, competition, mastery and control over nature, a unitary and static conception of time, religion based on Christianity, and separation of science and religion (Katz, 1985). All these values transcended into the fabric of the counseling profession, which led to, at its gate goal, a biased, monocultural practice. A culturally biased practice has a tendency to focus on rational more than relational, logic more than emotion, competition more than cooperation, independence more than interdependence, and an individualistic rather than a collectivistic interest.

In the context of our increasingly multicultural societies and communities, such practice, if unchallenged, is destined to look pale, incompetent, and eventually obsolete. To elucidate the ways in which our current counseling practice is culturally narrow focused, an examination of its cultural foundations and characteristics is detailed.

Individualistic and Egocentric Focus

Individualism is the basis for the dominant ideology in the United States, where individual rights are considered the most sacred. From political and legal systems to the institution of helping professions, the individual has been the unit of analysis, individual rights have been highly regarded, and individual welfare has been the sole focus of attention for interventions, preventions, and evaluations. This individualistic orientation has deep roots in the dominant cultural and political history in the United States. The deep roots and pervasive history of an individualistic orientation has resulted in most Americans (i.e., those who fit the term *Americans*—typically White and middle class) embracing an individualistic orientation. Consequently, the common ideological and behavioral patterns that are formed among the majority of the U.S. population have occupied dominant positions.

Psychological research has demonstrated an internalization of this cultural mentality and prevalence of self-focused behaviors in many aspects of American life. More specifically, the *fundamental attribution error* phenomenon (i.e., the tendency to place greater value on personality-based explanations for observed behaviors while undervaluing situational explanations; Ross, 1977), *self-serving biases* (i.e., the tendency to attribute success to one's personality factors and failure to external factors; Arkin, Appelman, & Burger, 1980), and the phenomenon of *in-group favoritism* (i.e., preference for one's in-group over anyone viewed as outside the group; Bobo & Zubrinsky, 1996) have been consistently observed and reflect psychological predispositions for high appraisal of self and low appraisal of others.

Individualism is clearly a culture-bound value that has formed the basis for most forms of counseling developed and practiced in past decades. For instance, the I-thou relationship is heavily emphasized by a number of theories, including psychodynamic, interpersonal, and person centered (D. W. Sue & Sue, 2008). Moreover, individuation is often seen as a healthy and normal developmental process (Ivey, D'Andrea, Ivey, &

Simek-Morgan, 2007), and individualism, autonomy, and ability to become one's own person are perceived as healthy and desirable goals for counseling (D. W. Sue & Sue, 2008). Therefore, counseling practice, from goal setting to specific interventions, has been about how to help clients feel better or solve their self-identified problems without sufficient consideration about their obligations or responsibilities to their social and cultural environments.

Although the premises of some counseling approaches are more group or collective focused such as the family systems perspective, individualism is still deeply rooted in how clinicians define and facilitate healthy systems, reflecting the values of individual rights, boundaries, independence, egalitarian relations, and so on. Individual autonomy is greatly promoted and seen as a condition for a healthy and mature system (Seeman & Seeman, 1983), while being dependent, enmeshed, and having unclear boundaries in the family network is often pathologized (Friedman, Utada, & Morrissey, 1987). For example, the concept of self-esteem is a cornerstone of Virginia Satir's experiential family therapy approach; the goals of that therapy are removing or correcting faulty communications and dysfunctional rules that are blocking one or more family members' growth and development of a positive self-esteem (Satir & Baldwin, 1983). Similarly, in Minuchin's (1974) structural family therapy, boundaries or the rules that regulate boundaries are critical elements and a central focus of treatment. In his conceptualization, family members are considered in regard to subsystems (i.e., smaller units of the system as a whole—spousal, parental, and sibling subsystems), and clear boundaries among them are perceived functional or healthy, whereas blurred boundaries are seen as dysfunctional.

In the case of Xilin, the counselor's approach was to focus on Xilin's anger toward her husband by encouraging her to talk about it, experience it, and eventually come to feel that her anger was as an important concern that warranted action. From an individualistic point of view, it could be argued that Xilin's "right" to be heard and respected by her husband was violated, and she, therefore, had the "right" to be angry and resentful. This individualistic approach lacked cultural sensitivity, and Dr. T. failed to understand Xilin in the context of her cultural background, by which pursuing personal relief of negative emotions at the expense of family unity is not supported. If clinicians do not consider or comprehend the values and cultural customs of their clients, they run the risk of devaluing, misunderstanding, and/or pathologizing the behaviors associated with their clients' belief systems and traditions. The counselor's individualistic approach and oversight in considering the social and cultural context that informed Xilin's thoughts, actions, and behaviors resulted in unintentional harm to the client.

Ethnocentric Perspectives

Ethnocentrism refers to the belief that one's worldview is the standard and is inherently superior and more desirable than that of others (Leininger, 1978). It is often manifested through judging other racial or cultural groups relative to one's own or holding one's own cultural group as the center of everything and a frame of reference for language, behavior, customs, and beliefs (Sumner, 1906). In U.S. history, the

European colonization efforts involved enculturating indigenous people, which reflected the ethnocentric view that European cultures and worldviews are superior. Indigenous people were viewed as uncivilized and forced to adopt European lifestyles, customs, beliefs, and values. This ethnocentric system persists as Western civilization has been taught in history books in the United States, while the other two thirds of the world population and their worldviews have been largely ignored. At the present time, ethnocentrism is still pervasive in the United States where the White middle-class values and worldviews tend to dominate social ideology and shape socially generated racial and cultural stereotypes against non-White or other culturally diverse groups. As pointed out by Neil Altman (2007), "One aspect of Whiteness in the American context . . . is that the culture associated with being a White American is considered the standard, the baseline from which other people diverge, as opposed to being one culture among many" (p. 20).

The counseling profession and mental health system are not exempt from the influence of ethnocentrism. In fact, they have been shaped by and in turn contributed to the dominance of the ethnocentric ideology. The theories and practices that are grounded in Euro-American monocultural perspectives are products of ethnocentric thinking, such as promoting individualistic rights and interests and pathologizing non-White cultural behaviors that are inconsistent with White values. In research conducted by Neuliep and McCroskey (1997), findings revealed that preference for one's in-group and use of one's own cultural system as a point of reference for treating culturally diverse clients can result in pathologizing client behaviors and/or cause unintentional harm. As a result of ethnocentrism, D. W. Sue & Sue (2008) pointed out the following:

> Our education systems and counseling/psychotherapy practices have often done great harm to our minority citizens. Rather than educate or heal, rather than offer enlightenment and freedom, and rather than allow for equal access and opportunities, historical and current practices have restricted, stereotyped, damaged, and oppressed the culturally different in our society. (p. 85)

Research has provided evidence of such harm done to ethnic minorities. Consider, for example, that consistent underuse of counseling services by ethnic and racial minorities (Ponterotto, Casas, Suzuki, & Alexander, 2001), overdiagnosis of various mental disorders of the culturally diverse (Schwartz & Feisthamel, 2009), higher levels of involuntary hospital commitments among ethnic minorities (Snowden & Cheung, 1990), lack of trust toward counseling among those who have experienced unjust social oppression (Nickerson, Helms, & Terrell, 1994), and overrepresentation of ethnic minority populations in prisons and other criminal systems where mental health issues are quite prevalent (Phillips & Bowling, 2003) have been unfailingly observed.

In the case of Xilin, ethnocentric conceptualization, as reflected in the counselor's intervention, hurt her in that the heavy focus on discussing her anger toward her husband implied that the problem was Xilin's inability to experience and articulate her anger, which Dr. T. obviously regarded as a sign of weakness and poor functioning. Dr. T. relied on her own ethnic or cultural system as a frame of reference for how Xilin should behave, which was to encourage expression of anger as a solution to her problems.

Monocultural Approaches Toward Human Behavior Evaluation and Change

Although worldviews or cultural values are neither right nor wrong, it is problematic when they are expressed through the process of ethnocentric monoculturalism (D. W. Sue & Sue, 2008). For instance, when treating Xilin, Dr. T. seemed to equate normality with individualism, a value highly regarded by the American culture, and overlooked the value of unity or harmony that Xilin's culture regards. It is recognized that counseling professionals who support mainstream cultural values and neglect minority or multicultural worldviews are practicing *ethnocentric monoculturalism*, which is quite common among American counseling and mental health delivery systems (Comas-Díaz, 2011). Due to the historical and cultural backgrounds of the counseling profession, counseling theories and practices in the United States have typically been based on monocultural traditions of thought that mainly reflect White, middle-class values. As a result, the cultures and cultural practices by racial, ethnic, social, and cultural minorities are often omitted or invalidated when considering how mental health is perceived, how goals for counseling are defined, and how behavioral changes are encouraged in the counseling process.

How Mental Health Is Viewed

In the United States, the *winner-take-all majority*, a form of majority tyranny, seems to have defined the U.S. democracy in past decades (Guinier, 1994). Similarly, the field of psychology and counseling is characterized by a tendency toward norm-defining meaning. In other words, U.S. psychology has not only treated the *norm* as a statistical entity representing the most common numerically but also as "the point of reference against which all else is measured" (Greene, 2007, p. 47). Statistical norms are equated with normality. Lorde (1984) pointed out that in the United States, the norm is "usually defined as White, thin, male, young, heterosexual, Christian, and financially secure" (p. 116). While society promotes mental health, what is considered as "normal" or healthy does not represent or reflect the cultures and experiences of American minorities to the same degree as it does the majority. Often people of color, sexual minorities, persons with disabilities, persons of low social class, or those with other minority status are stigmatized and their behaviors pathologized as their behaviors may deviate from those of the majority—the norm.

In defining mental health and diagnosing pathology, normality versus abnormality has been used as one major criterion in that *normality* has been viewed as ideal mental health and *abnormality* as the presence of pathology (D. Sue, Sue, & Sue, 2006). The problem inherited by this paradigm is apparent in that cultural-specific behaviors by racial, cultural, and social minorities would be more likely perceived as abnormal or pathological than those by the majority. As such, Asian American women who are over-compromising and highly tolerant of anger due to external pressure would easily be perceived as weak in ego-strength or low in self-esteem. Similarly, African American males "playing it cool" or possessing the belief that "The Man' is out to get them" would be viewed as paranoid or delusional (D. W. Sue & Sue, 2008.) Transgender individuals whose gender identity transgresses traditional definitions of *male* and *female* are at risk for societal discrimination and having their gender expression pathologized (Singh, Boyd, & Whitman, 2010). Sadly, normality or ideal mental health has historically represented those who conform to gender expression that is congruent with society's dichotomous, social constructions of gender rather than those who fall outside of the gender binary (Bullough, 2000). Persons who evidence a strong and persistent cross-gender identification and discomfort with their biological sex were often diagnosed with a gender identity disorder, which further elucidates a tendency to pathologize gender variance (i.e., nontraditional gender identities) and regard it as unhealthy and undesirable.

Another culturally biased criterion often used by mental health professions is the belief that it is only normal and healthy if one holds certain positive goals or ideals for life. In other words, the most popular humanistic philosophy of self-actualization (Rogers, 1961) or the highly regarded concepts of competence and autonomy (Allport, 1961) have dominated American professional psychology and mental health counseling practice. Any deviation from these notions is perceived as unhealthy or undesirable. However, such practice is discriminatory in that dominant cultural expectations are deemed as universally true, which pathologizes people with different cultural philosophies, worldviews, and beliefs. For instance, tribal Native Americans tend to value sharing and cooperation over individual autonomy and success, and some Latinas see their family responsibilities, not their career potential, as their primary life purpose. It is simply unjust and unfair to use the dominant American culture to define their mental health.

Additionally, pathology is often viewed as located within the minority individual or his or her cultural group to a much greater extent than would be suggested for majority group members. One major reason that pathology is viewed from within the minority individual is that social pathology (e.g., oppressive social conditions) is largely ignored when considering the behaviors of minority group members (Comas-Díaz, 2000). Social and cultural oppressions, hostility, and discriminations as well as poverty have undermined the mental health of the marginalized groups and restricted their access to resources and justices. Yet this part of the context is not adequately considered in how pathology is diagnosed and how mental health is defined. For example, if an African American male demonstrates mistrust and suspicious behavior, he may be labeled as "paranoid," even though his mistrust and suspicions may be indicative of his environmental circumstances.

In practice, the universal application of dominant theories of mental health and pathology is common. Many well-intentioned practitioners contribute to the victimization of racial, cultural, and social minorities by exercising inappropriate perceiving and thinking styles that lead to overpathologization of the socially marginalized. Jun (2010) identified three such common but harmful information-processing styles: linear, hierarchical, and dichotomous.

With *linear thinking*, one projects and generalizes on the basis of past experiences or cultural myths about certain groups and individuals. Racial profiling is an example of such thinking. It is dangerous for practitioners to view and judge people from diverse racial, social, and cultural groups on the basis of stereotypes of the group or past individual and isolated experiences. Perhaps this is one of the reasons why ethnic minorities have been more likely to be diagnosed with mental disorders as compared to White individuals.

Hierarchical thinking tends to be prevalent in individualistic and multiracial cultures (Black-Gutman & Hickson, 1996) in which individual achievements and competition (vs. collaboration or cooperation) are highly valued and deemed positive. This type of thinking reflects a superiority-inferiority orientation in perceiving and evaluating individual behaviors. Behaviors that are consistent with the dominant culture tend to be viewed as normal, desirable, healthy, or superior while those inconsistent with the dominant culture may be seen as abnormal, undesirable, unhealthy, or inferior. In the cultural context of the United States, being reserved and introverted is often perceived as undesirable and indicative of less positive personal traits such as low self-esteem or lack of self-confidence. Such hierarchical thinking contributes to the higher likelihood that the behaviors and practices of social and cultural minority groups will be viewed as abnormal and/or less desirable than those of majority group members.

Jun (2010) described *dichotomous thinking* as conceptualizing within an "either/or" mind-set, which contributes to "right/wrong" or "good/bad" judgments with most people perceiving what they believe or do as "right or good" and what others believe or do as "wrong or bad." In-group favoritism is an example of such thinking. In viewing mental health and psychopathology, this way of perceiving can victimize racial, social, and cultural minorities when their behaviors deviate from the behaviors accepted and valued by the majority. Viewing heterosexuality as normal and right behavior and same-sex attraction as abnormal and wrong is another example. Along with linear and hierarchical thinking, dichotomous thinking also contributes to ethnocentric biases and prejudices in our mental health delivery systems even when they are employed by well-intentioned and caring practitioners.

How Counseling Goals Are Conceptualized and Defined

Rooted in rugged individualism, the target of counseling practice is usually to help the individual feel better, get rid of negative symptoms, and/or become empowered. In support of this perspective, the Committee on Definition of the Division of Counseling Psychology of the American Psychological Association (1956) emphasized personal growth and defined counseling goals as "helping individuals to overcome obstacles to their personal growth, wherever these may be encountered, and toward achieving optimum development of their personal resources" (p. 283). Different theoretical perspectives in counseling also have implicit or explicit goals reflective of a mega theme of individualism. Consider, for example, all three traditional schools of thought in psychotherapy that endorse the notion of individual well-being and actualization. In the *insight-oriented* traditional psychodynamic treatment, the task of counseling or psychotherapy is to bolster clients' ego strength by helping them discover how their past physical and psychological experiences influence their present behaviors (Lake, 1985).

In *cognitive-behavioral* treatment, the goal is often about short-term symptom removal and observable behavioral changes (Feeley, DeRubeis, & Gelf, 1999). The *existential-humanistic* worldview focuses on helping clients make sense of their experiences toward the ultimate goal of self-actualization (Resnick, Warmoth, & Serlin, 2001). Although the goals of different theoretical orientations vary somewhat, there are some common themes that are clearly in line with mainstream culture in the United States. Perhaps this is one plausible explanation for why no empirical evidence has been found to show that any theoretical orientation is more or less effective than the others (Wampold, 2001).

The most obvious common theme is related to the individualistic nature of the conceptualization, which assumes that self-understanding or insight, freedom for self-actualization, and individuals' happiness or lack of negative emotions/symptoms are universally utmost important and desirable human conditions. This is supported by the dominant cultural values of individualism, individual autonomy, independence, and self-reliance. However, conceptualizing counseling goals in the context of counseling as working with one person at a time and with regard to the individual's struggles in life may misguide counseling effort toward ineffective outcomes when working with socially marginalized and culturally diverse persons.

We must consider that when the issue of power and privilege is introduced, many individuals' personal struggles become part of a cultural context where solutions to personal struggles may become impossible without systemic interventions. Moreover, from a multicultural perspective, the individualistic focus may not fit the values of many nonmainstream cultures where self-focused orientations may not be as highly valued. In fact, people from more collectivistic cultures may view the exclusive focus on the self as the problem rather than the solution to the problem (Zhang, 1994). This is evident in some older Chinese Americans who believe that people will have psychological problems if they think too much about themselves.

Another theme is the emphasis on immediate fixes or tangible changes. Counseling is aimed and evaluated by how it can help the client feel better or do better immediately after the counseling. From this perspective, counseling outcomes are often perceived and measured in terms of how clients feel immediately following the counseling sessions (Hill & Corbett, 1993). It is understandable that relief of pain is desirable, especially since pain is often what brought clients to counseling. It is noteworthy, however, that there are cultural variations in desirable outcomes. An example of this cultural variation can be seen among Eastern cultures in which there is a general appreciation for endurance of pain in order to achieve long-term and ultimate success. This practice was described in a qualitative study in which some Chinese therapists reported that in their counseling sessions they often focused on giving clients a few suggestions or profound ideas that they could think about and use to provide guidance over extended periods of time because they aimed at final healing rather than temporary relief (Lei, Hu, Chen, & Duan, 2012).

Finally, mental health counseling in the United States has historically treated mental illness and physical illness as separate but in a similar fashion, focusing on the parts or symptoms that are to be fixed or corrected. Wampold (2001) stated this:

> Mental health counseling is based on psychological principles and involves a trained therapist and a client who has a mental disorder, problem, or complaint; it is intended by the therapist to be remedial for the client's disorder, problem, or complaint; and it is adapted or individualized for the particular client and his or her disorder, problem, or complaint. (p. 3)

Again, this reflects the Western medical model that focuses care on identified pathology. In comparison, there are other cultures that would view human health as more of a holistic phenomenon and focus care on treating the person as a whole. For example, in the traditional Native American's view, the circle of life, represented by the Medicine Wheel, symbolizes Four Directions or components that include aspects of living: spirit (East), nature (South), body (West), and mind (North). Medicine refers to the *way of life* and represents one's search for balance between the four directions and between oneself and the universe. Reaching *harmony* means being in sync with the universe. The Medicine Wheel is at the heart of the Native American worldview and clearly illustrates the importance of a holistic orientation in which all aspects of living and of the person are attended to so that balance can be achieved. In terms of illness and according to Locust (1985), Native Americans believe the following:

> If one stays in harmony, keeps all the tribal laws and all the sacred laws, one's spirit will be so strong that negativity will be unable to affect it. . . . Once harmony is broken, however, the spiritual self is weakened and one becomes vulnerable to physical illness, mental and/or emotional upsets, and the disharmony projected by others. (p. 14)

Similarly, in traditional Chinese thinking, human health contains the integration of *yin* and *yang* energies. Illness is seen as a disturbance in the balance of these two energies, and therapy thus depends on accurate identification and harmonization of the sources of imbalance (Ebrey, 1981).

How Change Processes Are Pursued and Evaluated

Consistent with how mental health is defined and counseling goals set, the pursuit of client change in counseling and psychotherapy as recommended and outlined by various theories and systems also reflects monocultural and ethnocentric perspectives. One example is the heavy and exclusive emphasis, spoken or unspoken, on the internal locus of control and internal locus of responsibility of the client. The way in which our professional practice structures and delivers counseling services reflects this focus on the client, both for explanations of their experiences and for the solution to their problems.

According to Rotter (1966), *internal locus of control* refers to the belief that one can control the outcome of his or her actions and therefore has control over his or her fate, while *external locus of control* implies attribution of outcomes to external events, and thus one has less control over his or her fate. This theory has generated a large amount of research in various areas of psychology, including clinical, health, and counseling psychology. Results have largely favored internal locus of control as it is associated with higher achievement motivation, superior coping strategies, better mental health, higher quality of life, and so on (Maltby, Day, & Macaskill, 2007). On the other hand, research has also shown that ethnic minority members, individuals with low social class status, and women tend to have higher external locus of control than men and those from the middle class (D. W. Sue, 1978).

The individualistic orientation of the culture also tends to lead to assigning internal locus of responsibilities for both explanation of problems (e.g., fundamental attribution error; see Ross, 1977) and for solutions to the problem (e.g., the notion that changing our thoughts and behaviors will lead to changes in our feelings; see Glasser's [1965] *Reality Therapy*). In counseling practice, interventions are more often than not focused on how to help the client to change individual behaviors, assuming that it is the client's responsibility to "get better" or "correct what is broken." Clients' social and cultural realities have not been given due attention in regard to how we treat and counsel them. In fact, until recently when social justice counseling entered the discussion (Constantine, Hage, Kindaichi, & Bryant, 2007), internal locus of responsibility had been largely assumed and implied in all our counseling theories and systems.

The recent movement in promoting evidence-based treatment (EBT) further illustrates the fundamental principle and practice in mental health care in the United States. Although this movement is intended to promote quality of care by identifying and adopting psychological approaches and techniques that are based on the best available research evidence (Sackett, Straus, Richardson, Rosenberg, & Haynes, 2000), the application of EBT for understanding and evaluating psychological changes with culturally diverse clients is problematic for a number of reasons.

First, the EBT movement has been largely based on the Western empiricism of internal causal effects and fails to include specific cultural experiences of American minority populations (G. Hall, 2001). The exclusive reliance on objectively observable evidence in controlled clinical trials leaves little consideration for individual variations as related to different cultural contexts.

Secondly, when clinical trials are conducted, it is imperative that the samples observed are representative of the populations to which the findings will be generalized. Unfortunately, ethnic and cultural minorities have been much underrepresented in those clinical trials, which presents apparent issues when applying research findings and outcomes to inform practice for all populations (D. W. Sue & Sue, 2008). To observe the behavior of a specific group and then apply treatment recommendations to those whose cultural group was not included in the clinical trial calls into question the validity and appropriateness of the recommendation/intervention.

Finally, the recruitment of diverse and underrepresented populations for clinical trials could be problematic if the theoretical frameworks under investigation have known limitations for treating diverse and underrepresented groups in the first place. Additional concerns include the cultural differences between the Western medical model of health and treatment interventions and that of some minority cultures. Clinical trials that have not adequately addressed and accounted for the sociocultural context and experiences of diverse groups offer little benefit to treating the culturally diverse. Enhancing clinical trial participation with diverse populations and with relevant theoretical models is critically important to ensure that the research findings may be generalizable to diverse populations.

Communication Practices

Therapist-client communication is probably the most critical part of the counseling process. The "talking cure" can only be achieved when therapist and client are able to send and receive messages accurately, appropriately, and effectively. Due to the way in which counseling is most often conducted, it is no mystery that YAVIS (young, attractive, verbal, intelligent, and successful) clients are most liked by counselors and viewed as most likely to benefit from counseling (Jennings & Davis, 1977). However, it has also been recognized that clients who can do the best in counseling are most likely to be those who do not need counseling. The critical question about this phenomenon is this: Why does counseling practice lend itself to be effective for those who do not need it but not for those who need it the most?

Although the answers to this question can be multiple and perhaps multidimensional, one obvious answer to consider may lie in the communication characteristics of the traditional practice of counseling. Students of counseling are trained to use standard English and rely heavily on verbal communication in understanding the client and delivering interventions. Moreover, the Euro-American middle-class communication styles (rules of speaking, use of words, etc.) are often assumed and perceived as the proper and/or universal styles (D. W. Sue & Sue, 2008). The biases against various verbal communications (e.g., nonstandard English, foreign languages or accents, low vocabulary) can be translated as seeing the communicator as incompetent, uneducated, or low in intelligence. Clearly, such unexamined biases will influence counseling in that therapists may not understand clients from diverse cultural backgrounds or perceive them and their skills accurately.

Beyond language issues, communication is also heavily shaped by cultures. One way to distinguish cultures as directly related to communication styles is recognizing the level of context—namely, high and low contexts. "Proper" communication is very much determined by this context. Copeland and Griggs (1985) identified the United States along with other countries in North America and Western Europe as having low-context cultures and many cultures in the Eastern part of the globe as high in context. According to Edward Hall (1976), *low-context cultures* are generally linear, individualistic, and action oriented, and people in these cultures value logic, facts, and directness. Interpersonal communications in these cultures are expected to be straightforward, concise, and precise. But in *high-context cultures* that are more relational, collectivist, intuitive, and contemplative, interpersonal relationships, group harmony, and consensus to individual achievements are highly valued. Interpersonal communications in such cultures do not strive for precision or straightforwardness, but rather treat context (e.g., speakers' tone of voice, facial expression, gestures, personal status, family history) as more important than words. Yu and Gu (1990) pointed out that

Han Xu (implicit communication) is a social rule in Chinese culture, and effective communication should be contained, reserved, implicit, and indirect. Clearly, such communication is less governed by reason than by intuition or feelings. This example suggests that the dominant communication style in the United States may fail when applied to counseling ethnic minorities or internationals with different cultural backgrounds.

Another characteristic of communication in counseling is the focus on emotions in the process of healing. Although some theoretical approaches (e.g., cognitive, behavioral) do not rely on emotional sharing as much in establishing therapeutic relationships and pursuing corrective experiences and behavior changes, most counselors would view being emotional and emotional sharing as healthy behaviors indicative of trust and motivation to change. However, many cultures are not as emotive as the American culture. In fact, in some cultures emotional restraint is viewed as signaling psychological strength and is highly respected, and being emotional is viewed as weak or inappropriate in most interpersonal relationships (Yu & Gu, 1990).

Self-disclosure is another cultural behavior that is expected of counseling clients, and it is seen as a healthy personality trait, shows the ability to trust, and indicates a sincerity for change throughout the counseling process. In short, self-disclosure is regarded as a desirable counseling goal. Although research supports that self-disclosure could help with interpersonal relationship building (Barefoot et al., 1998; Steel, 1991), it is culturally insensitive and inappropriate to expect some ethnic minority clients to self-disclose. In fact, for some ethnic minority cultures, disclosing family information to strangers may be viewed negatively and withholding intimate material may be seen as a strength (LaFromboise, 1998). Yet the lack of self-disclosure or discomfort with self-disclosing demonstrated by some ethnic minorities is often interpreted negatively and believed to reflect their resistance, mistrust, or paranoia. Clearly, this perceived desirability for and reliance on self-disclosure in counseling may be disadvantageous or even victimize ethnic minority clients.

An example of how expected self-disclosure could work against some ethnic minority clients can be seen in a counseling context whereby a White counselor erroneously perceives an angry African American client's refusal to disclose personal information as passive aggressive, while the person's behavior can be explained by both cultural and sociopolitical considerations (Ridley, 2005). Although substantial importance has been given to self-disclosure in U.S. counseling practices, it is noteworthy that research has indicated that self-disclosure does not predict counseling outcomes for some ethnic minorities (Kim et al., 2003).

As discussed above, the monocultural nature of our counseling theories and practices has made the counseling profession unfit in serving the culturally diverse without some fundamental multicultural transformation of what we learn and what we do. As societies and communities become more and more culturally diverse, counseling professionals must be willing to adopt a culture-centered approach toward understanding the world and the people with whom they work.

A Reflection on the Critical Role of Culture

Culture influences our clients' dreams, attitudes, fears, desires, and so on. As a clinician, if I cannot understand my clients as cultural beings, I cannot understand the very essence of who they are as humans. How then can I serve them? On the most basic level, if I do not understand the ways in which culture influences my clients, it is very easy for me to make assumptions and allow my biases to guide my conceptualization and therapeutic work. This is not only harmful in that I distance myself from empathetic understanding of my client, but it is also dangerous.

Numerous times the question of whether or not we can fake empathy has arisen in my graduate training. My response is that one can fake sympathy, but one will never successfully fake empathy because empathy is true identification with our clients as we stand in their shoes and experience what they experience. And if someone were to tell me that he or she understands my experience yet makes inaccurate assumptions about my culture, I know the person is either speaking falsely or he or she is uneducated. I think this is one of the fastest ways to create an emotional and psychological distance between a counselor and a client. This is also dangerous in that a client may not return to counseling and will not receive the treatment that is needed. We may also unwittingly reinforce harmful and discriminatory stereotypes. Counseling is not a "one size fits all" process in which we ask our clients to mold their cultural identity based on our framework. Rather, we continuously stretch ourselves in our cultural awareness and understanding so that we can mold our framework based on their cultural identity.

—Florence F., an Armenian, female, counseling psychology student

A Call for Multicultural Professional Identity Development in Transforming the Field of Counseling

Ethnocentric monoculturalism is a dysfunctional perspective that is responsible for psychological colonization (Fanon, 1967). The failure of our counseling profession to effectively serve socially and culturally diverse individuals and communities in our pluralistic society of the United States can be explained by ethnocentric monoculturalism. Even with good intentions, practicing counseling without sufficient awareness, respect, acceptance, and understanding of cultural diversity can do great harm to marginalized groups, including persons who are racially, culturally, and socially diverse (Leininger, 1978). In addition, counseling practice informed by ethnocentric monoculturalism is both unethical and professionally unacceptable due to the potential to harm and ineffectively diagnose and treat diverse consumers of counseling and mental health interventions.

In the 21st century, monoculturalism and ethnocentrism must be eradicated as our communities within the United States and around the world are becoming more and more diverse. The time is now for the counseling profession to engage in unmasking and deconstructing the values, biases, and assumptions that are characteristic of ethnocentric monoculturalism. This process, however, cannot be accomplished by simply adopting the "melting pot" or "assimilation" guiding principles by blending the different cultures in the United States. The blending of cultures (i.e., assimilation) is just a glamorized form of monoculturalism that aims at a uniformed and homogeneous consolidation of cultures (D. W. Sue & Sue, 2008). Counseling theorists, educators, and practitioners will need to develop a multicultural professional identity so they can begin the process of reconstructing, transforming, and decolonizing the existing knowledge of theories and practices of counseling to include multicultural perspectives and a focus on multicultural contexts. We define *professional multicultural identity* as the following:

> Sense of self as a counselor who defines one's own personal and professional roles with a set of attitudes, beliefs, values, motives, experiences, skills, and practices that enable oneself to accurately understand and effectively intervene on behalf of clients and communities in our culturally pluralistic society. A necessary component of this identity is being a non- and anti-ist in all dimensions of diversity and supporting social justice for all.

A multicultural professional identity will allow the counselor to operate with a multicultural consciousness and become both intellectually and emotionally available in helping the socially oppressed and culturally diverse members of society. The development of this identity is an ongoing process that progresses throughout the life span and is continuously renewed as the environment changes.

Multicultural Professional Identity and the Profession's Ethical Standards

In our culturally diverse society, it is imperative that counselors have a sound ethical foundation and conscience from which to base their clinical judgments. The demographic landscape of the United States is rapidly changing from a nation where the majority of its members are White and from European American backgrounds to a society in which residents from non-European backgrounds represent the majority (D'Andrea & Arrendondo, 2002). It is predicted that Whites who represented three fourths of the U.S. population in 1990 will no longer be the majority group by the year 2050 (D. W. Sue, 1996). This changing face of America means that counselors will work with clients who are culturally different from themselves. Possessing a sound multicultural professional identity will help counselors to understand the nature of their ethical responsibilities as related to providing services to culturally diverse clients and promoting the values of the profession. Multicultural scholars have emphasized that counselors who provide services to culturally diverse clients but who are not trained or competent to do so are behaving unethically (D. W. Sue, Arredondo, & McDavis, 1992). Awareness and knowledge of one's own worldview and the worldview of ethnically, racially, and socially diverse others is of utmost importance when applying culturally appropriate treatment. Counselors must give consideration to culture-centered adaptations in their treatment response as our changing demographics will no longer allow for the minimization or trivialization of the role of culture in ethical reasoning.

In the early years of the counseling profession, the impact of cultural diversity was largely ignored. Specifically, Wrenn (1962, 1985) introduced us to the concept of *cultural encapsulation*, which refers to a tendency for people to treat others relative to their own cultural perspective while disregarding important cultural differences. To clarify further, the culturally encapsulated counselor embraces and imposes one set of assumptions that are based on dominant cultural values as being universal while disregarding any cultural variations or influences that might impact client progress. Cultural encapsulation, therefore, sets the stage for counselors to be insensitive to cultural variations and binds them to their own narrow perspective. According to Remley and Herlihy (2005), culturally encapsulated counselors often ignore evidence that challenges or disconfirms their own assumptions, which perpetuates stereotypical thinking. Scholars believe that cultural encapsulation may be the most predominant deterrent to the implementation of multiculturalism in counseling treatment and ethical decision making. Welfel (2010) noted that in order for the ethical ideals of the profession to be met, professionals must avoid cultural encapsulation, reject simplistic notions of culture and diversity, develop cultural awareness, and acknowledge that few counseling interactions are monocultural.

More recently, attention to multiculturalism and its impact on the counseling profession has become so intense that some have called this movement psychology's "fourth force" (Pedersen, 1999). Although much attention to cultural diversity has ensued, some scholars contend that this aspect of counseling practice has not yet achieved the attention it deserves (D. W. Sue & Sue, 2008). Therefore, it is not surprising that the ethical implications of a multicultural society on counseling practice have been extensively discussed as evidenced by multicultural considerations in the 2014 revision of the ACA 2005 *Code of Ethics*. Although cultural encapsulation may be the practice of some counselors today, it is believed that most counseling professionals recognize their professional obligation and responsibility to practice in a multiculturally sensitive manner (Lee, 2003). However, Remley and Herlihy (2005) noted that as members of the Western society, counselors have internalized many prejudicial attitudes and biases about the culturally diverse, and fighting and correcting these internalized prejudices is an indispensable process of learning and unlearning in order to reach and sustain multicultural competence. Therefore, helping counseling professionals and counselors-in-training develop a multicultural professional identity is critically important so that they do not fall prey to these internalized biases and thereby practice discrimination and social injustices unknowingly.

As counselors-in-training prepare themselves to practice ethically, it is imperative within the spirit of the code of ethics that all of the ethical standards be embraced as multicultural standards and not just those that explicitly focus on honoring diversity (Remley & Herlihy, 2005). We must acknowledge that the ethical reasoning of counselors is embedded within the counselor's worldview, which is influenced by sociocultural conditioning. Moreover, moral principles provide the foundation from which our ethical reasoning is based, and yet these principles—autonomy, nonmaleficence, beneficence, justice (Beauchamp & Childress, 1983), and fidelity (Kitchener, 1984)—that have risen to prominence and become known as "The Golden Five" are not universally endorsed by all cultures. In order to avoid culturally encapsulated ethical reasoning, these moral principles must be interpreted through a multicultural lens (Remley & Herlihy, 2005).

The principle of respect for *autonomy* (i.e., self-determination, and freedom to make choices for oneself) may be counter to some clients' cultural beliefs and practices, which inform making choices and decisions in the context of family, community, or other support networks. The principle of autonomy should therefore be viewed as multicultural autonomy (Burn, 1992) so that clients' cultural beliefs are considered in treatment planning, goal setting, and the overall counseling process.

Nonmaleficence as an ethical principle means "First, do no harm," which includes refraining from actions that risk hurting clients, either intentionally or unintentionally. Counselors working with culturally diverse clients who lack multicultural competence may unintentionally harm their diverse clients. The principle of nonmaleficence, which has been called the most fundamental ethical principle for medical and human service professionals, requires counselors to use only interventions that will not likely harm clients. Possessing a multicultural professional identity is critical to upholding the "First, do no harm" principle.

Counselors who intend to uphold the principle of *beneficence* recognize their responsibility to do good (i.e., duty to help their clients and society in general) and to engage in professional activities that promote the public welfare. Counselors who are unaware of their dominant power position and how to use it wisely when working with culturally diverse clients may assume they know better than their clients and their families what is in the best interest of their clients. Multicultural scholars have asserted that ethical decisions are made *with* the client rather than *for* the client and further encourage counselors not to replicate in their counseling relationships the power dynamics that are pervasive in society and create injustices for marginalized cultural groups (Remley & Herlihy, 2005).

The principle of *justice* is the counselor's obligation to act fairly and equitably in terms of access to resources and treatment and to not discriminate against others. This principle is particularly relevant when working with clients whose difficulties arise from discrimination and social injustices. The risk of violating this principle is greatest for counselors who stereotype a group and fail to implement strategies that will empower clients to cope with the adversities of their environment. Multiculturally competent counselors who are aware of inequalities in their process, agencies, and services determine the advocacy efforts needed to address injustice.

Faithful commitments to the promises made to our clients and to the truth are characteristic of the principle of *fidelity*. Counselors place clients' interests above their own. Because of the inherent power that the counselor holds, fidelity is of utmost importance. Clients of all backgrounds expect to be able to believe what the counselor says.

Summary

This chapter points out that counseling practice in the United States has largely been monocultural in nature, and it does not meet the needs of the culturally diverse. This recognition informs our call for counselors-in-training to begin their work toward developing multicultural competence, which is no longer a choice. It is unethical to practice counseling without multicultural competence in our diverse society. Further, we argue that multicultural competence development is largely rooted in the multicultural professional identity of the counselor.

Takeaway Messages

1. Current counseling practice is still largely monocultural in nature.
2. Failure to consider the role of social and cultural contexts of diverse clients may do harm.
3. It is the ethical and professional responsibility of counselors-in-training to become multiculturally competent.
4. To become multiculturally competent, one has to develop a multicultural professional identity.

A Reflection: My Formulation of a Multicultural Professional Identity

My formation of a multicultural professional identity started with my awareness of my own cultural identity. I particularly remember my realization that after the attack on the World Trade Center, walking through an airport as myself, a White man, was a very different experience than walking through that same airport as a Muslim or a person from the Middle East. This realization was earth-shattering for me. It caused me to question my assumptions and my beliefs. I realized that these same sorts of stigmas had influenced my ability to relate to others. As hard as this is to say, I had prevented myself from forming personal relationships with other people simply because of their religious or ethnic identity! I was determined to shift my paradigm of seeing and relating to people.

After entering my graduate counseling program, I was challenged by my professors and peers to continue pursuing my paradigm shift and realized that my ability to form relationships with others was dependent on my ability to recognize my own biases/privileges and be culturally sensitive. I chose to immerse myself in diverse environments whenever I could. For example, I intentionally got closely involved with the lesbian/gay/bisexual/transgender (LGBT) community on campus in order to better understand and experience the specific struggles of sexual orientation and gender identity minority students. Through this experience, I came face to face with the real suffering that many LGBT individuals encounter as the result of social oppression. I realized my own heteronormative views and was then able to change them.

I also owe my first African American male client for challenging my egocentric and ethnocentric worldviews. I walked into this therapeutic relationship feeling that I had a great deal of self-awareness of my own White privilege and significant sympathy for the struggles of racial/ethnic minorities. This therapeutic experience, however, brought a whole new level of cultural understanding. I listened to the heart and soul of this client and was able to empathically feel his deep fear and anger that was deeply rooted in his social experiences. I learned to listen to him and allow myself to be affected emotionally. As a result, he reported being surprised that he could talk to a White person and feel good about it, and I felt genuinely changed by him and started questioning my views on mental health and interventions for ethnic minority members.

—Bill T., European American, cisgender, male, counseling psychologist

Recommended Resources

Readings

American Counseling Association. (2014). *Code of ethics.* Retrieved from http://www.counseling.org/knowledge-center/ethics

Media

American Counseling Association. (n.d.). Archived Webinars. Dr. Courtland C. Lee's webinar *Why Does Culture Matter? Isn't Counseling Just Counseling Regardless?* Dr. Lee is director of the counselor education program at the University of Maryland–College Park. Available from http://www.counseling.org/Resources/Webinars.aspx

Gua Sha/The Treatment. (2009, September 9). Video clip portraying the different cultural values between Western society and a Chinese American family. Available from http://www.youtube.com/watch?v=gMq9FDq_A0s

References

Allport, G. W. (1961). *Pattern and growth in personality.* New York, NY: Holt, Rinehart & Winston.

Altman, N. (2007). Toward the acceptance of human similarity and difference. In J. Muran & J. Muran (Eds.), *Dialogues on difference: Studies of diversity in the therapeutic relationship* (pp. 15–25). Washington, DC: American Psychological Association. doi:10.1037/11500-001

American Counseling Association. (2014). *Code of ethics.* Retrieved from http://www.counseling.org/knowledge-center/ethics

Arkin, R. M., Appelman, A. J., & Burger, J. M. (1980). Social anxiety, self-presentation, and the self-serving bias in causal attribution. *Journal of Personality and Social Psychology, 38*(1), 23–35. doi:10.1037/0022-3514.38.1.23

Barefoot, J. C., Maynard, K. E., Beckham, J. C., Brummett, B. H., Hooker, K., & Siegler, H. C. (1998). *Trust, health, and longevity. Journal of Behavioral Medicine, 21*(6), 517–526. doi:10.1023/A:1018792528008

Beauchamp, T. L., & Childress, J. F. (1983). *Principles of biomedical ethics* (2nd ed.). Oxford, England: Oxford University Press.

Black-Gutman, D., & Hickson, F. (1996). The relationship between racial attitudes and social-cognitive development in children: An Australian study. *Developmental Psychology, 32*(3), 448–456. doi:10.1037/0012-1649.32.3.448

Bobo, L., & Zubrinsky, C. L. (1996). Attitudes on residential integration: Perceived status differences, mere in-group preference, or racial prejudice? *Social Forces, 74*(3), 883–909. doi:10.1093/sf/74.3.883

Bullough, V. (2000). Transgenderism and the concept of gender. *The International Journal of Transgenderism.* Retrieved from http://www.iiav.nl/ezines/web/ijt/9703/numbers/symposion/bullough.htm

Burn, D. (1992). Ethical implications in cross-cultural counseling and training. *Journal of Counseling and Development, 70*(5), 578–583. doi:10.1002/j.1556-6676.1992.tb01664.x

Comas-Díaz, L. (2000). An ethnopolitical approach to working with people of color. *American Psychologist, 55*(11), 1319–1325. doi:10.1037/0003-066X.55.11.1319

Comas-Díaz, L. (2011). Multicultural theories of psychotherapy. In R. J. Corsini & D. Wedding (Eds.), *Current psychotherapies* (9th ed., pp. 536–567). Belmont, CA: Brooks/Cole.

Constantine, M. G., Hage, S. M., Kindaichi, M. M., & Bryant, R. M. (2007). Social justice and multicultural issues: Implications for the practice and training of counselors and counseling psychologists. *Journal of Counseling and Development, 85*(1), 24–29.

Copeland, L., & Griggs, L. (1985). *Going international.* New York, NY: Random House.

D'Andrea, M., & Arredondo, P. (2002). Multicultural competence: A national campaign. *Counseling Today, 45,* 3, 31.

Division of Counseling Psychology, Committee on Definition. (1956). Counseling psychology as a specialty. *American Psychologist, 11,* 282–285.

Ebrey, P. B. (1981). *Chinese civilization and society: A sourcebook.* New York, NY: Free Press.

Fanon, F. (1967). *A dying colonialism.* New York, NY: Grove.

Feeley, M., DeRubeis, R. J., & Gelfand, L. A. (1999). The temporal relation of adherence and alliance to symptom change in cognitive therapy for depression. *Journal of Consulting and Clinical Psychology, 67*(4), 578–582. doi:10.1037/0022-006X.67.4.578

Friedman, A. S., Utada, A., & Morrissey, M. R. (1987). Families of adolescent drug abusers are 'rigid': Are these families either 'disengaged' or 'enmeshed,' or both? *Family Process, 26*(1), 131–148. doi:10.1111/j.1545-5300.1987.00131.x

Glasser, W. (1965). *Reality therapy: A new approach to psychiatry.* New York, NY: Harper & Row.

Glosoff, H. L. (2009). The counseling profession: Historical perspectives and current issues and trends. In D. Capuzzi & D. R. Grossi (Eds.), *Introduction to the counseling profession* (pp. 3–56). Boston, MA: Allyn & Bacon.

Greene, B. (2007). How difference makes a difference. In J. Muran & J. Muran (Eds.), *Dialogues on difference: Studies of diversity in the therapeutic relationship* (pp. 47–63). Washington, DC: American Psychological Association. doi:10.1037/11500-005

Guinier, L. (1994). *The tyranny of the majority.* New York, NY: Free Press.

Hall, E. T. (1976). *Beyond culture.* Garden City, NY: Anchor Books/Doubleday.

Hall, G. (2001). Psychotherapy research with ethnic minorities: Empirical, ethical, and conceptual issues. *Journal of Consulting and Clinical Psychology, 69*(3), 502–510. doi:10.1037/0022-006X.69.3.502

Hill, C. E., & Corbett, M. M. (1993). A perspective on the history of process and outcome research in counseling psychology. *Journal of Counseling Psychology, 40*(1), 3–24. doi:10.1037/0022-0167.40.1.3

Ivey, A. E., D'Andrea, M., Ivey, M. B., & Simek-Morgan, L. (Eds.). (2007). *Theories of counseling and psychotherapy: A multicultural perspective.* Boston, MA: Pearson Education.

Jennings, R. L., & Davis, C. S. (1977). Attraction-enhancing client behaviors: A structured learning approach for "Non-Yavis, Jr." *Journal of Consulting and Clinical Psychology, 45*(1), 135–144. doi:10.1037/0022-006X.45.1.135

Jun, H. (2010). *Social justice, multicultural counseling, and practice: Beyond a conventional approach.* Thousand Oaks, CA: Sage.

Katz, J. H. (1985). The sociopolitical nature of counseling. *The Counseling Psychologist, 13*(4), 615–624. doi:10.1177/0011000085134005

Kim, B. K., Hill, C. E., Gelso, C. J., Goates, M. K., Asay, P. A., & Harbin, J. M. (2003). Counselor self-disclosure, East Asian American client adherence to Asian cultural values, and counseling process. *Journal of Counseling Psychology, 50*(3), 324–332. doi:10.1037/0022-0167.50.3.324

Kitchener, K. S. (1984). Intuition, critical evaluation, and ethical principles: The foundation for ethical decisions in counseling psychology. *The Counseling Psychologist, 12*(3–4), 43–55. doi:10.1177/0011000084123005

LaFromboise, T. D. (1998). American Indian mental health policy. In D. A. Atkinson, G. Morten, & D. W. Sue (Eds.), *Counseling American minorities: A cross-cultural perspective* (pp. 137–158). Boston, MA: McGraw-Hill.

Lake, B. (1985). Concept of ego strength in psychotherapy. *British Journal of Psychiatry, 147*(5), 471–478. doi:10.1192/bjp.147.5.471

Lee, C. C. (2003). *Multicultural issues in counseling: New approaches to diversity* (3rd ed.). Alexandria, VA: American Counseling Association.

Lei, Y., Hu, B., Chen, J., & Duan, C. (2012, June). Therapists' views on why and how they use directives in therapy. In C. Duan (Chair). *Use of therapist directives in China.* Lecture conducted from the Society for Psychotherapy Research symposium, Virginia Beach, VA.

Leininger, M. (1978). *Transcultural nursing: Theories, research, and practice* (2nd ed.). New York, NY: Wiley.

Locust, C. (1985). *Native American Indian beliefs concerning health and unwellness.* Native American Research and Training Center Monograph. Flagstaff: University of Arizona Press.

Lorde, A. (1984). *Sister outsider: Essays & speeches.* Berkley, CA: Crossing Press.

Maltby, J., Day, L., & Macaskill, A. (2007). *Personality, individual differences and intelligence.* Upper Saddle River, NJ: Pearson Prentice Hall.

Minuchin, S. (1974). *Family and family therapy.* Cambridge, MA: Harvard University Press.

Munley, P. H., Duncan, L. E., McDonnell, K. A., & Sauer, E. M. (2004). Counseling psychology in the United States of America. *Counselling Psychology Quarterly, 17,* 247–271.

Neuliep, J. W., & McCroskey, J. C. (1997). Development of a United States and generalized ethnocentrism scale. *Communication Research Reports, 14,* 385–398.

Nickerson, K. J., Helms, J. E., & Terrell, F. (1994). Cultural mistrust, opinions about mental illness, and Black students' attitudes toward seeking psychological help from White counselors. *Journal of Counseling Psychology, 41*(3), 378.

Pedersen, P. (1999). *Multiculturalism as a fourth force.* Washington, DC: Taylor & Francis.

Phillips, C., & Bowling, B. (2003). Racism, ethnicity, and criminology: Developing minority perspectives. *British Journal of Criminology, 43*(2), 269–290. doi.org/10.1093/bjc/43.2.269

Ponterotto, J. G., Casas, J. M., Suzuki, L. A., & Alexander, C. M. (Eds.). (2001). *Handbook of multicultural counseling* (2nd ed.). Thousand Oaks, CA: Sage.

Remley, T. P., & Herlihy, B. (2005). *Ethical, legal, and professional issues in counseling.* Upper Saddle River, NJ: Pearson Prentice Hall.

Resnick, S., Warmoth, A., & Selin, I. A. (2001). The humanistic psychology and positive psychology connection: Implications for psychotherapy. *Journal of Humanistic Psychology, 41*(1), 73–101. doi:10.1177/0022167801411006

Ridley, C. R. (2005). *Overcoming unintentional racism in counseling and therapy* (2nd ed.). Thousand Oaks, CA: Sage.

Rogers, C. R. (1961). *On becoming a person.* Boston, MA: Houghton Mifflin.

Ross, L. (1977). The intuitive psychologist and his shortcomings: Distortions in the attribution process. In L. Berkowitz (Ed.), *Advances in experimental social psychology* (Vol. 10, pp. 173–220). New York, NY: Academic Press. Retrieved from http://www.sciencedirect.com/science/bookseries/00652601

Rotter, J. B. (1966). Generalized expectancies for internal versus external control of reinforcement. *Psychological Monographs: General and Applied, 80*(1), 1–28. doi:10.1037/h0092976

Sackett, D. L., Straus, S. E., Richardson, W. S., Rosenberg, W., & Haynes, R. B. (2000). *Evidence-based medicine: How to practice and teach EBM* (Vol. 2). London, England: Churchill Livingstone.

Satir, V., & Baldwin, M. (1983). *Satir step by step.* Palo Alto, CA: Science & Behavior Books.

Schwartz, R. C., & Feisthamel, K. P. (2009). Disproportionate diagnosis of mental disorders among African American versus European American clients: Implications for counseling theory, research, and practice. *Journal of Counseling and Development, 87*(3), 295–301.

Seeman, M., & Seeman, T. B. (1983). Health behavior and personal autonomy: A longitudinal study of the sense of control in illness. *Journal of Health and Social Behavior, 24*(2), 144–160. doi.org/10.2307/2136641

Singh, A. A., Boyd, C. J., & Whitman, J. S. (2010). Counseling competencies with transgender and intersex persons. In J. A. Erickson Cornish, B. A. Schreier, L. I. Nadkarni, L. Henderson Metzger, & E. R. Rodolfa (Eds.), *Handbook of multicultural counseling competencies* (pp. 415–441). New York, NY: Wiley.

Snowden, L. R., & Cheung, F. K. (1990). Use of inpatient mental health services by members of ethnic minority groups. *American Psychologist, 45*(3), 347–355. doi:10.1037/0003066X.45.3.347

Steel, J. L. (1991). Interpersonal correlates of trust and self-disclosure. *Psychological Reports, 68*(3, Pt. 2), 1319–1320. doi:10.2466/PR0.68.4.1319-1320

Sue, D., Sue, D. W., & Sue, S. (2006). *Understanding abnormal behavior* (8th ed.). Boston, MA: Houghton Mifflin.

Sue, D. W. (1978). Eliminating cultural oppression in counseling: Toward a general theory. *Journal of Counseling Psychology, 25*, 419–428.

Sue, D. W. (1996). Ethical issues in multicultural counseling. In B. Herlihy & G. Corey (Eds.), *ACA ethical standards casebook* (5th ed., pp. 193–197). Alexandra, VA: American Counseling Association.

Sue, D. W., Arredondo, P., & McDavis, R. J. (1992). Multicultural counseling competencies and standards: A call to the profession. *Journal of Counseling and Development, 70*, 477–486. doi.org/10.1002/j.1556-6676.1992.tb01642.x

Sue, D. W., & Sue, D. (2008). *Counseling the culturally diverse: Theory and practice* (5th ed.). New York, NY: Wiley.

Sumner, W. G. (1906). *Folkways*. Boston, MA: Ginn.

Wampold, B. E. (2001). *The great psychotherapy debate*. Mahwah, NJ: Erlbaum.

Welfel, E. R. (2010). *Ethics in counseling and psychotherapy: Standards, research, and emerging issues* (4th ed.). Belmont, CA: Brooks/Cole, Cengage Learning.

Wrenn, C. G. (1962). *The counselor in a changing world*. Washington, DC: American Personnel and Guidance Association.

Wrenn, C. G. (1985). Afterword: The culturally encapsulated counselor revisited. In P. B. Pedersen (Ed.), *Handbook of cross-cultural counseling and therapy* (pp. 323–329). Westport, CT: Greenwood.

Yu, D. H., & Gu, B. L. (1990). Zhong guo ren de qing mian jiao lu [Chinese face concerns]. In *Zhong guo ren de xin li*: Vol. 3. *Zhong guo ren de mian ju xing ge: Ren qing yu mian zi* (pp. 63–107). Taipei, Taiwan: Zhang lao shi chu ban she.

Zhang, W. (1994). American counseling in the mind of a Chinese counselor. *Journal of Multicultural Counseling and Development, 22*(2), 79–85. Retrieved from http://onlinelibrary.wiley.com/doi/10.1002/j.2161-1912.1994.tb00246.x/pdf

Demands for Multicultural Professional Counseling

If we cannot end now our differences, at least we can help make the world safe for diversity.

—John F. Kennedy

CHAPTER OVERVIEW

There was a time when counselors could expect that their next client to walk through the door would be female, most likely Caucasian, heterosexual, and from an upper-middle-class socioeconomic background. Although this was a common expectation of the past, we know for certain that counselors of the 21st century must not expect their clients to fit this description. Counselors, regardless of their employment setting, will encounter clients from varied racial, ethnic, cultural, and socioeconomic backgrounds. This increased diversity in our counseling consumers places demands on the profession to prepare counseling professionals to be multiculturally competent and responsive to the needs of a diverse society. The demands for multicultural competence serve as the focus of this chapter.

More specifically, this chapter provides a discussion of three major reasons why multicultural counseling competence and multiculturally effective counseling practices are indispensable to the provision of services to people and communities in the 21st century. Knowledge of these three topic areas—(a) presence and history of social oppression, (b) demographic changes in the United States, and (c) globalization movements in all areas of human lives—will help counselors understand the importance of culturally relevant information in the provision of services to their client populations.

SELF-ASSESSMENT OF PRE-EXISTING AWARENESS AND KNOWLEDGE

- What is my understanding of the role of culture in counseling?
- Is everyone influenced by cultures?
- Does social or cultural oppression really exist?
- To what degree do people's social and cultural positions influence their psychological behavior?

LEARNING OBJECTIVES

After reading this chapter, students will be able to do the following:

1. Recognize the need and necessity for multicultural competence in counselor training and development
2. Acknowledge the relevance of cultural and social experiences in individuals' behaviors
3. Articulate the challenges the counseling profession is facing in serving counseling consumers in the 21st century
4. Develop a sense of responsibility to become multiculturally aware, knowledgeable, and skilled

Taking a Moment to Reflect

Prior to beginning our discussion, it will be helpful to reflect on the complex and unique challenges faced by counselors of the 21st century in their provision of services to culturally diverse clients. Case Illustration 2.1 provides opportunity to engage in this moment of reflection.

CASE ILLUSTRATION 2.1

The Case of Dahab

Dahab (pseudonym) is a 19-year-old, African American male who presented to the inpatient psychiatric hospital for a suicidal statement and for auditory hallucinations. He reports being Christian, heterosexual, and a student working on his bachelor's degree in science. His appearance is neat and well maintained. When asked what his ethnicity is, he responded, "They insist that I am Sudanese." When asked what he considers himself, he responded, "That is not important."

Dahab reports that he longs to be with a fellow classmate even though he does not know he exists. At one point he stated, "I will never be happy if I can't be with him." Dahab was raised in the upper class since birth, and his father is believed to be a government worker for Sudan. He seems to have above-average intelligence and has very specific eating habits. Everything has to be placed in a very meticulous and certain way before he will start eating. He is also very focused on language and will not interact with someone whom he finds is not on his same level of education. When somebody tries to interact with him, he comes across as guarded and will point out the person's improper use of English.

Dahab's father and mother are from Sudan, and his father splits his time between Sudan and America. Dahab only sees him on average twice a year. He reports that since he is the oldest male child, he feels as if he needs to represent his family. While he admits to using marijuana daily for the last few years, he denies using alcohol or other drugs. Dahab tells staff members that he hears voices telling him that he will succeed and that he will win. He states that he likes these voices because they motivate him to do the best he can. When staff members try to get Dahab to take medication for the voices, he resists, saying the medications make him "feel stupid." He does not feel as if he needs treatment and feels that he is being held against his will. He has contacted various lawyers, but due to his lack of finances, none will take his case. When Dahab becomes insistent on leaving, his father obtains a lawyer and gains guardianship over him. Upon discharge 3 weeks later, Dahab is medicated and denies hearing voices even though it is apparent that he still is, due to his thought blocking and distant look. He appears groggy, and his overall demeanor is the same, except he speaks slower and sleeps more than initially.

This case demonstrates the complexity and challenge of working with the culturally diverse. Although we do not have specific information about Dahab's mental state and what specific situation or life events may have triggered his "suicidal statement" and his "auditory hallucinations" or how he was treated (including medications prescribed) in the 3 weeks he was hospitalized, we probably could conclude that he did not feel helped or understood and that the treatment provided did not seem to be effective. If we were to work with him in counseling, we may need answers to the following questions:

a. What is his experience as an African American male living in his community in the United States?

b. What questions arise regarding the inconsistency between his reported sexual orientation and interest in another man?

c. How is he viewed by people around him?

d. In what ways has his parents' "foreign" or "immigrant" status influenced him?

e. How is his family's high status in Sudan related to his behavior?

f. Is it possible that his "pathology" reflects cultural behavior or practices?

g. To what degree are his "problematic" behaviors due to his pathology or due to his enculturation?

h. Given our knowledge of counseling theories and practices, how competent are we to work with him?

Excerpt from a Reflection of a Nonbinary Transgender Person

Each individual has a very different way of experiencing his or her gender and sexuality, and a counselor imposing societal binary standards upon clients can do more harm than good. Counselors need to be educated on the lived experiences of transgender, queer, and gender-nonconforming individuals during their schooling/training. It is not just about medical transitions, surgeries, and hormones; it is about how those clients interact with the world, understand themselves and the experiences they have had as a gendered and sexed body, and how they identify rather than how they look. Counselors can understand very little about a person based on how that person looks. Someone who looks at me might think that I am a butch lesbian, but I don't identify as that at all. I identify as a queer, transgender person. I am attracted to multiple genders, and I do not accept the label of *woman* or *lesbian* for myself.

—Eli, a White, nonbinary, transgender person

Although there have not been sufficient answers, ample questions have been raised concerning the efficacy of professional counseling and competence of professional counselors in serving diverse clients effectively. What is known, however, is that professional counseling in the 21st century, whether practiced in the United States or in any foreign land, will need to meet the needs of culturally diverse individuals, groups, and communities. Due to the prevalence of cultural diversity in our nation and the importance of embracing diversity in order to provide effective counseling, our profession's ability to prepare multiculturally competent counselors and develop multiculturally efficacious counseling approaches will directly affect the sustainability of our profession as well as define its future. In order to meet the challenges of effective counseling in the 21st century, we must first comprehend the vast need for multiculturally sensitive and relevant counseling practices and understand the urgency and necessity of addressing multicultural competence in counselor training and theory development. In this chapter, we discuss three broad reasons that necessitate multiculturally competent counselors and efficacious practice if our profession is to remain indispensable.

The Presence and History of Cultural and Social Oppression

GUIDED CLASSROOM EXERCISE 2.1

Are We in the Same Social Reality?

Have 10 to 15 diverse students line up in a horizontal line. If there is no racial diversity among students, ask one student to take the role of an African American, one a Native American, one a Latino or Latina, and one an Asian American. Tell students that if a statement being read is "true" to them, they take a step forward. This continues until all statements are read in each section.

Section 1

1. If I should need to move, I can be pretty sure of renting or purchasing housing in an area that I can afford and in which I would want to live.
2. I can go shopping alone most of the time, pretty well assured that I will not be followed or harassed.
3. Whether I use checks, credit cards, or cash, I can count on my skin color not to work against the appearance of financial reliability.
4. If a traffic cop pulls me over or if the IRS audits my tax return, I can be sure I haven't been singled out because of my race.
5. I can go home from most meetings of organizations I belong to feeling somewhat tied in rather than isolated, out of place, outnumbered, unheard, held at a distance, or feared.
6. I can take a job with an affirmative action employer without having coworkers suspect that I got it because of race.

"Let's pause a moment and look at each other . . . are we in the same social reality?"

Section 2

7. In my work situation, I can reasonably believe that I am not underpaid because of my sex.
8. I am far less likely to face sexual harassment at work than are my other gender coworkers.

(Continued)

(Continued)

9. If I have children and a career, no one will think I'm selfish for not staying at home.
10. If I am heterosexual, it's incredibly unlikely that I'll ever be beaten up by a spouse or lover.
11. I can speak in public to a large group without putting my sex on trial.

"Let's pause a moment and look at each other . . . are we in the same social reality?"

Section 3

12. I have immediate access to my spouse in case of an accident or emergency.
13. I can raise, adopt, and teach children without people believing that I will molest them or force them into my personal sexuality preference.
14. I can share health, auto, and homeowners' insurance policies at reduced rates.
15. I can go wherever I wish and know that I will not be harassed, beaten, or killed because of my sexuality.
16. I do not have to "come out" to explain to people who I am and wait for their reactions.
17. I know that I will not be fired from a job or denied a promotion based on my sexuality.

Processing and Discussion

In a small group of four to five students, share how you feel about being in "ahead" or "behind" positions in the exercise in each section. How does it help us see the different social realities for different people? How does it help us see the privilege-oppression dynamics present in our society?

It is an undeniable fact that social and cultural oppression and injustice have been part of the recent history of the United States. A convincing example is that some people are provided with racial privilege while others suffer from racial oppression solely due to their color of skin (Johnson, 2006). Regardless of their social class, gender, sexual orientation, age, education, religion, disability status, and so on, the majority of people enjoy White racial privileges because they belong to the White racial group, and people of color are recipients of unearned disadvantages and oppression because they belong to non-White racial groups. White privilege (or White skin privilege) is an expression of power and social dominance of White individuals over racial/ethnic minorities in the same social, political, or economic spaces (e.g., community, workplace, income) through the attainment of unearned immunities and benefits (McIntosh, 1998). White privilege may be reflected in both obvious and less obvious unearned and unspoken advantages that White individuals may not recognize they possess or have access to. A more thorough discussion on White privilege and its role in perpetuating oppression and injustices that directly impact the mental health of our clients is provided in Chapter 7.

Oppression by Isms

From the "Are We in the Same Social Reality?" exercise, we can see that in our society individuals with different group memberships in race, gender, sexual orientation, and other diversity demographics have different social realities. Those with majority group memberships enjoy unearned advantages while those with minority group memberships are put in disadvantageous positions. The ideological foundation for such social injustice in the United States includes racism, sexism, heterosexism, and other isms. Such isms directly and indirectly influence the mental health of our nation and mental health services by our profession. For example, although many have hoped and believed that racism is a phenomenon of the past, it has been one of the reasons that social oppression and injustice persist and continue to plague our society (Thompson & Neville, 1999). President Clinton's Advisory Board to the President's Initiative on Race (1998) conducted a thorough investigation and concluded that racism was one of the most divisive forces in the United States; racial legacies of the past continued to haunt current policies and practices that created unfair disparities between minority and majority groups; and racial inequalities were so deeply ingrained in society that they were nearly invisible. Researchers and theorists generally agree that modern racism is more and more likely to be disguised or concealed and is also presented in ambiguous and nebulous forms (Sue et al., 2007).

The presence of racism and other isms is why our democratic society has an unjust side in terms of its members' access to resources, wealth, and opportunities. Various minority statuses, for instance, are often the bases for undue disadvantages and even lack of basic rights. Some people may suffer from such disadvantages due to multiple minority statuses even if they may benefit from privileges due to some of their cultural identities. For instance, White people benefit from White privilege, but they may experience other forms of oppression due to reasons other than being White, such as sexual orientation, age, social class, disability, and so forth. Lesbians, gay men, and same-sex couples, for example, do not have the same access to rights and resources that heterosexual individuals and couples enjoy. Of course, the intersections of these different types of social oppression would further victimize individuals who fall into multiple categories of disenfranchisement. For instance, racism and heterosexism may intersect to further disadvantage a gay person of color. Sexism, racism, and classism have a combined negative effect on a woman of color and of low social class.

Such oppression has been maintained through mechanisms at various levels, including the individual level, where marginalized people experience discrimination and stereotypes, and the societal or structural level, where marginalized people suffer from institutionalized inequality (McNamee & Miller, 2004). As a result, individuals from socially marginalized minority groups face significant prejudice and discrimination as well as lack of accesses and resources in society. Such inequalities have pervasive influence on the psychological health of Americans with minority statuses because they have created negative social experiences and polluted social environments. Living in an unsupportive and even hostile environment, people from underrepresented cultural and social backgrounds may understandably experience more psychological stress and traumatization and be more likely to suffer from decompensation and emotional difficulties (Sue & Sue, 2013).

GUIDED CLASSROOM EXERCISE 2.2

Self Reflection: How Aware Am I?

Reflect and share your answers to the questions with which you identify.

For White students

a. When was my first personal encounter with a person of color? What was that experience like for me?
b. In what ways do I agree or disagree with this statement: *Not all people can "just be themselves" in our society due to their skin color.* How do I feel about it?

For students of color

a. How do I feel about White people and about myself in relation to White people?
b. In what ways do I feel that I am better prepared to work as a counselor in the 21st century than White students?

A Reflection of an Asian American on Racial Identity

If anyone had asked me to discuss my racial identity development 2 years ago, I would not have known what to say besides the fact that I had to acculturate to the North American way of life when my family and I moved to the United States from South Asia 20 years ago when I was in second grade. It was relatively easy for me to transition into the new culture since I came here at such a young age. We moved around to a few different states, and despite this whole process, I never truly was able to see how my race played a factor in my experiences here. Before coming to graduate school, I worked hard at being Americanized—in other words, "acting White"—in order to fit in with society, and I was unintentionally able to avoid any significant aversive consequences due to my race. While this may have made me blind to the racism that ethnic minorities face in the United States, having the perception that we, despite our race, all truly have equal opportunities gave me the confidence to handle situations as if my race would never work against me and that all people's lives are affected solely by their actions, no matter their race.

This worked very well for me until I began experiencing instances (which I am now realizing began as early as elementary school) in which I was not treated as well as my Caucasian colleagues or friends. At first, I began internalizing these instances and thought it was something I did or something I was lacking that made people treat me this way. Now, due to my experiences as a doctoral counseling psychology student and other professional positions I have held in the field, I realize that ethnic minorities all around the country have faced situations similar to mine. Through my education and stories of racial discrimination experienced by my family for decades, I slowly realized that these acts were not committed due to my personal flaws but because of my race.

Never had I felt *so powerless* than the day I realized that no matter how hard I try at something, there are going to be instances in which my race is going to work against me. There were times that the feelings of injustice or anger I experienced were so powerful that I felt hopeless. I reached out to other ethnic minorities for support and realized that due to the resources I have available to me, it is my responsibility to advocate not only for myself but also for other ethnic minorities who may not have the same resources as I do.

Over time, I have learned not only which of my White friends understand these racial dynamics that exist in our society but also which of them fail to see—or even deny—the existence of these issues. Having these realizations and interactions has given me hope that maybe one day we can all accept and be proud of who we are and what group we belong to, peacefully coexist with one another, and live in a world where it is not only the law that says that everyone should have equal rights and opportunities but also that all people themselves *truly do have* equal rights and opportunities.

—Meera G., a cisgender, female, Asian American, counseling psychology doctoral student

Culturally Diverse Clients and Needed Counseling Services

Logically, individuals who suffer from social oppression and inequality need more, not less, psychological support and counseling service. Yet it has been well documented that there has been significant underuse of professional mental health services by ethnic and racial minorities and those of low socioeconomic status while the mental illness prevalence rates among these minorities are similar to those of the majorities (Sue & Sue, 2013). It is not hard to understand why mental health service did not reach those who need it. The two related and obvious reasons are (1) individuals with socially disenfranchised group memberships did not trust the mental health profession, including providers of service and the service they provide and (2) the mental health services were culturally biased and failed to meet the needs of the culturally diverse.

In discussing the longtime criticism of the counseling profession for its failure to serve the ethnic minorities, Remy (1995) pointed out that "ethnic minorities continue to be largely underrepresented and underserved in mental health agencies across the nation" and blamed "the prejudicial practices toward minority groups; the lack of knowledge on the part of mental health providers, of the negative impact of poverty and discrimination on the psychological well-being of ethnic minorities; and the unavailability of adequate counseling services" (p. 14). In a study of counseling use by ethnic minority students on college campuses, Kearney, Draper, and Baron (2003) had 1,166 African American, Asian American, Caucasian, and Hispanic help-seeking students from over 40 universities nationwide fill out a counseling outcome measure. They found that Caucasian students attended significantly more sessions than all other groups. Further, the greatest distress was found at intake in Asian American clients, followed by Hispanic, African American, and Caucasian students.

These observations should be seen as a call for our profession to mend itself and train competent practitioners to do better with what we have failed—serving all members of our society effectively. Multicultural counselor competence is necessary, and multicultural efficacy of the counseling practice is imperative to sustain our profession in the diverse world of the 21st century. It should be recognized that the psychological care for culturally oppressed and socially disenfranchised individuals, groups, and communities must offer corrective experiences so that culturally diverse clients can feel truly understood and validated and be provided with effective interventions. In order to meet this demand, counselors have to develop themselves to be multiculturally competent persons and improve counseling practice to be multiculturally effective. Otherwise, counseling could be another venue for continuing and reinforcing social oppression, which is in violation of our profession's fundamental ethical principle of beneficence and is counter to the basic humanitarian value and ethical principle of doing no harm.

An Experiential Learning Activity

Watch *Color of Fear*, a film produced by Lee Mun Wah (1994), a community therapist and diversity trainer. In the film, eight men share their thoughts and experiences about race and ethnicity. The film is 90 minutes long and can be viewed in its entirety or in parts, followed by discussions. Some possible discussion topics:

1. Could you describe your emotions at this moment? Whose experiences affected you the most?
2. With whom do you identify the most? In what ways? What is your agreement or disagreement with him?
3. With whom do you least agree? What do you think are the reasons?
4. What did you learn about race that you were not aware of (or did not believe) before?
5. Who would post the most challenge for you if he were your client? Why?

6. Who would be the least challenge for you to work with as a client? Why?
7. In what ways does the film demonstrate the need for multicultural counseling?
8. In what ways does the film demonstrate the need for the counseling profession to address social justice?

Is Multicultural Competence Really Needed?

To illustrate how multiculturally effective care by multiculturally competent counselors is necessary, let's consider Dahab from Case Illustration 2.1 again. No matter what criteria we use, we probably see that the treatment he received (mainly confinement and medication) was not optimal, at least not in terms of engaging him and helping him improve his overall well-being. We discussed this case along a series of questions earlier in this chapter. Now let's switch the focus to ourselves. In what ways are we feeling that we are ready and competent to help him in a multiculturally sensitive and efficacious way?

a. What is my first impression of Dahab?
b. Do I feel genuine respect toward him? Why?
c. How do I see him as "abnormal" or "sick" according to what I consider as normal and healthy?
d. How confident do I feel that I can earn his trust? Why?
e. What do I think is the importance of having a good therapeutic relationship with him?
f. Is my race or other cultural identities (e.g., American citizenship, gender, sexuality, socioeconomic status, education) influencing how I see and react to him? In what ways?
g. How likely is it I would have a different perception of Dahab if he were a White man from a middle-class family? Why?
h. How do I feel about his interest in men if I have a nonconforming sexual orientation?

These questions lead us toward the awareness that who we are and how multiculturally aware and competent we are will influence how we work with our culturally diverse clients. Due to the presence of social oppression and privilege, our work with clients can't be "one size fits all" or consist of "treating everyone the same." The history and experience of social oppression and privilege have created different levels of consciousness for people in different social positions, which may lead people to see different realities. Unless we devote ourselves to developing our multicultural selves and multicultural competence, we will not be able to help and will likely harm our culturally diverse clients. G. Talib Wright (2014), the director of the counseling resource center at Morehouse College, offered this in an article in the *Chronicle of Higher Education*:

> Black people in America are united, in part, by a shared experience of oppression. . . . Oppression-related assumptions often play out within a larger societal context. For some young black men, the shooting death of Michael Brown, an unarmed black teenager in Ferguson, Missouri, is a reminder of the depths of second-class citizenship in an unjust law enforcement system. Black men are often very reluctant to share personal stories of trauma because of the associated indignation and humiliation. So the trauma often goes untreated or is ignored but continues to disrupt personal and professional life. We have found that discussing a significant news event with students, both in therapy and during campus-wide events, can help build rapport and lead to the uncovering of important personal trauma relevant to the therapeutic relationship. (para. 8)

We can't overemphasize the negative role of oppression and social injustice in our diverse clients' mental health. Traditionally, psychotherapy has failed to reach people with minority racial, ethnic, social, and cultural backgrounds and has also let down diverse clients by failing to account for the effects of their experience of social oppression. Failure to recognize the negative impact of social oppression and injustice on individuals' psychological health not only contributes to ineffective clinical treatment but also has potential to do harm. McLellan (1999) articulated nicely our counseling profession's shortcomings: "Created by the mainstream to serve the mainstream, psychotherapy has failed marginalized people in fundamental ways" (p. 315).

Research has shown that inadequate services for the culturally diverse have resulted in consistent underuse of counseling services by ethnic and racial minorities (Ponterotto, Casas, Suzuki, & Alexander, 2001), overdiagnosis of various mental disorders of the culturally diverse (Schwartz & Feisthamel, 2009), and lack of trust toward counseling among those who have experienced social oppression (Nickerson, Helms, & Terrell, 1994). No doubt these observations suggest a lack of culturally responsive services, which runs the risk of harm and targets the counseling profession as multiculturally insensitive and ineffective.

Not fully recognizing the damage of social oppression on our clients as well as our personal and professional biases may result in unintentional harm to our clients. It is quite dangerous that counselors, without awareness, carry the oppressive messages under the cover of professional service to diverse clients. Let's examine this illustration:

Ruben is a Latino male who cross-dresses, and his story (see Case Illustration 2.2) demonstrates the counselor's failed attempt to understand his presenting concerns or accept his gender-variant behavior. By focusing on his cross-dressing behavior in isolation of emotional and cultural contexts and by suggesting to Ruben that he not tell his family but rather work harder to subscribe to behaviors that are congruent with a male identity, the counselor has unintentionally contributed to the negative social experiences Ruben encounters in his environment. These negative social experiences might possibly include (a) denial that Ruben experiences cultural discrimination and that it influences his psychological health, (b) invalidation of his emotional experiences in coping with the situation, and (c) pathologization of his gender-variant behavior. In addition, advising Ruben not to tell his family reflects the counselor's value of privacy, independence, and boundaries that are rooted in American mainstream culture. The counselor's inability to embrace Ruben's multiple cultural identities led to premature termination and, perhaps more damaging, the experience of further marginalization and oppression.

CASE ILLUSTRATION 2.2

The Case of Ruben

Ruben is a 52-year-old Latino male who has been happily married 27 years and has three young-adult children (19, 21, and 22 years old). Ruben, who is a computer software trainer, had been seeing his counselor for work-related stress and conflict with his supervisor. During his eighth counseling session, he disclosed to his counselor that he engages in cross-dressing behavior two to three times monthly during his out-of-town business travel. He stated that he cross-dressed when he was young but had not done so since getting married 10 years ago. He further explained that cross-dressing seemed to provide comfort during out-of-town travels when his two cotrainers, who traveled with him, were "out socializing at night" or "being bossy" to him "in front of others" or when the trainees/clients they worked with "were more critical" of him "than the other two trainers." He expressed interest in no longer wanting to hide this behavior from his wife and maybe even disclose it to his children. He requested the advice of his counselor about how to disclose his behavior to his wife and children as he feels bad about keeping it a secret and also because he would like to cross-dress more often.

The counselor listened attentively to Ruben's story and asked many follow-up questions concerning his strong desire to cross-dress more often and also to his concern about keeping this behavior from his wife. The counselor then responded by advising Ruben not to tell his wife and certainly not to tell his children. The counselor further advised Reuben to stop cross-dressing so that he does not risk losing both his marriage and his relationship with his children. Ruben's counselor suggested that he work harder to adhere to behaviors and identities that are congruent with his male biological sex and that they address this as a counseling goal for next week and future counseling sessions. Ruben did not return to counseling.

a. Discuss how the counselor's response and treatment approach demonstrated a breach of nonmaleficence.

b. What would have been the response of a counselor with a well-formulated multicultural professional identity?

c. Discuss the ways in which Ruben's social and cultural backgrounds need to be considered in order for the counselor to understand him accurately.

d. Do you think your multicultural awareness and knowledge play important roles in working with Ruben? If yes, how?

(Continued)

(Continued)

e. What assumptions do you make about clients based on sex and gender, and what are the practice implications of these assumptions?

f. Discuss how knowledge of gender identity and expression is an important aspect of multicultural counseling competency.

g. Reflect on your own stereotypes and biases toward gender-variant identities and expression. How might you explore and challenge these assumptions?

To do culturally diverse clients justice and to promote humanity and mental health for all people, we as a profession need to renew our counseling theories and methods and train for counselor multicultural competencies. We need to realize that there are people who are not only marginalized by society but also feel sidelined, even relegated, by the mental health profession. This has to change.

An excerpt from a recent interview with an African American male graduate student follows:

In what ways do you believe our counseling profession has inadequately served African American and transgender individuals?

I think the counseling profession hasn't considered diversity enough in trans communities. Trans people of color (also trans individuals living with disabilities) have unique challenges to overcome, and our experience doesn't mirror White, trans, able-bodied individuals. Stereotypes stemming from long-held racial assumptions can be heightened when undergoing transition (i.e., transitioning from an African American female identity to an African American male identity). The therapists and counselors I've spoken to are woefully inadequate in helping me simultaneously deal with transition and racial matters. I would feel more comfortable speaking to a person-of-color counselor, but I can rarely find any who are versed on trans identities.

What do you hope the counseling profession will do to advance its focus in order to ensure that effective services are provided to African American and trans consumers?

Always use and continue to improve on best practices. It's not strictly about the medical transition; there is a social aspect of trans masculinity that erects barriers in terms of dating partners and forming friendships with cisgender people. Also be aware that not everyone who identifies as transgender will undergo hormone treatment. Some are comfortable existing outside of the gender binary and run into problems with appearance and social interactions due to their lack of assimilation.

Finally, having a counselor who is knowledgeable enough to counsel about issues that relate to intimacy and sex is paramount. In matters of dating and intimacy, there are many cisgender people who believe that trans individuals are being deliberately deceptive and misleading when it comes to revealing their status. When do you reveal your status to a cis dating partner? Hopefully, prior to sex, but how do you reveal while maintaining a sense of personal safety and remaining datable? This is my current Everest.

Demographic Changes in the United States

CASE ILLUSTRATION 2.3

Shouldn't We Take Care of Ourselves?

Marie is a Latina, 36-year-old, stay-at-home mom who emigrated from Mexico with her family when she was 4 years old. She completed the tenth grade before she quit school and became a full-time mom. She was married after the birth of her second child, and now she and her husband are raising four children with the oldest daughter in the tenth grade. She was invited to talk to a multicultural class of counselors-in-training. She started out sharing her life and culture, but with students' questions, she got into some rather personal subjects, including her hardworking but emotionally distant husband who is also an immigrant and works as a carpenter, her oldest daughter's decision to quit high school after the tenth grade to start a family, her middle son's academic and behavior difficulties in middle school, her youngest daughter's degenerative conditions, and so on. She was obviously in distress when talking about some of the difficulties in her life. A student in the class wanted to help and engaged her in the following conversation:

Student: It sounds as if your husband hasn't been very helpful in dealing with all these difficult situations. Did you ever tell him that you need his support?

Marie: (a long silence) I don't know . . . I didn't . . .

Student: That must be very hard.

Marie: (looks confused) I'm not sure . . . not really.

Student: You are a good mom and you take care of everyone. What do you do for yourself to cope with stress?

Marie: (pause; noticeably feeling lost and uncomfortable) I am sorry that I have said too much.

Marie stopped talking after this verbal exchange. When the instructor thanked her and walked her to the door, she said, "I feel very bad for talking about myself."

From a specific angle, the exchange between Marie and the student (see Case Illustration 2.3) seems to demonstrate cultural differences among people from different cultural backgrounds. The student's intent to be helpful and seemingly appropriate questions from a traditional counseling theoretical view did not work well and instead led to Marie's verbal shutdown and inability to comfortably share further as well as feelings of self-blame. Not all cultures share the central individualistic focus of counseling that is reflective of Euro-American cultural values. Latinas often experience conflict when they perceive they are not fulfilling their traditional roles well, including being selfless in taking care of their husband and children (Sue & Sue, 2013). They may also feel uncomfortable with negative emotions and be unable to express them (Lopez-Baez, 2006). Doing something for one's self may not be perceived as acceptable as it is in Euro-American culture, and thinking about it may lead to negative self-evaluation.

It is extremely likely that counselors will find themselves in situations where they need cultural knowledge and skills to avoid such miscommunication or ineffective communication. Demographic changes in the United States have been significant and are continuing, which underpins the urgency and necessity for the counseling profession to acknowledge its responsibility for ensuring multicultural counseling competence and effective mental health care for all consumers. An increase of ethnic and cultural minorities in the numeric sense does not mean an increase in their social power; their large presence will, however, lead to increased interactions between the majority and minority cultures. Therefore, the field of counseling and its affiliated training programs and professional organizations must ensure that counselors possess multicultural competencies to serve a diverse U.S. population in the 21st century.

Increasing Trend of Racial and Ethnic Minorities

The census data have provided insights regarding our racially and ethnically diverse nation. Specifically, data from the 1995 Bureau of the Census predicted that approximately one third of the country's population would be people of color by 2000. This number was confirmed by the 2006 census data, which documented that one third of the country's total population was minority, and the number of people of color was projected to continue to increase (U.S. Bureau of the Census, 2006).

Estimates on the U.S. population's growth for 2011 indicated that racial and ethnic minorities for the first time in history comprised more than half (50.4%) of all children younger than one year old. This figure was an increase from the 49.5% reported in the 2010 census. Similarly, for a population younger than age 5, 49.5% were minority in 2011 compared to 49% in 2010 (U.S. Bureau of the Census, 2012).

A continued and steady increase in the number of minorities in this country is further evidenced by the 36.6% (114 million) of the U.S. population being made up of minorities in 2011 compared to 36.1% in 2010. By the year 2050, the percentage of minorities is expected to rise to 50%. According to the 2010 census, a population greater than 50% minority is now referred to as *majority-minority*. United States public schools became majority-minority for the first time in the fall of 2014 with 49.8% White, 15.4% Black, 25.8% Latino, 5.2% Asian, 1.1% Native American, and 2.8% biracial ("U.S. Public Schools," 2014). This trend is expected to continue.

The population growth change estimates provided by census data support our urging that counseling professionals must be prepared to work with diverse clients. To clarify, these data inform that non-Hispanic Whites are the slowest-growing group and contributed 35% of the population growth between 1990 and 2000, 23% between 2000 and 2010, and an expected 14% between 2010 and 2030. This declining trend is projected to result in the non-Hispanic White population contributing nothing to the population growth after 2030 because it is expected to decline in size (Day, n.d.).

The vast majority of growth in the total population reflects an increase in persons who reported their ethnicity as Hispanic or Latino as well as those who reported an ethnic category other than White alone. As the fastest-growing group, the Hispanic population is expected to double its 1990 size by 2015 and quadruple its 1990 size by the middle of the 22nd century. The census data projects the Hispanic-origin population to contribute 60% of the nation's population growth from 2030 to 2050 (Day, n.d.).

A Reflection of a Latino Gay Man on His Cultural Community

It makes sense that *familia* would be used to describe my community. After all, many Latino communities place much importance on the traditional family unit; in other words, *familismo* is a fact of life. *Familismo* defines the tendency for an individual to make decisions that are beneficial to the entire family. At times, gay Latino men grow up thinking that they need to keep certain aspects of themselves hidden in order to better suit the well-being and happiness of their family. Within this frame of thinking, being *machismo* is also largely present. Our community, whether they realize it or not, works in a way that provides more power, status, and opportunity to its males. For this reason, the Latino male is taught that a man should possess certain behavioral characteristics. Latino men learn early that they are to do everything they can to provide for and maintain order within their families. To achieve this, men within my culture are taught that they must be confident, protective, strong, intelligent, noble, and straight. Within our community, homosexuality does not fall within the framework used to describe a desirable man. My community is one that holds on to the idea that for a boy to "end up" gay (or questioning), something must have "gone wrong" throughout his development. Therefore, when one disregards or crosses the strict guidelines of *machismo*, he runs the risk of shaming the rest of the family and working against *familismo*.

This has the potential to be very hurtful to the individual. Often, oppressed communities cohabit and spend their time within certain areas of town. Despite differences in economic status, these areas of town are always beautiful, colorful, and lively. When people live within a country that they feel is not their own, it makes sense to associate and spend time with others who look like them and speak their language. It is comforting to find people who come from similar experiences and upbringings. Still, these communities are often small, or at least they feel that way. Not unlike other small communities, tight-knit Latino communities can be breeding grounds for gossip. If a community finds out that a family has a gay relative, the family can be marked by controversy. Many gay Latino males are cognizant of this risk and as a result internalize homophobia, guilt, and shame.

—Artemio, a Latino American gay man

Increasing Trend of Openly Sexual Minorities

Although the number of gay men and lesbians in the United States is hard to verify, the nonexclusive heterosexual population may be increasing due to the rising acceptance of bisexuality among America's youth (Leland, 1995). Approximately 581,000 U.S. same-sex-couple households were reported in 2009 (Lofquist, 2011), and although not a statistically significant difference, approximately 594,000 same-sex-couple households lived in the United States in 2010 (Lofquist, 2011). Similarly, Glosoff (2009) reported estimates of 4% to 18% of the U.S. population being lesbian, gay, bisexual, or transgender (LGBT). The variance reflected in these numbers illuminates the difficulty of obtaining accurate demographics for sexual orientation. It is known and documented in the literature that LGBT individuals are bullied and discriminated against in their schools and workplaces; consequently, they may be reluctant to identify themselves as such in surveys and elsewhere.

Increasing Religious Diversity

Religious diversity is also growing in the United States, and spiritual concerns are ever more likely to be a focus of counseling (Cecero, 2010). Religion and spirituality have been largely absent from the history of professional counseling development. It has only been in recent decades that the counseling profession has clearly acknowledged the important role and influence of both religion and spirituality on individuals' cultural practices and psychological behavior. This recognition is credited to the multicultural movement and its theorists and practitioners who became increasingly aware of the significant roles that religion and spirituality play in human life and therefore must play in counseling (Frame, 2003). Certainly, awareness of religion and spiritual diversity is both a necessity and a challenge due to significant differences between and among regions. According to an American Religious Identification Survey conducted in 2008, about 80% of Americans reported having an identifiable religion; among them, 76% self-identified as Christian. The survey also showed that religious diversity has increased in recent years. For instance, compared with 1990 data, 2008 witnessed a decrease in the percentage of the U.S. adult population that self-identified as Catholic, Baptist, Mainline Christian, or Jewish by 1.1%, 3.5%, 5.8%, and .6%, respectively and an increase in Eastern Religion, Buddhism, and Muslimism by .5%, .3%, and .3%, respectively (Kosmin & Keysar, 2009). What may complicate the picture further is that religious identification and prevalence may intersect with ethnicity, age, and regions of residence in the United States.

Considering all these demographic changes in our society, the field of counseling faces the challenges of producing competent counselors and providing effective practices. Once again we are reminded that the "typical" client in terms of race/ethnicity, sexual orientation, gender, religion, and socioeconomic status no longer exists, and instead our profession is challenged with serving consumers who are diverse and have salient multiple cultural identities. Acquiring multicultural competence is no longer a choice; it is without doubt our fundamental professional and ethical responsibility.

Immigration and Globalization

It is rather clear that an accurate evaluation of Dahab's (see Case Illustration 2.1) mental status and the delivery of effective interventions that can help alleviate the negative effects of his psychological distress involve our understanding of how his international background (as well as other background variables) informs his experience. In other words, what is it like to be a son of a government worker in Sudan? How does his international identity influence his experience in the United States? In what ways is it possible that hearing voices that "motivate me to do the best I can" is not a pathological expression of auditory hallucinations? How should we view his use of marijuana, which is illegal in the majority of the United States? Many questions pertaining to Dahab's international background need answering before we can effectively work with him. The professional responsibility of counselors in the 21st century demands multicultural and international competence in order to effectively work with Dahab and to minimize any potential for doing harm.

As our world is becoming increasingly globalized and peoples and nations of the world experience greater connectedness, the probability of counselors facing international issues and contexts in practice is much greater. This increased globalization will command our counseling profession to train and promote international counseling competence and address cultural specific issues related to individuals' international identity. Whether in the United States or in the international communities, our profession will be tested for its ability to serve people with international backgrounds, people with exposure to international cultures, and people in international contexts. Moreover, it has become and will continue to be a higher mission of the profession to assist, interact, and learn from international colleagues and communities that are developing counseling professions in their countries and to share our knowledge of the role of social justice and cultural plurality in counseling.

Increasing Presence of Immigrants

Recent immigrant statistics from the Migration Policy Institute (n.d.) online data hub show that the United States has the largest number of international migrants. In 2012 alone, 42,813,000 migrants entered the country, and in the past 10 years, 11,150,000 individuals from various countries have taken residency in the United States. The statistics on international students showed a similar fast-increasing trend. Project Atlas (n.d.) data showed that new international students' enrollment in the United States was 764,490 for the 2011 to 2012 academic year, with an increase of 5.7% from the previous year (723,277). These international students were from all over the world with China (194,029) and India (100,270) contributing the largest numbers.

Immigrants' experiences in the United States are diverse as well. Those from European countries may not experience as much scrutiny in terms of their legitimacy, intelligence, and ability as compared to those from other parts of the world (e.g., South America, Middle East). People with certain accents when speaking

English (e.g., British, German) may be more accepted and respected than others (e.g., those with Mexican or Native American accents). Stereotypes about immigrant groups pose different challenges and obstacles for them. Such international context-related privilege and oppression have both individual and collective impact on people with different cultural, country, language, social, economic, and faith origins in and outside of the United States.

A Reflection of Growing Up as a Daughter of Immigrant Parents

As the daughter of immigrant parents, I often feel a push/pull toward both my family's culture and becoming more acculturated to what is around me. It's definitely been difficult at times, especially when trying to communicate with my parents when they are very entrenched in their own way of thinking. There were times when I was singled out in grade school as being the one with "slanty eyes" or "chinky." This mainly occurred when I was the minority in upstate New York. I do notice that some people stare at me, almost accusingly, if I am in more rural areas of the Midwest, particularly when I am with my boyfriend (who is White). I consider more subtle racism to be unintentional, such as children pointing at me and stating, "Mom, look! It's an Oriental!" Another experience I often have is people asking, "Where are you from?" and "What kind of Asian are you?"

—A female graduate student in psychology whose parents are immigrants from Taiwan

Counseling Becoming International

Conducting international work could happen directly (e.g., interacting with foreigners in the counselors' homeland, as foreigners in other countries) or indirectly (e.g., interacting with people whose lives are affected by international connections, experiences in the United States, beyond its borders) and at an individual level (e.g., working with migrants, refugees) or societal level (e.g., working toward policies related to immigrants). When working with a client like Dahab, it is evident that we are dealing with international issues. There may be times when we deal with international issues indirectly, even without awareness. Our clients may present concerns that are related to their environment in which international people or issues are present. For instance, as a result of a large presence of international visitors, immigrants, and students, including those who are working or visiting abroad, there have been more international marriages, which will introduce different family system dynamics and influence individuals' communities. Further, with the convenience of the Internet, interconnections between people and countries, migration of citizens, and the ease of global communications and travel, counseling professionals can expect to interface and interact with people in cross-national contexts who hold differing worldviews. Although traveling to different countries may not be feasible for most, training programs are nonetheless encouraged to modify their curriculum with focus on integrating information and course-related material from cultures around the world. This might be accomplished by reviewing information on websites, watching movies, and establishing cross-national collaborations with scholars, practitioners, and students. Whether or not we like it, cultural value conflicts among different peoples and nations in the world have entered every corner of the world, and it is difficult to imagine how individuals' lives would be exempt from the influences of different cultures.

In response to the growing need for psychological care around the globe and the infusion of international issues within the United States, an internationalization movement has occurred in the field of counseling, which has been viewed as part of the "fifth movement" in the history of multicultural counseling (Ponterotto, 2008). The internationalization of counseling requires cross-cultural collaboration and "the inclusion of cross-national and cross-cultural perspectives in the predominant Western perspectives of counseling practice and research as traditionally operationalized in the United States" (Heppner, Leong, & Chiao, 2008, p. 68). This effort will prepare the counseling profession to better serve the mental health needs of an increasingly diverse U.S. society and further enhance our service to all clients because it challenges our natural tendency toward the status quo and ethnocentrism. Gerstein, Heppner, Ægisdóttir, Leung, and Norsworthy (2009) commented on the future of the counseling profession in the context of internationalization:

> It is rather evident that we are in the midst of a renaissance period in the counseling profession worldwide. Without a doubt, this period of reflection, evaluation, innovation, and cross-national collaboration will continue and evolve for decades into the future. It is difficult to predict how the field of counseling might change, how psychological services may be delivered, and how the texture and content of our collaborative professional relationships might develop and blossom. In the years ahead, however, we are absolutely convinced that new, refined, and creative approaches to counseling grounded in diverse cultural contexts and incorporating traditional forms of healing will continue to emerge and thrive. (p. 519)

Necessary Multicultural Ethics

The increasing need for multicultural counseling and our profession's commitment to serving the culturally diverse require counselors in the 21st century to adhere to the highest standards of multicultural ethics. As pointed out by Mays (2000), our service needs to ensure that "no one should have their future, their health, or their well-being compromised for reasons of class, gender, national origin, physical and psychological abilities, religion, or sexual orientation, or as a result of unfair distribution of resources" (p. 236). This has been taken as an ethical mandate by counseling professional groups such as the American Counseling Association (ACA, 2014) and the American Psychological Association (APA, 2010). The knowledge that "a monocultural psychology is not simply less accurate or generalizable, but positively distortive and oppressive" (Fowers & Davidov, 2006, p. 581) demands that psychological counselors develop multicultural ethical competence, and there is no alternative.

Fisher (2014) offered this description of multicultural ethical competence for psychologists that also applies to counselors:

> Multicultural ethical competence is a process that draws on psychologists' human responsiveness to those with whom they work and awareness of their own boundaries, competencies, and obligations. It requires flexibility and sensitivity to the context, role responsibilities, and stakeholder expectations unique to each work endeavor. Good intentions, confidence in one's ability to adapt traditional training to distinct groups and individuals, or a belief that personal experience is professionally sufficient to understand clients who share some of the psychologist's demographic characteristics are ethically insufficient in the absence of relevant multicultural knowledge and training. The individual, ecological, social, cultural, economic, institutional, systemic, and historical differences that shape the human condition affect the expression of and solution to ethical challenges in the practice of psychology. (p. 37)

To practice multiculturally efficacious counseling, all counselors must show multicultural ethical commitment in developing multicultural ethical competence. Counselors need to demonstrate commitment to social justice, understanding privilege and oppression, resisting stereotypes and biases, and openness to multiple worldviews (Fisher, 2014).

Summary

This chapter reviews the historical, current, and future direction of our society in terms of its demographics, cultural dynamics, and international interactions points to the importance of multicultural competence in our counseling profession. In past decades, the counseling profession and professionals as well as mental health delivery systems were not effectively serving the culturally diverse. To a significant degree, this failure to serve the needy reflects the ethnocentric and monocultural nature of counseling and counseling profession. Regrettably, this cultural deficiency may indirectly support racism and social injustice as imposed onto our diverse clients. Socially disempowered and oppressed individuals, groups, and communities have not been but deserve to be the recipients of competent counseling practice.

Knowledge of the diverse landscape of the United States in the 21st century calls for a commitment from our counseling profession to address the immense need for multiculturally effective psychological care with multiculturally competent professionals and services. We have little margin for error when it comes to the psychological care of those who are culturally and socially marginalized. Failure to serve them effectively may be accompanied with further oppression either by invalidating the harm of social oppression or by imposing culturally biased values. Such practices contribute to the public's negative images of oppressed groups and perpetuate the internalized isms held by all individuals in this society. In some sense, only multiculturally competent professionals and culturally responsive counseling practices can provide the corrective experiences that are due to those who have been victimized by the monocultural worldview reflected in the history of counseling practice. This is our profession's multicultural ethical responsibility and mandate.

Takeaway Messages

1. The sustainability of the counseling profession will require that counselors are multiculturally competent and prepared to meet the needs of culturally diverse populations both within and outside the United States.
2. Professional counseling practices of the past have been inadequate for serving culturally diverse populations and to some extent have even perpetuated the internalized isms practiced by all members of society.
3. Social and cultural oppression and injustices have profound influence on individuals' psychological health and also inform the social realities for different groups of people.
4. Continuous demographic changes in the United States necessitate that the counseling profession addresses multicultural competence and demonstrates commitment to serving the culturally diverse and socially marginalized.
5. International counseling competence is necessary for counselors in the 21st century.
6. It is the multicultural ethical mandate that counselors serve the culturally diverse with cultural competence.

Recommended Resources

Readings

Abu-Bader, S. H., Tirmazi, T. M., & Ross-Sheriff, F. (2011). The impact of acculturation on depression among older Muslim immigrants in the United States. *Journal of Gerontological Social Work, 54*, 425–448.

Bausum, A. (2009). *Denied, detained, deported: Stories from the dark side of American immigration.* Washington, DC: National Geographic Society.

McNamee, S. J., & Miller, R. K., Jr. (2004). *The meritocracy myth.* Lanham, MD: Rowman & Littlefield.

Miles, J. R., & Fassinger, R. E. (2014). Sexual identity issues in education and training of professional psychologists. In W. B. Johnson & N. Kaslow (Eds.), *The Oxford handbook of education and training in professional psychology* (pp. 452–471). New York, NY: Oxford University Press.

Sue, D. W. (2003). *Overcoming our racism: The journey to liberation.* New York, NY.: Wiley.

Media and Websites

Abani, C. (2007, August). *Telling stories from Africa.* (TED Talk). Retrieved from http://www.ted.com/talks/chris_abani_on_the_stories_of_africa.html

Adelman, L. (2003). *Race: The power of an illusion.* Retrieved from http://www.pbs.org/race/000_General/000_00-Home.htm

American Psychological Association. Answers to your questions about people with intersex conditions. http://www.silc.ku.edu/sites/silc.drupal.ku.edu/files/docs/LBGT/PDF%20Documents/Intersex.pdf

American Psychological Association. Answers to your questions for a better understanding of sexual orientation and homosexuality. https://www.apa.org/topics/sexuality/orientation.pdf

http://unfaircampaign.org

Levy, E. (Writer), & Glatter, L. L. (Director). (2010). The Chrysanthemum and the Sword [Television series episode]. In M. Weiner (Executive Producer), *Mad Men.* Los Angeles, CA: AMC Studios.

The latest news within the immigration benefit world handled by U.S. Citizenship and Immigration Services (USCIS). Both news media and general public can find important information about updates, alerts, and events that impact legal immigration. It also provides resources specifically for the news media. http://www.uscis.gov/news

Various documentaries on race and racism. http://www.aspeninstitute.org/policy-work/community-change/racial-equity-society-peer-learning-forum/documentaries-race-racism

References

Advisory Board to the President's Initiative on Race. (1998). *One America in the 21st century: Forging a new future.* Retrieved from http://clinton2.nara.gov/Initiatives/OneAmerica/PIR.pdf

American Counseling Association. (2014). *Code of ethics.* Washington, DC: Author. Retrieved from www.counseling.org

American Psychological Association. (2010). *Ethical principles of psychologists and code of conduct.* Washington, DC: Author. Retrieved from http://www.apa.org/ethics/code/index.aspx

Cecero, J. J. (2010). The spiritual exercises in counseling and therapy. In J. G. Ponterotto, J. M. Casas, L. A. Suzuki, & C. M. Alexander (Eds.), *Handbook of multicultural counseling* (pp. 479–490). Thousand Oaks, CA: Sage.

Day, J. C. (n.d.). *National population projections.* Retrieved from http://www.census.gov/population/pop-profile/adobe/2_ps.pdf

Fisher, C. B. (2014). Multicultural ethics in professional psychology practice, consultation, and training. In F. T. L. Leong (Ed.), *APA handbook in psychology* (Vol. 2, pp. 37–58). Washington, DC: American Psychological Association.

Fowers, B. J., & Davidov, B. J. (2006). The virtue of multiculturalism: Personal transformation, character, and openness to the other. *American Psychologist, 61*, 581–594.

Frame, M. W. (2003). *Integrating religion and spirituality into counseling.* Pacific Grove, CA: Brooks/Cole.

Gerstein, L. H., Heppner, P. P., Stockton, R., Leong, F. T. L., & Ægisdóttir, S. (2009). The counseling profession in and outside the United States. In L. H. Gerstein, P. P. Heppner, S. Ægisdóttir, S. A. Leung, & K. L. Norsworthy (Eds.), *International handbook of cross-cultural counseling: Cultural assumptions and practices worldwide* (pp. 53–68). Los Angeles, CA: Sage.

Glosoff, H. L. (2009). The counseling profession: Historical perspectives and current issues and trends. In D. Capuzzzi & D. R. Grossi (Eds.), *Introduction to the counseling profession* (pp. 3–56). Columbus, OH: Pearson/Merrill.

Heppner, P. P., Leong, F. T. L., & Chiao, H. (2008). A growing internationalization of counseling psychology. In S. D. Brown & R. W. Lent (Eds.), *Handbook of counseling psychology* (4th ed., pp. 68–85). Hoboken, NJ: Wiley.

Johnson, A. (2006). *Privilege, power, and difference.* New York, NY: McGraw-Hill.

Kearney, L. K., Draper, M., & Baron, A. (2003). *Counseling utilization by ethnic minority students.* Retrieved from http://cmhc.utexas.edu/pdf/ethnicmin.pdf

Kosmin, B. A., & Keysar, A. (2009). *American Religious Identification Survey (ARIS) 2008 summary report.* Hartford, CT: Institute for the Study of Secularism in Society & Culture. Retrieved from http://commons.trincoll.edu/aris/?s=survey+2008&submit=

Lee, M. W. (Director). (1994). *Color of fear* [Film]. United States: StirFry Seminars. Available at http://www.stirfryseminars.com/store/products/cof1.php

Leland, J. (1995, July 17). Not gay, not straight: A new sexuality emerges. *Newsweek, 126*(3), 44–50.

Lofquist, D. (2011). *Same-sex couple households: American Community Survey briefs.* Retrieved from http://www.census.gov/prod/2011pubs/acsbr10-03.pdf

Lopez-Baez, S. L. (2006). Counseling Latinas: Culturally responsive interventions. In C. C. Lee (Ed.), *Multicultural issues in counseling* (3rd ed., pp. 187–194). Alexandria, VA: American Counseling Association.

Mays, V. M. (2000). A social justice agenda. *American Psychologist, 55*, 326–327.

McIntosh, P. (1998). White privilege: Unpacking the invisible knapsack. In M. McGoldrick (Ed.), *Re-visioning family therapy: Race, culture, and gender in clinical practice* (pp. 147–152). New York, NY: Guildford Press.

McLellan, B. (1999). The prostitution of psychotherapy: A feminist critique. *British Journal of Guidance and Counselling, 27*, 325–337.

McNamee, S. J., & Miller, R. K., Jr. (2004). *The meritocracy myth.* Lanham, MD: Rowman & Littlefield.

Migration Policy Institute. (n.d.). *U.S. immigration trends.* Retrieved from http://www.migrationpolicy.org/programs/data-hub/us-immigration-trends

Nickerson, K. J., Helms, J. E., & Terrell, F. (1994). Cultural mistrust, opinions about mental illness, and Black students' attitudes toward seeking psychological help from White counselors. *Journal of Counseling Psychology, 41*(3), 378–385. Retrieved from http://search.proquest.com/psycinfo/docview/62824639/139976F969C311C3705/1?accountid=14556

Ponterotto, J. G. (2008). Theoretical and empirical advances in multicultural counseling and psychology. In S. D. Brown & R. W. Lent (Eds.), *Handbook of counseling psychology* (4th ed., pp. 121–140). Hoboken, NJ: Wiley.

Ponterotto, J. G., Casas, J. M., Suzuki, L. A., & Alexander, C. M. (Eds.). (2001). *Handbook of multicultural counseling* (2nd ed.). Thousand Oaks, CA: Sage.

Project Atlas. (n.d.). International students in the United States. Retrieved from http://www.iie.org/en/Services/Project-Atlas/United-States/International-Students-In-US

Remy, G. M. (1995). Ethnic minorities and mental health: Ethical concerns in counseling immigrants and culturally diverse groups. *Trotter Review,* 9(1), 5. Retrieved from http://scholarworks.umb.edu/trotter_review/vol9/iss1/5

Schwartz, R. C., & Feisthamel, K. P. (2009). Disproportionate diagnosis of mental disorders among African American versus European American clients: Implications for counseling theory, research, and practice. *Journal of Counseling & Development, 87*(3), 295–301. Retrieved from http://search.proquest.com/docview/61852297?accountid=14556

Sue, D. W., Capodilupo, C. M., Torino, G. C., Bucceri, J. M., Holder, A. M. B., Nadal, K. L., & Esquilin, M. (2007). Racial microaggressions in everyday life: Implications for clinical practice. *American Psychologist, 62*, 271–286.

Sue, D. W., & Sue, D. (2013). *Counseling the culturally diverse: Theory and practice* (6th ed.). Hoboken, NJ: Wiley.

Thompson, C. E., & Neville, H. A. (1999). Racism, mental health, and mental health practice. *The Counseling Psychology, 41*, 155–161.

U.S. Bureau of the Census. (2006). *The 2006 statistical abstract.* Retrieved from http://www.census.gov/compendia/statab/2006/2006edition.html

U.S. Bureau of the Census. (2012, May 17). *Most children younger than age 1 are minorities, Census Bureau reports* [Press release]. Retrieved from http://www.census.gov/newsroom/releases/archives/population/cb12-90.html

U.S. public schools become majority minority. (2014, August 11). *Inside Higher Ed.* Retrieved from https://www.insidehighered.com/quicktakes/2014/08/11/us-public-schools-become-majority-minority

Wright, G. T. (2014, October 27). Counseling Black men: The thousand-piece puzzle. *Chronicle of Higher Education.* Retrieved from http://chronicle.com/article/Counseling-Black-Men-The/149577/

Multicultural Movement: The Fourth Force

Tolerance and understanding won't "trickle down" in our society any more than wealth does.

—Muhammad Ali

CHAPTER OVERVIEW

This chapter presents a history of multicultural counseling development and discusses its historical and social background. Readers will be reminded that the development of the counseling profession needs to reflect the advancement of our understanding of related issues and keep up with the changes and development of our society. Specific focus will be on understanding the social injustice of leaving certain groups and people in oppressed positions and the necessity of providing effective service to those who have been socially oppressed and marginalized. To keep students informed of the advancement of the multicultural movement, this chapter will describe multiple cultural contexts in which our profession is enriched and discuss the critical role of social justice advocacy in counseling diverse clients in the 21st century.

SELF-ASSESSMENT OF PRE-EXISTING AWARENESS AND KNOWLEDGE

- What are the reasons that we need to be talking about multicultural counseling?
- How did the "multicultural movement" start? Who have been leaders?
- What are focal points of the multicultural movement?

- What are my roles as a counselor in this multicultural movement?
- What do I think about social justice advocacy and its role in working with diverse clients in therapeutic relationships?

LEARNING OBJECTIVES

After reading this chapter, students will be able to do the following:

1. Acquire knowledge about the history of the multicultural movement in the field of counseling
2. Understand the complexity and challenges of multicultural counseling
3. Recognize social injustice and its negative impact on culturally and socially marginalized communities, groups, and individuals
4. Understand the importance of social advocacy in helping those who have been victimized by social oppression
5. Develop a sense of responsibility to engage in multiculturally competent counseling practice and to promote social justice advocacy

CASE ILLUSTRATION 3.1

The Case of Amber and Patty

Amber and her mother Patty were brought to a free counseling clinic in a small town near a Navaho reservation in New Mexico by Milton Hillman, who was the social worker assigned to their case. Milton explained that Amber and Patty needed help because they have had a lot of "fights," and Amber had a recent suicide attempt. Milton reported being very concerned about Amber's stability and the effect of Patty and Amber's volatile relationship on Amber's two younger sisters who both have cognitive and developmental problems.

Amber is a 16-year-old, Native American, female, high school student from the Navajo tribe. She was born in California but, when she was 7 years old, moved back with her mother and two younger sisters to the reservation where her mother's family resides so her mother could get family help with raising her three children. Up until a month ago, Amber had been a straight A student and an accomplished cross-country and softball athlete at school. She planned to be the first of her family to attend college and play a college sport. Her mother, who works in janitorial services at Amber's school, was extremely proud of her. Amber has never met her biological father or his family and is

(Continued)

(Continued)

very close to her mother's side of the family. She and her family participate in many of the traditional spiritual ceremonies and traditions of the tribe.

Amber began dating 17-year-old Chris, who lives in the same community and is her first boyfriend, about four months ago. Patty was very unhappy that Amber started dating this young. Patty has talked to her on several occasions, asking her to "please stop" and "concentrate on your studies." According to Milton, Patty had reportedly taken Amber's dating "very hard" because it probably reminded herself of the "pain" she had endured before she moved back to the reservation. However, Amber (out of her "character") became more and more reactive and would talk back to Patty with much anger in her voice: "You had me when you were 15! How can you say anything about me starting to date at 16?" Patty became very upset and sad as Amber had never talked to her like that; she also began having a lot of physical problems, including pain all over all body.

About five weeks ago, Amber found out that Chris had been cheating on her with one of her friends. She felt devastated and broke up with him. A few days later, Amber became ill during a softball practice and was sent to a local clinic. During the clinic visit, Amber and her mother were provided the shocking news that Amber was 3 months pregnant. Over the next few days, Amber and her mother barely spoke to each other. Amber felt overwhelmed with emotions; she cried often, experienced a loss of appetite, skipped classes, and isolated herself from her friends. Patty also isolated herself from her friends and was very moody when interacting with her other children. As a result, Amber's younger sisters were unhappy and exhibited increased behavioral problems at school.

One evening Patty returned from church to find Amber sprawled out on the floor with a pill bottle. She immediately called 911, and Amber was rushed to the emergency room. The doctors were able to save both Amber and the baby. Unfortunately, the doctors were unable to determine if any permanent damage was done to the baby, and they have prescribed bed rest for the remainder of the pregnancy as a result.

GUIDED CLASSROOM EXERCISE 3.1

Understanding Amber and Patty's Experiences

Group Discussion

Imagine yourself as the counselor assigned to treat Amber and Patty, then answer the following questions:

1. What is your first impression of their "problems?"
2. In what ways are the issues that plague Patty and Amber not just between the two of them?

3. What initial thoughts do you have about possible reasons why Patty views Amber's dating as unacceptable?
4. How might their problem be related to their social or cultural contexts?
5. What hypotheses can you offer to explain their experiences?
6. What would you first address in working with them and why? What other areas would you want to focus on and why?
7. What are possible goals you think would be beneficial and would guide your work with them?

INDIVIDUAL AND SMALL-GROUP CLASS ACTIVITY 3.1

How Am I Related to Amber's Social and Cultural Context?

Complete Table 3.1 by writing *dominant/privileged* or *subordinate/disadvantaged* in each box to describe Amber's, Patty's, and your own social and personal status. Then, in small groups of three to four students, share your observations and thoughts about the following questions:

- In what way do you think Amber's social and cultural identities contribute to her experience?
- In what way do you think Patty's social and cultural identities contribute to her experience?
- What role has social oppression played in their difficulties? How does your social and cultural status interact with Amber and Patty's?
- How might you understand Amber and Patty's experience from a culturally sensitive and validating perspective?

One of the major markers of multiculturally competent and efficacious counseling is not attributing all symptoms or problem-causing experiences of our clients solely to their inner psyche (Sue & Sue, 2008). Instead, we view individuals in their cultural contexts and strive toward understanding the role of cultural patterns, social environments, and interpersonal dynamics and circumstances in their experiences. Perceiving, diagnosing, and treating individuals based on isolated symptoms without considering the social and cultural environmental input can do more harm than good. This is especially true for the culturally diverse because counseling in its traditional form supports the "mainstream cultural values, neglecting multicultural worldviews" (Comas-Díaz, 2011, p. 536) and was basically "created by the mainstream to serve the mainstream" (McLellan, 1999, p. 325).

Table 3.1 How Do I Relate to Amber and Patty?

	Amber's Social/ Cultural Categories	Patty's Social/ Cultural Categories	My Social/ Cultural Categories	What Role Did I Play in Their Contexts?	My Challenges in Working With Them	Privilege or Oppression?	Observations, Thoughts, or Comments
Navaho tribe							
Living on reservation							
Female							
Low social class							
Heterosexual							
Religion							
Having siblings with disability							
Other							
Other							
Other							

From a historical point of view, society and the world are aware of the need for multicultural competence. Counseling can only remain pertinent and effective as a helping profession with continuous progression and self-improvement in order to keep up with the needs of people living in diverse communities. Consequently, the multicultural movement within the field of counseling has developed in the past decades as our society has witnessed significant social, cultural, and political changes and advances. This movement has advanced our understanding of the impact of social experiences and the role of culture in understanding individuals' psychological functioning and in the efficacy of psychological interventions.

The Context and History of the Multicultural Movement

Colonization and Its Psychological Effects

Although it has not been discussed much, the greatest historical context for discussions of modern cultural differences and power differentials among people and in the world is probably the colonization between the 16th and 20th centuries when Europeans colonized most of the earth's territory. According to Monk, Winslade, and Sinclair (2008), this colonization significantly impacted the lives of all people everywhere in the world:

> Colonization has been a major shaping influence in the modern world on the entitlements that people claim, the privileges or disadvantages that they enjoy or suffer, the expectations of life that they can "realistically" expect or not expect, the shape of family relations that they might grow up in, the identity stories that they might enact in life, the careers that are possible for them to enter, the ways in which they might make sense of adversity and respond to it, and the feelings that accompany all of these experiences. (p. 56)

Clearly, it is not only the land that was colonized, as people's experience of colonization is largely psychological. Such psychological influences of colonization have persisted and are sometimes difficult for counselors to understand. Much of today's interracial, ethnic, and national cultural differences are extensions of cultural relations produced by colonization. Slavery, for instance, was a part of the accumulated wealth of the European empire. British colonization was accompanied by the transportation of millions of Africans to the New World, where Europeans viewed enslaved Africans as "a separate and subhuman species of human kind" (Ponterotto, Utsey, & Pedersen, 2006, p. 30). Theorists have noted that racism developed as a way to rationalize the world exploration by European powers and that racial prejudice was permanently incorporated into the psychological and social consciousness of White America and Black America (Ponterotto et al., 2006).

From a cultural perspective, the colonizing power imposed its political, moral, religious, and economic will on the subjugated peoples and societies above and beyond exploitation of the physical recourses. Examples of the impact of such imposition and exploitation are clear in the United States. The British colonization generated decisive and lasting impact on the culture and institutions of our society. From religion and language to traditions and legal structures, British influence is visible. The American creed of liberty, individualism, independence, and so on reflects British settlers' principles and philosophies (Huntington, 2004).

Effects of colonization are significantly reflected in people's mental health. Due to the power differential between the colonizer and the colonized, the colonizer would impose values and judgments onto the colonized, which posted a real danger of internalized degradation. Research has shown an overrepresentation of Native Americans, African Americans, and Latino/Latinas with mental health and drug and alcohol problems and who are incarcerated (Monk et al., 2008). Viewing and treating the distress of those clients as individual problems reflects the failure in recognizing the historical effect of colonization. Such practice will not only be ineffective but could also harm the client by causing retraumatization and denigration, which is "truly unethical" (Robinson-Zañartu, 2008, p. 79).

Decolonization is a relatively new phenomenon that started only in the 20th century. The multicultural movement in counseling may be viewed as an effort to decolonize the traditional counseling theories and practices that were built upon ethnocentrism in which the worldview of the socially powerful (e.g., those of European descent) is viewed as superior and more desirable than that of the socially oppressed (e.g., racial and ethnic minorities). Given the history of colonization, the multicultural movement is necessary for the counseling profession's continuous survival and credibility in the future.

SMALL-GROUP CLASS ACTIVITY 3.2

1. In thinking about your own family history, in what ways has your family's life been affected by the history of colonization and decolonization?
2. In thinking about the case of Amber and Patty, in what ways have their lives been affected by colonization?
3. How should we conceptualize Amber and Patty's concerns or issues so that our counseling approach is helpful for them and others who share their cultural experiences?
4. In what ways may the history of colonization influence your treatment and interventions in working with Amber and Patty?

Civil Rights Movement: Race, Ethnicity, and Identity

Prior to the civil rights movement in the 1960s, the counseling field was in its early years of development. The American Personnel and Guidance Association (APGA), the first name for the American Counseling Association that is recognized today, was established in 1952. During the first few decades of the 20th century, counseling was mainly a vocational guidance practice. Due to racial inequality, discrimination, and prejudice, "vocational counselors could not counsel minorities to enter the professions of their choice: It would be illogical for them to do so when discrimination routinely denied minorities access to those professions" (Jackson, 1995, p. 5). This reality led many counselors to either exclude minority clients or match them to the types of jobs they were most likely to get (Aubrey, 1977). Undoubtedly, such practice perpetuated social inequality and compromised minority Americans' mental health.

The civil rights movement seemed to be a wake-up call for the counseling profession. It incited discussion about the role of culture and racial pluralism in counseling. In fact, it was the racial upheavals that led to the substantial debate regarding the "counseling needs of culturally different clients, as well as the efficacy of services available to certain populations" (Robinson & Morris, 2000, p. 239). In 1962, Wrenn's article "The Culturally Encapsulated Counselor" warned the field that counselors who were insensitive to cultural characteristics and worldviews of clients could do harm. Unfortunately, the message was loud at the time, but it was not heard or followed with much intensity. In hindsight, it is clear that a human rights issue existed from the very beginning since the counseling field was developed without a clear plan and/or a directive to incorporate the needs of the racially and culturally diverse.

The passage of the Civil Rights Act of 1964 further fueled the energy and attention toward concerns of racial minorities. Citizens of the United States started to discuss and raise questions about the notion of minorities as inferior to the majority race, European Americans. It was during this time period that a multicultural movement in the field of counseling was born, which led to "an era of revolution, change, and growth in the counseling profession" (Jackson, 1995, p. 8). Leading the movement to recognize the racial biases and cultural encapsulation inherent in our counseling practices were Black counseling psychologists and professionals.

Recognition that the counseling profession had failed to provide "guidance for all" gained during this time period. This recognition further stimulated theoretical evaluation and empirical research for decades. Theorists have acknowledged and argued that it was impossible to provide effective service for all if the counseling theories and practice continued to focus on the average homogeneous White American as had been the case in the past (Copeland, 1983). By the mid-1970s, research showed some clear observations, including that racial and ethnic minority clients tended to underuse voluntary mental health services, African American clients preferred to see African American counselors, and racial and ethnic minorities were underrepresented in the counseling profession (Atkinson & Thompson, 1992). These research findings contributed to the advancement of multicultural research for the following decades.

Another noteworthy milestone of the counseling profession's recognition of multiculturalism and diversity was the 1972 formation of the Association for Non-White Concerns (ANWC) and the accompanying publication of the *Journal of Non-White Concerns in Personnel and Guidance* the same year. The ANWC was the ninth division of APGA, and its mission was to promote greater understanding of its ethnic minority group members. Scholarly writings on multiculturalism proliferated the 70s and 80s. Derald Wing Sue, a Chinese American scholar and educator, was the first and only person of color to serve as editor of the *Personnel and Guidance Journal* (from 1975 to 1978). Many articles that focused on multiculturalism were published during Sue's editorship, including his (1977) seminal special issue of the journal titled *Counseling the Culturally Different: A Conceptual Analysis*.

The term *multiculturalism* did not have much of a presence until the 1970s and 1980s, which was largely due to the assumption that conceptual, theoretical, and methodological frameworks already developed would be applicable to people of color. The inclusion of people of color in national leadership roles was further noted in 1971 when Thelma Daley, an African American woman from Maryland, was elected as president of the American School Counseling Association and in 1975 as the president of the Association for Counselor Education and Supervision (ACES), a division of APGA. In 1977, ACES drafted the Standards for the Preparation of Counselors and Other Personnel Services Specialists, which mandated that training programs prepare counselors to address the needs of a racially and ethnically diverse society (ACES Commission on Standards and Accreditation, 1977). The standards further required that graduate training programs include a common core of eight general areas considered necessary to counselor preparation, including social and cultural foundations. The inclusion of coursework or curricular experiences that attended to social and cultural foundations was to ensure that counselors-in-training had understanding of diverse groups and cultures, urban and rural communities, the changing roles of women, sexism, and population patterns. The impact of this standard resulted in the increase of multicultural coursework and experiences in counselor training programs across the country.

The multicultural movement experienced unprecedented growth and maturity in the 1980s and 1990s. It earned the name "the fourth force in counseling" (Pedersen, 1999), following the first three forces of psychoanalytic/psychodynamic, behavioral/cognitive-behavioral, and humanistic counseling. During this period of time, diversity of race and ethnicity became more forefront. All major ethnic minority groups became the foci of empirical research and theoretical writings. More significantly, there were researchers and writers of all races, including Anglos, who were studying and writing about not only their own ethnic groups but also other groups (Jackson, 1995). This advancement in the multicultural movement contributed to the starting of the shift from a monolithic perspective to a pluralistic view of counseling.

A Reflection: What It Means to Be an African American in Society

I am an African American woman and training to become a counseling psychologist. In a multicultural counseling class, I was asked to reflect on what it means to be an African American in this society. I was intrigued and realized that my life has created in me an answer to guide my pursuit.

Being Black means being strong, resilient, able to endure struggle and oppression, but still smile, and it means balancing being proud of my heritage while understanding that such feelings are met with strong opposition from those who choose to not see the beauty of my race. It also means, unfortunately, to be seen as a problem in this country, ignored, and have my history minimized and some of my contributions stripped. I have to constantly fight and counter the racist messages, overt or covert, that aim to tell me what social position I can hold and what I am allowed to achieve, while simultaneously having to shout and show my self-worth and competence to those who choose not to see me and/or create their own incorrectly informed image of me. Survival and progress are crucial. They are our ultimate homage to our foremothers and forefathers that fought so hard for our equality.

Being African American also means being responsible to my family, loved ones, and the Black community because my achievement is their achievement. We are a collective. My being is their being. Dedication to the advancement of our people and constantly investing in and enriching *our* culture is imperative. It means enduring disconnect from our true ancestry and in many cases still fighting to break the psychological shackles of slavery and reconciling what this means; at the same time, it means having much honor and pride in the rich heritage and traditions established by my people in this country that is overflowing with beauty, talent, success, spirituality, passion, creativity, pride, and greatness.

Speaking up and out against racial oppression and injustice means survival and strengthening the community but risks being labeled "angry, aggressive, a troublemaker, or an attacker." In fact, being African American means grappling with this double-edged sword while seeking a balance to fulfill the much-needed call to bring awareness to the injustices in this society. It means being a part of a race and culture that is bigger than the individual, and it means joining in the fight for equality and harmony—a rich legacy.

—Shaneice J., an African American, female, counseling psychology student

Women's Movements: Sex, Sexual Orientation, and Identity

Women's movements, especially the second wave of the feminist movement, also played a role in strengthening attention to inequality and diversifying the multicultural emphasis. After the first wave removed some legal obstacles for gender equality and achieved women's suffrage in 1920, the second wave of the women's rights movement (initially called the women's liberation movement) started in the 1960s and broadened the scope of discussions and debates concerning women's rights in relation to sexuality, family, workplace, reproductive, and other de facto inequalities.

Coinciding with the civil rights movement and the anti-Vietnam War upheavals, this time period became a new age of activism in dealing with both legal and cultural gender inequality. In such a context, "the voice of the second wave was increasingly radical . . . sexuality and reproductive rights were dominant issues" (Rampton, 2014, para. 5). Issues of rape, domestic violence, abortion, and access to child care also came to the forefront of the feminist platforms. Moreover, the movement focused on passing the Equal Rights Amendment to the Constitution, guaranteeing social equality regardless of sex. Notably, unlike the first wave of feminism that was mainly propelled by middle-class White women, the second wave engaged women of color and made efforts to demonstrate that race, class, and gender oppression were all related. This recognition was evident by the increased awareness of issues related to addressing the unique counseling needs of women.

During this time, one of the most significant developments was the birth of the feminist theory that aims at understanding the nature of gender inequality by examining women's social roles and experience. *Feminist therapy* emerged in counseling women, focusing on understanding the effect of women's experiences in society on their difficulties in growth and development. It was the first time in counseling that the negative impact of sexism on women's psychological health was acknowledged and addressed in psychological interventions. Although there were variations, feminist therapies tended to focus on empowering women by helping them recognize sex roles and minority status/socialization in society as possible sources or causes of psychological difficulties. The refreshing new notion was that the goal of counseling was changing (rather than adjusting to) the sexist culture and reclaiming personal power (Mahaney, 2007).

It should be noted that contemporary feminist theories and therapies have been deemed applicable not only to women but also to men. While gender disparity often exists in society with men being on top of the power hierarchy, men, especially men with other minority status, can experience exploitation and abuse by those holding power or control over them. Feminist therapies support equal value and worth of all people and respect individuals' rights to be conforming or nonconforming or choose traditional or nontraditional identities and roles. To achieve the therapeutic goal of empowering clients, many feminist therapists emphasize egalitarian therapeutic relationships and are also social justice activists to help create and promote social changes outside of the counseling office to ultimately improve the mental health of all individuals.

Gay Rights Movement: Sexual Orientation and Identity

The gay rights movement, in the bigger context of the multicultural movement, aimed at changing the hierarchical social structures that allow the powerful to marginalize and oppress the powerless. In addition, the gay rights movement served as an impetus for counseling professionals to embrace sexual orientation in working with lesbian, gay, bisexual, and transgender (LGBT) individuals. In U.S. history, same-sex attraction was perceived as deviant and illegal, and LGBT individuals were not given equal rights. Instead, they faced dangers of being punished by the law or deemed as psychologically abnormal. In 1779, Thomas Jefferson proposed a law that would mandate castration for gay men and mutilation of nose cartilage for gay women (Head, 2014). One hundred years later, lawmakers at both state and federal levels continued to target lesbians and gay men with draconian legislation and hateful rhetoric. It was not until 1961 that Illinois repealed its sodomy law. In 1969 the Stonewall Riots marked the beginning of the gay rights movement. The 3-day riots were violent demonstrations against a police raid at the Stonewall Inn, a gay bar in Greenwich Village in New York City. These riots became a defining event in American history and represented a turning point in the struggle for gay and lesbian equal rights.

The monumental event that significantly instigated the interest in integrating LGBT-affirmative counseling within the multicultural movement was the removal of homosexuality from the second edition of the *Diagnostic and Statistical Manual of Mental Disorders* (*DSM-II*) in 1973 by the American Psychiatric Association (Rothblum, 2000). Two years later in 1975, the American Psychological Association implemented a resolution supporting LGBT-affirmative practice. However, these events, although significant and positive, did not end the discrimination of LGBT individuals in society. The social-historical contexts of negatively constructing LGBT communities and individuals and pathologizing LGBT identities have manifested in stigma and social marginalization (Wilton, 2010). The counseling profession has taken leadership in recognizing the social oppression associated with lesbian, gay, bisexual, transgender, and queer (LGBTQ) identities and developing LGBTQ-affirmative counseling in recent years.

Globalization: Nationality and Identity

The multicultural movement in counseling has been fused by the globalization movements in all areas of human life starting in the late 20th century and continuing at full speed in the new millennium. As countries and nations have become more and more interconnected through the development of international economy, technology, and an ever higher rate of immigration, the awareness has grown that many issues closely related to human health are shared across cultures and nations, such as poverty, human rights, social injustice, environmental pollution, and so forth. The possibilities as well as challenges for mental health professions have become endless. The counseling profession in the United States has responded to this emergence of "a worldwide system of countries and cultures all mutually affecting one another" (Gerstein, Heppner, Ægisdóttir, Leung, & Norsworthy, 2012, p. 3) with excitement and realization of the challenges facing us.

On one hand, scholars and practitioners of counseling have enthusiastically recognized the great opportunities embedded in an internationalization movement of counseling and have felt a calling for addressing important international issues and helping the rest of the world develop a profession that the United States has experience with. For example, many influential members of the American Counseling Association (ACA) have chosen to travel to foreign lands to serve as resources and offer counseling-related services, which the need for became particularly obvious after WWII. Moreover, individual divisions of the ACA have also become active in supporting efforts toward international work and in providing international outreach. Additionally, international counselors throughout the world have been invited and welcomed to the ACA annual conventions. Such efforts have undoubtedly contributed to the formation of the internationalization movement within the counseling field and have unprecedentedly highlighted the role of culture in psychological health for the counseling profession in the United States.

On the other hand, one of the less formally acknowledged areas that can attest to the profound impact of globalization is how the counseling profession suddenly found itself being challenged to serve people who either have international backgrounds or are influenced by international cultures. With the presence of international visitors, immigrants, refugees, and students along with that of international intellectual, cultural, and material products in the United States, the American diversity landscape has been further enriched and cultural pluralism further increased. It is becoming less and less likely that anyone living in the United States can claim being free of international cultural influences. Both in the international communities and in the United States, the threat of the tendency for cultural homogenization (Arnett, 2002) or intellectual neocolonization (G. Adams, Kurtiş, Salter, & Anderson, 2012) is to be fought against. This reality has encouraged forward thinking in the theory and practice of counseling in multicultural contexts. As a result, culturally competent counselors in the 21st century will have to develop an identity that allows them to understand, respect, and integrate international cultures to facilitate recovery, healing, development, and growth of all clients.

Social Class, Age, Disability/Ability, and Other Dimensions of Diversity

It continues to be a process for the counseling profession to fully recognize the multidimensional nature of cultural diversity. As we have seen in this chapter, political and cultural movements have often been responsible for awakening and leading the counseling profession toward addressing the role of individuals' cultures, social status, identities, and socially created life environments. In recent years, researchers and scholars further recognized the complexity of diversity and advocated for attention to the influence of several other forms of isms on individuals and the intersections of individual diverse cultural identities. Jun (2010) noted that multicultural counseling emphasizes understanding clients from their sociocultural contexts (e.g., race, gender, class, sexual orientation, disability, age, religion, language, region).

Such consideration of individuals' multicultural identities and their intersections strengthened the awareness and understanding of the harm that classism, ableism, and other isms can cause. Any of these isms represents a system that puts some individuals in unearned advantageous positions and others in unearned disadvantageous ones. More specifically, *classism* "constitutes a form of oppression that is structural, maintained by practices that constitute 'business as usual,' and played out at the individual, institutional, and cultural levels" (M. Adams, 2000, p. 380). Campbell (2001) defined *ableism* as a "network of beliefs, processes, and practices that produces a particular kind of self and body . . . projected as the perfect, species-typical, and therefore essential and fully human. Disability, then, is cast as a diminished state of being human" (p. 44). *Ageism* refers to "systematic oppression by which governmental and institutional policies and regulations give power to the dominant age groups" (Jun, 2010, p. 224).

It is clear to us that these and other isms are socially constructed and operate to rank social identities, permitting dominant groups to have systematic privilege and power over nondominant groups. All the isms are based on ethnocentrism, which creates in-groups and out-groups, with in-groups being viewed and treated as superior and better than out-groups (Jun, 2010). The recognition of these isms as sources of social oppression and privilege commands the counseling profession to address cultural and individual diversity in its practice.

SMALL-GROUP CLASS ACTIVITY 3.3

In small groups of three to four students, read Request for Counseling, then discuss and share your reflections regarding the questions that follow.

Request for Counseling

Two parents brought Tracy to you for counseling. They reported that 14-year-old Tracy, a first-year high school student, had run into troubles (failing classes, getting into fights, missing classes, disobeying campus police, etc.) in school several times during the first 3 months of the current semester. Her parents said the high school experience had changed Tracy because she had not behaved this way before. They were angry at Tracy for causing problems and unhappy that the teachers at school did not appear helpful. They wanted you to help Tracy be a better student.

Discussion Questions

1. What is your initial impression of Tracy?
2. What additional information do you want to know?
3. How would you conceptualize Tracy's issues? What do you think are the key problems?
4. What are your thoughts about how Tracy's environment plays a role in her problems?
5. What interventions are you thinking about?
6. How might the client information below inform your thinking about Tracy's issues? How would you integrate it into your conceptualization and intervention?
   a. Tracy is Latina, attending a predominantly White high school.
   b. Tracy has some visual impairment due to an accident on the playground when in kindergarten.
   c. Both parents are women (one White and one Latina), who are adoptive parents to Tracy and two other children.
   d. Although one parent has a job, the family uses food stamps and other forms of public support to get by.

Reflection Questions

1. What assumptions did you have about a high school student and possible age-related difficulties?
2. What roles do contextual factors play in an individual's psychological health and behavior?
3. What are our responsibilities in attending to clients' social and cultural contexts in our clinical work?
4. What will happen if we make the mistake of ignoring the economic, social, health, and historical factors that Tracy brings to counseling?

The Focus and Scope of Multicultural Counseling

The multicultural nature of counseling practice is usually described by terms such as *multiculturalism*, *diversity*, and *pluralism*. These terms literally imply that individuals' cultural background and identity can be multiple or plural due to the inclusive nature of the scope of diversity, including race, ethnicity, sex, gender identity, sexual orientation, social class, age, ability/disability, international status, and so on. However, recognition of the pluralistic nature of our clients' cultural diversity and seeing individuals as members of social groups are not sufficient actions to ensure the efficacy of counseling practice to people with different cultural identities because human diversity does not exist in isolation. Social and cultural groups are always relating to and interacting with each other in society, which contributes to the formation of *cultural contexts* for all individuals and social groups.

What signifies multicultural counseling is first the belief that clients' experiences are shaped and determined by their cultural context and that any of their internal struggles reflect the larger cultural context they live in. Therefore, understanding the cultural context is a necessary condition for counselors' comprehension of their individual clients and requires that counselors recognize (a) the issue of power and privilege and its impact on different social groups, (b) cultural values and worldviews specific to members of social groups and to individuals' specific cultural identity, and (c) the complexity of cultural diversity unique to each individual. Second, multicultural counseling aims at providing culturally sensitive therapeutic service to empower those who have been socially disadvantaged or disempowered due to their social and cultural memberships (see Chapters 8 through 12). Because counselors are always a part of their clients' social contexts due to their cultural group memberships, it is imperative that counselors recognize their roles in client context and serve as helping agents in providing corrective and empowering experiences for clients.

The Issue of Power and Privilege

The issue of power and privilege is a foundational theme of diversity; its uneven distribution among different groups of people underpins a variety of cultural discrimination, prejudice, and social injustice in the United States and in the world. It is no secret that inequalities and differential opportunities for social and cultural identities exist, and "the ideal situation in which members of all identifiable social groups are equally regarded and have equal opportunities in their community has never really existed anywhere" (Monk et al., 2008, p. 142). Any claim that such a situation exists is usually made from a position of power and privilege.

Power can be generally defined as the ability to control or influence others' behaviors and is owned by those in structural positions of privilege in society (Monk et al., 2008). *Privilege* refers to an invisible package of unearned advantages, assets, and benefits (McIntosh, 1989; see Chapter 7 for more details) and is granted to people who have membership in one or more of the dominant groups along the line of race, ethnicity, gender identity, sexual orientation, class, age, ability/disability, nationality, religion, and so on. These characteristics of power and privilege create hierarchical social structures "with those experiencing the worst oppression on the bottom and their oppressors on the top" (Monk et al., 2008, p. 159). In the United States, some individuals enjoy privileges in a wide range of domains; White, middle- or upper-class, heterosexual, able-bodied, and Christian males typically accumulate more power than people in nondominant or marginalized groups, such as people of color, LGBTQs, those with lower social class status, and non-Christians. Others may have privileges in a few domains, such as Asian American females as well educated professionals or young African Americans as athletic celebrities. There are others who have very few privileges, such as a Latina, disabled, single mother living in poverty or an older lesbian refugee from Vietnam who speaks poor English.

It should be noted that privilege is most likely invisible to those who have it, and it is granted to them automatically as dominant-group members by society and institutions. On the other hand, those from nondominant or marginalized groups have to endure unearned disadvantages to maintain the privileges for the powerful. Once during a multicultural conversation, a White, female, graduate student in counseling shared the following:

> I had always thought that my family's low SES (socioeconomic status) exempted me from privileges, and I resented people using racism as an excuse for not trying hard. One day it all changed when my Native American client asked me, "As a White woman, do you have to worry about raising your children in ways other people may not like? Speaking up in the professional circles of counselors? Receiving a surprised look from your realtor when you ask to see a house for sale in an affluent neighborhood?" I was shocked! For the first time, I felt convinced that having White skin does mean privilege, which is probably at the cost of others.

In another example, the first author of this book (an Asian American) saw that Diane, a young, African American, female instructor, dressed professionally each time she went to teach class, even in the hot summer, so she commended Diane by saying, "You always dress nicely when you teach." Here is what Diane said in return:

> It is all because of my skin color. When you teach, students listen because you are a smart Asian American. You do not need to dress up because your high intelligence is assumed. That is not going to happen to me. Students have no reason to listen to me. What does a fat African American woman know? I know they are thinking, "If it weren't for affirmative action, she wouldn't even be here!" Thus, I need to dress up for power. It is sad that I have to use clothing to boost my credibility, but I need to use any help I can.

These examples depict an unjust social environment. It is clearly a myth that everyone has an equal opportunity to succeed in this society. Moreover, from a psychological point of view, minority members experience much more than just the real lack of opportunities or visible hostility. The hidden messages that go along with the tangible unfairness may undermine their sense of being and hurt their self-concept and mental health.

In another example of injustice, *The Race Card Project*, hosted by National Public Radio, reported that a White mother of two African American boys learned in the process of adopting her sons that "Black babies cost less to adopt" (National Public Radio Staff, 2013), with the adoption of White babies costing almost twice as much. This is appalling and heartbreaking and is even more unspeakable if we think what messages these children were told about their self-worth even before they came to this nation. Is the world a just one for them?

Because oppression exists for some members of society at such a deeply harmful level and because it can be invisible to those who do not experience it or to those who are the perpetrators of injustice, we must first and foremost deal with the issue of power and privilege if we are to succeed in becoming multiculturally competent counselors for our diverse world. If we are members of dominant groups, we need to recognize the influence of our privileges in clients' social contexts as well as the negative influence of the unjust system in our clients' lives.

Cultural Values and Worldviews

It is absolutely necessary that multicultural counselors recognize the unfairness and injustice in the distribution of social and cultural power and privilege. Moreover, *multicultural counseling* refers to the interaction between and among counselors and clients across cultures. Such interactions can be among people representing diversity in race, ethnicity, gender, sexual identity and orientation, age, ability/disability, nationality, and so on. Due to the distinct and different cultural values and worldviews held by people from various groups along these dimensions, conducting counseling in a business-as-usual manner is a disservice to people from nondominant social groups due to the ethnocentric worldviews embedded in traditional counseling theories and practice. Both cultural misunderstanding and lack of understanding are likely if counselors are not aware of how their clients differ in cultural values and worldviews and how their clients' cultural values and worldviews interact with their social experiences as minorities in the society.

Cultural values refer to beliefs and practices that members of a culture share and that exist in various areas of human life. Hofstede (2001) observed significant differences among diverse countries and identified five dimensions for understanding cultural values: power distance, individualism, uncertainty avoidance, masculinity, and long-term orientation. The value differences are not only limited to being across nations but also serve as the basis for individuals' thinking and behavior. In a multicultural society such as the United States, cultural value differences among various social and cultural groups and individuals are especially salient because the distinctive values are constantly in contact or conflict with each other, which may further highlight disparities and associate them unfairly with being right or wrong or good or bad.

Similarly, *worldview* is a cultural phenomenon that can be described by how individuals define themselves and how they relate to each other (Triandis, 1989). Viewing cultures as individualistic or collectivistic is one way to describe different cultural orientations or worldviews. The cultures in which individuals are mainly identified by their relationships with others are *collectivistic*, while those in which individuals primarily identity themselves by internal features such as personality traits, attitudes, or abilities are described as *individualistic*. Ample research has shown that individuals do differ in the degree to which they subscribe to collectivism or individualism both between groups, cultures, and nations, as well as within themselves. There are general patterns, however, that suggest Western societies tend to be more individualistic and less collectivistic than the rest of the world, and European Americans tend to be more individualistic and less collectivistic than other people (Oyserman, Coon, & Kemmelmeier, 2002).

Characteristics of individualism include valuing independence and autonomy, focusing on individual rights over collective duties, emphasizing self-fulfillment, and basing one's identity on personal accomplishment (Hofstede, 2001). People with strong individualist values tend to give priority to personal goals over collective ones. Horizontal interpersonal relationships are honored more than vertical ones, and small power distance between people is desired in individualistic cultures. In contrast, collectivism values interdependence in relationships, focusing on duties to the collective over individual rights, emphasizing self-sacrifice for the common good, and defining the self in relational terms (Triandis, 1989). Strong collectivists tend to subordinate personal to collective goals, be concerned about the effect of their behavior on others, show conformity, and honor the high power distance in interpersonal relationships.

The term *celebrating diversity* is often used to promote the awareness of and respect for different cultural values and worldviews. It is easier said than done because cultural values, value orientations, and worldviews among people from different cultures/nations, those with different physical and ethnic backgrounds, or individuals from various social groups can be quite divergent and often conflictual. Being able to appreciate and respect the diverse values and perceptions that are different than one's own can be challenging, especially for those with dominant-group membership in a variety of dimensions. In the United States, for example, the majority's views, values, and worldviews have always been treated as the norm in defining the good, the normal, or the standard, and the deficit hypothesis (Brammer, 2012) has driven theories and practices in the area of psychology and counseling. When not of the mainstream, cultural practices and views can be perceived as less than, problematic, or even pathological.

IN-SESSION COUNSELING INTERACTION 3.1

The following counseling session excerpt involves a White female counselor and a 42-year-old, Japanese American, single woman (Rose) who is a middle school math teacher.

Rose: It has been a struggle for me to get up in the morning and go to work: I am so tired of teaching and doing the same thing every day. I try hard to avoid running into the principal because I do not want to face her.

(Continued)

(Continued)

Counselor: That must be hard. I can feel the heaviness in your mood. It sounds as if you feel tired and burned out from teaching. Perhaps it is time to consider another career. Meanwhile, maybe you can learn to practice relaxation exercises so you will feel better.

Rose: Oh, no, I am not changing my career! I do not think relaxation helps either.

Counselor: Well, don't be so quick to say no. You know removing stressors is the best way to feel better.

Rose: I can't quit teaching, really, because math teachers are in shortage right now.

Counselor: But you have been unhappy with teaching. You can't just be altruistic and not take responsibility for your own mental health. I wonder if it is a convenient excuse for you to not take the necessary action for change. I know change is hard.

Rose: Well, I don't know. Our principal . . . you know . . . she is actually good . . . I just don't know.

Counselor: Are you afraid of talking to your principal? I think I can help you learn to be more assertive. You can't let her control your life. Again, ultimately you are responsible for yourself, and you have to overcome your psychological weaknesses to take care of yourself.

As this example shows, when the counselor is not aware of the difference between her own worldview and that of the client, misunderstandings and misconceptions may occur. Rose sees staying in a job she dislikes and treating the principal as an authority as her duty to the collective, but the counselor perceives those actions as inappropriate. The counselor, who seems to value independence and autonomy, tries to empathize with Rose but fails to understand and appreciate Rose's perspective and mistakes Rose's cultural behavior as unhealthy behavior. As a result, the counselor's lack of cultural knowledge predetermined that her good intention to help Rose will fail and perhaps even do harm.

Complexity of Diversity

The complex nature of diversity and multiculturalism is apparent. The following three facts, among many others, may contribute to this complexity in obvious ways: (a) All individuals have multiple cultural and social identities; (b) the saliency of each identity is not static and may change with time, place, and social environment; and (c) individuals with the same social and cultural group memberships may differ in their sense of identity, cultural values, and worldviews.

In counseling, when we consider the interaction between the counselor and clients, other counselor variables (e.g., the counselor's cultural identities, worldviews, past experiences) will further contribute to the complexity of addressing diversity in our work. These conditions challenge the common position that "I do not see differences (e.g., color), and I treat every individual as unique," as well as the positions that stereotype minorities according to their group memberships. Both the disparities across individuals' social and cultural identities (between-group differences such as how Latinos differ from Caucasian Americans, Asians from Africans, etc.) and differentiations among individuals from the same social and cultural groups (within-group differences such as how gay men are dissimilar from each other, how African Americans contrast from each other, etc.) need to be considered and understood because they are all the ingredients of the person's social and cultural context.

A Necessary Multicultural Competency: Social Advocacy

People have a tendency or wish to see the world as a fair and just place for all—a place in which individuals are held responsible for their own problems. However, as painful as it is, it is difficult to deny the fact that oppressed groups experience exploitation, marginalization, powerlessness, cultural imperialism, and violence, although the degree and form of these aspects of oppression may vary across different groups (Israel, 2006). There are intentional and unintentional perpetrators and victims as well as dominant or subordinate social positions in this unjust system. Individuals' psychological experiences are not separable from their social and cultural experiences. Thus, mental health counseling does not, and should not, occur in a vacuum. The larger sociopolitical influence of our societal climate not only underlies our diverse clients' suffering or pain but also influences the effectiveness of our counseling interventions and practice.

Oppression operates at multiple levels, including individual, institutional, societal, and international, and all levels of oppression hurt. The individual level of oppression is reflected in individuals' attitudes and actions toward people in lower power positions (e.g., people of color, low social status, minority sexual identities, foreign heritage). As counselors, lack of awareness of our own biases and prejudice toward people with lower social power may make us instruments for perpetration through counseling practice because counseling across power lines (e.g., a White counselor counseling a client of color, a male counselor working with a woman, a straight counselor treating a gay client) mirrors the nature of social and cultural relations involving dominant-subordinate relationships. For instance, if we are not aware of our own tendency to see immigrants who speak with heavy accents as unintelligent or feel fearful of Black males as potentially violent beings, our work with those individuals could do more harm than good. Counseling serves as a microcosm of society.

Oppression at the institutional level is responsible for policies, laws, rules, or other standards that favor individuals in dominant groups or some social positions and limits the freedom and access to resources for members from minority or marginalized groups (McNamee & Miller, 2004). This level of oppression is extremely damaging to the mental health of members of socially margined groups. They may suffer from unjust oppression, but the laws or rules are not on their side to protect them. For example, since the implementation of the prominent *Rockefeller Drug Laws* in New York in 1992, the racial disparity in the prison system increased dramatically. According to a report by the New York Civil Liberties Union, African and Latino American representation among persons incarcerated for drug offenses grew from 67% prior to the law to over 90% 15 years after the laws were implemented, while 72% of the 1.3 million adults who reported using illegal drugs were White ("Rockefeller," n.d.). Such gross injustices have direct, indirect, individual, and collective impact on minority communities and play a significant role in their members' mental health.

At the societal level, oppression can be observed in social codes, norms, and other practices endorsed by the society as good or bad that unfairly demonize people in lower power, such as people of color or low social class, sexual minorities, women, and people with disabilities. Various isms and superiority-inferiority differentials are fertilized in such contexts where people from dominant groups have the privilege to use their standards to measure, judge, and evaluate the unprivileged and determine what is normal, acceptable, or valued in our society.

When cultural behaviors and norms are demonized as wrong, backward, unprofessional, inferior, and so on, individuals from these cultural groups are victimized psychologically as well as socially. Even worse, social and cultural biases and prejudices enter various areas of life, including employment and the workplace, education and training, and mental health and other services. For example, from public media outlets (e.g., *No Talking Point Talk* on CNN, July 18, 2013) to public elections (e.g., see www.webpronews.com/baggy-pants-illegal-in-louisiana-town-opponents-say-law-is-slippery-slope-2013-04), the wearing of baggy pants has often been used to pathologize and discredit African American youth who are blamed for their personal failure and problems in their community. We can imagine the kind of indirect or implied negative messages such a position presents to African American youth. In reality, the negative impact of oppression at the societal level is pervasive on every individual of the society (people from all social groups with high or low powers), but it tends to compromise the psychological health and well-being of racial, social, and cultural minorities.

Social and cultural oppression are not contained within U.S. borders nor are they exclusive to citizens of the United States. The influence of oppression at the international level has a serious presence domestically in the United States. Domestic and international oppression may interact inside and outside of the country. Due to the dynamics of world politics, immigrants and/or refugees in the United States may experience different treatment, including various levels and forms of discrimination. For example, after the 9/11 tragedy, the Federal Bureau of Investigation reported that violence and hate crimes against Muslims surged and continued to spike 10 or more years later with the unsettled U.S./Middle East relationship ("FBI," 2012).

It is obvious that the experience of oppression constitutes a major part of the social context pertaining to the psychological suffering or mental health issues experienced by some members of society. To help these individuals heal, recover, or become empowered, interventions need to include the promotion of social justice. From a psychological point of view, if environmental factors that are responsible for the individuals' distress are not recognized and addressed, then interventions that target the individual and his or her symptoms will be counterproductive and even harmful. As pointed out by McLellan (1999), counseling and therapeutic endeavors should involve working for change through pursuing justice rather than adjusting to an unjust system.

Summary

This chapter discusses the development of multicultural counseling as a historical phenomenon. It reflects and deals with social realities in microcosmic counseling settings. The challenging nature of multicultural counseling is due not only to the complexity and diversity of individual and cultural differences but also to the fact that privilege and power are intimately involved in the experiences of clients and counselors. Counselors themselves are part of the social system in which social injustice exists and have a social role to play in clients' healing processes. Therefore, whether or not the counseling profession fully recognizes the necessity of integrating social and cultural contexts into clinical practice and whether or not counselors are in touch with their own cultural identities and experiences will determine whether we help or hurt diverse clients. One necessary multicultural competency in the 21st century is engaging in social advocacy to promote social justice for all.

Takeaway Messages

1. The multicultural counseling movement reflects social changes and advances that have occurred in the United States. The movement must continue with great force in order to meet the needs of a diverse society.
2. The system of social oppression is real and harms people, communities, and society. As counselors, we need to recognize oppression and the various isms that exist in society.
3. Everyone plays a role in the unfair social system of oppression. As counselors, it is critical that we understand that oppression is the result of others' exercise of unearned privileges.
4. As counselors, we must understand that our worldview is not necessarily shared by our clients. Unintentional invalidation of our clients' values and worldviews may do harm.
5. Positive changes in individuals' lives are influenced by positive changes in their social and cultural environments. As multiculturally competent counselors, engaging in social justice advocacy is a necessary component of counseling practice in the 21st century.

Recommended Resources

Readings

Díaz-Lázaro, C. M., Verdinelli, S., & Cohen, B. B. (2012). Empowerment feminist therapy with Latina immigrants: Honoring the complexity and sociocultural contexts of clients' lives. *Women & Therapy*, *35*(1–2), 80–92. doi:10.1080/02703149.2012.634730

Escobar, J. I., Nervi, C. H., & Gara, M. A. (2000). Immigration and mental health: Mexican Americans in the United States. *Harvard Review of Psychiatry, 8*(2), 64–72.

Guthrie, R. V. (1998). *Even the rat was White: A historical view of psychology* (2nd ed.). Needham Heights, MA: Allyn & Bacon.

Novels

- *The Big Sea* by Langston Hughes
- *The Help* by Kathryn Stockett
- *The Kite Runner* by Khaled Hosseini
- *A Long Way Gone* by Ishmael Beah

Websites

http://www.apa.org/pi/lgbt/resources/history.aspx
http://www.history.com/topics/black-history/civil-rights-movement
http://www.immigrationpolicy.org
https://implicit.harvard.edu/implicit/takeatest.html
http://www.researchgate.net/publication/5414559_Antiimmigration_rhetoric_in_the_United_States_veiled_racism/file/3deec51956d20a6f17.pdf
http://www.scholastic.com/teachers/article/brief-history-womens-rights-movements

References

Adams, G., Kurtiş, T., Salter, P. S., & Anderson, S. L. (2012). A cultural psychology of relationship: Decolonizing science and practice. In O. Gillath, G. Adams, & A. D. Kunkel (Eds.), *Relationship science: Integrating evolutionary, neuroscience, and sociocultural approaches* (pp. 49–70). Washington, DC: American Psychological Association.

Adams, M. (2000). Classism. In M. Adams, W. J. Blumenfeld, R. Castaneda, H. W. Hackman, M. L. Peters, & X. Zuniga (Eds.), *Readings for diversity and social justice* (pp. 379–382). New York, NY: Routledge.

Arnett, J. J. (2002). The psychology of globalization. *American Psychologist, 57*, 774–783.

Association for Counselor Education and Supervision Commission on Standards and Accreditation. (1977). Standards for the preparation of counselors and other personnel services specialists. *Personnel and Guidance Journal, 55*, 596–601.

Atkinson, D. R., & Thompson, C. E. (1992). Racial, ethnic, and cultural variables in counseling. In S. D. Brown & R. W. Lent (Eds.), *Handbook of counseling psychology* (2nd ed., pp. 349–382). New York, NY: Wiley.

Aubrey, R. E. (1977). Historical development of guidance and counseling and implications for the future. *Personnel and Guidance Journal, 55*, 288–295.

Brammer, R. (2012). *Diversity in counseling* (2nd ed.). Belmont, CA: Brooks/Cole.

Campbell, F. (2001). Inciting legal fictions: Disability's date with ontology and the ableist body of the law. *Griffith Law Review, 10*, 42–62.

Comas-Díaz, L. (2011). Multicultural theories of psychotherapy. In R. J. Corsini & D. Wedding (9th ed.), *Current Psychotherapies* (pp. 536–567). Belmont, CA: Brooks/Cole.

Copeland, E. J. (1983). Cross-cultural counseling and psychotherapy: A historical perspective, implications for research and training. *Journal of Counseling and Development, 62*, 10–15.

FBI: Dramatic spike in hate crimes targeting Muslims. (2012, Spring). *Intelligence Report, 145*. Retrieved from http://www.splcenter.org/get-informed/intelligence-report/browse-all-issues/2012/spring/fbi-dramatic-spike-in-hate-crimes-targetin

Gerstein, L., Heppner, P., Ægisdóttir, S., Leung, S. A., & Norsworthy, K. L. (2012). *Essentials of cross-cultural counseling*. Thousand Oaks, CA: Sage.

Head, T. (2014). *The American gay rights movement: A short history*. Retrieved from http://civilliberty.about.com/od/gendersexuality/tp/History-Gay-Rights-Movement.htm

Hofstede, G. (2001). *Culture's consequences: Comparing values, behaviors, institutions, and organizations across nations* (2nd ed.). Thousand Oaks, CA: Sage.

Huntington, S. P. (2004). *Who are we? The challenges to America's national identity*. New York, NY: Simon & Schuster.

Israel, T. (2006). Marginalized communities in the United States: Oppression, social justice, and the role of counseling psychologists. In N. Fouad, L. Gerstein, G. Roysircar, R. L. Toporek, & T. Israel (Eds.), *Handbook for social justice in counseling psychology: Leadership, vision, action* (pp. 149–154). Thousand Oaks, CA: Sage.

Jackson, M. L. (1995). Multicultural counseling: Historical perspectives. In J. G. Ponterotto, J. M. Casas, L. A. Suzuki, & C. M. Alexander (Eds.), *Handbook of multicultural counseling* (pp. 3–16). Thousand Oaks, CA: Sage.

Jun, H. (2010). *Social justice, multicultural counseling, and practice: Beyond a conventional approach*. Thousand Oaks, CA: Sage.

Mahaney, E. (2007, September 13). Theory and techniques of feminist therapy [Web log post]. Retrieved from http://www.goodtherapy.org/blog/theory-and-techniques-of-feminist-therapy/

McIntosh, P. (1989, July/August). White privilege: Unpacking the invisible knapsack. *Peace and Freedom*, 10–12. Philadelphia, PA: Women's International League for Peace and Freedom.

McLellan, B. (1999). The prostitution of psychotherapy: A feminist critique. *British Journal of Guidance and Counselling, 27*(3), 325–337.

McNamee, S. J., & Miller, R. K., Jr. (2004). *The meritocracy myth*. Lanham, MD: Rowman & Littlefield.

Monk, G. D., Winslade, J. M., & Sinclair, S. L. (2008). *New horizons in multicultural counseling*. Thousand Oaks, CA: Sage.

National Public Radio Staff. (2013, June 27). Six words: "Black babies cost less to adopt" [Audio podcast]. In *The race card project*. Retrieved from http://www.npr.org/2013/06/27/195967886/six-words-black-babies-cost-less-to-adopt

Oyserman, D., Coon, H. M., & Kemmelmeier, M. (2002). Rethinking individualism and collectivism: Evaluation of theoretical assumptions and meta-analyses. *Psychological Bulletin, 128*, 3–72.

Pedersen, P. (1999). *Multiculturalism as a fourth force*. Washington, DC: Taylor & Francis.

Ponterotto, J. G., Utsey, S. O., & Pederson, P. B. (2006). *Preventing prejudice: A guide for counselors, educators, and parents*. Thousand Oaks, CA: Sage.

Rampton, M. (2014). The three waves of feminism. *Magazine of the Pacific University*. Retrieved from http://www.pacificu.edu/magazine_archives/2008/fall/echoes/feminism.cfm

Robinson, D. T., & Morris, J. R. (2000). Multicultural counseling: Historical context and current training considerations. *Western Journal of Black Studies, 24*, 239–253.

Robinson-Zañartu, C. (2008). A response to a short history of colonization and decolonization. In G. Monk, J. Winslade, & S. Sinclair (Eds.), *New horizons in multicultural counseling* (pp. 78–80). Thousand Oaks, CA: Sage.

Rockefeller Drug Laws cause racial disparities, huge taxpayer burden: Hearing before the Committees on Codes, Judiciary, Correction, Health, Alcoholism and Drug Abuse, and Social Services, New York State Assembly (n.d.) (testimony of Robert A. Perry). Retrieved from http://www.nyclu.org/content/rockefeller-drug-laws-cause-racial-disparities-huge-taxpayer-burden

Rothblum, E. D. (2000). Somewhere in Des Moines or San Antonio: Historical perspectives on lesbian, gay, and bisexual health. In R. M. Perez, K. A. DeBord, & K. J. Bieschke (Eds.), *Handbook of counseling and psychotherapy with lesbian, gay, and bisexual clients* (pp. 57–80). Washington, DC: American Psychological Association.

Sue, D. W. (1977). Counseling the culturally different: A conceptual analysis. *Personnel and Guidance Journal, 55*, 422–425.

Sue, D. W., & Sue, D. (2008). *Counseling the culturally diverse: Theory and practice* (5th ed.). Hoboken, NJ: Wiley.

Triandis, H. C. (1989). The self and social behavior in differing cultural contexts. *Psychological Review, 96,* 506–520.

Wilton, L. (2010). Where do we go from here? Raising the bar of what constitutes multicultural competence in working with lesbian, gay, bisexual, and transgender communities. In J. Ponterotto, J. M. Casas, L. A. Suzuki, & C. Alexander (Eds.), *Handbook of multicultural counseling* (3rd ed., pp. 313–328). Thousand Oaks, CA: Sage.

Wrenn, C. G. (1962). The culturally encapsulated counselor. *Harvard Educational Review, 32,* 111–119.

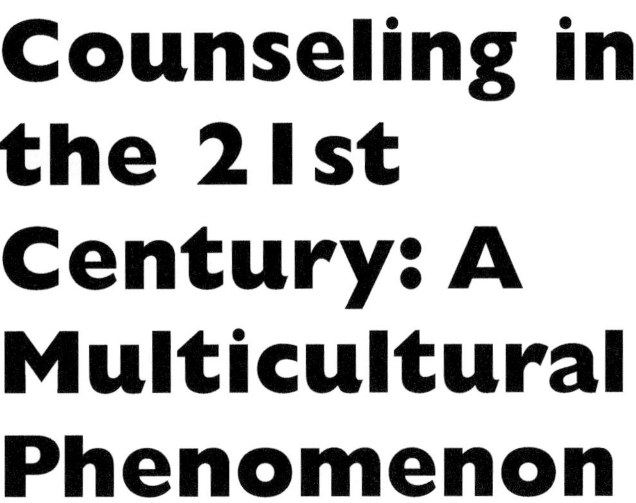

Section 2

Counseling in the 21st Century: A Multicultural Phenomenon

Major CACREP Standards for the Section

CACREP Standard 2a: Social and Cultural Diversity—multicultural and pluralistic trends, including characteristics and concerns between and within diverse groups nationally and internationally

CACREP Standard 2c: theories of multicultural counseling, identity development, and social justice

Specific Competencies Identified by CACREP Diversity and Advocacy Standards for Clinical Mental Health Counseling Addressed in Section 2

CACREP Knowledge 5: Understands the implications of concepts such as internalized oppression and institutional racism, as well as the historical and current political climate regarding immigration, poverty, and welfare

After Reading Section 2, Students Will Be Able to Do the Following:

a. Recognize the complexity of cultural identity at the individual, societal, and international levels (Chapter 4)

b. Understand the importance of attending to the intersection of clients' multiple cultural identities in the delivery of culturally relevant counseling (Chapter 4)

c. Understand the connection between social injustices and oppression and their clients' problems (Chapter 4)

d. Understand the necessity for internationalizing our counseling discipline (Chapter 4)

e. Recognize that the viability and progression of the counseling profession is contingent upon effective counseling for the culturally diverse (Chapter 5)

f. Recognize that the continued renewal of the counseling profession will require professionals to be ethically responsible by appropriately attending to the culturally diverse (Chapter 5)

Section Introduction

This section is focused on helping students understand that to remain as a viable profession in the 21st century, counseling has to be multiculturally efficacious. Due to the diversity in the cultural context at individual, societal, and international levels, counseling practice needs to address cultural and diversity issues without exception, including the intersection of multiple cultural identities, the presence of social oppression and discrimination, and cross-cultural variation in values and worldviews. Additionally, increased global migration also calls for renewal of the profession.

Chapter 4 discusses the presence and challenge of integrating individual, societal, and international multicultural contexts into counseling practice respectively. It argues that cultural context is a determining factor for the experience of the culturally diverse. The recognition of multilevel diversity will help prepare counselors-in-training to appreciate the complexity of multicultural differences so they can readily validate their client experiences.

Chapter 5 describes barriers for multicultural counseling inherent in the theories and systems of counseling due to their biased dominant cultural values. Professionals' beliefs and thinking styles can be obstacles for multicultural counseling as well. Finally, the lack of equity and access by some members of society limits the efficacy of counseling for them. This chapter promotes redefinition of counseling practice and defines multicultural counseling. It offers the perspective that professional renewal is necessary and the intersection of multiple dimensions of cultural identity deserves significant attention.

Multicultural Contexts of Professional Counseling in the 21st Century

America is more like a quilt—many patches, many pieces, many colors, many sizes, all woven together by a common thread.

—Rev. Jesse Jackson

CHAPTER OVERVIEW

This chapter considers the multicultural contexts of counseling in the 21st century with particular attention to understanding the complexity of cultural identity at the individual, societal, and international levels. Knowledge of the complexity of cultural identity at these three levels is critical to fully understand the issues and circumstances that plague our clients and to further provide a meaningful context for being able to intervene effectively on their behalf.

SELF-ASSESSMENT OF PRE-EXISTING AWARENESS AND KNOWLEDGE

- What is my awareness level of the complexity of individual cultural identity?
- How well am I able to integrate the complexity of individual cultural identity into understanding clients?
- How well do I understand the impact of social inequality on individuals' psychological functioning and well-being?
- How prepared am I to advocate on behalf of those who are directly and indirectly affected by social inequalities?
- How aware am I of the cultural context of the culturally diverse at the societal level in the United States?
- How well do I understand the influence of globalization in individuals' behaviors in the United States?
- How prepared am I to operate as a professional counselor in an international context?

LEARNING OBJECTIVES

After reading this chapter, students will be able to do the following:

1. Understand the complexity of individual cultural identity and its role in counseling
2. Acknowledge the relevance of social inequality in the psychological experiences of diverse consumers of the 21st century
3. Recognize the relevance of international issues in the behaviors and experiences of all citizens and immigrants of the United States
4. Become aware of the need to consider the role of larger social and cultural contexts in every individual's life

GUIDED PRACTICE EXERCISE 4.1

How Do You Identify?

From the list of cultural aspects that follows, select the three that are most salient to your identity and then do the following:

a. Describe the ways in which they are important to you.
b. In considering the intersection of your multiple cultural identities, discuss what it would be like to choose only *one* aspect of your identity as being core

to your being. What are the implications of minimizing other important aspects of your identity?

c. Share an example of how focusing on your salient cultural identities in isolation, rather than attending to their overlapping and interactive effects, fails to accurately reflect your life experiences.

d. Think about someone who is different from you in terms of your three cultural identities, and imagine how those aspects of his or her identity are important to him or her.

e. Why would failure to recognize the intersection of a client's multiple cultural identities (i.e., race, ethnicity, gender, and social class) be incongruent with the practice of effective multicultural counseling?

1. Race/Ethnicity
2. Sex
3. Gender
4. Sexual orientation
5. Class
6. Marital status
7. Religion
8. Professional/Career role
9. Family role
10. Age
11. Ability/Disability status
12. Health status
13. Political affiliation
14. Nationality
15. Geographic region
16. Education level
17. Professional activity
18. Leisure activity
19. Other (please specify)

CASE ILLUSTRATION 4.1

The Case of Multiple Cultural Identities

Syria and James have been married 20 years (unhappily the past 13 years); she is 38 and Vietnamese with a 2-year college degree, and he is 41, European American, and a high school graduate. James, who is of the Christian faith, left his wife and son and moved back to the United States from Vietnam 6 years ago to find stable employment. Four years later, Syria, who is Buddhist, immigrated to the United States from Vietnam with their 19-year-old son Kyle, who was diagnosed with autism at age 5. Although both James and Syria report praying daily that Kyle be healed from autism, they have not been spared the daily and insurmountable stressors of caring for an emotionally and mentally challenged son who they fear will never be able to leave home and consequently will forever be dependent upon them.

Syria is a stay-at-home mom who expressed disappointment that she is unable to work or to have a life outside the home due to being Kyle's primary caretaker. James has been unemployed off and on the past 4 years due to layoffs and seasonal work; recently, he was hired as a technician for a heating and cooling company, making $8.23 hourly with insurance benefits provided (although at a high premium that he cannot afford and has thus declined). Due to James's intermittent employment history, low income, lack of insurance, and the expenses incurred for Kyle's mental health treatment, the family has been strapped for money and living in poverty throughout their marriage.

Syria and James's marriage was in trouble prior to her migrating to the United States, and it has continued to deteriorate. They have reached out for counseling support at a low-cost community agency with a sliding fee scale. According to James, their family and marital problems stem from Syria not understanding or trying to understand the "American way." James shared that Syria, who has limited English skills, refuses to acculturate to this country. Syria explained that she does not know how to dismiss (nor does she want to abandon) her Vietnamese behaviors and traditions, and she was surprised at how quickly her American husband resumed his American ways (i.e., values, belief systems, communication styles, and behaviors). She pointed out that while living in Vietnam they socialized with her family, and James seemed quite comfortable doing as the Vietnamese did. She further shared how much she misses her family's support and how alone and misunderstood she has felt the past 2 years, especially during outings to the store and doctors' appointments for her son. In exasperation, she commented on her failed attempts to connect with others, her experiences with racial microaggression in the health care system (e.g., when visiting the restroom during her son's doctor appointment, she was mistaken for a custodial worker by a White female nurse practitioner and was asked to refill the soap dispenser) and in her surrounding community (e.g., being overlooked at the pharmacy counter while the White male behind her was attended to), and her belief that even her own husband has given up on her despite her efforts to nurture and salvage their marriage.

Syria appeared distressed and doubtful about her life and broke into tears when she spoke about her adult autistic son and her worries about who would care for him if something unexpected happened to her. She said she had been made to feel that his autism is her fault, so consequently, he is her responsibility. She appeared saddened, anxious, and fearful with evidence of low energy and a large distaste for life.

Clearly, this couple's life realities are rooted in a complicated cultural context in which each one has a set of unique cultural identities and values that may potentially complement or conflict with each other. Their life experiences are further complicated by the social reality they must face individually and also deal with as a couple. Although it is unlikely that James will be viewed and treated as an immigrant, it is likely that being married to an immigrant woman and fathering an immigrant child will expose him to discrimination or prejudicial biases toward immigrants either directly or indirectly through his wife and son. The counselor who works with Syria and James will have to understand and attend to their cultural contexts at the individual, societal, and international levels and specifically consider how the social constructions of race, gender, class, and immigration status have resulted in unfair and unjust social treatment.

The design and delivery of effective interventions are contingent upon addressing the simultaneity of social oppressions (e.g., racism, sexism, classism, immigrationism) that Syria is experiencing, the ethnicity and gender dynamics that are at play in this marriage, the couple's cultural conflict and ensuing power struggles, and other social and cultural issues. Moreover, attention is needed to understand the interactions between this couple's individual cultural negotiations and adjustments and the cultural context they live in at the societal and international levels. For instance, James followed the Vietnamese traditions while in Vietnam and did not think it unreasonable to expect Syria to follow the American Christian way now. However, in the societal context where White people enjoy unearned privileges and in the international context where the United States has a higher status in international affairs than Vietnam, demanding Syria to adopt the American Christian way of life may have the effect of invalidating her experiences and devaluing her culture.

SMALL-GROUP CLASS ACTIVITY 4.1

Integrating Knowledge About Multiple Cultural Identities for Clinical Practice With Syria and James

In a small group, discuss how you would work with this couple while attending to the intersection of their multiple cultural identities and what it means to you to be in tune with the history, values, and perspectives related to the couple's racial and ethnic group memberships, social class positions, and international background.

Cultural Context at the Individual Level

As discussed in Chapter 2, the United States has and will continue to become increasingly diverse. Reflected in this U.S. diversity is the recognition that every individual has a multicultural context, especially those with minority status in one or more domains of diversity (e.g., race, ethnicity, gender, sexual orientation/identity, age, disability. All individuals' worldviews are rooted in their relevant social and demographic identities.

Therefore, "an individual can be fully understood only in a holistic manner that includes understanding the influences and interactions of the individual's multiple sociodemographic groups, some or all of which may be salient identities for the individual" (Croteau & Constantine, 2005, p. 162). Needless to say, counselors' development of their own multicultural identity becomes a necessary condition for them to be able to understand, appreciate, and validate clients' personal and social experiences. In discussion of multicultural counseling in the 21st century, Jun (2010) identified a holistic perspective in "simultaneously examining one's multiple identities and how they intersect" (p. 12) as an essential ingredient of counselor multicultural competence.

Effective multicultural counseling demands that counselors understand clients and their worldviews from their social, cultural, and historical contexts with multiple identities and integrate this understanding into the delivery of culturally relevant services. Specifically, counselors must consider the intersection of multiple cultural identities when working with clients, particularly those whose worldviews may differ from their own. Race, ethnicity, social class, gender, sexual orientation, and social class represent salient cultural group memberships and are therefore the relevant lenses through which one's experiences and circumstances should be viewed (Constantine, 2001; Wilton, 2010). We risk our counseling services being ineffective when we consider these multiple cultural identities in isolation.

In order to accurately capture the complexities of one's life experiences and to understand the meaning one assigns to various issues and life circumstances, counseling professionals must focus on the intersection of their clients' salient cultural identities and the social oppression associated with every identity. Failure to consider the unique relationships among multiple cultural identities such as race, ethnicity, social class, gender, and sexual identity in our work with clients is antithetical to multiculturally competent counseling (Constantine, 2002; Jack, Ali, & Dias, 2014).

Historically, not only has the mental health field failed to attend to issues that are specific to various racial, ethnic, and cultural groups, but it has also failed to consider the interaction of various identity statuses. As a positive development in the past decades, the multicultural movement in the counseling field has raised awareness about the role of individual cultural identity in mental health, but the dominant approach used in addressing identity issues has by and large been single-identity based. As a result, an ethnic minority woman may be attended to as either a person of color or a woman, so her social experiences associated with the intersection of these two identities are often neglected. Failure to attend to the intersection of her identities is at the very least unfortunate and counterproductive. To further illustrate, if the counselor working with Syria focused only on her experience of being Vietnamese while trying to solve her marital problems, it is quite likely that Syria would feel misunderstood and perhaps even invalidated. Being forced to choose only one aspect of her identity minimizes and/or silences other important aspects of her being and may imply that she must declare allegiance to one cultural community rather than promote herself as a wholly integrated individual. The interplay of her identities significantly shapes her experiences and realities and consequently cannot be ignored (Fukuyama & Ferguson, 2000). In short, we can no longer risk compartmentalizing our clients' multiple identities into separate cultural categories that do not accurately reflect their experiences and real-life circumstances.

Attending to the Intersection of Multicultural Identities: Working With Syria

There are many multiple and overlapping layers of cultural identities that can be underscored and should be taken into consideration when conceptualizing Syria's social and life experiences (e.g., race, ethnicity, gender, language, physical disability, social class, sexual orientation, nationality). The distress that Syria described can be best understood in the context of her multiple experiences: She is a female immigrant of color and low socioeconomic status with Buddhist beliefs, and she is in a strained marital relationship with a White male while being the primary caretaker of a son with a disability. Her salient ethnic and national identities suggest that she may encounter discomfort, rejection, and even persecution due to her "foreigner" status that is accompanied by different customs, traditions, attitudes, and beliefs. In addition, she is poor, female, and Buddhist, which means she is not a member of the dominant culture (e.g., White, male, middle/upper class, Christian), so she is not the bearer of power or a developer of policy. Although she is unable to enter the workforce due to her caretaking responsibilities, if she were able to do so it is likely that her options would be limited to gender-segregated, low-wage, and stressful occupations with limited opportunity for advancement as this is a common position for the majority of women (Harley, Jolivette, McCormick, & Tice, 2002).

For immigrant women of color, poverty is likely to be an inherent part of their identity. Syria's support for her multiple cultural identities may be limited given her noted difficulties with establishing meaningful connections with others, including her husband, James, who believes her distress and their marital conflict can be resolved by her becoming more acculturated. Unintentionally, James's expectation for Syria to adopt the American Christian way compounds the negative rejection she experiences in the larger environment and reinforces the negation of her cultural heritage. When working with Syria, considering only one aspect of her multiple cultural identities (i.e., immigrant) does not allow her distress to be understood within the complex interplay of race, class, and gender, which has historical roots that reinforce oppression, discrimination, and devaluation of women.

In what follows, we provide an example of dialogue between Syria and a White female counselor who is not paying particular attention to the intersection of Syria's multiple cultural identities:

Syria: There are times when I wake in the morning and dread getting out of bed. I often wish I could sleep forever and in peace.

Counselor: You sound very depressed. Can you tell me if you have other symptoms of depression?

Syria: Am I depressed? I can't be depressed. I have a son to take care of.

Counselor: You are right that you have important responsibilities. Maybe you can let your husband share a bit more responsibility with caring for Kyle.

Syria: Maybe I should, but I would feel terrible about myself.

Counselor: Feel terrible for asking your husband to do more? You know James should understand that you both share the responsibility. Women should not feel bad for asking to be treated equal to men.

Syria: I know, but I don't know.

When counselors fail to conceptualize client issues in their complex cultural context, they are more likely to treat the client as "any client" with generic interventions applied, even if these interventions may have been ineffective to other clients. In this situation, the counselor seemed unaware of Syria's value for peace, her belief in the responsibility of motherhood, her expectations for her marriage, and her gender identity within a Vietnamese context. Such generic interventions may "miss the target" and fail to effectively empower clients and/or address client concerns.

Challenges of Integrating Individual Multicultural Contexts in Counseling Practice

What explanations are available regarding the challenges and/or difficulties counseling professionals may encounter with integrating meaningful elements of multiple identities? Constantine (2002) noted that our counseling training practices have historically relied on viewing each identity status separately and have failed to recognize the value of considering their potential interactions. The history of the multicultural movement in the counseling field represents developmental stages. As we learned in Chapter 3, multicultural counseling development started with the influence of the human rights movement and was subsequently fused by other cultural movements, including women's and gay rights movements. Each of these forces concentrated on addressing one area of diversity. In the past decades, this single-diversity focus resulted in literature being generated by multicultural scholars and researchers that was segregated among different dimensions of diversity. In recent years, however, the voice for promoting a holistic approach and attention to intersections of individual cultural identities in multicultural counseling has become stronger. Some scholars even proposed treating "multiple identities of an individual and intersections of multiple identities equally" (Jun, 2010, p. 8). We understand that this approach is yet to become mainstream thinking and recognize the validity of fear that an emphasis on "other diversities" may take away from the importance of addressing the negative impact of racism and discrimination on people of color. An important consideration is that the emotional salience varies among different dimensions of diversity in society, and so does the level of hurt associated with individual experiences related to different dimensions of diversity. Therefore, in applying a holistic perspective to understanding individuals' multicultural identities, we face the challenge of not minimizing any aspect of an individual client's experiences while being sensitive to the implications of the social and cultural contexts within society.

In practice, Constantine (2002) noted that some counselors may be reluctant to embrace the complexities of the interaction of multiple cultural identities for fear of feeling overwhelmed or uninformed about how to assist clients whose concerns may be rooted in societal injustices such as institutional oppression. To competently manage this overwhelming task, counseling professionals are challenged to develop their multicultural identities (Section 3) and learn to understand the cultural contexts of clients at the societal and international levels. Without a multicultural identity, it is extremely difficult for counselors to understand client experiences related to all multicultural identities. Further, to offer effective and fair assessments and treatments to clients with diverse cultural backgrounds, counselors have to be aware of the larger cultural contexts clients live in as they have a role in shaping and responding to client behaviors. It is probably true that the diversity context at the individual level contributes to the individual client's subjective and unconscious experiences, and the diversity contexts at the societal and international levels shape the cultural climate and collective unconscious in which clients' personal experiences are housed.

GUIDED PRACTICE EXERCISE 4.2

My Contributions to the Practice of Isms

Consider ways in which you have talked yourself out of feeling responsible for ethnocentrism, cultural racism, classism, sexism, homophobia, discrimination, and unexamined professional privilege. For example, maybe you recycled the myth of equal opportunity and merit or suggested that the problems of marginalized group members can be resolved by them working harder to include themselves rather than acknowledging their oppressive environments or assumed that our counseling consumers who are from racial and ethnic minority groups are to blame when our counseling interventions are ineffective.

Cultural Context at the Societal Level

Although a society that reflects diversity across race, ethnicity, gender, religion, sexual orientation, and age attests to the strengths of a heterogeneous culture, the United States with its vast diversity continues to struggle with equality for all. This struggle is described by the numerous historical movements and laws that have taken place in the fight for justice, access, and opportunity, including movements for civil rights, Asian rights, Chicano rights, gay rights, and women's rights and laws like the Americans with Disabilities Act (ADA). The diverse identities reflected in our nation (i.e., race, ethnicity, gender, age, sexual orientation, religion, and physical ability) are identity constructs that in conjunction with one another inform making meaning of life (Robinson & Howard-Hamilton, 2000). As previously noted, identities are multiple and simultaneous and affect a client's problem orientation.

Due to the lack of equity for members of various domains of diversity, individuals may live in the same society in the United States but face different social and life realities, which is significantly attributable to the cultural context that society has created and maintained. This context has awarded the "privileged" members, groups, and classes with more rights and resources than the unprivileged. Victor Lewis, who is a cast member of the famous diversity-training film *Color of Fear* (Lee, 1994), used an eloquent analogy that on the road toward opportunities and resources, the "spikes" of the roadblock would go flat for some people and up for others, making success possible or easier for some and impossible or harder for others. This unjust social reality is the context in which all Americans live. It is a fact that is hard to deny—that members of minority groups, such as people of color, women, lesbian/gay/bisexual/transgender/queers, nondominant-religion followers, immigrants/refugees, and those with low social class status are confronted with more obstacles and have to work harder than those with majority statuses in our society. For this reason, counseling practices have to address issues related to cultural contexts at the societal level for all clients in order to offer them effective, fair, just, and culturally relevant services.

To adequately address the influence of the societal level of cultural contexts for our diverse clients, professional counselors need to first recognize the unjust social reality that members of minority groups have to face and understand that the mental health of minorities is closely tied to the social injustice imposed onto them. Secondly, counselors need to examine their own multicultural identities, acknowledge their own unearned privileges and disadvantages, and acknowledge their roles in the unfair and unjust social oppression minority members of society experience. They need to understand how their cultural identities interact with those of their diverse clients (Section 3 of this book is devoted to these topics in detail) and how their ability to help diverse clients is based on their appreciation and fathom of clients' cultural and social experiences. Moreover, respecting cultural pluralism in society is a critical step for counseling professionals who expect to respond to the mental health needs of clients who differ from themselves in terms of race, culture, ethnicity, and social class. Pluralism challenges the history of oppression in the United States and emphasizes the value of cultural diversity. Sadly, though, the field of counseling is not exempt from the influence of ethnocentrism, classism, cultural racism, sexism, and discrimination (Utsey, Ponterotto, Reynolds, & Cancelli, 2000).

Numerous multicultural scholars (Greenleaf & Williams, 2009; Prilleltensky, 2008; Ratts, 2009) have written about the failed ethical responsibility of helping professions to address societal barriers due to the viewpoint that psychological distress and mental disorders are solely biologically or psychologically based and therefore originate and exist internally (Greenleaf & Bryant, 2012). This conceptualization of human problems does not help counselors to understand the effects of historical and current oppression, nor does it support counselors in making the connection between external social injustices and oppression and their clients' problems (Greenleaf & Williams, 2009). For example, the minority client whose mental and physical health are negatively impacted by racial profiling or inequities in health care is clearly the victim of failed systemic and discriminatory social policies, yet the mental health professional's training may direct him or her to concentrate on the problem at the individual level rather than address the systemic and large-scale changes that are needed. The experiences of prejudice and discrimination are a social reality for racial/ethnic minorities and other marginalized groups such as women, gays and lesbians, sexual minorities, and disabled persons who encounter social, economic, cultural, and political forces that deny them equal access and opportunity.

Attending to the Societal Cultural Context: Working With Syria and James

If the counselor who works with Syria and James shares James's worldview that at the root of the couple's marital problems is Syria's "unwillingness to acculturate and accept the American way," the counselor may be guilty of ethnocentric monoculturalism (i.e., assessing the client from only one cultural lens and failing to question his or her own biases), which is dysfunctional and unacceptable in a pluralistic society. To hold the belief that one group's history, values, language, and traditions are superior to another risks perpetuating the long-standing harm that has been done to minority citizens. Sue and Sue (2013) reminded us that much work remains if we are to successfully eradicate the historical practices of the counseling profession that have restricted, stereotyped, damaged, and oppressed the culturally diverse in our society. Moreover, they pointed out that it is the well-intentioned individuals who regard themselves as moral, decent, and fair-minded who may experience the greatest challenge with understanding how their beliefs and actions may be biased and prejudiced. For example, the White female nurse practitioner who visited the restroom at the same time as Syria made a judgment initially based on skin color and gender. The process of judging by appearance may be largely unconscious but undeniably occurs not only outside of the counseling event but also may be reenacted in our counseling sessions as well.

Assuming the counselor who works with Syria and James considers the convergence of multiple identity constructs in each of their lives, she or he would understand that their problems have been shaped by a constellation of factors that include ethnicity, gender, culture, geographic region, family, religion, and other dimensions such as ethnic identity. It is imperative that the counselor focus on all the identities that profoundly shape Syria's presenting concerns such as being a woman, wife, Buddhist, mother of an emotionally challenged son, and an immigrant living in the United States. All of these dimensions are critical to understanding Syria holistically, and none should be minimized or neglected. For example, only recently has the mental health profession removed its skepticism about the importance of religion/spirituality in the counseling milieu. Nonetheless, counselors have tended to avoid discussing this topic for reasons that include (a) lack of feeling comfortable or competent, (b) fear of proselytizing or judging their clients, (c) concern of usurping the role of clergy, and (d) belief that atheist or agnostic values held by the counselor challenge the authenticity of discussing spiritual or religious issues (Sue & Sue, 2013). Should the counselor fail to consider Syria's religious values, he or she runs the risk of overlooking important aspects of her cultural experience that may serve a role in helping her make meaning in life and cope with stress, particularly during turbulent and conflictual times. We acknowledge, however, that for some clients, religion may represent a form of oppression and bondage that hinders rather than helps to resolve problems, and this too must be explored with the client. To be effective, the counselor must consider Syria's multiple identities that exist simultaneously without being judgmental or engaging in stereotypical thinking. Listening to Syria's personal and unique story is essential.

The counselor will also need to effectively communicate with clients about their cultural values so that such values and worldviews are considered when making treatment decisions. It is important to know that a discussion of values common to various ethnic and cultural groups is not intended to place people into discrete categories, nor do we encourage the multiculturally competent counselor to memorize a list of values regarded as common to a particular group, regardless of how reassuring this practice may be for the counselor trainee. To do so implies a cookie-cutter approach, which is insensitive and offensive to the clients' uniqueness and intersection of their multiple cultural identities.

REFLECTION AND DISCUSSION QUESTIONS 4.1

An important aim of developing a multicultural professional identity is to recognize and appreciate the diversity that exists among people.

1. What are your attitudes regarding differences?
2. What perceptions do you hold about marginalized groups?
3. What is your own motivation for developing a multicultural professional identity?
4. Why are identifying and understanding the strengths of a client's culture important?
5. On which identity constructs might an inexperienced counselor working with Syria and James focus?

Multicultural Counseling Considerations for Working With Syria and James

Multicultural counseling with Syria and James must give simultaneous attention to family and community/systemic concerns. Specifically, the following issues must be addressed:

a. The level of acculturation for the family and each of its individual members
b. The value patterns being expressed and those that are characteristic of the family's cultures of origin

c. The family's understanding of mainstream values and the impact of them on their family dynamics

d. What conflicts exist in their cross-cultural marriage and what compromises can and have been made to compensate for potential value differences

Challenges of Integrating Societal Multicultural Context in Counseling Practice

What are some of the challenges or difficulties counseling professionals may encounter regarding the integration of societal cultural contexts in understanding individual clients' experiences? The greatest challenges are probably associated with the fact that we, counseling professionals, are part of the societal cultural contexts of our clients. Depending on the counselor's specific salient cultural identities, she or he may represent oppressors without awareness and perpetrate on clients of diversity unintentionally. For instance, a counselor who is White, male, heterosexual, Christian, able-bodied, or American born may represent unearned privilege, high social power, and majority group status to his clients who fall on the minority side of the various diversity dimensions. If the counselor is not fully aware of these dynamics or does not take responsibility to correct societal injustices experienced by the client, he could exacerbate the cultural and social victimization of the client. Sue and Sue (2013) stated the following:

> Perhaps the greatest obstacle to a meaningful movement toward a multicultural society is our failure to understand our unconscious and unintentional complicity in perpetuating bias and discrimination via our personal values/beliefs and our intuitions. The power of racism, sexism, and homophobia is related to the invisibility of the powerful forces that control and dictate our lives. In a strange sort of way, we are all victims. Minority groups are victims of oppression. Majority group members are victims who are unwittingly socialized into the role of oppressor. (p. 124)

Moreover, many of the dominant cultural values and beliefs that most individuals in our society are socialized with often reflect ethnocentric perspectives and distort the reality for minority members of the society. An example is the strong American value of meritocracy that implies that the United States offers a system of pure democracy in that the talented are awarded with power and privilege on the sole basis of their achievement. This belief has been deeply ingrained in America's value system since it is taught in schools and by society. The fascination with the meritocracy myth is exhibited by political leaders, corporate leaders, and the media, primarily in the perpetuation of the claim that meritocracy already exists (Thomas, 2013). This claim of meritocracy leads to the "no excuses" rhetoric that minimizes the experience and reality of people of color, women, and those in poverty. Individuals are led to believe that if one does not succeed, it is because the person is lazy, stupid, of weak character, or immoral. The meritocracy myth ignores the social inequality inherent in support and resources as well as the lack of level playing fields for minority or socially marginalized individuals. This myth, if unchallenged, can color and bias the counselors' perception of their clients with diverse backgrounds, and if unchecked, the counselor may revictimize them by failing to validate their experiences and/or blaming them for their plight.

To overcome these challenges, counselors must engage themselves in the lifelong pursuit of unlearning the isms that they have been socialized into believing, taking action to reduce their contribution to social oppression of others, and demystifying meritocracy for themselves and others. Developing a multicultural identity and nurturing a multicultural consciousness will allow individuals to see, hear, believe, and validate clients' social reality and take deliberate action to deconstruct Western assumptions of counseling that result in bias against racial/ethnic minorities, women, gays/lesbians, and others who are culturally diverse. From the perspective that our clients' experiences are rooted in cultural contexts at the societal level, counselors have the responsibility not only to help individuals in their counseling room but also to engage in social justice advocacy to promote, create, and facilitate social and cultural changes in society.

Again, developing a multicultural identity is a critical preparation for counselors to become multiculturally competent. Because the values, traditions, beliefs, and practices of our society are structured to mostly one segment of the population (i.e., European Americans or Western cultures), the oppression of the indigenous people of this country remains a social reality. The mental health delivery system and the counseling professionals it employs must be deliberate in their actions.

A Reflection of Cultural Identity by a Mexican Immigrant

I am a heterosexual Mexican male who identifies as a Hispanic and Latino person. I identify as a Hispanic because it resonates with my Spanish cultural and genetic heritage. I identify myself as Latino because Mexico is part of the Americas that was conquered by people from Western European Latin cultures (those whose language is derived from Latin such as Italian, French, Spanish, Portuguese, and Romanian). However, none of those two terms resonates as strong with me as the term *Mexican*; I am first and foremost Mexican.

Being Mexican to me (and probably to many of my family and friends) means being friendly, joyful, brave, celebrating life and death, eating traditional Mexican food, and listening to traditional music (my favorites are autochthonous music, huapangos, and mariachi, in that order). Because there is not a division of people by race in Mexico, as all Mexicans, I grew up without a racial identity; this has been an issue ever since I moved to the United States 10 years ago where I am required to define myself racially every time I fill out a form at a doctor's office, school, bank, federal government office, and so on. This pressure to define myself racially motivated me to research my family history—my Mexican history—and pay for an ancestry DNA test to compare and contrast with what

> my family and the history books said. It has not been easy to match my findings with the current American racial taxonomy. It seems extremely artificial to define myself racially in any specific way using the current racial categories in the United States. I wonder if I will ever find personal meaning in a racial term used in the United States (other than *human*) in a way that resonates with me strongly enough to identify with it. On the other hand, I still feel like an outsider, even after 10 years of being a permanent resident in the United States.
>
> –*Diego, a graduate student*

Cultural Context at the International Level

In its most recent training standard, the Council for Accreditation of Counseling and Related Educational Programs (CACREP) emphasizes understanding "characteristics and concerns between and within diverse groups nationally and internationally" (CACREP, 2009, p. 10) as one core area of knowledge necessary for the professional identity of 21st century counselors. This standard reflects the progressive nature of the organization's training expectations for meeting the needs of the public both in the United States and in the global village. Indeed, in today's globalized world, the boundaries between countries are shrinking and international exchanges increasing. The cultural context at the international level, which once existed in the far distance for many people, has entered the lives of American counselors, American consumers of counseling, and residents of the global village. Thus, counselor competence in addressing the role of international cultural contexts in working with clients domestically or internationally has become relevant, important, and necessary.

The internationalization of counseling is viewed by some scholars as having started as early as the 1940s when U.S. counseling experts began to collaborate with counselors in other countries (Heppner, Leong, & Chiao, 2008). It gradually formed a recognizable movement in the field of multicultural counseling (Ponteratto, 2008). Many writers describe this movement as being marked by an increase in the number of counseling scholars and practitioners who have extended their work beyond the U.S. and Canadian borders by offering services such as consulting, teaching, training, and research efforts (Gerstein, 2006) and the global growth of the counseling profession (Heppner et al., 2008). Commendably, these writers expressed awareness of the power differential between the scholars from the United States and those in international communities and warned the counseling field that internationalization efforts are not exempt from prejudice and biases inherent in the Western counseling theories and practice. In some ways, this movement can be described as "internationalizing domestic counseling products," which no doubt contributed to form the new international cultural context for people who are involved either directly or indirectly.

There is another side of this internationalization phenomenon that can be seen as reflecting a "globalization of identity" emerging from the ever-increasing level of migration across the globe and influenced by mass media and new technology (Monk, Winslade, & Sinclair, 2008). Compared to just a few decades ago, people living in the United States (and in the global village) have become much more internationalized, both in influencing and being influenced by foreign peoples, cultures, and products. Perhaps we can call it "integrating international influence domestically." In addition to being vertically shaped by their inherited cultures (e.g., racial, class, nationality/heritages), individuals are exposed to and influenced by, more than ever, international cultures horizontally (e.g., through immigration, media, technology). This phenomenon has made cultural context at an international level relevant and significant for all residents in the United States.

Along with the entry of international cultures into the United States, the complexity level of the cultural context of individuals, groups, families, and communities increases. It is likely that people within the same ethnic group, same social class, or even the same family will have different perceptions and experiences of their cultural contexts because individuals, especially young people, are prone to horizontal cultural influences. For instance, an immigrant family from Mexico will likely bring with them their traditional cultural values and practices. While the parents could raise their children consistent with their beliefs, children will grow up in communities where they are exposed to values in gender roles, religion, individual freedom, and so on. Likewise, this dynamic could happen with any other American family. People of all ages or racial backgrounds in different social classes are subject to what is brought about by the globalization of identity. To various degrees, families and individuals may be confronted by a "cultural war" (Monk et al., 2008, p. 253) as the result of horizontal cultural impact through immigration, media, and technology advancement. One familiar example would be an international marriage entering a family system that contains diverse opinions, which will set or create a new cultural context.

The counseling profession is caught in this phenomenon and challenged to provide effective service to discrete and connected cultural groups and peoples in the United States or across the borders. From the perspective that individual behavior can only be understood accurately in the context of the person, it is not hard to see why it is getting increasingly difficult for the counseling profession to sustain or operate from a set of existing descriptions of client needs or theoretical approaches. We need to recognize that individuals' cultural lives are shaped by contemporary social and cultural forces in which globalization, internationalization, and international exchanges have undeniable and significant roles. More and more likely, everyone's lives will be influenced by international cultural dynamics and interactions in some way. Therefore, being aware of and understanding the cultural context at the international level is critical for counseling in the 21st century. We believe that how individuals interact and operate domestically will contribute to their interactions with the rest of the world, and how the rest of the world relates to the United States and its citizens will influence individuals' lives within the country borders.

Attending to the International Cultural Context: Working With Syria and James

There is no question that being Vietnamese is one aspect of Syria's identity that brings her certain experiences. These experiences will be related not only to her Vietnamese cultural values but also to how others view her country and culture and treat her as a Vietnamese immigrant. Although it is possible that Syria might not present her Vietnamese identity as a problem or even a source of stress, the counselor who works with Syria should be sensitive to the potential influence of her international background.

Let's assume that Syria's counselor is an African American female. When working with Syria, the counselor needs to be aware of the power differential not only between Syria and herself but also between Vietnam and the United States. Being an ethnic minority, the counselor may be able to relate to Syria as a minority person; however, the counselor should be aware that she also represents U.S. citizenship, which places her in the higher power position. If Syria has difficulty trusting or sharing at the beginning of counseling, the interpretation should not be simply about client resistance or her inability to trust. When an immigrant lives in a country that holds higher power than his or her home country, psychological adjustment usually involves a period of time to feel comfortable or worthy of being in the country. Part of it is adjusting to a new place and new culture, but a significant part of it is the unavoidable consistent reminder by people and the surrounding environment that he or she is an outsider and from a country that has less power than the United States.

The counselor needs to consider this context in conceptualizing Syria's concerns, including all those related to language, values, worldview, communication style, faith, and so on. From goal setting to evaluation of counseling outcomes, Syria's experiences will have to be understood at both micro and macro levels, the latter including her feelings and experiences as an immigrant. With sensitivity, the African American counselor may be able to ease Syria's fear and distress by showing her understanding of the minority experience as well as acknowledging her power of being a member of a country that is hosting Syria's migration. The counselor's demonstrated respect for Syria and acceptance of her multiple cultural identities may have healing powers toward easing Syria's anxiety about not belonging.

Challenges of Integrating International Multicultural Context in Counseling Practice

Internationalizing Counseling and International Power Structure

Conducting international work will move the counseling profession beyond the U.S. borders, which shows the good intentions of American counseling professionals who want to share themselves and what they know with the rest of the world. However, viewed in the context of the world power structure, this effort is faced with the challenge not to blindly exercise the power and privilege that the United States possesses over other countries and impose on countries that are lower in power. Scholars have observed that "the globalization of cultural influences can be understood as a subtle new vehicle for political, economic, and cultural domination, a colonizing movement of the 21st century that recapitulates the colonization of previous centuries" (Monk et al., 2008, p. 229). Bound by the professional ethics of the field and guided by the desire to be truly helpful, it is the responsibility of counselors and mental health providers who engage in direct international work to acquire fluent knowledge of the targeted international culture, be aware of the potential power differential, and to offer services with cultural sensitivity.

International Counseling and Cultural Encapsulation

As we learned in Chapter 1, the counseling practice as we know it is largely developed from a monocultural perspective, focusing on individualistic and egocentric needs and using ethnocentric approaches toward change. This reality presents challenges for our efforts in contributing to the development and practice of counseling in international communities. Multicultural scholars have suggested that the counseling profession meet the challenge by closely examining the culturally encapsulated assumptions that inform our theories, training models, research paradigms, and counseling practice (Pedersen & Leong, 1997). Counseling professionals will need to focus on countering their personal and professional ethnocentrism as they "are no less ethnocentric than the general public" (Pedersen & Leong, 1997, p. 382). Confronting our ethnocentrism and cultural encapsulation can be accomplished by examining our own attitudes. Due to the maturation and success of the counseling profession in the United States, counseling professionals may see little value in looking elsewhere for alternative models and approaches, especially if they see the counseling discipline in the United States as a state-of-the-art model for others around the world to emulate (Leung, 2003). A better-than-thou attitude only perpetuates encapsulation and discourages counseling professionals from collaborating with their colleagues in other countries and learning about the indigenous aspects of counseling among various cultures.

Working With Visible and Invisible International Contexts in the United States

With the fast speed by which the world becomes international or globalized, international cultural context will enter every corner of our practice. We may work with clients who are directly or indirectly influenced by immigration, immigration policies, and/or the attitude toward immigrants/refugees/foreign visitors. The lives of citizens of the United States may be influenced by international contexts through media, traveling, marriage, collaboration, interpersonal encounters, and so forth. Taking client international backgrounds and connections into consideration has a role in deriving an accurate understanding of the person. However, it can be challenging for counselors to be aware of how their own feelings and thoughts about immigration issues in general and about specific countries and international cultures in particular influence their clinical judgment and interventions. The international dynamics among countries and cultures could influence how we perceive individuals from particular countries. Thus, it is important that counseling practitioners develop self-awareness as well as awareness of domestic climates for individuals with foreign backgrounds or associations. As a helping profession, the counseling practice is guided by the professional standard that the national and international multicultural and pluralistic trends be followed and that individuals be respected no matter what their national or international backgrounds and connections.

GUIDED PRACTICE EXERCISE 4.3

Curriculum Development

In groups of five to six students, consider this scenario:

You are a member of the curriculum committee at your graduate institution and have been given the charge to ensure that the counseling program's curriculum includes opportunities for students to learn about the approaches to counseling practiced in other cultures. In other words, you and members of your committee must develop courses, coursework, and/or course-related activities and projects that will (a) enhance students' knowledge about counseling in other cultural contexts, (b) develop their skills for international and intercultural counseling-related activities, (c) increase their understanding of the benefits of facilitating and supporting joint projects and activities on a global scale, and (d) challenge them to confront their own personal and professional ethnocentrism and their cultural encapsulation. Once your committee has discussed and completed its charge, share your ideas with the larger classroom for feedback and further discussion.

Summary

Recognition of the intersection of race, ethnicity, gender, social class, and other diversity identities is critical to the practice of effective multicultural counseling. This chapter focuses on the relevance of cultural contexts in understanding our culturally diverse clients. The complexity of culture as reflected at individual, societal, and international levels needs to be fully considered to ensure the effectiveness of treatment plans and clinical decisions that we make in working with diverse clients. Moreover, the integration of salient and meaningful aspects of multiple identities implies that we are interested in our clients as wholly integrated individuals.

Takeaway Messages

1. The intersection of all dimensions of diversity, including race, ethnicity, gender, sexual identity, social class, ability, age, and nationality is critical to the practice of effective multicultural counseling.
2. Social inequality assumes a critical role in the psychological experiences of diverse consumers and must not be overlooked in our counseling practice and interventions.

3. Clients' everyday experiences are informed by their social and cultural contexts and therefore must not be minimized when developing and implementing treatment strategies.
4. International issues in the behaviors and experiences of all citizens and immigrants of the United States warrant our full attention and consideration.
5. Multiculturalism has evolved as the fourth force of psychology, but much work remains in order to prepare students to be able to meet the challenges of globalization.
6. Global learning is critical to the continued progression and renewal of the profession and challenges the assumption that all good and useful knowledge comes from only the United States and can be universally applied.

Recommended Resources

Readings

Comas-Díaz, L. (2013). Multicultural psychotherapy. In F. T. L. Leong, L. Comas-Díaz, G. C. Nagayama Hall, V. C. McLoyd, & J. E. Trimble (Eds.), *APA handbook of multicultural psychology: Vol.2—Application and training* (pp. 419–441). Washington, DC: American Psychological Association.

Fazel, M., Wheeler, J., & Danesh, J. (2005). Prevalence of serious mental disorder in 7,000 refugees resettled in Western countries: A systematic review. *The Lancet, 365*(9467), 1309–1314.

Grant, K. J., Henley, A., & Kean, M. (2001). The journey after the journey: Family counseling in the context of immigration and ethnic diversity. *Canadian Journal of Counseling, 35*(1), 89–100.

Greenleaf, A. T., & Bryant, R. M. (2012). Perpetuating oppression: Does the current counseling discourse neutralize social action? *Journal for Social Action in Counseling and Psychology, 4,* 18–29.

Triandis, H. (2001). Individualism-collectivism and personality. *Journal of Personality, 69,* 907–924.

Websites

http://www.celt.iastate.edu/celt-resources/international-resources/cultural-differences/
http://www.culturalorientations.com/Our-Approach/Six-Levels-of-Culture/National-Societal-Culture/86/
http://geert-hofstede.com/countries.html
http://www.joe.org/joe/2001december/tt1.php

References

Constantine, M. G. (2001). Addressing racial, ethnic, gender, and social class issues in counselor training and practice. In D. B. Pope-Davis & H. L. K. Coleman (Eds.), *The intersection of race, class, and gender in multicultural counseling* (pp. 341–350). Thousand Oaks, CA: Sage.

Constantine, M. G. (2002). The intersection of race, ethnicity, gender, and social class in counseling: Examining selves in cultural contexts. *Journal of Multicultural Counseling and Development, 30,* 210–215.

Council for Accreditation of Counseling and Related Educational Programs. (2009). *2009 standards.* Retrieved from http://www.cacrep.org/for-programs/resources-for-programs/

Croteau, J. M., & Constantine, M. G. (2005). Race and sexual orientation in multicultural counseling: Navigating rough waters. In J. M. Croteau, J. S. Lark, M. A. Lidderdale, & Y. B. Chung (Eds.), *Deconstructing heterosexism in the counseling professions* (pp. 1–15). Thousand Oaks, CA: Sage.

Fukuyama, M. A., & Ferguson, A. D. (2000). Lesbian, gay, and bisexual people of color: Understanding cultural complexity and managing multiple oppressions. In R. M. Perez, K. A. DeBord, & K. A. Bieschke

(Eds.), *Handbook of counseling and psychotherapy with lesbian, gay, and bisexual clients* (pp. 81–105). Washington, DC: American Psychological Association.

Gerstein, L. H. (2006). Counseling psychologists as international social architects. In N. Fouad, L. Gerstein, G. Roysircar, R. L. Toporek, & T. Israel (Eds.), *Handbook for social justice in counseling psychology: Leadership, vision, action* (pp. 377–387). Thousand Oaks, CA: Sage.

Greenleaf, A. T., & Bryant, R. M. (2012). Perpetuating oppression: Does the current counseling discourse neutralize social action? *Journal for Social Action in Counseling and Psychology, 4,* 18–29.

Greenleaf, A.T., & Williams, J. M. (2009). Supporting social justice advocacy: A paradigm shift towards an ecological perspective. *Journal of Social Action in Counseling and Psychology, 2,* 1–14.

Harley, D. A., Jolivette, K., McCormick, K., & Tice, K. (2002). Race, class, and gender: A constellation of positionalities with implications for counseling. *Journal of Multicultural Counseling and Development, 30,* 216–238.

Heppner, P. P., Leong, F. T. L., & Chiao, H. (2008). The growing internationalization of counseling psychology. In S. D. Brown & R. W. Lent (Eds.), *Handbook of counseling psychology* (4th ed., pp. 68–85). New York, NY: Wiley.

Jack, D. C., Ali, A., & Dias, S. (2014). Depression in multicultural populations. In F. T. L. Leong, L. Comas-Díaz, G. C. Nagayama Hall, V. C. McLoyd, & J. E. Trimble (Eds.), *APA handbook of multicultural psychology: Vol. 2. Application and training* (pp. 267–287). Washington, DC: American Psychological Association.

Jun, H. (2010). *Social justice, multicultural counseling, and practice: Beyond a conventional approach.* Thousand Oaks, CA: Sage.

Lee, M. W. (Director). (1994). *Color of fear* [Film]. United States: StirFry Seminars. Available at http://www.stirfryseminars.com/store/products/cof1.php

Monk, G., Winslade, J., & Sinclair, S. (2008). *New horizons in multicultural counseling.* Thousand Oaks, CA: Sage.

Pedersen, P. B., & Leong, F. T. L. (1997). Counseling in an international context. *The Counseling Psychologist, 25,* 117–122.

Ponterotto, J. G. (2008). Theoretical and empirical advances in multicultural counseling and psychology. In S. D. Brown & R. W. Lent (Eds.), *Handbook of counseling psychology* (4th ed., pp. 121–140). Hoboken, NJ: Wiley

Prilleltensky, I. (2008). The role of power in wellness, oppression, and liberation: The promise of psychopolitical validity. *Journal of Community Psychology, 36,* 116–136.

Ratts, M. J. (2009). Social justice counseling: Toward the development of a "fifth force" among counseling paradigms. *Journal of Humanistic Counseling, Education, and Development, 48,* 160–172.

Robinson, T. L., & Howard-Hamilton, M. F. (2000). *The convergence of race, ethnicity, and gender: Multiple identities counseling.* Columbus, OH: Merrill/Prentice Hall.

Sue, D. W., & Sue, D. (2013). *Counseling the culturally diverse: Theory and practice* (6th ed.). New York, NY: Wiley.

Thomas, P. L. (2013). *Unmasking the meritocracy myth.* Retrieved from http://radicalscholarship.wordpress.com/2013/01/06/unmasking-the-meritocracy-myth/

Utsey, S. O., Ponterotto, J. G., Reynolds, A. L., & Cancelli, A. A. (2000). Racial discrimination, coping, life satisfaction, and self-esteem among African Americans. *Journal of Counseling & Development, 78,* 72–80. doi:10.1002/j.1556-6676.2000.tb02562.x

Wilton, L. (2010). Where do we go from here? In J. G. Ponterotto, J. M. Casas, L. A Suzuki, & C. M. Alexander (Eds.), *Handbook of multicultural counseling* (3rd ed., pp. 313–327). Thousand Oaks, CA: Sage.

5

Redefining and Renewing the Counseling Profession in the 21st Century

It is never too late to give up your prejudices.

—Henry David Thoreau

CHAPTER OVERVIEW

This chapter directs attention to the need to redefine and renew the counseling profession in the 21st century. The progression of the counseling profession requires that we focus on understanding human behavior in social and cultural contexts and that our delivery of services encompasses promoting cultural diversity and social justice for all. It is essential that we recognize and overcome the barriers toward effective multicultural counseling and make our practices culturally appropriate and meaningful in order to renew the profession as a viable helping profession. In describing how we should proceed to fulfill this challenging task, we specifically discuss the ethical responsibility of practitioners to provide culturally relevant counseling and counseling-related services and illuminate the specific codes of ethics (American Counseling Association [ACA], 2014) and accreditation standards (Council for Accreditation of Counseling and Related Educational Programs [CACREP], 2009) that require respect for the cultural worldviews and traditions of culturally diverse clients. Moreover, we emphasize that practicing ethically and effectively will require being sensitive to cultural variations and understanding clients' problems from a cultural context.

SELF-ASSESSMENT OF PRE-EXISTING AWARENESS AND KNOWLEDGE

- What warrants the effort to redefine counseling?
- Why is it critical that counseling practice and theories be renewed for the 21st century?
- What are some obstacles in offering efficacious counseling to racially, socially, and culturally diverse individuals?
- Why is multicultural competence a necessary aspect of professional counseling renewal?
- What are professionals' ethical responsibilities and obligations for renewing our counseling profession?

LEARNING OBJECTIVES

After reading this chapter, students will be able to do the following:

1. Recognize the obstacles for advancing the counseling profession as a multicultural phenomenon
2. Understand the role we play in perpetuating the ethnocentric and monocultural focus of professional counseling
3. Understand that our professional responsibilities in practicing counseling are an instrument for promoting cultural diversity and social justice
4. Recognize that serving the culturally diverse plays an important role in renewing our counseling theories and advancing our counseling profession
5. Articulate the profession's ethical responsibility for renewing the counseling profession

CASE ILLUSTRATION 5.1

The Case of Jess

Jess is a slightly overweight, 30-year-old African American heterosexual woman. She sought counseling with a White male therapist who specializes in affirmative therapy for cultural and gender diversity. In her intake session, Jess told the therapist that she had experienced several romantic relationships with married men in the past and was very frustrated with herself for always being the "other woman." She wanted to understand why she put herself in these situations and how she could change her behavior so that she could have a healthy relationship with an available man.

Jess had a long history of weight problems and had struggled with her self-esteem. Her father, a middle-level manager in a large hotel business, frequently told her that she would not amount to much unless she was successful at losing weight. Jess went to medical school and became a doctor, thinking that she could prove her worth by becoming a successful doctor. She also made several attempts at different weight loss programs but did not have any long-term success. At this point in her life, she said that she felt convinced she would never be accepted in the same way as her White peers at work and in her personal life. She was bitter that her efforts to become successful in her career and to manage her weight did not result in better relationship outcomes and that few men had been attracted to her.

As therapy progressed, Jess shared that she had enjoyed a liberating experience when she decided during her college years to wear her hair naturally and unstraightened. As a child, her father had insisted that she straighten and relax (use chemicals to straighten) her hair. She felt she won in standing up to her father about this, but she became angry when receiving feedback from friends and potential romantic partners that she would be more attractive with straight "White-person" hair. She noted that she was the only African American woman in her medical school and at her current workplace and had been told that she appeared arrogant and mean, which only added greatly to her upset.

Jess expressed a great amount of anger during the initial counseling sessions. Much of the anger was directed at her father, who had frequently insulted her about her appearance, and some was at specific men she had dated for not having left their spouses for her. She also expressed anger and frustration that "they" (the world she lived in) really did not like her, her race, and her appearance. She felt as if everyone had lied to her by telling her that she would be liked and loved if she could make herself more attractive and successful.

GROUP DISCUSSION QUESTIONS 5.1

Understanding Jess's Experiences

Group Discussion

After reading Jess's presenting concerns and life experiences, discuss the following questions:

1. What important considerations come to mind that inform your understanding of Jess's presenting concerns?
2. What would be an effective approach for the counselor to take in working with Jess?
3. In what ways are Jess's issues related to her life experiences in her and her family's social and cultural contexts?
4. What are some possible contextual factors that play a role in Jess's experience?
5. Why might it be dangerous or harmful to treat Jess without considering the social and cultural factors?
6. How would a counselor use himself or herself as a helping agent in working with Jess? What would be the answer if the counselor was a European American male, European American female, African American male, African American female, or other person of color?

Redefining and Renewing: Now Is the Time

In the previous chapters, we illustrated the necessity for multiculturally efficacious counseling if professional counseling is to continue to exist and serve the consumers of the 21st century. Now is the time that we discuss how to redefine and renew the counseling profession so it will remain a culturally relevant phenomenon in culturally diversified communities in the United States and around the world. We argue that students and professionals of counseling have the professional and ethical responsibility to practice counseling with multicultural sensitivity and competence and to contribute to the culturalization of the counseling profession in which the application of theories and methods is culturally relevant and the professionals who practice them are multiculturally competent. The extent to which the counseling profession will effectively promote mental health for all consumers is dependent upon its ability to successfully address the issue of diversity and the role of culture in the service we provide and among the people we serve. We as a profession must identify and overcome barriers that have prevented the practice of counseling from being just and efficacious for all.

A Reflection by a Latino Gay Man on His Cultural Community

Some populations within the Latino community view homosexuality as a "White people" thing. Homosexuality is seen as frilly and eccentric. From most Latinos' perspective, homosexuality is a lifestyle belonging to light-skinned and wealthy communities who have been

(Continued)

(Continued)

in some way warped by materialism and power. I'm unsure as to why this association exists. Could it have anything to do with the fact that light-skinned persons of power can afford to maintain lives of secrecy? Or perhaps persons of power can afford to be outspoken with less risk of backlash? For some, this view is slowly dissolving, but in many circles this association still rings true.

Many Latinos still believe that they can reverse homosexuality in their male children by putting them to work, teaching them the ways of the man, or toughening them up in some way. Even for *familia* who have managed to come out, their sexual identity is often not acknowledged or talked about within the home. I feel as though many counselors do not take into consideration the complex experiences of lesbian/gay/bisexual (LGB) Latinos. I feel that when counselors have a client who is LGB and Latino, they expect these identities to have been already "dealt with." I believe that many counselors fail to remember that identity development is an ongoing process and thus may be influencing a client's presenting concerns.

Our identities are fluid—they change, they aren't always as constant as they appear. For this reason, for some LGB Latino clients it may be important to discuss their various identities. Perhaps this minimization of the experiences of *familia* is a result of inadequate knowledge or even a tendency toward color blindness within the counseling relationship. In addition, I believe that LGB Latino clients would find it difficult to express these concerns to a counselor who they did not feel would understand such issues.

—*Artemio V., a Latino, gay, male graduate student*

Barriers to Multicultural Counseling

In the past several decades, scholars and practitioners have demonstrated efforts toward understanding and promoting the importance of multicultural counseling. Although substantial progress has been made, significant barriers still exist as we progress through the 21st century. These barriers, if left unaddressed, will impede efforts to deliver efficacious counseling to culturally diverse consumers in various communities of the United States and beyond its borders. Some of the barriers are due to the monocultural nature of existing counseling theories (inadequate tools), some are due to our personal beliefs and resistance (lack of readiness of practitioners), and some are due to differential access and lack of equity in society (lack of access and equity for the socially marginalized).

Ethnocentric and Monocultural Values of Counseling Theories

As described in Chapter 1, most existing counseling theories are, by and large, developed by people representing the mainstream European American cultures, rooted in the mainstream context, and suited for privileged people of similar cultural backgrounds. The bias that mainstream cultural norms are the model for universal standards is engrained from goal setting to outcome evaluation in counseling practice. Thus, in counseling settings, many diverse clients may find themselves in prescribed disadvantageous positions whereby their behaviors are more likely to be pathologized or used as reasons for their negative life experiences. This tendency to be blamed by others for their negative life events or to have their behaviors pathologized is often a replication of their experiences in life. In Jess's experience, for instance, her hairstyle (which mainstream culture has labeled as "ethnic") and weight have been used against her, resulting in difficulties with her life and career pursuits. If the counselor did not empathize with her or failed to recognize her experience as due to discrimination, it is likely that Jess's weight issue and hairstyle would be addressed in a way that would imply she was to blame for the hostility and lack of acceptance she experienced in her environment.

The ethnocentric and monocultural nature of our counseling theories has seriously limited the use of mental health services by underprivileged people who have different cultural, social, and economic contexts than that of the mainstream culture. For instance, most college campuses offer free counseling services to students, but research has shown that students of color or other minority statuses tend to underuse or prematurely terminate counseling. The researchers have pointed to the biased nature of counseling service itself as one explanation (Kearney, Draper, & Baron, 2005) and concluded that many minority students have not found counseling helpful or friendly to them.

Counseling practice often reflects culture-bound values such as exclusive emphasis on the individual and his or her interests, heavy reliance on client emotional and verbal expressiveness (including self-disclosure), and the view of mental health and physical health as separate. Many minority people who do not share these values may not seek counseling. There are also class-bound values that would discourage people with poor economic resources to benefit from counseling. In addition to the resource issues related to money and time, traditional counseling's focus on insight, intrapsychic self-exploration, or interpretation of behaviors may post further barriers to keep certain people from seeking counseling. Additionally, language can be a barrier for some immigrant or refugee groups. Due to these inherent value biases, counseling service can be culturally insensitive, antagonistic, or inappropriate to the experience of people from nonmainstream cultures or groups, which may further the discrimination and oppression they experience in society (Cokley, 2006).

To provide fair, helpful, and effective counseling to the culturally diverse, we face the challenge of not having adequate tools or guides from counseling literature. This fact further highlights the importance of training counselors in multicultural identity development and fostering multicultural consciousness building. In counseling, the counselors are the most important helping agents, and their cultural competence matters. With or without adequate existing tools, they must shoulder the responsibility to expand and strengthen the fourth force in counseling. Moreover, this generation of counselors also has the responsibility to continuously renew efforts in developing multiculturally efficacious counseling theories and methods.

Counseling Professionals' Personal Beliefs and Thinking Styles

There is little doubt that most counselors-in-training choose the counseling profession because of their interest in helping people, including people from underprivileged social, cultural, and economic positions. They are challenged, however, when they start the journey toward multicultural competence and realize that they have been socialized into certain beliefs and thinking styles that are incompatible with the life experiences of people from various minority groups. In fact, due to such socialization, they likely have unintentionally perpetrated and contributed to the institutional discrimination experienced by others who are members of socially marginalized and underprivileged groups.

One example of a belief that all of us hold that can have serious unjust and discriminatory consequences is that of the famous "American dream" or *meritocracy myth*. We are all familiar with and mostly buy into the image and notion that the United States is "a land of limitless opportunity in which individuals can go as far as their own merit takes them" (McNamee & Miller, 2004, para. 1). Is this a myth or a truth? Perhaps for some it is true, and for others it is not. There has been research documenting the ways in which meritocracy not only is impossible but also is used to maintain the system of discrimination and oppression for individuals of minority groups. From political/legal systems and educational opportunities to housing and employment, ethnic and cultural minorities have been discriminated against systemically. This so-called meritocracy "assumes" that people all start from the same place and compete on an even playing field, which is far from what has been the case in the United States (Takaki, 1993). The lack of access and equity for minority groups is simply undeniable, both presently and historically. Consequential to this lack of resources, the system of discrimination and oppression makes it difficult for the oppressed to develop merit and reduces the likelihood that their merit be recognized and/or rewarded (McNamee & Miller, 2004).

Because we live in the United States, the biased beliefs based on meritocracy and its associated discriminatory ideology and practices are all around us. Deliberate and intentional efforts are needed to combat them and to prevent us from being blind beneficiaries of this unjust system. Most importantly, the recognition of how meritocracy has been used to create and perpetuate social injustice will prevent us from doing harm to our clients. We need to develop a new consciousness that allows us to see and experience the world from others' perspectives and to acknowledge their experiences and reactions to oppression. Failure to validate our clients' experiences as victims of discrimination and oppression means we run the risk of perpetuating injustices and oppression in our counseling sessions.

GUIDED PRACTICE EXERCISE 5.1

Make it Personal and Relevant

Personal Thoughts and Relevance to Your Work as a Counselor

In small groups of four or five students, do the activities that follow.

1. Share your personal thoughts and questions about these phenomena:
   - Affirmative action in college admission
   - Mortgage loan eligibility
   - Gender gap in wages and salaries
   - Desegregation of schools
   - The belief that everyone has the right to be himself or herself
2. How are your thoughts on these issues relevant to your work as a counselor?
3. What are the dangers or risk of harm to our clients if we hold personal beliefs without awareness of our own biases?
4. Why does it matter whether or not we become aware of our attitudes and beliefs?
5. What type of self-reflection and/or other work must we do if we are to examine our personal beliefs and accept others' views?

After the small-group discussion, reconvene as a class. Consider and discuss the following statements regarding *merit*:

1. Affirmative action policy was enacted only to correct the long-standing "affirmative action for White males" so people of color could start developing merit.
2. Mortgage loan eligibility limits access to resources for the poor, which perpetuates the lack of merit.
3. Gender gap in wages and salaries reflects lack of equity, which hurts women in their development of merit.
4. Desegregation (although not yet accomplished) without integration does not provide equity, which continues to hinder African Americans' merit development.

Another example of a personal barrier to developing multicultural competence is how we are socialized and educated to think, including scientific thinking. In his book on social justice and multicultural counseling, Jun (2010) pointed out that some scientific thinking styles such as linear, hierarchical, and dichotomous thinking that have helped us succeed in academics and other areas may be a barrier in our understanding of cultural diversity.

Linear thinking views the behavior or attitude of a group at a particular moment as constant, and then uses it to predict the future behavior or attitude of the group. Such thinking tends to neglect the role of social and cultural contextual changes, time changes, or developmental changes in individuals' behavior, especially in the behavior of those from nonmainstream groups. Linear thinking underlies discrimination, prejudice, and isms related to race, gender, class, sexual orientation, disability, age, language, religion, and so forth because these isms "are based on the past experience or cultural myths that have been perpetuated generation after generation" (Jun, 2010, p. 29).

Hierarchal thinking places people in superior or inferior positions by believing that some groups are superior to others and that norms and values of one group are better than those of other groups. "Men are more capable than women" or "Heterosexuality is normal and heterosexuals are better" are examples of hierarchal thinking used to support discrimination. Similarly, *dichotomous thinking* (viewing things as either good/bad or right/wrong) also contributes to putting "the other" on the negative side because of the belief that "if I am right, you have to be wrong" (Jun, 2010). Both hierarchical and dichotomous thinking tend to lead to classifying values or worldviews of the dominant group as superior instead of viewing both dominant and nondominant groups equally. Thus, Jun (2010) promoted a holistic thinking style that adopts multilayered and multidimensional perspectives and a nonjudgmental attitude because "unintentional marginalization or minimization stems from practitioners' inappropriate thinking styles and not from their lack of care" (p. 37).

What adds to the challenges we face is rooted in professional training itself. Although most counselor-training programs require one or more courses on multicultural counseling, the fact remains that the general knowledge base on which counselors are trained does not sufficiently reflect multiculturalism and requires continuous learning, unlearning, and relearning. This demand can make the process of multicultural-competence development emotionally difficult for counselors-in-training. They often have to deal with feelings of frustration, disappointment, and even resentment. Every time they see a new client with different cultural backgrounds, they will have to construct, deconstruct, and reconstruct what they learned. Failure to perform these tasks successfully could lead to difficulties in sessions. Table 5.1 shows some communication blockers that mark low competence in working with diverse clients.

A Reflection on the Challenges of Developing a Multicultural Identity

When I was in graduate school, I sometimes felt an impulse to disengage or "shut down" when delving into my own multicultural incompetence (or that of my fellow classmates) that became too painful. I remember thinking, "I am doing better than most in this area; why should I subject myself to this stuff?" With encouragement from one of my multiculturally competent role models, I forced myself to stay open to the process and definitely benefited from the additional self-exploration and assessment.

Now that I have completed my graduate training, one of the greatest challenges I face is not being too comfortable with the knowledge and skills I have acquired. I think the risk of feeling overconfident is especially salient for individuals like me who have identified multiculturalism as an area of professional interest. It is essential to have ongoing reassessment and development for one's knowledge and skills to remain relevant.

Another challenge is making time to effectively intervene on behalf of clients and communities. Social justice is a foundation of multicultural counseling, and I need to create space in my schedule for service to the community. I constantly remind myself to do the following things:

1. Remember that my status as an African American woman does not automatically make me multiculturally competent
2. Remain open to the process of developing multicultural competence even when it is personally uncomfortable
3. Acknowledge my own faulty beliefs regarding multiculturally diverse individuals
4. Demonstrate willingness to engage myself in social justice advocacy
5. Remember that development of multicultural competence and multicultural professional identity is a lifelong journey

—J. B., a practicing counseling psychologist

Table 5.1 Multicultural Communication Blockers

- Blaming (victim or perpetrator)
- Feeling guilty, which immobilizes (as opposed to guilt, which is part of the process of unlearning and learning)
- Dominant (majority) group members struggling with group membership
- Targeted (minority) group members thinking they know total experience
- Telling to the exclusion of listening
- Listening to the exclusion of telling
- Only asking questions
- Not owning "your own stuff"
- Focusing only on one social group identity

(Continued)

Table 5.1 (Continued)

- Struggling to deal with other people's feelings and your own feelings
- Thinking dichotomously (either/or)
- Wanting answers to solutions in a hurry
- Separating or isolating from other people
- Lashing out
- Expecting others to "teach me"
- Working toward multiculturalism only to help minorities
- Withdrawing or exiting prematurely from a process because it is too uncomfortable

Source: Fukuyama, M. A., & Sevig, T. D. (1999). *Integrating spirituality into multicultural counseling.* Thousand Oaks, CA: Sage.

Lack of Equity and Access by Some Members of Society

It is a known fact that there is insufficient mental health service for all who need assistance and particularly a lack of access to quality service for ethnic and cultural minorities. In his report to the nation, U.S. Surgeon General Dr. David Satcher (2001) described the striking disparities in mental health care for racial and ethnic minorities. Evidence showed that ethnic minorities had less access to and availability of mental health services. There were common barriers such as cost, fragmentation of services, lack of availability of services, and social stigma toward mental illness, but "there are extra barriers deterring racial and ethnic minorities" (U.S. Department of Health and Human Services, 2001, p. 28), including mistrust and fear of treatment, racism and discrimination, and differences in language and communication. Several years later, empirical evidence once again demonstrated that ethnic minorities do not have a higher rate of mental illness but a lower level of access to and use of mental health care than White Americans (McGuire & Miranda, 2008). The researchers pointed out, "Among adults with a diagnosis-based need for mental health or substance abuse care, 37.6% of Whites, but only 22.4% of Latinos and 25% of African Americans, receive it" (p. 396). Among the mechanisms that contribute to such disparities are providers' bias, stereotyping, and discrimination, provider differences, and health insurance variations. Increasing diversity in the mental health workforce and providing culturally appropriate education for providers are identified as necessary for decreasing this disparity.

Poverty is also a known factor associated with both the prevalence of mental health needs and lack of access to service. Research has shown that mental illness is overrepresented in high poverty neighborhoods, and people with mental illness—members of minority racial/ethnic populations in particular—are disproportionately concentrated in high-poverty areas (Wolch & Dear, 1993). In terms of patterns of mental health service use, research has shown that racial/ethnic disparities in the use of mental health services are more salient in low-poverty areas than in high-poverty areas, and the use of emergency and inpatient hospitalization for mental health problems was more frequent for minority clients than for White clients (Chow, Jaffee, & Snowden, 2003).

Language barriers can be extremely problematic for immigrants, refugees, or visitors who are in need of adequate counseling and therapy service. The inability to communicate with a health care provider may undermine trust in the quality of care received, decrease the likelihood of appropriate follow-up (Brach & Fraser, 2000), and even result in diagnostic errors and inappropriate treatment (Woloshin, Bickell, Schwartz, Gany, & Welch, 1995). Therefore, the lack of bilingual counselors in our profession can result in no service or inferior service for language minorities. One negative consequence of a lack of bilingual counselors is the common practice of using children as translators for their parents in medical or legal matters. The danger and potential damaging effects of this practice have been documented (Sue & Sue, 2013). In 2005, the National Council on Interpreting in Health Care published national standards for interpreters of health care.

This lack of access and equity in receiving mental health services encountered by the underprivileged challenges the counseling profession to reach out to these underserved populations and to deliver culturally appropriate services. In other words, counseling professionals must not rely on underprivileged groups seeking them out; rather, they must reach out and offer assistance to potential clients who do not have the benefit of accessing services while also ensuring that their services are appropriate and efficacious when they do reach out. Counselors in the 21st century should see it as their responsibility to facilitate elimination of racial, cultural, and class disparity in health care through service, advocacy, and social justice. To avoid the unintentional perpetuation of social oppression of the underprivileged in our counseling services, all counselors must become multiculturally competent.

Effective Service to the Culturally Diverse

Why Must We Redefine Counseling Practice?

The counseling profession has emerged as a viable mental health profession with numerous accomplishments (e.g., accreditation, licensure, credentialing, third-party billing, use of technology in counseling, emerging international presence) and significant growth in its membership and diversification among its consumers, so it sounds bold and radical that we argue for redefining counseling. We offer the reflection by a White male therapist who saw Jess for several months to illustrate what we mean by redefinition.

A Reflection From Dr. K. About Working With Jess

Operating from a primarily psychodynamic perspective, I helped Jess get in touch with her anger, especially her anger toward her father who never really "accepted" her as who she was. This realization seemed to bring insight that Jess welcomed, but her general emotional state did not seem to improve. In fact, on a few occasions she indicated hating herself for being angry at her father. Our work took a positive turn one day when we got into a discussion about racism in the United States and how her father had tried so hard to act White in order to maintain a job to support his family. She was visibly relieved when I acknowledged how I benefited from racism and White privilege at her expense. Her overall anger decreased, including that toward her father and that toward society. She commented to me that it was completely out of her expectation that I, a White male, was able to start a conversation with her about race, take responsibility for the victimization of people of color in our society, and show unconditional acceptance of and high respect to her while she was stuck in the "generalized and nasty anger" that could "destroy" her and others.

Jess reached an insight that she was not crazy to be so angry, but perhaps she had let her anger be the front of her lack of self-acceptance and self-respect that reflected the message she received from society and her father. She also realized that one expression of this lack of self-acceptance was her tendency to get involved with married men. Jess's progress was very encouraging, but when I reviewed our work together, I felt surprised by how little I did in terms of using conventional interventions and by the degree to which addressing relevant macro social and cultural issues is critical in the healing of those with little or no social power. At the same time, I felt more responsibility on my shoulders to use my "social power" to help the powerless by promoting social justice.

–Dr. Robert K., a practicing counseling psychologist

One clear indication in the case of Jess is that counseling needs to go beyond the traditional approach that focuses exclusively on internal processes and individual-level dynamics when working with the culturally diverse who have experienced social and cultural isolation, discrimination, and oppression or whose cultures have been perceived as less than, abnormal, or out of the norm. Multicultural counseling should include the role of the counselor, the intervention, and the evaluation of outcomes in its definition. Counselors need to recognize their role in all diverse clients' social experiences and serve as advocates for them in society. Counseling interventions need to be rooted in clients' social contexts as well as in their individual contexts. The role of the collective unconsciousness resulting from social injustice in individuals' lives has to be addressed to allow and promote healing. The desired outcome of counseling should be viewed to include an improvement of social context as well as a decrease of individual symptoms. Thus, we define *multicultural counseling* as counseling practice in which the counselor recognizes the significant influence of social and cultural contexts in client experiences (including symptoms); conceptualizes, interprets, and intervenes accordingly; validates client cultural experience; and advocates for reduction of social oppression for the client.

As illustrated in Chapter 2, regardless of work settings, counselors will be confronted more often with the challenge of effective multicultural counseling. Failure to conduct multicultural counseling will risk doing harm to pluralistic clientele. Moreover, in order for the counseling profession to become a viable member of the global mental health network, we will need to think differently about our existing models and practices. The applicability of traditionally taught theories to diverse clientele must be closely examined as well as the profession's primary approach to delivering services. For example, 50-minute sessions, counseling provided in the counselor's office, and counseling that focuses on intrapsychic processes must be explored for their effectiveness with culturally diverse clients (Glosoff, 2009).

Given the global interconnectedness that is present and growing among counseling professionals, we can no longer afford to rely on U.S. conceptions of theory, research, and practice; rather, we must join collaborative efforts that consider mental health and human behavior in a broad global context. We echo the thoughts of Courtland Lee, professor of counselor education at the University of Maryland and a past president of the ACA, who emphasized that counselors must become globally literate human beings who need to "think globally and act locally" and specifically declared the following belief:

> I believe that counseling practice over the next decade must be predicated on counselors becoming globally literate human beings. Global literacy is the breadth of information that extends over the major domains of human diversity. It consists of the basic information that a person needs to possess in order to successfully navigate life in the technologically sophisticated, globally interconnected world of the 21st century—a world in which people from diverse cultural backgrounds interact in ways that were previously inconceivable. Global literacy implies an understanding of the contemporary world and how it has evolved over time. It encompasses important knowledge of cultural variations in areas such as geography, history, literature, politics, economics, and principles of government. Global literacy is the core body of knowledge that an individual gains over a lifetime about the world in which he or she lives. The driving force behind the development of global literacy is the commitment one makes to ensure that openness to cultural diversity is the cornerstone of his or her life. While the development of multicultural competency should continue to be an important goal for professional counseling training and practice, global literacy must be the goal for a life lived in a culturally competent manner. It logically follows, therefore, that one cannot be a culturally competent counselor if he or she is not a globally literate person, and a wider understanding of the world will be crucial for counselors in the decades to come. (as quoted in Shallcross, 2012)

The Intersection of Multiple Dimensions of Cultural Identity in Counseling Practice

The complexity of individual diversity has continued to increase and expand with social and cultural changes in the United States and in the world. Especially among the residents of the United States, every individual has multiple cultural identities. Some of these identities may provide the individual with unearned privileges, and others may leave the person in unearned disadvantaged positions. However, it should be noted that there are significant differences in terms of the specific nature and impact of discrimination, oppression, and disadvantage associated with each of the multiple dimensions of cultural diversity. For instance, *hate crimes* are mostly those "criminal offense(s) against a person or property motivated in whole or in part by an offender's bias against a race, religion, disability, ethnic origin, or sexual orientation" (Federal Bureau of Investigation, 2013). Thus, being inclusive in addressing cultural identity is not meant to equalize individual experiences due to each dimension of diversity; instead, it is meant to respect all individuals' cultural identities and validate their social experiences due to their cultural identities. It is harmful and unjust to compare different experiences due to culturally different identities and view them as the same, which will intentionally or unintentionally minimize or invalidate some clients' experiences.

It is the reality of the 21st century that counselors have to work with individuals' multiple cultural identities, namely the intersection of identity. Understanding the impact of the intersection of relevant cultural identities on our clients' behaviors provides counselors a greater contextual perspective that enhances their potential for accurate assessment and diagnostic validity. Moreover, the unique interrelationships among clients' cultural identities illuminate how they experience and make meaning of their culture and thereby minimize the counselor's tendency to assume that all members of a certain cultural group are the same or behave similarly (Constantine, 2002).

SMALL-GROUP CLASS ACTIVITY 5.1

What Are Your Thoughts and Reactions?

Read this reflection by Artemio V., a Latino gay male graduate student, and share your thoughts with the group on the questions that follow.

Within gay-themed television programs, films, and even pornography, Latinos are depicted as the "dangerous minority." I believe this lack of adequate representation helps to reinforce existing hierarchies within the LGB community that place LGB Latinos as a racialized subgroup of a larger, well-established, seemingly Caucasian queer community.

I once heard a speaker who explained that her parents learned to accept her after she urged them to "read on the subject." Almost immediately I realized how different coming-out experiences must be for ethnic-minority LGB individuals. I thought to myself that there is no way I could tell my family to "read on the subject" when many of my family members have trouble reading in their native Spanish, let alone English. I can recall another situation in which I overheard a high school classmate say, "There are gay

Mexicans? That's gross." It was during these years that I began to understand the vast amount of misinformation and insensitivity that is present within our society, especially within rural communities.

LGB individuals of color can internalize this "minority status," which can in turn influence the individual's sense of belonging, identity development, and interpersonal or intimate relationships. For example, often when a Caucasian man is interested in a gay Latino, the Latino may question whether the Caucasian male is only interested in him because he wants to fulfill a fetish or experience for himself what it is like to be with a "fiery" Latino. Another example would be that in the past, I thought that I could lessen the blow to my parents by presenting to them a partner of Mexican heritage with a traditional upbringing and strong family values.

Again I feel that these are topics that would be difficult to discuss within a counseling setting, especially if the counselor and client each self-identify with different communities. Similarly, *machismo* may come into play here if the client is struggling to discuss certain topics for fear of appearing weak or unstable. Thus far, I believe that the counseling profession has failed our community by not presenting to counselors or counselors-in-training specific scenarios that LGB Latino clients may experience throughout their lives.

1. How do you describe Artemio's cultural context?
2. How do you feel about the noted lack of acceptance of LGB individuals within Latino American communities?
3. How do you feel about the noted negative attitude toward LGB Latinos by the mainstream culture?
4. If you were his counselor, in what ways do you think your cultural identities would play a role in his experience of negative perceptions and prejudice?
5. How would you help him?

In recognition of diverse and multiple cultural identities, Hays (1996) developed a model for organizing and systematically attending to nine main cultural influences that counselors need to consider in their work with clients and that have been named important by the American Psychological Association (APA) and the ACA Division of Multicultural Counseling and Development. The ADRESSING model refers to the influences of age, disability, religion, ethnicity (including race), social status, sexual orientation, indigenous heritage, national origin, and gender and also includes the corresponding minority groups and forms of oppression that have been documented as important in counseling and psychology literature (see Table 5.2).

Counselors and educators are encouraged to apply Hays's ADRESSING model as a framework for examining their own biases and areas of inexperience regarding minority cultures and for considering the salience of clients' multiple cultural identities. For instance, trainees could be asked to think about their own identities as related to the nine cultural influences of the model. In other words, how do one's age, religious upbringing, social status, and so on affect his or her beliefs about the world? The model further serves as a mechanism to expand counselors' understanding of racism, ethnocentrism, and other forms of oppression that are pervasive and widely experienced by minorities and marginalized groups and also to remind counselors that everyone has biases and stereotypes. Hays (1996) explained that when biases held by dominant-group members are reinforced by political, social, and economic power, the presence of isms emerge as indicated by the following equation: "Racial Bias + Power = Racism; Gender Bias + Power = Sexism; Age Bias + Power = Ageism" (p. 335). She further clarified that minority members' isolated acts of discrimination against majority members cannot be considered racism because minorities and marginalized groups do not hold the power to systematically enforce their biases.

Although the ADRESSING model encourages assessment of the relative salience of cultural influences, the model does not determine the importance (i.e., weighting) of one cultural influence in relation to others; this is because a determination of salience is specific to each individual. Counselors should employ culture-specific knowledge and skills to draw hypotheses about their clients' salient cultural identities and/or to assist them with discussing salience with their clients. Application of the

Table 5.2 The ADRESSING Model: Nine Cultural Factors, Related Minority Groups, and Forms of Oppression

Cultural Factor	Minority Group	Biases With Power
Age/generational	Older adults	Ageism
Disability	People with disabilities	____[a]
Religion	Religious minorities	____[b]
Ethnicity/race	Ethnic minorities	Racism
Social status	People of lower status	Classism
Sexual orientation	Sexual minorities	Heterosexism
Indigenous heritage	Native peoples	Racism
National origin	Refugees, immigrants, and international students	Racism and colonialism
Gender	Women	Sexism

[a]Prejudice and discrimination against people with disabilities. [b]Religious intolerance includes anti-Semitism (i.e., against both Jewish and Muslim people) and oppression of other religious minorities (e.g., Buddhists, Hindus, Mormons).

Source: Hays (1996).

ADRESSING model can also include calling attention to any cultural identities that the client has omitted, assuming there is good reason/justification for doing so (i.e., that it fits with the presenting problems and goals and because rapport and trust have been established). The ADRESSING model provides an organizational framework for counselors to use while working continually to overcome their biases, and it illuminates the complex and overlapping cultural identities that provide meaning in our clients' lives.

Emerging and Necessary: Developing International Competence

Both the fast growth of international populations in the United States and the continuous increase of American counseling professionals' involvement in international communities mandate that we take into consideration international diversity in defining the meaning and mission of the counseling practice in the 21st century. As they are limited to serving domestic minorities, current counseling theories and methods are inadequate in serving either international people or international communities. However, the internationalization movement in the counseling field seems to have reached a higher level of momentum, and more and more individual practitioners, researchers, and educators have engaged themselves in international work. It is imperative that international competencies are integrated in the definition of our counseling profession.

Training counseling professionals to respond to the needs of a diverse U.S. society as well as a diverse world is part of the mission of counseling and will require exposing trainees to both multicultural and cross-cultural training strategies (Heppner, Leong, & Chiao, 2008). Furthermore, the multicultural training literature informs that there is a synergistic effect on counselor trainee cultural competencies when they are provided training that addresses both multicultural and cross-cultural competencies (Heppner, Ægisdottir, et al., 2008). To elaborate, research suggests that exposure activities such as brief but intense cultural immersion programs and studying abroad deepen cultural awareness, enhance cultural sensitivity, and lead to further involvement and participation in cross-cultural experiences. Intercultural learning and other international educational activities are also likely to reduce ethnocentric worldviews, which is critical in preparing the next generation of counseling professionals to be culturally competent.

The underlying principles of an array of multicultural competency guidelines emphasize valuing the socialization process of people in their cultural contexts, acknowledging the negative effects of one's minority status (i.e., examining clients' behaviors and psychological processes within a larger social context), and recognizing that the provision of services to the culturally diverse requires understanding of one's own racial and cultural dynamics (Heppner, Ægisdottir, et al., 2008). In consideration of cross-cultural competence, Heppner, Ægisdottir, et al. (2008) discussed nine challenges and opportunities that face the counseling profession. We believe their noted challenges and opportunities, as adapted and described in Table 5.3, play a direct role in advancing the profession and promoting effective services for the culturally diverse, which must include an international and global perspective.

Table 5.3 The Challenges and Opportunities for Cross-Cultural Competence and the Future of the Counseling Profession

Challenges and Opportunities	Description
1. Overcoming our ethnocentrism	Engaging in cross-cultural experiences may be an important first step in transcending ethnocentric biases. Counseling practitioners must examine their own attitudes and read about and learn from communities worldwide.
2. Enhancing cross-cultural competence	Building mutually beneficial and collaborative relationships with professionals in other geographic regions will aid in the promotion of cross-cultural competence.
3. Cultural sensitivity versus imposed ethics in theory development	We can no longer assume that our U.S. theories and models of counseling are universal and applicable to other cultural groups (i.e., imposed ethics).
4. Supporting and extending indigenous psychologies	We must not only examine the cultural relevance of our Western models of counseling in other countries, but we must also support and consider indigenous models of helping as equally effective healing approaches.
5. Promoting the integration of multicultural and cross-cultural foci	The integration of multicultural and cross-national activities enhances understanding of the role of culture in human behavior and further emphasizes the important role that cultural context plays in our delivery of culturally relevant services.
6. Promoting cross-national research collaboration	Cross-cultural knowledge can be accomplished by composing cross-national research teams and by conducting research on international and immigrant populations in the United States.
7. Promoting culturally valid practice around the globe	The viability of the counseling profession will require that we demonstrate that our U.S. counseling knowledge, philosophy, and techniques are culturally relevant in different environments.
8. Enhancing and promoting international education	Developing effective cross-cultural learning opportunities for U.S. students (and international students enrolled in U.S. training programs) will help to ensure that our students are competent to work not only with clients from U.S. cultures but other cultures as well. International and U.S. students and faculty can learn from each other about cross-cultural issues through their interactions and discussions, which will contribute to the internationalization of the counseling profession.
9. Collaboration among counseling organizations	Collaboration among counseling organizations worldwide has become increasingly important as there is much to gain from global sharing and alliances. Collaboration only among U.S.-based counseling organizations is no longer sufficient, and the future of the counseling profession will require that we share and learn across national boundaries.

Source: Heppner, Leong, and Chiao (2008).

Many factors such as globalization and an increase in immigration and migration of world citizens provide the need to enhance counseling professionals' skills in the development of indigenous psychology and the ability to interact effectively with people of different worldviews. Therefore, counseling programs are encouraged to develop cross-culturally appropriate training models that will prepare counseling students to work in international settings. Of critical importance to such a training program initiative is that faculty members in counseling programs around the world employ available technologies such as web-based conferencing that will allow them to collaborate with one another and with students and further discuss how course-related issues may be influenced by culture (Gerstein, Heppner, Ægisdottir, Leung, & Norsworthy, 2009).

The very limited and culturally encapsulated information that counselors-in-training receive about the models and approaches relevant to their field suggests that internationalizing the training curriculum in the counseling field will be critical to doing culturally appropriate international work. We cannot assume that our current models and theories of counseling are culturally relevant for clients from other countries and with differing worldviews. The counseling field and its training programs will need to continually assess the cultural validity and generalizability of its models and theories of counseling to ensure their relevance for a global practice of counseling. To expose trainees only to counseling theories, models, and interventions that are written and practiced in the United States is to further perpetuate the cultural encapsulation of the profession (Leung, 2003). Leung discussed the necessity of programs to instill a global perspective by requiring trainees to read counseling literature that is published from around the world with the intent to broaden and expand trainees' knowledge about counseling beyond the U.S. borders.

Effectively Serving the Culturally Diverse: A Process of Renewing the Profession

As the counseling profession responds to the need to prepare students for a multicultural and global society, counselor training programs will need to be more intentional about addressing cultural competency as related to counseling theories, practice, and research. The profession's advocacy for pluralism can no longer be framed through a Western mindset. Our multicultural and cross-cultural training paradigms must be universally defined and supported by a conceptual framework that is entrenched in universal culture. The renewal of our profession depends on this universal framework, and so do our consumers. The counseling profession's adaptation to the external demands of offering and maintaining culturally relevant training programs and securing a global, multicultural presence will determine its success and viability. Shannon Hodges (2011), a counseling professor at Niagra University, a prolific contributor to counseling journals, and a past member of the ACA Ethics Review Task Force, commented on the future success of the profession:

> To flourish, the counseling profession must chart a bold, progressive, global, strategic course of action to address postmodern challenges. An effective course of action is likely to result in numerous changes both for counselor education training and in the delivery of counseling services to an increasingly diverse, global clientele. (p. 198)

As the counseling profession heeds the call for globalization while also embracing a social justice stance, practitioners must be prepared to address the inherent and variant social and cultural norms around the globe that may present challenges for the profession in terms of its advocacy efforts. In other words, some restrictive and social caste system societies have limits on gender roles, religious identity, and sexual orientation, which may make it difficult to advocate for equality without appearing culturally insensitive. Hodges (2011) explained the predicament with the following example:

> Saudi Arabia, for example, is an absolute monarchy that prohibits men and women from sharing the same classroom, restricts women's movement outside the home, prohibits women from divorcing their husbands, and provides no legal protection against domestic abuse. Furthermore, homosexuality and a Saudi's practice of a religion other than Islam are potentially punishable by death. (p. 196)

Hodges (2011) further directed our attention to whether it is realistic to expect that social and cultural issues spread across diverse cultures can be unilaterally agreed upon and whether there are universal social justice principles (e.g., gender and sexual equity, religious freedom) that the counseling profession should promote. Hodges recommends that professional counseling organizations such as the ACA discuss the parameters and applicability of Western, social justice, and advocacy counseling expectations for non-Western societies. Because the profession's advocacy for pluralism is framed through a Western mind-set, Hodges encourages training programs to be mindful of the applicability of our social justice model on non-Western societies, particularly in light of the profession's efforts toward global expansion. These considerations illuminate the need for counselor education programs to adequately prepare students to engage in culturally responsive care of a multicultural and global society, which is essential to the continued viability of the counseling profession.

A Reflection by a Mexican Immigrant Counselor-in-Training

In the past 10 years, living in the United States as a Mexican has given me opportunities to create relationships with people from multiple nationalities and cultural backgrounds.

As a counselor-in-training, I am always open to reflecting on the multicultural aspects of my interactions with my clients and strive to capture and integrate the cultural aspects related to my clients' presenting concerns. I cherish the opportunity to see the world from my clients' vantage point while actively attempting to integrate their stories with theory I have learned. I find the process of becoming a multicultural counselor exciting, challenging, and rewarding. It is exciting because I get to reflect and learn many interesting things about myself, my culture, and many other human cultures (whether it is from books, trainings, or firsthand from my clients). It is challenging because it requires a great deal of effort and courage to learn and grow in this field (reflecting, finding out, and taking responsibility about my own biases as well as becoming aware and learning to cope with common biases in the American culture and advocate for positive change).

> Both my own and my clients' cultural background have significant roles in our therapeutic relationships. When I work with Caucasian clients, for instance, I use my international background as an excuse to have them explain to me aspects of their cultural background relevant to their presenting concerns. This allows both of us to get greater awareness and deeper insight into their cultural strengths and limitations, which are valuable resources/tools to help them reach their goals. When I work with clients of color (or from any other minority status such as gender, sexual orientation, etc.), in addition to having them help me understand their cultural background (the values and roles their culture dictates for them and the significant people around them), I also stay tuned for any stories that involve discrimination or oppression, which helps me better connect/empathize with them and their struggles and be more prepared to act in their best interest (validating their stories, processing painful experiences, and advocating on their behalf).
>
> —*B., a Mexican immigrant counselor-in-training*

Working With Cultural Diversity: A Basic Ethical Responsibility

The provision of services to culturally diverse others without adequate preparation and appropriate competencies raises concerns about our ethical responsibility. Both the body that establishes ethical codes for our discipline (ACA) and the professional accrediting body (CACREP) clearly emphasize that counseling programs have an ethical duty to educate both their faculty and students about their responsibility to respect individuals and groups with cultural aspects different from their own as unique and worthwhile and to become culturally skilled educators and counselors. It is critical that faculty and students of all cultural backgrounds experience the academy as an institution where culturally diverse perspectives are valued and commensurate with their program's training philosophy and curricula development.

If practitioners fail in their ethical responsibility to integrate diversity into their practice, they will most likely fail at being helpful, which subsequently risks the continued renewal of the counseling profession. Multiculturalism and diversity considerations are infused throughout the ACA (2014) *Code of Ethics* as well as other professions' ethics codes (e.g., APA, American School Counseling Association, National Association for Social Workers, Canadian Counselling Association) and require practitioners to understand the diverse cultural backgrounds of the clients with whom they work. Specifically, and related to personal values, advocacy, and boundaries of competence, counselors have an ethical responsibility to

- be aware of their own values, attitudes, beliefs, and behaviors and refrain from imposing values that are inconsistent with counseling goals (Personal Values, A.4.b.);
- advocate on behalf of their clients at individual, group, institutional, and societal levels and examine barriers that inhibit client growth and development (Advocacy, A.7.b); and

- gain knowledge, personal awareness, sensitivity, and skills that will allow them to work effectively with diverse clientele (Boundaries of Competence, C.2.a.).

Further, ACA ethical mandates pertinent to multicultural and diversity considerations include that counselors

- be respectful of approaches to counseling services that differ from the professional group in which one works (Different Approaches, D.1.a.);
- be cautious when selecting assessments for culturally diverse clients (Culturally Diverse Populations, E.6.a.);
- recognize that culture affects the way in which clients' problems are defined and diagnosed (Cultural Sensitivity, E.5.b.);
- do not perpetuate historical and social prejudices in the diagnosis and treatment of certain individuals and groups (Historical and Social Prejudices in the Diagnosis of Pathology, E.5.c.); and
- recognize the effects of culturally relevant factors (i.e., age, color, culture, disability, ethnic group, gender, race, language preference, religion, spirituality, sexual orientation, and socioeconomic status) when administering tests and interpreting results (Multicultural Issues/Diversity in Assessment, E.8.).

Finally, the ACA's (2014) *Code of Ethics* informs counselor educators and supervisors about their responsibility to address the role of multiculturalism and diversity in their training and supervision practices (see F.2.b. Multicultural Issues/Diversity in Supervision and F.11.c. Multicultural/Diversity Competence). Furthermore, we believe counseling training programs have an ethical responsibility to provide students practicum experiences that will allow them to work with culturally diverse others. Field experiences that challenge students to address cultural concerns and other areas of diversity will help them to develop self-awareness and examine attitudes associated with diversity competence. In addition to practicums, internships, and extended group activities in cultural communities, students can also benefit from living in different cultural environments.

Experiencing the culturally diverse not only provides an opportunity to understand another culture and the impact of oppression on the lives of its members but also challenges one to undergo his or her own culture shock and self-analysis (Vontress, 1976). Moreover, we agree with Gunnings (1971), who asserted that many of the problems that clients bring to counseling are perpetuated by an unjust system. The ethically and culturally competent counselor must, therefore, be willing to acknowledge and challenge a system that has historically dehumanized and oppressed society's diverse clientele (Gunnings, 1971).

In addition to practitioners' ethical responsibility to be multiculturally competent, the guidelines of CACREP (2009) also require that students who are preparing to work as counselors in the mental health field demonstrate knowledge, skills, and practices in the areas of diversity and client advocacy. More specifically, the standards call for supervised practicum/clinical experiences with varied cultural groups and in particular, exposure to clients from those environments in which the student is preparing to work. According to the standards, it is expected that students will be provided training opportunities with varied ethnic groups, subcultures, urban and rural societies, and other diversity aspects (e.g., religion, sexual orientation, gender identity). Training programs must therefore provide evidence that student learning has occurred in terms of the effect of racism, discrimination, sexism, power, privilege, and oppression on the lives of clients who are seeking counseling services. We risk the continued renewal of our profession if counselors are allowed to behave as if all their clients are the same and can be treated equally despite the social inequities and impediments that have been a large part of their history. The influence that culture has upon the self, society, and the helping process warrants our continued attention, and the viability of our profession is contingent upon understanding our clients in a cultural context.

Summary

This chapter promotes that counseling practitioners of the 21st century must meet their ethical obligation to provide culturally responsive care to the culturally diverse. To this end, counseling professionals must recognize the barriers and challenges rooted in both the people who provide service and in the existing theories and methods of counseling. A working definition of multicultural counseling is provided. Counselors-in-training have the responsibility to develop competencies in renewing the profession and counseling practice by practicing and improving multicultural counseling. Training programs must give serious consideration to how to facilitate multicultural counseling competency development and how such competencies are assessed. Additionally, understanding human behavior in a global context is critical to the progression of the counseling profession.

Takeaway Messages

1. The counselor is a particularly important helping agent in counseling the culturally diverse and must be prepared to enter clients' realities in order to understand their views and experiences. The counselor's own awareness, consciousness, and understanding of his or her clients' social and cultural issues play a critical role in client recovery, healing, and growth.

2. Exclusive focus on clients' internal psychological processes may lead to biased or inaccurate understanding of clients' experiences. Macro social and cultural issues influence clients' life experiences and need to be addressed in counseling them.

3. It is the basic ethical and professional responsibility of counselors to become multiculturally competent.

4. The future of our profession will be determined by how successful we are in the provision of competent psychological services to the culturally diverse.

Recommended Resources

Readings

Arredondo, P., & Arciniega, M. (2001). Strategies and techniques for counselor training based on the multicultural counseling competencies. *Journal of Multicultural Counseling and Development, 29*, 263–273.

Arredondo, P., & Rosen, D. (2007). Applying principles of multicultural, social justice, and leadership in training and supervision. In E. Aldorando (Ed.), *Advancing social justice through mental health practice* (pp. 443–456). Mahwah, NJ: Erlbaum.

D'Andrea, M., & Daniels, J. (2006, January 7). Embracing the deep structure of multicultural counseling. *Counseling Today*. Retrieved from http://ct.counseling.org/2006/01/ct-online-dignity-development-diversity/

McCreary, M. L., & Walker, T. D. (2001). Teaching multicultural counseling pre-practicum. *Teaching Psychology, 28*(3), 195–198.

Pieterse, A. L., Evans, S. A., Risner-Butner, A., Collins, N. M., & Mason, L. B. (2009). Multicultural competence and social justice training in counseling psychology and counselor education: A review and analysis of a sample of multicultural course syllabi. *The Counseling Psychologist, 37*(1), 93–115.

Media and Websites

Abani, C. (2007, August). Telling stories from Africa [TED talk]. Retrieved from http://www.ted.com/talks/-chris_abani_on_the_stories_of_africa.html

Implicit Association Tests: Project Implicit. (2011). Project Implicit is a non-profit organization and international collaboration between researchers who are interested in implicit social cognition—thoughts and feelings outside of conscious awareness and control. Available at https://implicit.harvard.edu/implicit/takeatest.html

Lee, M. W. (Director). (2003). *Last chance for Eden* [Film]. United States: StirFry Seminars. Available from http://www.stirfryseminars.com/

Peters, W. (Producer). (1970). Brown eyes, blue eyes. *ABC News*. Video retrieved from https://www.youtube.com/watch?v=VeK759FF84s

References

American Counseling Association. (2014). *Code of ethics*. Washington, DC: Author. Retrieved from http://www.counseling.org/knowledge-center/ethics

Brach, C., & Fraser, I. (2000). Can cultural competency reduce racial and ethnic disparities? A review and conceptual model. *Medical Care Research & Review, 57*, 181–217.

Chow, J. C., Jaffee, K., & Snowden, L. (2003). Racial/ethnic disparities in the use of mental health services in poverty areas. *American Journal of Public Health, 73*, 792–797.

Cokley, K. (2006). The impact of racialized schools and racist (mis)education on African American students' academic identity. In M. G. Constantine & D. W. Sue (Eds.), *Addressing racism* (pp. 127–144). Hoboken, NJ: Wiley.

Constantine, M. G. (2002). Predictors of satisfaction with counseling: Racial and ethnic minority clients' attitudes toward counseling and ratings of their counselors' general and multicultural counseling competence. *Journal of Counseling Psychology, 49*, 255–263.

Council for Accreditation of Counseling and Related Educational Programs. (2009). *2009 standards*. Retrieved from http://www.cacrep.org/for-programs/resources-for-programs/

Federal Bureau of Investigation. (2013). Hate Crime: Overview. Retrieved from http://www.fbi.gov/about-us/investigate/civilrights/hate_crimes/overview

Fukuyama, M., & Sevig, T. (1999). *Integrating spirituality into multicultural counseling*. Thousand Oaks, CA: Sage.

Gerstein, L. H., Heppner, P. P., Stockton, R., Leong, F. T. L., & Ægisdóttir, S. (2009). The counseling profession in- and outside the United States. In L. H. Gerstein, P. P. Heppner, S. Ægisdóttir, S. A. Leung, & K. L. Norsworthy (Eds.), *International handbook of cross-cultural counseling: Cultural assumptions and practices worldwide* (pp. 53–68). Thousand Oaks, CA: Sage.

Glosoff, H. L. (2009). The counseling profession: Historical perspectives and current issues and trends. In D. Capuzzi & D. R. Grossi (Eds.), *Introduction to the counseling profession* (pp. 42–43).

Gunnings, T. S. (1971). Preparing the new counselor. *The Counseling Psychologist, 2*, 199–201.

Hays, P. A. (1996). Addressing the complexities of culture and gender in counseling. *Journal of Counseling & Development, 74*, 332–338.

Heppner, P. P., Ægisdottir, S., Leung, S. M. A., Duan, C., Helms, J. E., Gerstein, L. H., & Pedersen, P. B. (2008). The intersection of multicultural and cross-national movements in the United States: A complementary role to promote culturally sensitive research, training, and practice. In L. H. Gerstein, P. P. Heppner, S. Ægisdottir, S. M. A. Leung, & K. L. Norsworthy (Eds.), *International handbook of cross-cultural counseling: Cultural assumptions and practices worldwide* (pp. 33–52). Thousand Oaks, CA: Sage.

Heppner, P. P., Leong, F. T. L., & Chiao, H. (2008). The growing internationalization of counseling psychology. In S. D. Brown & R. W. Lent (Eds.), *Handbook of counseling psychology* (4th ed., pp. 68–85). New York, NY: Wiley.

Hodges, S. (2011). Through a glass darkly: Envisioning the future of the counseling profession—A commentary. *The Professional Counselor: Research and Practice, 1*(3), 191–200.

Jun, H. (2010). *Social justice, multicultural counseling, and practice: Beyond a conventional approach*. Thousand Oaks, CA: Sage.

Kearney, E. M., Draper, M., & Baron, A. (2005). Counseling utilization of ethnic minority college students. *Cultural Diversity and Ethnic Minority Psychology, 11*, 272–285.

Leung, A. S. (2003). A journey worth traveling: Globalization of counseling psychology. *The Counseling Psychologist, 31*, 412–419.

McGuire, T. G., & Miranda, J. (2008). New evidence regarding racial and ethnic disparities in mental health: Policy implications. *Health Affair, 27*, 393–403.

McNamee, S. J., & Miller, R. K., Jr. (2004). The meritocracy myth. *Sociation Today, 2*(1). Retrieved from http://www.ncsociology.org/sociationtoday/v21/merit.htm

Satcher, D. (2001). *U.S. surgeon general report on mental health: Culture, race, and ethnicity*. Retrieved from: http://www.wkkf.org/resource-directory/resource/2001/08/us-surgeon-general-releases-report-on-mental-health-culture-race-and-ethnicity

Shallcross, L. (2012, March). What the future holds for the counseling profession. *Counseling Today*. Retrieved from http://ct.counseling.org/2012/03/what-the-future-holds-for-the-counseling-profession/

Sue, D. W., & Sue, D. (2013). *Counseling the culturally diverse: Theory and practice* (6th ed.). New York, NY: Wiley.

Takaki, R. T. (1993). *A different mirror: A history of multicultural America*. Boston, MA: Little, Brown.

U.S. Department of Health and Human Services. (2001). *Mental health: Culture, race, and ethnicity—A supplement to mental health: A report of the Surgeon General*. Rockville, MD: Author. Retrieved from http://www.ncbi.nlm.nih.gov/books/NBK44243/pdf/TOC.pdf

Vontress, C. E. (1976). Racial and ethnic barriers in counseling. In P. Pedersen, W. J. Lonner, & J. G. Draguns (Eds.), *Counseling across cultures* (pp. 42–64). Honolulu: University Press of Hawaii.

Wolch, J. R., & Dear, M. J. (1993). *Malign neglect: Homelessness in an American city*. San Francisco, CA: Jossey-Bass.

Woloshin, S., Bickell, N. A., Schwartz, L. M., Gany, F., & Welch, H. G. (1995). Language barriers in medicine in the United States. *Journal of the American Medical Association, 273*(9), 724–728.

Section 3

Becoming Multiculturally Competent

Major CACREP Standards for the Section

CACREP Standard 2c: theories of multicultural counseling, identity development, and social justice

CACREP Standard 2e: counselors' roles in developing cultural self-awareness, promoting cultural social justice, advocacy and conflict resolution, and other culturally supported behaviors that promote optimal wellness and growth of the human spirit, mind, or body

Specific Competencies Identified by CACREP Diversity and Advocacy Standards for Clinical Mental Health Counseling Addressed in Section 3

CACREP Knowledge 5: Understands the implications of concepts such as internalized oppression and institutional racism, as well as the historical and current political climate regarding immigration, poverty, and welfare

After Reading Section 3, Students Will Be Able to Do the Following:

a. Recognize the importance of developing a multicultural identity (Chapter 6)

b. Become aware of their privileges in areas where they hold dominant group memberships (Chapters 6–7)

c. Understand how various isms affect their cultural identity and social experiences (Chapters 6–7)

d. Understand the relationship between social oppression and privileges (Chapters 6–7)

e. Recognize the existence and pervasive impact of social oppression (Chapter 7)
f. Gain knowledge of cultural pluralism (Chapter 7)
g. Understand that attention is needed to both the roles of social oppression and cultural value differences in understanding the culturally diverse (Chapter 7)

Section Introduction

This section focuses on counselor multicultural identity development and understanding of the negative impact of social oppression and marginalization on the culturally diverse.

Chapter 6 methodically describes multicultural identity development along a number of diversity dimensions, focusing on the development process for majority group memberships. However, it is important to acknowledge that (a) the dimensions of diversity discussed in this chapter are not exhaustive; (b) we are not assuming that all counselors-in-training have dominant group membership in all the dimensions (minority group identity development will be discussed in Section 4); (c) focusing on these categorical identities in cultural values and worldviews presents only half of the whole picture—namely, between-group differences (the other half, within-group differences, will be integrated into Section 4); and (d) the separate discussion of identities is for the sake of clarity and does not intend to take away our holistic view of multicultural identity development.

Chapter 7 focuses on promoting an understanding of the pervasiveness of social oppression in society and its impact on the culturally diverse. Counselors may or may not experience some or any of these oppressive social treatments themselves (depending on their diversity demographics), but it is critical that they allow this knowledge to enter their consciousness and develop ability to validate such experiences of their culturally diverse clients. This knowledge is also the foundation of culturally efficacious interventions and social justice efforts.

Developing a Multicultural Identity

The paradox of education is precisely this—that as one begins to become conscious one begins to examine the society in which he is being educated.

—James A. Baldwin

CHAPTER OVERVIEW

This chapter encourages readers to understand the self as a multicultural being. A person living in the United States needs to see that the self is a product of one or more specific cultures and interaction of cultures. Multicultural competencies are not just skills or methods that we use in counseling. Based on a multicultural competence development model, developing a multicultural identity is the foundation and indispensable first step for counselor multicultural competence development. Along each of the dimensions of diversity, there are dominant and subordinate groups, and there are systems of privilege and oppression. The identity development for members of dominant and subordinate groups faces different challenges. This chapter focuses on the multicultural identity development for those who have a dominant-group membership in a given area (minority identity development will be covered in Section 4). It is critical that counselors-in-training (especially when they have dominant-group membership) develop new social and cultural consciousness about the existence and harm of isms and move from being oblivious to them to taking responsibility to eliminate them and advocate for the victims.

SELF-ASSESSMENT OF PRE-EXISTING AWARENESS AND KNOWLEDGE

- What cultures do I have?
- In what ways can I see myself as a cultural being?
- How is my identity (the sense of who I am) related to any cultural variables in my life?
- How do I categorize or label myself in terms of race, ethnicity, nationality, sexual identity, social class, religion, age, and ability/disability?
- What "social experience" do I encounter as a result of my identities?
- What dimension of my identity is most significant for me?
- What does it mean to be (my race or ethnicity), (my gender), (my social class), (my sexual orientation), (my age), (my ability/disability status), and so on?
- What unearned privileges have I enjoyed? For what reasons?
- What experiences of social oppression have I had? For what reasons?

LEARNING OBJECTIVES

After reading this chapter, students will be able to do the following:

1. Recognize the diverse dimensions of their own cultural identity
2. Become aware of the fact that everyone has a cultural identity along each dimension of human diversity
3. Recognize the need for further development of each one of their own identities in the cultural contexts of society
4. Articulate some of the implications of each dimension of one's identity on others
5. Recognize some of the unearned privileges and disadvantages they experience as the result of being who they are
6. Recognize that each individual plays a role in the society that treats individuals differently based on their personal, cultural, and social identities
7. View oppression and discrimination that people experience in the context of a diverse society
8. Take responsibility for their own contribution to the social oppression of others

CASE ILLUSTRATION 6.1

The Case of Samuel

Samuel is a 42-year-old successful Caucasian male lawyer who presented to therapy with the expressed desire to overcome his "social anxiety" and depression and develop a healthy romantic relationship. In the intake session, he said he was not sure who he was and did not feel comfortable with who he was. It was apparent that despite having had many successes, he felt a deep sense of dissatisfaction with his life. When asked specifically about his sexual orientation, he said he was gay but had never been in a long-term relationship with another man. He said that he had two sexual encounters with men in the past and a number of short-term relationships with women but never any sort of long-term romantic relationship. Samuel also reported that he frequently felt nervous in social settings and wondered if there was something "wrong" with him. He had a number of supportive friendships, yet he was haunted by general feelings of loneliness that he could not banish. His mood was generally low, and he had great difficulty articulating his feelings.

Samuel was generally active with coworkers and friends, frequently going to local social events such as parties, concerts, and sports games. He reported that he had liked these events in the past, but they have grown increasingly uncomfortable for him, though he did not really know why. Samuel said that his professional peers generally like him, but he did not trust that they would like him if they knew he was gay. He said he experienced significant work-related stress. He no longer felt comfortable around his coworkers and found his work to be boring and unrewarding. Samuel drank about eight to 12 servings of alcohol nearly every night but stated that he did not feel like it was much of a problem.

Samuel is an only child and has a strained relationship with both of his parents. His father was a hard worker and provider, but he had a significant problem with alcohol and was not emotionally present. He described his mother as overly critical and a perfectionist. He was raised in a small rural town where there were literally no openly gay people that he was aware of. He has not disclosed his sexual orientation to anyone except for one close friend. He felt that his law partners would not accept his sexuality, and he was afraid that his family would reject him, too. He stated that he was motivated for therapy, and money was not an issue for him, but he did not know how therapy can work for him.

GUIDED PRACTICE EXERCISE 6.1

How Do You Feel About Samuel?

Read Case Illustration 6.1 about Samuel. In small groups of three to four classmates, use the following questions as your guide to share with the group how you feel about him. Please challenge and help each other in this process.

(Continued)

(Continued)

1. What are your reactions and impressions of Samuel after reading this description?
2. Do you feel empathic toward him? In what ways?
3. Do you feel his pain? To what degree?
4. In what ways do you feel that you can relate to Samuel? Why?
5. In what ways do you feel it is hard to empathize with Samuel? Why?
6. Do you feel in any way you may have contributed to his fear of not being accepted by his professional peers as a gay person?
7. Consider your own identities. If you were a White woman, a White man, a person of color, or someone who had lived in poverty, how might you feel his pain?

If we compare how we each feel about this client and his concerns, it will probably become apparent that who we are and how we interpret and view ourselves does influence our perception of and experience with our clients. Although we may tell ourselves that our task is to empathize with the client and work for him, we may inadvertently miss signs, pay too much or too little attention to certain aspects of his life, or let our life experience color our perception and assessment of his experiences. Any aspect of our cultural identity, such as our gender, sexual identity, racial/ethnic background, age, or our social class status, may influence how we see and conceptualize Samuel's concerns and how we feel his pain.

Although we may not be fully aware, we bring ourselves as cultural beings into the relationship with our clients. Our attitudes, beliefs, and values along with our own life experiences will influence our perceptions and evaluations of and experiences with our clients. Obviously, if we want to help the culturally diverse, we need to be able to hear their stories accurately, validate their experiences, respect their identities, and advocate for their well-being without letting our own biases block the way. This can be challenging and even impossible if we do not feel the relevance of culture and cultural context in our own lives or view ourselves as cultural beings, especially if we are not aware of how our life experiences have biased our perceptions, shaped our worldviews, and contributed to others' social experiences. Thus, developing a multicultural identity is critical and necessary on our journey toward multicultural competence.

A Model of Multicultural Competence Development

Based on our knowledge of the literature on multicultural competence development and years of experience in offering teaching and training activities in this area, we developed a model of multicultural competence development (Figure 6.1).

Figure 6.1 Multicultural Competence Development Model

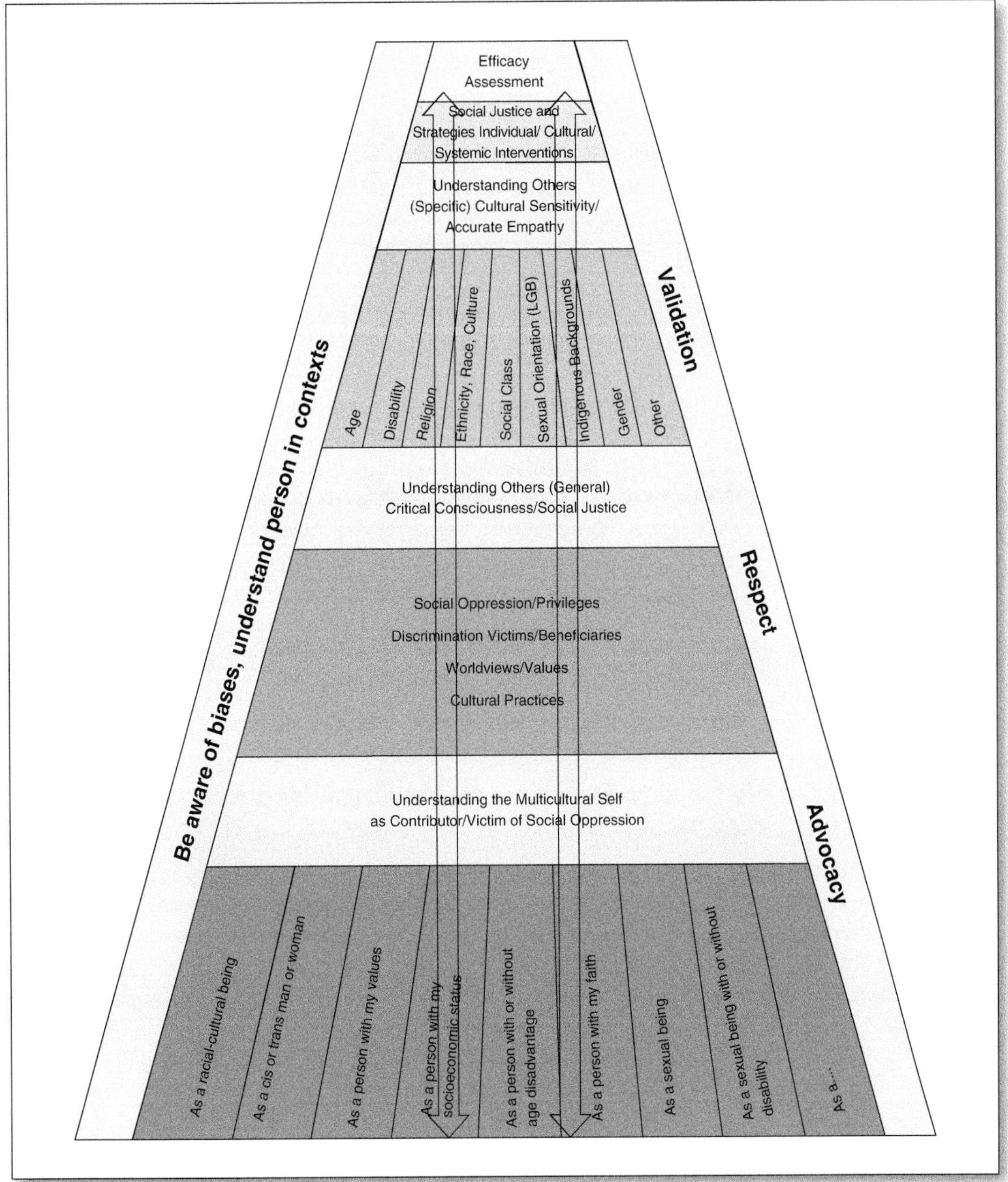

Source: Adapted from the integrated training model from Miville, M., Duan, C., Nutt, R., Waehler, C., Suzuki, L., Pistole, C., Arredondo, P., Duffy, M., Mejia, B., and Corpus, M. (2009). Integrating practice guidelines into professional training: Implications for diversity competence. The Counseling Psychologist, 37, 519–563.

As illustrated, the foundation (Stage 1) of multicultural competence is a *multicultural identity*. To offer effective counseling, competent counselors have to know who they are, what they stand for, how they have experienced society, and what roles they play in the society where they and their clients cohabit. With a multicultural identity, the counselor will be able to identify with and understand the culturally diverse or socially marginalized.

At Stage 2, a *multicultural consciousness* will be developed, based on the understanding of social structure and systems of privileges and social oppression. This multicultural consciousness will allow the counselor to hear clients' life narratives unfiltered by personal bias and see the world from the perspectives of others, especially the culturally diverse and socially marginalized.

At Stage 3, a *multicultural personality* is developed; it shows interest and effort in learning about individual differences in social contexts for all people, including the culturally diverse and socially marginalized. With a multicultural identity as the foundation and understanding of the system of oppression and privilege, the counselor will be able to address the intersection of client identities when working with the culturally diverse.

Finally, in Stage 4 *multicultural ability* is developed to facilitate social justice advocacy and therapeutic prevention and intervention strategies.

While a desired developmental process from the lower stages to higher stages is implied by the model, counselor development may not always be linear and will move back and forth among stages. As the world changes, multicultural competence needs to progress, resulting in a lifelong enrichment process. Notably, the development of basic counseling skills (e.g., validation, respect, advocacy) and the practice of multicultural counseling (e.g., being aware of one's own biases, understanding clients in social contexts) are always ongoing accompanying processes.

Why Do We Need to Develop a Multicultural Identity?

In our culturally diverse society, individuals' cultural identities are formed and exhibited through interactions with others with different cultural backgrounds. In these interactions, individuals may consciously or unconsciously contribute to each other's sense of self, social position, and relationships. Due to the power differential between groups that is rooted in history as well as present social structures domestically and internationally, those who are in high social power positions may let their biased attitudes and beliefs influence their perceptions of others who are in lower power positions and are racially or culturally different from them, favoring those who are similar to themselves (in-groups) and stereotyping dissimilar others (out-groups). There is certainly no exception in counseling settings, where such conscious or unconscious acts of cultural biases may have detrimental impact on culturally diverse clients.

The traditional identity theories (e.g., Freud's psychosexual development, Eric Erikson's ego and social identity development) seemed to imply universality in identity development and failed to take into full consideration the influence of individuals' cultural and social statuses, positions, and experiences. It has to be recognized that the diverse makeup of the United States and its international connections automatically makes every resident multicultural, although many have the privilege not to recognize this fact. Those who are in the dominant and privileged groups along any diversity dimension often do not acknowledge that they have cultures like those who are in minorities. The reason is that the dominant groups are in the position of power, and their culture and cultural values fill all areas of life (including the science and practice of counseling), which becomes the standard and the norm on which their sense of right or wrong, good or bad, acceptable or unacceptable, or healthy or unhealthy is based. It is difficult for individuals born into these privileged positions to see or feel the need to view themselves as cultural beings or even see culture as relevant to them. What they are brought up believing is the background, history, and context of their lives, and they may not be able to recognize the relevance of culture without a deliberate and concerted effort to see it.

One example of the privilege of not seeing culture as relevant is the color-blind attitude and ideology regarding difference in skin color. White people, who are not disadvantaged due to race, can choose to be color-blind or deny that race matters. It is not uncommon for White people to say that they do not see skin color and that they treat everyone the same. While this belief may reflect self-perceived good intention, it in fact serves to justify the current unjust social order and makes White people feel more comfortable with their relatively privileged standing in society (Fryberg, 2010). Clearly, most persons of color do not feel supported by this color blindness because it denies their negative experiences due to racism, rejects their cultural heritage, and invalidates their perspectives (Williams, 2011). They likely feel that race does matter to them as they regularly encounter difficulties due to race in various areas of life, including employment, income, access to education and health care, and so forth. Color blindness does not foster equality or respect, and it is a form of racism (Neville, Awad, Brooks, Flores, & Bluemel, 2013).

Another familiar example is the "Don't Ask, Don't Tell" attitude and military practice regarding gay and lesbian individuals. Military policy from 1993 to 2011, it denied the very basic rights of thousands of military servicemen and women. They could not present themselves honestly, take care of their partners and families with recognition, protection, or health/housing benefits, or reunite with loved ones in public upon returning from deployment. The emotional and psychological effects of this policy also permeated civilian parts of the society. Those who are not members of the lesbian/gay/bisexual/transgender/queer (LGBTQ) communities place the same injustice onto LGBTQ individuals. Because they do not have to examine what their sexuality or gender identities mean to them, heterosexual individuals minimize LGBTQs' psychological existence by claiming that "no one wants to know, so you don't tell."

Individuals tend to act to verify their conceptions of who they are in their existing social context with others; in turn, their individual acts not only reflect society but also reinforce the patterns of behavior and interaction among all coexisting people and groups that constitute the social context (Stets & Burke, 2003). Without conscious efforts, it is often difficult for some individuals to see that it is the social structure or context that gives them the privilege to act, to achieve, or to succeed in certain ways, and their behaviors further strengthen this structure. The more the privileged exercise their privileges, the more struggles the marginalized have to endure. One example is attributing lack of success among the oppressed to personal failures rather than to the unjust system that offers differential access to individuals for success. For instance, the "glass ceiling" that prevents women from reaching positions of power, the lack of access to health service for those with low socioeconomic status (SES), and the "illegality" for gay couples to marry exemplify the fact that individuals are shaped by social structure. If those longtime country-club-goers are not aware (or unwilling to recognize) that their social identity as the rich made them beneficiaries of U.S. political institutions' biased economic policies (Enns, Kelly, Morgan, Volscho, & Witko, 2013), it will be hard for them not to view the poor as less hardworking, less intelligent, or less capable than they are. This view is consistent with the identity theory that sees *self* as the product of society, and there is a reciprocal relationship between the self and society (Stryker, 1980).

Counselors' perception and understanding of their multicultural self may directly influence how they view and understand their clients' experiences and how their clients experience them. The essence of multicultural counseling is viewing clients within cultural contexts in which both the counselor and the client play a role; for example, the roles may be in opposition, such as oppressor versus victim (Duan & Smith, in press). The danger is obvious if the counselor fails to recognize himself or herself as a multicultural being. It will be all too easy and convenient to readily conceptualize an African American male's "black rage" as an intrapsychic issue, a Latino's low graduate record examination (GRE) score as reflecting low intelligence, a transgender or "in-questioning" person's gender identity as abnormal, a person in a wheelchair as less capable, an individual with a foreign accent as incompetent, a client complaining about hostility he sensed when using food stamps in an affluent town as feeling insecure, and so on.

In order to help our culturally diverse clients heal and gain corrective experiences from negative consequences of oppression, it is unacceptable and intolerable that we as counselors act out our own isms. It is not even good enough that we claim to be *non-ists* (such as nonracists, nonsexists, and nonheterosexists) who recognize that isms exist and are harmful but then fail to confront, challenge, or correct them. We as counseling professionals must be *anti-isms* (i.e., antiracism, antisexism, and anticlassism) and actively combat social oppression. In doing so, individuals from marginalized and oppressed groups can feel safe with us, validated by us, and with our help, understand their own experiences in ways that will not further push them down but encourage them to rise up. In order to achieve this level of therapeutic gain, we must have a clear sense of our own cultural identities and become multiculturalists who readily perceive (and help our clients perceive) client experiences in social and cultural contexts. As multiculturalists, we are expected to assist in the pursuit of social change and social justice so clients can heal and grow.

GUIDED PRACTICE EXERCISE 6.2

My Views and My Consciousness

In groups of five to seven students, read each of the following statements and share with each other your views and reactions.

- A real estate developer who is among the top 1% of asset holders said this to a news interviewer: "The poor should try to emulate, not envy, the rich—we work harder" (Bloomberg, 2014).
- One White male said to a group of men of color: "You give us White men a hard time for blocking your progress—we don't. The question is about you—why don't you go out and make a place for yourself? I see you equal to us" (Lee, 1994).
- Born a biological male, Nicole identified as a female at the age of 2. When she was in the fifth grade, she was banned from using the girls' bathroom, which led to a high-profile legal battle (Jeltsen, 2014).

Questions for Reflection

1. What are the different reactions to these statements among your group members?
2. What correct answers were you looking to apply?
3. How might you address any defensiveness you are experiencing?
4. Describe any pain you may have experienced for any party involved. If you did not feel any pain, why do you think that might be?
5. In what ways do you feel that your reactions reflect your cultural identity and/or consciousness?
6. Which of your reactions/feelings do you think will be helpful/unhelpful if you are the counselor for the person(s) of lower power in these stories?

A Definition of Multicultural Identity

The definition of *multicultural identity* as it applies to a professional counselor is multidimensional; what it means to develop a multicultural identity can be explained as follows:

> *Defining one's personal and professional roles with a set of attitudes, beliefs, values, motives, experiences, skills, and practices that enables one to accurately understand and effectively intervene on behalf of clients and communities in our culturally pluralistic society. A necessary component of this identity is being a non- and anti-ist in all dimensions of diversity and supporting social justice for all.*

A multicultural personal identity allows the individual to recognize himself or herself as a cultural being who experiences unearned social and cultural privileges and/or disadvantages while also acknowledging the prejudices and biases that he or she holds toward others. A multicultural professional identity informs the formation of a multicultural consciousness and prepares the counselor to develop both intellectual and emotional capacity for helping those who are socially oppressed and/or culturally diverse. The development of a multicultural identity (personal and professional) is a lifelong journey that requires continuous learning.

Dimensions of Multicultural Identity

Individuals with different demographic characteristics, such as age, sex, skin color, SES, or religious affiliations, may experience different social and cultural contexts within the same society. With or without open acknowledgement, people are perceived, treated, and evaluated differently simply because of their demographics. Such social contexts and experiences may trigger individuals to think, feel, and act in certain ways and derive a sense of self in relation to their perceived group memberships (Hogg & Vaughan, 2002). According to social identity theories, this is how an individual's social identity is formed, and all individuals have multiple identities due to their group memberships along different dimensions of human diversity. For instance, individuals may have a racial identity, sexual identity, religious identity, national identity, and so on, reflecting the sense of self derived from their perceived social group memberships.

Our cultural and social identities do not exist in isolation, in static mode, or in single dimension. The meaning of individuals' identities is determined not only by the individuals but also by how others treat them, interact with them, or view their social statuses. For example, being a Latino immigrant may or may not lead a youth to feel as if he doesn't belong depending on the situation, such as the neighborhood he lives in or school he goes to. Also, the saliency of each individual's identities may change at different places or times. An international Chinese female student in a wheelchair on a college campus may feel her disability as most salient in some situations (e.g., when she has to rely on the campus transportation service to move between buildings), but in others the most salient might manifest as her being non-American and Chinese (e.g., in-class discussions on topics related to cultural values). Additionally, social identity theorists point out that individuals may experience different levels of identity, such as personal, family, and national (Turner, Hogg, Oakes, Reicher, & Wetherell, 1987). Being an American may have different meaning when the person is in the United States versus when the person is overseas.

Regardless of the complexity and nuances discussed above, all individuals who live in this diverse country have to face the issue of cultural identity whether or not they choose to recognize it. It is because no one has the choice not to interact directly or indirectly with others from different cultural backgrounds. Only those who are in the dominant group can afford the privilege of ignoring their cultural identity. An understanding of our cultural and social experiences as related to each of our group memberships, including membership in both privileged and disadvantaged positions, and the roles we play in others' social and cultural experiences is critical to our multicultural identity development. Moreover, the development of a multicultural identity both personally and professionally is imperative if counselors are to succeed in understanding clients' multiple cultural identities.

Challenges of Multicultural Identity Development: Dominant Group Identities

A significant aspect of group identity is the issue of power or social dominance. There are always dominant and subordinate groups, and social power is distributed accordingly with the dominant group having more power over the subordinate groups. This power differential is translated into privileges for the dominant group and unfair treatment and oppression for the subordinate groups. Unfortunately, both in literature and in people's everyday lives, the dominant-group identities tend to be less visible than those of nondominant groups, which is due to the privilege of the "no-need-to-know" attitude of the dominant-group members. Multicultural researchers have pointed out that the dominant-group identity development is integral to a true understanding of the nature of privilege and oppression and genuine appreciation of multiculturalism (Worthington & Mohr, 2002). To illustrate how a dominant group such as an ethnic or racial group has the power of maintaining its role of dominance in the system of social and cultural stratifications, Doane (2005) stated the following:

> I define a dominant ethnic group as the ethnic group in a society that exercises power to create and maintain a pattern of economic, political, and institutional advantage, which in turn results in the unequal (disproportionately beneficial to the dominant group) distribution of resources. With respect to intergroup relations, a key element of dominance is the disproportionate ability to shape the sociocultural understandings of society, especially those involving group identity and intergroup interactions. (p. 376)

Although there is a developmental process for members of society to develop their cultural or group identity—dominant or subordinate—it is most challenging, yet critical, for counselors-in-training to develop a multicultural identity that challenges the existence of isms for any of their dominant-group memberships, such as being a White American, a male, a cisgender person, a heterosexual, a person without disability, a member of middle or upper class, and so on. A generic social identity development stage model by Jackson and Hardiman (1994) can be used to describe common attributes of individuals at different levels of dominant-group identity. This model identified five stages—*no social consciousness, acceptance (passive and active), resistance (passive and active), redefinition, and internalization*—that are progressive in nature and describe a journey from no or low social consciousness to high social consciousness regarding the existence and impact of social privilege and oppression. This generic model, along with several other existing specific identity development models, will be used in our discussion of dominant cultural group identity development in several selected areas that are emotionally salient for many people, especially subordinate-group members. This discussion will help us envision a path toward a multicultural identity.

A Reflection About the Meaning of Being White by a White Professor

Historically, being White—a category that expands and contracts with our political will—has meant the ability to be a citizen and own property, access to immigration, owning or renting in the most desirable and profitable neighborhoods, access to the best schools, and a whole host of other legal, political, and financial benefits. Whiteness also provides individuals the "benefit of the doubt." A key dynamic of White privilege in everyday life is the ability to be seen as an individual, supposedly unmarked by race. (Burke, 2013; see more at http://thesocietypages.org/specials/colorblindness-vs-race-consciousness/#sthash.mhMphLEz.dpuf)

—*A White professor*

Racial and Ethnic Identities

Most White European Americans are not particularly aware of their racial identity, which is clearly a privilege, but their attitude and behavior in relation to people of color reflect their racial identity and contribute to the cultural climate for subordinate racial and ethnic groups. Thus, it is critical that White counselors strive toward developing an antiracist identity so that they can relate to clients of color in a truly respectful manner and provide them with effective care. To describe the process of White racial identity development, several theoretical models identify progressive stages, from lower to higher, as markers of development. Although individuals generally move from lower to higher stages, there is fluidity between stages, and individuals can stay at more than one stage at a time or regress from higher to lower stages. Environmental factors such as place and time, social climate, and significant political or cultural events play an important role in individuals' experience of their racial identity. Based on a number of previous theoretical models, Sue and Sue (2013) present a 7-step descriptive model that is focused on the following basic assumptions:

1. Racism is an integral part of U.S. life, and it permeates all aspects of our culture and institutions (ethnocentric monoculturalism).
2. Whites are socialized into the society and therefore inherit all the biases, stereotypes, and racist attitudes, beliefs, and behaviors of the larger society.
3. How Whites perceive themselves as racial beings follows an identifiable sequence that can occur in a linear or nonlinear fashion.
4. The status of White racial identity development in any multicultural encounter affects the process and outcome of interracial relationships.
5. The most desirable outcome is one in which the White person not only accepts his or her Whiteness but also defines it in a nondefensive and nonracist manner. (p. 331)

Seven Phases of Development

Naïveté phase. White persons at this phase feel relatively neutral toward people with racial and ethnic minorities and tend to be innocent, open, and spontaneous regarding racial differences. This phase may be brief with individuals who show little racial awareness (i.e., young children) but are starting to "associate positive ethnocentric meanings to his or her own group and negative ones to others" (Sue & Sue, 2013, p. 331).

Conformity phase. Ethnocentric attitudes and beliefs dominate this phase in which individuals show minimal self-awareness about their own racial identity and strong belief in the universality of their cultural values and norms. Some characteristics of the naïveté phase and uncritical acceptance of White supremacist notions may be present. "Consciously or unconsciously, the White person believes that White culture is the most highly developed and that all others are primitive or inferior" (p. 332).

Dissonance phase. White persons enter this phase when they are forced "to acknowledge Whiteness at some level, to see the conflict between upholding humanistic nonracist values and their contradictory behavior" (p. 332). Oblivion to racial issues breaks down, they feel conflicted over irresolvable racial moral dilemmas, and they become increasingly conscious of Whiteness. Individuals at this phase often experience feelings of guilt, depression, helplessness, or anxiety.

Resistance and immersion phase. Whites begin to notice, question, and challenge the realities of oppression and their racism, feeling anger at individuals, institutions, and societal values for failed practice of democratic ideals and guilt for personally having been a part of the oppressive system. The "White liberal syndrome" (p. 334) may develop in which they either take a paternalistic protector role or overidentify with minority groups. Later they learn that neither of these roles is appreciated by minority groups. They may resolve this dilemma by moving back to the conformity phase or moving forward to the introspective phase.

Introspective phase. Individuals no longer deny that they have participated in oppression and have benefited from White privilege, entering a state of relative quiescence, introspection, and reformulation of what it means to be White. They recognize that racism is an integral part of U.S. society, ask painful questions regarding their racial heritage, confront prejudices and biases, and accept responsibility for contributing to social oppression. They accept Whiteness and understand the concept of White privilege and feel increased comfort in relating to racial and ethnic minorities.

Integrative awareness phase. This phase is marked by an understanding of self as a racial/cultural being, awareness of sociopolitical influences with respect to racism, appreciation of racial/cultural diversity, and commitment to eradicating oppression. A nonracist, White Euro-American identity becomes internalized, and an inner sense of security emerges in a society "that is only marginally accepting of integrative, aware White persons" (p. 335).

Commitment to antiracist action phase. This phase is characterized by social action. White persons give up the ultimate White privilege of seeing racism but not doing anything about it. They are actively working to correct the wrong made by racism and form alliances with persons of color and other liberated Whites to validate and encourage continuance to the struggle against individual, institutional, and societal racism.

It is clear that due to the society we live in, it can be challenging for White European Americans to develop a positive and nonracist/antiracist racial identity. As the author of a famous article on White privilege, Peggy McIntosh (1989) reflected the following:

> My schooling gave me no training in seeing myself as an oppressor, as an unfairly advantaged person, or as a participant in a damaged culture. I was taught to see myself as an individual whose moral state depended on her individual moral will. . . . Whites are taught to think of their lives as morally neutral, normative, and average, and also ideal, so that when we work to benefit others, this is seen as work which will allow "them" to be more like "us." (p. 10)

However, for culturally competent counselors, there is no option not to take on this challenge. Counselors' attitudes and beliefs regarding racism play a direct role in how they view, understand, and work with clients of color. For themselves, progress toward a positive and nonracist/antiracism White identity can be freeing as well, as Shawn T., a graduate student in counseling psychology, reflected. It is not hard to imagine that a client of color will find it comforting to have a counselor who is able to acknowledge his or her role in social oppression and does not focus on changing the client toward being "correct" or "right" according to White standards.

A Reflection: I Can't Deny Being a Racist

One of the most profound personal discoveries of my life is that I, whether I intend to be or not, am a racist. For most of my 24 years, my definition of *racism* was a way of being characterized by slander, slurs, hatred, distrust, violence, and self-declared superiority. Until recently, my definition of *racism* and the vision that term and its various iterations conjured, never included covert methods and expressions. As my multicultural consciousness has developed, my vision of what is and is not racist has evolved to a much broader and inclusive view. The view I hold now is what leads me to say that I am a racist.

This is a fact from which I cannot run, nor can I any longer justify and ignore. I am a White person, and I live in a society that places its highest value on the characteristics, aspirations, and successes of White culture. I have never experienced invalidation of my person, heritage, or future because the standard set forth by society at large is woven from the fabric of White history. Knowingly or not, intentionally or not, my life plays a part in maintaining a systemic process that is flawed and skewed, established and maintained in such a way as to empower one type of person over another.

This new discovery, this new level of awareness opens my eyes to the flaws of my past beliefs. I am not called to bring people of color up to my level. It is not my place to show people of color the right and proper aspirations and values. It is not my duty to make the world more White. A piece of me is broken by the knowledge that I am the oppressor that I disdain. My conscience is guilty as a result of the actions of my world and of myself. With my awareness, my new consciousness, I am called to respect and empower people to seek their own truths and values in whatever direction or form that may take. I am to be an ally and advocate to all, regardless of the color of their skin. I am called to recognize the distinct nature of all heritages and attempt to understand how those heritages inform the perception and experience of life in the context of a world that favors me and not people of color.

—Shawn T., a graduate counseling student

SMALL-GROUP CLASS ACTIVITY 6.1

Because whites have great privilege and sociopolitical power in society, they can more readily avoid working through issues of racial identity development. (Helms, 2004, p. 5)

Questions for White students

What emotions does this statement stir in you?

Why might you agree or disagree with Helms in your actual experience related to avoiding or committing to racial identity development?

Why might you agree or disagree that White people's avoidance of developing a racial identity is a reflection of their privilege and power?

Why do or don't you think it is relevant for White people to develop a racial identity?

How do you think non-White people may feel about White people's avoidance of racial identity development?

Questions for students of color

What emotions does this statement stir in you?

How do you think White people may feel regarding the assertion that they are avoiding their racial identity development?

How do you think White people may be affected by avoiding their racial identity development?

Why do you think "power and privilege" are relevant in terms of racial identity development for individuals in society?

How do you think White people's racial identity may influence your (and other people of color) existence and experience in this society? Why?

How about your own racial identity? How is it related to White people's racial identity?

How might this awareness about Whites' avoidance of their racial identity help you understand racial relationships in our society?

Sex, Gender, and Sexual Orientation Identities

Individuals' sex, gender, and sexual orientation identities are formed through socialization and the influence of societal institutions in which their identities reflect both how they see themselves and how others see and define them. Their group memberships, dominant or subordinate, influence their social experiences and the role they play in others' experiences. Socially constructed sexism, genderism, and heterosexism reflect individual, social, and institutional beliefs that the dominant groups in each of these identities are the norm and are superior to those in the minority groups, which is the foundation for social privileges and oppressions. It can't be overemphasized that counselors must not permit their personal identity to bias their clinical judgment and decision making about their clients. Therefore, counselors-in-training need to purposefully develop healthy sex, gender, and sexual orientation identities toward a multicultural identity that positions them to recognize and eliminate the negative influence of sexism, cisgenderism, and heterosexism.

Although it is not without controversy, *sex* is often viewed as a physical or biological characteristic (e.g., male, female) and *gender* a socially constructed and/or personally experienced identity (e.g., masculine, feminine, genderqueer, bi-gender). *Gender development* is a process in which the person is socialized with gendered norms the society assigns. *Cisgender* is a gender identity that society deems to match the person's assigned sex at birth. *Sexual orientation* refers to "an enduring emotional, romantic, sexual, or affectionate attraction or non-attraction to other people. Sexual orientation is fluid, and people use a variety of labels to describe their sexual orientation" ("Sexual orientation," n.d.).

Each of these identities can be viewed as a continuum along which individuals identify themselves. There are expected social roles that are built upon these identities. For instance, while sex can be seen as biological, socially constructed *sexism* gives social power and privilege to men, views women as subordinate and inferior, and "denigrates values and practices associated with women" ("Sexism," n.d.). *Genderism* recognizes only two genders (men and women) and believes gender is inherently tied to one's sex assigned at birth. *Genderists* believe that cisgender people are the dominant group and superior to transgender people, and they exclude those who don't conform to society's expectations of gender ("Genderism," n.d.). Similarly, *cisgenderism* assumes every person is cisgender and holds people to traditional expectations based on gender, marginalizes those who identify as transgender in some form, and punishes or excludes those who don't conform to traditional gender expectations ("Cisgenderism," n.d.).

Becoming Aware of Sexist Privileges

Sexism is prejudice based on biological sex, and it creates systematic privileges and advantages for men on the sole basis of their being men in our society. Jun (2010) said that because of sexism "governmental, institutional, and organizational policies, laws, and rules are written to favor men and unfairly discriminate against women" (p. 136). The profound negative effect of sexism on women has been well documented and is in fact visible in the everyday life of our society, including terrible situations in which sexism leads to sexual harassment or violence. What has not been specifically discussed is how cisgender men (individuals with social and institutional power associated with their sex and/or gender) develop their sex and gender identity. Similar to other dominant-group identity development, this process requires that men become aware of their social positions of power and the injustice inflicted on women, understand the meaning of being men in society, and recognize their role in sustaining sexism and gender discrimination.

It may be difficult for some men to see their privileges or recognize their roles in oppression of women because they themselves may feel oppressed due to other reasons. For instance, a White man in poverty may feel more oppressed than privileged. It is important to know that this person's disadvantage or oppression due to his socioeconomic status does not mean that he is not privileged in relation to his being male. In fact, "White men in the United States are systematically gender privileged, which allows them to have easier access to education, housing, health care, and jobs compared with women and men in other racial groups" (Jun, 2010, p. 137). Developing an antisexist identity in the sexist context of our society is challenging but necessary for all counselors.

If we use the generic social identity model by Jackson and Hardiman (1994), men likely go through some or all of the following stages of identity development:

No social consciousness—be oblivious to differences between men and women in their social experiences due to their sex

Acceptance—consciously or unconsciously accept the dominant group's views about men and women, act upon sexual stereotypes against women, and deny that the societal culture is oppressive for women

Resistance—start to question the dominant group's views that are inconsistent with previous beliefs when encountering or learning about women's experiences, notice the existence of privileges for men and discrimination against women, and recognize their own role in the oppression women experience

Redefinition—reexamine own identity as men, realize the responsibility for recognizing and eliminating sexism, and feel good about being men who are antisexist and believe in egalitarianism for men and women

Internalization—reach an understanding of social power and privilege associated with being men and be motivated to use the power of being men to advocate for social justice for women

Gender and Cisgender Identity Development

Gender is a personal expression and is separate from sex or sexual orientation. *Gender identity* is the extent to which one identifies as being either masculine or feminine and is often shaped through a process of differentiation—interactions of biological, social, and cognitive learning factors that occur over time. For cisgender people, gender identity is in accord with physical anatomy, and for others, gender identity may differ from physical anatomy or expected social roles. Due to genderism and cisgenderism, male gender is often viewed as intrinsically superior to female or other genders (including third gender, genderqueer, and other nonbinary-identified people), and those who identify their gender according to the sex assigned at birth (cisgender) are seen as more healthy or normal than those whose gender identity does not conform to the designated sex at birth. Thus, gender discrimination and oppression on the basis of actual or perceived gender identity exist in various forms, and the significant lack of equality in employment, higher education, and economic opportunities hurts women and individuals who are not gender conforming.

The presence of discrimination and oppression for some individuals and groups lays the responsibility of promoting justice and fairness on those who are in the dominant groups. For counselors, their sense of their own sex and gender identities, recognition of privilege, and willingness to give up undue power will influence how they view and work with clients. The process of this identity development involves active learning and likely consists of the five stages Jackson and Hardiman (1994) identified previously. Individuals would move forward from being unaware of or oblivious to the system of privilege and oppression related to genderism and cisgenderism (stage of *no social consciousness*) toward recognition of social injustice for minority groups (stages of *acceptance* and *resistance*). Their acceptance of responsibility for contributing to the unjust system and desire to see justice would motivate them into action to promote positive changes for the marginalized gender minorities (stages of *redefinition* and *internalization*).

A Reflection by an African American Trans Male

My interactions with cisgender men have been positive and negative. It's difficult to make friends with cisgender men because I feel that my trans masculinity causes conflict in areas of socialization and bonding. Because I wasn't socialized as male growing up, I lack the sense of male privilege and am often surprised when I'm made aware of the fact that my male privilege has influenced a situation. Some cis-men I have met exert their male privilege in situations where it serves them well. My inability to healthily bond with cisgender men has caused my social group to exist primarily in the trans community and its allies. Although this is comforting, I would like to expand my social interactions outside of the trans community.

Public bathrooms (on or off campus), gyms, and locker rooms always present an issue of safety. I can never use these facilities without being actively observant of my surroundings, which is both distracting and inconvenient.

—Langston, an African American trans male

Heterosexual Identity Development

In society where the dominant sexuality patterns tend to be viewed as healthy or normal and minority sexuality as unhealthy and/or deviant (Warner, 1991), individuals' sexual identity is directly linked to social power. For instance, protecting the current marriage law that excludes same-sex marriage gives heterosexual individuals the privilege of being legal, normal, or healthy, which directly affects the well-being or social status of those who identify with same-sex attraction.

By definition, *heterosexual identity development* refers to "the process by which people with a heterosexual sexual orientation (i.e., heterosexually identified individuals) identify with and express numerous aspects of their sexuality" (Worthington, Savoy, Dillon, & Vernaglia, 2002, p. 497). In literature, distinction has been made between sexual orientation and sexual identity. *Sexual identity* is "the comprehensive process involving self-definition more broadly as a sexual being" (p. 497), and *sexual identity development* is the process by which an individual conceptualizes one's sexuality, sexual identity, and sex value system regardless of sexual orientation. Due to the interactive nature of social identity development, sexual identity formation involves attitudes and behaviors toward in-group and out-group members with similar or different sexual orientation and/or identity.

Multidimensional heterosexual identity development. Focusing on both psychological and social processes, Worthington et al. (2002) conceptualized heterosexual identity development as a process that is far beyond the confinement of sexual orientation and that is impacted by privilege and group affiliation. Being a stable component of one's sexual identity, sexual orientation is also a socially constructed phenomenon, and according to Worthington et al., it contains the following five heterosexual identity statuses:

> *Unexplored commitment* status reflects "microsocial (e.g., familial) and macrosocial (e.g., societal) mandates for acceptable gender roles and sexual behavior and/or avoidance of sexual self-exploration, which may preempt legitimate active exploration" (p. 515). Individuals tend to follow prescribed norms in our culture and depreciate sexual minority groups, showing unexamined heterosexist and homonegative biases.
>
> *Active exploration* status is marked by "purposeful exploration, evaluation, or experimentation of one's sexual needs, values, orientation, and/or preferences for activities, partner characteristics, or modes of sexual expression" (p. 516). Dominant-group identity enters the consciousness, leading to either questioning or asserting the privileges of a dominant status.
>
> *Diffusion* status reflects an "absence of exploration or commitment and often results from crisis" (p. 518). Individuals at this status may reject social conformity and extend noncompliance to other social and cultural prescriptions in their sexual life. There is a lack of self-understanding and sense of identity. Active exploration may occur and professional assistance may be needed.
>
> *Deepening and commitment* status is characterized with the "movement toward greater commitment to one's identified sexual needs, values, sexual orientation and/or preferences for activities, partner characteristics, and modes of sexual expression" (p. 519). Individuals become more aware of their attitudes toward sexual minorities, perspectives of the dominant-subdominant relationships, and privilege and oppression related to sexual orientation.

Synthesis is the most natural and adaptive status of sexual identity development, characterized by a state of congruence among the dimensions of individual identity. Individuals come to "an understanding and construction of heterosexuality that fulfills their self-definitions and carries over to their attitudes and behaviors toward other heterosexually identified individuals and lesbian/gay/bisexual (LGB) persons" (p. 519). This status allows individuals to experience a synthesis of their own multiple identities (e.g., gender, race/ethnicity, religion), understand the continua of human sexuality, and be more affirmative toward lesbian/gay/bisexual/transgender (LGBT) individuals.

A Reflection by a Latino Gay Counselor-in-Training: Sense of Responsibility

Navigating within the two worlds can be difficult, and my goal is to serve as a counselor, mentor, and friend. Whether we want to acknowledge it or not, many of us gay Latino males need a supportive and validating voice. At times we need to hear that we are good enough, normal enough, Latino enough, gay enough, or straight-acting enough. At multiple points in our lives, we will worry about each of these things. Some of these thoughts are adaptive, and some are obviously maladaptive. Still, at one point or another they are considered or desired.

—*A Latino American counselor-in-training*

Social Class Identity Development

Although individuals' social class is often defined by income, classism is much more than individual differences or individual prejudice toward each other. *Classism* is socially constructed and is a form of "oppression that is structural, maintained by practices that constitute 'business as usual,' and played out at the individual, institutional, and cultural levels" (Adams, 2000, p. 380). It systematically assigns characteristics of worth and ability based on social class and maintains a system of beliefs and cultural attitudes that ranks people according to economic status, family lineage, job status, level of education, and other divisions. As a result, classism creates and supports "the systematic oppression of subordinated groups (people without endowed or acquired economic power, social influence, or privilege) by the dominant groups (those who have access to control of the necessary resources by which other people make their living)" (Collins & Yeskel, 2005, p. 143).

Intersecting with other dimensions of individual diversity (e.g., race, sexual orientation, ability/disability), one's social class is certainly a source of unearned privileges and/or undeserved disadvantages. Those from middle or high class (dominant groups) are seen not only as smarter and more capable than working-class and poor people (subordinate groups) but also as having the power to define for everyone else what is "normal" or "acceptable" in the class hierarchy. Unless they have a multicultural identity that includes non- and anticlassist attitudes and understanding, counselors may even do unintentional harm to clients from lower social classes who may internalize the classism and dominant groups' beliefs about them. Using Jackson and Hardiman's (1994) generic model, social class identity development for class-dominant-group members can be described in the following stages:

No social consciousness—be oblivious to differences due to social class and see the privilege of middle or higher classes as normal or standard

Acceptance—consciously or unconsciously accept the dominant groups' views about people in low social class, act upon classist stereotypes against them, and deny that the societal culture is oppressive to them

Resistance—start to question the dominant groups' views that are inconsistent with previous beliefs when encountering or learning about people from low social class, notice the existence of privileges for middle or high social classes and discrimination against people of low social class, and recognize their own role in the oppression related to social class

Redefinition—reexamine own identity as privileged, realize the responsibility for recognizing and eliminating classism, and feel good about being anticlassist

Internalization—reach an understanding of social power and privilege associated with being in middle and high classes and be motivated to advocate for social justice for people in low social class

Ableism and Multicultural Identity Development

Ableism is based on "a belief that impairment [irrespective of 'type'] is inherently negative which should, if the opportunity presents itself, be ameliorated, cured, or indeed eliminated" (Campbell, 2008, p. 154) and is a form of oppression and discrimination against individuals with physical, mental, or developmental disabilities. It is socially constructed to give power and control to people without disabilities who set the norm and standards, according to their way of doing, for determining what is good or normal or superior (Storey, 2007). As a result, those with disabilities are often viewed by ableists as abnormal or inadequate persons whose problems and solutions lie within them. Ableism uses a medical model to view disability as something to be fixed or cured and ignores the social model that views ableism as giving power to those without disabilities. It is noted that "systematic privilege has been maintained by the exclusion of individuals with disability/impairment, resulting in unequal access to power and justice" (Jun, 2010, p. 209).

Counselors must develop a multicultural identity that includes a non- and anti-ableist identity in order to serve those with disability. Following the generic cultural identity development model by Jackson and Hardiman (1994), those temporarily without disability (all persons may become disabled physically or mentally at some point in time) would go from the *no social consciousness* stage (many people are in this stage in the ableist society) through the *acceptance, resistance,* and *redefinition* stages. They need to recognize and give up their privilege of being ignorant or oblivious about discrimination against persons with disability and the roles they play in the negative social experience inflicted on those with disability. Eventually, they will be able to turn the feelings of guilt and powerlessness (unable to help those with disability) into action to remove barriers and eliminate ableism (the *internationalization* stage).

Other Isms and Multicultural Identity Development

Any beliefs that give power and privilege to some people and force social oppression onto others on the basis of individual characteristics or identities are examples of socially constructed *isms*. In developing a multicultural identity, counselors need to intentionally gain awareness, recognition, and understanding of their social positions in relation to those of others in *all* areas of individual diversity.

Age and Ageism

Age is one personal characteristic that everyone has, but ageism has unfairly discriminated against some and benefitted others. The term *ageism* was coined by Robert Neil Butler in 1969 to describe discrimination against seniors, including prejudicial attitudes and discriminatory practice against older people and institutional practices and policies that perpetuate negative stereotypes about older people. In recent years, theorists have defined ageism as a system of privilege and oppression that marginalizes, discriminates against, and takes away power, responsibility, and dignity from older adults; it also prejudices and discriminates against children and adolescents, ignoring their ideas or voices or assuming that they should behave in certain ways because they are too young.

The valuation of youth and devaluation of age contribute to ageism and lead to poor treatment of older adults. Many older adults experience mistreatment by society, including the health care system (Burbank, 2006). On the other side of the age spectrum, children may also suffer from ageism. Children often are not heard and become victims of domestic violence, neglect, or physical/emotional/sexual abuse (Jun, 2010). Our society, governmental institutions, and health care systems have not done an adequate job to protect children from harm, violence, and mistreatment. As noted by Westman (1991), "Institutional juvenile ageism exists when social systems ignore interests of children. Individual juvenile ageism exists when developmental interests of a child are not respected" (p. 237). In the mental health field, we have witnessed too many and too painful facts about children who suffer from various forms of abuse and harm.

Counselors who are to serve the diverse in the 21st century ought to be aware of and sensitive to how ageism has provided them privileges and has negatively impacted the autonomy, dignity, and quality of life for so many individuals at both ends of the age spectrum. With a multicultural identity that includes the recognition of age privileges and disadvantages, counselors will be able to understand client experience related to ageism and avoid using age-related centrism in evaluating clients.

Religion and Religious Prejudice

Religion is one area of human life where individuals easily find themselves facing in-group and out-group memberships and experiences. Individuals in one religion may see those in another religion or those who are atheists or agnostic as out-groups. Although many religions teach love and tolerance and are sources of strength for their members (Hunsberger & Jackson, 2005), there are also groups where religious ethnocentrism and in-group loyalty are promoted and religious intolerance toward out-groups is permitted. These groups have the tendency to minimize, marginalize, or discriminate against others with different beliefs, values, and identities (Altemeyer, 2003). According to the FBI, religious intolerance accounted for 19% of hate crimes across the nation in 2012 (Federal Bureau of Investigation, 2013).

Religious privilege that favors religion, religious beliefs, and religious figures is accompanied by the disadvantages imposed on those who are atheists or agnostic. In the United States, *Christian privilege* is a type of dominant religious group privilege:

> [It] views that non-Christian faiths are inferior or dangerous, or that adherents of other faiths are immoral, sinful, or misguided. These beliefs infiltrate established social institutions, are reinforced by broader American society, and are societal/cultural norms that have evolved as part of a society's history. . . . Oppression occurs when a dominant Christian group imposes its cultural norms, values, and perspectives on individuals with differing beliefs. ("Christian Privilege," n.d., para. 2, 5)

In the United States, Christian privilege is based on the presumption that Christian beliefs are social norms and associated with institutional support. Christian holy days are sanctioned as official state holidays, and nondominant religious groups are forced to incorporate Christian holy days into their lives.

Religion or faith identity can't be ignored in counselors' multicultural identity development. For those with a membership in the dominant group (e.g., Christian), development of a healthy religious identity without religious prejudice requires them to become aware of existing discriminative attitudes and practice against out-groups within their own religion and acknowledge the dominant-group privileges that benefit them while putting members of out-groups in disadvantages. They need to develop themselves as supporters of respect for other religions and for the irreligious. Advocating for equality among people with different religions will mark a high level of faith identity.

Nationality and Nativism

The United States is a country of immigrants. However, due to both historical and current sociopolitical reasons, over 30 million immigrants and refugees generally face challenges because of their nationality and/or their status of being non-U.S. citizens. *Nativism* demands favored status for U.S. citizens and supports efforts to lower the political or legal status and rights of various immigrant groups. While there are both xenophobic and xenophilic attitudes toward immigrants or refugees in the American public, there have been immigration policies and legal practices that allow immigrants "reduced rights and freedom" (Cole, 2003, p. 368). Therefore, nationality is one area of individuals' identity in which some people are privileged and some discriminated against. At the institutional level, U.S. citizens have the privilege of having access to rights, freedom, and opportunities protected by the law that are sometimes not available to noncitizens. Noncitizens with various immigration statuses (e.g., with or without permanent residence status, documented or not) also have different rights and accesses. At the societal, intercommunity, and interpersonal levels, immigration statuses along with race (e.g., European Caucasians vs. non-White people), region (e.g., developed countries vs. poor countries), language (e.g., English vs. other languages), education (e.g., intellectuals vs. blue-collar workers), wealth (e.g., investors vs. wage earners), and other factors become a basis for different levels of access and for discrimination and prejudice.

For nonimmigrant counselors-in-training, a multicultural identity involves a good understanding of the self as a member of the group of power that contributes to the discrimination inflicted upon immigrants and refugees, especially those from poor, non-White, and non-Christian countries. They have to allow the non-nativist view that immigrants deserve dignity and just treatment to enter their consciousness. The recognition of the dominant-group privilege one has and the role one has played in oppression to others is critical in the individual effort to develop a positive and antinativist cultural identity. This developmental process includes progression from being oblivious to being aware of experiences of self and others related to nationality, to becoming willing to accept responsibility and learn about others, and to committing oneself toward social justice for immigrants.

Self-Assessment of Multicultural Self

Table 6.1 Systems of Social Privilege and Oppression: My Social Position, Role, and Responsibility

Cultural & Social Identity	Dominant Groups	Subordinate Groups	Bases of Power
Race/ethnicity	White European American	People of color/ethnic minorities	Racism
Social class/SES	Middle or high social/ economic class	Low SES	Classism
Gender	Cisgender	Transgender	Genderism
Sex	Male	Female	Sexism
Sexuality	Heterosexuality	Homosexuality, bisexuality, asexuality	Heterosexism
Ability	People without disability	People with disability	Ableism
Age	Young adults	Older adults	Ageism
Religion	Religious majorities	Religious minorities (including people without religion)	Religious prejudice & oppression

Cultural & Social Identity	Dominant Groups	Subordinate Groups	Bases of Power
Nationality	Citizens of the United States	Refugees, immigrants, & internationals	Colonialism & nativism
Other identities salient to you			

SMALL-GROUP CLASS ACTIVITY 6.2

Reflecting on My Positions, Experience, and Consciousness

In the context of systems of social privilege and oppression (Table 6.1), self-reflect and share within a small group.

1. My social/cultural positions
   a. Am I a member of the dominant or subordinate group along each of these identities?
   b. What does this specific membership in a dominant or subordinate group mean to me in society?
   c. What does this specific membership in a dominant or subordinate group mean to others in society?
   d. In what ways have these social positions shaped my cultural being?
2. My social/cultural experiences
   a. In what ways am I benefiting from unearned privileges due to my membership in dominant groups? What are the implications of these privileges on others who are in subordinate groups?
   b. In what ways am I experiencing undeserved oppression due to my membership in subordinate groups? What change would I hope for in a just and fair world?
   c. How do I wish to be viewed and treated by the dominant or subordinate groups considering my identities along all these dimensions?
3. My social/cultural consciousness
   a. How aware am I about all the isms?
   b. What emotions do I experience in relation to the isms?
   c. What do I do with those emotions?

(Continued)

(Continued)

4. My professional and social responsibilities as a counselor in the 21st century
   a. How should or could I develop a positive and an anti-isms identity along each one of these dimensions?
   b. What challenges do I face in developing a multicultural identity?

Summary

This chapter focuses on multicultural identity development in relation to dominant-group memberships—namely White, cisgender, male, heterosexual, middle or high social class, temporarily able, Christian, and nonimmigrant. Developing a multicultural identity out of dominant-group membership is challenging, but it is the unwavering personal, social, and professional obligation of counselors in the 21st century. We will be personally irresponsible and professionally negligent if we fail to engage ourselves in this lifelong learning and development process. The discussion of this chapter is heavily focused on the personal aspect of identity development; multicultural professional identity development will be discussed in more detail in the following chapters.

Takeaway Messages

1. In preparing to serve the culturally diverse, counselors' multicultural identity development is the first step.
2. Counselors should strive to develop a healthy, positive, and anti-isms multicultural identity.
3. One needs to start with examining and understanding one's dominant-group memberships, asking, "What does my dominant-group membership mean to me and to others (who do not have this dominant membership) in our society?"
4. A personal multicultural identity is the foundation of a professional multicultural identity.
5. Always remember that we are training ourselves to effectively serve others, which is most likely the primary reason that we are in the counseling field.

Recommended Resources

Readings

Chung, R. C.-Y., Bemak, F., Ortiz, D. P., & Sandoval-Perez, P. A. (2008). Promoting the mental health of immigrants: A multicultural/social justice perspective. *Journal of Counseling and Development, 86,* 310–317.

Ferris State University. (n.d.). Using objects of intolerance to teach tolerance and promote social justice. *Jim Crow Museum of Racist Memorabilia at Ferris State University*. Retrieved from http://www.ferris.edu/jimcrow/

Ford, Z. (2012, July 12). *Study: Forty percent of homeless youth are LGBT, family rejection is leading cause.* Retrieved from http://thinkprogress.org/lgbt/2012/07/12/515641/study-40-percent-of-homeless-youth-are-lgbt-family-rejection-is-leading-cause/

Hoffman, R. M. (2004). Conceptualizing heterosexual identity development: Issues and challenges. *Journal of Counseling and Development, 82*, 375–380.

Leigh, Debra. (n.d.). *Twenty-eight common racist attitudes and behaviors.* St. Cloud State University Community Anti-Racism Education Initiative. Retrieved from http://shitrichcollegekidssay.tumblr.com/post/74373594065/28-common-racist-attitudes-and-behaviors-by-debra

Letourneau, N. L., Duffett-Leger, L., Levac, L., Watson, B., & Young-Morris, C. (2011). Socioeconomic status and child development: A meta-analysis. *Journal of Emotional and Behavioral Disorders, 21*(3), 211–224.

McNamee, S. J., & Miller, R. K., Jr. (2004). *The meritocracy myth.* Lanham, MD: Rowman & Littlefield.

Menning, C. (2013, February 21). Black history month for white people [Blog post]. Retrieved from http://misscellania.blogspot.com/2013/02/black-history-month-for-white-people.html

Smith, L., Foley, P. F., Chaney, M. P. (2008). Addressing classism, ableism, and heterosexism in counselor education. *Journal of Counseling & Development, 86*, 303–309.

References

Adams, M. (2000). Classism. In M. Adams, W. J. Blumenfeld, R. Castanda, H. W. Hackman, M. L. Peters, & X. Zuniga (Eds.), *Readings for Diversity and Social Justice* (pp. 379–382). New York, NY: Routledge.

Altemeyer, B. (2003). Why do religious fundamentalists tend to be prejudiced? *International Journal for the Psychology of Religion, 13*, 17–28.

Bloomberg Television Staff. (2014, February 7). Zell: The 1% work harder and should be emulated. *In the loop* [Television program]. Retrieved from http://www.bloomberg.com/news/videos/b/75f58b37-90f1-42f0-86c1-014aeb39a3e9

Burbank, P. M. (Ed.). (2006). *Valuable older adults: Heath care needs and interventions.* New York, NY: Springer.

Burke, M. (2013, July). Colorblindness vs. race-consciousness: An American ambivalence. *The Society Pages.* Retrieved from http://thesocietypages.org/specials/colorblindness-vs-race-consciousness/#sthash.mhMphLEz.dpuf

Butler, R. (1969). Age-ism: Another form of bigotry. *The Gerontologist, 9*, 243–246.

Campbell, F. A. K. (2008). Exploring internalized ableism using critical race theory. *Disability & Society, 23*(2), 151–162.

Christian privilege. (n.d.). In *Wikipedia.* Retrieved March 2, 2015, from http://en.wikipedia.org/wiki/Christian_privilege

Cisgenderism. (n.d.). In *LGBTQIA Resource Center glossary.* Retrieved from http://lgbtqia.ucdavis.edu/lgbt-education/lgbtqia-glossary

Cole, D. (2003). Are foreign nationals entitled to the same constitutional rights as citizens? *Thomas Jefferson Law Review, 25*, 367–388.

Collins, C., & Yeskel, F. (2005). *Economic apartheid.* New York, NY: New Press.

Doane, A. W., Jr. (2005). Dominant group ethnic identity in the United States: The role of "hidden" ethnicity in intergroup relations. *Sociological Quarterly, 38*, 375–397.

Duan, C., & Smith, S. (in press). Multicultural training and supervision in research and service. In M. Casas, L. Suzuki, C. Alexander, & M. Jackson (Eds.), *Handbook of multicultural counseling* (4th ed.). Thousand Oaks, CA: Sage.

Enns, P., Kelly, N., Morgan, J., Volscho, T., & Witko, C. (2013). Conditional status quo bias and top income shares: How U.S. political institutions benefited the rich. *Journal of Politics, 76*, 1.

Federal Bureau of Investigation. (2013, November 25). *Latest hate crime statistics: Annual report shows slight decrease.* Retrieved from http://www.fbi.gov/aboutus/investigate/civilrights-/hate_crimes/overview

Fryberg, S. M. (2010). When the world is colorblind, American Indians are invisible: A diversity science approach. *Psychological Inquiry, 21*(2), 115–119.

Genderism. (n.d.). In *LGBTQIA Resource Center glossary.* Retrieved from http://lgbtqia.ucda-vis.edu/lgbt-education/lgbtqia-glossary

Helms, J. (2004). Racial identity development and its impact in the classroom. *Reaching Through Teaching, 16*, 5.

Hogg, M. A., & Vaughan, G. M. (2002). *Social psychology* (3rd ed.). London, England: Prentice Hall.

Hunsberger, R., & Jackson, L. M. (2005). Religion, meaning, and prejudice. *Journal of Social Issues, 61*, 807–826.

Jackson, B., & Hardiman, R. (1994). Social identity development model. In M. Adams, P. Brigham, P. Dalpes, & L. Marchesani (Eds.), *Diversity and oppression: Conceptual frameworks* (pp. 19–22). Dubuque, IA: Kendall/Hunt.

Jeltsen, M. (2014, February). Why this transgender teen's big victory matters. *Huffington Post.* Retrieved from http://www.huffingtonpost.com/2014/02/03/transgenderrights_n_4705613.html?-utm_hp_ref=mostpopular

Jun, H. (2010). *Social justice, multicultural counseling, and practice: Beyond a conventional approach.* Thousand Oaks, CA: Sage.

Lee, M. W. (Director). (1994). *Color of fear* [Film]. United States: StirFry Seminars. Available from http://www.stirfryseminars.com/store/products/cof1.php

McIntosh, P. (1989, July/August). White privilege: Unpacking the invisible knapsack. *Peace and Freedom* (pp. 10–12). Philadelphia, PA: Women's International League for Peace and Freedom.

Neville, H. A., Awad, G. H., Brooks, J. E., Flores, M. P., & Bluemel, J. (2013). Color-blind racial ideology: Theory, training, and measurement implications in psychology. *American Psychologist, 68*, 455–466.

Sexism. (n.d.). In *LGBTQIA Resource Center glossary.* Retrieved from http://lgbtqia.ucda-vis.edu/lgbt-education/lgbtqia-glossary

Sexual orientation. (n.d.). In *LGBTQIA Resource Center glossary.* Retrieved from http://lgbt-qia.ucdavis.edu/lgbt-education/lgbtqia-glossary

Stets, J. E., & Burke, P. J. (2003). A sociological approach to self and identity. In M. R. Leary & J. P. Tangney (Eds.), *Handbook of self and identity* (pp. 128–152). New York, NY: Guilford Press.

Storey, K. (2007). Combating ableism in schools. *Preventing School Failure: Alternative Education for Children and Youth, 52*, 56–58.

Stryker, S. (1980). *Symbolic interactionism: A social structural version.* Redwood City, CA: Benjamin-Cummings.

Sue, D. W., & Sue, D. (2013). *Counseling the culturally diverse: Theory and practice* (6th ed.). Hoboken, NJ: Wiley.

Turner, J. C., Hogg, M. A., Oakes, P. J., Reicher, S. D., & Wetherell, M. S. (1987). *Rediscovering the social group: A self-categorization theory.* Oxford, England: Blackwell.

Warner, M. (1991). Introduction: Fear of a queer planet. *Social Text*; 9(4 [29]), 3–17.

Westman, J. C. (1991). Juvenile ageism: Unrecognized prejudice and discrimination against the young. *Child Psychiatry and Human Development, 21*(4), 237–256.

Williams, M. T. (2011, December). Colorblind ideology is a form of racism: A colorblind approach allows us to deny uncomfortable cultural differences. *Psychology Today.* Retrieved from http://www.psychologytoday.com/blog/colorblind/201112/colorblind-ideology-is-form-racism

Worthington, R. L., & Mohr, J. J. (2002). Theorizing heterosexual identity development. *The Counseling Psychologist, 30*(4), 491–495.

Worthington, R. L., Savoy, H. B., Dillon, F. R., & Vernaglia, E. R. (2002). Heterosexual identity development: A multidimensional model of individuals and social identity. *The Counseling Psychologist, 30*, 496–531.

7

Understanding Social Oppression and Cultural Pluralism

We don't see things as they are, we see them as we are.

—Anais Nin

CHAPTER OVERVIEW

This chapter provides a discussion of the presence, prevalence, and persistence of social oppression and its damaging impact on the lives and experiences of culturally diverse and socially marginalized individuals, groups, and communities. This context of oppression is the result of unearned social privilege by dominant groups and has had damaging effects on minority groups. Many of today's clients represent minority status in terms of race, ethnicity, religion, spirituality, gender, sex, national origin, physical ability, sexual orientation, age, education, socioeconomic status, and geographic origin. Counselors must recognize and understand their social experiences. Moreover, we need to recognize the cultural pluralism that occurs when the culturally diverse have worldviews and cultural values that are different from those of the mainstream culture. As counselors, we must fully embrace our social and ethical responsibility toward eliminating social oppression and its devastating effects, and we must respect cultural pluralism.

SELF-ASSESSMENT OF PRE-EXISTING AWARENESS AND KNOWLEDGE

- What does social oppression or social injustice mean to me?
- To what extent do I believe that social oppression or social injustice exists or is prevalent in today's society?
- To what extent do I believe that the issue of social oppression is relevant to counseling when many clients come in due to psychological difficulties?
- To what extent do I believe that counseling should address the issue of social oppression or social injustice in understanding our clients?
- How do I perceive individuals' experiences as a result of their diverse identities?
- How aware am I of cultural differences in worldviews among people with diverse cultural backgrounds?
- How comfortable am I working with individuals who have different cultural values than mine?
- Am I aware of my social, ethical, and professional responsibility in eliminating social oppression?

LEARNING OBJECTIVES

After reading this chapter, students will be able to do the following:

1. Understand the presence, relevance, and persistence of social oppression and social injustice in our society
2. Understand the unjust, unfair, and damaging nature of social oppression and social injustice
3. Understand the importance of considering the negative role of social oppression and injustice in working with the culturally diverse and socially marginalized individuals, groups, and communities
4. Understand that worldviews differ among people with different cultural backgrounds
5. Understand the importance of respecting clients' cultural values and traditions
6. Understand our social, professional, and ethical responsibility in eliminating social oppression

A Reflection: What Does It Mean to Be an African American Trans Male in This Society?

As an African American trans male, I wasn't socialized as a man. I dropped one minority criterion (female) for another. Once I transitioned, I *immediately* felt the societal pressure that African American males face even more strongly than I did prior to transitioning. White women cross streets or clutch their purses or poodles when I walk around my own (predominantly White) neighborhood. White men (especially those in positions of authority and power) are now more aggressive and competitive with me, and my intelligence level is constantly prejudged before I speak. One time I had a White male clerk at a wine store refuse to wait on me while helping my White male trans friends. I remained a minority when I transitioned, whereas my trans male counterparts gained White male privilege. I often wonder, "What does it feel like to be respected strictly based on the color of your skin without having to jump through all of the hoops to prove that you're a person of worth and respect?" I deal with microaggressions toward me every single day, and I can easily see why it would be tempting to give into the resentment and become the stereotype. I understand now the anger that heatedly lies beneath the surface of a lot of African American men in this society.

What does it mean to be an African American male in this society? It means having to put in 110% all of the time and never dropping the ball, knowing that as soon as you do, someone who isn't African American is ready and willing to slap you with a stereotype—whether outwardly or in the privacy of their minds. It also means dealing with cisgender African American males in a manner that I wasn't socialized for. It can make social interactions with any of the aforementioned groups challenging.

—Langston, an African American trans male

REFLECTION AND DISCUSSION QUESTIONS 7.1

1. In what ways did Langston's reflection impact you?
2. What potential internalized negative attitudes toward transgender people (known as transphobia) do you hold, and how might such attitudes affect your ability to work with transgender clients?
3. Do you believe mental health practitioners have a responsibility to confront the binary categorization of sex and gender? Why or why not?
4. How might you be contributing to the propagation of a gender binary system (i.e., what are your values and beliefs about gender, gender roles, and gender identity)?
5. Given the discrimination (microaggressions) and oppression that Langston noted he encounters as an African American trans male, how might you address oppression directly in your counseling work so that you do not perpetuate the injustices that Langston and other marginalized individuals have already experienced?

GUIDED PRACTICE EXERCISE 7.1

Advocacy Work With Transgender Clients

Advocating for social change is a part of mental health practitioners' professional responsibility. In a small group, discuss advocacy efforts that could be directed at changing systems that create injustices and cause psychological distress for transgender clients. Which ones would you recommend implementing and why?

CASE ILLUSTRATION 7.1

Case of Kevin

Kevin, a 42-year-old, African American, single, male attorney specializing in environmental law, was greeted by a 39-year-old White female counselor, Laurie. Laurie started by telling Kevin apologetically that she was aware that Kevin had requested an African American or other racial minority counselor, but unfortunately, the center was short staffed, and no counselor of color was available for him at this time. She also said that she believed she could help him.

Laurie respectfully asked Kevin what had prompted him to seek counseling at this time. Kevin replied that he relocated to the area 3 years ago, works long hours, and is a dedicated and diligent worker who has given his all-White firm 110%. He further explained that he is now questioning whether he made the right decision to accept the position with this law firm. He shared his extreme dissatisfaction and the toll the work stress and work climate are taking on him.

After hearing more about his successes and challenges as an attorney, including being the only ethnic minority person in the firm, Laurie immediately requested that Kevin complete a Strong Interest Inventory (SII) to determine if being an attorney is a compatible career choice. Kevin explained that he is very satisfied with his chosen career and that his current dissatisfaction is more related to the work environment. He was reluctant but eventually said, "I think it is the environment." Laurie responded, "I know that being an African American in this town is hard because most people have biases toward Black people." She quickly added, "Regardless of what others say, you should have a clear idea what you want to do and are fit for doing. You should take control of your life." Laurie continued to explain how the SII can both confirm his interest in choosing a career as an attorney and also identify other careers both within and separate from the legal field.

Kevin reluctantly agreed to schedule an appointment to take the SII. Two days before his appointment he called to cancel and stated work conflict as the reason and that he would call in a few days to reschedule, which he never did.

Questions to Consider

1. What thoughts do you have about Kevin's premature termination?
2. What thoughts do you have about Laurie's intervention strategy (i.e., the SII)?

3. If Kevin were your client, what approach would you have taken to demonstrate your understanding of the impact of Kevin's oppression on his work-related stress?
4. If Laurie were to consult with you about Kevin terminating prematurely, what would you say to her and what recommendations might you offer?
5. What if you were provided the following information that Kevin did not have a chance to tell Laurie in their first session?

Kevin accepted a position at a high-profile and well-respected law firm in this predominantly White region of the United States 3 years ago. In the 2 weeks after his arrival, he worked late hours, which seemed to be an unspoken expectation of this particular law firm. Upon leaving work late at night on three different occasions over a two-week period, he was pulled over by the same White male officer during his drive home.

The first time he was pulled over, he was told that he needed a light bulb to illuminate his license plate, apparently a requirement in this state. He was given a verbal warning and urged to get the required lighting. When he was pulled over the second time, the officer stated he was conducting a routine check to ensure that Kevin and others were not driving with expired tags. Kevin had current tags and was allowed to proceed without receiving any citation.

Having grown up in a part of the country where racial profiling was a daily occurrence for African Americans, Kevin began to doubt the officer's sincerity. Kevin had flashbacks of the days when he was a high school and college student and was pulled over for driving in suburban neighborhoods in his well-maintained and upper-middle-class car, something that came to be known in the African American community as being pulled over for "driving while Black."

Finally, similar to the two previous incidents, Kevin left the office around 11 p.m. and once again was pulled over by the same White officer. Kevin respectfully expressed his concern and bitterness with being pulled over every 4 to 5 days, to which the officer smiled and confessed that the intent of pulling him over was to have him roll down his car window so the officer could smell for any marijuana that Kevin may have been smoking. Kevin was irritated by the officer's suspicion that he might be smoking marijuana, but he was not shocked by the officer's behavior because racial profiling was something that his skin color triggered, despite his professional demeanor and career success.

Having been passed over twice for a promotion at the law firm, Kevin felt mental anguish. Not wanting to ruin his professional career, he sought counseling.

Social Oppression: Results of Unearned Privileges by Dominant Groups

Although most diverse clients do not seek counseling for discussing how to challenge racism or any other isms that have plagued their lives, their clinical concerns can't be understood accurately without full consideration of their experience of social oppression. As much as Laurie showed good intention and professional confidence, her ignorance of the negative impact of social oppression some members of our society experience created a wall between Kevin and herself. What is at stake is not only that she offered an ineffective intervention but also that her action perpetuated the very social oppression that African Americans suffer due to White privileges. Laurie has the privilege of not being aware that racism exists, but Kevin does not.

A Reflection by an African American Student

At (college), I had an issue with a professor on the first day of class who regaled us with a story of how a former student asked her to be lenient with her grading because she (the student) was African American. The professor used this anecdote as a teaching point of how she doesn't do special favors for students and that all of us had to put in the effort for the grade. I dropped the class the next day.

–An African American student

Agents of Social Oppression

Oppression is defined in *Webster's Third International Dictionary* as "unjust or cruel exercise of authority or power," and "oppresses, especially in being an unjust or excessive exercise of power" ("Oppression," n.d.). Oppressed individuals or groups are devalued, exploited, and deprived of privileges by an individual or group that has more power (Barker, 2003). Different opportunities for minority people and inequities in power are expressions of social oppression that have had a long-standing history in the United States. Those who call for equal treatment and access usually do so from a position of privilege (Monk, Winslade, & Sinclair, 2008). Substantial literature documents that oppression is continuous and undermines the progress and well-being of those who are affected (Ridley, 2005).

The oppressions experienced by some groups are well-known. For example, African American community members bore a disproportionate share of the Hurricane Katrina aftermath; women receive less pay for the same jobs as men; patients of color are less often recipients of organ transplants than White patients; a large number of the poor do not receive adequate health care; persons who are obese are commonly overlooked for employment; sexual minorities (e.g., gay, transgender) are targeted for violent hate crimes; prostitutes are arrested, but their clients are not (Monk et al., 2008), and African Americans are overrepresented in the criminal justice system (Hartney & Vuong, 2009).

On the opposite end of social oppression is social privilege. In other words, there are people who enjoy privileges at the expense of those who suffer from oppression. Social oppression is maintained and deepened by those who have power, privilege, and don't act to change the status quo of oppression-privilege structure. Positions in the privilege-oppression continuum impact individuals' identity development, their views and experience of the world, and their psychological and mental health. Based on the original work of Hardiman and Jackson (1997) and today's social environment, we can see that there are agents and targets of social oppression. In the United States, these pervasive and systemic hierarchies consist of at least the following demographic categories and agents and targets in each of them (see Table 7.1).

Table 7.1 Targets and Agents in Each Diversity Area

	Agents	**Targets**
Race/ethnicity	Whites	People of color
Gender	Cisgender men	Women & transgender people
Sexuality	Heterosexuals	Lesbian/gay/bisexual/ transgender people
Physical/mental/ developmental disability	Persons without disability	Persons with disability
Class	Owning class & middle or upper class	Poor & working class
Age	Middle-aged adults	Children & the elderly
Nationality	U.S. citizens	Immigrants & refugees

Source: Adapted from Hardiman and Jackson (1997).

The negative impact of these unfair systems is reflected in multiple levels, including individual, institutional, and societal levels. In everyday life, the experience of the agents and that of the targets clearly differs as the agents benefit from unearned privileges that keep the targets in undeserved disadvantages.

White Privilege

White privilege is an invisible and weightless knapsack of unearned assets granted to White people that can be cashed in each day for advantages that are unavailable to those who do not resemble the people who are in power. The power embedded in White privilege translates into a belief of White superiority, and, in the name of White superiority, it may be difficult for White Americans to experience the full impact of what has been done to racial/ethnic minorities and other marginalized groups in this country (Wildman & Davis, 2002). The belief that White Euro-American cultural heritage (history, values, languages) is more favorable and advanced represents White superiority and is reflected in terms of physical characteristics such as blond hair, blue eyes, and light complexion and cultural characteristics such as Christianity, individualism, standard English, emotional control, and capitalism (Sue & Sue, 2013). See Box 7.1 for McIntosh's (1989) discussion of White privilege.

BOX 7.1 WHITE PRIVILEGE: UNPACKING THE INVISIBLE KNAPSACK BY PEGGY MCINTOSH

Through work to bring materials from Women's Studies into the rest of the curriculum, I have often noticed men's unwillingness to grant that they are over-privileged, even though they may grant that women are disadvantaged. They may say they will work to improve women's status, in the society, the university, or the curriculum, but they can't or won't support the idea of lessening men's. Denials which amount to taboos surround the subject of advantages which men gain from women's disadvantages. These denials protect male privilege from being fully acknowledged, lessened or ended.

Thinking through unacknowledged male privilege as a phenomenon, I realized that, since hierarchies in our society are interlocking, there was most likely a phenomenon of white privilege that was similarly denied and protected. As a white person, I realized I had been taught about racism as something that puts others at a disadvantage, but had been taught not to see one of its corollary aspects, white privilege, which puts me at an advantage.

I think whites are carefully taught not to recognize white privilege, as males are taught not to recognize male privilege. So I have begun in an untutored way to ask what it is like to have white privilege. I have come to see white privilege as an invisible package of unearned assets that I can count on cashing in each day, but about which I was "meant" to remain oblivious. White privilege is like an invisible weightless knapsack of special provisions, maps, passports, codebooks, visas, clothes, tools and blank checks.

Describing white privilege makes one newly accountable. As we in Women's Studies work to reveal male privilege and ask men to give up some of their power, so one who writes about white privilege must ask, "Having described it, what will I do to lessen or end it?"

After I realized the extent to which men work from a base of unacknowledged privilege, I understood that much of their oppressiveness was unconscious. Then I remembered the frequent charges from women of color that white women whom they encounter are oppressive. I began to understand why we are justly seen as oppressive, even when we don't see ourselves that way. I began to count the ways in which I enjoy unearned skin privilege and have been conditioned into oblivion about its existence.

My schooling gave me no training in seeing myself as an oppressor, as an unfairly advantaged person, or as a participant in a damaged culture. I was taught to see myself as an individual whose moral state depended on her individual moral will. My schooling followed the pattern my colleague Elizabeth Minnich has pointed out: whites are taught to think of their lives as morally neutral, normative, and average, and also ideal, so that when we work to benefit others, this is seen as work which will allow "them" to be more like "us."

I decided to try to work on myself at least by identifying some of the daily effects of white privilege in my life. I have chosen those conditions which I think in my case *attach somewhat more to skin-color privilege* than to class, religion, ethnic status, or geographic location, though of course all these other factors are intricately intertwined. As far as I can see, my African American co-workers, friends, and acquaintances with whom I come into daily or frequent contact in this particular time, place and line of work cannot count on most of these conditions.

1. I can if I wish arrange to be in the company of people of my race most of the time.
2. If I should need to move, I can be pretty sure of renting or purchasing housing in an area which I can afford and in which I would want to live.
3. I can be pretty sure that my neighbors in such a location will be neutral or pleasant to me.
4. I can go shopping alone most of the time, pretty well assured that I will not be followed or harassed.
5. I can turn on the television or open to the front page of the paper and see people of my race widely represented.
6. When I am told about our national heritage or about "civilization," I am shown that people of my color made it what it is.
7. I can be sure that my children will be given curricular materials that testify to the existence of their race.
8. If I want to, I can be pretty sure of finding a publisher for this piece on white privilege.
9. I can go into a music shop and count on finding the music of my race represented, into a supermarket and find the staple foods that fit with my cultural traditions, into a hairdresser's shop and find someone who can cut my hair.
10. Whether I use checks, credit cards or cash, I can count on my skin color not to work against the appearance of financial reliability.
11. I can arrange to protect my children most of the time from people who might not like them.
12. I can swear, or dress in second-hand clothes, or not answer letters, without having people attribute these choices to the bad morals, the poverty, or the illiteracy of my race.
13. I can speak in public to a powerful male group without putting my race on trial.
14. I can do well in a challenging situation without being called a credit to my race.
15. I am never asked to speak for all the people of my racial group.
16. I can remain oblivious of the language and customs of persons of color who constitute the world's majority without feeling in my culture any penalty for such oblivion.
17. I can criticize our government and talk about how much I fear its policies and behavior without being seen as a cultural outsider.

(Continued)

(Continued)

18. I can be pretty sure that if I ask to talk to "the person in charge," I will be facing a person of my race.
19. If a traffic cop pulls me over or if the IRS audits my tax return, I can be sure I haven't been singled out because of my race.
20. I can easily buy posters, postcards, picture books, greeting cards, dolls, toys, and children's magazines featuring people of my race.
21. I can go home from most meetings of organizations I belong to feeling somewhat tied in, rather than isolated, out-of-place, outnumbered, unheard, held at a distance, or feared.
22. I can take a job with an affirmative action employer without having co-workers on the job suspect that I got it because of race.
23. I can choose public accommodations without fearing that people of my race cannot get in or will be mistreated in the places I have chosen.
24. I can be sure that if I need legal or medical help, my race will not work against me.
25. If my day, week, or year is going badly, I need not ask of each negative episode or situation whether it has racial overtones.
26. I can choose blemish cover or bandages in "flesh" color and have them more or less match my skin.

I repeatedly forgot each of the realizations on this list until I wrote it down. For me, white privilege has turned out to be an elusive and fugitive subject. The pressure to avoid it is great, for in facing it I must give up the myth of meritocracy. If these things are true, this is not such a free country; one's life is not what one makes it; many doors open for certain people through no virtues of their own.

In unpacking this invisible knapsack of white privilege, I have listed conditions of daily experience that I once took for granted. Nor did I think of any of these prerequisites as bad for the holder. I now think that we need a more finely differentiated taxonomy of privilege, for some of these varieties are only what one would want for everyone in a just society, and others give license to be ignorant, oblivious, arrogant and destructive.

I see a pattern running through the matrix of white privilege, a pattern of assumptions that were passed on to me as a white person. There was one main piece of cultural turf; it was my own turf, and I was among those who could control the turf. *My skin color was an asset for any move I was educated to want to make.* I could think of myself as belonging in major ways and of making social systems work for me. I could freely disparage, fear, neglect, or be oblivious to anything outside of the dominant cultural forms. Being of the main culture, I could also criticize it fairly freely.

In proportion as my racial group was being made confident, comfortable, and oblivious, other groups were likely being made unconfident, uncomfortable, and alienated. Whiteness protected me from many kinds of hostility, distress and violence, which I was being subtly trained to visit, in turn, upon people of color.

For this reason, the word "privilege" now seems to me misleading. We usually think of privilege as being a favored state, whether earned or conferred by birth or luck. Yet some of the conditions I have described here work systematically to overempower certain groups. Such privilege simply *confers dominance* because of one's race or sex.

I want, then, to distinguish between earned strength and unearned power conferred systemically. Power from unearned privilege can look like strength when it is in fact permission to escape or to dominate. But not all of the privileges on my list are inevitably damaging. Some, like the expectation that neighbors will be decent to you, or that your race will not count against you in court, should be the norm in a just society. Others, like the privilege to ignore less powerful people, distort the humanity of the holders as well as the ignored groups.

We might at least start by distinguishing between positive advantages, which we can work to spread, and negative types of advantage, which unless rejected will always reinforce our present hierarchies.

For example, the feeling that one belongs within the human circle, as Native Americans say, should not be seen as privilege for a few. Ideally it is an *unearned entitlement.* At present, since only a few have it, it is an *unearned advantage* for them. This paper results from a process of coming to see that some of the power that I originally saw as attendant on being a human being in the United States consisted in unearned advantage and conferred dominance.

I have met very few men who are truly distressed about systemic, unearned male advantage and conferred dominance. And so one question for me and others like me is whether we will be like them, or whether we will get truly distressed, even outraged, about unearned race advantage and conferred dominance, and, if so, what will we do to lessen them. In any case, we need to do more work in identifying how they actually affect our daily lives. Many, perhaps most, of our white students in the U.S. think that racism doesn't affect them because they are not people of color; they do not see "whiteness" as a racial identity. In addition, since race and sex are not the only advantaging systems at work, we need similarly to examine the daily experience of having age advantage, or ethnic advantage, or physical ability, or advantage related to nationality, religion, or sexual orientation.

Difficulties and dangers surrounding the task of finding parallels are many. Since racism, sexism, and heterosexism are not the same, the advantages associated with them should not be seen as the same. In addition, it is hard to disentangle aspects of unearned advantage which rest more on social class, economic class, race, religion, sex, and ethnic identity than on other factors. Still, all of the oppressions are interlocking, as the Combahee River Collective Statement of 1977 continues to remind us eloquently.

(Continued)

(Continued)

One factor seems clear about all of the interlocking oppressions. They take both active forms, which we can see, and embedded forms, which as a member of the dominant group one is taught not to see. In my class and place, I did not see myself as a racist because I was taught to recognize racism only in individual acts of meanness by members of my group, never in invisible systems conferring unsought racial dominance on my group from birth.

Disapproving of the systems won't be enough to change them. I was taught to think that racism could end if white individuals changed their attitudes. But a "white" skin in the United States opens many doors for whites whether or not we approve of the way dominance has been conferred on us. Individual acts can palliate, but cannot end, these problems.

To redesign social systems, we need first to acknowledge their colossal unseen dimensions. The silences and denials surrounding privilege are the key political tool here. They keep the thinking about equality or equity incomplete, protecting unearned advantage and conferred dominance by making these taboo subjects. Most talk by whites about equal opportunity seems to me now to be about equal opportunity to try to get into a position of dominance while denying that *systems* of dominance exist.

It seems to me that obliviousness about white advantage, like obliviousness about male advantage, is kept strongly enculturated in the United States so as to maintain the myth of meritocracy, the myth that democratic choice is equally available to all. Keeping most people unaware that freedom of confident action is there for just a small number of people props up those in power and serves to keep power in the hands of the same groups that have most of it already.

Although systemic change takes many decades, there are pressing questions for me and I imagine for some others like me if we raise our daily consciousness on the perquisites of being light-skinned. What will we do with such knowledge? As we know from watching men, it is an open question whether we will choose to use unearned advantage to weaken hidden systems of advantage, and whether we will use any of our arbitrarily awarded power to try to reconstruct power systems on a broader base.

Source: McIntosh, P. (1989, July/August). White privilege: Unpacking the invisible knapsack. *Peace & Freedom*, pp. 10–12. Reprinted with permission.

Male Privilege

Male privilege is an invisible and weightless knapsack of unearned assets granted to cisgender men that can be cashed in each day for advantages that are unavailable to women or transgender people. There is unearned social, economic, and political power embedded in male privilege that translates into superiority and domination over women or transgender people. For example, a male worker can expect not to be paid less than his female coworkers, not to be seen as incapable because of his gender, not to worry that his outfit will be seen as sexual, and not to be blamed for not staying home with children. Most significantly, males have the privilege of not being aware of their male privilege. These are just a few examples of male privilege; on his blog, *Alas! A Blog* (see www.amptoons.com), Barry Deutch, using McIntosh's (1989) approach in identifying White privilege, compiled a list of 46 possible male privileges that are generally shared by male members of the American society (Deutch, n.d.).

Heterosexual Privilege

Similarly, heterosexual privilege is an invisible and weightless knapsack of unearned assets granted to heterosexual people that can be cashed in each day for advantages that are unavailable to nonheterosexual people. There is unearned social, economic, and political power embedded in heterosexual privilege that translates into superiority and domination over nonheterosexual people. For example, a heterosexual person can be public about his or her sexual orientation anytime and anywhere, doesn't have to go through the coming-out process, or answer any questions concerning why he or she "chooses" to be heterosexual. Most significantly, a heterosexual person has the privilege of not being aware of his or her heterosexual privilege. To help raise awareness of the privileges afforded to heterosexuals in a heterosexist society, Griffin, D'Errico, Harro, and Schiff (2007) listed 44 examples of personal, social, psychological, economic, and legal privileges that accrue to heterosexuals. Various examples in social media are also presented. One such list of 40 heterosexual privileges was developed by the MIT School of Architecture and Planning (Diversity Learning Tree, n.d.-a.).

Ability Privilege

Ableism is the systemic disempowerment of persons with disability for the advantages of able-bodied persons or persons without cognitive or mental disability. Persons without disability benefit from the embedded ableism in politics, organizational practices, and institutional structures and enjoy an invisible and weightless knapsack of unearned assets that can be cashed in each day for advantages that are unavailable to persons with disability. There is unearned social, economic, and political power embedded in ability privilege. For example, an able-bodied person does not need to worry about whether the evening event he or she wants to attend is accessible, can go shopping alone without assistance, or can easily leave an uncomfortable interpersonal situation without being limited by the physical setting. A person without learning disability does not risk being seen as stupid for taking extra time to complete tests. Most notably, persons without disability have the privilege of not being aware of their ability privilege. To help raise the public's awareness, different authors have identified many ability privileges. Focusing on physical ability, the activist Melissa Graham (2009) listed 15 able-bodied privileges.

Class Privilege

Similarly, middle- to upper-class privilege is an invisible and weightless knapsack of unearned assets granted to middle- to upper-class people that can be cashed in each day for advantages that are unavailable to lower-class people. There is unearned social, economic, and political power embedded in class privilege that translates into superiority and domination over lower-class people. For instance, a person in middle or upper class can go to a doctor when sick, call an attorney when having legal trouble, and can have many "successful" people in his or her life circle. With economic resources, a middle- or upper-class person can focus on learning and skill building that lead to career and financial success. Obviously, middle- or upper-class people have the privilege of not recognizing their class privileges and attribute their "success" to their intelligence and ability. Using McIntosh's (1989) approach in identifying White privileges, the MIT School of Architecture and Planning (Diversity Learning Tree, n.d.-b.) developed a list of 31 class privileges.

U.S. Citizen Privilege

Nationality is one identity that brings individuals different social experience and treatment in U.S. society. Due to nativism and colonialism, U.S. citizens benefit from various privileges that are unavailable for immigrants and/or refugees. These privileges are associated with social, economic, and political rights and power that translate into superiority and domination over non-U.S. citizens. As U.S. citizens, people may apply for a job without worrying whether their immigration status will have a negative effect on their chances, they may be sure that it was not their perceived immigration status that made them wait longer than others to be served in a restaurant, and they may purchase a house anywhere without fear that others may think their family's presence will devalue housing in the neighborhood. To help the public recognize the victimizing effect of such privileges on immigrants/refugees, the Coloradans for Immigrant Rights identified a list of 18 U.S. citizenship privileges (Coloradans, 2010).

SMALL-GROUP CLASS ACTIVITY 7.1

In groups of three to four students, reflect and share your thoughts regarding these questions.

1. Imagine you are a member of the dominant group in each of the areas of race, gender, sexual orientation, class, ability, and citizenship; how do you feel when you read these lists of privileges?
2. Imagine you are a member of the minority group in each of these areas of race, gender, sexual orientation, class, ability, and citizenship; how do you feel when you read these lists of privileges?

Complexity of Privilege and Responsibility of the Agent

These forms of privileges by no means reflect an exhaustive list, and there are other forms of privileges due to isms and/or prejudice. It should be noted that most individuals have privileges due to some of their identities and may experience oppression due to other identities. For instance, a White gay man may experience White privileges but disadvantages due to being gay, and a cisgender male in low social class may experience disadvantages due to social class but have privilege as a cisgender man. We know that all privileges translate into inequality, which is a social reality that is ever present in the daily existence of the culturally diverse. It is the responsibility of the privileged in each area of diversity to understand the negative impact of their privilege on the unprivileged. Although those who are in the dominant groups cannot really give up their privilege (i.e., it cannot be given away), they can become aware of its existence, recognize its role in their lives, show willingness to share power with those who do not have it, and advocate for justice for the unprivileged. They have the ultimate social responsibility and power to eliminate oppression.

GUIDED PRACTICE EXERCISE 7.2

Determining Privileged or Oppressed Status

In a small group of three to four students, indicate whether you belong to a privileged or an oppressed group based on your (a) race/ethnicity, (b) gender, (c) sexual orientation, (d) language, (e) physical ability/disability, (f) religion, (g) region, and (h) socioeconomic status, regardless of whether or not you feel privileged or oppressed in each of these social identities. Once you have determined your status as privileged or oppressed for each identity listed, describe your personal experiences with privilege and/or oppression across numerous settings (e.g., community, work, school), how you handled it, and how you feel about your privileged and/or oppressed status.

Social Oppression: Unjust, Unfair, and Damaging

Literature supports the relationship between social injustice, oppression, and the mental health problems of persons upon which injustices and oppressions have been perpetuated (Satcher, 2001). Individuals who experience socially condoned mistreatment in society typically experience it on a daily basis, which has a profoundly negative and debilitating effect on their mental health and psychological development. Clearly, the experience of oppression is felt among groups outside the straight, White, Christian, middle-to upper-class male group. Although there is no hierarchy or distinction made regarding the intensity or level of oppression one experiences (i.e., how could we define one oppression as better or worse than another?), for some groups of people the experience of social injustices and oppression are a very familiar and everyday occurrence. Sadly, there are many groups of people who are oppressed in the United States, a country they regard as home.

The Myth of a Just-Society Perspective

Oppressed groups may internalize their injustices due to exposure to systematically negative social conditions. Moreover, the media has been known to suggest that the only obstacles to success and perhaps good mental health are one's own inadequacies (Penelope, 1994), which is a viewpoint that blames the victim and is based on the idea of a just society. A *just society* assumes that people get what they deserve and any failure is due to a lack of effort and ability. This just society perspective ignores the realities of systematic oppression and discrimination, which affects mental health. It is therefore inconceivable that counselors would ignore the sinister impact of social oppression on the lives and well-being of their clients.

Pervasive Oppression Due to Isms

The isms ideology/practice supports various forms of injustice and generates pervasive oppression at various levels. While oppressors have the privilege not to notice the existence of oppression, those who are in the marginalized groups have no escape from it. We are using racism to illustrate the multilevels of unjust, unfair, and damaging impacts of social oppression.

Racism is a universal phenomenon that has existed throughout human history and has been mutually reinforced at all levels of society—institutional, individual, and cultural. It is seen as a complex phenomenon and can be viewed as "a social attitude propagated among the public by an exploiting class for the purpose of stigmatizing some group as inferior so that the exploitation of either the group itself or its resources or both may be justified" (Cox, 1959, p. 393). It contains a relationship of domination in a system whereby one race is privileged and has more social power (e.g., White race) and the other is oppressed and systematically subordinated (e.g., African Americans, Latinos and Latinas, Asian Americans, Native Americans). There are different forms of racism.

Institutional Racism

Institutional racism involves a mechanism of domination and manipulation of societal institutions that provide preferences and advantages to the politically and socially dominant racial group (i.e., Whites), while justifying the oppression of racial and ethnic minorities. Although institutional racism can be either subtle or overt, it serves to restrict the rights of and deny access to those whose physical features and cultural patterns differ from the dominant group. In order for racism to exist, the institutional power of the dominant group must be imposed, as succinctly described by Smith (1995):

> One racial group must have the relative power—the capacity to impose its will in terms of policies. . . . Without this relative power relationship, racism is a mere sentiment because although group A may wish to subordinate group B, it lacks the effective power to so [therefore] it remains just that, a wish. (p. 143)

Thompson and Neville (1999) maintain that the negative effects of oppression in the forms of sexism and classism are experienced by Whites, but they do not experience the demoralizing impact of structural racism because racial and ethnic minorities do not hold positions of power that allow them to set policies that discriminate against Whites. They further clarified that although people of color can discriminate against Whites as individuals, these individual acts of discrimination do not translate into institutional practices that determine the outcomes for Whites. Race and racism have profound implications on the mental health of our clients (Carter 2005), and the professional dominance of White counseling practitioners and researchers also has significant implications for the perpetuation of racism and oppression (Thompson, Shin, & Stephens, 2005).

Individual Racism

Individual racism refers to personal beliefs, attitudes, and actions of individuals that humiliate or degrade another based on racial group membership. These acts support or perpetuate racism. In terms of the dynamics of individual racism, Diller (2007) questioned why it is so easy for individuals to develop and retain racial prejudices. He determined that humans have exhibited racism throughout history, and based on human history, they always will. He then directed our attention to the writings of Allport (1954) for a more complete answer to his question: Allport determined that racism continues to grow because prejudice has its roots in the normal and natural tendencies of people to feel more comfortable with others who are like them while being suspicious of differences, to develop beliefs that support their values while avoiding those that challenge them, and to scapegoat those who are most vulnerable while rationalizing their racist behavior. Sadly, differences are often perceived as threatening and result in a tendency to separate oneself from those who are perceived as different. This separation only intensifies the threat because separation limits communication, which heightens misunderstanding and also creates and sustains myths about other group members (Diller, 2007).

Cultural Racism

Cultural racism refers to the conscious or unconscious belief that the cultural values of one group are superior to those of another. In the United States, cultural racism takes the form of practices that embrace White cultural values as the norm and superior to the values of racial and ethnic minorities. According to Thompson and Neville (1999), cultural racism does the following:

> [It] often results in limiting, pathologizing, exoticizing, or entirely omitting the cultural practices or values and contributions of racial minorities. A simple example of cultural racism is when educational institutions refer to classical European music and literature as "high culture" and either omit or diminish the musical and intellectual contributions of other groups. (p. 167–168)

The adoption and domination of White European culture in the United States means that behaviors outside its parameters will be judged harshly and regarded as different, inappropriate, and/or bad. As an example of cultural racism, the second author of this book is reminded of a meeting initiated by an African American, female, counseling psychology doctoral student, whom we will call Jerrie, to discuss her preparation for predoctoral internship interviews.

Jerrie expressed concern that that her opportunity to secure an internship placement might be jeopardized by her hairstyle (i.e., dreadlocks), which is often perceived by

Whites as "ethnic." As such, she contemplated changing her hairstyle for the interviews in order not to risk her chances of securing a placement. The fact that Jerrie was worried about any potential negative effect of her hairstyle illuminates the real and lived experiences of racism that individuals of color encounter daily and the steps they sometimes take to try to minimize the horrendous effects of racism. Specifically, Jerrie explained:

> I ultimately decided to keep my dreadlocks. However, I tried several different styles in an attempt to find the most mainstream look possible for interviews. I finally mastered a curly, soft look that I thought seemed nonthreatening. As a matter of fact, I still use that style when I plan to be in conservative or unfamiliar professional settings. I've met other professional African American women with dreadlocks (several in academia) who talk about having a particular style they use when they don't want to bring attention to their hair in professional settings. (personal communication, October 12, 2012)

Cultural racism has implications for counseling professionals who must be aware of their cultural values and the extent to which their values may be different from those of their clients. Specifically, the counseling relationship and accompanying goals must make sense to the client while also falling within the scope of what the counselor conceives as therapeutic. Also important is that traditional counseling training and models are based on the dominant Western culture, which begs the question of what relevance do these Western values and cultural imperatives have for clients who have different cultural worldviews.

A Reflection by an African American Trans Male

In school, I've always had to strive harder than my peers, present my best self, and try not to take it too personally when others in my own trans community don't understand my struggles. I often find myself being the lone voice of reason and critical thought when it comes to issues that pertain to the African American community and other marginalized groups. Sometimes, I get exhausted defending myself and other African Americans around people who don't understand why their comment or off-centered joke has offended me or is just downright offensive to all. I can never stop being African American, and I'm proud of my cultural heritage, but I just want to have moments where I don't have to defend and/or deflect. I just want to be more than my race.

—Langston, an African American trans male

Environmental Racism

Environmental racism has been noted to be the fourth form of racism (Thompson & Neville, 1999) and addresses the impact of discrimination in environmental policy-making that differently affects the health risks of Whites and racial minorities. For example, environmental racism is evident when housing is built in predominantly low-class minority neighborhoods where contamination in the building areas has been previously documented. See Table 7.2 for further description of these forms of racism that are commonly referred to in literature.

Table 7.2 Common Forms of Racism

Form	Description	Example
Institutional racism	Policies, practices, and norms that perpetuate inequality and thereby result in significant economic, legal, political, and social restrictions	Media portrayal of acts of discrimination as incidents rather than experiences of pervasive racism Media coverage of such events is often conveyed from the perspectives of the powerful and the elite. People of color receive harsher sentences than Whites, and prisoners of color are more likely to be sent to solitary confinement than receive appropriate psychological treatment compared to White prisoners (Kupers, 1999).
Individual racism	Personal acts which humiliate or degrade a person based on his or her racial group membership	Name-calling or physical abuse
Everyday racism as a corollary to individual racism	The habitual occurrence of racism that racial minorities experience in their day-to-day living	Being followed in a department store Being ignored or mistreated by vendors or gatekeepers of certain services
Cultural racism	The conscious or unconscious belief that White cultural values and practices are the norm and superior to the values and practices of racial minorities	Emphasizing individualism or a future orientation as opposed to a collective ideology Measuring standard of dress and hairstyle against European criteria Regarding vocabulary and expressions that are used by specific ethnic groups as substandard Acknowledging holidays such as Christmas and Thanksgiving and ignoring holidays associated with non-European cultures Using Band-Aids called "skin color" in shades that approximate only White skin color
Environmental racism	Racial discrimination that occurs in environmental policy-making and is reflected in the official sanctioning of life-threatening poisons and pollutants in communities of color	Allowing housing developments that are occupied by low-income minorities to be built in contaminated areas, resulting in medical illnesses for the residents

SMALL-GROUP CLASS ACTIVITY 7.2

Overcoming Racism Discussion

According to Charles Ridley (2005), failing to confront racism is a form of racism itself. It is like having the ability to rescue a drowning child but failing to do so.

With this statement in mind and in a small group, engage in the following directives:

a. Share experiences of the various forms of racism described in this chapter that you have directly experienced, witnessed, or been informed of from others.

b. Consider situations where you may have failed to address racism or have been the perpetrator of racism and how you would handle the same situation today.

c. Discuss how you think people learn to behave in racist ways and whether/how they can change their behavior.

d. Identify and discuss useful strategies that counselors from all cultural backgrounds can employ to circumvent racist practices.

Microaggression

Microaggression refers to those interactions between people of different racial, social, and cultural backgrounds and identities that can be interpreted as small acts of mostly nonphysical aggression. Sue et al. (2007) describe racial microaggressions as "brief and commonplace daily verbal, behavioral, or environmental indignities, whether intentional or unintentional, that communicate hostile, derogatory, or negative racial slights and insults toward people of color" (p. 271). They usually involve perceived demeaning implications and other subtle insults against individuals due to race, gender, sexual orientation, social class, ability, age, and other demographics. Acts of microaggression are expressions of isms and shown in subtle, often automatic, and nonverbal perpetrations that are put-downs of the socially oppressed by offenders. Examples of this include color blindness (saying to a Black person, "I do not see color, and you are a normal person to me"), denial of personal bias (telling a gay person, "I am not homophobic—I have several gay friends"), and minimization of prejudice (saying to a woman, "I know you feel it is unfair that you did not get any raise while John has gotten two, but I am sure it is not a gender issue").

Sue et al. (2007) identified three forms of microaggressions—namely, microassault, microinsult, and microinvalidation. A *microassault* denotes "an explicit racial derogation characterized primarily by a verbal or nonverbal attack meant to hurt the intended victim through name-calling, avoidant behavior, or purposeful discriminatory actions" (p. 274). This form is similar to individual racism (although it generally happens in private situations) in which an offender can intentionally or deliberately be hurtful to others, such as calling persons of color "colored."

The second form, *microinsult*, is "characterized by communications that convey rudeness and insensitivity and demean a person's racial heritage or identity" and represents "subtle snubs, frequently unknown to the perpetrator, but [which] clearly convey a hidden insulting message to the recipient of color" (p. 274). An example of this is saying to a student of color, "I am sure that all the universities would recruit you. You are lucky." This is a microinsult because it implies that a student of color is not qualified but gets into college because of affirmative action or other reasons.

Lastly, *microinvalidations* refer to "communications that exclude, negate, or nullify the psychological thoughts, feelings, or experiential reality of a person of color" (p. 274). An example is saying to person of color who felt he was turned down for a job because he was not White, "You may be too sensitive." These aggressions are considered micro, but the effects are by no means minor. It is the offenders' privilege to perceive such acts as having no or minimal harm. Recipients of microaggressions are often told to "get over it" or "not to take it too seriously."

In therapeutic settings, microaggressions are also present and likely go unrecognized by clinicians who have dominant-group memberships and may unintentionally and unconsciously express unexamined biases (Sue et al., 2007). If we take a look at some of the examples of microaggressions identified in counseling settings (see Table 7.3), it is not difficult to see how such unintentional verbal behavior may harm minority clients and interfere with therapeutic treatment.

Table 7.3 Examples of Racial Microaggressions in Therapeutic Practice

Theme	Microaggression	Message
Alien in own land When Asian Americans and Latino Americans are assumed to be foreign-born	A White client does not want to work with an Asian American therapist because "she will not understand my problem." A White therapist tells an American-born Latino client that he/she should seek a Spanish-speaking therapist.	You are not American.
Ascription of intelligence Assigning a degree of intelligence to a person of color on the basis of their race	A school counselor reacts with surprise when an Asian American student had trouble on the math portion of a standardized test. A career counselor asking a Black or Latino student, "Do you think you're ready for college?"	All Asians are smart and good at math. It is unusual for people of color to succeed.
Color blindness Statements which indicate that a White person does not want to acknowledge race	A therapist says, "I think you are being too paranoid. We should emphasize similarities, not people's differences" when a client of color attempts to discuss her feelings about being the only person of color at her job and feeling alienated and dismissed by her co-workers.	Race and culture are not important variables that affect people's lives.

(Continued)

Table 7.3 (Continued)

Theme	Microaggression	Message
	A client of color expresses concern in discussing racial issues with her therapist. Her therapist replies with, "When I see you, I don't see color."	Your racial experiences are not valid.
Criminality/assumption of criminal status A person of color is presumed to be dangerous, criminal, or deviant on the basis of their race	When a Black client shares that she was accused of stealing from work, the therapist encourages the client to explore how she might have contributed to her employer's mistrust of her.	You are a criminal.
	A therapist takes great care to ask all substance abuse questions in an intake with a Native American client, and is suspicious of the client's nonexistent history with substances.	You are deviant.
Denial of individual racism A statement made when Whites renounce their racial biases	A client of color asks his or her therapist about how race affects their working relationship. The therapist replies, "Race does not affect the way I treat you."	Your racial/ethnic experience is not important.
	A client of color expresses hesitancy in discussing racial issues with his White female therapist. She replies, "I understand. As a woman, I face discrimination also."	Your racial oppression is no different than my gender oppression.
Myth of meritocracy Statements which assert that race does not play a role in succeeding in career advancement or education.	A school counselor tells a Black student that "if you work hard, you can succeed like everyone else."	People of color are lazy and/or incompetent and need to work harder.
	A career counselor is working with a client of color who is concerned about not being promoted at work despite being qualified. The counselor suggests, "Maybe if you work harder you can succeed like your peers."	If you don't succeed, you have only yourself to blame (blaming the victim).
Pathologizing cultural values/ communication styles The notion that the values and communication styles of the dominant/White culture are ideal	A Black client is loud, emotional, and confrontational in a counseling session. The therapist diagnoses her with borderline personality disorder.	Assimilate to dominant culture.
	A client of Asian or Native American descent has trouble maintaining eye contact with his therapist. The therapist diagnoses him with a social anxiety disorder.	
	Advising a client, "Do you really think your problem stems from racism?"	Leave your cultural baggage outside.

Theme	Microaggression	Message
Second-class citizen Occurs when a White person is given preferential treatment as a consumer over a person of color	A counselor limits the amount of long-term therapy to provide at a college counseling center; she chooses all White clients over clients of color. Clients of color are not welcomed or acknowledged by receptionists.	Whites are more valued than people of color. White clients are more valued than clients of color.
Environmental microaggressions Macro-level microaggressions, which are more apparent on a systemic level	A waiting room office has pictures of American presidents. Every counselor at a mental health clinic is White.	You don't belong/Only white people can succeed. You are an outsider/ You don't exist.

Source: Sue, D. W., Capodilupo, C. M., Torino, G. C., Bucceri, J. M., Holder, A. M. B., Nadal, K. L., & Esquilin, M. (2007). Racial microaggressions in everyday life: Implications for clinical practice. *American Psychologist, 62*, 271–286.

Understanding the Culturally Diverse

Impact of Social Oppression

It is unfortunate that identifications or group memberships of people are often used to perpetuate oppression and deny individuals their rights. Some are regarded as too old (ageism), some too poor (classism), some not exclusively heterosexual (heterosexism), some members outside the dominant group (ethnocentrism), some disabled (ableism), some women (sexism), and some not non-Hispanic White (racism) to name a few. Multicultural writers have pointed out that traditional counseling theorists ignored the roles that oppression played in the psychological development and overall functioning of our clients (Sparks & Park, 2000). They further acknowledged that social oppression contributes to the mental health problems of our clients and that their survival responses, which manifest due to oppressive conditions, are often mistaken for pathology (Comaz-Diaz & Greene, 1994). Therefore, in multicultural counseling, counselors must recognize that the experience of oppression is a context of life for the culturally diverse and not minimize the magnitude of its impact on diverse clients' mental health and overall development. To illuminate the association between psychological problems and one's social context, Prilleltensky (1999) wrote the following:

> Psychological problems tend to be reified into categories such as personality disorders, character flaws, or thought disturbances. However prevalent these problems might be, they do not exist on their own, nor do they come out of thin air; they are connected to people's social support, employment status, housing conditions, history of discrimination and overall personal and political

> power . . . promoting complete health means promoting *social justice*, for there cannot be health in the absence of justice. (p. 106)

The negative and damaging impact of oppression on diverse groups has been described by Duran, Firehammer, and Gonzalez (2008) as *soul wounding* (i.e., deep psychological and spiritual pain), and they remind us that operating from culturally biased views and utilizing intervention strategies that are incongruent with the values of our culturally diverse clients place us at risk of perpetuating injustices and institutional racism. In order to understand and meet the psychological needs of the culturally diverse, counselors must first acknowledge that oppression exists and that it negatively contributes to the mental health of their clients. Otherwise, counseling practitioners could be propagating isms and invalidating diverse clients' experiences.

Cultural Pluralism

As the world is becoming more integrated and the country more diverse, cultural pluralism becomes more and more present and integrated into all areas of human life. Although there has been disagreement in defining *cultural pluralism*, the concept generally refers to the coexistence of multiple cultures that participate fully in the dominant society but maintain their cultural distinctiveness. Some definitions specifically refer to ethnic groups that exist on their own terms within a larger society. A culturally pluralistic society would place high expectations of integration on its diverse member cultures rather than on assimilation. Cultural pluralism counteracts various isms and cultural discriminations.

To distinguish cultural pluralism from multiculturalism in the context of this book, we made an intentional differentiation between these two concepts. As discussed earlier, we believe in equality across diverse cultural groups and promote multiculturalism, arguing that racially, socially, and culturally diverse people deserve social justice. Regarding cultural pluralism, we will focus our discussion on diverse cultures, worldviews, and values shared by people with or without different racial or ethnic backgrounds. We believe that diversity in both individuals' cultural identities and their cultural values and worldviews contributes to individual and cultural differences and could be used as basis for discrimination. It is important that counselors understand and respect their clients' multicultural identity development and their worldviews and cultural values.

Worldviews

A dictionary definition treats *worldview* as "the fundamental cognitive orientation of an individual or society encompassing the entirety of the individual or society's knowledge and point of view" ("Worldview," n.d.-b.) or a "collection of beliefs about life and the universe held by an individual or a group" ("Worldview," n.d.-a.).

There are different ways in which worldviews have been categorized and described. From a religious perspective, Noebel (2006) believes that every person bases his or her decisions and behaviors on a particular worldview, even if the person may not be able to articulate it. He defined worldview as "any set of ideas, beliefs, or values that provide a framework or map to help you understand God, the world, and your relationship to God and the world" (para. 5) and views it as containing a particular perspective from any of the 10 disciplines—theology, philosophy, ethics, biology, psychology, sociology, law, politics, economics, and history. Specifically, he discussed six existing worldviews—namely, the Christian worldview, the Islamic worldview, the secular humanist worldview, the Marxist worldview, the cosmic humanist worldview, and the postmodern worldview; the Christian-versus-others dynamic seems to be reflected among these worldviews.

Also from a religious point of view, Dennis McCallum (1997) described five worldviews—naturalism (atheism, agnosticism, existentialism); pantheism (Hinduism, Taoism, Buddhism, other faiths, new age, and consciousness); theism (Christianity, Islam, Judaism); spiritism and polytheism (thousands of religions); and postmodernism. However, it should be noted that there are also arguments that the most basic differences exist between scientific-versus-religious worldviews, which are "diametrically opposed at their deepest philosophical levels" (Hall & Hall, 1986, para. 2). Scientific worldviews are in the realm of naturalist, rationalist, humanist, and evolutionary views of the world.

It is beyond the scope of this book to discuss each of these worldviews in detail, and it is inconsistent with the purpose of this book to get into discussions concerning the quality of any or each worldview. Our emphasis is on the belief of multiculturalism and goal of promoting social justice and cultural inclusiveness. We believe that developing awareness of diverse worldviews subscribed by diverse people and respecting people whether or not they subscribe to one worldview or another is critical in serving the culturally diverse. We do need to acknowledge, however, that there are systems of discrimination that are based on worldview prejudice and present a threat to those who are in minorities or out-groups (Major, Kaiser, O'Brien, & McCoy, 2007). In terms of religious worldviews, for instance, Christianity apparently has a dominant position in the United States, and those of Christian faith are given unearned privileges.

Cultural Values and Traditions

Cultural value systems are broadly shared by members of a cultural group or a society and probably encompass a wide range of norms (e.g., what is appropriate behavior), standards (e.g., what is good or bad), beliefs (e.g., meaning of life), or ideologies (e.g., what behavior should be punished). There are between-group differences as well as within-group differences in cultural values. Table 7.4 shows some examples of different values that are *generally* shared by people between cultural groups. It should be noted, however, that not all individuals in any group equally share all the values common for the group, nor are all the values identified representative of the group all the time. There are significant within-group differences as well as situational differences. This table is meant to heuristically remind us of the importance of taking into consideration individuals' cultural values when we try to understand their behavior.

Table 7.4 Examples of Cultural Differences Between Ethnic Groups

	Euro-American View	**Native American View**	**Afrocentric View**	**East Asian View (e.g., Japan, China)**
Relationship with universe/nature	Distinct from Attempt to control it	Interconnected to Harmony with it	Interconnected to Rhythm in nature	Interconnected to Harmony with it Fatalistic
Social unit	Individual	Family/community	Family/community	Family/country
Worldview	Individualism Competition	Cooperation Responsibility to community	Cooperation Responsibility	Familial Interclan relationship Humility
Basis of conduct	To control Governed by rules	Transformation	Transformation	To follow social expectations Governed by Tao (ethics)
View of self	Self-esteem Responsible for self	Part of group/community	Self in group/community	Part of family Familial face as priority Self-criticism
View of success	Winning Competition Efficiency Material assessment	Collective survival	Collective survival	Furthering relationship
View of group	On basis of fairness/equality for members Expectation for group support to individuals	Group as part of self-identity	Group as part of self-identity	Obligation to group Group interest higher than individual interest
Change	Change through confrontation	Change through transformation	Change through transformation	Change through following leadership
Time orientation	Future oriented High adherence to time/schedules	Present oriented Low adherence to time/schedules	Present oriented Low adherence to time/schedules	Past & present oriented Low adherence to time/schedules

To approach within-group differences, it may help to look at each cultural value as a continuum, from weak to strong, and see both interindividual differences and intraindividual differences in terms of their chosen spot on the continuum. As an example, Americans may value "individuality" to various degrees, depending on their life experiences, specific circumstances, age, relationship status, and so on. Some individuals may see it as utmost and sacred, and others may see it as only somewhat important; some may see it as extremely important at some points of life (e.g., in young adult stage) and as only somewhat important at other points (e.g., when starting a new family life).

The concept of individualism versus collectivism (Triandis, 1995) has been used to differentiate values held by individuals. Individualism is associated with a variety of values: independence, personal achievement, self-knowledge, individual uniqueness, privacy, assertive communication, competition, collectivism with a sense of duty to in-group (i.e., family, relatives, and friend circle), respect for decisions of the group, relatedness to others (i.e., relationships are more important than individual accomplishments, seeking others' advice, and a sense of belonging), harmony and working in groups, having a contextualized self, and valuing in interpersonal relationships. Individuals may endorse both individualism and collectivism but to different degrees. A less individualistic and more collectivist individual is more likely to give priority to a collective group such as family or company than to the self in decision making, while a more individualistic and less collectivistic person would do the opposite.

Another useful way to examine within-group differences is using the concept of dependent and interdependent self-construal (Markus & Kitayama, 1991). Cross-cultural studies, mainly between Anglos and Asians, have demonstrated that individuals from largely collectivistic cultures tend to have self-concepts that are more relationship oriented and more interdependent in nature, while those from largely individualistic cultures would emphasize personal independence and uniqueness in their self-concepts. Of course, within-group (e.g., among Anglos, among a particular Asian group) differences exist in the degree to which one defines the self as independent or as interdependent. Although the focus on the self and on interpersonal boundaries is very much emphasized in almost all counseling theories and systems, it is critical that counselors are mindful that not all individuals value the independent self-construal, at least not to the same degree, and defining oneself in relationships is not necessarily a deficiency in "self" development or low self-esteem.

Let's examine this verbal exchange between a therapist and a 24-year-old, single, male, Vietnamese American, college senior in the United States:

Therapist: Paul, thank you for coming to see me. Tell me why you are here.

Client: I don't know. Really. My mother asked me to come after I talked to her last week on the phone.

Therapist: What has happened that your mother would ask you to come?

Client: Not much. Really.

Therapist: What did you talk about over the phone?

Client: Not much. We talked about my roommate. Larry is getting engaged, and we went out for dinner the other day.

Therapist: Maybe your mother was thinking about you when you talked about Larry?

Client: Probably. I think she spends a lot of time thinking about me. I feel guilty.

Therapist: You feel guilty because . . . .

Client: Because I am not feeling right if my mother is not happy.

Therapist: Do you feel responsible for your mother's happiness?

Client: I never thought about it that way, but maybe that is right.

It appears that his mother is an integral part of Paul's self-identity in which the relationship overweighs the individual self. A competent counselor would respect that and conceptualize the client accordingly. Interventions will not be effective and may even be harmful if the client's cultural values are not considered.

Counselors' Social and Professional Responsibility in Eliminating Oppression

Counseling professionals must challenge the systems of oppression and not be afraid to address the actions that occur in society that support the maintenance of such systems. At the very least, we owe it to our clients to consider how their race/ethnicity, class, sex, age, and sexual orientation as a systematic identification have determined their placement in society—a placement which for many of our clients may reek of oppression and injustices that are directly related to their mental health. Counselors have the responsibility to avoid cultural biases embedded in our theories and practice and to function as agents of social change in confronting social injustice on behalf of our clients. A social justice perspective, also known as the fifth force in counseling (Lee & Hipolito-Delgado, 2007), is directly in line with multicultural competence. From an ethical point of view, consideration of historical injustices and oppressions on the mental well-being of our clients is clarified in the 2005 ACA *Code of Ethics*, Standard E.5.c (Historical and Social Prejudices in the Diagnosis of Pathology), which informs counselors to "recognize historical and social prejudices in the misdiagnosis and pathologizing of certain individuals and groups and the role of mental health professionals in perpetuating these prejudices through diagnosis and treatment."

Summary

This chapter discusses the relationship between privilege and social oppression and focuses on raising awareness about the negative impact of privilege (directly and indirectly) on the lives of those who are oppressed. To work with culturally diverse clients, counselors first need to understand the pervasive oppression and social injustice some populations have to endure due to various isms.

Moreover, cultural pluralism is reality, and it requires counselors to be sensitive and comfortable with differences in individuals' worldviews and cultural values. Effective helping has to fit the culture of the client. The chapter also emphasizes counselors' social and professional responsibility in joining the effort to eliminate social oppression and in serving the oppressed members of society.

Takeaway Messages

1. Counselors have to recognize their privileges in any area of diversity in which they have dominant-group membership and the negative impact of their privileges on the lives of the oppressed.
2. Counselors who have unearned privileges have the responsibility to address the issue of privilege and oppression, directly or indirectly, with their clients so they can be helpful to those clients.
3. Cultural pluralism is reality, and differences in worldviews and cultural values are present in all human interactions.
4. Counselors have to consider social oppression and cultural pluralism as important contexts for understanding culturally diverse clients.
5. Multiculturally competent counselors need to take responsibility in eliminating social oppression in all areas of their work.

Recommended Resources

Readings

Allen, T. W. (2012). *The invention of the White race: Racial oppression and social control.* Brooklyn, NY: Verso.
Bornstein, K. (1998). *My gender workbook.* New York, NY: Routledge.
Bronski, M. (2012). *A queer history of the United States.* Boston, MA: Beacon Press.
Lee, C. C. (Ed.). (2007). *Counseling for social justice* (2nd ed., pp. xiii-xxvii). Alexandria, VA: American Counseling Association.
New York Times Editors. (2009, December 7). Food stamps: The economies of eating well [Web log post]. Retrieved from http://roomfordebate.blogs.nytimes.com/2009/12/07/food-stamps-the-economics-of-eating-well/?_php=true&_type=blogs&_r=0

Media and Websites

Daniels, L. (Producer), & Daniels, L. (Director). (2013). *Lee Daniels' The Butler* [Motion picture]. United States: The Weinstein Company.
Wiseman, F. (Director). (1987). *Blind* [Documentary]. United States: IMDbPro.
www.lgbtqnation.com

References

Allport, G. W. (1954). *The nature of prejudice.* New York, NY: Doubleday.
American Counseling Association. (2005). *2005 code of ethics.* Washington, D.C.: Author.
Barker, R. L. (2003). *The social work dictionary* (5th ed.). Washington, DC: NASW Press.

Carter, R. T. (2005). Teaching racial-cultural counseling competence: A racially inclusive model. In R. T. Carter (Ed.), *Handbook of racial-cultural psychology and counseling: Theory and research* (Vol. 1, pp. 36–56). Hoboken, NJ: Wiley.

Coloradans for Immigrant Rights. (2010, March 31). Citizenship privileges. Retrieved from http://afsc.org/resource/coloradans-immigrant-rights-0

Comaz-Diaz, L., & Greene, B. (Eds.). (1994). *Women of color: Integrating ethnic and gender identities in psychotherapy*. New York, NY: Guilford.

Cox, O. C. (1959). *Caste, class, & race: A study in social dynamics*. New York, NY: Monthly Review.

Deutch, B. (n.d.). The male privilege checklist [Web log post]. Retrieved from http://amptoons.com/blog/the-male-privilege-checklist

Diller, J. V. (2007). *Cultural diversity: A primer for the human services* (3rd ed.). Belmont, CA: Thomson Brooks/Cole.

Diversity Learning Tree. (n.d.-a). *Heterosexual privilege checklist*. Retrieved from http://www.sap.mit.edu/content/pdf/heterosexual_privilege.pdf

Diversity Learning Tree. (n.d.-b). *Social class privilege checklist*. Retrieved from http://www.sap.mit.edu/content/pdf/class_privilege_checklist.pdf

Duran, E., Firehammer, J., & Gonzalez, J. (2008). Liberation psychology as the path toward healing cultural soul wounds. *Journal of Counseling & Development, 86*, 288–295.

Graham, M. (2009, October 12). The invisible backpack of able-bodied privilege checklist [Web log post]. Retrieved from https://exposingableism.wordpress.com/2009/10/12/the-invisible-backpack-of-able-bodied-privilege-checklist/

Griffin, P., D'Errico, K. H., Harro, B., & Schiff, T. (2007). Heterosexist curriculum design. In M. Adams, L. A. Bell, & P. Griffin (Eds.). *Teaching for diversity and social justice* (2nd ed., pp. 195–218). New York, NY: Routledge.

Hall, N. F., & Hall, L. K. B. (1986, May/June). Is the war between science and religion over? *Humanist*, 26. Retrieved from http://americanhumanist.org/humanism/Is_the_War_between_Science_and_Religion_Over

Hardiman, R., & Jackson, B. (1997). Conceptual foundations for social justice courses. In M. Adams, L. A. Bell, & P. Griffin (Eds.), *Teaching for diversity and social justice* (pp. 16–29). New York, NY: Routledge.

Hartney, C., & Vuong, L. (2009, March). Created equal: Racial and ethnic disparities in the U.S. criminal justice system. *National Council on Criminal and Delinquency*. Retrieved from http://www.nccdglobal.org/sites/default/files/publication_pdf/created-equal.pdf

Lee, C. C., & Hipolito-Delgado, C. P. (2007). Counselors as agents of social justice. In C. C. Lee (Ed.), *Counseling for social justice* (2nd ed., pp. xiii-xxvii). Alexandria, VA: American Counseling Association.

Major, B., Kaiser, C. R., O'Brien, L. T., & McCoy, S. K. (2007). Perceived discrimination as worldview threat or worldview confirmation: Implications for self-esteem. *Journal of Personality & Social Psychology, 92*, 1068–1086.

Markus, H. R., & Kitayama, S. (1991). Culture and the self: Implications for cognition, emotion, and motivation. *Psychological Review, 98*, 224–253.

McCallum, D. (1997). Christianity: The faith *that makes sense*. Retrieved from http://www.xenos.org/classes/papers/5wldview.htm#sthash.ez33GnVe.dpuf

McIntosh, P. (1989, July/August). White privilege: Unpacking the invisible knapsack. *Peace & Freedom*, pp. 10–12.

Monk, G., Winslade, J., & Sinclair, S. (2008). *New horizons in multicultural counseling*. Thousand Oaks, CA: Sage.

Noebel, D. A. (2006). *Understanding the times* (2nd ed.). Manitou Springs, CO: Summit Press. Retrieved from http://www.worldviewweekend.com/news/article/understanding-six-worldviews-rule-world

Oppression. (n.d.). In *Merriam-Webster's online dictionary* (11th ed.). Retrieved from http://www.merriam-webster.com/dictionary/oppression

Penelope, J. (1994). Class and consciousness. In J. Penelope (Ed.), *Out of the class closet: Lesbians speak* (pp. 12–98). Freedom, CA: Crossing.

Prilleltensky, I. (1999). Critical psychology foundations for the promotion of mental health. *Annual Review of Critical Psychology, 1,* 100–118.

Ridley, C. R. (2005). *Overcoming unintentional racism in counseling and therapy* (2nd ed.). Thousand Oaks, CA: Sage.

Satcher, D. (2001). *U.S. surgeon general report on mental health: Culture, race, and ethnicity.* Retrieved from: http://www.wkkf.org/resource-directory/resource/2001/08/us-surgeon-general-releases-report-on-mental-health-culture-race-and-ethnicity

Smith, R. C. (1995). *Racism in the post-civil rights era.* New York: State University of New York.

Sparks, E., & Park, A., (2000). The integration of feminism and multiculturalism: Ethical dilemmas at the border. In M. M. Brabeck (Ed.), *Practicing feminist ethics in psychology* (pp. 2203–2224). Washington, DC: American Psychological Association.

Sue, D. W., Capodilupo, C. M., Torino, G. C., Bucceri, J. M., Holder, A. M. B., Nadal, K. L., & Esquilin, M. (2007). Racial microaggressions in everyday life: Implications for clinical practice. *American Psychologist, 62,* 271–286.

Sue, D. W., & Sue, D. (2013). *Counseling the culturally diverse: Theory and practice* (6th ed.). Hoboken, NJ: Wiley.

Thompson, C. E., & Neville, H. A. (1999). Racism, mental health, and mental health practice. *The Counseling Psychologist, 27,* 155–223.

Thompson, C. E., Shin, C. E., & Stephens, J. (2005). Race and research evidence. In R. T. Carter (Ed.), *Handbook of racial-cultural psychology and counseling: Theory and research* (Vol. 1, pp. 277–294). Hoboken, NJ: Wiley.

Triandis, H. C. (1995). *Individualism & collectivism.* Boulder, CO: Westview Press.

Wildman, S. M., & Davis, A. D. (2002). Making systems of privilege visible. In P. S. Rothenberg (Ed.), *White privilege: Essential readings on the other side of racism* (pp. 89–95). New York, NY: Worth.

Worldview. (n.d.–a.). In *The free dictionary by Farlex.* Retrieved from http://www.thefreedictionary.com/worldview

Worldview. (n.d.–b.). In *Wikipedia.* Retrieved February 8, 2015, from http://en.wikipedia.org/wiki/World_view

Section 4

Exercising Multicultural Competencies: Working With the Culturally Diverse

Major CACREP Standards for the Section

CACREP Standard 2d: individual, couple, family, group, and community strategies for working with and advocating for diverse populations, including multicultural competencies

CACREP Standard 2e: counselors' roles in developing cultural self-awareness, promoting cultural social justice, advocacy and conflict resolution, and other culturally supported behaviors that promote optimal wellness and growth of the human spirit, mind, or body

Specific Competences Identified by CACREP Diversity and Advocacy Standards for Clinical Mental Health Counseling Addressed in Section 4

CACREP Knowledge 4: Understands effective strategies to support client advocacy and influence public policy and government relations

CACREP Knowledge 5: Understands the implications of concepts such as internalized oppression and institutional racism, as well as the historical and current political climate regarding immigration, poverty, and welfare

After Reading Section 4 (Chapters 8–12), Students Will Be Able to Do the Following:

a. See the social and cultural contexts of diverse populations and understand the disadvantages that society has imposed onto them

b. Learn the implication of cultural value and worldview differences between diverse populations and mainstream culture embedded in traditional counseling practice

c. Understand the minority cultural identity development process and its implication in individuals' mental health and worldviews

d. Appreciate the importance of seeing cultural and psychological strengths of minority groups given that their environment is biased and discriminative toward them

e. Be open-minded toward traditional cultural healing methods

Section Introduction

This section focuses on working with clients from diverse backgrounds, especially those who have been impacted by social oppression. The continued development of a multicultural identity and enriched understanding of the social, cultural, and political contexts of society are emphasized in this section. The previous sections have described the processes and challenges of the first two stages of counselor multicultural competence (see p. 133 for Multicultural Competence Development Model). In this section, the reader is introduced to the third and fourth stages where learning and development occur. Competent counselors demonstrate a developing multicultural consciousness and are committed to understanding clients in their specific social contexts.

We believe strongly that clients' diverse cultural identities do not operate in isolation in shaping their social experience and that everyone is multicultural, but we choose to organize our discussion of specific social contexts into five areas in this section—racial and ethnic, gender and sexual, social class, ability and age, and religion and spirituality. We chose this approach because (a) these are salient dimensions of diversity for those who are in subordinate groups and deserve significant attention, (b) the institutional oppression in these areas is obvious and keen and has had significant negative impact on members of subordinate groups, and (c) the inclusion of these dimensions of diversity are ripe for discussion. However, we emphasize that counselors need to adopt a holistic view of every client (considering the intersection of their identities) and client contexts (influenced by multiple cultural factors). Extensive knowledge about the role of each aspect of the multicultural identity of clients contributes to the holistic understanding of them and facilitates multicultural preventions and interventions.

It is also critically important we recognize that within each cultural group there are significant differences, partially due to their intersection of identities and partially due to their cultural values and worldviews. We encourage readers to position themselves in this context when they read the five chapters in this section. Your cultural identity (either as a member of the dominant or subordinate group) in a particular dimension will influence how you read that particular chapter.

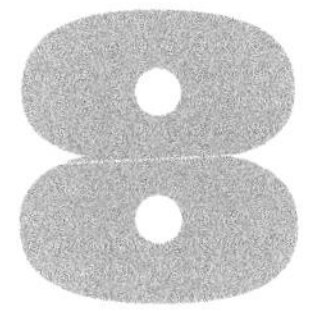

Working With Diversity in Racial, Ethnic, and Nationality Contexts

We hate each other because we fear each other. And we fear each other because we do not know each other. And we do not know each other because we are separated from each other.

—Martin Luther King Jr.

CHAPTER OVERVIEW

This chapter focuses on issues specific to working with racial and ethnic minority clients. Multiculturally competent counselors understand those clients' social and cultural contexts, including the negative influence of racism, discrimination, and microaggression they have to endure and the implications of their cultural values that are not shared by the mainstream culture. Moreover, counselors should understand the ongoing processes of cultural identity development of those clients with racial and ethnic minority statuses. In clinical services to those clients, counselors should pay attention to the cultural strengths of racial and ethnic minorities, respect their worldviews and perspectives, support traditional cultural healing methods, and advocate for social justice.

Due to the page limit, we can't present sufficient information that is specific to each racial and ethnic minority. At times we selected some groups to make the point, but in no way does that imply that only the selected groups deserve our discussion. We encourage readers to focus on the theoretical points and questions implied by the presented information and continue to seek further understanding.

SELF-ASSESSMENT OF PRE-EXISTING AWARENESS AND KNOWLEDGE

- What is my level of competency in addressing issues related to race, ethnicity, and nationality with culturally diverse clients?
- How well do I understand the important roles of race, ethnicity, and nationality in the psychological health of culturally diverse clients?
- How competent am I at integrating the racial, ethnic, and nationality experiences of my clients when attempting to understand them and their issues?
- How competent am I at providing interventions that effectively address clients' concerns in the context of their racial, ethnic, and nationality identities?
- How competent am I at using my own racial, ethnic, and nationality context as a helping agent in working with clients?
- What is my stage of racial identity development?
- How does my racial identity development influence my work with people of different racial, ethnic, and national backgrounds from me?

LEARNING OBJECTIVES

After reading this chapter, students will be able to do the following:

1. Understand the relevance of counselors' and clients' race, ethnicity, and nationality in establishing effective therapeutic relationships

2. Conceptualize clients' concerns and understand their racial, ethnic, and nationality experiences even if they do not come to counseling to address those specific experiences per se

3. Recognize and consider the relevance of race, ethnicity, and nationality when delivering psychological interventions

4. Understand the unjust and damaging impact of racism on the life and health of racial and ethnic minority group members

5. Recognize the importance of racial identity development in one's ability to provide effective counseling to racial and ethnic minority populations

CASE ILLUSTRATION 8.1

The Case of Samantha

Samantha is a 17-year-old Native American female high school junior in a predominantly White school. She was brought in by her adoptive parents to a community mental health center in a midsized city. Her parents reported that Samantha had attempted to run away from home in the previous week. Her parents appeared very stressed and worried about her. They were received for intake by a White male counselor who saw Samantha with her parents for half of the session and Samantha alone for about 20 minutes. With Samantha in the room, the mother repeatedly said to the counselor, "Please help her! She is our only child, and we are willing to do anything to help her." The intake counselor was able to gather the following information about Samantha through the interviews:

Samantha was adopted by a Caucasian family living in a middle-class White neighborhood when she was 6 years old. Her family of origin was unable to care for Samantha due to substance abuse, and she experienced multiple forms of abuse and trauma during her early years. Her family of origin identified as Native American and prior to Samantha's birth had spent time living on a Native American reservation. Samantha presented with multiple psychiatric diagnoses, including bipolar disorder, PTSD, and attachment disorder. Her parents said that she had received psychiatric care before, but she did not cooperate well with the psychiatrist. Samantha had engaged in self-harming behaviors, multiple suicide attempts, and substance abuse. Several days before, Samantha had a verbal fight with her parents and was grounded, but at midnight her mother found her gone. The family called the police, but Samantha came home on her own the next day. When the counselor asked Samantha what made her want to run away and what brought her back, she said, "They are unreasonable and never like any of my friends, but I don't want to hurt them because they have done a lot for me." When asked about her experiences at school, she said she was OK with her school but not a big fan of many school activities. She said she preferred hanging out with a smaller circle of friends. She also said she was OK with being a C student.

In describing Samantha's behavior in the session, the intake counselor reported that she was quiet and appeared disinterested or disconnected. She would respond to the counselor's questions with very brief answers and showed annoyance at times. At the end of the intake session, Samantha said to the counselor, "I do not need to come next week. It did not help anyway." Samantha's parents, however, assured the counselor that they would bring her back every week until the counselor thought she did not need to come anymore.

In this case, neither Samantha nor her parents mentioned anything about Samantha's cultural background as relevant to the situation. In fact, the reported difficulties Samantha was experiencing could easily be seen as "normal" for any teenager, especially a teenager with her diagnosis. To effectively help her, however, the counselor needs to conceptualize Samantha's experiences in the context of being Native American by birth, an adopted child by a White family, living in a community where few people are like her, a teenage girl, and so on. To help her effectively, however, the counselor needs to view Samantha and conceptualize her experiences in the context that she is a Native American by birth, an adopted child with a White family, living in a community where few people are like her, a teenage girl, and so on. Her experiences with school, family, and community are probably connected to all her identities because there are visible and invisible social expectations, perceptions, and views related to who she is that she probably can't avoid. Whether or not she is aware of it or able to articulate it, the role of her cultural identities can be significant in how she experiences and is perceived by her environment. It is worthwhile that we brainstorm possible ways in which Samantha's cultural identities may be related to her "symptoms" as reported and possible interventions that are sensitive to the cultural contexts she is in.

SMALL-GROUP CLASS ACTIVITY 8.1

Discussion and Exploration of the Case of Samantha

Form small groups with three or four students each. Discuss and explore answers to the following questions:

1. What do you think are the major issues that Samantha may be having? What is the degree to which they are age appropriate or inappropriate? Culturally appropriate or inappropriate?
2. What are the significant areas of her life that you want to explore with her?
3. What are the possibilities that Samantha's multiple ethnic identities (both Native American and White American) are sources of stress or resources for her at this time?
4. In what ways may Samantha's Native American heritage have contributed to her psychological difficulties at this time?
5. What roles may Samantha's White American family background play in how she experiences life in school, home, and community?
6. What kind of challenges does Samantha have to face in developing a healthy multicultural identity?
7. In what ways does your multicultural identity influence how you view Samantha and her "symptoms?"

It is likely that after attempting to answer these questions you find it hard to deny that Samantha's racial and ethnic backgrounds may have a role in her experiences, including her "symptoms." To say the least, her different skin color and her cultural background probably bring her interpersonal and social treatment that is different than that received by her White peers. You probably also became curious about the reasons that she preferred "a small circle of friends," her lack of enthusiasm about school activities, her running away but coming back (not wanting to hurt her parents), her satisfaction with being a C student, and so forth. Being adopted cross-racially may present additional demand on her psychological adjustment to her environment; thus, it will be another identity that she needs to integrate into her sense of self.

From the brief description, you probably did not know if the racial differences between her and her parents and most schoolmates is openly recognized or discussed. Was this a sensitive area or a taboo topic? How did Samantha feel about her being different and others' color-blind attitude? Did she feel accepted and respected? How did she deal with any possible obvious or subtle rejections? A culturally sensitive counselor would surely be interested in Samantha's developmental process of racial and cultural identity and how her difference from others in several identities had brought her both positive and negative experiences. Additionally, the diagnosis she received in the past would be reviewed with consideration of her culture and cultural identities.

Understanding the Cultural Contexts of the Racially and Ethnically Diverse

Working with racially and ethnically diverse clients, counselors must be aware of and attend to their social and cultural contexts as well as individual characteristics and life narratives. In Chapter 7, we discussed various forms of racism and racial privileges and oppression that exist in American society, which make it clear that social experiences due to racial group memberships matter in the individual's life. In this section, we selectively discuss a few areas in which racial disparity and inequality are obvious and persistent. We hope to strengthen the belief that we can't understand client clinical symptoms accurately without viewing the symptoms in social contexts.

Effect of Racism, Discrimination, and Microaggression

Racism is the root of racial and ethnic discrimination and microaggression and pollutes the social environment with all forms of racial/ethnic inequalities and stratifications that disadvantage people of color. A few examples are provided in this section. If we agree that individuals' growth and development processes interact with contexts, we will have to recognize that our conceptualization and treatment of clients must be rooted in the specific cultural contexts they are in. Although emphasizing individuals' responsibilities for themselves is a high value of the American culture and of the counseling profession, we can't neglect the fact that people of color are confronted by a lot more negative, aversive, and even denigrating conditions than their majority counterparts in our society. Applying this understanding in our clinical work is not meant to discourage people of color from taking responsibility for themselves but to encourage them to view their experiences in context so to limit the harm from them.

Racial Disparities in Economics

Abundant statistics and observations are available to show a grossly unfair and hard-to-accept picture. In 2006, White households had incomes that were two thirds higher than those of African Americans and 40% higher than those of Hispanics; in addition, Whites were more likely to own their homes and have a college degree (U.S. Bureau of the Census, 2006). As pointed out by Ohlemacher (2006), "Home ownership creates wealth, which enables families to live in good neighborhoods with good schools. It also helps families finance college, which leads to better paying jobs, perpetuating the cycle" (para. 2). Further, there are many other indicators of racial disparities in economics, such as the 2006 median household income that was $50,622, $30,939, and $36,278 for White, Black, and Hispanic households respectively (para. 13).

The consequences of economic inequality can be deep. To say the least, they make the notion "everyone has equal chance to succeed" a fallacy. Many racial and ethnic minority people are in the "losing" position at the starting line—they are already behind in various ways. In order to reach "equal" success, those who are in the disadvantaged positions have to do and achieve so much more than those with privileges. This aspect of social context deserves our attention in counseling racially and ethnically diverse clients.

Racial Disparities in Education

In discussion of the inequality of education, the topic of segregation or desegregation often comes up. Following the Jim Crow Laws (racial segregation laws enacted between 1876 and 1965 in the United States at the state and local levels), the segregation of Whites from Blacks in education (and in all other areas of life) legally lasted until 1954 when the Supreme Court of the United States ruled in *Brown v. Board of Education* to end it. However, around the 60th birthday of this important Supreme Court ruling, it was observed that "separated along socioeconomic and racial lines, schools are less diverse than at any other time in the past four decades" (Mullins, 2013, para. 1). The 2012 study by the Civil Rights Project at the University of California, Los Angeles, revealed that 74% of African American students and 80% of Latino students attended schools in 2009 to 2010 where at least half of the student body was from one minority. Further, in these segregated schools, teachers' salaries are lower, more teachers are uncertified, and advanced courses (e.g., Algebra II) are less likely offered than at other schools (U.S. Department of Education, 2014).

Racial disparity occurs in other areas such as school discipline, early learning, college readiness, and teacher quality (Hsieh, 2014). In school discipline, for example, the "zero tolerance" disciplinary policy adopted by many schools since 1990 has not only been proven to be ineffective but also "disproportionately target(s) students of color and students with disabilities" (Mokhtari, 2014, para. 2). Black students are expelled at three times the rate of White students. Native American and Native Alaskan students represent less than 1% of students but 3% of expulsions. Furthermore, over 50% of students who are involved in school-related arrests or referred to law enforcement are Hispanic or African American (U.S. Department of Education, 2014).

Racial Disparities in Employment

The disparity in unemployment between White workers and workers of color has long persisted. While economic recession hurts many people, it is not "an equal-opportunity victimizer" (Mishel, 2009, p. 1). Certain racial groups are hurt more than others. During the recent recession in August 2013, "Blacks ha[d] it the worst, with an unemployment rate at 16.7%—its highest level since 1984. The unemployment rate for Latinos was unchanged at 11.3%, and the unemployment rate for Whites fell slightly to 8%" (Censky, 2011). In December 2014, after a year of strong job growth, the Economic Policy Institute, an American think tank in Washington, D. C., reported that the national unemployment rate was almost twice as high for Blacks (10.4%) than it was for Whites (4.8%). When broken down by state, the White unemployment rate ranged from 2.1% (North Dakota) to 6.7% (Nevada), but the Black unemployment rate varied from 7.5% (Virginia) to 16.3% (Michigan), and nationally, the Black unemployment rate ranged from 1.7 to 5.3 times higher than the White unemployment rate (V. Wilson, 2015).

Research has shown that being unemployed can be stressful and exposes the individual to psychological challenges as well as economic difficulties. Unemployed persons show more distress than employed persons, and 34% of unemployed persons experience psychological problems such as depression, anxiety, and psychosomatic symptoms, while only 16% of employed persons had these problems (Paul & Moser, 2009). This context probably has another layer of negative impact on the psychology of those who see more people in their racial and social groups suffering from psychological problems in addition to being poor and unemployed due to racial inequality in employment. It can hurt self-concept.

Racial Disparities in Health and Health Care

In the larger context of the polarization of income and wealth and inequality in education and other areas of life in the United States, it has been a longtime fact that African Americans have higher rates of death, disease, and disability than White Americans. Additionally, it is also a known fact that "racial and ethnic minorities, especially African Americans, often receive a lower quality of care and have worse outcomes" (Jha, 2013, para. 1). This racial disparity is significantly due to a socially constructed stratification of races that "emerged in the context of social and economic oppression and [has] been used to perpetuate economic, cultural, ideological, political and legal systems of inequality" (Williams, Jackson, & Anderson, 1997, p. 336). Researchers have noted that individuals' social conditions may not only produce physiological differences between races but may also interact with any innate biological differences to affect health. In terms of actual health care and care quality, two major issues have been the foci of discussion: patient access to care and care providers' cultural competence.

Racial and ethnic minorities are known to have had poorer access and lower quality of health care compared to that experienced by White populations. Among the recommendations documented in the landmark report by former Surgeon General Dr. David Satcher in 2001 addressing the various barriers and inequalities that racial and ethnic minority communities endure, provider cultural competence was highly emphasized. Their cultural competence is the foundation for reaching other goals, such as increasing minority-specific research, diversifying the mental health workforce, training new providers in cultural diversity, and empowering consumers and families.

SMALL-GROUP CLASS ACTIVITY 8.2

Discussion and Exploration of the Case of Samantha

In the same small groups, brainstorm and describe Samantha's social context by listing specific social and cultural obstacles she has to overcome compared with her White peers.

Implication of Cultural Value Differences

Due to historical and current social, political, and international events, mainstream Americans have values that may be unique to them and may or may not be shared by culturally diverse populations. The strong values of freedom, fairness, and independence, for instance, are rooted in the history that Americans fought for freedom from the British during the American Revolution, and the high pride that defines American patriotism upkeeps the belief that other countries should model themselves after the United States in how to run the country and relate to other countries (C. C. Wilson & Gutierrez, 1995). These and other dominant cultural values are reflected in traditional counseling theories and practice. Those who do not share such history and national status may have different values and may not find counseling as helpful. It is the responsibility of counselors to understand and respect these minority groups' cultures, values, and worldviews and provide culturally sensible and effective services.

Family Structures, Communities, and Relationship Patterns

The genetic characteristics of counseling clash with how we view individuals and understand their relationships with family, community, and others. The mainstream culture acknowledges nuclear family structure as the legal standard in defining *family* and views adult family members as independent from each other. The family structures of ethnic minorities tend to be different, and so are the relationships between the individual and the family. The differences are reflected in inclusiveness, importance, and power structure of family.

African American families. Historically, those coming from Africa to the United States as slaves brought their value of kinship. Any individual is considered "a member of a people, a clan, a family, and a household. . . . The family was extended to include grandparents, aunts and uncles, cousins, and other relatives that wanted to be part" ("African American Family," n.d.). The saying "It takes a village to raise a child" describes many traditional African American families. Due to social and economic oppression in the second half of the 20th century, African American families, especially those in working or lower social class, suffered, and the family structure changed. A decline in the marriage rate, an increase in single-mother households, and enlarged roles of grandparents in child care are a few examples of the change. Although the middle class of African Americans is growing, poverty has been a common background for many Black families. As a result, African American families are increasingly headed by single parents, Black women have been less likely to marry than other women in the United States in recent years, and individual family members are often expected to adopt multiple roles within the family (see "African American Family," n.d.).

Spirituality and religion have an important position among African American families and communities. Black churches serve as great social and economic support and provide opportunities for self-expression, leadership, community involvement, and organized effort in combating racism (Rowles & Duan, 2012). Working with individuals and families in counseling, our professional practice is challenged to (a) recognize the strength of African Americans living in such family constellations and (b) recognize the limitations and biases of our theories and practice in assessing and treating African American individuals and families. Being aware of and respecting their cultural and spiritual practices that may or may not be consistent with our own is essential.

Hispanic or Latino/Latina families. Hispanics or Latino/Latinas are a diverse group (e.g., Mexican, Central and South American, Puerto Rican, Cuban). There are family characteristics that are often seen as representative of most of the diverse subgroups, such as strong kinship, the role of extended families, and emphasis on family well-being (vs. individual well-being). At the current time, one important aspect of understanding Hispanic families is the impact of socioeconomic disadvantages on family life (Vega, 1995). Due to a complex set of factors (including the hardships involved in immigration, low levels of human capital, racial discrimination, and settlement patterns), Hispanic poverty rates remain high, ranging from 16.2% (for Cubans) to 26.3% (for Dominicans) according to census data from 2007 to 2011 census data (Macartney, Bishaw, & Fontenot, 2013). Associated with poverty, many families suffer due to low skill levels, job instability, and inadequate earnings for males, which leads to the phenomena of retreat from marriage, nonmarital childbearing, and female family headship (Oppenheimer, 2000).

Native American families. The concept of extended family is a strong feature among diverse Native American families, and children being raised by relatives living in separate households is common (Garrett, 2006). Multiple family members such as aunts and uncles may take on child care responsibilities and discipline children, and grandparents often play significant roles in decision making in child rearing. Another characteristic of many Native American families is the matrilineal heritage by which women can inherit power, such as taking on the positions of tribal rulers. Socially and economically, Native Americans are one of the most disadvantaged groups in the United States and have the highest (27%) national poverty rate (Macartney et al., 2013) as shown in U.S. census data.

Cultural Values, Traditions, and Strengths

Differences among racial and ethnic populations are present in all areas of life. One significant variance is around the moral principle of individual "rights" or freedom to action—in other words, how to position one's own benefit or interest in the individualism/collectivism continuum. While mainstream American culture distinctively values individual rights and freedom to the greatest degree (more on the individualistic side), many racial and ethnic minorities emphasize the importance of responsibilities and obligations to others, especially families. In Chinese families, for instance, filial piety is an expected imperative moral conduct. Individuals are to be loving, respectful, polite, considerate, loyal, helpful, dutiful, and obedient to their parents even if self-sacrifices have to be made. Those who are not pious about it are often condemned. A traditional saying asks this: How can a person be loyal to friends, country, or others if he or she does not have piety toward his or her own parents?

Hispanics or Latin Americans are often characterized as honoring and practicing *familism*, a strong commitment to family life that is qualitatively distinct from that of non-Hispanic whites (Vega, 1995). It entails the subordination of individual interests to those of the family and group and encompasses structural/demographic, behavioral, and attitudinal dimensions (Valenzuela & Dornbusch, 1994). Including extended kin and having a large family size reflect the structural configuration of familism. Individuals are expected to fulfill family role obligations by sharing resources, showing mutual assistance and support, and keeping frequent contact among family members. In the socioeconomic hardship that many Hispanics or Latino and Latina Americans have to face, familism has been viewed as a protective factor (Landale, Oropesa, & Bradatan, 2006). This value is often challenged as individuals and families acculturate and adapt to U.S. family norms. Notably, this value may also conflict those of independence and autonomy, which are honored highly by our counseling theories and practice. Thus, a deliberate deconstruction and reconstruction process of knowledge needs to happen when we work with Hispanic or Latino and Latina individuals and families.

Although diverse, Native American and Native Alaskan cultural and spiritual values generally include high emphasis on sharing and giving (vs. taking or accumulation of material), cooperation (valuing harmony and family, taking precedence over individual), noninterference (rights of others are respected), present-time orientation (focus on the present rather than future), spirituality (focused harmony among spirit, mind, and body), and respect for and learning from elders (learning by respecting and listening to elders) (Garrett & Portman, 2011). These values may be the foundation of some of Native Americans' behavior that may appear "hard to understand" or "abnormal" from a European perspective. For instance, some Native Americans may not appear driven or motivated to work hard to accumulate wealth or be outstanding in career or school, some youth may not be active in some school activities because they do not want to be competitive, some parents may be more indulgent and less punitive than parents of other ethnicities, some individuals may not work well with deadlines, and some people may not make eye contact or other direct communications.

Communication: Cross-Cultural Dynamics

Regardless of clinicians' expertise, clinical interventions can help only when they are communicated to clients effectively. Communication is a complicated process; cross-cultural communication needs to deal with different styles and practices. In counseling sessions, counselors need to send messages to and receive messages from clients accurately, which requires that counselors understand client communication styles as well as their own. In a cross-cultural counseling setting, a lack of knowledge of each other's communication styles may lead to misunderstandings or negative consequences. Let's examine this example:

Counselor: Tell me what brought you in today.

Client: (long pause, head down) I don't know. I just feel low (in low voice).

Counselor: I can see that. You sound low. What has happened?

Client: (long pause) Nothing. Nothing bad, I mean.

Counselor: OK, just tell me what is on your mind at this moment.

Client: (long pause) I don't know.

Counselor: That is OK. (silence)

Client: (getting visibly uncomfortable)

This not-so-productive communication can be a meaningful clinical phenomenon, such as the client not being ready for or clear about the counseling process, the client being resistant, the client testing the counselor, and so on. However, it may also be an example of ineffective communication due to the counselor's failure in understanding the client's communication style that reflects implicit and non-self-focused styles. For a traditional East Asian person, for instance, right-to-the-point, explicit, and problem-centered communication can be viewed as rude, uncomfortable, and inappropriate, thus ineffective. Starting with small talk, sharing words that are agreeable to the other person's ears, saying things that clarify the status of the parties, and using nonverbal behavior to make the other person comfortable may be good ways to start a conversation. Moreover, communication may vary in how nonverbal behaviors are interpreted, how meanings are presented (implicitly or explicitly), and how communicators' social and interpersonal statuses are portrayed. Additionally, different cultures may have different taboo subjects as well as preferred topics.

Nonverbal Communication

Nonverbal behavior is meaningful for people in all cultures. Many individuals' emotions, such as high levels of anger, frustration, or happiness, can be ascertained from their facial expressions and/or body language by people familiar with the culture. However, that may not be the case in cross-cultural settings because there are cultural differences to the degree that people let their emotions show or in the way they show their emotions through proxemics, kinesics, and paralanguages (Sue & Sue, 2013).

Proxemics refers to "perception and use of personal and interpersonal space" (Sue & Sue, 2013, p. 214). Different racial and ethnic groups may have different comfort levels concerning personal space or conversational distances. Euro-Americans generally require larger personal space to feel comfortable than Latin Americans, African Americans, South Americans, Arabs, and many Asians. Latin Americans' preference for physical closeness may make others uncomfortable. In counseling relationships, this presents an area of attention for the counselor.

Kinesics refers to "bodily movement" (p. 215), including facial expressions, postures, gestures, eye contact, and so on. Cultural variations in kinesics can be quite significant. Smiling, for instance, is generally seen as friendly, positive, or likeable in our society, which may add positivity in the psychological assessment of the person. However, in some cultures (e.g., Japanese culture), smiling may not always convey positive emotions or approval but embarrassment or shyness. Being "serious" in some Asian cultures is viewed as reflecting capability or competence, and smiling can be seen as showing weakness or immaturity. Moreover, expression of emotions with kinesics is generally discouraged among East Asian cultures, but being reserved and restrained is highly valued.

Paralanguage refers to "other vocal cues that individuals use to communicate" (p. 217). Many cues such as "loudness of voice, pauses, silences, hesitations, rate of speech, and inflection" (p. 217) are very communicative about the person. Cross-culturally, such cues may communicate different messages. Use of silence is an example. In North America, silence is often viewed as a floor-yielding cue and dealt with by the listener filling in the conversation. It can also be seen as an expression of giving up, lack of words/ideas, or impatience. In Asian culture, however, silence is often a sign of respect, deference, or politeness, and rather than an invitation for someone to take the floor, it actually is a gesture for permission to continue speaking. With this understanding, a counselor may be less inclined to conceptualize Asian clients who don't say much as not knowing or not cooperating in counseling.

Context-Driven Communication

Any given verbal or nonverbal behavior can have different meanings in different cultural contexts. A *yes* may not be a confirmative answer and may even mean *no* when it is used in certain cultural context. In more collectivistic or more ethics- and morality-centered cultures (e.g., Chinese), saying the "right thing" is highly expected and desired because of its implication for relationships. To understand such contextual differences, world cultures have been described as having high or low contexts (Hall, 1976). Although this high-low context is a relative concept (not absolute high or low, but on a high-low continuum), there are cultures that clearly have high context (e.g., Middle East, Asia, Africa, South America) and others low context (North America and much of Western Europe). As briefly discussed in Chapter 1, higher-context cultures tend to be more "relational, collectivistic, intuitive, and contemplative," while lower-context cultures more "logical, linear, individualistic, and action-oriented" (B. Wilson, n.d.). See Table 8.1 for a comparison between these two types of cultures along a number of dimensions. People from high-context cultures emphasize interpersonal relationships, and those from low-context cultures value logic, facts, and directiveness.

In high-context cultural communication, words and word choices are important because using few words could communicate a complex message through being implicit, indirect, and vague or by being accompanied with tone of voice, facial expression, gestures, or postures. Sometimes many things are left unsaid, leaving the culture to explain and the listener to figure them out. Some communication theorists point out that the primary goal of verbal communication in high-context cultures is not for accuracy in messages but for establishing and maintaining an appropriate relationship with the listener (Gao & Ting-Toomey, 1998). On the other hand, communication in low-context cultures is expected to be straightforward, explicit, concise, and accurate. Precise words are to be used and to be taken literally. Legal documents count more than the trust between people. The responsibility of precise communication is on the speaker.

The counseling implication of cultural communication differences is that counselors need to avoid using their own communication styles as the standard in evaluating client behavior, and they need to learn to communicate with diverse clients by understanding clients' communication styles.

Table 8.1 Examples of Differences Between High- and Low-Context Cultures

High Context (HC)	Low Context (LC)
Association	**Association**
• Relationships depend on trust, build up slowly, are stable. One distinguishes between people inside and people outside one's circle. • How things get done depends on relationships with people and attention to group process. • One's identity is rooted in groups (family, culture, work). • Social structure and authority are centralized; responsibility is at the top. Person at top works for the good of the group.	• Relationships begin and end quickly. Many people can be inside one's circle; circle's boundary is not clear. • Things get done by following procedures and paying attention to the goal. • One's identity is rooted in oneself and one's accomplishments. • Social structure is decentralized; responsibility goes further down (is not concentrated at the top).
Interaction	**Interaction**
• High use of nonverbal elements; voice tone, facial expression, gestures, and eye movement carry significant parts of conversation. • Verbal message is implicit; context (situation, people, nonverbal elements) is more important than words. • Verbal message is indirect; one talks around the point and embellishes it. • Communication is seen as an art form—a way of engaging someone. • Disagreement is personalized. One is sensitive to conflict expressed in another's nonverbal communication. Conflict either must be solved before work can progress or must be avoided because it is personally threatening.	• Low use of nonverbal elements. Message is carried more by words than by nonverbal means. • Verbal message is explicit. Context is less important than words. • Verbal message is direct; one spells things out exactly. • Communication is seen as a way of exchanging information, ideas, and opinions. • Disagreement is depersonalized. One withdraws from conflict with another and gets on with the task. Focus is on rational solutions, not personal ones. One can be explicit about another's bothersome behavior.

(Continued)

Table 8.1 (Continued)

High Context (HC)	Low Context (LC)
Territoriality	**Territoriality**
• Space is communal; people stand close to each other, share the same space.	• Space is compartmentalized and privately owned; privacy is important, so people stand farther apart.
Temporality	**Temporality**
• Everything has its own time. Time is not easily scheduled; needs of people may interfere with keeping to a set time. What is important is that activity gets done. • Change is slow. Things are rooted in the past, slow to change, and stable. • Time is a process; it belongs to others and to nature.	• Things are scheduled to be done at particular times, one thing at a time. What is important is that activity is done efficiently. • Change is fast. One can make change and see immediate results. • Time is a commodity to be spent or saved. One's time is one's own.
Learning	**Learning**
• Knowledge is embedded in the situation; things are connected, synthesized, and global. Multiple sources of information are used. Thinking is deductive, proceeds from general to specific. • Learning occurs by first observing others as they model or demonstrate and then practicing. • Groups are preferred for learning and problem solving. • Accuracy is valued. How well something is learned is important.	• Reality is fragmented and compartmentalized. One source of information is used to develop knowledge. Thinking is inductive, proceeds from specific to general. Focus is on detail. • Learning occurs by following explicit directions and explanations of others. • An individual orientation is preferred for learning and problem solving. • Speed is valued. How efficiently something is learned is important.

Source: What's Up With Culture? School of International Studies, University of the Pacific, Bruce La Brack, ed. (2003) available at http://www2.pacific.edu/sis/culture/

SMALL-GROUP CLASS ACTIVITY 8.3

Discussion and Exploration of the Case of Samantha

In the same small groups, discuss/explore the following areas:

1. Describe and list possible cultural strengths that Samantha or her family may have.
2. What do you think about her communication style? Do you see differences between your and Samantha's communication styles?
3. How do you want to work with her?

Cultural Identity Development of the Racially and Ethnically Diverse

The knowledge of how racial and ethnic minority clients are influenced by larger societal factors, including racism, discrimination, and inequality may guide counselors to exercise sensitivity in acknowledging the relevance of contexts in client experiences. However, we must not ignore within-group differences. One of the areas where clients of color may differ from each other is how they experience the larger social context (interaction between subjective and objective experiences), which would determine how they see themselves and how they identify with their group(s).

Members of racial and ethnic minority groups in the United States have to face the adversity of various forms of racism, and their identity development is unavoidably confined in this racist context. Living in an environment where one's own race is not as respected as that of others, a racial minority individual has to go through a series of stages from denial of racial difference between the self and others and not liking being a member of a minority race toward immersing oneself in the culture and eventually gaining a secure racial and cultural identity. Additionally, having a positive and healthy minority racial identity has to involve commitment to eliminating racism and promoting social justice for all. In the text that follows, we review a few racial/cultural/ethnic identity development models (there are many more) to illustrate the process that non-Caucasians experience.

Black Racial Identity Development

The *nigrescence* (French, meaning "the process of becoming black") theory by Cross (1995) is the most seminal theoretical foundation of Black identity development models. Through several revisions, Cross described five stages through which Black individuals living in the United States develop a sense of self as a Black person and as a multiculturalist by overcoming negative attitudes toward self and others and move from "a White frame of reference to a positive Black frame of reference" (Sue & Sue, 2013, p. 291):

> *Pre-encounter stage.* Individuals absorb beliefs and values of the dominant White culture and devalue their own Blackness. They tend to perceive the world from a White frame and consider their Blackness as undesirable. As a result, they seek to assimilate and be accepted by Whites and may distance themselves from other Blacks. Individuals at this stage often experience self-hatred and poor mental health.
>
> *Encounter stage.* Individuals begin to gain awareness that is typically precipitated by experiences that force them to acknowledge the impact of racism in life. Profound crises or events that challenged their previous thinking are often involved, such as being rejected by White friends in their social life or (in the national spectrum) the murder of Dr. Martin Luther King Jr. They realize that Whites will not view them as equals and experience a shift in worldview to focus on identifying with Blacks and feeling angry at White racism.

Immersion-emersion stage. Individuals reject White values and become immersed in African American culture. They actively seek out opportunities to explore aspects of their own history and culture, which leads to gradual development of Black pride, "but internationalization of positive attitudes toward one's own Blackness is minimal" (Sue & Sue, 2013, p. 291). The sense of pride grows, anger and guilt decrease, and a newly defined and affirmed sense of self emerges.

Internalization stage. African American individuals develop a secure and self-confident Black identity. They become comfortable being a member of a minority racial group while not feeling the need to be anti-White. They appreciate both Afrocentricity and multiculturalism and are willing to establish meaningful relationships with Whites and build coalitions with members of other oppressed groups.

Internalization-commitment stage. The commitment element at this stage refers to individuals taking action in bringing positive social changes toward equality and social justice. They attempt to translate their "personal sense of Blackness into a plan of action or a general sense of commitment" to the concerns of Blacks as a group, which is sustained over time (Cross, 1991, p. 220).

This model shows that race is an important part of a Black person's self-concept. At different stages of development, feelings about being Black may have positive or negative valance. Counselors need to consider the racial identity of African American clients and understand their experiences in context. Often confirmation, education, and empathy may be more helpful than pathologizing, correcting, or being indifferent.

To illustrate is a short dialogue between a White male counselor and a Black male client:

Counselor: At the end of our last session, you talked about the fight with your boss when he asked to see your daily record. How is that situation now?

Client: You know, he is just a piece of shit. I don't look at him. I don't look at anyone—they are all damn annoying! They think I am crazy. They don't know they are crazy!

Counselor: Who are "they?"

Client: "They" are all White dudes. They got no brain and only follow him.

Counselor: Were you able to completely avoid him without problems for your work?

Client: I don't damn care! He asked me to stay after work to talk to him. I didn't give a shit!

Counselor: Were you not afraid of being punished or even losing your job?

Client: Damn them! Dare they! I would let them have it if they do!

If we do not consider this client's racial status and racial identity stages, our clinical intuition may lead us to see a number of "problems" with him, such as a tendency of being antisocial, a lack of self-control, a generalizing thinking style, anger, and being irrational in decision making. However, the knowledge that the client is an African American from a poor neighborhood should remind us to view his behavior in his social and cultural context. There are different directions the counselor can potentially take in diagnosing and treating the client. One is the "business as usual" approach—exploring the diagnosis of antisocial behavior, focusing on anger issues and anger management, and teaching him proper thinking (e.g., avoiding generalization) and decision-making skills (e.g., not letting disliking the boss jeopardize his job security). Another direction could be the "person-in-culture" approach—focusing on validating his experiences of being treated poorly by a White boss, understanding his perspectives in the context of his Black identity and his past experience of racism, showing respect to his effort in dealing with the situation the best he could, and using the counselor's "power" as a White male to acknowledge the fight the client has been in against racism and the social oppression that the client's group (Black people) have had to endure. These two approaches no doubt will lead to different results in terms of diagnosis, intervention, and therapeutic relationship.

Minority Racial/Cultural Identity Development

To illustrate the experiences and struggles of all oppressed people in understanding themselves in the United States, Atkinson, Morten, and Sue (1998) developed a general model of minority identity development. This model assumes that cultural oppression is a common theme of nondominant minority group members' social experience and the individuals' need to understand their own heritage culture, the dominant culture, and the relationship between the two in developing their cultural identity. Five stages of development are identified, and common attitudes at each of the stages toward self, one's own minority group, others' minority groups, and the dominant group are described (see Table 8.2).

Table 8.2 The Racial/Cultural Identity Development Model

Stages of Minority Development	Attitude Toward Self	Attitude Toward Others of the Same Minority	Attitude Toward Others of a Different Minority	Attitude Toward Dominant Group
Stage 1—Conformity	Self-depreciating or neutral due to low race salience	Group-depreciating or neutral due to low race salience	Discriminatory or neutral	Group-appreciating
Stage 2—Dissonance	Conflict between self-depreciating and group-appreciating	Conflict between group-depreciating views of minority hierarchy and feelings of shared experience	Conflict between dominant-held and group-depreciating	Conflict between group-appreciating

(Continued)

Table 8.2 (Continued)

Stages of Minority Development	Attitude Toward Self	Attitude Toward Others of the Same Minority	Attitude Toward Others of a Different Minority	Attitude Toward Dominant Group
Stage 3—Resistance and immersion	Self-appreciating	Group-appreciating experiences and feelings of culturocentrism	Conflict between feelings of empathy for other minority	Group-depreciating
Stage 4—Introspection	Concern with basis of self-appreciation	Concern with nature of unequivocal appreciations	Concern with ethnocentric basis for judging others	Concern with the basis of group depreciation
Stage 5—Integrative awareness	Self-appreciating	Group-appreciating	Group-appreciating	Selective appreciation

Source: Atkinson, D. R., Morten, G., & Sue, D. W. (1998). *Counseling American minorities: A cross-cultural perspective* (5th ed). Dubuque, IA: William C. Brown. © McGraw Hill Education.

Stage 1—Conformity: acceptance of the belief of White superiority and minority inferiority. Minority individuals desire to assimilate with the dominant culture and escape from their own cultural heritage. They feel shameful for not being White and do not want to be associated with others of their own group. Low self-esteem and negative perceptions of other minority groups are common.

Stage 2—Dissonance: gradually or suddenly via a traumatic event become aware of the inconsistence between the belief-held value at the conformity stage and experienced cultural reality. Individuals experience conflict between both self-depreciating and self-appreciating attitudes about themselves and group-depreciating and group-appreciating beliefs toward members of their own minority group; additionally, they question the stereotypes previously held about other minority groups.

Stage 3—Resistance and immersion: tendency to adopt views and beliefs of own group completely and reject the dominant social and cultural values. Individuals endorse self-appreciating attitudes toward the self and group-appreciating beliefs toward others in the same group. Immersion in their own culture, ethnocentric feelings about other minority groups, and group-depreciating attitudes toward the dominant group are present at this stage.

Stage 4—Introspection: a need for a positive self-definition and autonomy emerges, and intense negative emotion (e.g., anger toward the White society) subsides. Individuals reflect on the basis of previous self-appreciating toward self, ethnocentric views of others, and group-depreciating attitudes toward the dominant group.

Stage 5—Integrative awareness: inner sense of security and freedom to appreciate aspects of diverse cultures emerges with conflicts/discomforts experienced at previous stages resolved. Individuals develop a positive self-image, strong confidence, and group pride and reach out toward different minority groups. They also experience openness to the constructive elements of the dominant culture and recognize White racism as a sickness in society and that White people are also victims.

A Reflection by a Biracial Person: Learning Who I Am

My cultural identity is important to me, but it has been a journey to understand it. As a biracial individual, I have always been conflicted as to which side of my heritage I consider my cultural identity. This conflict has often led me to feel frustrated and guilty because I sometimes do not know if I understand who I really am.

When I was growing up, I lived in a predominantly Native American community. I always knew I was Cherokee, but I did not realize how important my cultural identity was until my family moved away from our community. Suddenly, I went from being part of the majority to being the minority and in many cases the "only." After the move, I found it difficult to relate to my classmates. Even though we were the same age I felt completely different from them.

As I grew older (into junior high and high school), this feeling became increasingly more difficult to deal with. As a result, I felt angry a lot of the time because I did not understand why I always felt different. It was during this time that I realized that every part of me, from the way I thought to the way I dressed, was different from my peers. All I wanted was to feel that I fit in again, so I decided to change the way I dressed in an effort to be part of the crowd. The turquoise jewelry that I once wore with pride was replaced with something found from a local boutique. I cut my hair short and had a more stylish hairdo rather than having long hair that was symbolic of my culture. I changed everything with the hope that looking different on the outside would change the feelings that I was experiencing on the inside. Despite having changed the outside, I could never change who I was on the inside. My peers accepted me as "one of them," but I never felt like a part of the group. For many people of color, this act of changing for a world that is not theirs is an everyday occurrence. It is something they feel they must do to be accepted.

I attended an all-Native American college and once again felt at home. It was also during this time that I realized this constant difference I felt was due to my cultural identity. I began to embrace my identity as being an important part of my life and understand its effects on how I conceptualize the world around me. Today, I still feel as if the world around me tries to change me rather than accept my cultural differences. As a result, I must have a great deal of patience with those around me because of the ignorant and insensitive comments said in my presence. For this reason, when I return to my hometown I truly feel that I leave America and go home. I go home to where individuals share my cultural values and where I do not need to explain/educate those around me.

—Leigh V., a cisgender, female, biracial doctoral student in counseling psychology

Biracial and Multiracial Identity Development

A racial/ethnic/cultural identity is an integral part of any individual's identity, whether the person is a minority or majority group member. This identity development becomes more complicated if the person has two or more racial/ethnic backgrounds by birth, such as biracial or mixed or multiracial individuals. Earlier efforts by Poston (1990) and Root (1990) resulted in two widely cited biracial identity development models (mainly for White/Black biracial people).

Poston's model described five levels of experiences of biracial people. *Personal identity* refers to the identity that is independent of either parents' racial/ethnic background. *Choice of group categorization* describes those who mainly choose one parent's group membership as primary identification. Multiple factors may influence the decision about which parental background is chosen, including the social status of the specific cultural heritage, level of social support, and personal decision. *Enmeshment/denial* is the stage where individuals experience confusion and guilt over the fact that they have two racial/ethnic heritages and/or have to choose one over the other. At this stage, individuals may experience self-hate. *Appreciation* marks the stage where individuals begin to appreciate having multiple identities. Finally, when individuals reach the *integration* stage, they are able to fully appreciate their multicultural identity and existence.

Root's biracial or multiracial identity development model proposed four positive resolutions of the tensions biracial people experience. *Acceptance of the identity society assigns* shows the conformity to the societal expectations of who they are. *Identification with both or all racial groups* would require the individuals to face potential resistance from others. *Identification with a single racial group* demonstrates individuals' ability to choose one group membership independent of social pressure. *Identification as a new racial group* allows the individual to move fluidly among racial groups and identify with other biracial or multiracial people.

More recently, scholars pointed out that linear models (such as those used in most identity development theories) do not work well for biracial or multiracial individuals, and ecological models should be used to explain factors contributing to identity development (Renn, 2003). Renn proposed five patterns of identity among multiracial college students in which students hold a *monoracial identity, multiple monoracial identities, a multiracial identity, an extraracial identity,* and a *situational identity* (identifying differently in different contexts).

Immigrant Acculturation and Identity Development

One of the greatest challenges for all immigrants, especially non-White and non-Western immigrants, is related to acculturation toward the dominant American culture. The level of acculturation not only has direct implication in immigrants' efforts of making a living in the United States but also has influence on their sense of social and cultural identity (Schwartz, Montgomery, & Briones, 2006). *Immigrant acculturation* refers to a process in which immigrants adopt the beliefs and behaviors of the dominant group and can be seen as "the process of cultural change and adaptation that occurs when individuals from different cultures come into contact" (Gibson, 2001, p. 19).

Coming into contact with an unfamiliar culture and social environment, immigrants may experience various psychological challenges, including managing possible acculturation shock and acculturation stress. *Acculturation shock* can be viewed as a set of emotional responses as the result of the "loss of perceptual reinforcements from one's own culture, to new cultural stimuli which have little or no meaning, and to the misunderstanding of new and diverse experiences" (Adler, 1975, p. 13). In a new culture, individuals may feel like outsiders, be unable to be themselves, have difficulty in receiving support, and not know what and how to do things to survive or succeed in life. They may feel some or all of the following emotions: strain due to the efforts required to make psychological adaptation to the new culture; sadness over the loss of friends, profession, status, and possessions; rejection by members of the new culture; confusion regarding role, role expectations, values, and self-identity; surprise, anxiety, and even disgust and indignation after becoming aware of cultural differences; and impotence in coping with the new environment (Taft, 1977). Acculturation shock may lead to loss of communication competence, distorted self-reflections regarding feedback from others, and feeling pressure to change identity-bound behavior (Zaharna, 1989). Cultural shock is generally greater at the beginning and decreases over time.

Immigrants' cultural adjustment processes can be described through a series of stages, and the length of each stage varies depending on the individual's situations and the level of acculturation pressure. Initially, there may be a "honeymoon" period where the sojourners feel fascinated by the new culture and environment. As time goes on, they may have to face real problems in life, such as issues regarding language, transportation, employment, and so on, which can result in their feeling frustration, anxiety, or anger. They eventually achieve a certain level of recovery and acculturation based on crisis resolution and cultural learning and gradually adapt to the new culture to various degrees. During such an adjustment process, immigrants often experience *acculturation stress*, which results from stressors that are rooted in the process of acculturation and manifests symptoms such as depression, anxiety, marginalization, alienation, and identity confusion when their attempts to cope fail (Berry, 2006).

The acculturation process is comprised of two dimensions (Berry, 1997): maintenance of original cultural identity and maintenance of relations with other groups. Within these two dimensions, four categories of acculturation strategies emerge: integration, separation, assimilation, and marginalization. *Integration* refers to those individuals who value both cultural maintenance and intergroup relations. *Separation* applies to those who advocate cultural maintenance but do not value intergroup relations. *Assimilation* refers to a rejection of cultural identity and the adoption of the host culture. *Marginalization* occurs when individuals value neither cultural maintenance nor intergroup relations. Those who practice the strategy of integration are hypothesized to experience the fewest difficulties in adaptation, indicating the highest level of mental health. In other words, both their acculturation level (the degree to which an immigrant can identity and practice the host culture) and ethnic identity (the degree to which the immigrant can identify with his or her racial/ethnic group) predict immigrants' wellness.

SMALL-GROUP CLASS ACTIVITY 8.4

Discussion and Exploration of the Case of Samantha

In the same small groups, discuss and explore the following questions:

1. How would you describe Samantha's racial/ethnic/cultural identity development at the present time?
2. What unique challenges or opportunities does she have at this stage of her identity development?

Assessment, Prevention, and Intervention

Recognizing Cultural Strengths of Racial and Ethnic Minorities

Because our counseling theories are largely rooted in European cultural values, it is too easy to misdiagnose minority cultural behaviors as negative or pathological if we do not recognize their cultural strengths. It is their strengths that helped them survive and thrive in the face of unjust and unfair racism and discriminations. As counselors who invest in the well-being of minorities that have been socially disadvantaged, we will need to adopt a positive view and not readily see behaviors that vary from what is expected from the European standard as problematic. Let "be aware of biases and see clients in context" guide our clinical assessments and "validate, respect, and advocate" direct our prevention and intervention efforts. Seeing cultural strengths can translate into accurate assessments and effective prevention and intervention efforts.

Major protective factors or cultural strengths of ethnic minority groups in the United States include positive racial/ethnic identity, familial patterns with extended kin, value of collective interest, and support from their own communities. Both White counselors and counselors of color need to be reminded that many of the diagnostic tools (e.g., *Diagnostic and Statistical Manual of Mental Disorders* [*DSM*]) we have are based on mainstream cultural norms and standards and reflect a White and middle-class worldview (Jun, 2010).

Before making any diagnosis, counselors need to consider cultural factors. For instance, for ethnic minorities, relying on other members of the family for decision making or holding relatively low differentiation or blurred boundaries among family members should not be automatically viewed as signs of dysfunction. Inability to compete or be assertive does not imply low self-esteem. Being raised in a single-mother household does not automatically indicate deficit, and being taught about racism (racial socialization) does not make individuals "angry Blacks" or "paranoid Latinos." In fact, the involvement of relatives, friends, and older siblings in child rearing contributes to the building of a supportive network, the flexibility of roles, kinship bonds, and strong work ethics (McCollum, 1997). The "strong Black woman" image exemplifies pride, self-reliance, and ability to handle challenges, and "machismo Latino" signifies manhood and implies taking responsibilities. Additionally, strong religiosity has played a significant and positive role in community building and individual health among African Americans and some other oppressed minorities, and some religious behaviors, such as hearing voices, may not be a psychotic feature.

There are cognitive variables that tend to create vulnerable spots for the counselor to either misread or be misinformed in understanding ethnic clients. Hypothesis-confirming tendency based on one's own worldview and stereotype is one of them. Osmo and Rosen (2002) found evidence that hypothesis-conformity strategies led to overdiagnosis among social workers. Counselors must check their hypothesis formulation and avoid basing it on stereotypical or biased theories without awareness. Fundamental attribution error is a real threat (Ross, 1977). Without conscious effort, counselors may make a fundamental attribution error by overattributing symptoms to personal characteristics of diverse clients rather than to their situations. Thus, counselors need to adopt an information-gathering mode and avoid using quick-decision rules to assess diverse clients with the intention of not minimizing any clients' experience in their social contexts.

Respecting Racial and Ethnic Minority Clients' Worldviews and Perspectives

As discussed in Chapter 7, people from different cultures or with different racial and ethnic backgrounds may have different worldviews and see the social environment differently. In psychological assessment and treatment, lack of awareness of worldview differences may lead to harm. For instance, viewing a Black client's inability to trust authorities as pathological will not lead to healing but instead will make counseling an instrument of further perpetration. Consider the story of a 9-year-old African American boy who was sent for psychological testing by a school authority. On the test, he received the question, *What would you do if, in a cinema, you saw smoke coming in from underneath a door and you thought, "Fire!"?* He chose the answer "I will run away as fast as possible" instead of the correct answer "inform the authorities." Upon probing, he said he answered as he did "because I am afraid when police come they will think I did it." This is an example of how individuals' social experiences shape their worldviews. If he receives negative and unfair feedback for the "wrong" answer, he would not only lose the point but also be hurt in self-confidence.

"Doing no harm" is one of the utmost critical, ethical principles for our profession. Not respecting racial/ethnic minority clients' worldviews can lead to unintentional harm by our well-meaning interventions; insisting on assertiveness training for a Japanese American client who values modesty and humbleness much more than assertiveness; promoting "self-care" behavior with a Latina client for whom self-care is an alien concept; asking an Arab woman to "stand up" to her husband to gain support from him; or demanding that a Chinese client recognize and talk about her anger toward her mother are a few examples. Although it is difficult for counselors to always know their clients' worldviews, it is ultimately their responsibility to find them out. It is critical that our counseling service is oriented toward respecting clients' worldviews even if they may be different from ours and may not even appear "right" to us.

Supporting Traditional Cultural Healing Methods

Many cultures have their traditional healing methods. They may or may not fit what Western counseling professionals would endorse as effective or credible practices, and we as counselors may have various attitudes toward them. Considering that racially and ethnically diverse clients may, to various degrees, practice or believe the effectiveness of those methods, it is sensible that we stay open-minded and show willingness to incorporate them in facilitating client healing.

There are some cultural healing practices that have gained significant support from the mainstream culture. Native Americans' spiritual ceremonies and rituals such as sweat lodges, sun dances, or ghost dances, once banned, have entered formal and informal counseling and self-care practices for both Native people and others. Other examples include Chinese herbal remedies, *qi gong* (气功), and many forms of holistic practice (treating physical, mental, and spiritual issues holistically in healing). Remarkably, the East Asian traditional and spiritual practice of meditation has been formally integrated into counseling theories and practice in Western countries (e.g., Dialectic Behavioral Theory [DBT]. Acceptance and Commitment Therapy [ACT]). Yoga, originally a spiritual practice of Hinduism and Buddhism in India, has become popular worldwide.

However, there are other forms of traditional healing methods that are less understood and less accepted, such as Shamanism in Native American culture, bullet-pouring in Bulgaria (Feng, 2013), and various "superstitious" or Shamanic practices in East Asia that reportedly execute invocation, divination, dream interpretation, driving off evil spirits, and so on. Our trained scientific minds most likely have difficulty accepting the "dual world" concept implied by these practices. Nonetheless, judging clients' cultural beliefs is not our purpose—facilitating healing is. Thus, being open-minded, nonjudgmental, and respectful in hearing client stories and finding ways to integrate all client resources into counseling interventions is what multiculturally competent counselors should do.

Advocating for Social Justice Through Psychological Prevention and Intervention

Previous chapters have illustrated ways in which racial and ethnic minorities in our society have experienced mistreatment, discrimination, and injustice; and their psychological health is closely related to their social and cultural experiences. Thus, social justice should be a theme in our prevention and interventions treatment both within and outside of counseling rooms. Clients' social experience of oppression needs to be validated and accounted for in our diagnoses. Moreover, any effective treatment needs to be linked to advocating for social justice for them. Otherwise, clinical gains obtained in counseling settings are difficult to transfer to real-life situations because the larger cause of their issues (their social and cultural environment) was not addressed. This topic will be discussed in detail in Section 6.

SMALL-GROUP CLASS ACTIVITY 8.5

Discussion and Exploration of the Case of Samantha

In the same small groups, discuss and explore the following questions:

1. How does the understanding of Samantha's social context, identity development, and cultural strengths inform your clinical assessment and treatment plan for her?
2. What changes do you see in how you think about this case now from what you thought at the beginning of the chapter?
3. What are your thoughts about the need to attend to client race or ethnicity in counseling?

Summary

This chapter highlights the essentiality of considering racial and ethnic factors in working with diverse people. These factors include clients' social contexts, their racial/ethnic/cultural identity development, and their values and worldviews. Counting these factors in our assessment, prevention, and intervention efforts is necessary and imperative. Such a clinical approach is the opposite of that of the color-blind ideology discussed in Chapter 6. Counselors have to pay attention to both the social context of every person of color and the within-group differences in racial/ethnic/cultural identity development and worldviews. Every individual of color will exhibit specific cultural characteristics. This challenges counselors to exercise their multicultural consciousness and communication skills to derive an accurate understanding of the client to guide all assessment, prevention, and intervention efforts. Moreover, social justice should be a theme in all counseling activities.

Takeaway Messages

1. Unlike the popular practice in mainstream culture of avoiding talking about race or racial issues, counselors should hold racial consciousness and antiracism attitudes when working with racial/ethnic minority clients.
2. Minority identity development is a complicated and ongoing process, and every counselor has a cultural identity that influences how he or she sees clients' identities.
3. Counselors should never conceptualize clients' concerns without considering their social contexts, identity development, cultural values, and worldviews.
4. Be aware that many existing tools that are used to assess clients are culturally biased; assessment tools should be used only with sufficient consideration of clients' cultural contextual factors.
5. Remember to see clients' cultural strengths and avoid pathologizing "abnormal" behaviors.

6. Be invested in understanding communications styles of diverse people.
7. Social oppression is an everpresent contextual factor for all clients of color; thus, multicultural counseling practice needs to integrate the theme of social justice in all service activities.

Recommended Resources

Readings

American Psychological Association. (2003). Guidelines on multicultural education, training, research, practice, and organizational change for psychologists. *American Psychologist, 58*, 377–402.

Carter, R. T. (2007). Racism and psychological and emotional injury: Recognizing and assessing race-based traumatic stress. *The Counseling Psychologist, 35*, 13–94.

Neville, H. A., & Awad, G. H. (2014). Why racial color-blindness is myopic. *American Psychologist, 69*, 313–314.

Nguyen, H.-H. D., & Ryan, A. M. (2008). Does stereotype threat affect test performance of minorities and women? A meta-analysis of experimental evidence. *Journal of Applied Psychology, 93*, 6, 1314–1334.

Nigatu, H. (2013, December 9). Twenty-one racial microaggressions you hear on a daily basis [Web log post]. Retrieved from http://www.buzzfeed.com/hnigatu/racial-microagressions-you-hear-on-a-daily-basis

Planas, R. (2013, November 20). Latino activists want Texas schools to address 'institutionalized racism.' Retrieved from http://www.huffingtonpost.com/2013/11/20/mexican-american-studies-texas_n_4309955.html

Films

Milchan, A., Grisham, J., Nathanson, M., Lowry, H. (Producers), & Schumacher, J. (Director). (1996). *A time to kill* [Motion picture]. United States: Warner Brothers.

Okuefuna, D. (Producer), & Tickell, P. (Director). (2007). *Racism: A history* [Documentary]. United Kingdom: BBC Four. Available from http://topdocumentaryfilms.com/racism-history/

References

Adler, P. S. (1975). The transitional experience: An alternative view of culture shock. *Journal of Humanistic Psychology, 15*, 13–23.

The African American family. (n.d.). Retrieved from http://www.history.org/almanack/life/family/black.cfm

Atkinson, D., Morten, G., & Sue, D. (1998). *Counseling American minorities: A cross-cultural perspective* (5th ed.). Dubuque, IA: William C. Brown.

Berry, J. W. (1997). Immigration, acculturation, and adaptation. *Applied Psychology: An International Review, 46*, 5–34.

Berry, J. W. (2006). Acculturative stress. In P. Wong & L. Wong (Eds.), *Handbook of multicultural perspectives on stress and coping* (pp. 287–298). New York, NY: Springer.

Brown v. Board of Educ., 347 U.S. 483 (1954).

Censky, A. (2011, September 2). August jobs report: Hiring grinds to a halt. In Time Warner (Producer), *CNN money*. Retrieved from http://money.cnn.com/2011/09/02/news/economy/jobs_report_unemployment/index.htm?iid=EL

Cross, W. E., Jr. (1991). *Shades of Black: Diversity in African-American identity.* Philadelphia, PA: Temple University Press.

Cross, W. E., Jr. (1995). The psychology of nigrescence: Revising the Cross model. In J. G. Ponterotto, J. M. Casas, L. A. Suzuki, & C. M. Alexander (Eds.), *Handbook of multicultural counseling* (pp. 93–122). Thousand Oaks, CA: Sage.

Feng, Y. Y. J. (2013, April 17). My experience with the bullet pourer [Web log post]. Retrieved from https://yinyangjinfeng.wordpress.com/2013/04/17/my-experience-with-the-bullet-pourer-%D0%BB%D0%B5%D0%B5%D0%BD%D0%B5-%D0%BD%D0%B0-%D0%BA%D1%83%D1%80%D1%88%D1%83%D0%BC/#more-665

Gao, G., & Ting-Toomey, S. (1998). *Communicating effectively with the Chinese*. Thousand Oaks, CA: Sage.

Garrett, M. T. (2006). When Eagle speaks: Counseling Native Americans. In C. C. Lee (Ed.), *Multicultural issues in counseling: New approaches to diversity* (pp. 25–53). Alexandria, VA: American Counseling Association.

Garrett, M. T., & Portman, E. A. A. (2011). *Counseling Native Americans*. Belmont, CA: Cengage.

Gibson, M. A. (2001). Immigrant adaptation and patterns of acculturation. *Human Development, 44*, 19–23.

Hall, E. T. (1976). *Beyond culture*. New York, NY: Anchor Books.

Hsieh, S. (2014, March 21). Fourteen disturbing stats about racial inequality in American public schools [Web log post]. Retrieved from http://www.thenation.com/blog /178958/14-disturbing-stats-about-racial-inequality-american-public-schools#

Jha, A. (2013, June 4). Racial disparities in health care: Justin Dimick and coauthors' June *Health Affairs* study [Web log post]. Retrieved from http://healthaffairs.org/blog/2013/06/04/racial-disparities-in-health-care-justin-dimick-and-coauthors-june-health-affairs-study

Jun, H. (2010). *Social justice, multicultural counseling, and practice: Beyond a conventional approach*. Los Angeles, CA: Sage.

Landale, N. S., Oropesa, R. S., & Bradatan, C. (2006). Hispanic families in the United States: Family structure and process in an era of family change. In M. Tienda & F. Mitchell (Eds.), *Hispanics and the future of America* (pp. 138–178). Washington, DC: National Academies Press.

Macartney, S., Bishaw, A., & Fontenot, K. (2013, February). *Poverty rates for selected detailed race and Hispanic groups by state and place: 2007-2011 American Community Survey Briefs*. Retrieved from http://www.census.gov/prod/2013pubs/acsbr11-17.pdf

McCollum, V. J. C. (1997). Evolution of the African American family personality: Considerations for family therapy. *Journal of Multicultural Counseling and Development, 25*, 219–229.

Mishel, L. (2009, July 15). State-by-state unemployment trends by race, ethnicity and gender: National overview [Conference call]. Retrieved from http://s3.epi.org/files/page//pdf/ib257_states.pdf

Mokhtari, R. (2014, June 2). Beyond zero tolerance: Promising alternatives in school discipline [Web log post]. Retrieved from http://www.hrc.org/blog/entry/beyond-zero-tolerance-promising-alternatives-in-school-discipline

Mullins, D. (2013, September 25). Six decades after Brown ruling, U.S. schools still segregated. *Aljazeera America*. Retrieved from http://america.aljazeera.com/articles/2013/9/25/56-years-after-littlerockusschoolssegregatedbyraceandclass.html

Ohlemacher, S. (2006, November 14). Persistent race disparities found. *The Washington Post*. Retrieved from www.washingtonpost.com

Oppenheimer, V. K. (2000). The continuing importance of men's economic position in marriage formation. In L. J. Waite (Ed.), *The ties that bind: Perspectives on marriage and cohabitation* (pp. 283–301). New York, NY: Aldine de Gruyter.

Osmo, R., & Rosen, A. (2002). Social workers' strategies for treatment hypothesis testing. *Social Work Research, 26*, 9–18.

Paul, K. I., & Moser, K. (2009). Unemployment impairs mental health: Meta-analyses. *Journal of Vocational Behavior, 74*, 264–282.

Pfeiffer & Company. (n.d.). *The 1993 annual: Developing human resources*. Retrieved from http://www2.pacific.edu/sis/culture/pub/Context_Cultures_High_and_Lo.htm

Poston, W. S. C. (1990). The biracial identity development model: A needed addition. *Journal of Counseling & Development, 69*, 152–155.

Renn, K. A. (2003). Understanding the identities of mixed-race college students through a developmental ecology lens. *Journal of College Student Development, 44*, 383–403.

Root, M. P. P. (1990). Resolving "other" status: Identity development of biracial individuals. In L. S. Brown & M. P. P. Root (Eds.), *Diversity and complexity in feminist therapy* (pp. 185–205). Binghamton, NY: Haworth.

Ross, L. (1977). The intuitive psychologist and his shortcomings: Distortions in the attribution process. In L. Berkowitz (Ed.), *Advances in experimental social psychology* (Vol. 10, pp. 173–220). New York, NY: Academic Press.

Rowles, J., & Duan, C. (2012, January). Perceived racism and encouragement among African American adults. *Journal of Multicultural Counseling and Development, 40*(1), 11–23. doi:10.1111/j.2161-1912.2012.00002.x

Satcher, D. (2001). *Mental health: Culture, race, and ethnicity, A supplement to mental health: A report of the surgeon general.* Retrieved from http://www.nami.org/Content/NavigationMenu/Find_Support/Multicultural_Support/Annual_Minority_Mental_Healthcare_Symposia/DisparitiesOverview.pdf

Schwartz, S. J., Montgomery, M. J., & Briones, E. (2006). The role of identity in acculturation among immigrant people: Theoretical propositions, empirical questions, and applied recommendations. *Human Development, 49,* 1–30.

Sue, D. W., & Sue, D. (2013). *Counseling the culturally diverse: Theory and practice* (6th ed.). Hoboken, NJ: Wiley.

Taft, R. (1977). Coping with unfamiliar cultures. In N. Warren (Ed.), *Studies in cross-cultural psychology* (Vol. 1, pp. 121–153). London, England: Academic Press.

U.S. Bureau of the Census. (2006, July 1). *Vintage 2006: National tables.* Retrieved from http://www.census.gov/popest/data/historical/2000s/vintage_2006/

U.S. Department of Education. (2014, January 8). *Joint "Dear Colleague" letter.* Retrieved from http://www2.ed.gov/about/offices/list/ocr/letters/colleague-201401-title-vi.html

Valenzuela, A., & Dornbusch, S. M. (1994). Familism and social capital in the academic achievement of Mexican origin and Anglo adolescents. *Social Science Quarterly. 75,* 18–36.

Vega, W. A. (1995). The study of Latino families. In R. Zambrana (Ed.), *Understanding Latino families: Scholarship, policy, and practice* (pp. 3–17). Thousand Oaks, CA: Sage.

Williams, D. R., Yu, Y., Jackson, J. S., & Anderson, N. B. (1997). Racial differences in physical and mental health: Socio-economic status, stress and discrimination. *Journal of Health Psychology, 2,* 335–351.

Wilson, B. (n.d.). *Chapter 1 lecture: High-context and low-context culture styles.* Retrieved from http://www.marin.edu/buscom/index_files/Page605.htm

Wilson, C. C., II, & Gutiérrez, F. (1995). *Race, multiculturalism, and the media: From mass to class communication* (2nd ed.). Thousand Oaks, CA: Sage.

Wilson, V. (2015, January 29). After a year of strong job growth, recovery remains uneven: Southern states lead with smallest racial unemployment rate gaps in fourth quarter of 2014. *Economic Policy Institute.* Retrieved from http://www.epi.org/publication/state-unemployment-by-race-fourth-quarter-2014/

Zaharna, R. (1989). Self-shock: The double-binding challenge of identity. *International Journal of Intercultural Relations, 13,* 501–525.

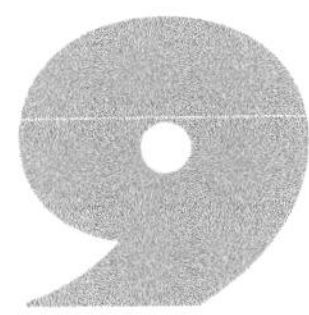

Working With Diversity in Gender and Sexual Orientation Contexts

No culture can live if it attempts to be exclusive.

—Mohandas K. Gandhi

CHAPTER OVERVIEW

This chapter provides a discussion of gender and sexual orientation diversity and further challenges counseling professionals to stay current and informed in order to practice ethically and effectively, which includes understanding the breadth of treatment concerns common to working with sexual orientation, gender, and multiple cultural identities. Scholars have noted a diverse population that now includes lesbian, gay, bisexual, transgender, queer, questioning, curious, interested, allied, and intersexed (LGBTQQCIAI) persons, and they have concluded that counseling practitioners may lack the necessary skills to work effectively in this rapidly changing domain of practice. As the number of gender- and sexual-identity-diverse clients who seek treatment continues to increase in school, community mental health, and university counseling settings, counseling professionals must be well trained and also be aware of the impact that societal discrimination and prejudice have on their clients' mental well-being. Therefore, in this chapter we consider the important role of gender and sexual orientation in working with culturally diverse clients and discuss strategies for assisting counselor trainees with providing ethically and culturally sensitive therapeutic interventions.

SELF-ASSESSMENT OF PRE-EXISTING AWARENESS AND KNOWLEDGE

- How competent am I at addressing issues related to gender and sexual orientation with culturally diverse clients?
- How well do I understand the important role of gender and sexual orientation in the psychological health of culturally diverse clients?
- How competent am I at integrating the gender and/or sexual orientation experiences of my clients when attempting to understand them and their issues?
- How competent am I at providing interventions that effectively address clients' concerns in the context of their gender and sexual orientation?
- How competent am I at using my own gender and sexual orientation context as a helping agent in working with clients?
- How do I describe the development of my gender and sexual identity?
- How does my gender and sexual identity development influence my work with people of different gender and/or sexual identities from me?

LEARNING OBJECTIVES

After reading this chapter, students will be able to do the following:

1. Understand the relevance of gender and sexual orientation statuses (for both the counselor and clients) in establishing effective therapeutic relationships
2. Conceptualize clients' concerns and understand their gender and sexual orientation experiences even if they do not come to counseling to address those experiences per se
3. Recognize and consider the relevance of gender and sexual orientation when delivering psychological interventions
4. Understand the unjust and damaging impact of genderism and heterosexism on the life and health of gender variant and sexual minority group members
5. Recognize the importance of counselors' gender and sexual identity development in their ability to provide effective counseling to gender variant and sexual minority populations

A Reflection of a White, Queer, Nonbinary Transgender Person

What does it mean to be a White, queer, nonbinary transgender person in this society?

I cannot ignore or deny the fact that I have White privilege and that I live in a society that offers unearned benefits to all White people regardless of their gender or sexuality. And I am grateful that I live in an era where female-bodied individuals are not required to wear dresses, elaborate hairstyles, and makeup. Just a few weeks ago I was looking at my mother's high school yearbooks, and she was telling me that there was no option for women to wear anything but skirts or dresses. She told me that a male teacher who walked with a cane would routinely slide his cane up the legs of female students. So I am grateful for the feminist movement and all activist movements that have fought for woman-identified and/or female-bodied equality.

While never taking for granted how far our society has come in terms of its perception and treatment of women, I still feel we have a long way to go before transgender and queer-identified people are taken seriously and treated with respect and understanding. Yes, it's great that same-sex marriage is gaining in popularity and "Don't Ask, Don't Tell" is gone, but in my opinion, there are other problems that are just as important, such as lesbian/gay/bisexual/trans/queer (LGBTQ) homelessness, transgender oppression, hyper-masculinity, and so forth. These problems cannot be solved by passing a law; they are deeply set in our society's prejudices and perceptions—based entirely on sexism and transphobia.

We have boxed ourselves into a binary system (gay/straight, male/female), and with that restrictive system comes expectations that few people can naturally live up to. I am one of those people. It is very difficult for me to live in this society as someone who does not identify with one of the two binary genders. I am constantly irritated by the "him or her," the "he or she," the "boys and girls," the "male/female" everything. Everything in our society is "this or that," and for someone who is neither this nor that, I feel completely invisible and ignored.

What experiences (e.g., school, home, community) have you had that made you feel different?

Before I knew what transgender or gender nonconforming meant, the only identity marker that made sense to me was lesbian. I knew I was attracted to women but I also knew that my gender identity did not fit neatly into the "butch" or 'femme" lesbian binary. Ever since I came out at the age of 19, I had this dilemma, and although the lesbian community welcomes gender nonconformity in the shape of butch women, I was a gender-nonconforming person without the hardness, without the dominance, without the uber-masculinity of the butch women I knew. I remember taking copious numbers of online quizzes in my college years to figure out what my lesbian label really was. Most of the time it came back with 'soft butch,' which I halfheartedly accepted as the most accurate (but not completely accurate) label for my gender identity/expression.

(Continued)

(Continued)

One particular instance stands out in my mind as a moment when I consciously realized that my gender was different from other women. About 10 years ago I was working for a political nonprofit with other progressive folks. One night we had a "girls night" gathering where we ate dinner and drank lots of wine and talked about things that women talk about when they get together. Even though sexuality was a nonissue (straight and lesbian women were both in attendance), I still felt entirely out of place, like an alien in a land where people assumed I was human. While the women talked exuberantly about dresses, high heels, makeup, and other feminine expressions/ways they move through the world as women, I just sat there dumbfounded. In that moment, I had a small revelation that my gender identity was not like theirs. Although my body is physiologically female, I had no other common ground with those women. Around that time in my life, I was trying really hard to fit into the feminine box. I would begrudgingly buy feminine clothing, I would attempt to wear makeup on occasion, and I would shame myself over the fact that I felt strongly against wearing a skirt or dress to formal events (What else was I supposed to wear? Dressing in drag was not my thing either.). Although this experience was a realization that I was very different, it also caused a lot of internal conflict, a lot of internalized shame and frustration that I didn't fit into the traditional "woman" box . . . even the "butch" one.

Just a couple of weeks ago I was standing in a parking lot with three new friends, and one of them commented on another's high-heeled boots. "I just love all of your shoes," she said. All three women continued to ooh and aah jealously over this woman's shoes, which are all high heeled and quite feminine. I just stood there in silence with an uncomfortable smile on my face. It's not that I think her shoes are ugly; I just have absolutely no interest in wishing I could wear them or thinking they are anything particularly important to emphasize.

I have lots of friends who are female-to-male (FTM) and have undergone medical transition. I feel as if they should be more accepting of me than the general public, but more often than not, they are not inclusive, and they refuse to accept me as a transgender-identified person. I once had a heated conversation with a trans man who insisted that trans people like me (female-bodied but not wanting to transition) are hurting the feminist cause *and* the transgender cause because we are inhabiting a space that is neither woman nor man. He argued, "How can the identity of woman become more inclusive if people like you refuse the label?" I tried to explain to him that even if the identity of *woman* was expanded to include and accept masculine women, I still would not feel like or identify as a woman. As sure as he is that he is not a woman, that is how sure I am. Yet because I do not feel a medical transition is the right solution for me, I am somehow doing a disservice to the feminist and transgender movements by not identifying as a woman. My identity is not a political choice—I truly do not feel gendered in either direction.

Because I do not feel a medical transition is the right solution for me, I am excluded from safe spaces that are only open to FTM individuals. Many of my friends are trans men, and I am constantly excluded from their gatherings and excursions that are exclusively for trans men. I feel entirely uncomfortable with gatherings that are exclusively feminine women; I am excluded from FTM spaces because I am not transitioning; I do not feel a shared experience with male-to-female (MTF) individuals. Where is my community? Where do I find kindred spirits, role models, or friends who understand and accept my gender identity?

What experiences have you had that are due to being different (in terms of your interactions with mainstream society)?

Shopping for clothes and shoes is a frustrating and sometimes even traumatic experience for me. Clothing stores are divided into women's and men's clothes, and almost every single clothing manufacturer assumes that female-bodied individuals want to wear frilly, low-cut, dainty, or otherwise assumedly "feminine" clothes. I do not want to wear any of these things, and yet most men's clothes do not fit me because I am only 5'3" and have very noticeable curves. And it is not true that I want to wear all men's fashion; I feel just as ridiculous in a three-piece suit as I do in a dress. I am grateful that casual clothes are typically more androgynous or nongender specific, which is probably why I highly prefer to wear a T-shirt and jeans or pants to almost any occasion, even if it is not appropriate attire. How do I dress formally and/or professionally if the gendered clothing options all feel ridiculous and uncomfortable?

Because I am not and do not wish to transition from female to male, it is very difficult for me to explain to new people that I meet at school and work that I do not wish to be called a "lady" or "miss" or "girl" and so forth. I often do not say anything and silently wince in discomfort when friends address me and a group of women as "ladies" or "girls." I am frustrated with myself for not speaking up and saying that I do not like being addressed as such, but at the same time, I am tired of calling attention to it over and over again, and there are no alternatives that are entirely appropriate—I don't want to be called "sir" or "boy" and so on. I just want to be called by my name, without a gendered pronoun or adjective attached. I don't want to be seen as being different or a contrarian, so most of the time I simply do not say anything at all. It frustrates me that there is such a lack of understanding about gender(s) beyond the binary and that I automatically get lumped into all things female/feminine.

—Eli, a graduate student

REFLECTION AND DISCUSSION QUESTIONS 9.1

Your Thoughts on the Gender Binary System and Culturally Competent Counseling

1. Given that the binary construction of gender (male/female) and sexuality (gay/straight) pervade American culture, what thoughts and attitudes do you hold about persons possessing a fluid gender and sexual identity?
2. If Eli were your client, how comfortable and competent would you feel working with someone who lives outside the dominant binary gender system? What challenges, if any, might you encounter and why?

(Continued)

(Continued)

3. Eli does not identify as either man or woman and consequently does not want to be called *lady*, *miss*, or *girl*, nor *sir* or *boy*. Instead Eli prefers to be called *Eli* without reference to a gendered pronoun or adjective. How might you use Eli's lived experiences to educate yourself and others about gender and sexual fluidity and especially those who identify as transgender, gender nonconforming, and/or genderqueer?
4. What would you say to your fellow counselor-in-training who expressed frustration when learning that his client identified as genderqueer? Your colleague believes that people fall into one of two boxes (i.e., male or female), and although you can switch the boxes such that you can be a boy who wants to be a girl and a girl who wants to be a boy, you can't ever fall outside the boxes (i.e., neither male nor female) or change the boxes constantly (go back and forth between maleness and femaleness).

Understanding Sexual Orientation and Gender Identity

The LGBTQQCIAI population is rapidly growing in the caseloads of counseling professionals, yet mental health professions have historically exhibited heterocentric and homophobic biases and prejudices toward nonsex or gender-normative orientations and often fail to validate lesbian/gay/bisexual (LGB) individuals (Pachankis & Goldfried, 2004). As discussed in earlier chapters, heterosexism has been a victimizing context for these individuals, and social injustice has inundated their life experiences. We have to make counseling one place where LGBTQQCIAI people can feel safe, understood, respected, and helped.

Sexual orientation and gender identity have become increasingly complex with everexpanding constructs (DeAngelis, 2002). More specifically, DeAngelis (2002) commented on the extended evolution of these constructs and particularly noted that many lesbian/gay/bisexual/trans (LGBT) youth now call themselves *queer* as a blanket term for their community, and the expression and acceptance of *genderqueer* or fluid gender identities are much more common for today's youth than in past decades. Counselors who fail to recognize and understand the complex and expanding constructions of gender and sexual identities will be limited in their work effectiveness and even risk causing harm.

Lesbian, Gay, and Bisexual Identity Development

The early understanding of LGB identity development was reflected in different stage models (e.g., Cass, 1979; Troiden, 1979) that captured the resolution of internal conflicts related to being LGB and the coming-out process. As described, LGB individuals typically begin with using multiple defense strategies to block recognition of personal feelings of same-sex attraction, which can cause negative consequences for their mental health. Many of them will experience a gradual process in recognizing and accepting their same-sex feelings, which is then followed by a period of emotional and behavioral experimentation with same-sex partners. They may experience identity crisis with the first same-sex-relationship breakup and move to a higher level of acceptance of nonheterosexual feelings after dealing with the crisis. Gradually, "a sense of identity as lesbian or gay becomes internally integrated and is viewed as a positive aspect of self" (Bilodeau & Renn, 2005, p. 26). Scholars tend to view coming out as a fluid process with starts, stops, and backtracking.

Criticisms about these stage models include that they do not reflect bisexual identity development process accurately and fail to address intersectionality of identities related to all dimensions of diversity. Research has revealed differences in LGB identity development across race and ethnicity, social class, gender, gender identity, nationality, faith development, and physical ability (Bilodeau & Renn, 2005). To account for the complexity and fluidity of nonheterosexual-identity development, D'Augelli (1994) presented a "life span" model that identified six identity processes:

- Exiting heterosexuality
- Developing a personal LGB identity
- Developing an LGB social identity
- Becoming an LGB offspring
- Developing an LGB intimacy status
- Entering an LGB community

These processes are not ordered in stages and can operate independently. Individuals may experience development in any of these processes at various degrees at a given time.

Gender Identity Development

Gender reflects the social norms of what is regarded as feminine and masculine. Carroll, Gilroy, and Ryan (2002) noted the important distinction between the terms *sex* and *gender*. Whereas sex refers to the cluster of biological, chromosomal, and anatomical determinants of male and female, gender, which is unrelated to anatomy, encompasses how people identify themselves as masculine or feminine and their understanding of their own biology and morphology (Fausto-Sterling, 2000; Roughgarden, 2004). *Gender identity* refers to one's self-identification as man, woman, transgender, or some other categorization. Specifically, Carl Bushong (1995), the pioneer of the Tampa gender identity program, explained gender identity as follows:

> Gender identity is one's *subjective* sense of one's own sex. Like pain, it is unambiguously felt but one is unable to prove or display it to others. One's subjective gender is just as real and immalleable as one's physical gender but unfortunately not recognized in our culture. When one's *gender identity* does not match their *physical gender*, the individual is termed gender dysphoric. Like minority sexual orientation, gender dysphoria is not pathological, but a natural aberration occurring within the population.

Scholars agree that gender is complex and that the rigid binary conceptualization of gender does not sufficiently explain the myriad ways of human experience (Davidson, 2007; Sausa, 2005). Counseling professionals must be careful not to draw conclusions about one's sexual orientation based on adherence to conventional notions of masculinity and femininity. In other words, counseling professionals should not assume a client is gay because he does not portray a conventionally masculine persona, nor should the practitioner assume that an atypical gender client is transgender (i.e., desires to be the opposite biological sex) (Schneider, Brown, & Glassgold, 2002).

Similar to sexual orientation being understood as a continuum, Eyler and Wright (1997) proposed a gender framework for understanding the multiplicity of gender identifications that exist. Their framework explains gender identification along a continuum ranging from female-based to male-based identities, with *bi-gendered* (i.e., alternating between feeling/acting like a woman and feeling/acting like a man) identities at the center. They refer to their model as an individually based gender continuum. In actuality, the authors' scheme represents nine discreet and separate possible categories of gender rather than a continuum with continuous gradations or overlap between individual differences of gender. Although the argument has been made that a continuous model is needed, Eyler and Wright's model represents a step forward and in the right direction. The authors also recognized the importance of including the "other-gendered" and "ungendered" options in their 9-point gender framework. See Table 9.1 for their gender identification scaled on a continuum with nine defining points.

Table 9.1 An Individually Based Gender Continuum

Female	I have always considered myself to be a woman (or girl).
Female with maleness	I currently consider myself to be a woman, but at times I have thought of myself as really more of a man (or boy).
Gender-blended, predominant female	I consider myself gender-blended because I consider myself (in some significant way) to be both a woman and a man, but I act somehow more of a woman.
Other-gendered	I am neither a woman nor a man but a member of some other gender.
Ungendered	I am neither a woman, a man, or a member of any other gender.
Bi-gendered	I consider myself bi-gendered because sometimes I feel (or act) more like a woman and other times more like a man or sometimes like both a woman and a man.
Gender-blended, predominant male	I consider myself gender-blended because I consider myself (in some significant way) to be both a man and a woman but somehow more of a man.
Male with femaleness	I currently consider myself to be a man, but at times I have thought of myself as really more of a woman (or girl).
Male	I have always considered myself to be a man (or boy).

Source: Eyler and Wright (1997). Gender identification and sexual orientation among genetic females with gender-blended self-perception in childhood and adolescence. *International Journal of Transgenderism,* 1(1), 37-51.

Transgender Identity Development

Scholars have viewed *transgender* as an inclusive category for a wide range of identities, including transsexuals, transvestites, male and female impersonators, drag kings and queens, male-to-female (MTF) persons, female-to-male (FTM) persons, cross-dressers, gender benders, gender variants, gender nonconformings, and ambiguously gendered persons (Bilodeau & Renn, 2005). It should be noted that these labels are commonly used in the United States and reflect Western medical and psychiatric perspectives. In some non-Western cultures, transgender identities are defined to reflect cultural norms (e.g., Besnier, 1993).

Transgender people have been greatly pathologized by the American psychiatric profession that deemed their identity as a *disorder* through various editions of its *Diagnostic and Statistical Manual of Mental Disorders* (*DSM*). This reinforces the gender binary (gender binarism) belief and ideology in our culture and disorders those who do not conform to this discriminatory system. As a result, there are instances of significant prejudice, negativity, violence, and social injustice toward transgender people in our society. Although in the most recent and fifth edition of the *DSM*, *gender dysphoria* replaced *gender identity disorder* to refer to transgender people, arguably, some trans people may still feel *disordered* and/or *pathologized* since a diagnosis is needed to pursue physical/legal transition. In a qualitative study conducted by Brown, Maragos, Lee, Davidson, and Dashjian (2015), some FTM adults regarded gender dysphoria as a medical condition (i.e., birth defect) rather than a mental health issue. Concerns such as this could make the identity development of trans people challenging.

Working Ethically and Effectively With Sexual Minorities

Scholars have noted that because of the transformations associated with sexual and gender identities, counseling professionals may be unprepared to work effectively and ethically with LGBTQQCIAI clients, including those who reflect gender blending and fluid gender identities (Anhalt, Morris, Scotti, & Cohen, 2003; Biaggio, Orchard, Larson, Petrino, & Mihara, 2003; Schneider et al., 2002). More specifically, as counseling professionals, we have been trained in a heterocentric society in a historically heterocentric profession, and our training programs have provided only minimal training on the clinical concerns presented by LGB clients in therapy (Anhalt et al., 2003).

Mental health professionals are thus challenged to develop and maintain competence in their delivery of services to culturally diverse clients. It is imperative that practitioners consider the distress that homophobic bias and antigay attitudes can cause LGB clients. Failure to do so may lead to unsubstantiated attributions regarding the cause and source of distress for the LGB individual seeking counseling. Counseling trainees and professionals who acknowledge their own homophobia and/or implicit bias against LGB individuals are encouraged to seek assistance from an experienced, gay-affirmative supervisor.

Training Issues

Developing competency for working with sexual orientation and gender identity issues requires that practitioners are familiar with terms and definitions that are essential to appropriate therapeutic responses. In other words, the counselor who is asked by a client, "Am I gay/lesbian/ bisexual/queer?" will be unprepared to help the client engage in the necessary exploration if the counselor is unfamiliar or uncomfortable with the terminology. Similarly, a counselor may not respond appropriately to clients who discuss the challenges they face in the workplace because of their fluid gender identity if the counselor is unclear about the meaning of this term.

Professional concern exists regarding the adequacy of counseling professionals' training and competency to work with LGBT clients. In a study conducted by Bidell (2005), counseling students revealed that their training programs did not prepare them to work competently with LGB clients. It is also important to note that limited research has considered the effectiveness of various interventions for working with LGB clients or the type and quality of training that is being delivered (Kocarek & Pelling, 2003). Researchers have pointed out that systematic training on LGBT issues is critical if mental health professionals are to provide quality services to these populations (Firestein, 1996; Greene, 1994).

In accordance with the core curriculum requirements set forth by the Council for Accreditation of Counseling and Related Educational Programs (CACREP, 2001), CACREP-accredited counseling programs must provide social and cultural diversity training and experiences (see Sec. 2, K2). Training that includes sexual and gender identity competency can decrease homophobic prejudice and raise support for the rights of lesbians, gay men, and other sexual and gender minority clients (Case & Stewart, 2010).

Given that sexual orientation and gender identity are different phenomena and require different competencies (Carroll et al., 2002), we will begin with a discussion of sexual orientation counselor competency followed by a discussion of competency related to gender identity concerns. Although transgender individuals are commonly included as members of the LGB community, their trans status is not about sexual orientation but rather gender congruence. As such, in our discussion of sexual orientation competency, we will be referring to clients who are LGB. Competency for working with transgender, intersex, and clients of gender fluidity will be considered when discussing gender identity.

Sexual Orientation

Numerous terms have been used to describe sexuality, and these terms are often used interchangeably: *sexual orientation, affectional identity, affectional preference, sexual identity,* and *sexual preference*, to name a few (APA, 2001; Worthington, 2004). Sexual orientation refers to the sex or sexes of persons to whom one is sexually and affectionally attracted (Schneider et al., 2002). Sexual orientation is further described by Schneider et al. as an innate predisposition and that although sexual orientation, in reality, is a continuous rather than a dichotomous variable, individuals of Western culture tend to identify with one of three sexual orientation categories: gay/lesbian, bisexual, or heterosexual (see Table 9.2).

Table 9.2 Sexual Orientation and Nonbinary Categories

Sexual Orientations	**Nonbinary Gender**
Asexual	Androphilia and gynephilia
Bisexual	Pansexuality
Heterosexual	Polysexuality
Gay/Lesbian	Intersexuality
	Third gender

Even though most people are primarily oriented toward one sex, they may possess some attraction toward the other sex. That is, a same-sex-pairing attraction does not presume the absence of attractions to the opposite sex or unwillingness to engage in heterosexual sexual behavior from time to time (Schneider et al., 2002). The second author of this text is reminded of a self-identified lesbian friend who, during a social outing, pointed to a man in the room and stated, "He is my male type." Substantial literature has documented that self-identified gay men and lesbians have had heterosexual encounters (Kinsey, Pomeroy, & Martin, 1948).

The notion that one's identified sexual orientation may not be consistently congruent with one's sexual behaviors, cognitions, and fantasies may be particularly common in certain cultures (Zamora-Hernandez & Patterson, 1996). For example, the term *on the down low* refers to Black men who have sex with men (MSM) and women (i.e., bisexually active) but who do not self-identify as gay or disclose their same-sex attraction and behaviors to their main female sex partners, families, or friends (Millett, Malebranche, Mason, & Spikes, 2005). It has also been noted that in some cultures a gay identity may be reserved for persons who take on specific sexual roles. For instance, a man who is sexually aroused only by men and is the one who penetrates and never allows men to orally or anally penetrate him does not identify as gay but rather identifies as a heterosexual man who allows gay men to have sex with him (Zamora-Hernandez & Patterson, 1996).

In his research on sexual orientation, Alfred Kinsey and his colleagues (1948) developed the Kinsey scale, which attempts to describe a person's sexual orientation using a 6-point scale based on behaviors, psychological responses, and physical attractions ranging from exclusively heterosexual to exclusively homosexual. The work of Kinsey et al. (1948) illuminated the complexities of sexual orientation and challenged the simplicity of a dichotomous model based primarily on physiological arousal. See Table 9.3 for a full description of the Kinsey scale categories.

Table 9.3 Kinsey Scale Classifications

Rating	Description
0	Exclusively heterosexual
1	Predominantly heterosexual, only incidentally homosexual
2	Predominantly heterosexual, but more than incidentally homosexual
3	Equally heterosexual and homosexual
4	Predominantly homosexual, but more than incidentally heterosexual
5	Predominantly homosexual, only incidentally heterosexual
6	Exclusively homosexual
X	Nonsexual

Source: Kinsey, A. C., Pomeroy, W. B., & Martin, C. E. (1948). Sexual behavior in the human male. *Journal of Clinical Psychology*, *4*, 314–314.

Sexual Orientation and Counselor Competency

In order for counselors to provide ethical and effective counseling services to LGB individuals, couples, and families, they must develop and demonstrate specific attitude, skill, and knowledge competencies (Fassinger & Richie, 1997; Israel & Selvidge, 2003; Kocarek & Pelling, 2003). Because LGB clients experience injustices and prejudices different from racial/ethnic minorities, it is extremely important that counseling professionals have knowledge of LGB sociocultural history and biases in the mental health system. Moreover, counselors' delivery of competent services to LGB clients will require that they are aware of their own attitudes and prejudices regarding same-sex pairings (Israel & Selvidge, 2003).

Counseling professionals are encouraged to obtain a copy of the *Guidelines for Psychotherapy with Lesbian, Gay, and Bisexual Clients* developed by Division 44/Committee on Lesbian, Gay, and Bisexual Concerns Joint Task Force on Guidelines for Psychotherapy with Lesbian, Gay, and Bisexual Clients. These guidelines originally appeared in the December 2000 issue of *American Psychologist* (Vol. 55, No. 12) and address attitudes toward LGB clients, diversity issues, relationship and family dynamics important to LGB clients, and ways to increase training in LGB issues. One very specific goal of these guidelines is to provide counseling professionals with basic information and references for working with LGB clients.

In a survey of clinical psychologists, Murphy, Rawlings, and Howe (2002) noted that although many of the clinical concerns of LGB clients are similar to those of heterosexual clients, special training on LGB concerns is still needed because of the significance of internalized homophobia with presenting issues such as low self-esteem, mood disorders, anxiety disorders, and sexual dysfunction. In other words, societal heterocentrism manifests itself at an individual level when the hostility and prejudice that society exhibits toward LGB persons is internalized (Pachankis & Goldfried, 2004). Therefore, practitioners are likely to do their clients a disservice if the underlying internalized homophobia is not addressed. Murphy and colleagues further noted that practitioners are relying on literature about lesbians and gay men to guess how to intervene effectively with bisexual clients. Certainly more research specific to the unique needs of bisexual clients is needed, and training programs are encouraged to include specific training for working with bisexual clients and also to be aware that some trainees and practitioners may hold dichotomous thinking about sexual orientation, which will need to be addressed.

Counseling Competencies

Issues that have been documented as important in the lives of LGB clients and which counseling professionals will need to know about when providing services to this population include LGB identity development, parenting, and romantic and family relationships (Pachankis & Goldfried, 2004). As previously noted, practitioners must not assume that their LGB clients' problems are rooted in their sexual orientation but instead must consider the extent to which their problems arise from society's negative reactions to nonheterosexual orientations. Increasing the multicultural competence of counselors working with LGB clients will first require that trainees familiarize themselves with basic knowledge regarding LGB issues. Simply gaining knowledge, however, does not necessarily translate to increased competency. Trainees must also demonstrate awareness and skill in working with LGB clients.

Knowledge

Counselors who are LGB-affirmative recognize that LGB clients present unique counseling issues, and they act as advocates for their LGB clients. Specifically, counselors help clients face the challenges of possessing a sexual minority status and support them in their efforts to act on societal issues that perpetuate their disenfranchisement. Moreover, LGB-affirmative counselors provide clients with coping skills for societal issues that cannot be successfully challenged and are aware of resources available to LGB clients. Examples of resources suggested by Pachankis and Goldfried (2004) might include (a) gay-straight alliances in middle and senior high schools and on college and university campuses; (b) religious groups such as LGB synagogues, the network of Roman Catholic LGB individuals, and Dignity/USA; (c) professional organizations that offer support and networking opportunities such as the National Gay Pilots Association; and (d) organizations for ethnic and racial minority LGB persons.

Specific subjects that counseling professionals will need knowledge of if they are to provide effective treatment to LGB clients include homophobia/heterosexism, identity development (i.e., the process of establishing and maintaining a positive LGB identity), the coming-out process, lifestyle issues (e.g., LGB individuals in heterosexual relationships), family-of-origin issues, couple relationships, parenting, religious conflicts and sexual identity, and workplace issues. It is imperative that counseling professionals have knowledge of LGB-related issues; knowledge without awareness or skill provides an incomplete picture of what is needed to become multiculturally competent. Practitioners must therefore demonstrate awareness and skills.

Awareness

The application of knowledge about LGB issues requires awareness of self and others. Being aware of one's reactions to LGB issues is extremely important because of the obvious and subtle ways that prejudice and bias against LGB individuals exists in society (i.e., heterosexism/homophobia). Such biases not only influence our clients' view of themselves but also our view of our clients. Awareness of others must also be accomplished and should include the ability to relate empathically and to demonstrate personal sensitivity and understanding of the common experiences and characteristics of members of the LGB community. Counseling professionals who demonstrate awareness of others are in good position to challenge negative stereotypes, which likely informs more effective treatment with LGB clients.

In line with the notion of awareness as related to cultural competence is S. Sue's (1998) discussion of *dynamic sizing*, which Sue refers to as the counselor's awareness and skill in "knowing when to generalize and be inclusive and when to individualize and be exclusive" (p. 446). Sue further explained that practitioners may avoid overt expressions of stereotypes but the stereotypes may, nonetheless, exist in their belief systems and thereby influence their behaviors. When such stereotypes manifest, the client's individual characteristics are muddled by the group's characteristics. The opposite mistake is made when practitioners fail to consider the cultural group characteristics affecting their individual client. According to Sue, appropriate dynamic sizing is imperative to multicultural competence and occurs when counseling professionals can avoid stereotypes of members of a group while also valuing the important role of culture. S. Sue (1998) offers the following clarification:

> In dynamic sizing, the therapist is able to place the client in a proper context—whether that client has characteristics typical of, or idiosyncratic to, the client's cultural group. Moreover, there is another important component of dynamic sizing that involves the ability to appropriately generalize one's own experiences. For example, a person who has experienced discrimination and prejudice as a member of one group may be able to understand the plight of those in another group who encounter the same experiences. An African American who has faced oppression may be able to more easily understand the feelings of women who are oppressed. All people have felt like outsiders at one time or another. If this experience can be used to understand the feelings of many minority group persons, then therapists can become more empathetic and understanding and better clinicians. They are able to see and understand common experiences. However, the mere fact that therapists have experiences as, for example, an outsider does not guarantee the ability to empathize. The ability to dynamically size—to appropriately categorize experiences—is important. (p. 446)

Skills

As related to skill building in working with LGB clients, scholarly literature has not addressed how to increase counselor skills to the same extent as areas of knowledge and awareness. Nonetheless, some scholars have suggested that various theoretical orientations can be effective in counseling LGB clients as long as counselors operate from an affirmative stance (Fassinger, 2000). Tasks specific to LGB affirmative counseling have been articulated by Clark (1987) and include (a) encouraging clients to establish a support network with other LGB individuals; (b) assisting clients with exploring how systemic oppression and prejudices have affected their well-being and mental health; (c) desensitizing shame and guilt associated with same-sex attraction; and (d) allowing permission for clients to express their emotions, including anger about being oppressed and the victims of hate crimes. Because of LGB clients' past experiences in the mental health system and those of their LGB family/friends, LGB clients may display skepticism regarding counselors' competence to effectively address their issues. As such, practitioners must gain proficiency with addressing LGB issues that may arise in counseling. As previously noted, an examination of one's own feelings and attitudes (awareness) toward LGB individuals is necessary, and counselors must also show respect for their clients' sexual orientation and lifestyle if they are to emerge competent and skilled in working with members of the LGB community.

Experiential exercises, and in particular the use of role-play, have a long history in counselor training. Because role-play is viewed as highly interpersonal and interactional, it is thought to enhance the development of interpersonal skills, which bodes well for working with culturally diverse groups (Kocarek & Pelling, 2003). Much research supports the powerful and rewarding benefits of role-play for the development of various skills (e.g., interpersonal-conflict reduction, assertiveness training, family reunification, understanding of research ethics, use of hypnotherapy) and also the documented advantages of increased empathy, student involvement and motivation, and immediate learning and feedback (Kocarek & Pelling, 2003). As such, role-play has been considered a beneficial exercise for increasing counselor skill in working with LGB clients. We refer our readers to Kocarek and Pelling's model of structured role-play exercises to increase skill in working with LGB clients.

Specifically, Kocarek and Pelling (2003) noted that as heterosexual allies who were interested in learning how to better work with LGB clients, they completed a course on LGB issues in partial fulfillment of their doctoral degree in counseling psychology and found the focus on knowledge and self/other awareness to be very helpful; however, it was actually the role-play experiences that provided the greatest benefit toward their multicultural competence in working with LGB clients. They explained that once knowledge and awareness have been achieved, the practical application of skill in working with LGB clients can be facilitated through a developmental approach of role-play exercises (developed from the LGB literature) that gradually exposes trainees to greater levels of feedback (one observer to a small group of observers who provide feedback) and scenario difficulty. In other words, a gradual increase in difficulty provides a less anxious experience, which is much more conducive to learning. In order to competently provide services to clients with complex multiple cultural identities, a discussion of gender must be considered when discussing sexuality.

Working With Nonbinary Gender Identity

Counseling professionals have an ethical responsibility to understand the complexities of both internalized and externalized oppressions that gender-variant individuals experience. Moreover, the counseling profession emphasizes practitioners' ethical obligation to support and advocate for justice and equity when working with sexual minorities, including gender-variant clients. The implications of changes in the traditional binary thinking about gender include how we focus treatment. To clarify, the focus of treatment, for example, no longer centers solely on assisting gender dysphoric clients with adjusting to their new gender or alleviating shame and distress for closeted cross-dressing clients; rather, treatment must also affirm their unique gender identities and target a culture that is broken by ignorance, prejudice, and strong hatred for differences. The focus, therefore, is to transform the cultural context in which gender-variant individuals live (Carroll et al., 2002).

To assist counselors with the delivery of multiculturally competent services to gender-variant clients, we consider the attitudes, knowledge, and skills that Carroll et al. (2002) regard as imperative for counselors and which they adapted from D. W. Sue and Sue (1999). In terms of attitudes, Carroll et al. suggested that practitioners rethink their assumptions about gender and sexual orientation and adopt a trans-affirmative/trans-positive approach to counseling that includes advocacy and education on behalf of gender-variant clients. Practitioners must recognize not only their role in helping clients alleviate the emotional distress they experience due to the traditional gender binary but also how they might be contributing to it. Historically, it is known that the mental health system has failed members of the LGBTQ community by pathologizing their sexual and gender identities; as such, counselors must affirm their gender-variant clients and advocate for their social, political, and economic rights.

Acquiring an adequate knowledge and skills base requires that counselors have information regarding the historical and psychological contexts in which gender-variant clients live, including familiarity with evolving technology. Counseling professionals who are able to communicate effectively about issues of gender convey openness, acceptance, and support of their clients' concerns. Affirming the identities of clients who possess nontraditional gender identities can help to alleviate any shame, fear, secrecy, and/or isolation experienced when attempting to embrace their nontraditional gender (Carroll et al., 2002). Counselors who believe in a traditional gender binary system and/or maintain that same-sex attraction is a sin against their religious convictions may believe reparative therapy is a necessary treatment option for clients of varied sex and gender identities. It is important to note that this approach is counter to multicultural counseling competencies and in direct opposition to the American Counseling Association *Code of Ethics* (2014).

In order to effectively intervene on behalf of gender-variant clients, counselors must suspend their own cultural biases and preunderstandings about gender and be willing to listen to clients' stories and experiences (Laird, 1999). In line with a social justice advocacy approach, Laird recommended that mental health professionals bring their clients' stories to the professional literature and into the political arena.

Effective counseling requires not only that counselors possess a multicultural professional identity but also that they acquire good consultation, referral, and case management skills. An important task of the counselor is to recognize the full spectrum of gender identities that exists and to have adequate knowledge of local, regional, and national organizations that offer support and networking opportunities for the gender-variant community.

Table 9.4 Counseling Issues for LGB Clients

i	Institutionalized discrimination related to marriage rights, equal employment opportunities, adoption rights, and limited work environments (e.g., individuals may appear "accepting" or "tolerant" of a same-sex attraction lifestyle but oppose sexual minorities working as teachers of young children because of their supposed sexual deviance)
ii	Assumed heterosexism (a belief system that positions the "superiority" of heterosexuality over nonheterosexual forms of behavior)
iii	Loss of support system from family and search for "new family" in the LGB community
iv	Stress associated with the transition of coming out, finding a suitable partner, internalized homophobia/heterosexism
v	Physical and emotional abuse by intolerant groups
vi	Feeling degraded as a result of microaggressions, which may lead clients to question whether they were truly discriminated against due to their sexuality (e.g., "If my performance has been good, was I fired for my sexuality?"); feelings of self-doubt as a result of covert forms of discrimination
vii	Subjected to reparative forms of therapy (mental health practitioners and church groups continue to offer these services to persons struggling with their sexual identities)

GUIDED PRACTICE EXERCISE 9.1

Discussion and Exploration of the Cases of Jacob, John, and Jamie

After reading the case illustrations of Jacob, John, and Jamie, respond to the questions provided in Table 9.5. These cases can also be used for role-play with one student as the client, one student as the counselor, and a third student as an observer.

(Continued)

(Continued)

Case Illustration: Jacob

Jacob is a 19-year-old, male, freshman college student who identifies as Puerto Rican. He recently came to the university counseling center, reportedly due to high levels of stress related to his schoolwork and concerns regarding his sexuality. Jacob also reports that he has begun suffering from panic attacks during which he experiences a racing heart, chest pains, and an inability to catch his breath. He is currently failing all of his courses and reported that he often struggles to understand his professors in class. He further explains at intake that he is not considered to be a United States citizen and often fears deportation for both himself and his family. He reports that he and his parents came to the United States about 17 years ago on temporary visas, but they never returned to Puerto Rico.

Jacob reports that he has recently begun perusing gay websites, chatting with men online, and then meeting these men for "casual sex." However, he adamantly denied identifying as gay and commented that neither he nor his family supports such a lifestyle. He reports feeling distrustful of counselors but decided to seek counseling because he is beginning to feel out of control, hopeless about life, and often thinks about dropping out of school. He denies prior or current suicidal ideation.

Case Illustration: John

John is a successful, single, middle-aged Caucasian businessman at a private company in a large metropolitan area. During the intake interview, he describes in great detail working his way to the top of the company, eventually becoming the chief executive officer. John reports that he identifies as heterosexual but states that approximately two years ago he began attending circuit parties on the weekends where he drinks and has sex with men he meets at these parties. He reports that this is "no big deal" because nothing bad ever happens. However, he is now concerned because he is experiencing difficulty keeping up with his normal pace at work and has missed several work days the past 6 months because he is either too tired or "hungover." He reports wanting to continue attending these parties because they make him feel "young and alive," and he meets interesting people.

Case Illustration: Jamie

Jamie is a 17-year-old Caucasian female who identifies as bisexual and is accompanied to counseling by her mother. Jamie reports that she was kicked out of her parents' home at the age of 15 after telling them that she might be attracted to both girls and boys. Upon disclosing her sexual attraction, her family enrolled her in reparative therapy at her church, where she reports being "subjected to mental torture" by her pastor. She was eventually thrown out of the house after her high school principal informed her parents that Jamie was seen at school holding hands with another female student. Jamie lived with friends for 3 months until her parents agreed that she could return home. Jamie describes her family as very religious and homophobic and reports that she still loves them. Finally, Jamie shares that in order for her to be able to live at home, her parents are requiring that she seek counseling so that she can become heterosexual.

Table 9.5 Clinician Considerations in Working With LGB Clients

i	Can I still work effectively with this client given our differing identities and experiences (e.g., discrimination)? Why or why not?
ii	Am I willing to seek out additional resources in order to strengthen my understanding of this population? Is yes, what is my plan for accessing additional resources?
iii	Am I prepared to be an active advocate rather than simply a proponent of the status quo? If, yes, what am I prepared to do?
iv	Am I willing to address any biases my client may have against me as a counselor due to past negative experiences with the mental health system?
v	What can I do to make my client feel understood and affirmed in his or her sexual identity exploration and/or partner choices?
vi	Am I willing to address complex issues in counseling (when appropriate) such as internalized homophobia and heterosexism? Why or why not?

Table 9.6 Counseling Issues for Fluid Gender Identity Clients

i	Discrimination from both LGB individuals and heterosexual individuals
ii	Being mislabeled/misunderstood/misdiagnosed as many people are unaware that *both* sexuality and gender identities fall along a spectrum
iii	Lack of services (e.g., counselors, support groups) that provide a safe place to explore and develop positive identities

Table 9.7 Clinician Considerations in Working With Fluid Gender Identity Clients

i	Am I aware of language/terminology biases that may promote intolerance of gender-minority individuals (e.g., referring to my client as one gender or the other, when in fact my client may not identify as one specific gender)?
ii	Am I willing to work with a client who does not subscribe to the traditional gender binary?

Table 9.8 Counseling Issues for Transgender Clients

i	Medical decision making: pre/post hormones, pre/post op
ii	Securing financial resources for sex reassignment surgery (SRS), if SRS is a desired goal
iii	Dealing with both gender and sexual orientation
iv	Discrimination and harassment
v	Career development

GUIDED PRACTICE EXERCISE 9.2

Discussion and Exploration of the Case of Melanie

After reading the case illustration of Melanie, respond to the questions provided in Table 9.9. This illustration can also be used for role-play with one student as the client, one student as the counselor, and a third student as an observer.

Case Illustration: Melanie

Melanie is a 16-year-old African American female who was brought to counseling by her parents after getting into another fight with a high school classmate. During the intake, Melanie's parents described their daughter as "confused," stating that Melanie often claims to be a boy. They stated that they are at a loss and asked the counselor to "fix" their daughter. Melanie reported feeling like a boy since about the age of 6 years, getting into fights with peers after they refer to her as a girl and having no friends at school. Melanie reported feeling "alone, as if no one understands." Melanie further explained that her mother has never allowed her to wear boys' clothes and has recently forced her to wear only dresses.

Melanie has been in trouble at school for getting into physical altercations with other students, entering the boys' bathroom on several occasions, and ignoring teachers who refer to Melanie as "her" or "she." Melanie's parents stated that their daughter recently began to sneak alcohol from the liquor cabinet at home. Melanie reported feeling "sad" and "moody" most days. During the intake interview, the counselor notices that Melanie's left eye is black from the fight with a male classmate, and several cuts on Melanie's wrists are exposed when she pulls at the sleeves of her jacket.

Table 9.9 Clinician Considerations in Working With Transgender Clients

i	Is SRS a desired end for my client? If not, how well do I understand gender outside of a binary system?
ii	What biases do I hold toward transgender persons, and how will I work to eliminate these biases?
iii	Am I familiar with both mental health and medical resources specializing in working with the transgender population?
iv	Am I capable of asking open-ended, affirming questions regarding my client's sexuality, gender, and relationships with others?
v	Can I provide my client with a referral for transgender support groups?
vi	Given that co-occurring disorders are often higher in gender and sexual minority populations, am I competent to address substance abuse issues?

Summary

This chapter discusses the importance of counselors' understanding the full spectrum of sexual orientation and gender identities in order to provide competent care to clients. Advocacy efforts are emphasized as a means to change systems that cause oppression and psychological distress. Nonheterosexual identity development is reviewed, as well as a framework for understanding the multiplicity of gender. The necessary attitudes, knowledge, and skills to work effectively with sexual minorities are explored to help counselors enhance their multicultural competency.

Takeaway Messages

1. Counselors must not assume that the binary construction of gender as male/female and sexual orientation as straight/gay applies to their clients.
2. The credibility of the counseling profession is predicated on counseling being a place where *all* clients can feel safe, understood, and respected.
3. Failure to recognize the complexity and expanding constructions of gender and sexual identities will render counselors ineffective in their provision of services to culturally diverse clients.
4. Knowledge of LGB sociocultural history and biases in the mental health system are critical to ethical and multiculturally competent services.
5. Counselors must consider the extent to which the issues presented by LGB clients arise from societal heterocentrism.
6. Developing gender identity competency requires understanding and familiarity with terms and definitions.
7. It is the counselor's ethical responsibility to advocate for justice and equity in the provision of services to gender-variant and sexual-minority clients.

Recommended Resources

Prevailing Models of LGB Identity Development	
Cass (1979)	Homosexual identity formation: A theoretical model. *Journal of Homosexuality, 4,* 219–235.
Coleman (1981/1982)	Developmental stages of the coming out process. *Journal of Homosexuality, 7,* 31–43.
Grace (1992)	Affirming lesbian and gay adulthood. In N. J. Woodman (Ed.), *Lesbian and gay lifestyles: A guide for counseling and education* (pp. 33–47). New York, NY: Irvington.
Ritter and Tendrup (2002)	*Handbook of affirmative psychotherapy with gay men and lesbians.* New York, NY: Guilford Press.
Troiden (1979)	Becoming homosexual: A model of gay identity acquisition. *Psychiatry, 42,* 362–373.

(Continued)

(Continued)

LGB Topics and Relevant Literature	
Heterosexism	Alden, H. L., & Parker, K. F. (2005). Gender role ideology, hate crimes and homophobia: Linking attitudes to micro-level anti-gay attitudes and hate crimes. *Deviant Behavior, 26*(4), 321–343. doi:10.1080/016396290931 614 *Smith, I., Oades, L. G., & McCarthy, G. (2012). Homophobia to heterosexism: Constructs in need of re-visitation. *Gay and Lesbian Issues and Psychology Review, 8*(1), 34–44. *Outlines all definitions of homophobia and heterosexism from 1960 to 2012
Identity Development	Bedard, K. K., & Marks, A. K. (2010). Current psychological perspectives on adolescent lesbian identity development. *Journal of Lesbian Studies, 14*(1), 16–25. doi:10.1080/10894160903058857 Comeau, D. L. (2012). Label-first sexual identity development: An in-depth case study of women who identify as bisexual before having sex with more than one gender. *Journal of Bisexuality, 12*(3), 321–346. doi:10.1080/15299716.2012.702611 dickey, l. m., Burnes, T. R., & Singh, A. A. (2012). Sexual identity development of female-to-male transgender individuals: A grounded theory inquiry. *Journal of LGBT Issues in Counseling, 6*(2), 118–138. doi:10.1080/15538605.2012.678184 Dillon, F. R., Worthington, R. L., & Moradi, B. (2011). Sexual identity as a universal process. In S. J. Schwartz, K. Luyckx, & V. L. Vignoles (Eds.), *Handbook of identity theory and research* (Vols. 1–2, pp. 649–670). New York, NY: Springer Science + Business Media. doi:10.1007/978-1-4419-7988-9_27
	Olive, J. L. (2012). Reflections on the life histories of today's LGBQ postsecondary students. *Journal of LGBT Youth, 9*(3), 247–265. Savin-Williams, R. C. (2011). Identity development among sexual-minority youth. In S. J. Schwartz, K. Luyckx, & V. L. Vignoles (Eds.), *Handbook of identity theory and research* (Vols. 1–2, pp. 671–689). New York, NY: Springer Science + Business Media. doi:10.1007/978-1-4419-7988-9_28 Shapiro, D., Rios, D., & Stewart, A. J. (2010). Conceptualizing lesbian sexual identity development: Narrative accounts of socializing structures and individual decisions and actions. *Feminism & Psychology, 20*(4), 491–510. doi:10.1177/0959353509358441 Telingator, C. J., & Woyewodzic, K. T. (2011). Sexual minority identity development. *Psychiatric Times, 28*(12), 39–42.
Coming-Out Process	Bates, D. (2010). Once-married African-American lesbians and bisexual women: Identity development and the coming-out process. *Journal of Homosexuality, 57*(2), 197–225. doi:10.1080/00918360903488848 Dunlap, A. A. (2011). *Changes in the coming out process over time* (Doctoral dissertation). Abstract retrieved from http://facultysites.etown.edu/dunlapal/dissertation-summar-changes-in-the-coming-out-process/

	George, S. (2011). Blogging bisexuals and the coming-out process. *Journal of Bisexuality, 11*(2/3), 320–328. doi:10.1080/15299716.2011.572013 Gragg, R. A. (2012). Working with sexual minority youth: Coming out. *Brown University Child & Adolescent Behavior Letter, 28*(10), 1–6. Grov, C., Bimbi, D. S., Nanín, J. E., & Parsons, J. T. (2006). Race, ethnicity, gender, and generational factors associated with the coming-out process among gay, lesbian, and bisexual individuals. *Journal of Sex Research, 43*(2), 115–121. Matthews, C. H., & Salazar, C. F. (2012). An integrative empowerment model for helping lesbian, gay, and bisexual youth negotiate the coming-out process. *Journal of LGBT Issues in Counseling, 6*(2), 96–117. doi:10.1080/15538605.2012.678176 Zamboni, B. D., Robinson, B. E., & Bockting, W. O. (2011). HIV status and coming out among African American gay and bisexual men. *Journal of Bisexuality, 11*(1), 74–84. doi:10.1080/15299716.2011.545309
Lifestyle Issues (e.g., LGB individuals in heterosexual relationships)	Buxton, A. P. (2001). Writing our own script: How bisexual men and their heterosexual wives maintain their marriages after disclosure. *Journal of Bisexuality, 1*, 155–189. Higgins, D. J. (2002). Gay men from heterosexual marriages: Attitudes, behaviors, childhood experiences, and reasons for marriage. *Journal of Homosexuality, 42*, 15–34.
Family of Origin Issues	Dahlheimer, D., & Feigal, J. (1994). Community as family: The multiple-family contexts of gay and lesbian clients. In C. H. Huber (Ed.), *Transitioning from individual to family counseling* (pp. 63–74). Alexandria, VA: American Counseling Association. Matthews, C. R., & Lease, S. H. (2000). Focus on lesbian, gay, and bisexual families. In R. M. Perez, K. A. DeBord, & K. J. Bieschke (Eds.), *Handbook of counseling and psychotherapy with lesbian, gay, and bisexual clients* (pp. 249–273). Washington, DC: American Psychological Association. Savin-Williams, R. C. (2001). *"Mom, Dad, I'm gay": How families negotiate coming out.* Washington, DC: American Psychological Association.
Couple Relationships	*Ard, K., & Makadon, H. (2011). Addressing intimate partner violence in lesbian, gay, bisexual, and transgender patients. *Journal of General Internal Medicine, 26*(8), 930–933. doi:10.1007/s11606-011-1697-6 *Recent literature has focused on LGBT couples and domestic violence. Fingerhut, A. W., Riggle, E. B., & Rostosky, S. (2011). Same-sex marriage: The social and psychological implications of policy and debates. *Journal of Social Issues, 67*(2), 225–241. doi:10.1111/j.1540-4560.2011.01695.x

(Continued)

(Continued)

	Gottman, J. M., Levenson, R. W., Gross, J. J., Fredrickson, B. L., McCoy, K., Rosenthal, L., . . . Yoshimoto, D. (2003). Correlates of gay and lesbian couples' relationship satisfaction and relationship dissolution. *Journal of Homosexuality, 45*, 23–44. Matthews, C. R., & Lorah, P. (2012). Domestic violence in same-sex relationships. In S. H. Dworkin & M. Pope (Eds.), *Casebook for counseling lesbian, gay, bisexual, and transgendered persons and their families* (pp. 307–317). Alexandria, VA: American Counseling Association. Rothblum, E. D., Balsam, K. F., & Solomon, S. E. (2011). The longest "legal" U.S. same-sex couples reflect on their relationships. *Journal of Social Issues, 67*(2), 302–315. doi:10.1111/j.1540-4560.2011.01699.x
Parenting	Bigner, J. J. (1996). Working with gay fathers: Development, postdivorce parenting, and therapeutic issues. In J. Laird & R. J. Green (Eds.), *Lesbian and gay couples and families: A handbook for therapists* (pp. 370–403). San Francisco, CA: Jossey-Bass. *Byrn, M. P., & Holcomb, M. L. (2012). Same-sex divorce in a DOMA state. *Family Court Review, 50*(2), 214–221. doi:10.1111/j.1744-1617.2012.01445.x *Divorce is just as tricky to navigate for the courts as marriage is with regard to same-sex couples. Fitzgerald, B. (1999). Children of lesbian and gay parents: A review of the literature. *Marriage and Family Review, 29*, 57–75. Goldberg, A., & Kuvalanka, K. (2012). Marriage (in)equality: The perspectives of adolescents and emerging adults with lesbian, gay, and bisexual parents. *Journal of Marriage & Family, 74*(1), 34–52. Hart, J. E., Mourot, J. E., & Aros, M. (2012). Children of same-sex parents: In and out of the closet. *Educational Studies, 38*(3), 277–281. doi:10.1080/03055698.2011.598677 Johnson, S. M., & O'Connor, E. (2001). *The gay baby boom: The psychology of gay parenthood.* New York: New York University Press. Johnson, S. M., & O'Connor, E. (2002). *For lesbian parents: Your guide to helping your family grow up happy, healthy, and proud.* New York: New York University Press. Lev, A. (2010). How queer!: The development of gender identity and sexual orientation in LGBTQ-headed families. *Family Process, 49*(3), 268–290. doi:10.1111/j.1545-5300.2010.01323.x *Mallon, G. P. (2011). The home study assessment process for gay, lesbian, bisexual, and transgender prospective foster and adoptive families. *Journal of GLBT Family Studies, 7*(1/2), 9–29. doi:10.1080/1550428X.2011.537229 *Many same-sex couples decide to adopt versus using a donor, thus parenting issues include adoption-related concerns. Unfortunately, same-sex couples are often only allowed to adopt children considered to be "less desirable" (e.g., ethnic minority). Their newly created family structure must then navigate issues related to transracial identities.

	Regnerus, M. (2012). Parental same-sex relationships, family instability, and subsequent life outcomes for adult children: Answering critics of the new family structures—Study with additional analyses. *Social Science Research, 41*(6), 1367–1377. doi:10.1016/j.ssresearch.2012.08.015 Rosenfeld, M. J. (2010). Nontraditional families and childhood progress through school. *Demography, 47*(3), 755–775.
Religious and Sexual Identity Conflicts	Anderton, C. K. (2011). A review of the religious identity/sexual orientation identity conflict literature: Revisiting Festinger's cognitive dissonance theory. *Journal of LGBT Issues in Counseling, 5*(3/4), 259. doi:10.1080/15538605.2011.632745 Dahl, A., & Galliher, R. V. (2012). The interplay of sexual and religious identity development in LGBTQ adolescents and young adults: A qualitative inquiry. *Identity: An International Journal of Theory and Research, 12*(3), 217–246. doi:10.1080/15283488.2012.691255 Green, M. S., Murphy, M. J., & Blumer, M. C. (2010). Marriage and family therapists' comfort working with lesbian and gay male clients: The influence of religious practices and support for lesbian and gay male human rights. *Journal of Homosexuality, 57*(10), 1258–1273. doi:10.1080/00918369.2010.517072 Wentz, J. M., & Wessel, R. D. (2011). The intersection of gay and Christian identities on Christian college campuses. *Journal of College and Character, 12*(2), 1–6.
Workplace Issues	Davis, D. (2009). Transgender issues in the workplace: HRD's newest challenge/opportunity. *Advances in Developing Human Resources, 11*(1), 109–120. Godfrey, D. (2012). Three legs on the ground: Retirement income essentials for LGBT adults. *Generations, 36*(2), 81–87.
	Lyons, H. Z., Brenner, B. R., & Lipman, J. J. (2010). Patterns of career and identity interference for lesbian, gay, and bisexual young adults. *Journal of Homosexuality, 57*(4), 503–524. Ragins, B. R., & Cornwell, J. M. (2001). Pink triangles: Antecedents and consequences of perceived workplace discrimination against gay and lesbian employees. *Journal of Applied Psychology, 6*, 1244–1261. Rostosky, S. S., & Riggle, E. D. B. (2002). "Out" at work: The relation of actor and partner workplace policy and internalized homophobia to disclosure status. *Journal of Counseling Psychology, 4*, 411–419.

Websites

Definition of terms: http://geneq.berkeley.edu/lgbt_resources_definiton_of_terms
Medical and psychological aspects of transgender care: www.trannsgendercare.com
P-FLAG (Parents Families and Friends of Lesbians and Gays) is a national non-profitally organization committed to advancing equality through its mission of support, education, and advocacy. It has over 300 chapters and hundred thousands of members. www.pflag.org
Encyclopedia of GLBTQ culture: http://www.glbtq.com/subject/social-sciences_a-e.html

The Midwest Trans and Queer Wellness Initiative (MTQWI) is an organization that provides community resources for Midwestern transgender, transsexual, genderqueer, gender variant, fluid, queer, questioning, and LGBTQQCIAI people. http://www.transqueerwellness.org/terms

Glossary of queer terms: http://daviscenter.williams.edu/about/history-of-the-mcc/queer-student-resources/glossary/

Glossary of trans terms: https://docs.google.com/document/edit?id=1YKAAZgij2Iyy CUWyZtcDz2N9cav2vH1kwaZWNDp3mSQ

The Intersex Society of North America is a resource for clinicians, parents, and persons who require information about disorders of sex development (DSDs).http://www.isna.org/

Gender Identity Disorder Reform includes medical professionals, caregivers, scholars, researchers, students, human rights advocates, and members of the transgender, bisexual, lesbian, and gay communities and their allies who are calling for reform of the classification of gender diversity as a mental disorder. www.gidreform.org

Transgender Films (Carroll et al., 2002; Singh, Boyd, & Whitman, 2010)

Boys Don't Cry (Pierce, 1999)

The Brandon Teena Story (Muska & Olafsdottir, 1998)

Ma Vie En Rose (Berliner, 1997)

Normal (Anderson, 2003)

Outlaw (Lebow, 1994)

Paris Is Burning (Livingston, 1991)

Southern Comfort (Davis, 2001)

TransAmerica (Tucker, 2005)

TransGeneration (2005)

Periodicals for Exploring the Culture of Transgender People

Chrysalis Quarterly

Gendertrash

Transgender Tapestry

References

American Counseling Association (2014). *Code of ethics.* Retrieved from www.counseling.org

American Psychological Association. (2001). *Publication manual of the American Psychological Association* (5th ed.). Washington, DC: American Psychological Association.

Anhalt, K., Morris, T. L., Scotti, J. R., & Cohen, S. H. (2003). Students' perspectives on training in gay, lesbian, and bisexual issues: A survey of behavioral clinical psychology programs. *Cognitive & Behavioral Practice, 10*, 255–263.

Besnier, N. (1993). Polynesian gender liminality through time and space. In G. Herdt (Ed.), *Third sex, third gender: Beyond sexual dimorphism in culture and history*. New York, NY: Zone Books.

Biaggio, M., Orchard, S., Larson, J., Petrino, K., & Mihara, R. (2003). Guidelines for gay/lesbian/bisexual-affirmative educational practices in graduate psychology programs. *Professional Psychology: Research and Practice, 34*, 548–554.

Bidell, M. P. (2005). The sexual orientation counselor competency scale: Assessing attitudes, skills, and knowledge of counselors working with lesbian, gay, and bisexual clients. *Counselor Education and Supervision, 44*, 267–279.

Bilodeau, B. L., & Renn, K. (2005). Analysis of LGBT identity development models and implications for practice. *New Directions for Student Services, 111*, 25–39.

Brown, C., Maragos, A., Lee, R., Davidson, B., & Dashjian, L. T. (2015). *Female-to-male transsexuals: Giving voice to their experience.* Manuscript submitted for publication.

Bushong, C. (1995). The multidimensionality of gender. *Tapestry J, 71*, 33–37. Retrieved from http://www.transgendercare.com/guidance/multi.htm#top

Carroll, L. C., Gilroy, P. J., & Ryan, J. (2002). Counseling transgendered, transsexual, and gender-variant clients. *Journal of Counseling & Development, 80*(2), 131–139.

Case, K. A., & Stewart, B. (2010). Changes in diversity course student prejudice and attitudes toward heterosexual privilege and gay marriage. *Teaching of Psychology, 37*(3), 172–177. doi:10.1080/00986283.2010.488555

Cass, V. C. (1979). Homosexual identity formation: A theoretical model. *Journal of Homosexuality, 4*, 219–235.

Clark, D. (1987). *The new loving someone gay.* Berkeley, CA: Celestial Arts.

Council for Accreditation of Counseling and Related Educational Programs. (2001). *CACREP accreditation manual: 2001 standards.* Alexandria, VA: Author.

D'Augelli, A. R. (1994). Identity development and sexual orientation: Toward a model of lesbian, gay, and bisexual development. In E. J. Trickett, R. J. Watts, & D. Birman (Eds.), *Human diversity: Perspectives on people in context* (pp. 312–333). San Francisco, CA: Jossey-Bass.

Davidson, M. (2007). Seeking refuge under the umbrella: Inclusion, exclusion, and organizing within the category transgender. *Sexuality Research and Social Policy, 4*(4), 60–80.

DeAngelis, T. (2002). A new generation of issues for LGBT clients. *APA Monitor, 33*, 42–44.

Eyler A. E, & Wright, K. (1997). Gender identification and sexual orientation among genetic females with gender-blended self-perception in childhood and adolescence. *International Journal of Transgenderism, 1*(1), 37–51.

Fassinger, R. E. (2000). Applying counseling theories to lesbian, gay, and bisexual clients: Pitfalls and possibilities. In R. M. Perez, K. A. DeBord, & K. J. Bieschke (Eds.), *Handbook of psychotherapy with lesbians, gay, and bisexual clients* (pp. 107–131). Washington, DC: American Psychological Association.

Fassinger, R. E., & Richie. B. S. (1997). Sex matters: Gender and sexual orientation in training for multicultural counseling competency. In D. B. Pope-Davis & H. L. K. Coleman (Eds.), *Multicultural counseling competencies: Assessment, education, and training and supervision* (pp. 83–110). Thousand Oaks, CA: Sage.

Fausto-Sterling, A. (2000). *Sexing the body: Gender politics and the construction of sexuality.* New York, NY: Basic Books.

Firestein, B. (1996). Bisexuality as a paradigm shift: Transforming our disciplines. In B. Firestein (Ed.), *Bisexuality: The psychology and politics of an invisible minority* (pp. 263–291). Thousand Oaks, CA: Sage.

Greene, B. (1994). Lesbian and gay sexual orientations: Implications for clinical training, practice, and research. In B. Greene & G. M. Herek (Eds.), *Lesbian and gay psychology: Theory, research, and clinical application* (pp. 1–24). Thousand Oaks, CA: Sage.

Israel, T., & Selvidge, M. M. D. (2003). Contributions of multicultural counseling to counselor competency with lesbian, gay, and bisexual clients. *Journal of Multicultural Counseling and Development, 31*, 84–97.

Kinsey, A. C., Pomeroy, W. B., & Martin, C. E. (1948). *Sexual behavior in the human male.* Philadelphia, PA: Saunders.

Kocarek, C. E., & Pelling, N. J. (2003). Beyond knowledge and awareness: Enhancing counselor skills for work with gay, lesbian, and bisexual clients. *Journal of Multicultural Counseling and Development, 31*, 99–112.

Laird, J. (1999). Gender and sexuality in lesbian relationships: Feminist and constructionist perspectives. In J. Laird (Ed.), *Lesbians and lesbian families: Reflections on theory and practice* (p. 47–89). New York, NY: Columbia University Press.

Millett, G., Malebranche, D., Mason, B., & Spikes, P. (2005, July). Focusing "down low": Bisexual Black men, HIV risk, and heterosexual transmission. *Journal of the National Medical Association, 97*(7 Suppl.), 52S–59S.

Murphy, J. A., Rawlings, E. I., & Howe, S. R. (2002). A survey of clinical psychologists on treating lesbian, gay and bisexual clients. *Professional Psychology: Research and Practice, 33,* 183–189.

Pachankis, J. E., & Goldfried, M. R. (2004). Clinical issues in working lesbian, gay, and bisexual clients. *Psychotherapy: Theory, Research, Practice, Training, 41*(3), 227–246.

Roughgarden, J. (2004). Evolution's rainbow: Diversity, gender, and sexuality in nature and people. London, England: University of California Press.

Sausa, L. A. (2005). Translating research into practice: Trans youth recommendations for improving school systems. *Journal of Gay and Lesbian Issues in Education, 3*(1), 15–28.

Schneider, M. S., Brown, L. S., & Glassgold, J. M. (2002). Implementing the resolution on appropriate therapeutic responses to sexual orientation: A guide for the perplexed. *Professional Psychology: Research and Practice, 33,* 265–276.

Singh, A. A., Boyd, C. J., & Whitman, J. S. (2010). Counseling competencies with transgender and intersex persons. In J. A. Erickson Cornish, B. A. Schreier, L. I. Nadkarni, L. Henderson Metzger, and E. R. Rodolfa (Eds.), *Handbook of multicultural counseling competencies* (pp. 415–441). New York, NY: Wiley.

Sue, D. W., & Sue, D. (1999). *Counseling the culturally different: Theory and practice* (3rd ed.). New York, NY: Wiley.

Sue, S. (1998). In search of cultural competence in psychotherapy and counseling. *American Psychologist, 53,* 440–448.

Troiden, R. R. (1979). Becoming homosexual: A model of gay identity acquisition. *Psychiatry, 42,* 362–373.

Worthington, L. (2004). Sexual identity, sexual orientation, religious identity, and change: Is it possible to depolarize the debate? *The Counseling Psychologist, 32*(5), 741–749.

Zamora-Hernandez, C. E., & Patterson, D. G. (1996). *Homosexually active Latino men: Issues for social work practice.* In J. F. Longres (Ed.), *Men of color: A context for service to homosexually active men* (pp. 69–91). New York, NY: Harrington Park Press.

10

Working With Diversity in Social Class Contexts

It is the place of feeling that binds us or frees us.

—Jack Kornfield

CHAPTER OVERVIEW

This chapter discusses social, cultural, and counseling issues related to social class, with an emphasis on understanding the social context and worldview of those who are marginalized by society because they are in lower social classes. We want to make readers aware that social class stratification is an unjust social and systemic practice, and people who suffer from low social class or poverty have been the victims, not the problem. We provide information on social class disparities in various areas of life to condemn classism and to increase readers' awareness concerning the injustice that our nation's poor have had to endure.

The chapter also discusses the issues related to identity development, values, and worldviews of those who are unjustly marginalized in our economic culture. We hope to help readers understand that White middle-class values are generally reflected in our counseling theories and practice. Effective multicultural counseling for marginalized social class groups requires respect for the fact that social context has a determining effect in those people's lives. We discuss how failure to understand the impact of classism and class-related worldviews could lead to victim blaming and doing harm. Moreover, in order to address the social problem of poverty, social justice advocacy is necessary.

SELF-ASSESSMENT OF PRE-EXISTING AWARENESS AND KNOWLEDGE

- How do I describe my class identity development?
- How does my class identity influence my work with people from lower social classes?
- What is my level of understanding of issues related to social class and poverty?
- How well do I understand my own social class and its impact on who I am and how I live my life?
- What privileges do I have due to my social class, and how might they affect my work with people in poverty?
- How well do I understand the impact social class status has on clients' psychological health, especially those from low social classes?
- How well do I understand the worldviews of those from low social classes?
- How competent am I at working with clients who suffer from poverty?
- How competent am I at providing interventions that effectively address concerns of those being marginalized by our society due to their socioeconomic status (SES)?

LEARNING OBJECTIVES

After reading this chapter, students will be able to do the following:

1. Recognize the importance of their class identity development in their ability to effectively counsel people from lower social classes
2. See that classism exists and how it unjustly affects people
3. Recognize the power and privilege held by those who are members of middle to high social classes
4. Recognize and start to overcome their personal prejudice related to social class
5. Understand the relevance of social class in establishing effective therapeutic relationships with clients
6. Conceptualize clients' concerns and understand their psychological needs in the context of their social class
7. Show interest in serving and advocating for those who are victimized by classism

CASE ILLUSTRATION 10.1

The Case of Anisha

Anisha, a 32-year-old biracial (White mother/Black father) woman, is a single mother of three children—a 15-year-old daughter and 6-year-old twin boys. She showed up with her three children at a community mental health free clinic with papers to show that she was ordered by a municipal court judge to receive counseling. She told the front desk clerk that she was "tired of dealing with the police," and "would not mind seeing shrinks for a change." Her 15-year-old daughter added, "My mother wants to do the right thing." In the waiting room, the daughter helped her mom fill out the client information form, on which she checked "middle school" for last grade completed.

An Asian American female counselor saw the family for the intake after Anisha refused to leave the children in the waiting area, saying, "I need them to be with me, or I will leave with them." During the session, the daughter seemed to play an important role. She tried to calm the twins down (they clearly were uninterested and did not want to be there) by getting them to work on the drawing books the counselor provided, and she also participated in answering the counselor's questions toward her mom every now and then. The session lasted for about 30 minutes and had to end due to the twins becoming noisy and physical with each other. The counselor was able to provide an intake report with the following information:

Behavior Observation: Anisha is a very skinny, short person with rather dark skin for a biracial person, but she had a strong presence in the room. She wore colorful clothes that were a bit dirty and looked young for her age. Although she did not volunteer to speak much, she had her opinions and was direct in expressing herself and did not show sensitivity to how others may feel (lack of empathy).

Family Background: Anisha lives in a housing project with her children. She was never married and had little contact with the two men who were her children's fathers and said, "Do not talk about them," when the counselor asked about their involvement in the children's lives. In terms of her work history, she has worked at different times but was not able to keep jobs. She said that "they always fire me"—twice from fast food stores for "stealing food" and once from a Laundromat for "bringing children to work." The most recent legal trouble she had was for theft; she was caught stealing clothing items from a local store (a scarf and a skirt). Anisha and her children were currently on welfare, receiving food stamps and an allowance for housing. Anisha said that the judge told her he would take the welfare income away. The daughter added, "He told Mom to come to counseling." When asked about her parents, Anisha said, "I refuse to talk about them." Her daughter murmured, "I never knew them."

Presenting Concerns: When asked what issues she wanted to work on in counseling, Anisha said, "Don't ask me. I have no problems. You can tell me or you can ask the judge." Her daughter jumped in at one time to say, "My mom doesn't sleep well. She often does not eat dinner." Anisha immediately said, "Shut up. What do you know?" After going around a few times, she eventually softened her tone and reported that she had a lot of headaches, poor appetite, and frequent nightmares. She said she was afraid that something was wrong with her and that she would not be able to raise her children. When asked about the most recent trouble with the law, she returned to her earlier demeanor with flat affect: "I have nothing to say." The daughter added, "Mom wants to do it right," then turned to her mother and said, "Mom, please."

SMALL-GROUP CLASS ACTIVITY 10.1

Discussion and Exploration of the Case of Anisha

Form small groups with three or four students in each. Discuss this case and share your thoughts on the following questions:

1. What is your initial impression of the client?
2. What are the "problems" you want to focus on in working with Anisha?
3. What is your assessment of her cognitive skills?
4. How do you describe her emotional health?
5. How would you approach the task of assessment/diagnosis?
6. What would be the general direction of your interventions?
7. How confident are you that you would be able to offer her effective counseling?

Social Class and Classism

Whether or not we recognize it, we are all part of a social class in a society where there are large variations among people in terms of wealth, material possessions, power, authority, and prestige. We live in certain neighborhoods, attend certain schools, shop in certain stores, and socialize with certain circles of people. We most likely recognize that we are members of a certain class and that there are others who would either choose not to "lower" themselves to move to our neighborhoods or do not have the resources to attend our schools. There is a hierarchy of social class in our society, including upper class (elite), upper middle class, lower middle class, working class, and poor (note: this is one of several ways to categorize and label the classes). In our professional literature, various terms/labels have been used to refer to those with lower than middle-class status, such as the poor, the working poor, people with low SES, low-income families, people in poverty, or those with extreme poverty (homeless). Theorists generally agree that social class is a social stratification that organizes people into this hierarchy on the basis of inequality and uneven distribution of resources and power (Lott, 2002).

The concept of social class is often conflated and interchangeably used with that of SES, while in fact they may bear different meanings (Liu, Ali, et al., 2004). *SES* is generally a person's position in an economic hierarchy and can be determined by an individual's or family's economic and social position in relation to others, based on objective indices such as income, education, and occupation. In research, SES is often measured as one's level of resources, control, or prestige (Gallo & Matthews, 2003). Social class, on the other hand, also contains a subjective element that "the person is conscious of others within the same social class group as well as others outside of the group" (Liu, Soleck, Hopps, Dunston, & Pickett, 2004, p. 96). This group awareness or class consciousness is considered the basis of *classism*, an ideology supporting differential treatment to individuals based on their social class or perceived social class.

Classism

Classism can be defined as "prejudice and discrimination that are directed toward and experienced from others to maintain homeostasis within one's own perceived status position . . . (and) can occur among any people and among any groups, regardless of actual social class" (Liu & Ali, 2005, p. 192). Classism is closely tied to the economic culture of our society, where people are stratified based on their SES. Although classist attitudes can be theoretically experienced and expressed by all socioeconomic classes with the intention of maintaining in-group and out-group boundaries, the differential social power each group has over others makes significant difference in the effect of such attitudes by different social strata. Downward classism (e.g., regarding members of other groups as inferior or deserving poverty) creates social injustice and unfair disadvantages for members of lower social classes. Additionally, internalized classism (Liu & Ali, 2005) can victimize oneself with feelings of frustration, emotional difficulties, and even low motivation due to inability to move upward in social class.

For the purpose of our discussion of counseling the marginalized groups in social class, we choose to focus on classism as the systematic oppression of subordinated class groups by the advantaged dominant class group. It "denotes negative attitudes, beliefs, and behaviors directed toward those with less power, who are socially devalued" (Lott, 2012, p. 654). Similar to racism, sexism, and heterosexism, classism can be expressed in the form of *institutional classism* and *interpersonal classism*. There are prejudice (negative attitudes toward the poor), stereotypes (shared negative beliefs about the poor), and discrimination (distancing, excluding, or denigrating behavior toward the poor) associated with classism. Williams (1993) further explained it when he wrote the following:

> Categorization of groups of people into upper and lower strata, into superior and inferior, is done by those who require such categorization to maintain their power, prevent others from obtaining an equal share of resources, and sustain the myth of superiority. (Lott, 2002, p. 101)

Expressed in everyday life, classism is the systematic assignment of characteristics of worth and ability based on social class, which is prejudicial, unfair, and unjust.

Social Class and Privilege

Although it is recognized as one dimension of cultural diversity, social class has not received its due attention in counseling research and practice, reflecting a "blind spot" (Liu, Pickett, & Ivey, 2007) of the American society. One of the reasons is that those who are in the position of power to expose the truth about social class (whether in politics, academic research, or professional practice) are the beneficiaries of the social class system—or at least are not in the disadvantaged positions in this hierarchy. There is "class privilege (i.e., unearned advantage and conferred dominance) and power" (Moon & Rolison, 1998, p. 132) that is assigned to those who have middle to high social class positions.

Class power translates into access to resources and control to "set the rules, frame the discourse, and name and describe those with less power" (Lott, 2002, p. 101). This power enables discrimination and grants members of high class unearned advantages and privileges that increase their power in relation to that of others. Similar to privileges due to other dominant social group memberships, class privilege is largely invisible to those who have it, but it benefits them in many ways, including financial or material recourses and access to education, housing, employment, health care, and so forth. Additionally, there are also various degrees of emotional or psychological benefits, such as feeling in control, self-confidence, a sense of belonging, and not being fearful of being perceived inferior due to being poor.

Similar to White privileges, middle- or upper-class privileges are difficult to acknowledge by those who have them. No one wants to believe that his or her professional or academic success, accumulation of wealth, or personal talent may be partially due to his or her position in society. For instance, growing up as a member of the middle class, a child is able to participate in various intellectual, athletic, artistic, social, or other extracurricular activities, which is a privilege that children from low social class do not have. This privilege no doubt places middle-class children ahead of children in poverty in terms of developing talent, skills, and knowledge for success later in life. In daily life, invisible privileges, such as shopping for groceries, turning up the heat in the house, or washing hands with running water, can be so pervasive that people take them for granted. Clearly, being a member of the middle or upper class comes with privileges in many areas of life. Comedian Sam Killermann developed a list of more than 30 examples of class privilege that will be useful for class discussion (see http://itspronouncedmetrosexual.com/wp-content/uploads/2012/10/Its-Pronounced-Metrosexual-Class-Privilege-List.pdf).

SMALL-GROUP CLASS ACTIVITY 10.2

Reflection on My Own Class Privileges

In small groups of three to four students, open the website for Sam Killermann's examples of class privileges (http://itspronouncedmetrosexual.com/wp-content/uploads/2012/10/Its-Pronounced-Metrosexual-Class-Privilege-List.pdf) and read them one at a time. Each member uses the self as the reference and answers "true" or "false," then shares his or her answers to the following questions with the group:

1. Was I aware of this privilege?
2. In what ways do I benefit from it or have to deal with it?
3. What does it mean to those who would have the opposite answer?
4. In what ways do I feel bothered by the fact that people would have different answers to this item?
5. What other class privileges do I have?

Intersectionality of Social Class With Race and Other Dimensions of Diversity

Although all middle- to upper-class people enjoy class privileges, their intersectionality of identities leads to significant within-group differences. Middle-class individuals who have subordinate-group memberships in race, sex, gender, sexual orientation, ability, or citizenship may experience unfair and undeserved disadvantages imposed onto them due to their subordinate-group membership in those areas. By comparing a White, male, heterosexual, cisgender, able-bodied, middle-class American with a male, cisgender, able-bodied, middle-class Mexican immigrant, we can probably infer that their life experiences and experienced privileges will be different. For any given individual living in the United States, multiple systems of privileges/oppression are at work in shaping their lives.

BOX 10.1 A VIEW OF INTERSECTIONALITY OF CULTURAL IDENTITY AND MULTIPLE SYSTEMS OF OPPRESSION

On www.huffingtonpost.com, author and advocate Gina Crosley-Corcoran (2014) shared her personal view of social class privilege:

I came from the kind of poor that people don't want to believe still exists in this country. Have you ever spent a frigid northern Illinois winter without heat or running water? I have. At twelve years old, were you making ramen noodles in a coffee maker with water you fetched from a public bathroom? I was. Have you ever lived in a camper year round and used a random relative's apartment as your mailing address? We did. Did you attend so many different elementary schools that you can only remember a quarter of their names? Welcome to my childhood.... My white skin didn't do shit to prevent me from experiencing poverty.... After one reads [Peggy] McIntosh's powerful [1988] essay, it's impossible to deny that being born with white skin in America affords people certain unearned privileges in life that people of another skin color simply are not afforded. . . . I know now that I am privileged in many ways. I am privileged as a natural born white citizen. I am privileged as a cis-gendered woman. I am privileged as an ablebodied person. I am privileged that my first language is also our national language.... But thankfully, intersectionality allows us to examine these varying dimensions and degrees of discrimination while raising awareness of the results of multiple systems of oppression at work.

White, Middle-Class Privilege

Social class, classism, and privilege are closely related to race and racism. The known "American culture" mostly represents the values and worldviews of the White middle class, which in turn suffuse our counseling theories and practices (Liu et al., 2007). The dominant values such as independence, autonomy, and freedom that are mostly from White middle-class traditions are highly regarded and followed in counseling. Thus, those who fit in the box of White middle class may find themselves well served by a helping profession, which is clearly a privilege.

To the pervasiveness of the White middle-class privilege phenomenon, Liu et al. (2007) presented examples of possible White middle-class self-statements that "illustrate a middle-class person's sense of worth and entitlement in various contexts, expectations, and assumptions" (p. 199). These statements cover eight areas—namely, housing and neighborhood, economic liberty, social structural support, power, familiarity with middle-class behavioral norms, self-satisfaction, leaving a heritage, and leisure (see Table 10.1). It is not difficult to see that the exercise of each of these privileges is at the expense of others who are unfairly placed in disadvantageous positions.

Table 10.1 Sample Self-Statements About White Middle-Class Privilege

The Privileges of Housing and Neighborhood
I can be assured that I have adequate housing for myself and my family.
I can be reasonably assured of the safety of my neighborhood.
I can be sure that most people that live in my neighborhood have the same privileges that I do.
I can easily stay away from parts of my town or areas where those who have less money live and have all my needs met.
My neighborhood is well maintained, and I can expect city or county services to be helpful to me.
To the best of my knowledge, those who live in my neighborhood are making their living legally.
Those who live in my neighborhood are unlikely to get into trouble with the law.
The Privileges of Economic Liberty
I can be assured of three meals a day with variety of choice and good nutrition.
I do not have to worry about surviving from day to day.
I can buy not only what I need to have but also what I want.
Given my background and the work I've done, I feel it is my right to be financially comfortable.
I feel able to obtain loans and manage my debts.
My child does not have to take on the responsibilities of an adult to keep the household running smoothly.
I expect to be able to retire with sufficient income.
I can work one job.
My family can survive an illness of one or more members.
I am pleased that I have enough money that I can comfortably give some away to charity.
The Privileges of Sociostructural Support
I can be reasonably certain that the government has my best interests in mind.
I can be reasonably certain that my elected representatives actually represent *me*.
I expect police to protect me and my interests.
When politicians speak of the middle class, I know they are referring to me.
The Privileges of Power
I am unaware of the lives of the "invisible working poor" and the impact of their low salaries on whom my middle-class privilege depends.
I feel able to influence schools and other institutions to treat my family fairly and give them advantages when they deserve it.
If my child runs into a problem in school, I feel that my concerns as a parent will be heard.

I have the monetary or human resources to get myself or my family out of legal trouble. I have the resources to make choices regarding my medical care. I have the power and prestige to reject those in a lower class. I can demand respect from others. I feel entitled to a good education. I can see a doctor when I want and expect reasonably fast and good service. I expect to receive reasonable respect and attention when I am shopping or interacting with a stranger. I feel I have the right to judge the service people provide me.
Familiarity With Middle-Class Behavioral Norms
I do not have to learn the social class behaviors of others. My life experience has been such that I feel comfortable in most social settings. The idea of a lawsuit is not foreign to me. Using a credit card is easy and normal. I know proper behavior and etiquette when dining in public. I feel uncomfortable when I come into contact with poor people or those who are homeless.
The Privileges of Self-Satisfaction
I can look at my life and feel that it has been reasonably successful. I feel I am what others strive to be. Because of what I have, others may be envious of me. I can feel sorry for others who have less than me. I can be ignorant of the hardships of others.
The Privileges of Leaving a Heritage
I can be reasonably assured that my status and influence will allow greater opportunities for my family. I can be reasonably certain that my child will be as or more prosperous than I am. I can be reasonably assured that I might receive an inheritance or leave one for others. The saying "follow in my footsteps" does not have a negative connotation. I assume that my child(ren) will have at least as good a life as mine or better.
The Privileges of Leisure
I can leisurely engage in activities that do not supplement my income. I can spend time and money on superficial concerns. I can expect to have vacation time each year.

Source: Liu, Pickett, and Ivey (2007). White middle-class privilege: Social class bias, and implications for training and practice. *Journal of Multicultural Counseling and Development, 35*, 194-206.

Social Class and Poverty

Poverty is a consequence of a society's unequal distribution of resources (Lott & Bullock, 2001) and can be generally defined as the lack of the minimum food and shelter necessary for maintaining life or a state of being extremely poor. The U.S. Census Bureau defines it by setting poverty thresholds in dollar amounts as the minimum income, and any individual or family who fails to meet the minimum is deemed as living in poverty. A few examples of poverty thresholds used in 2011 included the following:

- For an individual under 65 years old, it was $11,702.
- For a two-person household (both being 65 years and over), it was $13,609.
- For a family of four (with two children under 18), it was $22,811. ("Poverty," n.d.)

With these thresholds, 15.3% of the U.S. population (about 46.2 million people) in 2011 had income below the poverty level. It was also reported that the poverty rate had been increasing for four consecutive years (Bishaw, 2012). Moreover, some ethnic minorities had higher levels of poverty (see Figure 10.1).

Women, especially minority women, are more likely to be poor than men, and single women with children are most vulnerable to poverty (Cawthorne, 2008). Data collected in 2007 showed that 26.5% of African American women, 23.6% of Hispanic women, 11.6% of

Figure 10.1 U.S. Poverty Rates by Race and Hispanic or Latino Origin: 2007 to 2011

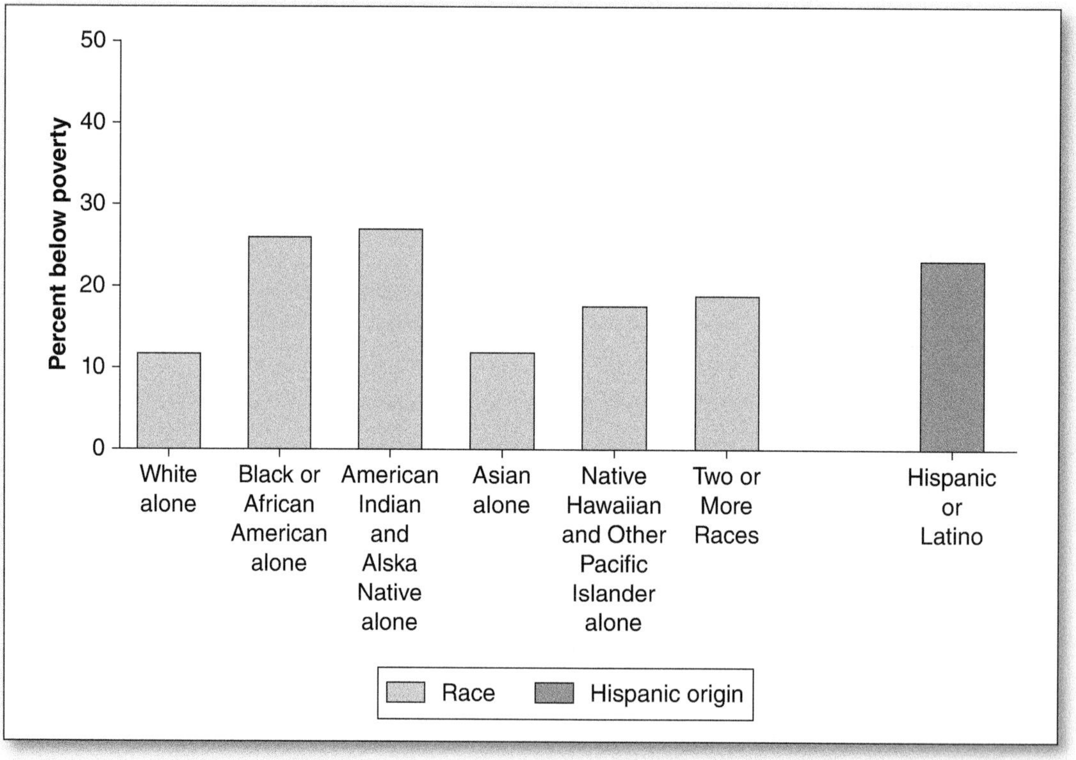

Source: Macartney, Bishaw, and Fontenot (2013).

Note: Persons who report only one race among the six defined categories are referred to as the race-alone population, while persons who report more than one race category are referred to as the Two or More Races population. This figure shows data using the race-alone approach. Use of the single-race population does not imply that it is the preferred method of presenting or analyzing data. The Census Bureau uses a variety of approaches. Because Hispanics may be of any race, data in this figure for Hispanics overlap with data for race groups.

White women, and 10.7% of Asian women were in poverty. Although there are many possible reasons, the gender pay gap may be one of the unfair phenomena that contribute to the high poverty rate among women. According to a 2013 report by the Institute of Women's Policy Research (Hegewisch, Williams, Hartmann, & Hudiburg, 2014), the ratio of women's and men's median annual earnings for full-time year-round workers was 76.5% in 2012, which means the annual gender wage gap for full-time year-round workers was 23.5%.

The largest group of poor people in the United States currently is the working poor, not people on welfare (Lott, 2012). Working-class and low-income individuals and families suffer in myriad ways from lack of access to many necessities for life due to their SES, such as adequate housing, health insurance, quality education, and so on. Additionally, the gross inequality due to social class often exposes the poor to many other kinds of exploitation or abuse. Lott and Bullock (2001) presented evidence that being poor not only means having inadequate life necessities but also entails being treated as "less than full citizens" by congressional leaders (p. 201), being blamed for their poorness by upper social classes, being perceived as incompatible to middle class in "parental style, cognitive style, problem-solving skills, speech systems, and so on" (p. 201), and being victimized by various negative perceptions, attributions, and attitudes. In media, for instance, the middle class is always portrayed as the norm or as characters of fictional programs. The poor, on the other hand, tend to appear on daytime talk shows and reality-based crime shows that convey distorted images and messages about the poor by showing "dysfunctional relationships, infidelity, and unruly, promiscuous teenage girls" (Bullock, Wyche, & Williams, 2001, p. 232). Differential representations of crime and social class, such as reality-based police dramas, "reinforce the stereotype that low-income men, particularly poor men of color, are involved with drugs" (p. 232). Such exploitation and abuse exacerbate the suffering of the poor and contribute to the power of middle or upper classes.

Understanding the Social Context of the Poor

To prevent ineffective or harmful interventions, counselors working with people of low social class must recognize their own class privileges, understand the social context of the poor, and avoid automatic application of the White middle-class values embedded in counseling theories. In Chapter 7, we discussed classism in the context of counselors' self-work in multicultural identity development in regard to social class. It is likely that most counselors-in-training at this time are members of the middle class. A multicultural consciousness is needed in understanding the experiences of those clients who are working poor or live in poverty. For counselors-in-training who have experienced being poor or poverty, caution is needed not to generalize their own experiences of surviving poverty to every client. Accurate understanding is needed for both broad and specific cultural and social contexts for every client.

Effects of Poverty

Effects of poverty are serious and grave for individuals, communities, and society. The growth of "urban ghettos" and the homeless population are results of chronic poverty and joblessness. These communities become "problems" or places to avoid for the larger society. People in these communities, especially families and children, are vulnerable to violence, criminal activities, and various threats to their well-being, health, and development. A report by the American Psychological Association points out, "Deepening poverty is inextricably linked with rising levels of homelessness and food insecurity/hunger for many Americans, and children are particularly affected by these conditions" (APA, n.d., para. 1). According to a report by the National Center on Family Homelessness, more than 1.6 million children (one in 45 children) in the United States were homeless in 2010, and approximately 650,000 were below age 6 (Bello, 2011). Children and youth who live in poverty are at greater risk for poor academic achievement, higher school dropout rates, abuse and neglect, behavioral and socioemotional problems, physical health problems, and developmental delays. Being homeless makes these risks even higher.

Psychologically, poverty also has a significant impact on individual behaviors and decision making. Research has documented an inverse relationship between SES and unhealthy behaviors such as tobacco use, physical inactivity, and poor nutrition, which then is related to higher health risks and mortality (see Pampel, Krueger, & Denney, 2011, for a comprehensive review). People with low SES are more likely to engage in such unhealthy behaviors than middle-class people. We want to encourage our readers to consume such information with multicultural consciousness and to be aware of the pitfall of blaming the victim. Often their decisions tend to be unproductive or self-destructive according to the White middle-class standard, but while it is in their best interest if healthier behaviors are adopted, we need to understand that sometimes their circumstances make healthy actions impossible or extremely difficult.

In a recent news report, an African American woman, Shanesha Taylor, was arrested for leaving her 6-month-old and 2-year-old sons alone in her car while she was interviewing for a job nearby in Scottsdale, AZ. Taylor did not have child care. When asked in a TV interview how she made the decision to leave her children in the car, she responded, "It's making a choice out of desperation. It's choosing what is the best option, what is the best thing for me to do in this particular situation—being able to provide food, a roof, clothes, shoes for them, or take this moment and care for them" (Kim, 2014). This is an example that individuals should not be judged out of their context, including their social class context.

SMALL-GROUP CLASS ACTIVITY 10.3

Discussion and Exploration of the Case of Anisha

In the same small groups, reflect on the following questions related to Anisha:

1. How does learning about classism and social class privileges/disadvantages change how you view Anisha and her circumstances?
2. At an emotional level, how do you feel about Anisha and about working with her in counseling?
3. What do you see as your challenges in working with her?

Effect of Classism, Discrimination, and Microaggression

Classism is real, negative, and has demoralizing effects on those who are on the bottom of the social class hierarchy. In daily life, classism supports discrimination and microaggression and creates a hostile environment for many.

Disparities Due to Social Class

The gaps between the rich and the poor in the United States are significant and are deepening in many cases and in myriad ways. In education, it has been a known fact that children from low social class families do not perform as well as their counterparts from affluent families. "As the income gap between high- and low-income families has widened, the achievement gap between children in high- and low-income families also widened" (Reardon, 2011, p. 91).

Research has shown that from early childhood, parental investments (money and time) in children's learning affect reading, math, and other skills later in life (Duncan & Magnuson, 2011). These investments are closely related to and restricted by the family SES. Education has always been a great society equalizer that improves individuals' chances of success in life, but now the advantages that money can buy on tests and school performance have become so great that they threaten the American ideal that education enables anyone who works hard to succeed. In today's American society, not everyone has the equal chance to succeed—the rich have a lot more opportunities than the poor. Social class status is one of several dimensions of diversity that can dictate what one can or can't achieve in education.

Classism has also contributed to class disparities in health and health care. The Centers for Disease Control and Prevention pointed out, "In the United States . . . the risk for mortality, morbidity, unhealthy behaviors, reduced access to healthcare, and poor quality of care increases with decreasing socioeconomic circumstances. . . . This association is continuous . . . and cumulative over the life course" (Beckles & Truman, 2011, p. 1). In fact, cancer mortality rates are largely related to race and social class (Byers, 2010). Research shows that the greatest influence on the improvement of health (with longer life expectancy and low infant and maternal mortality) has been due to improved social conditions (Wilkinson & Pickett, 2008). It is clear that the inequality in social conditions translates into unjust disparities in health outcomes and life expectancy for the poor.

Access to health care is obviously an area where the poor find themselves in a severely disadvantaged position. Due to the high cost of health insurance, about 47 million nonelderly Americans were uninsured in 2012, and the majority of them were in low-income working families; additionally, people of color were at higher risk of being uninsured than non-Hispanic Whites ("Key facts," 2014). Without health insurance, the uninsured are gambling with their lives, according to Dr. Sherry Glied (n.d.) from Columbia University:

> They're at risk of not getting regular care when they need it. They're at risk of not catching real problems before they get serious enough to not be treatable. They're at risk of not getting the best treatment when they actually do get sick. And they're at tremendous financial risk. They could lose everything that they've saved in their lives because of some even fairly minor health problem. (para. 6)

SMALL-GROUP CLASS ACTIVITY 10.4

Reflection on My Thoughts and Feelings About Meritocracy

In the same small groups, share and discuss your thoughts and feelings about the following questions:

1. Why do you think poor people are poor?
2. What comes to your mind when you think about the "American dream?"
3. Do you see different "realities" for different people when it comes to realizing the "American dream?"
4. In what ways do you think meritocracy is true or a fallacy? Why?
5. What emotions are you feeling when you think/talk about these questions?

Stereotypes of the Poor

The belief of meritocracy is deeply rooted in the American value system. It is often translated into attributions of the fate and marginalization of the poor to their own deficiencies—namely, they did not work hard, were not capable, or made bad choices. Entrenched in this biased and linear thinking about meritocracy are the stereotypes about the poor. As a result, when we hear that some poor students used drugs and missed school, we tend to think, "No wonder those poor students do not do well in school," while it is much less often that we would make such generalizations toward others. Such stereotypes lead to discrimination and microaggression against people who are poor.

In his recent book, Gorski (2013) provided evidence to dispute five common stereotypes about poor people—namely, poor people do not value education, poor people are lazy, poor people are substance abusers, poor people are linguistically deficient and bad communicators, and poor people are ineffective and inattentive parents. We all know that there are many other negative stereotypes about poor people being "less than" or "inferior to" the rich. Psychologically, these stereotypes further victimize the poor (above and beyond tangible material and access disadvantages). The research on *stereotype threat* (Steele, 2010) shows consistent evidence that people who are stereotyped tend to behave in a way that is consistent to the stereotype.

To help people understand low social class, we need to combat the unfair stereotypes and show genuine respect to them and their life experiences. Operating from a multicultural consciousness, let's not forget the following:

> Most poor people work every day. . . . Most poor people are . . . invisible and without national leaders. Most poor people are not on welfare. They raise other people's children. They work every day. They put food in our children's schools. They work every day. They clean our offices. They work every day. They work in fast food

> restaurants. They work every day. They cut grass; they water our flowers. They work every day. They comb our beaches. They work every day. They pick lettuce. They work every day. They work in hospitals, as orderlies and the like, and when we are sick, they wash our bodies, cool our fevers, launder our diseased sheets, empty slop jars; no job is beneath them. And yet, when they get sick, they cannot afford to lie in the bed that they made up every day. It's time for a change. (J. Jackson, 2000, p. 329)

Upward Mobility Expectations and Biases

Upward mobility is defined by dictionaries as the movement from one social level to a higher one, such as from lower social class to middle class, and is generally believed possible for every American. In his 2014 State of the Union Address, President Barack Obama reiterated that belief:

> Here in America, our success should not depend on accident of birth but the strength of our work ethic and the scope of our dreams. . . . it's how the son of a barkeep is the Speaker of the House, how the son of a single mom can be president of the greatest nation on Earth. (White House, 2014, para. 15)

While we recognize that many individuals have beaten the odds and have overcome challenges to achieve significant success in life, and we agree that it is great to have the hope that greater social equality will come, such drastic upward movement on the social ladder is certainly the exception rather than the norm (Clark, 2014). Due to various systemic reasons or reasons out of individuals' control, this may be more like a fantasy than a possibility for many. This way of promoting the meritocracy myth of the American dream (McNamee & Miller, 2004), while potentially motivating, has unintended consequences. Those who fail to move up on the SES ladder are blamed for their failure while the role of the unjust system of maldistribution of wealth and power is not recognized.

Upward mobility biases rooted in meritocratic reasoning may be present in our counseling practice. In order to be helpful, we often focus on helping those with low social class to move toward what is considered better according to the middle-class standard. For instance, in vocational psychology and counseling, counselors often operate from a definition of a *good society* as "one in which all people have opportunities to work in safe, humane conditions with compensation that affords a sufficient standard of living" (Blustein, McWhirter, & Perry, 2005, p. 148). Yet it is not clear what constitutes a good job or whether or not it is tied to the location or social class (Liu & Ali, 2005). There is a tendency to view high-status jobs as good, prestigious, and superior, and "push for upwardly mobile occupations" (p. 190). Liu and Ali cited research showing that "aspirations of material and monetary success . . . are associated with poor adjustment and behavioral disorders" (pp. 190–191). As a society, we do not value the work that is deemed as low paying or the low-level job, while in fact such jobs are necessary for everyone's survival.

Hostility of Microaggression

Cognitive and behavioral "distancing is the dominant response to poor people on the part of those who are not poor, and that distancing, separation, exclusion, and devaluing operationally define discrimination. Such responses, together with stereotypes and prejudice, define classism" (Lott, 2002, p. 100). Classism hurts people no matter how it is expressed, either bluntly or subtlety. However, the subtle forms of expression often go without being noticed, and we counselors are often unintentional perpetrators. Here is a counselor's summary of a client presented to a supervisor:

> So we spent some time talking about how he could be prepared for the upcoming job interview in a grocery store. We started with how he should prepare his look and what answers he needed to some common questions he might run into. He wore an old collar shirt and dark blue jeans that day and asked me if that was good enough. I told him that although he looked OK for someone from his neighborhood, he may want to wear maybe a pair of khaki pants, that is, if he had them. I also told him that I was sure the interviewer would understand if he did not dress properly because they knew his address; somehow he became noticeably quiet and his voice lowered. . . . I was at a loss.

With this description, could you see where the microaggression occurred and how it may have hurt the client? The passage sounds patronizing and demeaning and indicates lower expectations and perceptions of the client being "less than."

Social Class Identity, Values, and Worldviews

Social class status is a major contextual factor that determines individuals' social experiences. The poor are treated by our society as invisible to those who are not poor, even though it is widely known that poverty is one of the most devastating problems that our country faces. Deliberate efforts are needed to understand how people in low social classes develop their social identity and what values and worldviews they may have.

Social Class Identity

Social class matters; it intersects with other diversity demographics in any American's social identity development. One's social class identity is socially constructed and a product of the interaction between the in-group (e.g., the poor) and out-group (e.g., middle class, the rich). Similar to other cultural identities, an individual in the oppressed group (low social class) may go through stages to reach a healthy social class identity. Research has shown that being able to claim a firm working-class identity may provide a "place" in the class culture of our society for the individual to negotiate a "self" and to practice certain values in life, which is especially possible for those who have been successful in upward mobility on the SES ladder (Jones, 1998, p. 160).

Using B. Jackson and Hardiman's (1994) model, individuals with low social class may experience five stages of identity: naïve, acceptance, resistance, redefinition, and internalization. At the *naïve stage*, individuals (young children) have no consciousness about social class differences or different codes of behaviors specific to their group (the poor). As they become aware that others do not share their group identity, they leave this stage and move into the *acceptance stage*. They accept and identify with, consciously or unconsciously, the dominant group (middle class or the rich) along with their worldviews, including the view about the poor. Usually the conflicts between the dominant group's view and the positive attributes of their own group lead them to the *resistance stage*. The awareness of social class oppression and its impact is more acknowledged, and individuals start questioning classist assumptions and practice. The *redefinition stage* is when individuals focus more attention to people and their experiences in their own group and lessen association with the dominant group. Finally, individuals enter the *internalization stage* where they view their in-group members positively and understand classism.

Theoretically, upward mobility, if it happens, can happen at any stage. We believe, however, individuals at later stages have better understanding of the social and institutional factors associated with the class stratification and the impact of classism. Therefore, they are more likely to succeed in the face of classism and are more capable of dealing with discrimination and prejudice after they succeed. For counselors, working with individuals requires consideration of both emotional and cognitive experience differences between stages and choices of different intervention strategies.

SMALL-GROUP CLASS ACTIVITY 10.5

Reflection on My Social Class Background and Worldview

In your same small groups, share your thoughts and feelings about the following questions:

1. When you were growing up, what was your family's financial situation?
2. Describe the neighborhood(s) you lived in when growing up.
3. Describe your educational experiences and those of your parents and grandparents.
4. How did your family spend time together? Did you take vacations? Have leisure times?
5. How was your family's social life? With whom did you socialize?
6. How would you describe your family's social class status?
7. In what ways do you think your social class plays a role in your achievements up to this point?
8. In what ways have your social class and achievements shaped your current worldview—your attitudes, behaviors, and feelings about money, work, interpersonal relationships, sense of self, expectations of life, political positions, and so on?
9. Describe how you view and feel about people in other social classes.
10. How do you view classism?

Social Class Values and Worldviews

Social class is a cultural phenomenon in the economic culture of the United States. Social class status differences and associated experiences are the bases of different cultural values and worldviews, which in turn influence individuals' behaviors and experiences. To help understand how to integrate social class context into counseling and how to facilitate individual growth in different social classes, Liu and Soleck, et al. (2004) presented a social class worldview model (SCWM). This model is comprised of five interrelated domains:

a. *Consciousness, Attitudes, and Salience*: Individual's capacity to articulate and understand the relevance and meaningfulness of social class in his or her environment

b. *Referent Groups*: People (past, present, and future) in an individual's life who help guide the development of an SCWM and mediate social class behaviors

c. *Property Relationships*: Materials that people value, use to define themselves, expect as a part of their worldview, and use to exclude others

d. *Lifestyle*: The way individuals choose to organize their time and resources within a socially classed context to remain congruent with their economic culture

e. *Behaviors*: Learned and socialized, purposeful and instrumental actions that reinforce an individual's social class worldview (pp. 104–106)

This model helps us understand the differences across social classes as well as those within each social class. To work with people with low social class in counseling, we need to understand their behavior in the context of their life environment, references groups, views on material aspects of life, life habits, and so forth. Most importantly, we need to assess how they view their own social class and their socioeconomic environment. Very often, internalized classism is a real influential factor. Individuals may sometimes internalize the dominant society's negative beliefs about them and play them out against themselves and others of their class. They may engage in behaviors out of feelings of inferiority to higher-class people, shame for their own family, hostility and blame toward other working-class or poor people, or even beliefs that classist institutions are fair. This is the result of experienced classism.

There have been attempts to describe the value differences related to one's social class. Payne (1996, 2012) discussed a number of "hidden rules among classes." She identified differences between those in poverty, the middle class, and the wealthy in 15 areas: possessions, money, personality, social emphasis, food, clothing, time, education, destiny, language, family structure, worldview, love, driving forces, and humor; she showed that people may have different values or follow different decision-making rules due to their difference in social class. For instance, regarding money, it is likely that people living in poverty would focus on how to spend it, while middle class might focus on how to manage it, and the rich on how to invest it. Regarding worldview, the rich may be more likely to discuss international issues than the middle class or the poor since what is happening locally and nationally may be more relevant to their lives.

Although we think describing value differences among people in relation to their different social class statuses without considering their class consciousness or social class identity posts the danger of stereotyping, this awareness helps us to take into consideration the role of individuals' social class in their values, priorities, and worldviews in the economic culture of our society. In counseling, when the counselor and the client are from different social classes, extra sensitivity is needed for the counselor not to use his or her own values to evaluate the client. In fact, we would also promote focusing on strengths and positive characteristics and behaviors of the underprivileged. With a multicultural consciousness, we will not automatically deem spending money as less smart or less responsible than managing or investing money. We believe the psychological value of different rules is not determined by the social class, but it reflects different levels of privileges.

SMALL-GROUP CLASS ACTIVITY 10.6

Discussion and Exploration of the Case of Anisha

In the same small groups, reflect on the following questions related to Anisha:

1. In what ways does your knowledge of the social contexts of the poor influence how you view Anisha and her situation?
2. How does your knowledge of social class related to identity development, values, and worldviews inform your understanding of Anisha and her situation?
3. How do you conceptualize Anisha's lack of empathy?
4. How do you describe and view her communication style?
5. What are some of the strengths Anisha exhibited?

Assessment, Prevention, and Intervention

Overcoming Social Class Biases

Social class biases in assessment and selection of people and their merits and skills have been documented for a long time and in many areas, including education, employment, legal affairs, medical services, and so on. The gross injustice to members of low social classes is apparent and long lasting. They are unfairly seen as having fewer desirable characteristics or merits and perceived as being less achieved, less qualified, less deserving, and more blamable and punishable than the rich or the middle class. People in low social class have little or no voice in defending themselves. The rules, norms, and standards are set by the middle or upper class in all areas, including education and psychology. In mental health–related professions such as counseling, assessment biases can lead to serious consequences, including over- or misdiagnosis, failed interventions, or even retraumatization of socioeconomically marginalized people.

To conduct a fair assessment, counselors should first and foremost be aware of their own social class and the ways in which they have benefitted from or have been impacted by their position on the social class ladder. It is probably safe to say that the majority of us who have made it to graduate school have received help that is not available to everyone in our society. Second, counselors need to be aware that most assessment tools we have were designed by and for the White middle class. The normal-abnormal or healthy-unhealthy standards do not reflect the worldviews and values of those who have low SES or live in poverty. Third, counselors, with a multicultural consciousness, need to listen to and hear client stories as attentively and thoroughly as possible. Due to social class differences, we may live in two Americas and often do not share a common "reality." Our assessment of what is normal, right, or healthy is context driven. For instance, we would think intrinsic motivation toward work is healthy and desirable, but extrinsic motivation is equally respectful and reflects strength in the context that survival needs outweigh self-actualization efforts.

Last but not least, we need to develop a positive view of and genuine passion for the people who are socioeconomically disadvantaged. They may not play by our playbook or may not even appear motivated to change, but they have a lot that we can learn from. No matter how "abnormal" their circumstances or "symptoms" may be, they are doing their best to survive and succeed. In fact, recent studies by the Pew Research Center found no evidence that "lower-income and less-well-educated Americans value patriotism, religion, or family any less than they ever have" and they "haven't undermined their values and long-term optimism . . . there is little evidence that they feel sorry for themselves, or see themselves as economically doomed or morally adrift" (Kohut & Dimock, 2013, para.19). Only by being positive and genuinely interested in them can we get accurate information for a fair assessment.

Eliminating Unintentional Victim Blaming

Both overt and covert victim blaming is common when considering issues related to poverty. Rather than acknowledging and examining the uncomfortable truth concerning systemic issues about poverty, using the poor as scapegoats happens in government policies, media, and even in professional services. We are all aware of the national dialogues on social welfare-related issues in which the poor are portrayed publicly as lazy, unmotivated, reliant on government welfare, and so on. In fact, most people living under the poverty line are not welfare recipients, and the majority of them want to work and be productive members of society (Kohut & Dimick, 2013). The poor are mostly presented in the media as associated with crime, disease, substance abuse, mental illness, and low academic achievements. Even when the subject of the show is positive (e.g., improving school retention of students from low-income families), such repeated and abundant negative associations reinforce stereotypes and carry a victim-blaming message.

In many professional prevention programs such as parent education, reading programs, and drug abuse preventive activities, the attitude that "You have this problem, and we are here to help you fix it" may convey a victim-blaming message as well. How we determine the problem and choose the method and delivery services (e.g., focusing only on the individual and not the systemic issues) could make the targeted people feel that they are the problem. For instance, schools may want to help students from low-income families to succeed by assigning them more readings and doing more tests without addressing the fact that the school is terribly unsupported, and the teaching staff is not qualified because of its location in a poor neighborhood. Similarly, in working with individuals and communities by providing psychoeducational programs, counselors need to be thoughtful and not treat the people as the problem. Many of their behavioral problems are reflections of the neglect and unfair treatment by the larger system and society.

SMALL-GROUP CLASS ACTIVITY 10.7

How Well Could You Survive in Poverty?

First, rate the following statements on your own using the scale below; then share your answers and reflect on them with your small group. Make sure to focus on your emotional experiences.

1	2	3	4	5
Not At All				Very Much

1. I know which churches and sections of town have the best rummage sales.
2. I know when Wal-Mart, drug stores, and convenience stores throw away over-the-counter medicine with expired dates.
3. I know which pawn shops sell DVDs for $1.
4. In criminal courts in my town, I know which judges are lenient, which ones are crooked, and which ones are fair.
5. I know how to physically fight and defend myself.
6. I know how to get a gun, even if I have a police record.
7. I know how to keep my clothes from being stolen at the Laundromat.
8. I know what problems to look for in a used car.
9. I/my family use a payday lender.
10. I know how to live without electricity and a phone.
11. I know how to use a knife as scissors.
12. I can entertain a group of friends with my personality and my stories.

(Continued)

(Continued)

13. I know which churches will provide assistance with food or shelter.
14. I know how to move in half a day.
15. I know how to get and use food stamps or an electronic card for benefits.
16. I know where the free medical clinics are.
17. I am very good at trading and bartering.
18. I can get by without a car.
19. I know how to hide my car so the repo man cannot find it.
20. We pay our cable TV bill before we pay our rent.
21. I know which sections of town "belong" to which gangs.

Source: Payne (2012).

Respect, Validate, and Be Strength Based

Validating clients' experiences and respecting their humanity are the top golden rules of counseling. However, efforts and skills are needed when we work with clients whose social context (with socioeconomic disadvantages) is different from ours and from what our theories reflect. We need to be able to accept that how they feel is real, reasonable, and valid, that their thoughts and ideas reflect their strength, and that the way they are living their life is the best way they can see. It can be difficult if we are not able to challenge the White middle-class worldview that is deeply embedded in our knowledge as well as in our personal life.

It is extremely disturbing that socioeconomic inequality in the United States has seriously undermined Americans' health (Weir, 2013). Research has consistently shown that socioeconomic inequalities have adverse effects on health behaviors (e.g., smoking, physical activity, diet) and physical (e.g., high blood pressure, obesity, heart disease, infectious diseases, mortality) and mental (e.g., depression, anxiety, mood disorders) health (Phelan, Link, & Tehranifar, 2010). It is important that when we work with individuals or families, we understand this context and show respect to them even if their behaviors may be "dysfunctional" from our cognitive point of view of psychological health. Individuals' poor health behaviors are often seen and talked about as "risk factors," but we need to understand the underlying cause and not blame individuals. It is not their choice to eat unhealthily or be malnutritioned, live under stressful conditions, or have social isolation. Even unhealthy behaviors such as smoking and inactivity need to be viewed in the context of lack of resources and opportunities. With a multicultural consciousness, perhaps counselors can conceptualize "risk" and "protective" factors as a continuum along which people in disadvantageous positions exercise their strength and do the best they can to survive, succeed, and contribute to society.

There have been observed psychological characteristics of people from low-income families or in poverty in counseling. Socioeconomically disenfranchised clients may show difficulty in trusting counselors who are not members of their social class, lack of interest in the counseling process, low motivation for change, or an inability to be engaged in therapeutic activities (Monk, Winslade, & Sinclair, 2008). These behaviors should not be seen as deficits or obstacles but rather understood as reflecting their ability to protect themselves or survive in difficult life conditions. Their resilience, strength, and perseverance need to be acknowledged. Only through validation and respect can we build helpful therapeutic relationships with them.

Working with this population, counselors may find themselves feeling disbelief or extreme sadness (for what they learn about clients' actual situations), hopelessness (for not being able to change things for them), or frustration (for not being therapeutically helpful to them). These feelings often lead to a tendency to distance themselves (emotionally or physically) from clients and their environments. We need to remember that our distancing behavior is quite familiar to them because they have been treated with it by society, and it can do harm. With a nonclassist cultural identity, we need to show our multicultural consciousness and bring our heartfelt compassion into the therapeutic work with them.

Social Advocacy

Medical sociologists have addressed a timeworn but basic and critical social problem that our society has faced for a long time: "Society's poorer and less privileged members live in worse health and die much younger than the rich and more privileged ones" (Phelan et al., 2010, p. 528). Based on years of research, Phelan et al. pointed out that "socioeconomic inequalities in health and mortality are very large, very robust, and very well documented" (p. 528). They argue that to solve the problem of health disparities, the link between resources (money, knowledge, prestige, power, beneficial social connections, and medical and health-promoting advances) has to be weakened or broken. Efforts are needed at policy levels. What should multiculturally competent counselors in the 21st century do? Advocate! We need to advocate for systemic changes through policies, as well as serve the population at individual, family, or community levels. Section 5 will be devoted to this topic.

SMALL-GROUP CLASS ACTIVITY 10.8

Discussion and Exploration of the Case of Anisha

In the same small groups, reflect on the following questions and brainstorm how to best help Anisha:

1. What would you do to establish an effective therapeutic relationship with her?
2. How would you prepare yourself to validate her and her experiences?

(Continued)

(Continued)

3. What about her and what specific experiences would you want to validate?
4. How would you gain genuine respect and express it to her?
5. What would be the areas of treatment that you would focus on?
6. What are some advocacy actions that you think you would want to explore to help Anisha?

Summary

This chapter discusses poverty as a social phenomenon that reflects systemic injustice. In the economic culture of our society, some people not only have to endure hardship due to low income or lack of access to opportunities, but they also have to face classism, a negative attitude and belief system that plays a significant role in making the poor poorer and making it difficult for the poor to survive and succeed. Under the belief system of meritocracy cherished by the middle and upper class, the poor suffer from psychological stress and abuse in our society. Counselors of the 21st century need to be cognitively knowledgeable and emotionally prepared to help the poor in ways that will not reinforce negative societal messages about them. For this, we need to be aware of and overcome our biases and avoid victim blaming. Exercising our multicultural consciousness, we will feel passionate in validating, respecting, and advocating for them.

Takeaway Messages

1. Social class is socially constructed and awards middle- and upper-class privileges but puts low classes in disadvantageous positions.
2. Social inequality in power and access to resources is responsible for economic and psychological suffering of the poor.
3. As counselors, we need to recognize our own class privileges and biases and appreciate the strength of clients with low social class status.
4. Counseling theories and systems mainly reflect middle-class values, and blind application of them can lead to victim blaming.
5. Multiculturally competent counselors will use a strength-based approach and focus on respecting, validating, and advocating for their clients.

Recommended Resources

Readings

Black, L. L., & Stone, D. (2005). Expanding the definition of privilege: The concept of social privilege. *Journal of Multicultural Counseling and Development, 33*, 243–255.

Fernandez, M. A., Butler, A. M., & Eyberg, S. M. (2011). Treatment outcome for low socioeconomic status African American families in parent-child interaction therapy: A pilot study. *Child & Family Behavior Therapy, 33*(1), 32–48.

Grimes, M. E., & McElwain, A. D. (2008). Marriage and family therapy with low-income clients: Professional, ethical, and clinical issues. *Contemporary Family Therapy, 30*, 220–232.

Johnson, L. (2012, February 21). Eating near the poverty line [Web log post]. Retrieved from http://www.wholefoodsmarket.com/blog/whole-story/eating-near-poverty-line

Kim, S., & Cardemil, E. (2012). Effective psychotherapy with low-income clients: The importance of attending to social class. *Journal of Contemporary Psychotherapy, 42*(1), 27–35. doi:10.1007/s10879-011-9194-0

Sachs, J. D. (2005). *The end of poverty: How we can make it happen in our lifetime.* New York, NY: Penguin Press.

Media and Websites

Gantz, J., & Gantz, H. (Producers), & Gantz, J. (Director). (2013). *American Winter* [Documentary]. United States: HBO. Available from http://www.americanwinterfilm.com/buy-dvd

APA website: http://www.apa.org/pi/ses/resources/publications/factsheet-education.aspx

Class action: http://www.classism.org

http://factfinder2.census.gov/faces/nav/jsf/pages/index.xhtml

http://heinonline.org.www2.lib.ku.edu:2048/HOL/Page?handle=hein.journals/josf87&collection=journals&page=325#335

References

American Psychological Association. (n.d.). *Effects of poverty, hunger, and homelessness on children and youth.* Retrieved from http://www.apa.org/pi/families/poverty.aspx

Beckles, G. L., & Truman, B. I. (2011, January 14). Education and income: United States, 2005 and 2009. *Morbidity and Mortality Weekly Report, 60*(Suppl.), 13–19. Retrieved from http://www.cdc.gov/mmwr/preview/mmwrhtml/su6001a3.htm?s.cid_su6001a3_w

Bello, M. (2011, December 31). Report: Child homelessness up 33% in 3 years. *USA Today.* Retrieved from http://usatoday30.usatoday.com/news/nation/story/2011-12-12/homeless-children-increase/51851146/1

Bishaw, A. (2012, September). *Poverty: 2010 and 2011 American Community Survey Briefs issued.* Retrieved from http://www.census.gov/prod/2012pubs/acsbr11-01.pdf

Blustein, D. L., McWhirter, E. H., & Perry, J. C. (2005). An emancipatory communitarian approach to vocational development, theory, research, and practice. *The Counseling Psychologist, 33,* 141–179.

Bullock, H. E., Wyche, K. F., & Williams, W. R. (2001). Media images of the poor. *Journal of Social Issues, 57,* 229–246.

Byers, T. (2010). Two decades of declining cancer mortality: Progress with disparity. *Annual Review of Public Health, 31,*121–132.

Cawthorne, A. (2008, October 8). The straight facts on women in poverty. Retrieved from https://www.americanprogress.org/issues/women/report/2008/10/08/5103/the-straight-facts-on-women-in-poverty/

Clark, G. (2014). *The son also rises: Surnames and the history of social mobility.* Princeton, NJ: Princeton University Press.

Crosley-Corcoran, G. (2014, May 8). Explaining White privilege to a broke White person [Web log post]. Retrieved from http://www.huffingtonpost.com/gina-crosleycorcoran/explaining-white-privilege-to-a-broke-white-person_b_5269255.html

Duncan, G. J., & Magnuson, K. (2011). The nature and impact of early achievement skills, attention skills, and behavior problems. In G. J. Duncan & R. J. Murnane, (Eds.), *Whither opportunity? Rising inequality, schools, and children's life chances.* (pp. 47–70) New York, NY: Russell Sage Foundation.

Gallo, L. C., & Matthews, K. A. (2003). Understanding the association between socioeconomic status and physical health: Do negative emotions play a role? *Psychological Bulletin, 129*, 10–51.

Glied, S. (n.d.). The uninsured. *Healthcare Crisis: Who's at Risk? (PBS)*. Retrieved from http://www.pbs.org/healthcarecrisis/uninsured.html

Gorski, P. C. (2013). *Reaching and teaching students in poverty: Strategies for erasing the opportunity gap*. New York, NY: Teachers College Press.

Hegewisch, A., Williams, C., Hartmann, H., & Hudiburg, S. K. (2014, March). *The gender wage gap: 2013—Differences by race and ethnicity, no growth in real wages for women*. Retrieved from http://www.iwpr.org/publications/pubs/the-gender-wage-gap-2013-differences-by-race-and-ethnicity-no-growth-in-real-wages-for-women#sthash.9PUU26oc.dpuf

Jackson, B., & Hardiman, R. (1994). Social identity development model. In M. Adams, P. Brigham, P. Dalpes, & L. Marchesani (Eds.), *Diversity and oppression: Conceptual frameworks* (19–22) Dubuque, IA: Kendall/Hunt.

Jackson, J. (2000). What ought psychology to do? *American Psychologist, 55*, 328–330.

Jones, S. J. (1998). Subjectivity and class consciousness: The development of class identity. *Journal of Adult Development, 5*, 145–162.

Killermann, S. (2014, August 10). Thirty-plus examples of class privilege. Retrieved from http://itspronounced-metrosexual.com/wp-content/uploads/2012/10/Its-Pronounced-Metrosexual-Class-Privilege-List.pdf

Kim, E. K. (2014, July 24). 'Moment of desperation' led Arizona mom to leave kids in hot car during job interview. *USA Today*. Retrieved from http://www.today.com/parents/moment-desperation-led-shanesha-taylor-leave-kids-hot-car-1D79969954

Kohut, A., & Dimock, M. (2013, May 9). U.S. poor express strong values, not self-pity. *Bloomberg View*. Retrieved from http://www.bloombergview.com/articles/2013-05-09/u-s-poor-express-strong-values-not-self-pity

Liu, W. M., & Ali, S. R. (2005). Addressing social class and classism in vocational theory and practice: Extending the emancipatory communitarian approach. *The Counseling Psychologist, 33*, 189–196.

Liu, W. M., Ali, S. R., Soleck, G., Hopps, J., Dunston, K., & Pickett, T. (2004). Using social class in counseling psychology research. *Journal of Counseling Psychology, 51*, 3–18.

Liu, W. M., Pickett, T., Jr., & Ivey, A. E. (2007). White middle-class privilege: Social class bias, and implications for training and practice. *Journal of Multicultural Counseling and Development, 35*, 194–206.

Liu, W. M., Soleck, G., Hopps, J., Dunston, K., & Pickett, T. (2004). A new framework to understand social class in counseling: The social class worldview model and modern classism theory. *Journal of Multicultural Counseling and Development, 32*, 95–122.

Lott, B. (2002). Cognitive and behavioral distancing from the poor. *American Psychologist, 57*(2),100–110. doi:10.1037/0003-066X.57.2.100

Lott, B. (2012, November). The social psychology of class and classism. *American Psychologist, 67*(8), 650–658. doi:10.1037/a0029369

Lott, B., & Bullock, H. E. (2001). Who are the poor? *Journal of Social Issues, 57*, 189–206.

Macartney, S., Bishaw, A., & Fontenot, K. (2013, February). *Poverty rates for selected detailed race and Hispanic groups by state and place: 2007–2011 American Community Survey Briefs*. Retrieved from http://www.census.gov/prod/2013pubs/acsbr11-17.pdf

McNamee, S. J., & Miller, R. K., Jr. (2004). *The meritocracy myth*. Lanham, MD: Rowman & Littlefield.

Monk, G. D., Winslade, J. M., & Sinclair, S. L. (2008). *New horizons in multicultural counseling*. Thousand Oaks, CA: Sage.

Moon, D. G., & Rolison, G. L. (1998). Communication of classism. In M. L. Hecht (Ed.), *Communicating prejudice* (pp. 122–135). Thousand Oaks, CA: Sage.

Pampel, F. C., Krueger, P. M., Denney, J. T. (2011). Socioeconomic disparities in health behaviors. *Annual Review of Sociology, 36*, 349–370. doi:10.1146/annurev.soc.012809.102529

Payne, R. K. (1996). *A framework for understanding poverty: Modules 1–7 workbook*. Highlands, TX: aha! Process.

Payne, R. K. (2012). *A framework for understanding poverty: 10 actions to educate students.* Highlands, TX: aha! Process.

Phelan, J. C., Link, B. G., & Tehranifar, P. (2010). Social conditions as fundamental causes of health inequalities: Theory, evidence, and policy implications. *Journal of Health and Social Behavior, 51*, 528–540.

Poverty. (n.d.). *U. S. Bureau of the Census.* Retrieved from https://www.census.gov/hhes/www/poverty/methods/definitions. html

Reardon, S. F. (2011). The widening academic achievement gap between the rich and the poor: New evidence and possible explanations. In G. J. Duncan & R. J. Murnane (Eds.), *Whither opportunity? Rising inequality, schools, and children's life chances*, pp. 91–116. New York, NY: Russell Sage.

Steele, C. M. (2010). *Whistling Vivaldi and other clues to how stereotypes affect us.* New York, NY: W. W. Norton.

Weir, K. (2013). Inequality in the United States is undermining Americans' health and longevity, say experts. *Monitor on Psychology, 44*(9), 37–41.

White House Office of the Press Secretary. (2014, January 28). *President Barack Obama's state of the union address.* Retrieved from http://www.whitehouse.gov/the-press-office/2014/01/28/president-barack-obamas-state-union-address

Wilkinson, R. G., & Pickett, K. E. (2008). Income inequality and socioeconomic gradients in mortality. *American Journal of Public Health, 98*, 699–704.

11

Working With Diversity in Physical Ability

We must recognize the whole gamut of human potentialities, and so weave a less arbitrary social fabric, one in which each diverse human gift will find a fitting place.

—Margaret Mead

CHAPTER OVERVIEW

This chapter provides discussion of diversity in physical ability with attention to the increasing number of persons with disabilities (PWDs) in the U.S. population. Counselors of all specialties and orientations will need to be competent in their service delivery to clients with disabilities. Disability is a complex and multifaceted issue that transcends all social divides, including racial/ethnic, sexual orientation, gender, religion, and class strata (McDonald, Keys, & Balcazar, 2007). We encourage the understanding of disability as an element of human diversity and discuss the predominant models of disability that provide varying definitions and causal attributions of disability. We give consideration to what constitutes ethical practice when providing services to individuals with disabilities with emphasis on elements of competency. If counseling professionals are to provide competent and ethical mental health services, they must be prepared to advocate on behalf of all underrepresented or marginalized groups—including persons with disabilities.

SELF-ASSESSMENT OF PRE-EXISTING AWARENESS AND KNOWLEDGE

- How do I describe my physical ability/disability identity development?
- How does my ability/disability identity influence my work with persons with disabilities?

- What is my level of competency regarding physical ability in working with culturally diverse clients?
- How do I understand the role of my clients' physical ability in their psychological health?
- How competent do I feel integrating their physical ability experiences in my understanding of them and their issues?
- How competent do I feel providing interventions that effectively address clients' concerns in the context of their physical ability?
- How competent do I feel utilizing myself (in terms of my physical ability) as a helping agent in working with clients?

LEARNING OBJECTIVES

After reading this chapter, students will be able to do the following:

1. Understand the marginalizing impact of ableism on the life and health of persons with disabilities
2. Recognize the importance of counselors' ability/disability identity in their competence to effectively counsel persons with disabilities
3. Understand the relevance of counselors' and clients' physical ability statuses in establishing effective therapeutic relationships
4. Conceptualize clients' concerns and understand their physical ability experiences even if they did not come to counseling to address those experiences per se
5. Be sensitive to the physical ability relevance of psychological interventions that counselors plan and/or deliver
6. Understand the necessity of counselors being comfortable using their own physical ability in building effective theoretical relationships with culturally diverse clients

The Reflections of Anthony

What does it mean to be an African American, blind male in this society?

It means to be seen as different and separate from everyone else in society. In group discussions, I am rarely asked a direct question, and many times people seem to forget that I am in the room. My participation in activities, like sports, storytelling, or thoughtful recourse is seen as "special" because my blindness and ethnic origin are the only two

(Continued)

(Continued)

things that make me exceptional. I am never viewed as a hardworking, ambitious person who excels because he wants to pursue the American dream. In fact, is it possible for blind people to dream at all? In summary, being a blind African American means to constantly fight against stereotypes and tirelessly attempt to get people to accept my normalcy.

What experiences (e.g., school, home, community) have you had that made you feel different?

One day while waiting for the bus, I was approached by a bus driver from a different bus. The man had stopped not to check if I needed to catch his bus but rather to update me on my current appearance. This bus driver wanted to know if I knew what I looked like. I told him that I did; I explained that I had not always been blind. I informed him that I was married and had two children who always commented on my slowly greying hair. At this point, I assumed the conversation was finished. The bus driver then said, "Do you know how dark-skinned you are?" I responded that I was aware of this and did not have a problem with my dark skin—after all, my wife loves it! He then continued with, "You are really a dark, ebony man." He said he too was dark-skinned, though not nearly as dark as I. I had suspected this man was African American because of the sound of his voice and the vernacular of his speech. His informing me of his skin tone confirmed it for me, and I really was not in the mood for this bizarre conversation. I then asked him to leave me alone because I was getting angry. At this point, he invited me to his church, which he indicated was Baptist with a lot of praising, shouting, and singing, which I would probably enjoy because you know, me being blind and all. Needless to say, I never went to the church. I do not think this stranger would have approached me with this thoughtlessness if I were sighted. My disability made me feel vulnerable, and I believe the only reason the absurdity ended was his necessity to get back to work.

What experiences (e.g., school, home, community) have you had due to being different (in terms of your interaction with mainstream society)?

I lived life as an African American male with sight until I was 23 years old. I am twice that age now, so I have lived more than half of my life as a blind person. It was much easier to engage and be part of general society prior to my 23rd birthday. A minority with a disability has been an eye-opening experience, no pun intended. As a newly blind person, I assumed that prejudice and racism were a function of the sighted world. Experience has taught me otherwise.

Many years ago I was a participant in a selective placement program at a nonprofit center in Arkansas. The Internal Revenue Service (IRS) uses this facility to select vision-impaired people for employment. The nonprofit agency's mandate was to train and develop blind people for possible employment with the IRS. The IRS would conduct interviews at the agency as positions within their call centers became available. There were always more people seeking employment than positions available, so we had to compete for the jobs.

My job coach at the agency asked me to skip the first round of interviews in order to work on my braille skills, even though I was the only one within the group who had a college degree and had experience at a call center. The job at the IRS was over-the-phone tax collections. I told her that I believed I could do the job and work on my braille skills at the same time. By this time, I had been informed by current blind IRS employees that having braille skills was not as important as it had been in the past because most of the resources were online through the IRS computer network, and this could be tapped by using a computer loaded with speech software. My job coach continued to insist that I not interview even though I felt I had good reasons to at least attempt an interview.

To make a long story short, I did interview, and I worked at the IRS for over 10 years. I honestly believe she did not want me to interview because she wanted the less-qualified White people to have a better shot at getting the job. She thought I should have waited my turn, so to speak. After everyone was informed that I was selected, I had several blind people approach me with the "Gosh, I did not know that you were Black" statement. I wondered who told them and why they were so surprised.

In what ways do you believe our counseling profession has inadequately served African Americans with disabilities?

I think the prime issue is the continued belief that anyone who is disabled needs to see a rehabilitation counselor and not just a counselor. Counselors need to strive to understand that people are individuals with group classifications, and those classifications may or may not fit the individual's identity. African Americans and the disabled continually deal with stereotype bias, and it is very insulting when trusted professionals engage in this behavior.

I have an acquaintance who, after graduating from college, started working at a bank, telemarketing credit cards. He quickly grew tired of peddling credit card applications to people while they attempted to enjoy dinner with their family. Within a 1-year period, he abruptly quit the job, stating he could no longer handle the stress and the work environment. He went to see a career counselor and was told that because of his demographic classification (African American and blind), it would be nearly impossible for him to get a job, and he should strongly consider trying to work out things with his previous employer. My friend told her he hated doing sales work, and this was a source of excessive anxiety for him. He told her that the anxiety the job caused him contributed to his marriage difficulties because he was so angry and disgusted when he got home. He said he told her, "I really want to seek other employment." My friend said that it seemed as if the counselor did not hear what he said and just wanted him to consider going back to the job. I am glad to say he did find other employment by doing his own job search.

(Continued)

(Continued)

There are two things that bother me about the interaction between my friend and the career counselor. Number one is why would she think his employer would take him back so readily? I believe she saw the job as a gift to him, and all he needed to do was ask for the present back. The counselor seemed to operate under the assumption that this job was granted to him, that it was not something he earned by his own merit. The other issue with this interaction is how little the counselor listened to the stated needs of my friend. She never did address his anxiety and the problems in his marriage. I think this is because my friend had been stereotyped by the counselor, and the counselor was not aware she was doing this. His counselor seemed to operate from only within his demographic and could not think outside of the box. She seemed to think that his marriage was not that important to him.

What do you hope the counseling profession will do or how might it advance its focus in order to ensure that culturally and socially effective services are provided to blind African Americans?

I believe that the profession needs to make a stronger effort to encourage blind or otherwise disabled African Americans to seek employment in the counseling profession. Nothing helps people feel more understood and included than when people in the helping services look like them and share some of their history and issues.

More needs to be done to engage the blind African American community. I think counselors need to put more effort into understanding their prejudices in dealing with the blind and how these prejudices can be harmful to blind African Americans. The counselor should strive to understand that, in general, African Americans deal with oppression in some form daily, and this feeling of oppression is amplified when the person is blind.

It is an uphill battle to successfully thrive and enjoy life as an African American because of the weight of oppression. This battle is made more difficult when blindness is added to ethnicity because both groups separately deal with oppression daily. When a person is both blind and African American, he or she has to deal with oppression from society explicitly and within his or her family and community implicitly. In other words, his African American family and community may agree that they all live in an oppressive state, but this same community may not recognize how their behavior and actions oppress their blind family members. It is important for a counselor to understand the effect this dichotomy can have on a person's psychological makeup. Unintentional, unrecognized oppression can cause feelings of separation and isolation.

To develop a meaningful relationship with blind clients, counselors must strive to develop an empathetic relationship that communicates sincere compassion devoid of pity for the blind client. It is only possible to do this by understanding that blind African Americans may come to counseling for problems that have nothing to do with being blind and at the same time have everything to do with being blind. The only way to get to the root cause of the presenting issue is to listen with an open heart and understand that though the person lives without sight, there is light within. A counselor who can perceive this light is fully serving his or her blind African American client.

REFLECTION AND DISCUSSION QUESTIONS 11.1

Reflecting on How You Are Affected by Anthony's Experience

1. What emotional reactions are invoked in you in response to Anthony's experience as a person with a disability?
2. Do you think that life for those with disabilities has improved? Why or why not?
3. What thoughts and attitudes do you hold about the concept of disability?
4. Do you believe that a blind or deaf student is capable of being a psychotherapist? Why or why not?
5. If Anthony were your client, how comfortable and competent would you feel working with a client who is not sighted?
6. What would you say to your fellow counselor-in-training who expressed that Anthony's disability was a type of punishment or consequence for his wrongdoings?

Including Disability Diversity: Developing Multicultural Competence

Recent statistics indicate that approximately 56.7 million Americans (19% of the population) had a disability in 2010, and more than half of them rated their disability as severe (U.S. Bureau of the Census, 2012). Similarly, Brault (2012) noted that 20% of individuals residing in the United States are identified as having some form of disability—the largest minority group in the country—with an expected increase as the baby boomer population ages. Throughout the chapter, we refer to the term *persons with disabilities* (PWDs) so as to refer to the person first and not the disability. In other words, the person who is deaf, the person who uses a wheelchair, or the person with AIDS is preferred to the deaf person, the wheelchair-confined person, or the AIDS victim. It is not uncommon, however, for individuals of a disability group to self-identity as deaf persons, but this same terminology may be regarded as culturally insensitive if used by mental health professionals. Moreover, counselors must refrain from using language that would be deemed as inappropriate or insulting to PWDs. When uncertain about what terminology to use, it is always good practice to ask clients what they prefer (United Spinal Association, 2011).

Disability Defined

The questions of what is a disability and how PWDs perceive themselves are complex and difficult to answer (Olkin, 1999). Questions of disability status and identity are at the pulse of disability policy, and there is greater attention to create a more positive understanding of what it means to have a disability. The Americans With Disabilities Act (ADA) of 1990 defines an *individual with a disability* as "a person who has a physical or mental impairment that substantially limits one or more major life activities, or has a record of such an impairment, or is regarded as having such an impairment" (para. 3). Examples of major life activities include seeing, hearing, walking, breathing, and so forth. Using a definition different from the ADA, the United Nations defined *disability* as "any restriction or lack (resulting from an impairment) of ability to perform an activity in the manner or within the range considered normal for a human being" (United Nations Enable, 2007). The definition of disability under the Social Security Administration is based on ability to work, and persons are considered disabled under Social Security rules if (a) they cannot do work they previously did, (b) it is determined that they are unable to adjust to other work because of their medical condition, and (c) their disability has lasted or is expected to last for at least one year or to result in death (Social Security Administration, n.d.). Many definitions of disability exist, making a clear and consistent definition of disability rather elusive.

Olkin (1999) described disability identities on a 5-point continuum ranging from (a) not disabled, (b) disabled but no identity as a person with a disability, (c) identifies as a person with a disability, (d) feels a part of the disability community, and (e) disability rights activist. Olkin further noted that the first points of the continuum (i.e., locations *a* to *c*) refer to those who are more vulnerable to the effects of stigma, prejudice, and discrimination, whereas the end points of the continuum (locations *d* and *e*) are reflective of those whose disability is part of their self-identity; they are more likely to have friends and partners with disability and seek therapists with disability.

There are many different kinds of disabilities (e.g., physical, intellectual, cognitive, psychiatric), and it is important to note that disability is not necessarily a permanent classification as people can and do completely recover from some types of disabilities. The topic of disability encompasses a wide range of issues, including the basic question of what it means to be normal. The answer to this question is an important one because it has great impact on the self-concept of individuals and how we treat one another (Smart, 2001).

The correct terminology for talking about persons with disabilities is to refer to the person first and not the disability (Palombi, 2010). The "person who uses a wheelchair" is preferred over "wheelchair person." Palombi further clarified that this general rule may be less applicable in some communities such as with blind or deaf individuals who prefer to self-identify as "blind person" or "deaf person" (p. 56). Because persons who are blind or deaf may find it culturally insensitive for a mental health practitioner to use the same terminology (i.e., blind or deaf person), the practitioner should ask clients what terminology they prefer when referring to their disability (Palombi, 2010).

CASE ILLUSTRATION 11.1

Understanding Disability: The Case of Katrina

Katrina is in her mid-50s and works for the Social Security Administration as a union representative officer. She has been employed by Social Security for 31 years and enjoys her job. She is generally in good health but has a history of migraine headaches with onset 25 years ago. On average, she experiences about two migraines a month, which are severe enough to cause her to leave work or call in sick. She takes prescribed medication without much symptom relief and has received treatment from two different pain clinics with little to no success. The migraines are debilitating and may last 1 or 2 days. Given her long tenure on the job, she is able to take time off from work during migraine episodes without penalty; however, her direct supervisor has complained to her about her numerous and unplanned absences.

Discussion Questions

1. Does Katrina have a disability?
2. If yes, on what definition are you basing your decision? If no, what informs your decision?
3. If yes, how do you describe Katrina's disability identity using Olkin's (1999) theoretical frame?
4. Why do you think there are more disabilities than ever before?

Disability as a Multicultural Issue

Research informs that people's reactions toward PWDs are either extremely positive or negative (Katz, Hass, & Bailey, 1988), and the difference may be explained by discomfort, competing responses (e.g., avoid or assist), and the degree of anxiety experienced about one's own potential illness and/or death (Ryan, 1991). There is no doubt that PWDs need mental health services. They seek counseling for issues similar to their able-bodied peers and also due to barriers to independence, health separation and individuation from family, and development of a positive self-concept. Moreover, like racial/ethnic, sexual orientation, or religious minority groups, PWDs are often marginalized and stereotyped (Atkinson & Hackett, 1988). As such, mental health professionals can expect to reference this area of learning in their provision of services (Banks & Kaschak, 2003).

Persons who are not disabled may regard their nondisability status as superior—this attitude is referred to as *ableism* and is a form of discrimination and social prejudice against people with disabilities (Weeber, 1999). Consequently, the potential for bias toward PWDs among society members merits serious attention. Because mental health providers mirror larger society, there is potential to emulate and perpetuate society's negative biases and stereotypes (Asch & Rousso, 1985). More specifically, Asch and Rousso (1985) pointed out that literature written by mental health professionals who provided services to PWDs tended to reinforce negative or ambivalent attitudes about their psychological well-being.

A decade later, researchers noted that although mental health professionals' attitudes toward disability have become increasingly positive, there has not been the same improved perception in the way of service delivery (Marinelli & Dell Orto, 1999). For example, Kemp and Mallinckrodt (1996) conducted a study in which two videotaped analogues portrayed an intake interview with a client whose presenting issue related to sexual abuse. The two analogues were identical in every respect except the presence of an apparent disability: in one condition, the client was portrayed as nondisabled, and in the second condition, the client was portrayed using a wheelchair. Participants consisted of both counselors and graduate students who viewed one of the two conditions and completed a case conceptualization task. Findings revealed that therapists assigned different treatment priorities based on whether the client had a disability and whether they themselves had received training in disability issues. Specifically, counselors who lacked training in disability-related issues were less likely to focus on themes appropriate for treating a sexual abuse survivor with a disability (e.g., relationship, sexuality, affective issues) and instead tended to focus on extraneous issues (e.g., employment, financial needs). Common errors in counseling PWDs include having lowered expectations of client capability, imposing counselors' values, failing to address intimacy and sexual relationships, or failing to address the disability itself due to perceived irrelevance or when the disability is too anxiety provoking for the counselor to discuss (Kemp & Mallinckrodt, 1996).

Hosie, Patterson, and Hollingsworth (1989) have informed us that counselors' inability to identify disability-related themes may be an ethical issue. In other words, counselors must consider the effects of social stigma, pejorative treatment, discrimination experiences, and power and relationship issues with PWDs. This is especially important given society's focus on physical beauty and work and financial success. Attention to the impact of the disability on normal development is also warranted. That is, adolescent clients' healthy individuation from their parents, including their sexual exploration, must be considered in light of being physically dependent on their caregiver. Counselors must also be careful to not assume that any of these issues is a presenting concern for a client with a disability.

In order for counselors to be prepared to work with PWDs, they are encouraged to equate disability status with the effects of minority status, which means they would understand that similar to racial and ethnic minorities, the issues that PWDs present for counseling are also varied. Understanding of the common societal biases and interpersonal experiences of minority group individuals is a step in the right direction toward increasing the clinician's sensitivity and effectiveness (Ponterotto & Cass, 1991). Moreover, to meet the minimum standards of practice, counselors will be required to become competent in disability issues (Hayes, 2001). In past years, PWDs were treated primarily by rehabilitation counselors, most likely due to the attitude (without justification) that the client's disability was their sole concern, and the other aspects of the client's life such as their sexuality or interpersonal relationships were unimportant. Contrary to this viewpoint, PWDs require the services of counselors in all specialty areas, including aging, couples and family counseling, group counseling, school counseling, substance abuse counseling, career counseling, and sex counseling, to name a few.

Given the wide range of disabilities in American society and the fact that PWDs are a large and growing minority group—second only to combined ethnic groups (U.S. Census Bureau, 2003)—counselors must become familiar with the commonalities of the disability experience, which likely include oppression and discrimination (Olkin, 1999). Counselors who fail to recognize that PWDs want respect and not sympathy and that lowered expectations may be communicating that they do not perceive PWDs to be capable continue to perpetuate stigma and prejudicial attitudes (Smart & Smart, 2006). Of further import is recognition that the client's disability is simply one part of his or her identity. Similar to all others, PWDs have multiple identities and roles, and a complete understanding of their varied identities is crucial in the provision of competent service delivery.

Disability as a Social Construction

Disability is often referred to as a social construct because the disability is understood in terms of how society perceives it (Olkin, 1999). Traditional frameworks of disability have suggested a medical nature of disability with focus on individual-centered deficits and impairments. The conceptualization of disability as being solely located within the individual is changing with understanding that disability is an interaction among the individual, the disability, and his or her environment (Higgins, 1992). Some scholars of disability research have noted the paradigm shift from a medical framing to conceptualization of disability as socially constructed. In other words, disability is a function of an individual's impairment in context (Pledger, 2003). Smart (2001), citing Groce's book *Everyone Here Spoke Sign Language: Hereditary Deafness on Martha's Vineyard*, provided an example of individuals who had a disability but were not perceived as such due to the large proportion of community members who had the disability:

> In 1633, an inherited trait that causes deafness was brought to the island Martha's Vineyard. Geographic isolation and intermarriage resulted in deafness for many individuals; many families had members who were deaf. What is unusual about the story is a lack of a disability identity on the island. On Martha's Vineyard, deafness was a natural part of human existence. Deafness was unremarkable. Moreover, as the title of Groce's book suggests, the use of sign language was not regarded as an accommodation and, indeed, the widespread use of a communication system that everyone could understand probably contributed to the lack of a disability identity. Also, because telecommunications had not yet been introduced, most long-distance communication used the written word. Thus, people who were deaf were not disadvantaged. Many disability advocates have theorized that it is not biological conditions that "make" disabilities, but rather the lack of accommodations (Higgins, 1992; Liachowitz, 1988; Scott, 1969). And the story of Martha's Vineyard certainly lends support to this theory. (p. 6–7)

Scholars of disability policy and research emphasize that disability is not something that resides in the individual as the result of some impairment but rather it resides in society. For example, a person in a wheelchair may be confronted with employment challenges not because of his or her condition but due to environmental barriers in the workplace that obstruct or limit wheelchair access. Similarly, children with intellectual disabilities encounter difficulties in school due to the attitudes and perceptions of teachers who may be unwilling to adapt to different learning styles. These examples highlight that disability must be fully understood as an interaction between the person and his or her environment.

With an increasing proportion of the U.S. population experiencing some type of disability, we are challenged find out what disability is and whether the definition will change as more individuals identify with having a disability. For many members of society, being *healthy* means being "normal," and *illness* equates to "deviance" (Weeber, 1999). Because *normal* is often defined solely as the absence of deviance, illness, and disability, the definition of normal becomes one of exclusion—and no definition of exclusion is helpful (Smart, 2001).

Ableism

Ableism is the unique form of discrimination against PWDs based on their disability status alone (Keller & Galgay, 2010). Although ableism is seldom included when discussing modern forms of oppression (Keller & Galgay, 2010), discrimination against PWDs has a long-standing history in the United States. The negative attitudes and behaviors that PWDs have endured may be fueled by distorted assumptions and beliefs about disability (Wallace, Carter, Nanin, Keller, & Alleyne, 2003). Ablesim, according to Keller and Galgay (2010),

> favors people without disabilities and maintains that disability in and of itself is a negative concept, state, and experience. Implicit within ableism is an able-centric worldview which endorses the belief that there is a "normal" manner in which to perceive and/or manipulate stimuli and a "normal" manner of accomplishing tasks of daily living. Disability represents a deviation from these norms. (p. 242)

The elimination of systematically sanctioned ableism due to the passage of the ADA in 1990 and other recent amendments has resulted in more subtle, secretive, and covert formats of ableism referred to as disability microaggressions (Keller & Galgay, 2010). In their research, Keller and Galgay discussed the existence of disability microaggressions and, in particular, those that have been found in similar other research: denial of identity (i.e., denying the identity of a person with a disability) and second-class citizenship (i.e., denial of rights and respect of the person with a disability by the perpetrator). Specifically, denial of personal identity occurs when a salient aspect of the PWD's identity (other than the disability itself) is disregarded. In other words, a salient aspect of the PWD's identity remains invisible to the perpetrator, which leads to an overemphasis on the disability. An example of this denial is evidenced when one reacts with surprise upon hearing about the PWD's career or some other affiliation. Similarly, second-class citizenship occurs when PWDs' right for equal access is denied because it is considered to be bothersome, expensive, and not a good use of time, effort, and resources. To clarify, Keller and Galgay's research results yielded the following example of inequality: during a staff meeting the question is raised about improving accessibility to the restaurant, and the official plan is to wait until more PWDs eat at the restaurant before any changes are implemented. This example indicates that the PWDs' rights to equal access are not important.

Clearly it is the negligence and action of those who are able bodied that create microaggressions and cause psychological and emotional harm to PWDs. Precisely, the negative experiences of disability microaggressions provide evidence of perpetrators' ableist worldview, which promotes a lack of respect and value for PWDs (Keller & Galgay, 2010). To understand the experiences of PWDs, able-bodied individuals have to recognize their unearned privileges, become aware of any negative assumptions about disabilities, and accept responsibility to fight against ableism. Thus, mental health professionals must develop an ability/disability cultural identity (where one strives to become an activist in combating ableism) in order to show respect to PWDs, understand their vulnerability to abuse and harassment due to lack of social power and control, and validate their experiences of microaggressions and the treatment they receive from ableist members of society. Individual PWDs' psychological difficulties can't be effectively responded to without acknowledgement of and efforts to change their social context.

A Reflection by a Cisgender, Hispanic Female: Not All Types of Disability Are Visible

Deep levels of honest introspection and immersion are necessary tools for multicultural identity development. I do not think I had a good understanding of what it was like to be part of the disabled minority group until I recently suffered from chronic pain from a hip injury. I have a handicapped parking permit that I use when I am having difficulty walking. Observers who are not aware of my condition and perceive me as a young, healthy woman have left demeaning notes on my car like, "I thought handicapped meant physically disabled, not mentally." Recently, an older woman (and faculty member) approached me in a parking lot and began to harass me for parking in a handicapped spot. The old me would have ripped this lady a new one, but having developed my multicultural professional identity, I responded with poise. I used the opportunity as a teaching moment to explain to her that not all types of disability are visible. For all she knew, I could have cancer, be recovering from surgery, or have a brain tumor. I asked her to spend some time thinking about what it was like to be in my shoes and experience such harassment. I believe the experience was a reminder for her, and more importantly for myself, to never make automatic judgments and be willing to empathize with others.

–Frida M., a cisgender, Hispanic, female doctoral student in counseling psychology

Models of Disability

Although there are numerous models of disability, three major models typically used to conceptualize disability are the moral, medical, and social/minority models of disability. These models of disability provide a framework for understanding disability, determining who has a disability, and addressing the problem of disability.

The first and oldest model of disability is the *moral model*, which regards disability as the result of moral lapse or sin (Olkin, 1999). In this view, the individual is shamed by his or her disability, and if she or he is a member of a culture that values family and group over individuals, then the shame extends to the group. In essence, the person and/or the family bears the blame for straying from the path of the devout, and the punishment is the resulting disability. The moral model is predicated on the belief that disability is a consequence of wrongdoings by the individual, family, or community member, and entire families may be stigmatized and socially excluded. Others who embrace the moral model may see the disability as a test of faith (i.e., an affliction that must be endured before future reward can be obtained)—in other words, "God gives us only that which we can bear." PWDs are regarded as a blessing to others who would not have been able to endure the affliction (i.e., suffering). The moral model promotes feelings of shame and guilt to the extent that PWDs have been kept hidden by their families (Mackelprang & Salsgiver, 1999; Olkin, 1999). Although the moral model represents the oldest perspective of disability, it is still valued in some cultures (Mackelprang & Salsgiver, 1999; Olkin, 1999). Rhoda Olkin (1999) shared the following example of how outward manifestations of a disability reflect inner maleficence:

> I recently received a mail-order catalogue (*Wireless*, 1998) offering a "Gaelic blessing plaque" which had the following message: "May those who love us, love us. And those that don't love us, may God turn their hearts; and if he doesn't turn their hearts may he turn their ankles so we'll know them by their limping." (p. 25)

In sum, the moral model views disability as residing within the individual and carries with it a degree of stigma.

The *medical model* perspective, which has historically dominated the development of disability policy (Palombi, 2010), has removed the moral or sin aspect and replaced it with the view that disability results from the individual's physical and mental limitations and is unrelated to social and environmental barriers (Smart, 2001). That is, disability is a failure of a bodily system and thus is deemed abnormal and pathological. The treatment goals for this model are to cure or ameliorate the condition to the greatest extent possible, including rehabilitation. The medical model has been rejected by PWDs who do not accept the view of being abnormal. According to Olkin (1999), "The main contribution of the medical model is the repudiation of the view of disability as a lesion on the soul" (p. 26).

Both the moral and medical models maintain that disability resides within the individual; however, the *social model* (also known as the *minority model*) locates the disability in the environment and society and emphasizes the attitudinal barriers that restrict PWDs' full participation in society (Palombi, 2010). The minority model was an outgrowth of the actions employed by African Americans during the civil rights movement in the 1960s. More specifically, PWDs became aware of the need to advocate for their rights during the civil rights movement (Middleton, Rollins, & Harley, 1999). The shift from the individual model to the social model in understanding disability allows for consideration of oppression and environments that fail to accommodate PWDs. From this perspective, PWDs are regarded as a minority group that has been denied its civil rights, equal access, and protection (Olkin, 1999).

In the social/minority model, a person is not considered disabled when in an environment where she or he can access the same information as someone who is able-bodied. For example, a blind person with access to a book in braille is able to read much like a sighted person who has access to printed material. Barriers that exist in society and the environment must be altered in order to allow full participation of PWDs in society. Interestingly, when people without disabilities are asked what they believe will be the

A Reflection: My Story of Disability

My life path drastically changed 20 years ago at the age of 9 when I was paralyzed due to a spinal cord injury caused by a vehicle accident. I am still processing the relationship between the disability and who I am today. For a long time after the accident, I would wake up screaming from the same nightmare in which I walked to a cliff and was about to fall off. There was an outburst of inexplicable anger within me. I dropped out of school. I was trapped at home, and life was hopeless. But my mom, with her long-term vision and her relentless effort, revived my spirit by getting me to read books about how people with disabilities overcame barriers to become successful. I was inspired! I realized that I could still study, work, and contribute to society.

However, for the first 4 years after the accident, my mom and I both held the belief that I could walk again if I received appropriate treatment. The realization came after three major surgeries that I had to live with a wheelchair for the rest of my life. That was terribly hard! I started to face life with a wheelchair in a society where people place either extremely low or extremely high expectations on us. I started focusing on achieving in every opportunity I had, such as doing well in school. The discrimination and inequity in access to transportation, entertainment, employment, and so on made me upset and angry at first, but gradually, I realized that I could only do the best I could. I made a decision that surprised many people: I would study abroad in the United States after receiving my master's degree. I wanted to see more of the world and expand my vision and independence.

My life in the United States so far has been really refreshing and nurturing. The accessible environment freed me, and I can live on my own entirely. I have role models on campus, and some of them have more severe disabilities than I do. It helps me look at the disability from a new perspective. How disability affects a person's life depends more on the accessibility of the environment rather than the person himself or herself. I began to realize that for all those years I had never really accepted my disability. One of my identities was a person in wheelchair, not a person with disability. I am grateful that I finally realized it because it means a lot to me in terms of who I am and how I connect to the world. I had no choice about having a disability, but I can choose how I deal with it. My disability did not just bring me sadness and difficulty–it has provided me rich life experiences and contributed to who I am now.

–A cisgender, female graduate student from China

major challenges for PWDs, they report their impairment. To the contrary, when PWDs are asked the same question they cite social barriers and the negative attitudes of others toward PWDs; these barriers and negative attitudes require additional coping for PWDs (Olkin, 1999). The social/minority model emphasizes the elimination of social, environmental, and attitudinal barriers so that the lives of PWDs will be enhanced. Each of the models discussed contributes to the understanding of the disability experience. A comparison of the three models along seven dimensions, including meaning, intervention goals, and benefits, is included in Table 11.1. There are advantages and detriments to each style, but clients can benefit from the counselor's guided exploration of each model.

Table 11.1 Comparison of the Moral, Medical, and Social Models of Diversity

Measure	Moral	Medical	Social
Meaning of disability	Disability is a defect caused by moral lapse or sin, failure of faith, evil, test of faith.	A defect in or failure of a bodily system that is inherently abnormal and pathological.	Disability is a social construct. Problems reside in the environment that fails to accommodate people with disabilities.
Moral implications	The disability brings shame to the person with the disability and his or her family.	A medical abnormality due to genetics, bad health habits, person's behavior.	Society has failed a segment of its citizens and oppresses them.
Sample ideas	"God gives us only what we can bear," or "There's a reason I was chosen to have this disability."	Clinical descriptions of "patients" in medical terminology. Isolation of body parts.	"Nothing about us without us," or "Civil rights, not charity."
Origins	Oldest model and still most prevalent worldwide.	Mid-19th century. Most common model in the United States. Entrenched in most rehabilitation clinics and journals.	In 1975 with the demonstrations by people with disabilities in support of the yet-unsigned Rehabilitation Act.
Goals of intervention	Spiritual or divine, acceptance.	"Cure" or amelioration of the disability to the greatest extent possible.	Political, economic, social, and policy systems, increased access and inclusion.
Benefits of model	An acceptance of being selected, a special relationship with God, a sense of greater purpose to the disability.	A lessened sense of shame and stigma. Faith in medical intervention. Spurs medical and technological advances.	Promotes integration of the disability into the self. A sense of community and pride. Depathologizing of disability.
Negative effects	Shame, ostracism, need to conceal the disability or person with the disability.	Paternalistic, promotes benevolence and charity. Services for but not by people with disabilities.	Powerlessness in the face of broad social and political changes needed. Challenges to prevailing ideas.

Source: Olkin, R. (2002).

SMALL-GROUP DISCUSSION 11.1

Confronting My Bias

Society, media, our families, and our unique histories contribute to both collective and personal biases about disability as a construct and also toward persons with disabilities. A disability can and does engender emotional reactions that are deeply rooted. Similar to awareness of our biases in other categories of diversity, we are challenged to confront our biases and respect the diversity within disability.

In a small group of four to five students, examine your attitudes and potential biases (e.g., PWDs have a lesser quality of life compared to their able-bodied peers) by discussing what "disability" means and whether your preconceptions about disability prevent access to accurate evaluations about the experiences of PWDs.

To Which Model of Disability Does Your Client Subscribe?

Determining the model used by clients is important for several reasons. Olkin (1999) said that the model of disability that a client predominantly endorses reflects (a) how the problem is perceived, (b) how the problem is presented, (c) the locus of the problem, and (d) goals for treatment (p. 52). In other words, it is important for PWDs to recognize how the models of disability have influenced their perceptions about their disability status. Olkin also noted that the disability model permeates the counselor's work from the first interaction with the client (and his or her family) because knowing which model the client is most comfortable with and which provides the greatest degree of satisfaction and self-understanding is beneficial to treatment. Whereas some clients may be familiar with the models of disability and thereby ascribe to the social/minority model because they are in fact the persons who are reading and writing about the models, other clients may need to be introduced to the models. Table 11.2 provides questions that can be asked of clients about their disability experience in order to help them become familiar with the various models of disability. Specifically, Olkin (1999) suggested that clients and their families be given a copy of the table during the counseling session or as a homework assignment and requested to respond to the questions pertaining to each model. The counselor could make this request by stating the following:

> How you think about yourself as a person with a disability will affect greatly how you think about yourself overall. You may not even be aware that you have a model of disability. Take a few minutes to ask yourself some questions that can help bring your model to light. Use the questions in this table to help you, but also feel free to think of other questions or situations that the table doesn't address. (p. 170)

It is important that the counselor allow the client to determine where she or he feels most comfortable when responding to the questions and that the counselor is not invested in a particular outcome model. It is possible that a client might identify with and hold beliefs from more than one model, yet other clients might be bothered or uncomfortable with their fit in a particular model and find it distressing. The goal of the counselor in this regard is to remember that "there is no such thing as complete adjustment to disability. One is never *there*, only *traveling* there. Thus, the client's thoughts about disability will constantly change and evolve" (Olkin, 1999, p. 172).

Table 11.2 Assessing the Client's Models of Disability

Assessing the Client's Models of Disability	
Moral Model	Do you feel shame or embarrassed about your disability?
	Do you feel you bring dishonor to your family?
	Do you try to hide or minimize the disability as much as possible?
	Do you try to make as few demands on others as possible because it's "your problem" and hence your responsibility?
	Do you try to make your disability inconspicuous?
	Do you think your disability is a test of your faith, or is it a way for you to prove your faith?
	Do you think your disability is punishment for your family's failing?
Medical Model	Do you think that life for persons with disabilities has improved tremendously?
	Do you think a public figure, such as the president, wouldn't have to hide his or her disability today?
	Do you try to make as few demands as possible because you think you should be able to find a way to do it yourself?
	Do you dress in ways that maximize your positive features and minimize the visibility of the disability?
	Do you believe that persons with disabilities do best when they are fully integrated into the nondisabled community?
Minority Model	Do you identify yourself as part of a minority group of persons with disabilities?
	Do you feel kinship and belonging with persons with disabilities?
	Do you think that not enough is being done to ensure rights of persons with disabilities?
	When policies and legislation are new, do you evaluate them in terms of their effects on persons with disabilities?

Assessing the Client's Models of Disability	
	Do you think the major goal of research should be to improve the lives of persons with disabilities by changing policies, procedures, funding, and laws?
	Do you think that persons with disabilities do best when they are free to associate in both the disabled and nondisabled communities as bicultural people?

Source: Olkin (1998). Copyright 1998 by National Rehabilitation Hospital Press. Reprinted by permission.

SMALL-GROUP CLASS ACTIVITY 11.1

Applying Meaning to the Client's Models of Disability

After reading Case Studies A through 3, complete Table 11.3 and discuss your responses in a small group. Case Study A is provided with the answers as an example of how to complete Table 11.3.

Case Study A:

My 19-year-old son has traumatic brain injury from sustaining multiple concussions while playing football, with a major concussive episode occurring 3 years ago that resulted in his being in a coma for 2 weeks. Although he has made some improvement in his cognitive functioning, he is not the same as he was prior to the injury. My family has noticed deficits with his memory, problem-solving ability, language, and even his personality. He is frustrated and grief-stricken over his loss of functioning and skill, especially that he is no longer able to play football. His dad and I are also having a hard time because it was our son's dream to become a professional football player. We wanted him to be seen by you so that you could determine whether this injury will have a long-term impact now that he will never be able to play football. I know God never gives us more than we can bear, but I can't help but wonder if He is punishing my husband and me for having our son out of wedlock.

Case Study 1:

My 16-year-old son has Asperger's syndrome. Although he looks like a pretty normal adolescent, he has difficulty interacting with others and is often awkward in social situations. We are most saddened by the difficulty he has making and keeping friends. He seems to say things that are inappropriate or less mature than his age-related peers, and we thought it would be good for him to be seen by a counselor because now that

(Continued)

(Continued)

he is getting older and his peers are both older and more mature, my husband and I are concerned that our son will be left further behind developmentally.

Case Study 2:

My 28-year-old daughter was diagnosed with schizophrenia when she was 23 years old. She takes medication to help control the voices she hears and the thoughts that others are reading her mind. She wants to just sit for hours without moving or talking, which I understand is related to her disorder. Although she completed college, she is having difficulty finding a job, and she doesn't really have any friends and has not dated since college. I am concerned that she is missing out on the workforce, and as she gets older, it will become more and more difficult for her to find work.

Case Study 3:

My daughter is deaf due to a birth defect. We have tried very hard to help her learn how to live with being deaf, but it has been difficult, since both my wife and I and our youngest daughter are able to hear. We have told her that despite her profound hearing loss, she can do anything she wants. Recently, she applied to a graduate program in counseling and did not disclose that she is deaf. We worry that if she gets accepted to the program, she will be isolated and will not fit in with her classmates. We have inquired about whether there are other students in the program with a visible disability and were told that currently there are not. We know she is never going to be like all of the other students in a counseling program, so we want to help her find a program where she'll fit in. We are not sure what is best for her, so we'd like to talk about it. It feels as if it is our problem that we don't know how to best help her.

Table 11.3

Case Study	Theme(s)	Main Concern(s)	Explanation of Disability	Who Has the Problem	Model
A	Son has not completely recovered and has cognitive deficits	Will his injury have long-term impact on his functioning; will he be able to play football again	Punishment for having son out of wedlock	Mother, father, and son	Moral
1					
2					
3					

Source: Adapted from Olkin (1999).

Palombi (2010) emphasized the importance of knowledge and skill competency when working with PWDs and provided a list of activities to facilitate development of the counselor's knowledge and skills:

- Visit an organization/agency that provides services to PWDs (e.g., independent living center, office of vocational rehabilitation).
- Write a paper describing the beliefs and practices of two disability traditions.
- Invite community leaders who are PWDs to speak to the counselor's class/organization.
- Participate in and/or attend discussions about disability-related topics.
- Participate in the grand rounds of counselors at a rehabilitation facility related to visible and invisible disabilities.
- Research a model of disability and how it is addressed in societal attitudes.
- Get involved in disability experiences (e.g., book readings, movie festivals, lobbying for disability civil rights).

Disability and Ethical Practice

Counselors who practice ethically and are culturally responsive to the needs of PWDs should have a basic knowledge of the Americans With Disabilities Act of 1990, an understanding of the three predominant models of disability (e.g., moral, medical, social), and competence in advocacy skills and disability-related social justice issues (Cornish et al., 2008). Because PWDs live in a challenging sociopolitical context, it is crucial that counseling professionals embrace their advocacy roles, engage in social justice counseling, and support social justice issues as they have the potential to influence disability policies, which may have impact on the treatment and resources available to PWDs (Pledger, 2003). Similarly, the American Counseling Association (ACA) *Code of Ethics* (2014), Section C Professional Responsibility, Introduction, states the following:

> Counselors are expected to advocate to promote changes at the individual, group, institutional, and societal levels that improve the quality of life for individuals and groups and remove potential barriers to the provision or access of appropriate services being offered. (p. 8)

Although there are no ethical standards that specifically address counselors' provision of services to PWDs, the ACA published its advocacy competencies in a 2010 book titled *Advocacy Competencies: A Social Justice Framework for Counselors*. The ACA advocacy competencies provide a framework for implementing microlevel and macrolevel advocacy strategies. Specifically, the advocacy competencies are designed to help counselors attend to their clients' social context and to be skilled at both individual-level counseling and community-based work in order to successfully help clients achieve optimal psychological growth and development. Advocacy and social justice counseling are at the forefront of the profession, and counseling professionals will need to be prepared to engage in this important and timely work.

Ethical counselors seeking to work competently with PWDs must also be familiar with developmental issues (e.g., dating, sex, pregnancy, childbirth) and any medical considerations specific to their clients' condition (Asch & Fine, 1997). Ethical and competent counselors also understand what is means to hold multiple minority statuses should a client, for example, be African American, lesbian, and with disability (Sue & Sue, 2003). PWDs who are members of multiple marginalized groups have the experience of being "a minority within a minority" (McDonald Keys, & Balcazar, 2007, p. 148). Determining which identities are most important and how to categorize the experiences of multiple identities can be challenging. As such, counselors must understand the unique living experiences of PWDs who are also members of multiple marginalized groups (Palombi, 2010). Finally, counseling professionals bear a responsibility for honest self-reflection in order to assess their readiness for providing competent and ethical services to PWDs (Cornish et al., 2008). Equally important is for counseling professionals to examine their view of clients with disabilities and to question any preconceived attitudes and/or prejudicial assumptions (Sue & Sue, 2008).

Although ethical codes and practice guidelines require counseling professionals to practice in a multiculturally sensitive manner, Palombi (2010) noted several reasons why counseling professionals may find it difficult to incorporate disability-related factors in their treatment services. First, counselors may feel unprepared to address disability-related issues, particularly if they have not received academic instruction or training in disability. Second, counseling professionals may experience discomfort with the topic of disability because they may be unaware of their own biases and attitudes toward PWDs (Olkin, 1999). Third, counselors who have had limited interaction with PWDs may question their competency and feel unable to offer assistance. Finally, counselors who lack understanding about the prejudice and discrimination that PWDs experience may refrain from asking clients whether they have a disability, including onset, duration, cause, and how they experience the disability in their life. The consequence of the counselor's hesitancy to address the topic of disability may mean that the client is left feeling further marginalized and invalidated (Leigh, Powers, Vash, & Nettles, 2004).

Disability is a multicultural issue, and PWDs are named as a minority group in the counseling profession. We, therefore, encourage graduate training programs to include the topic of disability as a part of their core curricula. This will likely be necessary in order for counselors to receive the education and training needed to offer culturally responsive and ethical services to PWDs. Smart and Smart (2006) noted that most graduates of counseling programs do not possess competencies to provide services to clients with disabilities (p. 36). Components of training in graduate programs could focus on the cultural history of PWDs, including discrimination, oppression and biases, relevant mental health issues such as alienation, self-esteem, and relationship issues, and appropriate counseling strategies that will minimize therapeutic mishaps due to counselor naiveté or lack of knowledge.

Summary

This chapter discusses the increasing number of members of society with disabilities and calls upon counselors in the 21st century to provide multiculturally sensitive services to PWDs. Counselors will likely be presented opportunities to work directly with clients who have disabilities or secondarily through clients who are caregivers or family members of PWDs. To develop clinical competence, counseling professionals must acknowledge their own feelings and attitudes about disability issues, including how they feel and behave toward those with disabilities. They must engage in introspection to recognize deficiency areas and biases that they can then attend to and fully address.

The marginalization of PWDs stems in part from the moral and medical models of disability that locate the problems of disability within the person, thus pathologizing PWDs. An understanding of disability as a social construct is a necessary, although insufficient, step in the right direction toward including disability in diversity. "For the oppression of people with disabilities to be addressed within psychology, disability will have to board the diversity train" (Olkin, 1999, p. 136). It is, therefore, essential that counselors understand disability as a multicultural issue and be prepared to advocate on behalf of clients who have disabilities by understanding the challenging sociopolitical context in which they live and by minimizing barriers to care.

Takeaway Messages

1. As members of society, counseling professionals have been exposed to prejudices and negative attitudes toward PWDs, which they have likely internalized.
2. Counseling professionals must recognize that they are members of a society that oppresses and marginalizes PWDs.
3. PWDs are regarded as a minority group, which necessitates understanding disability as a multicultural issue and advocating on behalf of PWDs so as to eradicate oppressive conditions that impede human growth and development.
4. Models of disability provide a framework for how people think about disability and how they think about PWDs (i.e., they contribute to the understanding of the disability experience).
5. Disabilities are a social construct in that they are understood in terms of how society defines them.
6. PWDs must be helped to understand how their perspectives on disability have been shaped by three predominant models of disability and what the implications are of subscribing to one model over others.
7. Counseling professionals have an ethical obligation to confront the barriers that PWDs experience due to societal prejudices and discrimination.

Recommended Resources

Readings

The following two books address treatment for PWDs and were written for mental health professionals who have not received training in that dimension of diversity:

Mackelprang, R., & Salsgiver, R. (1999). *Disability: A diversity model approach in human service practice.* Belmont, CA: Brooks/Cole.

Olkin, R. (1999). *What psychotherapists should know about disability.* New York, NY: Guilford Press.

Media and Websites

Olkin, R. (2005). *Disability-affirmative therapy: A beginner's guide* [Video 460]. United States: Microtraining and Multicultural Development. Available from https://www.academicvideostore.com/video/disability-affirmative-therapy-beginners-guide

Neudel, E. (2011). *Lives worth living: The fight for disability rights* [Documentary]. United States: PBS. Available from http://www.pbs.org/independentlens/lives-worth-living/

Professional organization for individuals involved in policy development and the provision of quality services for PWDs—Association on Higher Education and Disability: www.ahead.org

People With Disabilities Foundation (PWDF): www.pwdf.org

Disability Information for Students and Professionals (DISP): www.abilityinfo.com

National Center for the Dissemination of Disability Research (NCDDR): www.ncddr.org

References

American Counseling Association. (2014). *Code of ethics*. Retrieved from www.counseling.org

Americans With Disabilities Act—Title I. (1990). *Definition of an individual with a disability*. Retrieved from http://health.hawaii.gov/dcab/files/2013/01/definition.pdf

Asch, A., & Fine, M. (1997). Nurturance, sexuality, and women with disabilities. In L. J. Davis (Ed.), *The disability studies reader* (pp. 241–259). New York, NY: Routledge.

Asch, A., & Rousso, H. (1985). Therapists with disabilities: Theoretical and clinical issues. *Psychiatry, 48*, 1–12.

Atkinson, D. R., & Hackett, G. (Eds.). (1988). *Counseling non-ethnic American minorities*. Springfield, IL: Charles C Thomas.

Banks, M., & Kaschak, E. (Eds.). (2003). *Women with visible and invisible disabilities*. New York, NY: Haworth Press.

Brault, M. W. (2012). Americans with disabilities: 2010. *Current Populations Reports*, 70–131. Washington, DC: U.S. Bureau of the Census.

Cornish, J. A. E., Gorgens, K. A., Monson, S. P., Olkin, R., Palombi, B. J., & Abels, A. V. (2008). Perspectives on ethical practice with people who have disabilities. *Professional Psychology: Research and Practice, 39*, 488–497.

Halstead, L. S. (Ed.). (2006). *Managing post-polio: A guide to living and aging well with post-polio syndrome* (2nd ed.). Washington, DC: MedStar National Rehabilitation Network.

Hayes, P. A. (2001). *Addressing cultural complexities in practice: A framework for clinicians and counselors*. Washington, DC: American Psychological Association.

Higgins, P. C. (1992). *Making disability: Exploring the social transformation of human variation*. Springfield, IL: Charles C Thomas.

Hosie, T. W., Patterson, J. B., & Hollingsworth, D. K. (1989). School and rehabilitation counselor preparation: Meeting the needs of individuals with disabilities. *Journal of Counseling & Development, 68*, 140–144.

Katz, I., Hass, R. G., & Bailey, J. (1988). Attitudinal ambivalence and behavior toward people with disabilities. In H. E. Yuker (Ed.), *Attitudes toward persons with disabilities* (pp. 47–57). New York, NY: Springer.

Keller, R. M., & Galgay, C. E. (2010). Microaggressions experienced by people with disabilities in U.S. society. In D. W. Sue (Ed.), *Microaggressions and marginality: Manifestation, dynamics, and impact* (pp. 241–268). New York, NY: Wiley.

Kemp, N., & Mallinckrodt, B. (1996). Impact of professional training on case conceptualization of clients with a disability. *Professional Psychology: Research and Practice, 27*, 378–385.

Leigh, I. W., Powers, L., Vash, C., & Nettles, R. (2004). Survey of psychological services to clients with disabilities: The need for awareness. *Rehabilitation Psychology, 49*, 48–54.

Liachowitz, C. H. (1988). *Disability as a social construct: Legislative roots.* Philadelphia: University of Pennsylvania.

Mackelprang, R., & Salsgiver, R. (1999). *Disability: A diversity model approach in human service practice.* Pacific Grove, CA: Brooks/Cole.

Marinelli, R., & Dell Orto, A. (1999). *The psychological and social impact of disability.* New York, NY: Springer.

McDonald, K. E., Keys, C. B., & Balcazar, F. E. (2007). Disability, race/ethnicity and gender: Themes of cultural oppression, acts of individual resistance. *American Journal of Community Psychology, 39,* 145–161.

Middleton, R. A., Rollins, C. W., & Harley, D. A. (1999). The historical and political context of the civil rights of persons with disabilities: A multicultural perspective for counselors. *Journal of Multicultural Counseling & Development, 27,* 105–114.

Olkin, R. (1999). *What psychotherapists should know about disability.* New York, NY: Guilford.

Olkin, R. (2002). Could you hold the door for me? Including disability in diversity. *Cultural Diversity and Ethnic Minority Psychology, 8*(2), 130–137.

Palombi, B. J. (2010). Disability: Multiple and intersecting identities—Developing multicultural competencies. In J. A. E. Cornish, B. A. Schreier, L. I. Nadkarni, L. H. Metzger, & E. R. Rodolfa (Eds.), *Handbook of multicultural counseling competencies* (pp. 55–92). Hoboken, NJ: Wiley.

Pledger, C. (2003). Discourse on disability and rehabilitation issue: Opportunity for psychology. *American Psychologist, 58,* 279–284.

Ponterotto, J. G., & Casas, J. M. (1991). *Handbook of racial/ethnic minority counseling research.* Springfield, IL: Charles C. Thomas.

Ryan, J. M. (1991). The relationship of selected variables on attitudes of vocational rehabilitation counselors, as measured by the Attitudes Toward Disabled Persons scale. *Dissertation Abstracts International, 52*(09), 3187A.

Scott, R. A. (1969). *The making of blind men: A study of adult socialization.* New York, NY: Russell Sage.

Smart, J. F. (2001). *Disability, society and the individual.* Austin, TX: Pro-Ed.

Smart, J. F., & Smart, D. W. (2006). Models of disability: Implications for the counseling profession. *Journal of Counseling & Development, 84,* 29–40.

Social Security Administration. (n.d.). *Disability planner: What we mean by disability.* Retrieved from http://www.ssa.gov/dibplan/dqualify4.htm

Sue, D. W., & Sue, D. (2003). *Counseling the culturally diverse: Theory and practice* (4th ed.). New York, NY: Wiley.

Sue, D. W., & Sue, D. (2008). *Counseling the culturally diverse: Theory and practice* (5th ed.). New York, NY: Wiley.

United Nations Enable. (2007). Frequently asked questions. Retrieved from http://www.un.org/esa/socdev/enable/faqs.htm#definition

United Spinal Association. (2011). *Disability etiquette.* Jackson Heights, NY: Author. Retrieved from http://www.unitedspinal.org/pdf/DisabilityEtiquette.pdf

U.S. Bureau of the Census. (2003). *Disability status: 2000.* Retrieved November 5, 2007, from http://www.census.gov/prod/2003pubs/c2kbr-17.pdf

U.S. Bureau of the Census. (2012). *Nearly 1 in 5 people have a disability in the U.S.* Retrieved from https://www.census.gov/newsroom/releases/archives/miscellaneous/cb12-134.html

Wallace, B. C., Carter, R. T., Nanin, J., Keller, R., & Alleyne, V. (2003). Identity development for "diverse and different others:" Integrating stages of change, motivational interviewing, and identity theories for race, people of color, sexual orientation, and disability. In B. C. Wallace & R. T. Carter (Eds.), *Understanding and dealing with violence: A multicultural approach* (pp. 41–92). Thousand Oaks, CA: Sage.

Weeber, J. E. (1999). What could I know of racism? *Journal of Counseling and Development, 77,* 20–23.

12

Working With Diversity in Religion and Spirituality

Christian, Jew, Muslim, shaman, Zoroastrian, stone, ground, mountain, river, each has a secret way of being with the mystery, unique and not to be judged.

—Rumi

CHAPTER OVERVIEW

This chapter provides understanding of the role of spirituality in counseling with attention to competent multicultural counselors being knowledgeable and accepting of the spiritual differences between themselves and their clients. The inclusion of a spiritual dimension in counseling practice may be met with reluctance by some counselors due to the lack of knowledge and skills. We therefore discuss this potential reluctance and the awareness, knowledge, and skills necessary to enhance counselors' religious and spiritual competencies with the aim of facilitating the treatment of the whole client–mind, body, and spirit. Strategies for including spirituality as an aspect of the client's culture are also provided.

SELF-ASSESSMENT OF PRE-EXISTING AWARENESS AND KNOWLEDGE

- What is my level of competency regarding religion and spirituality in working with culturally diverse clients?
- How do I understand the role of religion and spirituality in my clients' psychological health?
- How competent do I feel integrating clients' religion and spirituality in understanding them and their issues?
- How competent do I feel providing interventions that effectively address clients' concerns in the context of their religion and spirituality?
- How competent do I feel utilizing my own spiritual and/or religious experiences as a helping agent in working with clients?

LEARNING OBJECTIVES

After reading this chapter, students will be able to do the following:

1. Understand the relevance of counselors' and clients' religion and spirituality in establishing effective therapeutic relationships
2. Conceptualize clients' concerns and understand their religious and spiritual experiences even if they did not come to counseling to address those experiences per se
3. Understand religion and spirituality as being relevant to the treatment goals and psychological interventions counselors deliver

The Reflections of Lee Lynne: A Christian Counseling Professional

I am an African American female in my 40s and have been practicing as a licensed psychologist in a secular setting (private practice) since 2006. I have taught in a counseling program since 1999, conducted research and scholarship in the integration of religion and spirituality in counseling, and provided professional development workshops for mental health professionals on the topic. I am Protestant and was raised in a conservative faith

(Continued)

(Continued)

tradition, including attending elementary (nursery through eighth grade) and college at religious schools. I remain very active in church.

—Lee Lynne, an African American psychologist

Why is it important for counselors to integrate religion and spirituality into their therapeutic endeavors?

I believe that it is important for counselors to integrate religion and spirituality into therapeutic endeavors. For so many people in our society, religious and spiritual beliefs help to construct the lens through which they view the world. Whether deliberately and intentionally or inadvertently, many individuals consider the religious teachings and expectations to which they have been exposed when making decisions or making sense of their current circumstances. Even for people who no longer affiliate with a particular faith tradition, religious background may be important to explore because the decision to sever ties with a faith tradition is often a significant one in someone's life. For many people, their faith is a source of strength and can be a powerful resource to help them through emotional difficulties. For others, religion may be associated with feelings of rejection, confusion, or pain. Counselors should be open to exploring all that is significant in people's lives, and this exploration may include integration of the religious and spiritual beliefs and histories of their clients.

Although I wholeheartedly believe that religion and spirituality should be integrated into counseling (if it is indeed relevant for a particular client), I have sometimes struggled with doing this in my own practice. When we get into this realm, we are often talking about issues for which people have certain Truths (with a capital T). People simply believe what they believe, myself included. In my opinion, these beliefs are not up for debate. My role as a counselor is to explore the impact of those beliefs on my clients' mental health. Take, for instance, people's varied beliefs about what happens when people die. I may disagree with my clients' beliefs about the afterlife based on my own beliefs and may even think that my beliefs might allow for greater comfort in times of mourning. However, I do not challenge their belief systems. Rather, I explore their beliefs, how these beliefs affect the grieving process, and how to better cope given these beliefs.

When the root of suffering seems closely related to the belief system or confusion about a faith teaching, I believe that a referral to a religious leader is most appropriate. It is there where clients can receive assistance in understanding certain doctrines. This interpretation of beliefs or doctrines is beyond the scope of my professional expertise, and it is not what I am licensed to do. My challenge in making referrals is monitoring whether I am most likely to refer clients whose beliefs are most similar to or distal from my own. In other words, my biases may affect how quickly I suggest a clergy referral with different clients; as a counselor, I need to be aware of this. Note that although I am a Christian and will identify as such, if appropriate, I do not practice 'Christian counseling,' per se, and have always worked in secular settings.

What challenges, if any, have you encountered with integrating religion and spirituality in your practice (e.g., is it important to explore a client's religious background and beliefs and are you successful at doing so)?

One reason the integration of religious and spiritual beliefs in counseling is difficult for me is because I wasn't really trained how to do it. Religion and spirituality were (and still are) taboo topics in many training programs. Although we know that students come to programs with all types of beliefs, including those related to faith, too often there is not an open atmosphere where they are encouraged to share or explore them, particularly as they relate to how their beliefs might impact their work with clients. Depending on the institution or even the region of the country, some groups (e.g., conservative Christians, atheists) often feel criticized for having certain beliefs.

As this is a relatively new area in counseling programs, there is a strong likelihood that faculty-in-training programs also have not been trained in this area and therefore do not encourage open dialogue with students. Aside from reminding students that they should not impose their beliefs on clients, there may be little guidance in how to effectively and ethically explore and integrate a client's religious or spiritual beliefs in counseling. Luckily, the field has grown exponentially in the last several years, and there are several resources available to help clinicians provide ethically sound and clinically relevant services to clients and to help faculty train students to do so.

This is not an easy undertaking, and I am still learning. With everything that I learn, I feel more confident and competent. One reference that I found particularly helpful in clarifying the often blurred line between psychological and spiritual interventions by counseling professionals is an article by Gonsiorek, Richards, Pargament, and McMinn (2009). I think this article can be useful for both religious and nonreligious clinicians. There is also a host of books, articles, workshops, and videos that can be used to support training for professionals and students.

What recommendations do you have for how counseling programs can prepare students to be competent in addressing religion and spirituality in counseling (e.g., provide competent services that are sensitive to the religion/spirituality of clients)?

I would encourage faculty-in-training programs to recognize that religious and spiritual beliefs (of clients and of trainees) are present in every counseling session, spoken or unspoken, explored or not. Trainees will be better equipped to effectively manage their own belief systems (religious/spiritual or not) while exploring their clients' beliefs if trainees are encouraged to develop competence in this area as part of their training programs. Faculty-in-training programs should examine the spiritual competencies as identified by the Association for Spiritual, Ethical, and Religious Values in Counseling (and endorsed by the American Counseling Association) and determine whether their

(Continued)

(Continued)

curricula is designed to adequately address any of those competencies. If not, then review and possible revision of the training program is likely warranted. Trainees should be encouraged to increase their levels of awareness, knowledge, and skills in the area of spiritual and religious competencies. Whether through a multicultural counseling class, a separate class on religion and spirituality, or through practicums, this topic should be present in every curriculum. I am encouraged by the attention paid to this topic in recent years and hope that as a field we will become more prepared to deal with the breadth and depth of our clients' struggles, including those connected in subtle or obvious ways to their belief systems.

Religion and Spirituality: A Cultural Diversity Context

Religion and Spirituality Defined

Before proceeding with a discussion on the relevance of *religion* and *spirituality* in counseling practice, we must first consider how these two terms are defined and how the conceptualization of these terms may vary depending on how they manifest in our lives and the lives of our clients through personal background and life experiences (Bartoli, 2007). Numerous definitions of spirituality exist, which inform the complexity of this construct. The definitions reviewed suggest that spirituality includes one's values, beliefs, sense of purpose and direction, capacity for growth, pursuit of something greater than oneself, search for harmony and wholeness in the universe, and desire for betterment of the world (Frame, 2003). Religion, which is regarded as easier to understand, reflects the beliefs and practices of an organized institution (Shafranske & Maloney, 1990). Specifically, Shafranske and Sperry (2005) provided the following definitions, which have been supported by scholars in literature and which, for the purposes of this chapter, we have relied upon:

> *Spirituality* refers to an individualized, internal, and value-based connection to the transcendent dimensions of life, which brings new meanings and leads to growth. Spirituality also does not presume a connection to mainstream and organized religious institutions. *Religion*, however, implies affiliation with a religious institution and adherence to specific doctrines as well as some behavioral expectations. (pp. 13–14)

Persons who think of themselves as spiritual rather than religious may maintain that the institutions of religion interfere with their private experience of spirituality (Frame, 2003). It is therefore important to note that these two constructs are not mutually exclusive (i.e., religion is one form of spirituality). Some followers of religion may find that the institution, doctrine, rituals, and community of their religion are means through which their spirituality are supported and enhanced. Thus, Frame (2003) says one may be simultaneously religious and spiritual, spiritual without being religious—18% of U.S.

adults are "spiritual but not religious" (PEW Research Center, 2012)—or religious without being spiritual (e.g., going through the motions of being religious without taking the practices to heart).

My Client Is Religious or Spiritually Oriented: Shouldn't I Refer My Client to the Clergy?

Counselors and other mental health professionals may be hesitant or opposed to working with religious or spiritually oriented clients or consider clients' spiritual beliefs and values in their counseling practice. According to Frame (2003), one reason why counselors are hesitant and neglect to integrate religion and spirituality into work with culturally diverse clients has to do with competence. More specifically, and despite the profession's overwhelming interest in spiritual and religious diversity, Frame pointed out that until recently, few counseling professionals had received specialized training in their coursework and clinical experiences with regard to the integration of religion and spirituality. Essentially all ethical codes of the profession governing the practice of psychotherapy inform practicing only in areas in which one is competent. For example, the American Counseling Association (ACA) 2014 *Code of Ethics*, Standard C.2.a. Boundaries of Competence, states the following:

> Counselors practice only within the boundaries of their competence, based on their education, training, supervised experience, state and national professional credentials, and appropriate professional experience. Whereas multicultural counseling competency is required across all counseling specialties, counselors gain knowledge, personal awareness, sensitivity, dispositions, and skills pertinent to being a culturally competent counselor in working with a diverse client population. (p. 8)

Standard C.2.a. clearly dictates practicing within the boundaries of competence and also reminds us of the overall ethical requirement that counselors must be multiculturally competent in their provision of services. If we indeed conclude that counseling programs have an ethical responsibility to ensure that graduates demonstrate competence with respect for clients across the full range of diversity, including religion and spirituality, then program faculty and clinical supervisors must be knowledgeable about diverse religious and spiritual traditions (Schulte, Skinner, & Claibom, 2002) and competencies for addressing spiritual and religious themes in counseling.

Yet another explanation offered by Frame (2003) for counseling professionals' neglect or opposition to the inclusion of religion and spirituality in counseling practice is related to their personal experiences. In other words, counselors who have negative feelings and/or experiences with religion may have difficulty interacting with religious clients. Their negative religious incidents may result in a disapproving and cynical attitude toward spiritually and religiously oriented clients. Similar to other unresolved issues that might prevent or interfere with our effectiveness to be culturally competent, we are encouraged to engage in efforts to ensure continued clinical competence. Standard C.2.d. Monitor Effectiveness of the ACA (2014) *Code of Ethics* states, "Counselors continually monitor their effectiveness as professionals and take steps to improve when necessary. Counselors take reasonable steps to seek peer supervision to evaluate their efficacy as counselors" (p. 8).

The inclusion of religion and spirituality in multicultural counseling is vastly important; some scholars assert that to be multiculturally competent, a counselor should also be religiously/spiritually competent and vice versa (Evans, 2003). Furthermore, to effectively counsel individuals across cultures, counselors must have an understanding of the various spiritual and religious beliefs of their culturally diverse clients. Moreover, counselors must reach their own religious/spiritual maturity in order to effectively assist clients in their religious/spiritual journey. The journey toward developing spiritual competence is akin to what one would experience in the transition from monoculturalism to multiculturalism. In other words, it involves unlearning attitudes and behaviors that promote bias and misunderstanding (Fukuyama & Sevig, 1999).

CASE ILLUSTRATION 12.1

The Case of Leslie

Leslie is a 38-year-old unemployed Christian woman who sought counseling to discuss her recent (1 month) separation from her husband of 9 years. She explained that this was the fourth time she had initiated a separation from her husband, Calvin, who is also a Christian. Leslie sought counseling to garner emotional support and to receive help with identifying tools and resources that could assist her with becoming economically independent. Her goal was to be able to take care of herself so that she wouldn't have to return to her abusive marriage, which had been her pattern in the past. Leslie explained that now that her 7-year-old-daughter was in school, and she was separated from her husband (who objected to her working outside the home), she wanted to look for paid employment with health benefits so that she could provide a stable home and be able to care for her daughter. The counselor, Elbert, asked Leslie about the supports she had in her life, and she replied that her parents were deceased and that her two siblings, whom she had limited contact with, resided in other states; her church community and a lady friend had been her major sources of support.

She reported that she was raised in a Baptist church and has always endorsed the doctrines and beliefs of her religious tradition, but she expressed her confusion as to why her pastor would always encourage her to return home to her abusive husband after what he referred to as the "cooling off period." Moreover, he would remind her of the vows she took that stated "for better or worse." Leslie and Calvin attended a few counseling sessions with their pastor, but she explained that Calvin's success at doing better never lasted more than a couple of months.

She expressed feeling torn about giving up on her marriage, as that seemed somewhat contradictory to her religious convictions. Leslie told Elbert that she would like to explore the role of religion in her decision making both personally (as related to her marriage) and professionally (as related to her career) since her faith had played such an important role in her survival and personhood. In other words, she wants to feel comfortable that any decision she makes is consistent with her religious frame of reference and how said beliefs might also inform her career journey.

Discussion Questions

Keeping in mind the important role of religion in Leslie's personal and professional life, discuss the following questions:

1. What is your initial reaction to her presenting concerns, and what she is requesting from you as her counselor?
2. What is your level of comfort regarding the integration of religion in clinical practice?
3. Consider what, if any, unresolved religious or spiritual issues you might have that could impact how you would respond to Leslie.
4. Do you feel inclined to work with Leslie or refer her out? Please explain your choice.
5. What training is needed to bridge the gap between a secular counseling profession and a religious public so that counseling professionals can better understand the role of religion and spirituality in counseling?

What Do We Know About the Religious/Spiritual Orientation of Counseling Professionals?

According to survey data and relative to the general population, psychotherapists are less religious in terms of affiliation, attendance, beliefs, and values (Bergin & Jensen, 1990); thus, it is quite likely that they are far less religious than the clients they serve. Research that specifically examines the personal religiosity and spirituality of psychologists has indicated that psychologists (32%) compared to Americans in general (64%) are only half as likely to affirm a belief that "God really exists." Moreover, compared to 15% of the general population, 48% of psychologists regarded religion as unimportant in their lives (Delaney, Miller, & Bisonó, 2013). A conceptual distinction between religion and spirituality was noted in the Delaney et al. study in that psychologists ascribed much more importance to spirituality in their lives than to religion. This distinction is also seen in American society, when people describe themselves as spiritual but not religious (Fuller, 2001) and is also a common self-description of 12-step programs (e.g., Alcoholics Anonymous) where a set of guiding principles regarded by members as spiritual principles detail the course of action for healing. In addition, members are asked to recognize a Higher Power that can give them strength in overcoming their addiction or compulsion. The Higher Power might involve God, spirituality, or some form of meditation.

Counselors who have unresolved religious or spiritual issues may find it difficult to attend to religion and spirituality in the therapeutic encounter. Moreover, if a faith orientation has been absent or unimportant in the counselor's own life, then it is possible that the value of integrating religion and spirituality in the counseling relationship may be unclear. For example, counselors who were raised in orthodox religious homes and later questioned the validity of their family of origin's religion or have unresolved theological questions may feel anxious discussing religious or spiritual concerns. As such, the counselor may consciously or unconsciously redirect the client's religious or spiritual content to avoid feeling uncomfortable. Similarly, counselors without a religious or spiritual upbringing may not understand the potential impact of clients' faith background on their counseling goals and treatment and consequently fail to attend to it (Frame, 2003). Frame also explained that counselors who have experienced significant losses or trauma might also be experiencing crises of faith in that they are disappointed in or angry with God or their Higher Power for not preventing such atrocities from occurring. Specifically, she described the following challenge:

> When clients raise spiritual or religious questions about evil, death, and "why bad things happen to good people" (Kushner, 1981), counselors might feel unprepared to deal with the powerful emotions these topics unleash for them. They might also feel incapable of responding effectively to their clients' distress, and thus could attempt to minimize or avoid it. Such difficulty for the counselor signals the need for supervision, personal counseling, and perhaps referral of the client. (p. 27)

Yet another challenge presents itself for counselors when their clients' social and political positions, informed by a particular religious perspective, are in direct opposition to their own position. Examples of viewpoints that could potentially breed opposition include decisions about abortion, the rights of same-sex couples, counselors who may have been sexually abused by the clergy, and so forth. As such, counselors might find themselves in peculiar positions where they have assumed responsibility to free their clients from what they perceive to be flawed religious and spiritual convictions, or they may simply refuse to work with clients whom they perceive to have strong religious or spiritual dogma. Thus, counselors must reconcile their internal conflicts so their unresolved personal issues do not interfere with their counseling effectiveness.

Religion and Spirituality in Counseling

In the United States, more than 90% of individuals have reported that they are religious or spiritual (Princeton Religion Research Center, 1996; Richards & Bergin, 1997). Despite the prevalence of those who are spiritually or religiously affiliated, counseling professionals tend to be much less religiously oriented than clients (Worthington, 1989) and fail to address religious or spiritual issues in their work with clients (Kelly, 1995).

Given that a majority of U.S. individuals believe in some form of a Higher Power or being, and many are actively involved in religious institutions, it seems logical that a majority of clients will have some kind of religious or spiritual background that informs their attitudes, feelings, and behaviors. Moreover, empirical research has shown positive correlations between religious/spiritual faith and mental health (Hackney & Sanders,

2003; Koenig & Larson, 2001; W. R. Miller & Thoresen, 2003; Seybold & Hill, 2001). Thus, the salutary relationship between religion/spiritual involvement and mental health would seem to suggest that religion and spirituality are essential elements of the psychotherapeutic milieu.

We must also consider that our clients' religious and spiritual beliefs may be ancillary tools in their assessment and treatment planning (Frame, 2003). As such, we can no longer ignore the necessary preparation and training that counselors will need in order to competently explore the role of religion and spirituality in the lives of clients. Although counselors' interest in religion and spirituality as clinically relevant issues in the treatment environment has been documented (Faiver, Ingersoll, O'Brien, & McNally, 2001), their comfort and ability to address these issues is less clear. Unless training programs deliberately include issues of religion and spirituality in academic curricula, some counseling professionals may fail to include religious and spiritual discussion in relation to other therapeutic concerns (Constantine, 1999).

Given that counseling professionals have traditionally refrained from or been unwilling to include spiritual/religious discussions in therapy (Richards & Bergin, 1997), we must consider the impact of counselor reluctance on clients' perceptions about the appropriateness and/or desire to discuss such issues in therapy (Rose, Westefeld, & Ansley, 2008). In other words, clients who are concerned about how their counselors may respond to their religious or spiritual backgrounds and worldviews may be less willing to discuss their beliefs and may also conclude that the counseling setting is inappropriate for such discussion.

Accepting Clients as Spiritual and/or Religious Beings

An examination of counseling clients' beliefs about the appropriateness of discussing spiritual and religious in counseling revealed that 27% desired to discuss religious or spiritual issues because they regarded these experiences as essential to their healing or growth or because spirituality was an important coping mechanism. Rose et al. (2008) provided the following client statements to support this finding:

> I had been in therapy for years and could only heal to a certain level. It wasn't until my present counselor approached me about spirituality that I could receive healing at a deeper level. (p. 27–28)

> What you believe spiritually or religiously can help with solving problems. If the counselor doesn't know what you believe, how can they help? (p. 28)

Rose et al. (2008) further reported that approximately 8% of their sample made a distinction between religiosity and spirituality, with a stated preference for discussing spirituality in counseling and not religion:

> I think spiritual issues are more important because spirituality is more prevalent in everyone regardless of religion. (p. 28)

> God is spiritual—that's why I want it discussed. (p. 28)

It is also important to note that approximately 10% of participants in the Rose et al. (2008) study indicated that religious and spiritual issues were either unimportant in their lives or irrelevant to their presenting issues. Some of these participants also mentioned that they would feel more comfortable discussing their issues with a minister or member of the clergy. Other research also supports participants' beliefs that religion and spirituality are best discussed within an ecclesiastical setting (Thayne, 1998). It is worth noting that clients who believe a secular counseling setting is not the appropriate place to discuss spiritual/religious-related therapeutic content may also hold negative expectations about how their counselor will respond to their beliefs and experiences. Nonetheless, training programs are encouraged to prepare students to address the therapeutic aspects of religion and spirituality in their work with clients, which is consistent with the increased awareness of religion and spirituality as one aspect of our clients' culture and central to their identities. Evans (2003) summed it nicely:

> It is difficult for counselors to be multiculturally competent if they resist addressing the client's spiritual issues . . . counselors who are spiritually mature and include spirituality in their work with clients epitomize the culturally competent counselor. (p. 170)

Understanding Religion and Spirituality Development

Humans are spiritual beings. Whether or not one is religious, individuals go through a psychological developmental process toward a mature spiritual self, which William James (1968) viewed as "spiritual me" that is "the true, the intimate, the ultimate, the permanent me" (p. 46).

Although spiritual identity has not been studied as much as other human identities (e.g., psychosocial, racial, sexual, cultural) by psychological theorists of identity development, its importance in individuals' health and behavior is hard to ignore. In the area of professional counseling, it is particularly salient because one's spiritual and/or religious identity can serve as a source of strength in reaching inner peace or buffering against stress (G. Miller, 1999), or a source of prejudice or bias in relation to others with different religious beliefs (Altemeyer, 2003). To build healthy therapeutic relationships with clients, mental health professionals need to recognize their own level of spiritual identity development as well as that of their clients. As indicated by Evans (2003), counselors need to have spiritual maturity to work effectively with clients who are at different stages of their spiritual/religion identity.

There have been several faith or religion development models. The 7-stage model by James Fowler (1981) described a developmental sequence for faith, indicating that individuals must establish a secure sense of self (social self) before developing the secure spiritual self. This model describes faith development as a dynamic and genuine human experience with a meaning-making focus. The sequential nature of the stages predicts that individuals may not skip any stage but can potentially stay at a given stage for a long time. The seven stages are: *primal faith, intuitive-period faith, mythic-literal faith, synthetic-conventional faith, individuative-reflective faith, conjunctive faith, and universalizing faith.* It appears that the first four stages are targeted more toward an individual identity development process, and the latter stages indicate a spiritual development process of transcending the self to relate to God (Ford-Grabowsky, 1986).

In proposing a spiritual identity development model, Poll and Smith (2003) described a developmental process that individuals experience through "interacting with God and by recognizing divine within themselves and others" (p. 133). By integrating insights from other identity development theories with theistic insights, this model identified four stages of spiritual development, namely the following:

> *Pre-awareness stage.* Individuals in this phase have not had spiritual experience and do not consciously regard themselves in spiritual terms.
>
> *Awakening stage.* This stage often involves "a period of learning, crisis, or conflict that prompts an awakening of awareness of the self in relation to God" (p. 134). Individuals at this stage begin to view experiences or events in spiritual terms.
>
> *Recognition stage.* This stage "would entail recognition and recollection of other spiritual experiences, such that the initial awareness obtained in the previous stage is progressively generalized to an awareness of spiritual experiences in other settings and interactions" (p. 134). Individuals start to recognize a consistent spiritual identity and see spiritual themes in their experiences.
>
> *Integration stage.* This final stage typically "involves an integration of spiritual experiences with self-concept" (p. 134). Individuals at this stage see themselves as spiritual beings and attempt to weave spirituality into many aspects of their life.

Although spirituality identity development can be highly idiosyncratic, these theoretical models offer a structure and language for us to recognize our spiritual identity development process and become aware of our own views, biases, and perspectives on religion and spirituality. We need to know how such perspectives might impact our work with clients who may or may not share our spiritual and/or religious beliefs and whose stage of spiritual identity development may be different from our own. As noted by Frame (2003), we must understand how our own worldviews and history can greatly impact our work with clients:

> It is my judgment that confronting your own personal history with and current orientation toward religion and spirituality is critical. I believe that as counselors, one of the best tools we have to offer our clients is ourselves. In the therapeutic encounter, our humanness, authenticity, and empathy can be catalysts for change. If we are open to our own personal growth, are willing to move beyond our comfort zones, and are open to exploring what gives our lives meaning, then we are capable of being excellent role models for our clients. Likewise, if we are unaware of our own inner conflicts, have unresolved issues that are outside of our awareness, or are reluctant to confront our questions about meaning and values in our lives, we can severely limit or even harm our clients' growth process. (p. 1–2)

Given the relevance and importance of religion and spirituality for the majority of Americans and the growing diversity of religious and spiritual beliefs and traditions, counseling professionals must be prepared to respond to the religious and spiritual dimensions of clients' problems. Viewed from a developmental perspective, spirituality and/or religious identity development are germane to clients' values and worldviews and are also relevant considerations in counseling. Similar to other cultural identities, both counselor and client spiritual and religious identities may influence the therapeutic relationship and treatment process and outcomes. Thus, it is critical that counselors be aware of their own and their clients' spiritual identity developmental stages, understand potential counselor-client power dynamics (e.g., being members of different religious groups), and respect clients who embrace their spiritual and/or religious identities.

Integrating Religion/Spirituality Interventions

It can be challenging to integrate spirituality into counseling if the counselors are not trained due to the fact that "spiritual and religious themes appear to be minimally included in counseling program curricula" (Hage, Hopson, Siegel, Payton, & DeFanti, 2006, p. 217). To provide counselors who have a developing multicultural identity (including a religious and spiritual component) a place to start, Fukuyama and Sevig (1999, p. 161) offered some process suggestions:

- Develop a clear understanding of personal religious beliefs and worldviews
- Focus on client's spiritual concerns
- Sustain a study group or a supervision group for processing countertransference issues
- Be prepared since the level of integrating spirituality depends on the counselor's readiness
- Consider the counseling environment, as some settings (e.g., schools) may have restrictions

There can be different types of spiritual integration "ranging from philosophical positions to concrete behaviors" (p. 160). Fukuyama and Sevig (1999, p. 161) also presented some integrations used by clinical social workers revealed in a 1996 survey by Bullis, including the following:

- Explore client's spiritual background
- Explore client's religious background
- Help client clarify spiritual values
- Recommend participation in spiritual programs (meditation groups, 12-step programs)
- Use spiritual language or metaphors
- Pray privately for client
- Explore spiritual elements in dreams
- Use or recommend spiritual books

In 1998, Golston, Savage, and Cohen surveyed American Psychological Association (APA)-accredited internship training programs in clinical and counseling psychology and received data from 210 programs (Fukuyama & Sevig, 1999, p. 162). They found the following "top-rated goals" regarding religious and spiritual issues among those programs:

Becoming aware of ethical issues in supervising counselors-in-training who have specific religious beliefs (views on same-sex attraction, abortion, etc.)

Becoming aware of one's religious/spiritual biases

Becoming aware of limitations in one's competency in dealing with religious/spiritual issues (RSI) in therapy

Becoming sensitized to religion/spirituality as a component of clients' cultural contexts

Becoming aware of stereotypes one holds related to particular religions/spiritual traditions or adherents

Becoming aware of how one's own religious/spiritual belief system may influence the counseling process

Becoming aware of the role of religion and spirituality for special populations (i.e., ethnicity, disability, sexual orientation, sex, and age)

Becoming aware of one's own religious/spiritual values

Becoming aware of RSI as aspects of presenting issues in therapy (e.g., death of a loved one, low self-esteem, depression, relationship issues, feelings of guilt)

Learning to assess the role of RSI in client pathology

Learning when and how to refer clients to religious leaders for spiritual counseling or consultation

Increasing counselor comfort level and skill in raising and dealing with RSI

These research results seem to show that as a helping profession we have started and need to continue exploring ways in which spirituality can be integrated into counseling. In the overall context of multiculturalism, spiritual values are to be integrated because they are important contexts for people and communities in the United States. To strengthen the point that multicultural spiritual interplay can't be ignored, Fukuyama and Sevig (1999) offered a comparison of spiritual and multicultural values (see Table 12.1). Perhaps this is one way by which we can ease resistance or discomfort in integrating spirituality into counseling, and we can find more ways to integrate spirituality and multiculturalism to improve the efficacy of counseling for the culturally diverse.

Training for Religion/Spirituality Competencies

Despite the counseling profession's increased interest in religion and spirituality, there continues to be scarce and inadequate training in this area (Walker, Gorsuch, & Tan, 2004; Young, Cashwell, Wiggins-Frame, & Belaire, 2002), which means we are not adequately preparing mental health professionals to be competent in working with a religiously/spiritually diverse clientele. In short, unless we rethink our training curriculum and goals, our program graduates will be left on their own to develop relevant competencies; we therefore run the risk that emerging counseling professionals will lack the awareness, knowledge, and skills to address and incorporate spiritual and

Table 12.1 Comparison Between Spiritual and Multicultural Values

Spiritual Values	Multicultural Values
Connectedness w/ others	Cultural similarities
Contact & conflict with reality	Cultural differences
Compassion & love	Understanding & empathy
Relationship outside of self	Movement from ethnocentrism toward cultural pluralism
Social justice	Dealing with issues of oppression, advocacy
Faith	Flexibility & patience
Grace, intimacy, creativity	Commitment & humor
Sacredness & mystery	Tolerance of ambiguity
Detachment	Observational skills
Paradox	Bicultural & multicultural skills

Source: Fukuyama, M. A., & Sevig, T. D. (1999). *Integrating spirituality into multicultural counseling.* Thousand Oaks, CA: Sage.

religious concerns and perspectives in their clinical practice. Religion and spiritual competence typically follows the model of competencies in other multicultural areas and therefore includes three fundamental aspects: awareness, knowledge, and skills (Sue & Sue, 1990).

The Association for Spiritual, Ethical, and Religious Values in Counseling (ASERVIC, 2009) has developed a list of competencies to assist helping professionals as they address spiritual and religious themes in counseling. These competencies are guidelines that complement the values and standards espoused by the ACA *Code of Ethics* and include the following six competency domains: (a) culture and worldview, (b) counselor self-awareness, (c) human and spiritual development, (d) communication, (e) assessment, and (f) diagnosis and treatment (see Table 12.2 for the complete list of competencies).

Religion, Spirituality, and Ethical Considerations

As counseling professionals, we have an ethical responsibility to promote and protect client welfare and our profession's code of ethics (ACA, 2014) and present specific standards for how we are expected to relate and behave in concert with our clients. Although virtually all of the codes of ethics of the mental health profession (e.g., counseling, school, family therapy, psychology, social work) include standards referencing respect for human dignity and freedom of the client, specific guidelines for integrating religion and spirituality into counseling are not explicit. In consideration of the ethical

Table 12.2 Competencies for Addressing Spiritual and Religious Issues in Counseling *Endorsed by the American Counseling Association (ACA)*

The Competencies for Addressing Spiritual and Religious Issues in Counseling are guidelines that complement, not supersede, the values and standards espoused in the ACA *Code of Ethics*.	
Consistent with the ACA *Code of Ethics* (2005), the purpose of the ASERVIC competencies is to "recognize diversity and embrace a cross-cultural approach in support of the worth, dignity, potential, and uniqueness of people within their social and cultural contexts" (p. 3). These competencies are intended to be used in conjunction with counseling approaches that are evidence-based and that align with best practices in counseling.	
Culture and Worldview	
1.	The professional counselor can describe the similarities and differences between spirituality and religion, including the basic beliefs of various spiritual systems, major world religions, agnosticism, and atheism.
2.	The professional counselor recognizes that the client's beliefs (or absence of beliefs) about spirituality and/or religion are central to his or her worldview and can influence psychosocial functioning.
Counselor Self-Awareness	
3.	The professional counselor actively explores his or her own attitudes, beliefs, and values about spirituality and/or religion.
4.	The professional counselor continuously evaluates the influence of his or her own spiritual and/or religious beliefs and values on the client and the counseling process.
5.	The professional counselor can identify the limits of his or her understanding of the client's spiritual and/or religious perspective and is acquainted with religious and spiritual resources, including leaders, who can be avenues for consultation and to whom the counselor can refer.
6.	The professional counselor can describe and apply various models of spiritual and/or religious development and their relationship to human development.
Communication	
7.	The professional counselor responds to client communications about spirituality and/or religion with acceptance and sensitivity.
8.	The professional counselor uses spiritual and/or religious concepts that are consistent with the client's spiritual and/or religious perspectives and that are acceptable to the client.
9.	The professional counselor can recognize spiritual and/or religious themes in client communication and is able to address these with the client when they are therapeutically relevant.

(Continued)

Table 12.2 (Continued)

Assessment	
10.	During the intake and assessment processes, the professional counselor strives to understand a client's spiritual and/or religious perspective by gathering information from the client and/or other sources.
Diagnosis and Treatment	
11.	When making a diagnosis, the professional counselor recognizes that the client's spiritual and/or religious perspectives can a) enhance well-being; b) contribute to client problems; and/or c) exacerbate symptoms.
12.	The professional counselor sets goals with the client that are consistent with the client's spiritual and/or religious perspectives.
13.	The professional counselor is able to a) modify therapeutic techniques to include a client's spiritual and/or religious perspectives, and b) utilize spiritual and/or religious practices as techniques when appropriate and acceptable to a client's viewpoint.
14.	The professional counselor can therapeutically apply theory and current research supporting the inclusion of a client's spiritual and/or religious perspectives and practices.

Source: Association for Spiritual, Ethical, and Religious Issues in Counseling. (2009). *Competencies for addressing spirituality and religious issues in counseling.* Retrieved from http://www.aservic.org/resources/spiritual-competencies/

concerns that speak to religious and spiritual interventions in counseling, we discuss the following areas in which religion and spirituality raise unique challenges: client welfare, competence, and imposition of values.

Client Welfare

The primary ethical responsibility of counseling professionals is to respect the dignity and promote the welfare of clients (ACA, 2014). Counseling relationships with our clients include commitment, honesty, and respect for cultural differences. In order to practice ethically and ensure client welfare, we must address religious and spiritual issues when they arise in our counseling relationships. The ethical counselor values the clients' worldviews, which may include religious and spiritual frameworks. We do not have the prerogative to neglect any facet of our clients' experiences, identities, and worldviews—to do so is irresponsible, unethical, and runs the risk of doing harm to our clients.

In our efforts to protect client welfare, we are encouraged to work within our clients' belief systems (Tan, 1994). This means we work to understand clients' constructed realities that include their beliefs and practices and how such realities create distress and/or promote well-being in their lives. When we understand clients' religious and spiritual persuasions, we are in position to help them explore the extent to which these transcendent experiences create stress in their lives or serve as a buffer against it. Counselors who are multilingual in that they are able to communicate with their clients about relevant religious and spiritual concepts (e.g., grace, mercy, sins, salvation) demonstrate their respect for their clients' worldviews and traditions, which in turn informs trust and relationship building (Haug, 1998).

Professional Obligations

In addition to client welfare being a hallmark of ethical practice, competence is also an important goal. Our ACA (2014) *Code of Ethics* informs professional competence (C.2.a. Boundaries of Competence) and specifically states that "counselors gain knowledge, personal awareness, sensitivity, dispositions, and skills pertinent to being a culturally competent counselor in working with a diverse client population" (p. 8). The importance of the integration of religion and spirituality in counseling can be seen in the increased offerings that are designed to prepare students to work with clients who bring religious and spiritual concerns to counseling (Ingersoll, 1997).

Our field's professional literature, conferences, and workshops have also discussed and/or provided training opportunities for counseling professionals to learn how to work with clients' religious and spiritual concerns. Counselors must take advantage of these opportunities to develop their competence and to practice ethically. It is important to note that counselors do not need to share their clients' religious and spiritual orientations in order to help clients explore and use their belief systems in counseling (Propst, 1992). Consultation and supervision should be sought, however, when counselors employ novel religious and spiritual interventions (Frame, 2003).

Avoiding Values Imposition

Our ACA (2014) *Code of Ethics* commands that we respect our clients' diverse opinions and values. Specifically, A4.b. Personal Values states the following:

> Counselors are aware of—and avoid imposing—their own values, attitudes, beliefs, and behaviors. Counselors respect the diversity of clients . . . and seek training in areas in which they are at risk of imposing their values onto clients, especially when the counselor's values are inconsistent with the client's goals or are discriminatory in nature. (p. 5)

Because we do not enter counseling value-free (Corey, 2001), working with clients' religious and spiritual beliefs can make counselors vulnerable to violating the personal values standard. Frame (2003) differentiated between *imposing* one's values and *exposing* one's values and further noted the controversy in the professional field as to whether exposing one's values is simply a subtlety of imposing one's values. Whereas imposing one's values either overtly or covertly implies an attempt to influence the client's beliefs and choices, exposing one's values means counselors disclose their religious or spiritual perspectives to their clients.

In the spirit of informed consent, Aponte (1996) suggested that counselors make their values explicit so they can then refer clients to other providers if divergent values create unresolved conflicts. This stance is problematic in the sense that some referrals may be prompted by counselors' refusal to work with clients who have values different from their own. More recently, ethical standards have been interpreted to mean that refusing to counsel a client with whom the counselor has a values conflict is unethical, and legal proceedings support this (see *Keeton v. Anderson-Wiley et al.*, 2011; *Ward v. Wilbanks*, 2010).

Moreover, some clients such as children, adolescents, and adults with fragile egos may be influenced by their counselors' disclosure of their value orientations, resulting in clients adopting their counselors' belief systems due to not having formulated their own. In this scenario, exposing values could result in imposing values; counselors must, therefore, consider the extent to which disclosure of values is in the best interest of their clients (Frame, 2003). Counseling professionals may also be uncertain about the use of prayer in counseling sessions and in particular whether agreeing to pray for one's client out loud or silently is an imposition of values. Such challenges warrant attention, and supervision or consultation is encouraged to ensure the promotion of client welfare and respect for clients' values. It is within our ethical practice to assist clients to determine which beliefs support them in living meaningful lives or are destructive in their fulfillment of meaning. What we cannot do is to tell them what to believe or direct them toward a certain set of values; doing so is imposing our values and is in violation of our standard of practice.

Assessing Religion and Spirituality: The Clinical Interview

Conducting religious and spiritual assessments should employ multiple methods. When counselors assess clients' religious and spiritual backgrounds, they are seeking to understand their clients' beliefs, values, and worldviews and how these perspectives

Reflection on the Role of Spirituality and Religion in the Formation of a Multicultural Identity

First, being able to help myself, my family, and my friends understand changes in my behavior, my worldview, even my relationship with God is OK as I develop a refined multicultural personal and professional identity. For me, being a spiritual and religious person, one of the most difficult areas was reconciling things I had been taught by religious leaders, mentors, and the like with the values our field has for the LGBTQ population. Being able to talk through this with a counselor was very meaningful, and I have a supportive romantic partner as well. However, I recall pointing out things here and there to family or friends and feeling odd or misunderstood. At one point, a family member told me to "remember who I am" and not to let my training change my core beliefs. For me, this was the biggest obstacle.

—S. D., a White, male doctoral student in counseling psychology

are related to their presenting concerns and resources for solving their problems. Assessment methods that assist with providing a comprehensive picture of our clients' experiences include intake forms, clinical assessment interviews, genograms, and paper-pencil measures. For the purpose of this chapter and due to space, we will focus on the clinical interview since it is an integral part of the counseling process and a method used by all counseling professionals.

The clinical interview provides opportunity for counselors to gather information about clients' relevant religious and spiritual history, the role of faith in their life, including supports and barriers, and the resources available to them based on their religious or spiritual heritage. Noting the importance of religious and spiritual issues as a presenting issue in counseling, Kelly (1995) recommended that religion and spiritual beliefs be included on a checklist of presenting concerns (e.g., intake form) to be discussed during the clinical interview. In other words, it is imperative to assess clients' satisfaction with their current religious and spiritual practices. If clients respond affirmatively to a faith or spiritual background, the following questions can serve as discussion points:

> Do you believe that religious or spiritual influences have contributed to your problems?
>
> What religious or spiritual resources, if any, have you employed in the past to help you overcome your problems?
>
> Would you like your counselor to consult with your religious/spiritual leader if it appears this could help you overcome your problems (Richards & Bergin, 1997, p. 193)?

CASE ILLUSTRATION 12.2

The Case of Renee and Morris

Renee, 45, and her husband, Morris, 46, sought counseling with Sheila to deal with marital conflict that had existed for most of the 16 years of their marriage. Renee described their marital distress as stemming from poor communication and volatile arguments; she further expressed concern that Morris's bullying, intimidating, and verbally abusive behaviors and frequent outbursts of anger were the cause of her excessive alcohol consumption and ultimately her preference to not be around him. Morris told Sheila that he was a Christian and very involved in his church, which included serving as an usher and regularly attending Sunday worship services and weekly Bible study. He prayed daily and relied on his faith to help him be the best husband possible and to avoid the temptations of sin and mistreatment of his wife. He had been a good steward in terms of attending church regularly, but Morris expressed his frustration for Renee's lack of church involvement, complaining that

(Continued)

(Continued)

she rarely attended church on Sunday and never participated in Bible study or other church-related activities. He felt certain that if she got more involved in church, she could get her drinking under control.

Morris grew up in a family where religion was eschewed in favor of partying, socializing, and drinking, and he was puzzled at how he and Renee had essentially changed places, as she had grown up strict Pentecostal, with religion being at the forefront of everything in her childhood, adolescence, and young adulthood, and now he couldn't even get her to attend church on Sunday.

Renee often told Morris to not bug her about going to church, as she was without doubt a believer (Christian) who didn't need to participate in the formality of a church service to know that "Jesus was the son of God." After all, she had spent "every waking moment" of the years during her childhood and young adulthood in church and could recite Biblical scriptures that the average Christian would have to look up. "Get off my back!" she would scream.

Morris's goal was to get Renee involved in church so he could get her to stop drinking. Renee expected Morris to continue to attend church as often as possible so that his abusive and controlling demons could be confronted and eradicated.

Discussion Questions

Taking into consideration Renee and Morris's religious backgrounds and experiences, discuss the following questions:

1. How would you frame Renee and Morris's problem?
2. What role is religion and/or spirituality playing in their relationship?
3. What interventions would you consider relevant for working with this couple?
4. What resources, if any, would you need to assist you with this case?
5. What personal issues, if any, does this case raise for you?
6. How effective do you believe you could be working with this couple, and what are obvious facilitators and/or hindrances for you?

When Do Religion and Spirituality Become Harmful or Pathological?

The positive benefits of religion/spirituality and mental health have been well documented in literature. Some mental health professionals may express concern about the harmful effects of religion and spirituality on clients' emotional and physical well-being. Counselors may want to assist clients in exploring how religious or spiritual belief systems contribute positively to their lives and functioning. For the client who believes in reincarnation and consequently becomes a strict vegetarian, the belief itself is not necessarily the subject of scrutiny but whether the practice of being a vegetarian is a positive or negative life experience (Frame, 2003).

Mental health professionals have considered the religious cult phenomenon in the context of religion and spirituality and counseling treatment and more specifically the extent to which religious cults are maladaptive. Although a discussion of cult characteristics is beyond the scope of this chapter, we do describe Richards and Bergin's (1997) schema on adaptive versus maladaptive religion and spirituality, which includes dimensions of healthy and unhealthy religion. According to Richards and Bergin, *adaptive religion* involves a social dimension that includes networking and establishing supportive, kinship-type relationships. Religion that is adaptive is also described as healthy, growing, creative, and helpful in making its followers to make sense of the ambiguous aspects of their life. To the contrary, *maladaptive religion* is dependent, perfectionistic, and includes elements of manipulation and deception. Members of maladaptive religion tend to be anxious and overcontrolled.

Richards and Bergin (1997) distinguish between healthy and unhealthy religion by noting that healthy religion is characteristic of openness to reform, renewal, and change. Perhaps most important and of relevance to the practice of counseling is that those for whom religion is healthy tend to be more tolerant of differences. Moreover, *healthy religion* is characterized as nurturing, caring, empathic, inspiring, and prophetic; from a counseling perspective, religion that is healthy can be a resource from which clients can draw support when faced with difficult life issues. Conversely, *unhealthy religion* is rigid, authoritarian, intolerant, controlling, and abusive and may involve evil or supernatural and mystical beliefs and practices. Followers of unhealthy religion may feel judged and pressured to conform to the expectations and rules of their leaders (Richards & Bergin, 1997, p. 189).

GUIDED PRACTICE EXERCISE 12.1

My Spiritual Journey?

Reflecting on your earliest memories, describe what you recall about religion or spirituality in your home life, including any church experiences or spiritual traditions through childhood, adolescence, young adulthood, and beyond.

What, if any, faith or spiritual tradition do you embrace today, and how might it have changed or been challenged to this point?

What defining moments (decisions, events, and/or experiences) have shaped who you are today?

What direction, if any, are you hoping to take in your life as related to a religious or spiritual dimension?

SMALL-GROUP CLASS ACTIVITY 12.2

Counselor Competencies: Spirituality in Counseling

The Summit on Spirituality's list of competencies (see Table 12.3) addresses four knowledge domains: (1) general knowledge of spiritual phenomenon, (2) awareness of one's own spiritual perspective, (3) understanding of clients' spiritual perspective, and (4) spiritually related interventions and strategies. These competencies were the outgrowth of counselor educators who proposed to infuse spirituality into counselor education, which resulted in a 1999 summit meeting (Miller, 1999) and four subsequent sessions held during conferences of the ACA and Association for Counselor Education and Supervision.

In groups of four or five students, review and discuss one of the four domains with attention to (a) their current level of competency, (b) comfort with the competencies as related to fully engaging their clients' spiritual/religious worldviews, (c) how they will apply these competencies to help appreciate and respect their clients' religious/spiritual belief systems, (d) completeness of the competencies (i.e., they were developed in 1999—consider what updates are needed), and (e) what counseling training programs can do to ensure the competency domains are achieved.

Table 12.3 Counselor Competencies: Spirituality in Counseling

Counselor Competencies: Spirituality in Counseling

1. Believing that a general understanding of spiritual phenomena is important to the counseling process, the counselor can
   a. Explain how the varieties of spiritual phenomena are understood from the perspective of diversity.
   b. Discuss possible relationships, including similarities and differences, among various views of spirituality: psychospiritual, religious, spiritual, and transpersonal.
   c. Describe basic beliefs of various spiritual systems, including the major world religions, indigenous people's spirituality, agnosticism, and atheism.
   d. Explain at least two models of human spiritual development across the life span.
   e. Describe research, theory, and clinical evidence that indicate the relationships between spiritual phenomena on the one hand and mental health on the other.
   f. Explain how the potential power of combining spiritual issues with counseling methods compels the counselor to operate from a solid ethical base.
2. Believing the awareness of one's own spiritual perspective is important to the counseling process, the counselor can
   a. Describe one's own spiritual perspective.
   b. Identify key events in one's life that contributed to the development of one's own spiritual perspective and explain how those events contributed.

c. Identify specific attitudes, beliefs, and values from one's own spiritual perspective that may support or hinder respect for and valuing of different spiritual perspectives.

d. Actively engage in an ongoing process of challenging one's own attitudes and beliefs that hinder respect for and valuing of different spiritual perspectives.

e. Conceptualize oneself from two different models of human spiritual development across the life span.

f. Conceptualize oneself in terms of research, theory, and clinical evidence that indicate relationships between spiritual phenomena and mental health.

3. Believing that an understanding of the client's spiritual perspective is important to the counseling process, the counselor can

   a. Demonstrate openness to, empathy with, and acceptance of a variety of spiritual phenomena.

   b. Describe the role of the client's spiritual perspective in an understanding of the client as a whole.

   c. Acquire knowledge needed to better understand a client's spiritual perspective by requesting information from the client and/or from the outside resources.

   d. Identify when one's understanding and/or acceptance of the client's spiritual perspective is insufficient to adequately serve the client.

4. Believing that spiritually related intervention strategies and techniques are important to the counseling process, the counselor can

   a. Assess the relevance of the spiritual domain in a client's therapeutic issues.

   b. Use spiritual terms and concepts that are meaningful to the client.

   c. Use the client's spiritual perspective in the pursuit of his or her counseling goals as befits their expressed preferences.

   d. When relevant to the client's counseling goals and expressed preferences,

      (1) Apply spiritual developmental theory to facilitate client understanding of their present stage/status of life span spiritual development.

      (2) Share research, theory, and clinical evidence with the client to facilitate their understanding of the relationship between spiritual phenomena and their mental health.

   e. Demonstrate competent use of techniques for remediation of problems with, facilitation of, enhancement of, and psychological integration of spiritual phenomena.

   f. Consult with professionals in the area of spirituality, including professionals the client considers to hold spiritual authority, when such consultation would enhance service to the client.

   g. Having identified limits to one's acceptance or competence, seek consultation, seek further education or training, and/or demonstrate appropriate referral skills.

Source: Young, Cashwell, Wiggins-Frame, and Belaire (2002).

GUIDED PRACTICE EXERCISE 12.2

Counselor Interview Questions

Identify a licensed counselor to interview about the role of religion and spirituality in his or her practice of counseling. The goal of this interview is to understand the extent to which licensed counseling professionals attend to their clients' religious and spiritual beliefs in the provision of direct counseling services. This interview experience should familiarize you with the counselor's religious or spiritual framework and his or her perceived importance of the integration of religion and spirituality in counseling practice. The following questions are suggested to guide the interview:

1. What is your understanding of the differences between religion and spirituality?
2. Do religion and spirituality deserve a place in the practice of counseling? Why or why not?
3. How does your theoretical orientation inform working with clients' religious and spiritual issues?
4. Can you share an example of a client's problem involving religion or spirituality and how you worked with this client?
5. What has been your own religious or spiritual journey?

Summary

This chapter discusses the impact of religion and spirituality on a person's multicultural identify. Whereas religion indicates allegiance to the beliefs and practices of an organized institution, spirituality denotes beliefs, experiences, and practices in relating to a Higher Power. Religious and spiritual experience both have an impact on the relevance of counseling, and the link between personal faith and mental health is well documented in the literature.

Given clients' personal investment in their religious and spiritual experience and that religious commitment is an important expression of diversity, we can no longer ignore or minimize the importance of including religious and spiritual discussion in our counseling practice. Furthermore, we must help counseling professionals frame their assessments, treatment planning, and interventions in ways that are sensitive and responsive to clients' religious and spiritual backgrounds. Although counselors may not be actively attuned to their clients' spiritual and religious frameworks and feel ill prepared or show reluctance to understand the connections between client issues and religion, training programs are encouraged to provide counselor trainees with the necessary preparation and skills needed to competently explore the role of religion and spirituality in the lives of their clients. An informed appreciation of clients' spiritual/religious worldviews and use of spiritually/religiously sensitive approaches is consistent with our counseling profession's code of ethics.

In short, counselor educators and supervisors must ensure that trainee endorsement into the profession includes their responsiveness to potential client spirituality and religiosity discussions.

Religion and spirituality are defining aspects of cultural diversity, and we have an ethical obligation to seek an accurate and complete understanding of the world of the religious client.

Takeaway Messages

1. A majority of U.S. individuals are spiritual or religious.
2. Counseling professionals may be reluctant to integrate religious and spiritual beliefs in their counseling practice due to lack of training and competence, negative experiences with religion, and/or unresolved theological questions that cause anxiety.
3. To be multiculturally competent, counselors must also be religiously/spiritually competent.
4. Clients may conclude that the counseling setting is inappropriate for spiritual/religious discussions if they perceive their counselor's reluctance.
5. Given that religion/spirituality are central to our clients' identities, training programs are encouraged to deliberately include religion and spirituality in academic curricula and training goals.
6. Ethical counselors value their clients' worldviews, which include their spiritual and religious experiences.
7. Positive associations between spiritual/religious involvement and mental health have been documented in literature.

Recommended Resources

Readings

Burke, M. T., Chauvin, J. C., & Miranti, J. G. (2005). *Religious and spiritual issues in counseling: Applications across diverse populations.* New York, NY: Brunner-Routledge.

Plante, T. G. (2009). *Spiritual practices in psychotherapy: 13 tools for enhancing psychological health.* Washington, DC: American Psychological Association.

Post, B. C., & Wade, N. G. (2009). Religion and spirituality in psychotherapy: A practice-friendly review of research. *Journal of Clinical Psychology, 65,* 131–146. doi:10.1002/jclp.20563

Richards, P. S., & Bergin, A. E. (2005). *A spiritual strategy for counseling and psychotherapy* (2nd ed.). Washington, DC: American Psychological Association.

Media

Lathan, S. (Director). (1984). *Go tell it on the mountain* [Made-for-television move]. United States: ABC. (An African American family saga based on the 1953 semi-autobiographical novel by James Baldwin.)

McMinn, M. R. (2006). *Christian counseling* [Motion picture]. Available from American Psychological Association. 750 First Street, NE, Washington, DC 2002-4242.

References

Altemeyer, B. (2003). Why do religious fundamentalists tend to be prejudiced? *International Journal for the Psychology of Religion, 13,* 17–28.

American Counseling Association. (2014). *Code of ethics.* Retrieved from http://www.counseling.org/resources/aca-code-of-ethics.pdf

Aponte, H. J. (1996). Political bias, moral values, and spirituality in the training of psychotherapists. *Bulletin of the Menninger Clinic, 60*(4), 488–502.

Association for Spiritual, Ethical, and Religious Issues in Counseling. (2009). *Competencies for addressing spirituality and religious issues in counseling.* Retrieved from http://www.aservic.org/resources/spiritual-competencies/

Bartoli, E. (2007). Religious and spiritual issues in psychotherapy practice: Training the trainer. *Psychotherapy: Theory, Research, Practice, Training, 44*(1), 54.

Bergin, A. E., & Jensen, J. P. (1990). Religiosity of psychotherapists: A national survey. *Psychotherapy: Theory, Research, Practice, Training, 27*(1), 3.

Bullis, R. (1996). *Spirituality in social work practice.* Washington, DC: Taylor & Francis.

Constantine, M. G. (1999). Spiritual and religious issues in counseling racial and ethnic minority populations: An introduction to the special issue. *Journal of Multicultural Counseling and Development, 27*(4), 179–181.

Corey, G. (2001). *Theory and practice of counseling and psychotherapy* (6th ed.). Belmont, CA: Wadsworth.

Delaney, H. D., Miller, W. R., & Bisonó, A. M. (2013). Religiosity and spirituality among psychologists: A survey of clinician members of the American Psychological Association. *Spirituality in Clinical Practice, 1*(S), 95–106.

Evans, K. M. (2003). Including spirituality in multicultural counseling: Overcoming counsellor resistance. In G. Roysircar, D. S. Sandhu, & V. E. Bibbins, Sr. (Eds.), *Multicultural competencies: A guidebook of practices* (pp. 161–171). Washington, DC: United States Association for Multicultural Counseling and Development.

Faiver, C., Ingersoll, R., O'Brien, E., & McNally, C. (2001). *Explorations in counseling and spirituality: Philosophical, practical and personal reflections.* Belmont, CA: Wadsworth/Thompson Learning.

Ford-Grabowsky, M. (1986). What developmental phenomenon is Fowler studying? *Journal of Psychology and Christianity, 5*, 5–13.

Fowler, J. W. (1981). *Stages of faith: The psychology of human development and the quest for meaning.* New York: Harper & Row.

Frame, M. W. (2003). *Integrating religion and spirituality into counseling: A comprehensive approach.* Pacific Grove, CA: Brooks/Cole.

Fukuyama, M. A., & Sevig, T. D. (1999). *Integrating spirituality into multicultural counseling.* Thousand Oaks, CA: Sage.

Fuller, R. C. (2001). *Spiritual, but not religious: Understanding unchurched America.* New York, NY: Oxford University Press.

Golston, S. S., Savage, J. S., & Cohen, M. C. (1998, August). Internship training practices regarding religious and spiritual issues. Paper presented at the 106th American Psychological Association convention, San Francisco, CA.

Gonsiorek, J. C., Richards, P., Pargament, K. I., & McMinn, M. R. (2009). Ethical challenges and opportunities at the edge: Incorporating spirituality and religion into psychotherapy. *Professional Psychology: Research and Practice, 40*(4), 385–395.

Hackney, C. H., & Sanders, G. S. (2003). Religiosity and mental health: A meta-analysis of recent studies. *Journal for the Scientific Study of Religion, 42*(1), 43–55.

Hage, S. M., Hopson, A., Siegel, M., Payton, G., & DeFanti, E. (2006). Multicultural training in spirituality: An interdisciplinary review. *Counseling and Values, 50*, 217–234.

Haug, I. E. (1998). Including a spiritual dimension in family therapy: Ethical considerations. *Contemporary Family Therapy, 20*(2), 181–194.

Ingersoll, R. (1997). Teaching a course on counseling and spirituality. *Counselor Education and Supervision, 36*(3), 224–232.

James, W. (1968). The self. In C. Gordon & K. J. Gergen (Eds.), *The self in social interaction* (Vol. 1, pp. 41–49). New York, NY: Wiley.

Keeton v. Anderson-Wiley et al., 23 F. C 647 (D. Fla. 2011), *aff'd*, 664 F.3d 865 (11th Cir. 2011).

Kelly, E. W., Jr. (1995). *Spirituality and religion in counseling and psychotherapy: Diversity in theory and practice.* Alexandria, VA: American Counseling Association.

Koenig, H. G., & Larson, D. B. (2001). Religion and mental health: Evidence for an association. *International Review of Psychiatry, 13*(2), 67–78.

Kushner, H. S. (1981). *When bad things happen to good people.* New York, NY: Avon Books.

Miller, G. (1999). The development of the spiritual focus in counseling and counselor education. *Journal of Counseling & Development, 77,* 498–501.

Miller, W. R., & Thoresen, C. E. (2003). Spirituality, religion, and health: An emerging research field. *American Psychologist, 58*(1), 24–35.

Poll, J. B., & Smith, T. B. (2003). The spiritual self: Toward a conceptualization of spiritual identity development. *Journal of Psychology and Theology, 31*(2), 129–142.

Propst, L. R. (1992). Spirituality and the avoidant personality. *Theology Today, 49,* 163–172.

Richards, P., & Bergin, A. E. (1997). *A spiritual strategy for counseling and psychotherapy.* Washington, DC: American Psychological Association.

Rose, E. M., Westefeld, J. S., & Ansley, T. N. (2008). Spiritual issues in counseling: Clients' beliefs and preferences. *Psychology of Religion and Spirituality, S*(1), 18–33.

Schulte, D. L., Skinner, T. A., & Claibom, C. D. (2002). Religious and spiritual issues in counseling psychology training. *The Counseling Psychologist, 30*(1), 118–134.

Seybold, K. S., & Hill, P. C. (2001). The role of religion and spirituality in mental and physical health. *Current Directions in Psychological Science, 10*(1), 21–24.

Shafranske, E. P., & Maloney, H. N. (1990). Clinical psychologists' religious and spiritual orientations and their practice of psychotherapy. *Psychotherapy: Theory, Research, Practice, Training, 27*(1), 72.

Shafranske, E. P., & Sperry, L. (2005). Addressing the spiritual dimension in psychotherapy: Introduction and overview. In L. Sperry & E. P. Shafranske (Eds.), *Spiritually oriented psychotherapy* (pp. 11–29). Washington, DC: American Psychological Association.

Sue, D. W., & Sue, D. (1990). Counseling the culturally different: Theory and practice. New York, NY: Wiley.

Tan, S.-Y. (1994). Ethical considerations in religious psychotherapy: Potential pitfalls and unique resources. *Journal of Psychology and Theology, 22,* 389–394.

Thayne, T. R. (1998). Opening space for clients' religious and spiritual values in therapy: A social constructionist perspective. *Journal of Family Social Work, 2*(4), 13–23.

Walker, D. F., Gorsuch, R. L., & Tan, S. (2004). Therapists' integration of religion and spirituality in counseling: A meta-analysis. *Counseling and Values, 49*(1), 69–80.

Ward v. Wilbanks, 2010 U.S. Dist. LEXIS 127038 (E.D. Mich. July 26, 2010). Retrieved from http://www.lexisnexis.com

Worthington, E. L. (1989). Religious faith across the life span: Implications for counseling and research. *The Counseling Psychologist, 17*(4), 555–612.

Young, J. S., Cashwell, C., Wiggins-Frame, M., & Belaire, C. (2002). Spiritual and religious competencies: A national survey of CACREP-accredited programs. *Counseling and Values, 47*(1), 22–33.

Section 5

Social Justice and Multicultural Counseling

Major CACREP Standards for the Section

CACREP Standard 1j: knowledge of ethical and legal considerations

CACREP Standard 2e: counselors' roles in developing cultural self-awareness, promoting cultural social justice, advocacy and conflict resolution, and other culturally supported behaviors that promote optimal wellness and growth of the human spirit, mind, or body

CACREP Standard 2f: counselors' roles in eliminating biases, prejudices, and processes of intentional and unintentional oppression and discrimination

Specific Competencies Identified by CACREP Diversity and Advocacy Standards for Clinical Mental Health Counseling Addressed in Section 5

CACREP Knowledge 8: advocate for policies regarding community resources

CACREP Knowledge 9: demonstrate the ability to modify counseling systems and their techniques and interventions to make them culturally appropriate for diverse populations

After Reading Section 5, Students Will Be Able to Do the Following:

a. Understand the necessity of both social justice-oriented counseling and advocacy practice in improving positive social experiences for the culturally diverse (Chapter 13)

b. Understand the necessity of social justice orientation in counseling to avoid doing harm to clients who are members of the socially oppressed groups (Chapter 13)

c. Understand the role of social justice in counseling and appreciate the necessity that counselors adopt a social justice counseling paradigm in their work (Chapters 13–14)

d. Increase readiness to take personal, professional, and social responsibility in promoting social justice for all people (Chapters 13–14)

e. Obtain knowledge about how to conduct social justice counseling practice in and out of counseling rooms (Chapter 14)

f. Increase the sense of aspirational ethical responsibility that requires taking actions for social justice (Chapter 14)

Section Introduction

This section focuses on the necessity that counseling practice be social justice oriented and counselors be social justice minded in all they do to help the culturally diverse inside and outside of the counseling session.

Chapter 13 focuses on helping counselors-in-training to recognize the existence and negative effects of social inequality and injustice. In order to effectively counsel those who have suffered from social inequality, counselors need to conceptualize client experiences in their social context. If we believe that individuals' social environments may affect their psychological health, ignoring their experience of social injustice may lead to misperception, mistreatment, and even retraumatization. A socially responsive approach to counseling is necessary to help diverse clients, and social justice advocacy may help diverse communities by reducing inequality in their social environments.

Chapter 14 describes counselors' personal, professional, and social responsibilities in promoting social justice. Becoming an ally for oppressed groups may be one way to show personal commitment to social justice. Professionally, counselors may consider using social justice-informed counseling strategies. Finally, counselors are encouraged to engage in social advocacy to eradicate social injustice for all people.

13

Role of Social Justice in Counseling

Real peace is not the absence of conflict. It has always been the presence of justice.

—Martin Luther King Jr.

CHAPTER OVERVIEW

This chapter focuses on the necessary role of social justice in counseling and elucidates why the phenomenon of social inequality warrants social justice advocacy in our work with clients. The unjust nature of social inequality and its devastating impact on socially marginalized individuals and groups should motivate counselors in the 21st century to become committed to social justice and advocacy efforts. To adequately help clients who are victims of social injustice, social justice counseling and advocacy efforts must inform our work both within and outside of the counseling room. The American Counseling Association (ACA) has taken a leadership role and presented eight resolutions toward promoting a socially responsible approach to counseling. Counselors-in-training must be prepared to serve culturally diverse clients with attention to social justice.

SELF-ASSESSMENT OF PRE-EXISTING AWARENESS AND KNOWLEDGE

- How well do I understand the social injustice phenomenon in our society?
- How well do I understand the counseling profession's commitment to justice and social responsibility?

- How relevant is social justice in my social life?
- How willing am I to be an advocate for promoting social justice?
- What is my understanding of the role of social advocacy in counseling the culturally diverse in the 21st century?
- How competent am I at integrating social advocacy into counseling practice?
- How prepared am I to engage in social advocacy efforts?

LEARNING OBJECTIVES

After reading this chapter, students will be able to do the following:

1. Understand the relevance of the social injustice phenomenon in people's lives, especially those who experience social marginalization
2. Understand how diverse clients are affected by social injustice
3. Appreciate the importance of social justice and advocacy efforts in psychological interventions for the culturally diverse
4. Understand how to validate clients who are socially oppressed as a result of social injustice
5. Show respect to those who suffer from social injustice
6. Demonstrate readiness to engage in social justice advocacy

CASE ILLUSTRATION 13.1

The Case of Tonga

Tonga was a 14-year-old Latina student at a middle school located in a "terrible area" (as people often refer to it) of the city. She was relatively light skinned and had a compact body build. Tonga's academic performance was very poor, and she was currently repeating the sixth grade. She had reportedly said to classmates that she did not care about school or anyone at school, and if it were not due to the free lunch program, she would not be at school at all. It was public knowledge that she was unrealistic and dreamed the impossible—she wanted to be a model.

Tonga did not have many friends at school and had been a target of bullying. One time she was harassed by a group of boys for "appearing to look like a dude" to the point she had to beg the boys not to rip off her pants to check if she had a penis. Her mother told Ms. Brown, an African American English teacher and Tonga's homeroom teacher who was new to the school, that Tonga had attempted suicide three times in the previous 3 years by attempting to hang herself, taking many pain pills stolen from her mother's purse, and cutting her wrists.

Tonga had lived at home with her Guatemalan mother 35, Mexican stepfather, 41, stepsister, 9, and stepbrother, 7, for the past 3.5 years since her mother and stepfather got married. Prior to that, she and her mother were homeless, living on and off the streets. Tonga did not have contact with her biological father, whom she knew only as being "no good," according to her mother. Tonga was close to her mother, Marta, who had no formal education and no history of employment and was currently very sick, battling throat cancer. Tonga had reportedly said, "I will not live if my mother dies." Tonga did not feel close to her stepfather, Juan, but was "grateful to him for giving us a place to live." Juan had recently lost his job as a janitor for an apartment complex because the new owner, according to Marta, wanted to "improve" the quality of his staff and fired the only two Mexican workers. Tonga had reportedly wanted to stay away from home because "Juan was mad all the time."

Marta was very concerned about Tonga's poor school performance and suicidal tendencies and had been to school many times. She cried every time she talked to the teachers and would say, "She will never have a better life if she fails school." However, the school had not been able to do much to help Tonga with her school performance or the reported suicidal ideations other than offering additional academic tutoring by her homeroom teacher, which Ms. Brown voluntarily offered twice a week.

Ms. Brown took Tonga to see Mike, a counseling practicum student from a university nearby who had just arrived at the school for his first day. Ms. Brown said to Mike, "I am so glad that you are here, and I think you can help her better than I can." She went on to tell Mike that Tonga had psychological issues in addition to academic difficulties, and she was really not sure if there were any solutions to all of Tonga's problems.

SMALL-GROUP CLASS ACTIVITY 13.1

Discussion and Exploration of the Case of Tonga

In small groups of three to four students, imagine you were in Mike's position and discuss your thoughts related to the following questions:

1. What were some of Tonga's "problems?"
2. What were possible causes or sources of these problems?
3. Who or what factors were responsible for the problems?
4. What level of control did Tonga, her family, or her teachers have in managing the problems?
5. What resources were needed to help Tonga get rid of these problems?

Although this is by no means a worst-case scenario, Tonga's case provides a glimpse of the lives of those who live in poor neighborhoods in American cities. One can't help but ask, is it fair? Is it just? Is it her fault or her parents' fault? According to the United Nations, children have rights to life, survival, and development via healthy, free, and dignified methods ("Protecting Children's Rights, 2014). Why do or don't some children have these rights? Who tend to be the ones that are not afforded these basic rights (because of their gender, their racial/ethnic background, their social class status, and so on)? There is no doubt that unjust and unfair social inequalities plague our American society.

Social Injustice or Inequality

Social injustice is expressed by the unequal access (inequality) to resources, rights, and opportunities and is more prevalent in the United States than most people want to believe or choose to acknowledge. Certainly, if we were more mindful and attentive, we would recognize social injustice when reading the newspaper, listening to the radio or television, walking in certain neighborhoods in our city or town, or reviewing our governmental policies. Injustice in the areas of race/ethnicity, gender and sexual identity, social economic class, religion, nationality, and so on affect people in both tangible and intangible ways. The social problems of poverty, hunger, crime, and violence have roots in social injustice and further the oppression inflicted upon socially disenfranchised minority groups. Counseling practice in the 21st century must promote social justice when serving the culturally diverse.

Marginalized Communities

Although individuals may experience inequality due to various reasons, *social inequality* refers to the existence of structured and recurrent patterns of unequal opportunities and rewards for different groups of people due to social statuses or positions as related to who they are demographically. There are communities and cultural groups in the United States and around the world that are known to be oppressed and marginalized by society, and the lives of people from those communities reflect the impact of such social injustice. In the United States, for instance, people and communities from racial/ethnic backgrounds, low social class, nonheterosexual or noncisgender groups, nondominant religions, immigrant populations, or those with disabilities are examples of marginalized groups. Counselors who work with members of these groups have to begin by understanding their social context and emphasize respect and advocacy for social justice. Social contexts that are plagued with injustice because we choose to look the other way are unfortunately widespread and disenfranchise many communities. Counselors have to exercise their multicultural consciousness and become fully aware of the extent to which our culturally diverse clients are impacted by their social context.

As recently as August 9, 2014, headlines erupted with the news of another unarmed Black teenager shot and killed by a White policeman (KMOV Staff, 2014).

This tragedy struck a nerve in the nation, especially the African American community and its allies and empathizers, further stirring up the heartbreak and frustration that had stemmed from the trend of young Black men dying as a result of police brutality. In this event, Michael Brown of Ferguson, Missouri, was at least the fifth unarmed Black man killed by a police officer in the United States in a 1-month period (Harkinson, 2014).

According to a report by *USA Today* (Johnson, Hoyer, & Heath, 2014), the FBI's justifiable homicide data taken from 17,000 law enforcement agencies revealed that from 2005 to 2012, a White police officer killed a Black person nearly two times a week for an average of 96 killings per year in the United States. Further, the report showed that 18% of Blacks versus 8.7% of Whites who were killed were under the age of 21. With these statistics and consideration of the fact that James Eagan Holmes, the White gunman who killed 12 and wounded several dozen in a movie theatre in Aurora, Colorado, on July 20, 2012, was taken alive, one can't help but ask how such injustice could continue to exist in our democratic society. We should be able to see and understand why those who identify themselves as Black Men Walking (BMW) fear for their safety in American cities.

There are probably many aspects to any single incident like the Ferguson case that different individuals want to argue for or against, often reflective of their social positions, views, and biases. We want to remind our readers that as future counselors (not as bystanders or defense attorneys) they should use their multicultural consciousness to recognize the feelings of those who are hurt the most and to acknowledge the profound negative impact of social injustice on members of oppressed groups. It is not arbitrary that members of certain racial groups tend to be victims in such terrible events, and it is hard to deny that racism at both institutional and personal levels plays a role. The excessive brutality and killing of unarmed Black men by White police officers who are not indicted is an example of social injustice and inequality, which furthers the systemic discrimination that victimizes members of minority racial groups. Not everyone has the same access to safety, and not everyone can trust or be trusted by the country's law enforcement agencies. For many, vicarious traumatization and retraumatization are possible due to the systemic nature of such injustice.

An opinion piece titled "How Many Unarmed People Have to Die?" by LZ Granderson (2014), a CNN contributor, senior writer for ESPN, and lecturer at Northwestern University, was published on the CNN website the day after Michael Brown was shot to death. Granderson expressed concerns about the social injustice that runs rampant in our society and specifically gave voice to a number of thoughts likely prevalent in African American society, including that "he is tired" of the bodies of unarmed Black people lying in our streets, of armed assailants trying to justify their actions by describing how they feared for their lives, of being told that the killings "have nothing to do with race," of worrying about his 17-year-old son being shot "by some random White guy" who thinks he is playing his music too loud, of worrying that the same could happen to him, and of "waiting for verdicts and hoping for justice" (para. 1–4).

Many similar stories that do not make the national news also reflect the prevalence of racial injustice in our American society. Alex Landau, an African American man who was adopted by a White couple and grew up in a predominately White, middle-class suburb of Denver, and his mother, Patsy Hathaway, shared the following story on National Public Radio's (NPR) *Morning Edition.*

As she and her husband raised Alex, Patsy tried hard to use her love to conquer all potential problems associated with her son's skin color and never discussed the topic of race with him. Surrounded by White friends, neighborhoods and schools, Alex did not feel the need to discuss race until one day, when he was 19 years old, he was almost killed by a police officer for an alleged traffic violation. After being pulled over and told that he had made an illegal left turn, Alex got out of the car and was patted down by one of three police officers who were at the scene. Alex's White friend, who was a passenger in the car, was patted down and subsequently handcuffed when the officer discovered some weed in his coat pocket. Alex, who was not handcuffed, thought he was cleared with the pat down, so he asked the police if he could please see a search warrant. The next thing he could recall was being grabbed and hit on the face by the policeman, followed by a gun being placed against his head before he lost consciousness. "It took 45 stitches to close up the lacerations in my face alone," he said. "It was the point of awakening to how the rest of the world is going to look at you. I was just another Black face in the streets, and I was almost another dead Black male." (NPR Staff, 2014)

In addition to the social injustice of police brutality, of which minorities are unfairly targeted, hate crimes are yet another example of social injustice that injures and victimizes members from socially marginalized communities. The U.S. Department of Justice defines *hate crimes* as "the violence of intolerance and bigotry, intended to hurt and intimidate someone because of race, ethnicity, national origin, religion, sexual orientation, or disability" (U.S. Department of Justice, n.d.). Such crimes deprive individuals of their basic human right to safety. In 2006, the FBI reported 7,722 incidents of hate crimes, of which "about 52% were directed at people because of their race; 19% because of the victims' religion; 16% because of their sexual orientation; and 13% because of their ethnicity or national origin" (National Crime Prevention Council, n.d.). Hate crime laws are intended to protect citizens from such crimes.

Although all but five states in the United States have hate crime laws, only 15 states and the District of Columbia protect sexual orientation and gender identity in their legislation, and 15 more include only sexual orientation (Human Rights Campaign Foundation, 2014). This lack of protection for sexual minorities and gender-variant groups is accompanied by an increased rate of hate crimes against LGBT individuals. Data on violence against transgender people paint a picture of overt injustice: Transgender people are at risk for multiple types of violence, including sexual violence, throughout their lives (Stotzer, 2009). Further, the National Coalition of Anti-Violence Programs reported that the hate murder rate of lesbian/gay/bisexual/transgender/queer (LGBTQ) people was its highest, and among documented incidents of violence, transgender women and people of color faced the most severe hate violence (NCAVP, 2014).

Social inequalities are experienced in numerous ways, including denial of one's basic human rights. The right to marry is a fundamental human right that is denied to some groups of people in the United States as well as in other countries. There are a large number of benefits and rewards offered by the U.S. government for married people compared to those who are single, such as paid leave to care for an ill spouse, Social Security survivor benefits and spousal benefits, the right not to testify against one's spouse, and so forth.

Economic inequality and social injustice victimize individuals who have low income or live in poverty in the United States and around the world. Children and families from those communities suffer from lack of access to housing, food, education, health care, and other life necessities. Those from low income and/or impoverished communities also encounter lack of respect, understanding, and acceptance from mainstream society. Disparities in every area of life between these communities and others are noticeable and painfully present in today's society, which is unfair and should not be tolerated.

Additionally, there are other identified groups that suffer from systemic discrimination, including persons with disabilities, mental illness, or certain physical features (e.g., being overweight, too short), victims of domestic violence, immigrants from certain parts of the world, the aging population, and those with certain accents.

It is undeniable that social injustice has negative effects in our marginalized communities; thus, it is the goal of counselors of the 21st century to help promote social justice and equality for all members of society.

A Personal Reflection by a White Student

The Meaning of "Be Yourself"

When I was younger, whenever I was worried about fitting in with new people or into a new situation, I was told, "Be yourself." I was always told that if I was myself, people would like me, and I would fit in and have friends. I always took this statement for granted and thought that if we wanted to be accepted, all we had to do is be ourselves.

The painful reality is not all people share this same luxury. The phrase that put me at ease as a child means something entirely different to people of color. People of color cannot simply be told to be themselves in order to fit in because they live in a society that has unfairly and unjustly established norms that are not inclusive of minorities. People of color simply being themselves is opening themselves to being ostracized by the majority and pushed even farther from the ideal of fitting in. Someone like me, White, a racist, telling a person of color to be himself or herself in order to achieve the goal of being appealing or fitting in is in effect telling the individual to be more like me. Act White. This brings tears to my eyes because people should be able to be accepted for who they are at their core, not for who the majority wishes them to be. An adult certainly should have this right, but it is not just the adults of the world being told to repress their true selves—it is the children, too.

—Shawn T., a White, cisgender, male graduate student in counseling

Types of Social Injustice

There are two broadly interconnected types of social injustice. One type occurs in differential social treatment of diverse social and cultural groups due to racism, sexism, classism, ageism, heterosexism, and other isms. The chapters in Section 4 selectively presented evidence of social injustice that marginalized racial, gender, social class, physical ability, and religious groups endure. The presence of social inequality is real, whether or not we acknowledge it. Our multicultural origins and backgrounds place us at different social positions; we might experience social inequality in some areas but play a role in perpetuating the injustice that disadvantages others.

This type of inequality or injustice (i.e., differential social treatment) can be expressed directly or indirectly. Blatant discrimination against racial minorities in hiring practices, bigotry toward LGBT people, sexual exploitation through the trafficking of young women and girls, and violence perpetrated on the homeless are some examples. There are also relatively indirect or covert expressions of such social inequality or injustice even in our society's helping professions. Schoolteachers paying more attention to White students than to students of color, colleges making admission decisions using test scores known for having racial biases (Jaschik, 2010), psychiatrists trusting White patients' honesty more than that of African Americans (thus being three times more likely to assign a "schizophrenia" diagnosis to African Americans than to White Americans) (Escobar, 2012), counselors failing to maintain an LGBT-affirming environment at a counseling center and routinely referring LGBT clients out for "lack of expertise," social workers refusing to work in rural areas, and attorneys dropping clients who are unable to pay are some examples.

The second type of social inequality occurs in laws and governmental policies and regulations that discriminate against some groups of people by assigning or allowing unequal opportunities and resources to them based on their social and cultural identities. There are economic policies that perpetuate poverty for some groups, death penalty laws that inconsistently affect certain racial groups, marriage laws that do not grant LGBT individuals basic rights to marry or care for their loved ones, and policies that allow differential access to health care, education, and civil rights, just to name a few. These inequalities are harder to recognize because they can unfairly disadvantage groups of people "legally," but the impact on individuals' lives can be overwhelming and demoralizing. These types of inequalities reflect the influence of covert isms embedded in the lawmaking processes and have produced serious disparities in so many areas of life for millions of Americans.

The unfortunate truth about this type of social inequality is that discriminative laws or policies that impose inequality for various minority groups have existed throughout our nation's history. The following are a few examples of our government's laws and legislative actions that have contributed to the discrimination and disparity of racial/ethnic minorities, sexual minorities, and gender-divergent groups:

- Starting in 1830, indigenous communities were forced from their southeastern homelands by the Indian Removal Act. Over 10 years, more than 100,000 Native children and adults marched thousands of miles into unknown territory west of the Mississippi River to relinquish over 25 million acres of their homeland to White settlers. Thousands died on their westward trek, which became known as the "Trail of Tears" (History.com Staff, 2009).
- The 1862 Emancipation Proclamation led to the freeing of slaves in the District of Columbia, but former slave owners were "compensated for all losses by acts of the United States, including the loss of slaves" (Lincoln, 1862, para. 13).
- In 1882, the Chinese Exclusion Act banned immigration of both skilled and unskilled Chinese laborers (History.com Staff, 2009).
- The 1924 Johnson-Reed Act created an immigration quota system based on national origin, favoring "Nordics" over the "inferior" races of Asia and Southern and Eastern Europe (U.S. Department of State: Office of the Historian, n.d.).
- The creation of Japanese American concentration camps in 1942 forced 111,000 Japanese Americans into internment camps for the duration of World War II (Fiset, 2008).
- Racial segregation laws enacted by state and local governments between 1874 and 1975 were known as Jim Crow Laws. They promoted segregation under the label of "separate but equal" and condemned Black citizens to inferior treatment ("Jim Crow Laws," n.d.).
- In 1971, President Nixon's "war on drugs" initiative violently targeted and imprisoned poor people and people of color disproportionally ("Fighting Drug War Injustice," n.d.).
- The "Don't Ask, Don't Tell" policy that prevented gays, lesbians, and bisexuals from openly serving in the military was effective from 1993 to 2011 before being banned; as of March 2015, transgender individuals are still prohibited from serving openly in the military (Don't Ask, Don't Tell, 2015).
- Though formal law didn't dictate discrimination in the civilian workplace, it wasn't until 2007 that the Employment Nondiscrimination Act was first proposed by some members of Congress to outlaw discrimination of sexual orientation in the workplace, specifically during hiring (Employment Non-Discrimination Act, n.d.).
- Hate crimes against victims based on their race, color, religion, or national origin were selectively prosecuted after the 1969 Federal Hate Crimes Law, but it wasn't until 2009 that the Matthew Shepard Act brought about the law's expansion to include crimes motivated by the victims' perceived gender, sexual orientation, gender identity, or disability (Anti-Defamation League, n.d.).

As can be seen from these examples, our culturally diverse clients have had to endure a history of oppression created by inequality in our nation's laws and legislative actions. The pervasive negative impact of such inequality on the lives of those who are marginalized and disenfranchised can easily be seen throughout our nation's communities. Thus, multiculturally competent counselors need to work with diverse clients not only to combat personal issues but also to address systemic issues as a necessary step toward effective helping.

A Personal Reflection by a White Student

My Responsibility as a White Person

After taking a multicultural counseling class, the concepts of social justice to which I had been exposed in college suddenly took on new meaning when I realized their relevance to a career in counseling. If I did not endeavor to become a multiculturally competent counselor, then at best I would struggle to help to my clients, and at worst I would risk bringing them harm.

As a White person in America, I benefit daily from the unfairly obtained social advantages that White privilege confers. In essence, society privileges those who conform, and the parameters by which this conformity is measured are defined by the privileged. This self-sustaining, circular process operates under the guise of meritocracy. The belief in a just society that privileges the worthy and rewards those who work hard leads us to believe that if you do not succeed, it is because you are lazy, stupid, of weak character, or immoral. The worst part of this lie is that it is not just held by those whom it benefits. This fiction is insidiously imposed upon the hearts and minds of those it punishes.

For too long, White people, such as myself, have allowed each other to be oblivious to the plight of the disenfranchised and to make excuses for their social injustices. For this reason, it is my responsibility as a person in a helping profession, but more importantly as a person of privilege, to be outraged about racism because, as Sue and Sue (2013) put it, "The ultimate white privilege is the ability to acknowledge it but do nothing about it" (p. 335).

—Jean S., a White, cisgender, heterosexual, middle-class, female graduate student in counseling

SMALL-GROUP CLASS ACTIVITY 13.2

Discussion and Exploration of the Case of Tonga

In the same small groups, share your thoughts on the following questions about Tonga:

1. How would you describe Tonga's social context?
2. What are possible external factors that contribute to Tonga's problems?
3. In what ways do you think Tonga is a victim of social injustice?

Victimizing Effects of Social Inequality

Lack of Opportunity Toward Success

Social inequality has both obvious and not-so-obvious negative effects on its recipients. Experiencing dehumanization and unacceptance and having less or no access to power, resources, or opportunities leads to obvious negative experiences, such as not being able to meet basic survival needs, poor physical health, and psychological stress and symptoms. For instance, the Century Foundation (2004) reported the following:

> America has failed to make good on that promise of equal opportunity. The benefits of having a college education are greater than ever, but low-income students continue to lag in three major areas: their college enrollment rates are low; their degree completion rates are low; and their enrollment and graduation rates from selective colleges are particularly low. (p. 2)

This lack of equality is more pronounced for ethnic minorities. As a consequence of lack of preparation and economic resources, people of color are not getting adequate education, a believed condition for economic success. Based on three national longitudinal studies of high school graduates in 1982, 1992, and 2004, the Center for Education Policy Analysis at Stanford University reported that, "Black and Hispanic students are dramatically underrepresented in the most selective colleges, even after controlling for family income" (Reardon, Baker, & Klasik, 2012). The *Chronicle of Higher Education* reported in 2010 that on average, "60% of white students who start college have earned bachelor's degrees six years later. But only 49% of Hispanic students and 40% of black students do" (Gonzalez, 2010).

Lack of educational success for people of color and/or those in poverty does not start in higher education. Living in harsh realities of social inequality, the school performance of youth and children of color is not only tied to their family employment and income but also to how they are perceived and received in society. Social perceptions and treatments will in turn impact their self-concept and overall well-being. As observed, children living in poverty are 1.3 times more likely to have developmental delays or learning disabilities than those who don't live in poverty (Currie, 2007). By the end of the fourth grade, African American, Hispanic, and low-income students are already 2 years behind grade level, and by the 12th grade, they are 4 years behind (National Center for Education Statistics, 1999).

In his remarks regarding the "My Brother's Keeper" initiative (White House, 2014), which aims to bring together private sector and philanthropic organizations to improve the lives and outcomes of boys/young men of color in the United States, President Barak Obama said the following:

> As a black student, you are far less likely than a white student to be able to read proficiently by the time you are in 4th grade. By the time you reach high school, you're far more likely to have been suspended or expelled. There's a higher chance you end up in the criminal justice system, and a far higher chance that you are the victim of a violent crime. Fewer young black and Latino men participate in the labor force compared to young white men. And all of this translates into higher unemployment rates and poverty rates as adults. (para. 15)

Being Viewed as Problems

It is too often that our nation's problems, such as violence and crime, are perceived as linked to poverty; it stands to reason that Blacks and Latinos have been accused of committing higher levels of violent crimes than Whites (Kaufman, 2005). While much attention has been given to address these issues in various ways, including at policy levels, through scientific research, and in educational programs, significant improvement or positive outcomes have yet to come. One of the reasons may be the lack of focus on the macro social and societal factors that provide contexts for the problems; instead, the theme of victim blaming is prevalent. For instance, the infamous war on drugs during the last several decades of the 20th century enlarged the prison population to an unprecedented high and literally destroyed Black families and communities in the United States (McWhorter, 2011). Even scientific research often examines the relationship between race or ethnicity and crime without sufficient attention to macro societal context. As a result, the public perception of people of color or the poor is that they are the criminals, the problems of society. Such perceptions and beliefs contribute to the further stratification of society and victimize individuals who are not the problem but victims of the problem.

Social inequality unavoidably leads individuals to feel devalued and/or unaccepted. Moreover, the accompanying feelings of low self-confidence and internalized negative stereotypes add to their victimization and suffering, thereby creating a "vicious cycle" that overtly plagues their lives. As noted by Currie (2007), "Poor children are more likely than other children to suffer mental health problems, including learning disabilities and developmental delays in addition to their physical health problems" (p. 2). If they want to perform or achieve as those from unoppressed groups, they have to do so much more, often with so much less support and fewer resources. Yet they are often perceived as "losers" or responsible for the inequality created by society. Tonga's situation can be seen as an example. Due to a lack of resources and access to opportunities, she experienced psychological and academic problems, which reduced her chances for success. The cycle continues.

Vulnerability to Victimization and Revictimization

It is not hard to see that people who are confronted with chronic deprivation and harsh social conditions often feel unsafe, insecure, and powerless. Consequently, Abramovitz (2007) said that maladaptive behaviors may occur, including self-harm (e.g., self-medication, dropping out of school, unsafe sex, ineffective parenting, inability to hold a job, lack of self-care, suicide) and/or other harmful acts (e.g., crime, assault, battery, rape, homicide). In the context of social inequality, these behaviors only augment their cycle of victimization, both in visible domains (e.g., unemployment, imprisonment) and in invisible areas (e.g., lower self-concept/self-worth, depression/anxiety, aggression/anger). Unfortunately, due to that social inequality, their families and communities are often incapable of providing these individuals, especially children, with the necessary support to live mentally and physically healthy lives.

The oppressiveness of our societal culture, including its dominant ideology and public policies, has led to an epidemic of homelessness among LGBT youth, according to a report by the National Gay and Lesbian Task Force Policy Institute (Ray, 2006). Research has shown that about "26% of gay teens were kicked out of their homes," and these youth "face a multitude of ongoing crises that threaten their chances of becoming healthy, independent adults" (p. 5). Being homeless, ill cared for, and/or marginalized due to heterosexual prejudice and discrimination are the daunting circumstances of many LGBT youth. They are also especially vulnerable to loneliness, depression, and other psychological difficulties (McWhirter, 1990). It is clear that most of their difficulties are not caused by intrapsychic issues but rather by environmental hostility and abuse, which, if unchanged, continues to create and maintain an LGBT-youth victimization and revictimization cycle.

Gender inequality is a pervasive phenomenon. Women are universally more likely to be victims of violence and sexual crimes, less educated, and more prone to poverty (World Bank, 2001). Besides these obvious detrimental differences, gender inequality has a domino effect on all women physically, socially, and psychologically. For instance, women have to do much more than men to achieve some of the highly desirable traits in Western culture, such as autonomy, assertiveness, and high self-esteem. Their extra effort and hard work makes them vulnerable to stress and physical and psychological risk factors. The stress-induced emotional difficulties they encounter set off yet another unfair gender generalization, which is how they are perceived by others. These less-than-positive perceptions further stigmatize them and make it hard for them to achieve the success they deserve; unsurprisingly, women are more likely to experience depression than men due to certain stressors unique to their gender and due to sexism (Nolen-Hoeksema, 2001). Women's lack of social power makes them vulnerable to trauma, violence, poverty, and sexual exploitation, and their expected social roles (e.g., primary caretaker, peacemaker, emotional anchor in the household) impose added pressures on them that they try to juggle while maintaining high performance at work (where they often have to work harder than their male counterparts). These large contextual factors present unique difficulties to women and may negatively affect their lives.

The spilled-over effect of income inequality is hard to overlook. This inequality causes stress, frustration, and family disruption, which then increases the rates of crime, homicide, and violence (Wilkinson, 1996) and the instances of deteriorating health, leading to a higher rate of mortality for the poor (Wilkinson, 1997). On top of such tangible sufferings, individuals living in deprived communities where there is low and underinvestment in the social and physical infrastructure also suffer from being perceived as less than, lazy, inferior, deserving misery, or responsible for their social oppression. The effect of such psychological abuse and mistreatment is pervasive and serious, and it affects daily life as well as social and political involvement. Children from low social class who lack family support are more likely to be perceived as ill prepared when they start school; we can expect that they have to overcome more obstacles to succeed as compared to their age-related peers who are the beneficiaries of consistent family support. With more obstacles to overcome, they are less likely to be awarded the opportunity to pursue a higher level of education, which lessens the likelihood that they will obtain well-paid jobs; in turn, they will be less financially able to provide for their families. Additionally, even their democratic rights are often compromised, as the poor are less likely to vote due to the obstacles and challenges of their less than favorable life circumstances (e.g., inability to take time off from work, inconvenient polling locations, lack of transportation to them) and larger-scale injustices such as unfair voting restrictions and voter suppression tactics (e.g., requiring an address, multiple forms of identifications, imposing polling-place dress codes, or using actual physical intimidation at the poll area). Voting suppression techniques, legal and illegal, such as requiring photo identification or disallowing felons from voting after their sentences have been discharged, are used to deny eligible voters the right to vote and disproportionately affect poor minorities, especially African Americans and Latinos. The injustice continues.

Social injustice negatively affects millions of people and is unfortunately widespread in the United States and around the world. As responsible counselors, we must acknowledge and address in all our counseling services the larger issues of social injustice that our clients have to endure. Our therapeutic understanding of our clients and the interventions we design and employ to help them must take into consideration their social contexts. Otherwise, victim blaming is hard to avoid, and retraumatization through counseling becomes a reality.

A Personal Reflection by a White, Gender-Nonconforming Person

An Experience With a Counselor Who Is Unaware

I remember one particular counselor who was attempting to get me in touch with my "inner child," but she kept calling this inner child a "little girl." I felt so much discomfort around the thought that my inner child was a little girl that I stopped going to see her altogether. I was not brave enough to tell her why it upset me; I was just beginning to understand my own gender identity, and to be honest, the discomfort I felt with her phrasing pushed me toward a greater understanding of myself. But I think it is important for any counselor who is working with a transgender, gender-nonconforming, or queer client to be thoughtful about the pronouns and phrases they choose to describe that client, particularly if the client has not chosen or agreed to those words themselves.

—Eli, a gender-nonconforming person

Social Justice

What is social justice? There are different definitions and interpretations. According to Davis (1996), *social justice* is defined as the following:

> [It is] a basic value and desired goal in democratic societies and includes equitable and fair access to societal institutions, laws, resources [and] opportunities, without arbitrary limitations based on observed, or interpretation of, differences in age, color, culture, physical or mental disability, education, gender, income, language, national origin, race, religion, or sexual orientation" (p. 1).

Focusing on inclusion, Bell (1977) identified the goal of social justice as including a vision of a society in which individuals have "full and equal participation of all groups" and "the distribution of resources is equitable and all members are physically and psychologically safe and secure" (p. 3). But to highlight the essence of *access to social justice*, Reverend Jesse Jackson (2000) stated the following in an address to psychologists:

> If you think of African American history as a symphony in four movements, you have freeing the slaves, the first movement. The second movement is the end of legal segregation. The third movement is the right for all Americans to vote. And the fourth, the one we are in now, is about access. Access to capital; access to resources; access to information, to technology, to education; access to opportunity. All people in the U.S. do not have equal access to these things. (p. 239)

Despite different opinions concerning how to best define social justice, the following common elements are widely shared: (a) recognizing and acknowledging systematic differential access to power, information, or opportunity, and (b) attempting to correct the inequality through redistribution of these resources (Fouad, Gerstein, & Toporek, 2006). Although these goals sound grand, mental health professionals are actually uniquely positioned to address many social justice-related issues due to their focus on prevention, strength-based approaches, and multiculturally sensitive and relevant practice. As long as social injustice exists, pursuing social justice through counseling practice is an obligatory responsibility of multiculturally competent counselors.

A Reflection by a Counselor-in-Training

Living Out Social Justice: My Uncomfortable Companion of Growth

Being back in graduate school to become a counseling psychologist, I feel renewed energy and support for my commitment to the uncomfortable learning in understanding social justice. I am most thankful to my previous training in social work for the way it challenged me to practice social justice by beginning with critical self-reflection. In fact, I learned that to actively and consciously strive for social justice, it required that I not run from myself. Classroom content and practicum experiences necessitated my regular, firsthand encounters with my own classism, ableism, homophobia, sexism, and racism.

I worked as a therapist in a community mental health clinic where the majority of my clients dealt with the triple jeopardy of mental illness, poverty, and rural living. I am grateful for the countless ways this work shook me out of my cozy, privileged existence. On one important occasion, a social justice mantra came down to me from the least suspecting of sages, a client who quoted Krishnamurti: "It is no measure of health to be well adjusted to a profoundly sick society." That bit of social justice wisdom, in that context, continues to speak to me today.

(Continued)

(Continued)

The requirements of social justice often run counter to my reflexes as a counselor. I seek to mend, heal, and validate. But living out social justice demands action based in self-awareness that can feel prickly. Whether practiced within the context of a therapeutic alliance or on the streets of activism, social justice first asks that I explore identity-threatening questions: Am I brave enough to stand up for justice if it means being ostracized? How am I complicit in the oppression I claim to abhor? How might my words—intentional or not—"otherize" people? These questions require me not only to engage discomfort but to invite it in and to allow myself again and again to be transformed in the process.

—Michelle S., LCSW, a Caucasian, cisgender, female social worker and counseling psychology doctoral student

Social Justice and Counseling

The goal of mental health counseling is to help clients and to recognize that all clients' needs are determined by both internal and external factors. Due to existing power differentials and inequalities in society, the psychological health of the culturally diverse is unfairly and heavily influenced by social injustice. Often, being able to see a counselor is one of the best opportunities culturally diverse individuals can have; counseling is meant to be helpful to them and is offered by trained professionals. Counseling can be a healing process for them and facilitate their recovery, growth, and development. However, this outcome does not automatically occur, and counseling professionals need to exercise their professional responsibility and multicultural consciousness and deliberately engage in social justice counseling and advocacy efforts in order to achieve this goal. Some theorists have proposed that social justice counseling could be the "fifth force" of our profession (Ratts, 2009).

What is social justice counseling? *Social justice counseling* is based on the recognition that individuals' experiences, including suffering or symptoms, are impacted by social inequality in oppression, privilege, and discrimination. This recognition will shape counseling practices. Social justice counseling, according to Lewis, Ratts, Paladiono, and Toporek (2011), "represents a shift from traditional, individually-focused models" and "exemplifies a change in worldview from established psychological traditions" (p. 6). As we discussed earlier in this book, traditional counseling approaches are often ineffective and even harmful in the provision of services to our culturally diverse clients. A social justice-based paradigm is necessary to provide our oppressed clients with the corrective experiences needed to offset the negative effects of social injustice. As the Counselors for Social Justice (a division of the ACA) website shows (www.counselorsforsocialjustice.net), social justice counseling involves a multifaceted approach to counseling. The major components include promoting human development and empowering the individual "as well as active confrontation of injustice and inequality in society as they impact clientele as well as those in their systemic contexts" (para. 2).

As indicated, social justice practice can take different forms in counseling, including social justice-informed individual, family, group, and community preventions and interventions and social advocacy on a more macro level outside of counseling rooms (e.g., counselors acting as social advocates). Social justice work by counselors may happen inside and outside of counseling rooms and in different settings or content areas. It is important to note the following:

> Human development issues cannot be understood simply by assessing a client's affective, behavioral, or cognitive development or by requiring that change come exclusively from the client. Instead, counselors need to view client problems more contextually and use advocacy to remove oppressive environmental barriers (Lewis, et al., 2011, pp. 6–7).

In other words, counselors have to be the change agents who conduct "professional action designed to change societal values, structures, policies and practices, such that disadvantaged or marginalized groups gain increased access to tools of self-determination" (Goodman et al., 2004, p. 795).

Social Justice Counseling in Schools

Working with youth and adolescents in school, especially public schools, counselors have to face the larger issue of lack of equality in multiple areas. There are risk and protective factor constellations for our nation's youth that are the result of the interaction between individual and environmental influences. If we consider the "Case of Devonta," which is found in this chapter, we can see the role of social injustice in this student's life. Although Devonta is a good student graduating from high school, he is not prepared for college. Based on the location and demographics of its students, we can guess the condition of his high school in terms of teacher qualifications, school facilities, rigor of academic education, and role models. It is not news that funding gaps in our nation's schools are present at different levels, which contribute to differential and inequitable levels of human and material resources for schools. As counselors working with students like Devonta, how can we provide effective helping without addressing issues related to social injustice both in our sessions and in extratherapuetic encounters? Any exclusive focus on Devonta's personal problems would imply victim blaming and reinforce negative effects of social inequality.

CASE ILLUSTRATION 13.2

Case of Devonta

After his first 5 weeks of attending a state college, Devonta, a 19-year-old African American male student, was caught skipping school and "drinking and messing around" by his grandma, who has been his primary caretaker. Devonta was scolded, grounded, and told that if he did not straighten himself up, Grandma would not allow him in her house anymore. But a few days later, he was caught again.

(Continued)

(Continued)

Devonta was a good student, having mostly A grades in his high school that was described as a "high poverty" school with about 60% African American and 23% Hispanic students in the inner city of a metropolitan area. Devonta had a good relationship with his high school counselor Mr. Miles. Grandma and Devonta showed up to see Mr. Miles, whom Grandma knew and trusted. It was clear that Grandma wanted Mr. Miles to help fix Devonta's problems, and she said, "He has to go to college if he wants to live as a decent human being in the future."

Mr. Miles was surprised to see Devonta because few graduates visit after leaving the school. He immediately felt that Devonta had "changed a lot" and especially noticed he did not seem as "enthusiastic" as he used to be. After talking to him, Mr. Miles got a glimpse of Devonta's difficulties in adjusting to college. Devonta felt completely unprepared academically and unaccepted by his peers for being "stupid" because he did not know "many things that others all know" or "have the stuff they do" and had so little that he could share with others. In a very low voice, he said, "I really do not think I belong in college. I don't know what I should do. Grandma, please don't force me."

Social Justice Counseling in Career and Vocational Areas

Having the right to work and receive equitable pay is one ideal of our society. However, the lack of equality in work access, conditions, compensation, and environment is widely known across different groups along gender, race, sexual orientation, social class, and so forth (Toporek & Chope, 2006). For instance, Kaplan, Haan, Syme, Minkler, and Winkleby (1987) observed the following:

> It is the poor who are exposed to dangerous environments, who (if employed) often have stressful, unrewarding and depersonalising work, who lack the necessities and amenities of life and who, because they are not part of the mainstream of society, are isolated from information and support. (p. 126)

In an analysis of labor market characteristics of Mexican immigrants in the United States, the Center for Immigration Studies, a nonprofit research organization, reported that the occupations in which Mexican immigrants are most concentrated are service occupations (not private household), which include such jobs as security guards, cooks, waiters, and child care workers; farming positions (except managerial), primarily agricultural and horticultural laborers; precision production, craft, and repair vocations, which include mechanics, repairmen, metal workers, meat processors, and construction trades (e.g., masons); and operators, fabricators, and laborers, comprised mostly of factory workers, warehouse workers, and drivers (Camarota, 2002). These jobs are clearly not high paying and do not have high prestige from a broad public view.

In the field of career development and vocational guidance, counselors' ability to address issues related to disparities and inequalities is critical. We know that not everyone begins at the same starting line when seeking employment due to a variety of social factors; not everyone has equal opportunity to climb the "career ladder" (e.g., job promotion) regardless of their ability; not everyone is treated the same at the workplace due to many factors out of their control; and not everyone shares the same values that define the prestige or meaning of work. In fact, as shown by research, members of socially marginalized groups experience significant vocational barriers (Lent, Brown, & Talleyrand, 2002) and workplace discrimination (King et al., 2011; Root, 2003), that makes work or employment a different life experience for them. Additionally, many victims of discrimination don't receive protection from the judiciary system because microaggressions in the form of microinsults, microinvalidations, and microassaults are not evaluated by the legal system as discriminatory (King et al., 2011).

There are many forms of subtle discriminations that make the workplace unwelcoming or even hostile for nondominant groups. Ample research findings have shown that Black and Hispanic job applicants are less likely than Caucasian applicants to secure interviews and job offers; women are paid less and undervalued compared to men; and Black women are at a double disadvantage (Gedeon, 2013) due to their double minority status. To illustrate, in 2006, ABC's *20/20* television program conducted a social experiment by posting on a career website identical résumés with different names on the top (either the "Blackest" or "Whitest" names). The result showed that the résumés with the "Whitest" names were downloaded 17% more often by job recruiters than those with the "Blackest" names (para. 3). In 2014, the *Today Show* on NBC broadcasted a story called "What's in a Name When You Apply for a Job?" that made a similar point. A man named José spent 6 months applying for 50 to100 jobs a day online with no result, but when he dropped the "s" in his name and applied as Joe, multiple replies and offers started coming in from the same positions he applied for as José (para. 1).

SMALL-GROUP CLASS ACTIVITY 13.3

Discussion and Exploration of the Case of Tonga

In the same small groups, discuss and share your answers to the following questions:

1. What do you think about Tonga's suicidal ideations?
2. How does her family's situation play a role in her problems?
3. How would you approach the task on hand as her counselor?

Social Justice Counseling in the International Arena

Social injustice is a worldwide phenomenon, and it hurts people and communities in the United States even if it happens in other parts of the world. This is primarily due to the United States' close international connection with the world. International presence in the United States and that of Americans in other parts of the world is high, and the effects of social inequality experienced globally are applicable to our counseling work. For instance, working with immigrants, refugees, business visitors, or international students about what has happened in their home countries has become relevant to our work. If traveling to a developing country to offer help with disaster relief, emergency intervention, educational assistance, or to inform the development of a counseling profession, we must be knowledgeable of social justice-related issues. As responsible counselors in the 21st century, we need to answer the call to contribute to our profession's efforts "to effectively resolve systemic and structural issues through social justice, advocacy, and activism" in the United States and around the world (Gerstein, 2005, p. 379).

Another layer of unequal power is associated with individuals' nationality or home of origin. Although the United States has been a country of immigrants and its citizens are heavily involved in interactions with many other countries, the power differential exists both in the United States and in international communities. In working with individuals of other nationalities or conducting professional activities in other countries, an American counselor needs to be aware of the power inequality, show willingness to share power, and understand the impact of the power differential in relationships with people of other nationalities.

Promoting a Socially Responsive Approach of Counseling

Sensitivity to social injustice is only the first step, and the time has come that social justice be integrated into counseling practice. We the counselors will either be part of the solution to social injustice or part of the problem. Only socially responsible counseling can help individuals, groups, communities, and society heal and eliminate social injustice. To help counselors act responsively, the ACA passed a series of resolutions in 2005 to provide a direction for training programs. These resolutions clearly demonstrated the ACA's commitment to endorsing social justice counseling in eradicating toxic social environmental conditions in our society due to religious prejudice, racism, sexism and sexual violence, ableism, heterosexism, ageism, classism, and negative effects of war (ACA, 2005).

The Socially Responsive Practice Project reported by the Adler School of Professional Psychology (2012) is an example of training programs' responsibility and action in addressing social justice in mental health practice. The program clearly defined *socially responsive practice* as ensuring community health rather than simply providing service. It pointed out the following:

> The most pressing issues facing individuals and communities cannot be resolved with diagnoses or be addressed somewhere in the psyches of those involved. Oppression afflicts millions each day, and socially responsible practitioners must be prepared to engage at the intersection of power and resolve to end this affliction. (p. 5)

Acknowledgement and awareness of pervasive social inequality highlights the critical importance of attending to the social contexts of our clients and understanding their psychological experiences in order to avoid misdiagnosis, victim blaming, or social injustice. Unquestionably, it is not enough to work with individuals in the counseling room on how to improve self-esteem or build confidence while their reality is plagued by injustice and gives them little room to grow. Moreover, lack of self-esteem, confidence, or other desirable individual qualities should not be viewed as equal reflections of personal weakness for people who live in different social realities. Without full consideration of specific social and cultural contexts, no clinical judgments can be accurate and no interventions effective. It is unfortunate that social inequality is so prevalent in the social context of those who are marginalized, but the resulting damage of such inequality is significant to their psychological health. We want our readers to be reminded that those who suffer from the various forms of inequalities are the victims, and they are not the cause of their sufferings.

In order to be socially responsive and provide socially responsive service, counselors must see, hear, and experience the injustice that is inflicted on the oppressed. Viewing the world with a multicultural consciousness that is the result of a multicultural identity is indispensable in this process. Looking but not seeing, and listening but not hearing happens when the counselor and the client are operating from different consciousnesses, which makes socially responsive practice impossible. It is apparent that if the suffering of marginalized groups is rooted in or influenced by the inequality and injustice they experience in society, multiculturally competent counselors have to apply a multicultural consciousness in perceiving, understanding, and respecting those who are challenged by social injustices and fulfill their social responsibility to participate in advocacy efforts that promote positive social changes toward eradicating inequality.

SMALL-GROUP REFLECTIVE EXERCISE 13.1

What Does It Say About My Consciousness?

In small groups of three or four students, reflect and share your thoughts and feelings about this scenario and the following questions:

In late November 2014, word of civil unrest in Ferguson, Missouri, filled the news channels and media after the grand jury returned a decision of "no indictment" for the police officer who shot Michael Brown, an unarmed African American young man, to death. Brian Stelter (Nov. 30, 2014), the host of Reliable Sources *on CNN, noted that two different conversations were being reflected in the media following the incident. He pointed out that one conversation, which was more common among White people, was more about finding out exactly what happened at the scene and who was right or wrong legally, while the other conversation, which was more common among people of color, was more about how the incident reflected systemic racial discrimination in policing and in the larger social system of the country and ways in which Black people are hurt and victimized.*

(Continued)

(Continued)

1. Which conversation do you find yourself drawn to?
2. Do you agree that the type of conversation we invest our energy in reflects our social justice consciousness? Why or why not?
3. Which conversation do you see as more helpful to your effort of helping the socially oppressed?
4. How do you think your consciousness will affect how you hear your clients of color, especially African American clients?
5. In what ways does this consciousness determine your commitment to social justice?
6. How do you see the relationship between your multicultural identity and multicultural consciousness?

A Group Activity

Read the narrative "Counseling Student Refuses to Counsel Gay Client About Relationship Issues." Then in small groups of three to four students, have each student provide a response to the questions that follow the narrative. After members have shared their responses to the first question one at a time, all members can then ask questions and respectfully share their reactions to the responses provided. Following the same response and discussion format as Question 1, proceed through Questions 2, 3, and 4. Once all group members have responded and discussed the four questions, the small group provides a summary of their discussion and responses to share with the larger classroom.

Counseling Student Refuses to Counsel Gay Client About Relationship Issues

The counseling profession was recently confronted with issues of heterosexism when Julea Ward, a Christian graduate student at Eastern Michigan University's (EMU) counseling program, refused to counsel a gay client about relationship issues. Ward was a student in good standing with a 3.91 GPA and was scheduled to meet with a gay client on Jan. 26, 2009, during her counseling practicum. Two hours prior to the scheduled session she asked her supervisor if she could refer the client to another counselor. Ward believed that homosexuality is immoral and that being gay is a choice one makes; therefore, she could not in good conscience counsel the client. School officials interpreted Ward's refusal as a violation of professional standards, including failure to tolerate different points of view.

Ward was asked by members of the counseling department to complete a remediation plan that would require her to affirm and validate same-sex behavior in accordance with our profession's code of ethics. Ward refused the remediation plan and requested a formal hearing. On March 10, 2009, during the formal hearing, which included a 4-member review panel, Ward stated that she could not in good conscience and in an affirmative way counsel a gay client who has concerns about a gay relationship; she could, however, counsel gay clients about other issues. Ward maintained that she could not violate her religious beliefs by affirming gay relationships.

On March 12, 2009, Ward was notified in writing that the review panel had decided unanimously that she would be dismissed from the counseling program immediately due to violating the ACA *Code of Ethics* and in particular Codes A4.b. ("Counselors . . . avoid imposing values that are inconsistent with counseling goals") and C.5 ("Counselors do not condone or engage in discrimination based on age, culture . . . sexual orientation"). Ward appealed to the EMU School of Education dean, who upheld the panel's decision. In June 2009, Ward sued EMU and lost in lower courts. Judge George Steeh dismissed Ward's claims against the EMU Board of Regents and faculty members in the counseling program due to Ward's refusal to change her behavior, not her beliefs.

Jay Kaplan, staff attorney for the American Civil Liberties Union of Michigan, who litigates on behalf of LGBT individuals, agreed that EMU acted properly in dismissing Ward. He further stated that students in counseling programs need to learn to focus on the client and not impose their own values and maintained that Ward's values were at odds with the program's coursework requirements. Two days after the lawsuit was dismissed, Ward and her attorneys from the Alliance Defense Fund, a legal organization that works to uphold the rights of religious college students and faculty, appealed to federal court. In January 2012, the U.S. 6th Circuit Court of Appeals ruled in favor of the appeal, stating that the lawsuit deserved to have a jury trial.

On June 12, 2012, a state house committee approved a bill introduced by Representative Joe Haveman that would prohibit religious discrimination against students who are studying counseling, social work, and psychology. Bill 5040 (2011), also known as the Julea Ward Freedom of Conscience Act, was passed by the Michigan House of Representatives on June 2012 by a 59 to 50 vote. It was then referred to the Michigan Committee on Government Operations, where it remains at the time of this printing.

1. Do you believe that Ward was in violation of the ACA *Code of Ethics* and in particular Codes A4.b (Personal Values) and C.5 (Nondiscrimination)? Why or why not?
2. Do you support EMU's decision to dismiss Ward from the counseling program? Why or why not?
3. If Ward had consulted with you about her religious beliefs and interest in pursuing the counseling profession, what would you have discussed with her and what recommendations would you have offered?
4. Representative Joe Haveman argued that Ward's solution to refer the client was in the client's best interest as the client would not receive the best care/service from a counselor who had moral issues with the client's lifestyle. Therefore, Haveman believed Ward acted appropriately, and he further stated that students have a right to freedom of religious speech. Do you agree with Representative Haveman's arguments? Why or why not?
5. From a social justice perspective, what do you think will be the effect of the way this case is handled in the legal system on LGBT groups? On the faith community? On society?

Summary

This chapter discusses the prevalence of social inequality in the United States and around the world and its devastating impact on socially marginalized individuals. Without question, social inequality is unjust, unfair, and demoralizing to those who are marginalized by society due to their racial, social, and cultural group memberships. Multicultural counseling practice in the 21st century must employ a socially responsive approach toward counseling, and mental health professionals must integrate social justice advocacy into their provision of services both in and out of counseling sessions. In order to prevent harm and achieve positive counseling outcomes, multiculturally competent counselors must exercise their multicultural consciousness in recognizing the existence and impact of social inequality and understand their clients from oppressed groups in this context. Effective interventions have to be built on the basis of validating clients' experiences of social oppression. Socially responsive counselors will assume a more obvious role in the promotion of social justice and advocacy efforts in the larger societal context of their clients' lives.

Takeaway Messages

1. Social inequality exists in the United States and around the world, and it undermines the lives of those who are members of socially marginalized groups.
2. Individuals' psychological health is affected by their experience of social inequality.
3. Social justice is an important cause for all responsible citizens, especially for mental health counselors in the 21st century.
4. To effectively help culturally diverse people, issues related to social justice must be addressed both within and outside of the counseling setting.

Recommended Resources

Readings

Bemak, F., Chung, R. C.-Y., Talleyrand, R. M., Jones, H., & Daquin, J. (2011). Implementing multicultural social justice strategies in counselor education training programs. *Journal for Social Action in Counseling and Psychology, 3*(1), 29–43.

Schwartz, J. P., & Lindley, L. D. (2009). Impacting sexism through social justice prevention: Implications at the personal and environmental levels. *Journal of Primary Prevention, 30*, 27–41.

Stevenson, B. (2014). *Just mercy: A story of justice and redemption.* New York, NY: Spiegel & Grau.

Wronka, J. M. (2007). *Human rights and social justice: Social action and service for the healing and health professionals.* Thousand Oaks, CA: Sage.

Zalaquett, C. P., Foley, P. F., Tillotson, K., Dinsmore, J. A., & Hof, D. (2008). Multicultural and social justice training for counselor education programs and colleges of education: Rewards and challenges. *Journal of Counseling and Development, 86*, 323–329.

Media and Websites

Joseph, P. (2011). *Zeitgeist: Moving forward* [Documentary]. Available from https://www.youtube.com/watch?v 4Z9WVZddH9w

British Columbia "Social Justice" education materials: https://www.bced.gov.bc.ca/irp/pdfs/social_studies/support_materials/sj12_unitten.pdf

Counselors for Social Justice of ACA website: http://www.counselorsforsocialjustice.net/advocacy.html

My Brother's Keeper Initiative by the White House: http://www.whitehouse.gov/my-brothers-keeper Social Justice Action Plan

Social Justice Program Guides by the University of Arizona: http://www.life.arizona.edu/home/hall-living/social-justice-and-diversity/social-justice-program-guides

Stirfry Seminars and Consulting: http://www.stirfryseminars.com/

References

20/20 Staff. (2006, September 21). Top 20 "Whitest" and "Blackest" names. In ABC's *20/20*. Retrieved from http://abcnews.go.com/2020/story?id=2470131&page=1

Abramovitz, M. (2007). Poverty and economic injustice. *Social Work Today, 7*(2), 24. Retrieved from http://www.socialworktoday.com/archive/marapr2007p24.shtml

Adler School of Professional Psychology. (2012). *The socially responsible practice project.* Retrieved from http://www.adler.edu/resources/content/9/2/3/documents/Adler_SRP_LowRes.pdf

American Counseling Association. (2005). *Resolutions promoting a socially-responsible approach to counseling.* Retrieved from http://www.counselorsforsocialjustice.net/PDF/ResponsibleApproachCounseling.pdf

Anti-Defamation League. (n.d.). *Matthew Shepard and James Byrd, Jr. Hate Crimes Prevention Act (HCPA) What You Need to Know.* Retrieved from http://www.adl.org/assets/pdf/combating-hate/What-you-need-to-know-about-HCPA.pdf

Bell, L. A. (1997). Theoretical foundations for social justice education. In M. Adams, L. A. Bell, & P. Griffin (Eds.), *Teaching for diversity and social justice: A sourcebook* (pp. 3–15). New York, NY: Routledge.

Camarota, S. A. (2002, November). *Immigrants in the United States—2002: A snapshot of America's foreign-born population.* Retrieved from http://www.cis.org/

The Century Foundation (2004). *Left behind: Unequal opportunity in higher education.* Retrieved from http://tcf.org/assets/downloads/tcf-leftbehindrc.pdf

Counselors for Social Justice. (n.d.). *What is social justice in counseling?* Retrieved from www.counselorsforsocialjustice.net

Currie, J. (2007). Poverty among inner-city children. *Princeton Publications.* Retrieved from: http://www.princeton.edu/~jcurrie/publications/inman_june07.pdf

Davis, K. (1996). What is social justice? *Perspectives on Multicultural and Cultural Diversity, 6*, 1–3.

Don't Ask, Don't Tell (DADT). (2015). In *Encyclopædia Britannica.* Retrieved from http://www.britannica.com/EBchecked/topic/1553878/Dont-Ask-Dont-Tell-DADT\

Employment Non-Discrimination Act. (n.d.). *Human Rights Campaign.* Retrieved July 29, 2014 from http://www.hrc.org/resources/entry/employment-non-discrimination-act

Escobar, J. I. (2012, September 1). Diagnostic bias: Racial and cultural issues. *Psychiatric Services, 63*(9), 847. doi:10.1176/appi.ps.20120p847

"Fighting Drug War Injustice." (n.d.). *Drug Policy Alliance.* Retrieved from http://www.drugpolicy.org/fighting-drug-war-injustice

Fiset, L. (2008, September 16). The assembly centers: An introduction. *Discover Nikkei.* Retrieved from http://www.discovernikkei.org/en/journal/2008/9/16/enduring-communities/

Fouad, N. A., Gerstein, L. H., & Toporek, R. L. (2006). Social justice and counseling psychology in context. In R. L. Toporek, L. H. Gerstein, N. A. Fouad, G. Roysircar, & T. Israel (Eds.), *Handbook for social justice in counseling psychology* (pp. 1–16). Thousand Oaks, CA: Sage.

Gedeon, K. (2013). *Minorities and racial discrimination in the workplace: Are we exaggerating?* Retrieved August 23, 2014, from http://madamenoire.com/279178/minorities-and-racial-discrimination-in-the-workplace-are-we-exaggerating/

Gerstein, L. H. (2005). Counseling psychologists as international social architects. In R. L. Toporek, L. H. Gerstein, N. A. Fouad, G. Roysircar-Sodowsky, & T. Israel (Eds.), *Handbook for social justice in counseling psychology: Leadership, vision, and action* (pp. 377–387). Thousand Oaks, CA: Sage.

Gonzalez, J. (2010, August 9). *Reports highlight disparities in graduation rates among White and minority students.* Retrieved from http://chronicle.com/article/Reports-Highlight-Disparities/123857

Goodman, L. A., Liang, B., Helms, J. E., Latta, R. E., Sparks, E., & Weintraub, S. R. (2004). Training counseling psychologists as social justice agents: Feminist and multicultural principles in action. *The Counseling Psychologist, 32*, 793–837.

Granderson, LZ. (2014, August 12). *How many unarmed people have to die?* Retrieved from http://www.cnn.com/2014/08/11/opinion/granderson-missouri-police-shooting/index.html?hpt=op_t1

Harkinson, J. (2014, August 13). *Four unarmed black men have been killed by police in the last month.* Retrieved from http://www.motherjones.com/politics/2014/08/3-unarmed-black-african-american-men-killed-police

History.com Staff. (2009). *Chinese Exclusion Act.* Retrieved from http://www.history.com/topics/chinese-exclusion-act

History.com Staff. (2009). *Trail of tears.* Retrieved from http://www.history.com/topics/native-american-history/trail-of-tears

Human Rights Campaign Foundation. (2014). *A guide to state-level advocacy following enactment of the Hate Crimes Prevention Act.* Retrieved from http://www.hrc.org/resources/entry/a-guide-to-state-level-advocacy-following-enactment-of-the-matthew-she

Jackson, J. (2000). What ought psychology to do? *American Psychologist, 55*, 328–330.

Jaschik, S. (2010, June 21). New evidence of racial biases on SAT. *Inside Higher Ed.* Retrieved from https://www.insidehighered.com/news/2010/06/21/sat

"Jim Crow Laws." (n.d.). *United States history.* Retrieved from http://www.u-s-history.com/pages/h1559.html

Johnson, K., Hoyer, M., & Heath, B. (2014, August 15). Local police involved in 400 killings per year. *USA Today.* Retrieved from http://www.usatoday.com/story/news/nation/2014/08/14/police-killings-data/14060357/

Kaplan, G. A., Haan, M. N, Syme, S., Minkler, M., & Winkleby, M. (1987). Socio-economic status and health. In R. W. Amler & H. B. Dull (Eds.), *Closing the gap: The burden of unnecessary illness* (pp. 125–129). New York, NY: Oxford University Press.

Kaufman, J. (2005). Explaining the race/ethnicity-violence relationship: Neighborhood context and social psychological processes. *Justice Quarterly, 22*, 224–251.

King, E. B., Dunleavy, D. G., Dunleavy, E. M., Jaffer, S., Morgan, W. B., Elder, K., & Graebner, R. (2011). Discrimination in the twenty-first century: Are science and the law aligned? *Psychology, Public Policy, and Law, 17*(1), 54–75.

KMOV Staff. (2014, August 10). *Unarmed Ferguson, MO, teen Michael Brown shot multiple times, killed by cop: Community outraged.* Retrieved from https://www.youtube.com/watch?v=KFmiuwHCSfY

Lent, R. W., Brown, S. D., & Talleyrand, R. (2002). Career choice barriers, supports, and coping strategies: College students' experiences. *Journal of Vocational Behavior, 60*, 61–72.

Lewis, J. A., Ratts, M. J., Paladino, D. A., & Toporek, R. L. (2011). Social justice counseling and advocacy: Developing new leadership roles and competencies. *Journal for Social Action in Counseling and Psychology, 3*, 5–16.

Lincoln, A. (1862, September 22). Preliminary Emancipation Proclamation. *National Archives and Records Administration.* Retrieved from http://www.archives.gov/exhibits/american_originals_iv/sections/transcript_preliminary_emancipation.html

McWhirter, B. T. (1990). Loneliness: A review of current literature, with implications for counseling and research. *Journal of Counseling & Development, 68*, 417–422.

McWhorter, J. (Winter, 2011). How the war on drugs is destroying Black America. *Cato's Letter: A Quarterly Message on Liberty, 9*(1), 1–5. Retrieved from http://www.cato.org/sites/cato.org/files/pubs/pdf/catosletterv9n1.pdf

National Coalition for Anti-Violence Programs. (2014, May 29). *National report on hate violence against lesbian, gay, bisexual, transgender, queer and HIV-affected communities released today: Multi-year trends in anti-LGBTQ hate violence and homicides continue* [Media release]. Retrieved from http://www.avp.org/storage/documents/2013_mr_ncavp_hvreport.pdf

National Crime Prevention Council. (n.d.). Hate crime. Retrieved from http://www.ncpc.org/topics/hate-crime

National Public Radio Staff. (2014, August 15). After a traffic stop, teen was "almost another dead black male." In NPR's *Morning Edition*. Retrieved from http://www.npr.org/2014/08/15/340419821/after-a-traffic-stop-teen-was-almost-another-dead-black-male

"Protecting Children's Rights." (2014, May 19). *Unicef*. Retrieved March 17, 2015, from http://www.unicef.org/crc/index_protecting.html

Ratts, M. J. (2009). Social justice counseling: Toward the development of a "fifth force" among counseling paradigms. *Journal of Humanistic Counseling, Education, and Development, 48*, 160–172.

Ray, N. (2006). *Lesbian, gay, bisexual and transgender youth: An epidemic of homelessness*. New York, NY: National Gay and Lesbian Task Force Policy Institute and the National Coalition for the Homeless. Retrieved from: http://www.thetaskforce.org/downloads/reports/reports/HomelessYouth_Executive-Summary.pdf

Reardon, S., Baker, R., & Klasik, D. (2012, August 3). *Race, income, and enrollment patterns in highly selective colleges, 1982–2004*. Retrieved February 14, 2015, from http://cepa.stanford.edu/sites/default/files/race%20income%20%26%20selective%20college%20enrollment%20august%203%202012.pdf

Root, M. P. (2003). Racial and ethnic origins of harassment in the workplace: Evaluation issues and symptomatology. In D. B. Pope-Davis, H. L. K. Coleman, W. M. Liu, & R. L. Toporek (Eds.), *Handbook of multicultural competencies in counseling psychology* (pp. 478–492). Thousand Oaks, CA: Sage.

Stotzer, R. (2009). Violence against transgender people: A review of United States data. *Aggression and Violent Behavior, 14*, 170–179.

Sue, D. W., & Sue, D. (2013). *Counseling the culturally diverse: Theory and practice* (6th ed.). Hoboken, NJ: Wiley.

Today staff. (2014, September 4). What's in a name when you apply for a job? In NBC's *Today*. Retrieved from http://www.today.com/video/today/55986337#55986337

Toporek, R., & Chope, R. (2006). Individual, programmatic, and entrepreneurial approaches to social justice. In R. L. Toporek, L. H. Gerstein, N. A. Fouad, G. Roysircar, & T. Israel (Eds.), *Handbook for social justice in counseling psychology* (pp. 1–16). Thousand Oaks, CA: Sage.

U.S. Department of Justice. (n.d.). Hate crime. Retrieved from http://www.justice.gov/crs/hate-crime

U.S. Department of State: Office of the Historian. (n.d.). *Milestones 1921–1936: The Immigration Act of 1924 (The Johnson-Reed Act)*. Retrieved from http://history.state.gov/milestones/1921-1936/immigration-act

White House Office of the Press Secretary. (2014, February 27). *Remarks by the President on "My Brother's Keeper" initiative*. Retrieved from http://www.whitehouse.gov/the-press-office/2014/02/27/remarks-president-my-brothers-keeper-initiative

Wilkinson, R. G. (1996). *Unhealthy societies: The afflictions of inequality*. London, England: Routledge.

Wilkinson, R. G. (1997). Health inequalities: Relative or absolute material standards. *British Medical Journal, 314*, 591–595.

World Bank. (2001). *Engendering development*. New York, NY: Oxford University Press.

14

Developing Social Justice Counseling and Advocacy Skills

The individual must not merely wait and criticize. He must serve the cause as best he can. The fate of the world will be such as the world deserves.

—Albert Einstein

CHAPTER OVERVIEW

This chapter focuses on the ways in which counselors can develop advocacy and social justice counseling skills. Due to the nature of work as a health professional, counselors have a personal, professional, and social responsibility to help those who are socially disenfranchised through social justice counseling and advocacy initiatives. Although the literature in the area of social justice counseling has not been well developed, this chapter describes the various strategies counselors may use in social justice-orientated counseling activities, practices, and advocacy actions. On a personal level, counselors may develop an identity as an ally for the purpose of promoting social equality and social justice. Professionally, counselors need to adopt a social justice counseling paradigm and learn to use social justice-informed counseling strategies, such as strength-based or prevention-oriented approaches or empowerment-focused interventions. Finally, counselors have a social responsibility to engage in social advocacy efforts that extend beyond the counseling milieu in order to promote positive social change for all people. From an ethical point of view, our mandate of *do no harm* will be best accomplished via advocacy efforts and social justice counseling.

SELF-ASSESSMENT OF PRE-EXISTING AWARENESS AND KNOWLEDGE

- How much effort have I made to integrate social justice advocacy in my work with clients?
- How do I make myself an advocate for socially oppressed people?
- How do I deal with situations in which I feel my clients are using discrimination as an excuse for not being able to succeed?
- What skills do I possess to address social justice issues with my clients?
- What skills do I possess to engage myself in social advocacy for promoting justice for the socially oppressed?
- How well am I prepared to be an ally to the socially marginalized?

LEARNING OBJECTIVES

After reading this chapter, students will be able to do the following:

1. Understand the importance of taking personal responsibility in supporting the oppressed in society by becoming an ally
2. Understand the importance of taking professional responsibility in providing social justice-oriented services
3. Understand the potential harm that conventional counseling practice may cause to socially oppressed groups
4. Become aware of the necessity of adopting a social justice counseling paradigm in providing effective counseling services
5. Become interested in using strength-based counseling and focusing on prevention
6. Become invested in empowering diverse clients by employing social justice counseling
7. Become more ready to take action toward promoting social advocacy and positive social change for all people

CASE ILLUSTRATION 14.1

The Case of Alicia

Alicia is a 38-year-old computer engineer who just left her prior job with a large construction company on the West Coast and moved back home to a midsized town in the Midwest. Her racial and ethnic backgrounds include half Brazilian, a quarter

(Continued)

(Continued)

Irish Caucasian, and a quarter Native Hawaiian. Currently, she is unemployed and actively looking for a job. She came to counseling for help with depression and anxiety. She had called the clinic 2 days earlier, asking to see Ronda, a White female counselor.

In the first session, she appeared nervous and fidgety and told Ronda that she had a long history of depression and anxiety but seemed to feel worse recently since she had moved home. She then said nervously that she had wanted to wait (until she found a job) to seek counseling, but some recent nightmares and panic attacks scared her, and she did "not want to do anything stupid." It took about 20 minutes for Alicia to relax and start offering information about her life more comfortably. Alicia disclosed that she asked to see Ronda because she saw Ronda at a rally supporting lesbian/gay/bisexual/transgender/queer (LGBTQ) groups 2 weeks earlier, so she thought "that would make this a bit easier." Alicia is a transgender woman who transitioned before moving back home. She stated being very happy about the transition process as she successfully passed as female but also shared that the process was "really hard" in terms of having to deal with "a lot of crap" from some people in her life circle. She commented that although she had some understanding and supportive coworkers, two of her supervisors had really made life difficult for her. They would check her work products frequently, assign her tasks that others did not want, and give her low ratings for job performance. Alicia said that she was not fired but had been told several times that "you probably do not want to wait to be asked to leave." Eventually, Alicia decided to quit her job and move back in with her mother, who had been supportive of her and who lives alone and is suffering from early signs of dementia. Her father died several years ago, and Alicia said that "he would have had a hard time if he knew that I did this (transition from male to female)." Alicia also felt she would like to "start all over" with her mother, whom Alicia had problems with on and off during her gender incongruence years.

Alicia reported a number of severe depression and anxiety symptoms, including weight loss, crying for no obvious reason, sleep disturbances with frequent nightmares, difficulties concentrating, and fear of being alone in the house. She felt frustrated because she was not like this before she quit her job and moved back home. Although she expressed being very happy about her decision to transition, she explained that all the "practical aspects" of her life had turned worse and presented her with new challenges. She felt conflicted about her decision to move back home, realizing that it was harder for her to find a job in her field than when she was a man; the small-town culture did not help. When asked about her social support since being back in her hometown, she said, "I am not sure if I have any, although I am still talking to several high school friends. What hurts me the most, though, is that Mother is no longer invited to her knitting group and was asked to move to another group in the Bible study program in church; she also has not received any phone calls for helping out in a local school like she did before I came back."

SMALL-GROUP CLASS ACTIVITY 14.1

In small groups of three or four students, share your initial impression and thoughts about Alicia:

1. What emotions does Alicia's story elicit in you?
2. What is your general impression about the influence of Alicia's social context on her symptoms?
3. What are the issues at hand that you as a counselor need to be attentive to?
4. What does it say to you that Alicia sought Ronda out as her counselor?

As discussed in the last chapter, the profoundness of social inequality and injustice calls the counseling profession to respond to the mental health needs of the socially oppressed and marginalized by integrating social justice work into our provision of services. Clients who are afflicted by social oppression and marginalization deserve our professional recognition, respect, and competent service. Therefore, in addition to providing individualized culturally sensitive counseling, multiculturally competent counselors in the 21st century must also "function as change agents at organizational, institutional, and societal levels" (Vera & Speight, 2003, p. 255).

There are both personal and professional challenges to making the counseling profession an institution of positive social change and counselors its active change agents. As such, persistent efforts are necessary for the continuity and advancement of our profession in the 21st century. We believe this important work will need to commence with individual efforts from multiculturally competent and conscientious professionals. As counselors, we have personal, professional, ethical, and social responsibilities to integrate social justice into our provision of services with the goal of empowering culturally diverse clients and promoting their health and well-being.

Taking Personal Responsibility: Social Justice Competency Development

The personal work for counselors starts with the recognition of the fact that we live in a world where social inequality and injustice are part of the social structure and its norms. Socially responsible individuals will allow themselves to feel the emotions and develop passion associated with the belief that the status quo is not acceptable and has to change.

Those who are not members of oppressed groups have the power to influence change. Their attitude and behavior toward social inequality make them either contributors to or change agents against social injustice. In discussing the obvious and negative impact of social inequality on African American youth, President Obama noted that "the worst part is we've become numb to these statistics. We're not surprised by them. We take them as the norm. We just assume this is an inevitable part of American life, instead of the outrage that it is" (White House, 2014). Any ignorance, apathy, or denial about the existence of social injustice needs to be challenged. We need to allow ourselves to see that there are children who are hungry, who are not receiving proper education, who are not feeling safe in their neighborhoods. There are adults who are denied basic rights to love, to work, or to have basic survival needs met, and there are those who are wrongfully accused, persecuted, or punished just because of who they are. In this context, we either become part of the solution or remain part of the problem. We may deliberately develop competency in advocating for social justice or inadvertently contribute to maintaining the status quo—namely, perpetuation of an unjust system and social context for the disenfranchised.

Starting a Personal Journey

At a personal level, becoming an ally is one way that individuals can nurture and exercise a multicultural consciousness in effort to become "part of the solution." On her website, Anne Bishop, an activist and the author of *Becoming an Ally*, stated, "Allies are people who recognize the unearned privilege they receive from society's patterns of injustice and take responsibility for changing these patterns" (n.d., para. 1). A person from a dominant group can be an ally for those in a subordinate group, such as a person from a more privileged social class being a class ally. A class ally shows attitudes and behaviors that are anticlassist, is committed to increasing his or her own understanding of the issues related to classism, and works actively toward eliminating classism on many levels. Similarly, people can become allies of LGBTQ communities, racial minorities, immigrants, people with disabilities, women, the elderly, and so on.

In terms of how to act and live as an ally, Paul Kivel, a social justice educator, activist, and writer, provides a list of tactics that a White person can use to be an ally for people of color.

1. **Assume racism is everywhere, every day.** Just as economics influences everything we do, just as gender and gender politics influence everything we do, assume that racism is affecting your daily life. We assume this because it's true, and because a privilege of being white is the freedom to not deal with racism all the time. We have to learn to see the effect that racism has. Notice who speaks, what is said, how things are done and described. Notice who isn't present when racist talk occurs. Notice code words for race and the implications of the policies, patterns, and comments that are being expressed. You already notice the skin color of everyone you meet—now notice what difference it makes.

2. **Notice who is the center of attention and who is the center of power.** Racism works by directing violence and blame toward people of color and consolidating power and privilege for white people.

3. **Notice how racism is denied, minimized, and justified.**

4. **Understand and learn from the history of whiteness and racism.** Notice how racism has changed over time and how it has subverted or resisted challenges. Study the tactics that have worked effectively against it.

5. **Understand the connections between racism, economic issues, sexism, and other forms of injustice.**

6. **Take a stand against injustice.** Take risks. It is scary, difficult, and may bring up feelings of inadequacy, lack of self-confidence, indecision, or fear of making mistakes, but ultimately it is the only healthy and moral human thing to do. Intervene in situations where racism is being passed on.

7. **Be strategic.** Decide what is important to challenge and what's not. Think about strategy in particular situations. Attack the source of power.

8. **Don't confuse a battle with the war.** Behind particular incidents and interactions are larger patterns. Racism is flexible and adaptable. There will be gains and losses in the struggle for justice and equality.

9. **Don't call names or be personally abusive.** Since *power* is often defined as power over others—the ability to abuse or control people—it is easy to become abusive ourselves. However, we usually end up abusing people who have less power than we do because it is less dangerous. Attacking people doesn't address the systemic nature of racism and inequality.

10. **Support the leadership of people of color.** Do this consistently, but not uncritically.

11. **Learn something about the history of white people who have worked for racial justice.** There is a long history of white people who have fought for racial justice. Their stories can inspire and sustain you.

12. **Don't do it alone.** You will not end racism by yourself. We can do it if we work together. Build support, establish networks, and work with already established groups.

13. **Talk with your children and other young people about racism.** (pp. 1–3)

Kivel, P., Creighton, A. "Making the Peace." Hunter House (2002).Used by permission of Paul Kivel.

Becoming an ally is a personal journey. It will take courage and devotion from mental health counselors in the 21st century to view promotion of social justice as a personal responsibility. This personal effort will enhance counseling professionals' effectiveness in the provision of services to clients and communities. To become an ally, counselors need to be aware of their own multicultural identity (recognizing social oppression they may experience and privileges they enjoy), exercise their multicultural consciousness to unlearn various isms and develop social justice beliefs and attitudes, respect the leadership among the oppressed social groups for which they are seeking to be an ally, and stay connected with their own groups to show support and help each other in understanding oppression.

Reflection by a Counselor-in-Training

How I See My Middle-Class Privilege

Growing up, I never had to worry about when I would eat next. I could choose between private or public schooling. I could walk around my neighborhood without fear of crime or violence. If I was sick, I could go right to my family physician and receive help. More profoundly, I had the privilege of believing that my experience was the norm. After learning about the deeper structure of how social class can pervasively affect a person, I feel obligated to reevaluate my identity into a bigger cultural context. If I was not in the middle class, I would be a different person. Institutional and socioemotional barriers to succeed educationally, financially, and occupationally would have been a cloud over my head as soon as I woke up in the morning. However, acquiring a deeper understanding of how social class can affect someone should not be the end goal. I am obligated to give a concrete response–I need to not only recognize how my middle social class oppresses lower classes but also find a way to remove it from my life. I want to contribute to the hope that the trapping and draining of a person's potential that occurs due to low social class can be remediated by acts of charity and sacrifice. Being a mental health counselor, I will fulfill my responsibility and obligation to be part of positive social changes by being active politically and in the community as well as conducting multiculturally meaningful counseling services.

–Ryan L., a White, cisgender, heterosexual, male, middle-class graduate student with a Catholic faith in his mid-20s

Becoming an Ally for Social Justice

There have been warnings that sometimes supportive individuals—aspiring allies with good intentions—may not be effective in helping or may even be harmful through their efforts in the course of promoting social justice. That is because good-willed actions can perpetuate social oppression if the actors are not aware of their own multicultural identity and their unearned privileges and engage in actions for goals other than social justice. For instance, the following are all statements that reflect genuinely good intentions but will, to various degrees, perpetuate the unjust social system and negative perceptions of the recipients' diversity (being poor, a racial minority, or nonheterosexual):

> I really want to help that poor kid to succeed, so I bought him school supplies and told him that he should work hard and I would be watching him.
>
> By giving up a small portion of their assets, rich people can make life easier for many poor people.
>
> I want to help my clients of color feel as confident as their White peers.
>
> White counselors should teach low-income clients of color what to expect from counseling.

I told Jill that even if she is gay I still love her.

Straight people should try to talk to LGBT people without using language that disapproves of their sexual identity.

Seeing our own dominant group membership as superior (or as helpers) in itself is a perpetration on the members of the subdominant groups. This attitude not only furthers the "othering" of diverse group members (Duan & Smith, in press) but also keeps them down as recipients of dominant groups' charity, which may harm individuals as well as reinforce the oppressive social systems in the area of cultural diversity.

Now you probably want to ask the question, "How do we go about developing ourselves and becoming allies?" The answers to this question are similar to those we discussed in Chapter 6: In order to become a multiculturally competent counselor, we have to develop a non- and anti-ism multicultural identity along with a multicultural consciousness. To the specific goal of becoming an effective ally to promote social justice, individuals need to develop an ally identity. Although there are specific awareness, knowledge, skills, and actions required for allies for specific populations, the conceptual identity development model for aspiring social justice allies by Edwards (2006) may serve as a general guide for our discussion (see Table 14.1).

Table 14.1 Aspiring Ally Identity Development

	Aspiring Ally for Self-Interest	**Aspiring Ally for Altruism**	**Ally for Social Justice**
Motivation	Selfish—for the people I know and care about	Other—I do this for them	Combined selfishness—I do this for us
Ally to . . .	Ally to a person	Ally to target group	Ally to an issue
Relationship with Members of Oppressed Groups	Working *over* members of the target group	Working *for* members of the target group	Working *with* members of the target group
Victims of Oppression	Individuals with personal connection are or could be victims—my daughter, my sister, my friend	They are victims	All of us are victims—although victimized in different ways and unequally
Focus of Problem	Individuals—overt perpetrators	Others from the agent group	System

(Continued)

Table 14.1 (Continued)

	Aspiring Ally for Self-Interest	**Aspiring Ally for Altruism**	**Ally for Social Justice**
View of Justice	These incidents of hate are exceptions to the system of justice	We need justice for them	We need justice for all
Spiritual or Moral Foundation	I may be simply following doctrine or seeking spiritual self-preservation	I believe helping others is the right thing to do	I seek to connect and liberate us all on spiritual and moral grounds
Power	I'm powerful	I empower them—they need my help	Empower us all
Source of Ongoing Motivation	Motivator (my daughter, my sister, my friend) must be present	• Dependent on acceptance/praise from the other • Easily derailed by critiques by others • Often leads to burnout	Sustainable passion—for them, for me, for us, for the future
Mistakes	I don't make mistakes—I'm a good person, and perpetrators are just bad people	Has difficulty admitting mistakes to self or other[s]—struggles with critique or exploring own issues—highly defensive when confronted with own behavior	Seeks critiques as gifts and admits mistakes as part of doing the work and a step towards one's own liberation—has accepted own *isms* and seeks help in uncovering them
Relationship to the System	Not interested in the system—just stopping the bad people	Aims to be an exception from the system, yet ultimately perpetuates the system	Seeks to escape, impede, amend, redefine, and destroy the system
Focus of the Work	Perpetrators	Other members of the dominant group	My people—doesn't separate self from other agents
Privilege	Doesn't see privilege—wants to maintain status quo	Feels guilty about privilege and tries to distance self from privilege	Sees illumination of privilege as liberating and consciously uses unearned privilege against itself

Source: Edwards, K. E. (2006). Aspiring social justice ally identity development: A conceptual model. *NASPA Journal, 43*(4), 39–60. Table 1, p. 47. Reprinted by permission of Taylor & Francis LLC (http://www.tandfonline.com)

Conceptually, individuals may serve as allies for self-interest, for altruistic purposes, or for social justice. Those who become allies for self-interest "are primarily motivated to protect those they care about from being hurt" (Edwards, 2006, p. 46). They generally see the world as a fair and just place, feel powerful or self-actualized themselves, and focus their charity on helping suffering or mistreated individuals. Clearly, while their actions may be seen as charitable and commendable, they actually perpetuate the systems of oppression. Those who become allies for altruism begin to recognize the systemic nature of privilege and oppression (mainly intellectually) and seek "to engage in ally behavior as a means of dealing with the guilt" (p. 49) as members of a privileged group. The need to take on the role of "rescuer" is high, and the "we help them" mentality is strong. This motivation by guilt can be helpful for a while, but "when confronted with their own oppressive behaviors, they may become highly defensive . . . an attempt to maintain their status as exceptional members of the dominant group" (p. 49). Such "paternalistic nature of this altruism may lead to positive gains in the short term, but ultimately perpetuates the system of oppression by placing aspiring allies in the role of exceptional helper to the victims of oppression" (p. 49).

Being an *ally for social justice* means "to work with those from the oppressed group in collaboration and partnership to end the system of oppression" (Edwards, 2006, p. 51). Those allies are motivated by the mission and goal of social justice and recognize that in a different way members of the dominant groups are victims of social injustice as well. Allies who take actions toward social justice aim at not only freeing the oppressed but also at liberating themselves to "reconnect to their own full humanity" (p. 51). Allies for social justice have a clear sense of their own multicultural and ally identities, understand the deep structures of social oppression, commit themselves to fighting against various isms, and take responsibility in working with their own dominant groups as well as subordinate groups.

GUIDED SMALL-GROUP CLASS EXERCISE 14.1

Who Can Be My Ally? For Whom Can I Be an Ally?

Get into small groups of three to four people. Each person draws a circle, writes his or her name at the center, and fills the circle with all his or her identities to make it look as if many satellites (identities) surround the name in the center. Then each person picks one identity he or she feels most proud of and one that is associated with the most pain and shares one experience/story for each of them with the group.

After finishing that activity, reflect and share your answers to the following questions in the same small groups:

1. Would I appreciate having an ally among the group or in society? Who would be the most powerful allies for me? In what ways?

(Continued)

(Continued)

2. Do I want to be an ally to anyone in the group or in society? Why? What makes me powerful in being an ally for that person or that group?
3. In what ways do I believe or not believe it my personal responsibility to be an ally?
4. What are some of my past efforts at being an ally?
5. In what ways am I ready to develop my ally identity?
6. What are the paths, tasks, and challenges I have in developing a social justice ally identity?

Taking Professional Responsibility: A Social Justice Counseling Paradigm

Knowing that individuals' experiences and behaviors can only be understood accurately in context, we have the professional responsibility not to ignore clients' social and cultural contexts when working with them. It is also our responsibility to address these contexts directly or indirectly when they are the reasons or causes for the unfair and unjust social treatment that our clients have to face. It has been conceptualized that a psychologist or counselor has the professional responsibility to promote social justice both *via* and *in* their work (Kelman, 2010). In another words, our counseling service can be a vehicle for bringing about positive social changes, and it is the responsibility of the counselor to make it happen.

With a multicultural consciousness, counselors integrate social justice into services they provide, adopting a counseling paradigm that "uses social advocacy and activism as a means to address inequitable social, political, and economic conditions that impede the academic, career, and personal/social development of individuals, families, and communities" (Ratts, 2009, p. 160). This paradigm translates into counselors' awareness and knowledge that it is harmful and unethical to only assess client experiences and symptoms and then intervene to require changes exclusively from the client while the large social context is clearly a negative factor in or the cause of their symptoms. Counselors have to "view client problems more contextually and use advocacy to remove oppressive environmental barriers" (Lewis, Ratts, Paladino, & Toporek, 2011, p. 7).

Using a social justice counseling paradigm, counselors adopt a worldview that allows them to further appreciate our definition of multicultural counseling (see Chapter 6). Being able to see various obstacles and barriers our clients face in the context where we all play a role (as oppressors or victims) may motivate our social justice counseling effort and help us understand our clients and "the debilitating impact oppression has on clients' ability to reach their potential" (Lewis et al., 2011, p. 7). It is clearly articulated that "achieving social justice is both a goal and a process" through which social justice counseling practice would "ensure that every individual has the opportunity to reach her or his academic, career, and personal/social potential free from unnecessary barriers" (p. 7). Accordingly, our interventions and other services must be conducted with this goal in mind.

Social Justice-Informed Counseling Strategies

To avoid conducting remedial interventions that have been complicit in maintaining the status quo of an unjust social order, multiculturally competent counselors must reexamine counseling systems and strategies and focus on correcting negative effects of social injustice in the lives of those who have been oppressed due to their cultural diversity. In the field of counseling, we have the tradition of using several strategies that lend themselves well toward social justice-centered counseling. More work is needed to refine, enrich, and improve these strategies, and all of us are in a good position to contribute to this effort through research and practice.

Strength-Based Approach

Strength-based counseling challenges the medical model in mental health care, which often blames the victims for their victimization by focusing on what is wrong with them and their symptoms. The diagnosis, according to the *Diagnostic and Statistical Manual for Mental Disorders* (*DSM*), requires that clinicians match client symptoms with listed criteria. There is little room for considering individuals' contexts or differentiating similar symptoms caused by different contributing factors. For the socially oppressed, this diagnosis process pays little attention to how individuals have dealt with social injustice imposed upon their group or in what ways they have shown strength in surviving unfair social treatment and living with undue disadvantages (the opposite of social privilege) as a result of their social positions. For instance, it is most likely that Alicia's symptoms "qualify" her for major depressive or anxiety disorder. Such labeling implies that something is wrong with her, rather than with the discriminative and unjust social treatment she receives.

The emergence of strength-based counseling was initiated by cross-cultural scholars who questioned the assumptions of traditional counseling theories and practice in the context of minority cultures and contexts (Smith, 2006). Thus, the strength-based theory is rooted in the belief that culture has a significant role in shaping individuals and their psychological experiences. Smith stated, "All strengths are culturally based . . . cross-cultural counseling should focus on clients' cultural and individual strengths rather than on the victimization effects of racial or ethnic discrimination" (p. 17). In terms of achieving positive psychological changes and growth, individuals' motivation and positive emotions are important factors that could "trigger upward spirals toward emotional well-being" (Fredrickson & Joiner, 2002, p. 172). Therefore, strength-based interventions not only provide a sense of being valued or capable for the culturally marginalized but also encourage positive changes and actions for them to reach higher psychological well-being.

It should be noted that strength-based counseling does not mean to ignore symptoms and only focus on what is going well in our clients' lives. Rather, this approach recognizes and validates symptoms and views the symptoms from a strength-based perspective (vs. a pathology-focused perspective). Let's examine this example of a White female counselor in session with a young Vietnamese American nurse aide and single mother of 3-year-old twin daughters:

Counselor: You said you felt more depressed recently; tell me more about it.

Client: Recently, I have been having more and more difficulty concentrating, I can't sleep well at night, and sometimes I just want to cry. I am afraid that I will make some huge mistakes at work and hurt someone. I am really scared.

Counselor: Tell me what has happened in your life recently that might have led to these difficulties.

Client: I am not sure and don't know if that matters. I just want to be able to control myself. I want you to help me. If I could stop crying so much. . . . The other day when my mother called to tell me that my daughter fell off a chair, I lost it and yelled at her. I felt terrible afterwards. I cried and cried and cried. Please help me stop all this. I feel helpless.

We may speculate how counselors with different orientations would proceed and the types of possible interventions they may employ at this point. Some conventional approaches may lead to efforts to help the client eliminate depressive symptoms by using corrective strategies, such as focusing on insight by digging at the root of her depression, using relaxation exercises to help with sleep, doing various mental exercises to help with concentration, identifying and disputing maladaptive thoughts that may underlie her depression, and so on.

Instead, in using a strength-based approach, a counselor may focus on client awareness of her inner strengths and her strengths in coping with challenging external stressors, thus helping her to feel empowered to make changes. Some possible inner strengths the client presented in this short dialogue include her awareness of her need for change (she sought counseling), her care for her patients and/or coworkers (she was afraid of making mistakes to hurt them), her desire to be better (she wanted to control her symptoms), her willingness to take responsibility for her actions (she felt terrible after yelling at her mother), and so forth. The counselor also needs to listen for possible external stressors (her experienced cultural climate at work, her experienced prejudice due to being a single mother, possible economic hardship she might have, etc.) and identify her strengths in coping with such stressors. It is probably safe to say that it is her strength that has helped her succeed up to this point (in the face of social inequality), and it will be her strength again that helps her succeed in overcoming her current difficulties. Counselors need to be aware that conventional interventions aimed at fixing her symptoms may convey an implicit message that her deficits are the problem, ignoring the aversive impact of social inequality.

Preventive Focus of Counseling

Although prevention has always been viewed as one of the major tasks of mental health counselors, counselor training programs have not adequately attended to the role of prevention in preparing counselors to work with diverse clientele, nor have our counseling research agendas given prevention the attention it deserves. Although one-on-one counseling is one way of providing services to disenfranchised clients, it is limiting in that it does not promote social change. Similarly, our current training models are based primarily on a medical model, which can be problematic and potentially harmful for oppressed clients because a medical model of treatment conveys victim blaming and, like one-on-one counseling, it fails to account for the real cause of/solutions to the psychological problems that many clients experience. An accurate and complete understanding of the experiences of oppressed clients can only be achieved through validating their experiences in the larger social context in which they live. Moreover, our ability to promote positive systemic change will require that we embrace a social justice counseling perspective which emphasizes prevention and encourages the expansion of our professional activities beyond the counseling setting.

By definition, *prevention* means (a) stopping a problem behavior from ever occurring; (b) delaying the onset of a problem behavior; (c) reducing the impact of a problem behavior; (d) strengthening knowledge, attitudes, and behaviors that promote emotional and physical well-being; and (e) promoting institutional, community, and government policies that further physical, social, and emotional well-being (Romano & Hage, 2000). A number of current social realities, such as attitudes and beliefs (e.g., stigma about receiving mental health service), access (e.g., low remedial mental health service use and options for minorities and the poor), the increased problem of poverty (e.g., growing numbers of children, youth, and families in poverty), and increased risk factors such as violence, substance abuse, bullying, assault, and so on, make it clear that preventive service is necessary, critical, and significant.

From the perspective that aversive and unjust social, political, and cultural conditions play a role in individuals' mental health, it should be viewed as a professional mandate that we focus on preventive work. Symptom-driven interventions often connote victim-blaming messages, and preventive actions may provide the oppressed corrective experiences within the social and cultural environment. Prevention may include advocating for policies that are protective of the rights of those who have low social power, promoting public education to reduce prejudice and discrimination toward the culturally disenfranchised, and alleviating stigma associated with psychological reactions to negative social treatment, as well as reinforcing protective factors for and enhancing positive functioning of the individuals. One example of preventive care would be offering emotional and tangible safety support to those who may be negatively impacted by a hate crime against members of their minority group that is being broadcast in the news. Another example would be providing psychoeducational services to educate the public about how the experience of racism, heterosexism, or any other ism may cause psychological distress, symptoms, and reactions.

Empowerment: Validation and Education

Although empowerment may implicitly underlie many counseling interventions, social justice-oriented counseling focuses on it as a central component of counseling. In the literature of various helping professions, empowerment has been viewed both as a process and as an outcome of helping. For social work, Pinderhughes (1983) defined it as "the capacity to influence the forces which affect one's life space for one's own benefit" (p. 332) and as "the ability and capacity to cope constructively with the forces that undermine and hinder coping, the achievement of some reasonable control over [one's] destiny" (p. 334). By definition, *empowerment* involves a sense of gaining power for those who have felt powerless or who have had low power, or it involves a change of power balance. In her work with African American communities, Solomon (1976) described empowerment as making sure those "who belong to a stigmatized social category throughout their lives can be assisted to develop and increase skills in the exercise of interpersonal influence and the performance of valued social roles" (p. 6). When counseling the socially and culturally disenfranchised populations, counselors need to recognize the way in which power operates in society and "how individuals and communities are affected by the way power is used" (McWhirter, 1991, p. 70).

Counselors who recognize the role of social justice in the healing of the oppressed will validate client experiences and/or symptoms in the context of the unjust social reality in which the "powerless" minority groups live. Most clients do not come to counseling to discuss their suffering from racism or other isms; rather, they may come to ask for help with their symptoms, which may be viewed and evaluated as intrapersonal issues by conventional counseling approaches. It is counselors' responsibility to do them justice by conceptualizing their symptoms in context and offering interventions accordingly.

One intervention may be educating clients about the role of person-environment interaction in individuals' psychological experiences. In discussing counseling practice with clients of color, Courtland Lee (1991) articulated the following:

> People from ethnic groups of color, by and large, have experienced considerable frustration in their person-environment transactions with American society. The historic challenges inherent in the restricted and often extreme conditions confronting these groups in this country have undermined self-esteem, disrupted social relationships, caused frustration, and contributed to high levels of stress. Such challenges have often led to the development of maladaptive behavior patterns. The psychological effects of such maladaptive behavior have often been devastating, many times leading to a sense of intra- and interpersonal powerlessness. (p. 69)

This recognition mandates that counseling interventions focus on helping clients in "developing their ability to use resources to effectively combat the debilitating effects of negative environmental forces . . . [and] functional environmental mastery behaviors that lead to personal adjustment and optimal mental health" (Lee, 1991, p. 69). Helping clients understand contributing external factors to their experiences, engaging in positive activities to buffer the effect, and learning to use resources is important. Focusing on correcting their symptoms can only reinforce the sense of being the problem and being powerless. Again, conceptualizing client experience in social context is an antecedent of culturally effective interventions.

Empowerment: Outreach and Community Services

With the recognition that an unjust or hostile social environment contributes to the poor psychological health of those who are oppressed in society, counseling services need to extend beyond the counseling room and reach communities in an effort to change negative aspects of the environment. Professional counseling service needs to help break down institutional and social barriers and challenge long-standing traditions and notions that obstruct health and development for the culturally diverse (McWhirter, 1991). Counselors of the 21st century need to be advocates for positive social and community changes and "form proactive coalition with clients" (Lee, 1991, p. 69). Such efforts will result in the culturally diverse empowering themselves to "eradicate aspects of negative environmental press that impede upon development" (p. 69).

Outreach and community services can take different forms. Education, community organization, and consultation and collaboration are a few examples. A form of diversity education is providing communities (e.g., schools, churches, neighborhoods) with accurate information about how various isms have contributed to the psychological experience and behavior of the culturally diverse and how those who hold majority membership can help reduce inequality for the disenfranchised. For instance, many young African American males exhibited fear, anger, and even destructive behavior via community protests regarding the death of Michael Brown in Ferguson, Missouri, in 2014. Diversity education in communities such as Ferguson may help reduce negative reactions, increase empathy, and prevent marginalized youth from being further victimized. In addition, community organization may help to convey support and respect and encourage them to heal and grow.

Consultation is another cornerstone activity for professional counselors; it is most effective when paired with collaboration. Consultation and collaboration may help mobilize other professionals to assist with efforts in helping the culturally diverse. Such helping activity at a macro level may address both individual and contextual issues related to the targeted clients. For example, to help a child in poverty succeed in school, the consultation process would allow the consultant to focus on the child, the parents, the classroom, the school, the neighborhood, and the education system with full consideration of the environmental influences. Such services may avoid the pitfalls of a medical model of helping and emphasize a social justice perspective of the helping process.

Social Advocacy Practice

As we increase our understanding of the negative impact of social oppression on the socially marginalized, it is becoming more and more obvious that social advocacy is a necessary component of professional helping. We promote positive changes through counseling, but that is not enough. By focusing on interventions toward changing the individual exclusively, we are not only failing to eliminate the causes or contributing factors for the suffering of our culturally diverse clients but also joining "the forces that perpetuate social injustice" (Albee, 2000, p. 248). For instance, if we conceptualize Alicia's depression and anxiety as completely resultant of her personal issues (e.g., inability to stand up for herself with her supervisors, difficulty in adjusting to a new environment, relationship issues with her parents), we are reinforcing the idea that her difficulties are her own fault and leaving the negative impact of gender identity discrimination out of our consciousness. This practice will contribute to maintaining the status quo of social injustice. To help Alicia and many individuals like her, eliminating the biggest stressor, gender identity discrimination, is probably one of the most important elements of the helping/healing process. Therefore, counselors in the 21st century need to engage in social advocacy as part of their professional responsibility.

To inspire mental health counselors to engage in social justice practice, Charles Sheperis, a leader, educator, professional counselor, and social advocacy activist, offered the following encouraging and motivational remarks (quoted in Shallcross, 2010, pp. 29–30):

> The biggest misconception is that the effort of working toward social justice has to be a Herculean effort. The reason many individual counselors enter the profession is because they love being in the service of others. Simply looking for opportunities to address inequalities even on a smaller scale is a great act in the name of social justice.
>
> Taking a few small steps toward living the philosophy of social change can go a long way. By recognizing an injustice and taking a step to address it, counselors begin to live the philosophy.
>
> We shouldn't be on the bandwagon; we should lead the charge. . . . We (counselors) have a dedication to social justice interwoven throughout all aspects of our work. Social justice is inherent in our ethical code, our standards for accreditation, and throughout our work. Social justice is an overarching theme for what counselors do.
>
> Pay attention to the world around you and see where there is an opportunity to take an action. . . . If counselors pay attention to the world clients live in, they will see small places where they can take action.

Training for Social Justice Competencies

More and more, our counseling profession, scholars, and practitioners embrace a philosophy of social justice. However, implementing a social justice training agenda can be challenging for training programs, most of which still train counselors in a traditional way and focus on one-on-one counseling using classical theories. Ali, Liu, Mahmood, and Arguello (2008) discussed the pedagogy of social justice training, promoting "(a) holistic learning based in conscientization and consciousness raising; (b) a reliance on egalitarian methods such as participatory learning, dialogue, and self-reflection; and (c) an effort to equalize power inequities in the teacher-student relationship and classroom dynamics" (p. 3).

Being aware of the larger academic infrastructure of training, we have proposed two practical ways of including social justice into curriculum—namely, *service learning* and *creating unique practicum experiences*. Service learning, a deliberate, adaptable, and interdisciplinary practice based on civic education, would help counseling trainees connect academic coursework to community needs and concerns. Unique practicum experiences, such as those in a homeless shelter, would provide trainees opportunities to work with underserved populations and learn to be involved in public policy initiatives and other justice-promoting activities.

In 2003, the American Counseling Association (ACA) took leadership and endorsed an advocacy competencies model (see Figure 14.1).

Figure 14.1 Advocacy Competencies

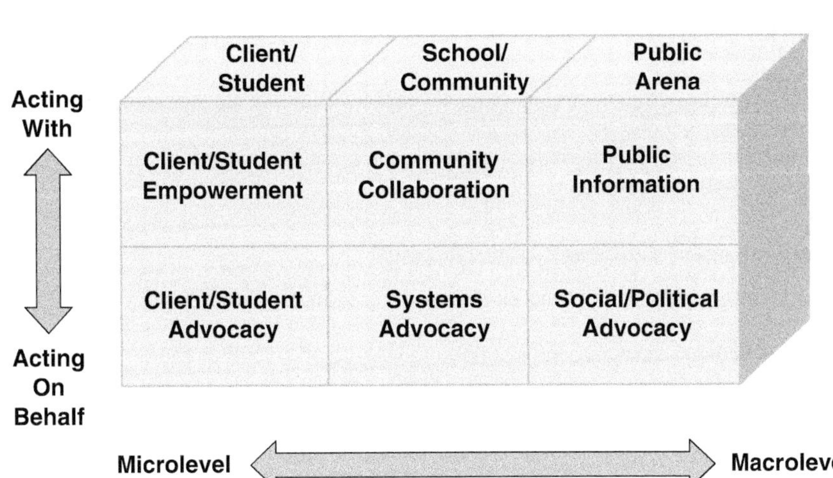

Client/Student Empowerment

- An advocacy orientation involves not only systems change interventions but also the implementation of empowerment strategies in direct counseling.
- Advocacy-oriented counselors recognize the impact of social, political, economic, and cultural factors on human development.
- They also help their clients and students understand their own lives in context. This lays the groundwork for self-advocacy.

Empowerment Counselor Competencies

In direct interventions, the counselor is able to

1. Identify strengths and resources of clients and students.
2. Identify the social, political, economic, and cultural factors that affect the client/student.
3. Recognize the signs indicating that an individual's behaviors and concerns reflect responses to systemic or internalized oppression.
4. At an appropriate development level, help the individual identify the external barriers that affect his or her development.

(Continued)

Figure 14.1 (Continued)

5. Train students and clients in self-advocacy skills.
6. Help students and clients develop self-advocacy action plans.
7. Assist students and clients in carrying out action plans.

Client/Student Advocacy

- When counselors become aware of external factors that act as barriers to an individual's development, they may choose to respond through advocacy.
- The client/student advocate role is especially significant when individuals or vulnerable groups lack access to needed services.

Client/Student Advocacy Counselor Competencies

In environmental interventions on behalf of clients and students, the counselor is able to

8. Negotiate relevant services and education systems on behalf of clients and students.
9. Help clients and students gain access to needed resources.
10. Identify barriers to the well-being of individuals and vulnerable groups.
11. Develop an initial plan of action for confronting these barriers.
12. Identify potential allies for confronting the barriers.
13. Carry out the plan of action.

Community Collaboration

- Their ongoing work with people gives counselors a unique awareness of recurring themes. Counselors are often among the first to become aware of specific difficulties in the environment.
- Advocacy-oriented counselors often choose to respond to such challenges by alerting existing organizations that are already working for change and that might have an interest in the issue at hand.
- In these situations, the counselor's primary role is as an ally. Counselors can also be helpful to organizations by making available to them our particular skills: interpersonal relations, communications, training, and research.

Community Collaboration Counselor Competencies

Regarding community collaboration, counselors will be able to

14. Identify environmental factors that impinge upon students' and clients' development.
15. Alert community or school groups with common concerns related to the issue.

16. Develop alliances with groups working for change.
17. Use effective listening skills to gain understanding of the group's goals.
18. Identify the strengths and resources that the group members bring to the process of systemic change.
19. Communicate recognition of and respect for these strengths and resources.
20. Identify and offer the skills that the counselor can bring to the collaboration.
21. Assess the effect of interaction with the community.

Systems Advocacy

- When counselors identify systemic factors that act as barriers to their students' or clients' development, they often wish that they could change the environment and prevent some of the problems that they see every day.
- Regardless of the specific target of change, the processes for altering the status quo have common qualities. Change is a process that requires vision, persistence, leadership, collaboration, systems analysis, and strong data. In many situations, a counselor is the right person to take leadership.

Systems Advocacy Counselor Competencies

In exerting systems-change leadership at the school or community level, the advocacy-oriented counselor is able to

22. Identify environmental factors impinging on students' or clients' development.
23. Provide and interpret data to show the urgency for change.
24. In collaboration with other stakeholders, develop a vision to guide change.
25. Analyze the sources of political power and social influence within the system.
26. Develop a step-by-step plan for implementing the change process.
27. Develop a plan for dealing with probable responses to change.
28. Recognize and deal with resistance.
29. Assess the effect of advocacy efforts on the system and constituents.

Public Information

- Across settings, specialties, and theoretical perspectives, professional counselors share knowledge of human development and expertise in communication.
- These qualities make it possible for advocacy-oriented counselors to awaken the general public to macro-systemic issues regarding human dignity.

(Continued)

Figure 14.1 (Continued)

Public Information Counselor Competencies

In informing the public about the role of environmental factors in human development, the advocacy-oriented counselor is able to

30. Recognize the impact of oppression and other barriers to healthy development.
31. Identify environmental factors that are protective of healthy development.
32. Prepare written and multimedia materials that provide clear explanations of the role of specific environmental factors in human development.
33. Communicate information in ways that are ethical and appropriate for the target population.
34. Disseminate information through a variety of media.
35. Identify and collaborate with other professionals who are involved in disseminating public information.
36. Assess the influence of public information efforts undertaken by the counselor.

Social/Political Advocacy

- Counselors regularly act as change agents in the systems that affect their own students and clients most directly. This experience often leads toward the recognition that some of the concerns they have addressed affected people in a much larger arena.
- When this happens, counselors use their skills to carry out social/political advocacy.

Social/Political Advocacy Counselor Competencies

In influencing public policy in a large, public arena, the advocacy-oriented counselor is able to

37. Distinguish those problems that can best be resolved through social/political action.
38. Identify the appropriate mechanisms and avenues for addressing these problems.
39. Seek out and join with potential allies.
40. Support existing alliances for change.
41. With allies, prepare convincing data and rationales for change.
42. With allies, lobby legislators and other policy makers.
43. Maintain open dialogue with communities and clients to ensure that the social/political advocacy is consistent with the initial goals.

Source: ACA Advocacy Competencies Model. (Web) The American Counseling Association. Reprinted with permission. No further reproduction authorized without written permission from the American Counseling Association.

While social advocacy has gradually become more and more expected in the work and competence of counselors, the need for professional advocacy is also recognized. The recognition and representation of our profession in the public eye requires professional advocacy. Based on the available literature, Hof, Dinsmore, Barber, Suhr, and Scofield (2009) summarized a set of professional advocacy competencies, including (a) promoting professional identity, (b) increasing the public image of counseling, (c) developing interprofessional and intraprofessional collaboration, and (d) promoting legislative policy initiatives.

Hof et al. (2009) proposed the T.R.A.I.N.E.R. model that "engages counselors in social advocacy and professional advocacy concurrently, facilitates counselor connection and collaboration with diverse communities, and raises the awareness of the counseling profession in the general marketplace" (p. 15). Counselors' social advocacy and professional advocacy are viewed as complementary and necessary. The T.R.A.I.N.E.R. model refers to the following processes (p. 18):

- *Target* advocacy needs of underrepresented client groups and their associated professional advocacy requirements
- *Respond* to the targeted needs by determining which social and/or professional advocacy competencies should be implemented to address those needs
- *Articulate* a plan to accomplish both social and professional advocacy
- *Implement* the plan
- *Network* for advocacy during the training
- *Evaluate* the training
- *Retarget* to address unmet social and/or professional advocacy needs

SMALL-GROUP CLASS ACTIVITY 14.2

In small groups of three or four students, brainstorm how to best conceptualize Alicia's presenting concerns and how to best assist her by addressing the following questions:

1. How would you conceptualize and assess Alicia's clinical symptoms (e.g., depression, anxiety)?
2. What potential hypotheses would you start with in understanding her symptoms?
3. How would you position yourself in establishing the therapeutic relationship with Alicia?
4. What types of "changes" in her would you pursue through counseling and why?
5. How could you help Alicia feel empowered?

Taking Social Responsibility: Community Advocacy for Social Justice

Albert Einstein once wrote, "The world is too dangerous to live in—not because of the people who do evil, but because of the people who sit and let it happen" (Sue, 2003, p. 14). To make the world a more fair and supportive place, every one of its residents has certain social responsibilities, especially mental health workers who are to assist people in reaching psychological wellness. We contend that multiculturally competent counselors will feel a sense of responsibility for eradicating the obvious wrongdoings and injustices that potentially victimize and compromise the mental and physical well-being of those who are disenfranchised. Ideologically, social inequality is generally condemned and social justice is desired in society today, but actions to eliminate the inequality are yet to be strengthened. It will take everyone's willingness and efforts to engage in social advocacy. Bottom-up advocacy efforts are necessary to lead to top-down law and policy changes, which are necessary for social justice. In fact, laws and policies that reduce inequality would promote psychological strength and well-being for all people.

In discussing the rewards and challenges of social advocacy for counselors, Zalaquett, Foley, Tillotson, Dinsmore, and Hof (2008) reminded our profession that we are overdue for concerted efforts in "fostering the types of multicultural/social justice initiatives that are necessary to forge major changes" (p. 327). They also pointed out that ultimately members of the dominant group in any of the diversity areas (e.g., White people in the area of race, cisgender straight persons in the area of gender and sexual identity) are the ones who have the power to change unfair and unjust systems. Therefore, culturally competent counselors are encouraged to pursue understanding of the part they play in contributing to their clients' cultural context. Moreover, they must take an active role in providing the cultural sensitivity, understanding, and advocacy actions both within and outside of counseling sessions that will help their diverse clients heal.

Using the context of supporting and working with lesbian/gay/bisexual (LGB) youth, Gustavsson and MacEachron (1998) outlined specific actions that counselors (or other helping professionals) may take to contribute to the course of social justice and the help that LGB youth deserve—namely, the following:

1. Make contact with service organizations that provide LGB-specific services.
2. Formalize the connections between your agency and these services to improve mutual referrals and to strengthen the credibility, support, and resources available to the organizations, if none exist.
3. Develop a program in your agency.
4. Start with a support group.
5. Have LGB-affirmative books, magazines, posters, community announcements, and other symbols of support in offices and waiting areas.

6. Advertise the service, specifically mentioning lesbian and gay youth.
7. Act as a liaison between the LGB community as a whole and your organization.
8. Be knowledgeable about HIV and AIDS and prepared to counter myths about LBG people.
9. Document by age, gender, and sexual orientation any services you provided and services that are needed but unfulfilled.
10. Bring the met and unmet needs to the attention of your agency's administrators.
11. Provide public education via speaking engagements that address lesbian and gay issues.
12. Help develop peer counseling and support telephone lines.
13. Help sensitize staff at youth shelters, foster care and adoption services, and residential and other programs to the needs of lesbian and gay youth and the special risks they face. (pp. 41–50)

Good, Ethical Practice in a Multicultural World

Becoming competent in social justice counseling and advocacy is a necessary dimension of the ethical practice of counseling. Good, ethical practice requires that counselors work effectively with cultural diversity in the therapeutic process by providing professional services that demonstrate respect for varied cultural worldviews (Corey, Corey, & Callanan, 2011) and no longer minimizing or ignoring the negative impact of social injustice inflicted upon diverse clients. Vera and Speight (2003) differentiated mandatory and aspirational ethics by pointing out that *mandatory ethics* involve the minimum of following the "rule" by attending to, being aware of, and developing sensitivity to issues of power, bias, discrimination, and oppression in counseling. To effectively serve oppressed populations, counselors need to strive toward fulfilling *aspirational ethics* by conducting social justice counseling and advocating for social justice inside and outside counseling rooms. That is, counselors should take actions toward "attaining the highest possible standard . . . advocate for the elimination of systems of oppression, inequality, or exploitation" (pp. 257–258).

Students often ask if they should refer clients who have cultural backgrounds they are unfamiliar with in order to not be accused of practicing unethically. Although referral is sometimes an appropriate course of action, it should not be considered the solution to counselors whose cultural backgrounds are less diverse than the clients they serve. Counselors should not be selecting clients based on their own views or values but should become multiculturally competent themselves, which demands a shift in thinking and attitudes. Certainly, we cannot know everything about every cultural group, and we do not believe that all counselors can work effectively with all clients, but we do expect that counseling professionals refrain from using their own value system as the basis and criteria for how clients should think and behave. Also, because clients belong to multiple cultures and because the salience of membership in any one cultural group changes by situation, counselors must operate from a multicultural identity and a multicultural consciousness. Too much focus on cultural group membership may result in stereotypical thinking (i.e., being too color conscious or attributing all problems to a client's cultural background); however, too narrow of a focus on the individual runs the risk of overlooking the impact of the cultural environment on the client's presenting issues (Haynes, Corey, & Moulton, 2003). We like the suggestion provided by Corey et al. (2011) as to how students can glean the most from their training and prepare to practice in a culturally ethical manner:

> You will not become more effective in multicultural counseling by expecting that you must be completely knowledgeable about the cultural backgrounds of all your clients, by thinking that you should have a complete repertoire of skills, or by demanding perfection. Rather than feeling that you must understand all the subtle nuances of cultural differences when you are with a client, we suggest that you develop a sense of interest, curiosity, and respect when faced with client differences and behaviors that are new to you. Recognize and appreciate your efforts toward becoming a more effective person and counselor, and remember that becoming a multiculturally competent counselor is an ongoing process. In this process there are no small steps; every step you take is creating a new direction for you in your work with diverse client populations. (p. 152)

CASE ILLUSTRATION 14.2

The Case of Juan

Juan is a 31-year-old Puerto Rican man who was recently released from prison following a 2-year sentence due to possession of an illicit drug (heroin). As a requirement of his parole, he must complete court-mandated counseling and find employment, which he has successfully done at a construction company. Juan moved from Puerto Rico to the United States at the age of 10 with his mother and siblings; his father remained in Puerto Rico. He is the father of three young children and is bilingual in English and Spanish. He identified as Catholic, has several tattoos, and wore a large metal cross around his neck during the counseling sessions. Juan admits to being a recovering heroin addict who has not used since being sentenced to prison.

Juan was seen for weekly counseling by Lorraine for approximately two months. During their sessions, Juan expressed his objections to the mandate and claimed he did not understand why he had to see a counselor. Moreover, Juan commented on the physical differences between Lorraine and himself, spoke a number of phrases in Spanish, and also mentioned several times that Lorraine must have grown up very sheltered, which she believed was Juan's way of pointing to reasons why a Caucasian 24-year-old female could never understand his experiences as a poor and uneducated male Puerto Rican. Juan was initially unaware that Lorraine spoke Spanish and thus was able to understand what he was saying. She remembered initially feeling very uncomfortable with their vast cultural differences. Not only was Juan opposed to seeking counseling, but it seemed to Lorraine that he had come to the conclusion that she would never be able to understand him.

Following their second session, she reflected on the dynamics of their therapeutic relationship and discussed with Juan their differences in culture and social contexts. She also disclosed that she understood Spanish. During subsequent sessions, Juan stopped complaining about having to come to counseling and discussed what he called the most important things in his life: family and faith. He loved spending time with his children and frequently talked about changing his ways for their benefit. Such discussion gave Lorraine the opportunity to validate the fact that part of him had to make wrong decisions (dealing heroin) to support his family and that he had to endure a lot of hardship to "succeed." They also discussed his past drug addiction and successes with remaining drug free; he accepted that he had made errors in his past, which he wanted to overcome.

Juan's strong faith and how he used it to overcome his past problems became a focus of counseling (instead of his sentence and probation). Lorraine believed focusing on Juan's cultural background and accompanying values strengthened their rapport as counseling progressed. Lorraine soon began to feel more comfortable in sessions with Juan, and he appeared more trusting of the therapeutic relationship and willing to share about his life experiences. Lorraine reflected on her counseling experience with Juan:

> Juan was my first experience during my training that involved vast cultural differences. When working with him, I always tried to do so through a cultural lens. I made sure to reflect on our cultural differences, acknowledge how our differences positioned us for privileges and disadvantages unfairly, and show Juan how interested I was in learning about his background and life experiences. In addition, appropriate self-disclosure (i.e., disclosing my familiarity with the Spanish language as well as my own sense of faith) turned out to be very helpful when working with Juan. We completed several successful sessions before having to terminate when I completed my academic program.

Used by permission of Genevieve Maliszewski

1. What skills did Lorraine employ that would demonstrate being a culturally competent counselor? What else could she have done to provide culturally responsive care, particularly if she were afforded additional counseling sessions?
2. What do you think about Lorraine's approach to counseling Juan?
3. Should Lorraine have referred Juan to a counselor trainee with a more similar cultural background? Why or why not?
4. Was it ethically appropriate for Lorraine to self-disclose about her faith and ability to speak Spanish? Why or why not?
5. How would you assess Lorraine's repertoire of multiculturally appropriate skills?

It is desirable that counseling practitioners develop a repertoire of culturally appropriate skills and intervention strategies, as serving in roles other than the traditional counselor (e.g., advocate, consultant, social change agent, liaison) also becomes necessary. Culturally responsive skills must be based on three basic premises: (a) diversity is real and should not be dismissed; (b) differences are simply differences and not deficiencies or pathology indicators; and (c) stereotypical and monolithic thinking must be avoided (Lee, 2001). In the case example of Juan, his counselor Lorraine acknowledged the role of diversity in her therapeutic relationship with him. In doing so, she embraced Juan's cultural beliefs, values, behaviors, and communication styles and appeared interested and open to continuing to learn. She did not avoid the issue of cultural differences or social contexts by claiming to be color-blind, thereby assuming that Juan was just like all of her other clients. Finally, she refrained from stereotypical thinking and instead seemed to look for a balance between Juan's cultural group membership and his individual uniqueness. She listened and understood that his religious faith was an important source of strength for him, and it does not appear that she pathologized his past and current behaviors.

When we look at Juan's situation, it becomes clear that not pathologizing but respecting client experience and focusing on cultural strength is important. A social justice orientation and an understanding of external/environmental factors underlying individual experiences help counselors to validate client experiences, and feeling validated may help clients feel freer to recognize their mistakes and their ability to overcome the mistakes. Multiculturally competent counselors will aim at eliminating the negative impact of social injustice on their diverse clients via ethical practice both in and out of the counseling setting, which is an important standard for doing no harm.

Summary

This chapter discusses the important role of social justice in our delivery of effective psychological services to the oppressed in our society, including the personal, professional, and social responsibilities that counselors in the 21st century will need to demonstrate in order to combat social inequality. Becoming a personal ally for social justice, using strength-based counseling with clients, engaging in outreach services, and taking action to advocate for positive social change are paths through which counselors may help culturally diverse clients. Based on the understanding that social context is an important determinant of individual behaviors, our counseling professional organizations have become more oriented toward social justice counseling than in years past. Inside and outside counseling rooms, counselors can serve as social advocates and must assume a vibrant role in the promotion of social justice for oppressed members of society.

Takeaway Messages

1. Development of a multicultural identity involves recognizing the influence of social oppression, injustice, and privileges and understanding individual behaviors and experiences in social context.
2. Becoming an ally for social justice is a personal journey that is consistent with the development of multiculturally competent counselors.

3. Social justice-oriented counselors challenge the medical model of conventional counseling practice, including diagnosis and treatment that perpetuates social injustice.

4. Strength-based counseling and social advocacy practice are effective ways to help clients from oppressed groups and to support positive social change for all people.

5. Without a social justice orientation, helping professionals may unintentionally do harm to those clients who have suffered from social injustice.

Recommended Resources

Readings

American Counseling Association. (n.d.). *Advocacy competencies: A social justice framework for counselors.* Retrieved from http://associationdatabase.com/aws/NCDA/pt/sd/news_article/27983/_PARENT/layout_details_cc/false

Bradley, J. M., Werth, J. L., Jr., & Hastings, S. L. (2012). Social justice advocacy in rural communities: Practical issues and implications. *The Counseling Psychologist, 40,* 363–384.

Kenny, M. E., Horne, A. M., Orpinas, P., & Reese, L. E. (2009). *Realizing social justice: The challenge of preventive interventions.* Washington, DC: American Psychological Association.

Kivel, P. (2002). *Uprooting racism: How White people can work for racial justice.* Gabriola Island, British Columbia: New Society.

Ratts, M. J., DeKruyf, L., & Chen-Hayes, S. F. (2007). *The ACA advocacy competencies: A social justice advocacy framework for professional school counselors.* Retrieved from: http://www.biomedsearch.com/article/ACA-advocacy-competencies-social-justice/172831285.html

Schwartz, J. P., & Lindley, L. D. (2009). Impacting sexism through social justice prevention: Implications at the personal and environmental levels. *Journal of Primary Prevention, 30,* 27–41.

Vasquez, M. J. T. (2012). Psychology and social justice: Why we do what we do. *American Psychologist, 67,* 337–346.

Media and Websites

Gantz, J., & Gantz, H. (Producers), & Gantz, J. (Director). (2013). *American Winter* [Documentary]. United States: HBO. Available from http://www.americanwinterfilm.com/buy-dvd

Joseph, P. (2011). *Zeitgeist: Moving forward* [Documentary]. Available from https://www.youtube.com/watch?v=4Z9WVZddH9w

Multicultural and Social Justice Competence Principles for Group Workers: http://www.asgw.org/pdf/asgw_mc_sj_priniciples_final_asgw.pdf

Rocero, G. (2014, March). *Why I must come out* [Video file] Retrieved from http://www.ted.com/talks/geena_rocero_why_i_must_come_out?language=en

References

Albee, G. W. (2000). The boulder model's fatal flaw. *American Psychologist, 55,* 247–248.

Ali, S. R., Liu, W. M., Mahmood, A., & Arguello, J. (2008). Social justice and applied psychology: Practical ideas for training the next generation of psychologists. *Journal for Social Action in Counseling and Psychology, 1*(2), 1–13.

Bishop, A. (n.d.). *Becoming an ally: Tools for achieving equity in people and institutions.* Retrieved from http://www.becominganally.ca/Becoming_an_Ally/Home.html

Corey, G., Corey, M., & Callanan, P. (2011). *Issues and ethics in the helping professions.* Pacific Grove, CA: Brooks/Cole.

Duan, C., & Smith, S. (in press). Multicultural training and supervision in research and service. In M. Casas, L. Suzuki, C. Alexander, & M. Jackson (Eds.), *Handbook of multicultural counseling* (4th ed.). Thousand Oaks, CA: Sage.

Edwards, K. E. (2006). Aspiring social justice ally identity development: A conceptual model. *NASPA Journal, 43*(4), 39–60.

Fredrickson, B. L., & Joiner, T. (2002). Positive emotions trigger upward spirals toward emotional well-being. *Psychological Science, 13*, 172–175.

Gustavsson, N., & MacEachron, A. (1998). Violence and lesbian and gay youth. In L. Sloan & N. Gustavsson (Eds.), *Violence and social injustice against lesbian, gay, and bisexual people* (pp. 41–50). New York, NY: Routledge.

Haynes, R., Corey, G., & Moulton, P. (2003). *Clinical supervision in the helping professions: A practical guide.* Pacific Grove, CA: Brooks/Cole.

Hof, D. D., Dinsmore, J. A., Barber, S., Suhr, R., & Scofield, T. R. (2009). Advocacy: The T.R.A.I.N.E.R. model. *Journal of Social Action in Counseling and Psychology, 2*, 15–28.

Kelman, H. (2010, July). *Becoming a socially responsible psychologist.* Paper presented at the annual conference of Psychologists for Social Responsibility, Boston, MA.

Kivel, P. (2006). *Guidelines for being strong White allies.* Retrieved from http://www.paulkivel.com/component/jdownloads/finish/1/23/0?Itemid=31

Lee, C. C. (1991). Empowerment in counseling: A multicultural perspective. *Journal of Counseling and Development, 69*, 229–230.

Lee, C. C. (2001). Defining and responding to racial and ethnic diversity. In D. C. Locke, J. E. Myers, & E. L. Herr (Eds.), *Handbook of multicultural counseling* (pp. 581–588). Thousand Oaks, CA: Sage.

Lewis, J. A., Arnold, M. S., House, R., & Toporek, R. L. (2002). *Advocacy competencies: Task force on advocacy competencies.* Alexandria, VA: American Counseling Association. Retrieved from http://www.counselorsforsocialjustice.net/Advocacy%20Competencies%20Domain%20Outline.pdf

Lewis, J. A., Ratts, M. J., Paladino, D. A., & Toporek, R. L. (2011). Social justice counseling and advocacy: Developing new leadership roles and competencies. *Journal for Social Action in Counseling and Psychology, 3*, 5–16.

McWhirter, E. H. (1991). Empowerment in counseling. *Journal of Counseling and Development, 69*, 222–227.

Pinderhughes, E. B. (1983). Empowerment for our clients and for ourselves. *Social Casework, 64*, 331–338.

Ratts, M. J. (2009). Social justice counseling: Toward the development of a "fifth force" among counseling paradigms. *Journal of Humanistic Counseling, Education, and Development, 48*, 160–172.

Romano, J. L., & Hage, S. M. (2000). Prevention and counseling psychology: Revitalizing commitments for the 21st century. *The Counseling Psychologist, 28*, 733–763.

Shallcross, L. (2010, June). Counselors taking a stand. *Counseling Today: An American Counseling Association Publication*, 28–35.

Smith, E. (2006). The strength-based counseling model. *The Counseling Psychologist, 34*, 13–79.

Solomon, B. B. (1976). *Black empowerment: Social work in oppressed communities.* New York, NY: Columbia University Press.

Sue, D. W. (2003). *Overcoming our racism: The journey to liberation.* New York, NY: Wiley.

Vera, E. M., & Speight, S. L. (2003). Multicultural competence, social justice, and counseling psychology: Expanding our roles. *The Counseling Psychologist, 31*, 253–272.

White House Office of the Press Secretary. (2014, February 27). *Remarks by the President on "My Brother's Keeper" initiative.* Retrieved from http://www.whitehouse.gov/the-press-office/2014/02/27/remarks-president-my-brothers-keeper-initiative

Zalaquett, C. P., Foley, P. F., Tillotson, K., Dinsmore, J. A., & Hof, D. (2008). Multicultural and social justice training for counselor education programs and colleges of education: Rewards and challenges. *Journal of Counseling and Development, 86*, 323–329.

Section 6

Applying Multicultural Competencies: Case Examples

This section provides case examples to illustrate ways in which a counselor attempts to integrate his or her multicultural understanding into clinical interventions. Counselor-client interactions are presented verbatim that reflect the counselor's intentional verbal and nonverbal behavior to address cultural or diversity aspects of the issue. The counselor also provides reflections pertaining to how he or she conceptualizes the client concerns and how he or she tries to reflect that conceptualization in practice. We hope that by reviewing these examples our readers will be able to deepen their understanding of how we define multicultural counseling (pp. 112–113) and why we emphasize the necessity of a multicultural identity. Please know that there is no one right way to conduct multicultural counseling nor a cookbook to provide you with a multicultural counseling recipe. With a multicultural identity, one can adopt a multicultural consciousness and exercise skills accordingly.

15

Helping Jermaine Feel "Normal"

Setting

We are at a counseling center at a community college that offers 2-year associate degree studies as well as career training, self-improvement, adult basic skills, and other classes for the general public. There is significant cultural diversity among the students, although the percentage of ethnic minorities is rather low.

Meeting Jermaine

As he was preparing to leave his office (located at the community college counseling center) at the end of the day on Monday, Mr. Scott, a White male counselor, heard a call from the intercom that there was a walk-in client that needed his immediate attention. Mr. Scott came out of his office and saw a young African American woman sitting on the floor in a corner of the waiting area with her head between her knees and her hands around them. The receptionist told Mr. Scott, "A male student walked her in but left before I was able to talk to him. She has been sitting like this since she came in and is not answering any of my questions." Mr. Scott walked closer and bent down to talk to the young lady.

Hi, I am Mr. Scott. I want to be of help to you.

(silence)

Can you tell me your name so I can address you properly?

(silence)

Can you tell me why you are here?

(silence)

Who is the male student who brought you here?

(silence)

You know we are about to close. We had better use the last few minutes. Please say something to me.

(silence)

If you do not talk to me, I won't be able to help you.

(silence)

After a few minutes, Mr. Scott sat down on the floor, too, facing the client, saying nothing. As the receptionist indicated that it was time to close, Mr. Scott said, "Jerry, could you please give us a few more minutes?"

After another few minutes, the client said, "I am sorry to keep you here. I should come tomorrow." She stood up without looking at Mr. Scott and walked toward the door.

Mr. Scott quickly stood up and grabbed a business card from the front desk, handed it to the client, and said, "Thank you for being so considerate. Please call me tomorrow."

The client took the card and said, "I am Jermaine."

Share your observations about the following questions:

1. What do you think Mr. Scott said or did that was effective? Why?
2. What do you think Mr. Scott said or did that was not effective? Why?
3. From a multicultural point of view, what cultural dynamics surfaced in this short encounter between Jermaine and Mr. Scott?
4. What situational factors do you see that might be worth the counselor's attention?

Mr. Scott's Reflection

Jermaine is apparently nervous, anxious, and very uncomfortable in a counseling facility. There must be reasons, probably out of her control, that she presented herself in this immature way. She looked to be in her 20s, but her voice sounded young. I wonder what her environment is like at home and in school. If she calls tomorrow, what can I say that is inviting and nonthreatening to her? How can I make it easier for her to come in and see me? I probably ought to use my "power" of being a White male to be of assistance to her. I should have asked Jerry what the man who brought Jermaine here looked like. Was he older? White? Authoritative or friendly looking? Regardless, my first goals are to make her feel welcome and confident that I have good intentions, that I have a strong interest in helping her, and that I won't make her feel blamed.

Mr. Scott's self-reflection showed his multicultural understanding in the following areas:

1. His being White means something in his potential therapeutic relationship with Jermaine. With this awareness, he may make his White identity work for him in helping Jermaine—of course, he must understand the privilege-oppression dynamics involved.
2. He is oriented toward learning about Jermaine's environment and social contexts. Staying away from the "What is wrong with her?" mind-set may allow him to address the factors that contribute to Jermaine's symptoms and empower her to act toward her goals.
3. He sets an initial goal to help Jermaine feel she can trust him not to blame her. As discussed in earlier chapters, a symptoms focus may carry a victim-blaming message when contributing contextual factors are overlooked.

The Brief Phone Call

Jermaine called the next afternoon.

Jermaine: I just want to let you know that I appreciated that you sat with me and stayed late for me. I am sorry.

Mr. Scott: I am thrilled that you called, Jermaine, because I want to thank you for allowing me to be with you yesterday afternoon.

Jermaine: (silence)

Mr. Scott: Also, I was touched by your sensitivity to others. I am sorry that we made you leave so soon.

Jermaine: (silence)

Mr. Scott: Jermaine, you are giving me a gift with this phone call.

Jermaine: No one likes me.

Mr. Scott: How about giving me a chance to get to know you more? I would really enjoy talking with you. I can see you tomorrow at 4:00.

Jermaine: (silence)

Mr. Scott: Are you giving me the opportunity?

Jermaine: I don't know. I just wanted to call to thank you. That's all.

Mr. Scott: Let's meet tomorrow then. I thank you for the opportunity.

Jermaine: Maybe . . . OK, just one time.

Share your observations about the following questions:

1. In what ways does this short conversation reflect Mr. Scott's multicultural competencies?
2. How would you describe and evaluate Mr. Scott's approach in getting Jermaine to agree to come to counseling?

Mr. Scott's Reflection

Jermaine is a considerate person and sensitive to others, strengths that can help her in some major ways. She appears to have difficulty in saying no to others, which must be shaped by her environment but makes her likable at the same time. I wonder if she was taken advantage of before. What will motivate her to stay in counseling (not come just once)? She needs to feel she is a contributor to the process. I'd better make the intake session a first session as well.

Intake and Session I

In the waiting room, Mr. Scott approached Jermaine, who was sitting in a corner, reading a magazine.

Mr. Scott: Hi, Jermaine!

Jermaine: Hi.

Mr. Scott: I am so glad to see you. I want to shake hands with you—is that all right?

Jermaine: (nervously giggles, then extends her hand)

In his office, Mr. Scott let Jermaine sit in the chair that faces the door to give her a sense of control. Mr. Scott sits in a chair that is not directly facing Jermaine's but is somewhat in line with hers to reduce the power differential. Mr. Scott hopes the setting may help Jermaine feel a bit more equal to him.

Mr. Scott: In this next hour, I want to get to know you as much as you will allow me to so I can be helpful to you, but you have the control to choose what to tell me. Could we have you start?

Jermaine: I don't know.

Mr. Scott: That is all right.

Jermaine: (silence)

Mr. Scott: Do you want me to ask you questions?

Jermaine: Yes.

Mr. Scott: OK, tell me about your day today.

Jermaine: Today was a better day. I didn't have to go to the criminal justice class, and I do not have that group project meeting for history class.

Mr. Scott: Hm. Is that a relief?

Jermaine: Yes. I am just not good enough.

Mr. Scott: It sounds as if there may be more . . . more about how you feel about those classes.

Jermaine: Um, no one likes me. I do not fit in. I feel I am crazy.

Mr. Scott: The class setting makes you feel crazy?

Jermaine: They see me as a criminal, I think. I am not. I am really not! (looking visibly distressed, about to cry)

Mr. Scott: You are not a criminal. I hear you.

Jermaine: My father was jailed for several years. Then my brother. They know it. But I love my father. I love my brother. I am not a criminal. I am not! (getting louder)

Mr. Scott: Being able to love is precious. It is no crime to love. (hands a tissue box to Jermaine)

Jermaine: (wiping tears) My father was arrested for selling cocaine, my brother for stealing. They were just not good, but they had to do it because my younger brother is developmentally delayed, and my mother died when giving birth to him. I know I am supposed to hate criminals, but I can't. I know others hate them. Mickey said one day that I would be an accomplice. I just lost it!

Mr. Scott: It must be terribly hard for you. When was that?

Jermaine: Three weeks ago. It's not just him—many others in class are like that, too. I feel crazy! I am stupid!

Mr. Scott: It sounds as if you had a clear understanding to disagree with them. Good for you. (a short silence) Somehow, you let what they say affect you this much even if you don't agree with them. I wonder if we can work together to figure that out.

Jermaine: (stops crying and looks puzzled but engaged) You really think I am right?

Mr. Scott: You are right to think on your own feet and disagree with them. You know yourself—and your father and brother—the best.

The intake and first session progressed smoothly and ended with a handshake between Jermaine and Mr. Scott and an appointment for the following week.

Share your observations about the following questions:

1. What impressions do you have of the intake and Session 1?
2. What do you think about Mr. Scott's decision to make the intake session the first counseling session as well?
3. What multicultural competencies shown by Mr. Scott can you identify?
4. What would you identify as effective interventions? Ineffective ones?
5. How successful do you think Mr. Scott is in validating, respecting, and advocating for Jermaine?

Client Profile

While focusing on therapeutic relationship building, Mr. Scott was able to collect sufficient information to complete the narrative for the intake report that indicates the following client profile:

> Jermaine is a 22-year-old African American heterosexual female. She was born and raised in the United States and self-identified as "atheist." She reported being healthy except for having had panic attacks a few times in the recent past. She reported no history of drug or alcohol abuse. She said she was around cocaine when her father was in the business, but she had no interest in it. She stated that her school performance was not so good, but "I graduated."
>
> She lives with her father and one younger brother who has a developmental disability. Her mother died 15 years ago during his birth. She has two older brothers who are "in and out of the house, sometimes bringing trouble and sometimes help." Her family lives in an apartment in a poor neighborhood. Due to his criminal history, her father never has had steady employment. They receive limited financial support from the government for her younger brother.
>
> Jermaine worked as an exotic dancer after high school for a few years before attending the community college. She said she has the longest work history in her family, and her job gave her joy as well as tears, but she said at this time she did not want to talk about that part of her life. She was glad that she was able to support her family financially and save some money for school now.
>
> Jermaine said the person who walked her to the counseling center the day before was a member of her history class project group. She said that she "lost it" again, wanting to yell and scream during the discussion about the human rights movement in the 60s. She reported, "I couldn't talk about that topic there. I probably said something that I don't remember, then they all looked at me. Then the next thing I knew was Steve saying, 'You have to go to the health center.'" She said she really didn't know how they got to the counseling center.

> Many times during the session, she commented, "What is wrong with me? I can't control myself anymore!" Jermaine said that she usually regretted them afterwards, but such incidents had become more and more frequent. She expressed, "I hate myself. I really want to feel normal."
>
> One thing Jermaine said toward the end of the session was, "I know I am in trouble, but I will not quit school. This is my only chance to get out of the bad situation my family and I have been in. I am really afraid I may fail."

Mr. Scott's Reflection

Jermaine is a strong fighter and a young person with hopes and goals. Psychologically, she appears to internalize outside negativity and is not aware that her symptoms (although not completely clear yet) are, to a significant degree, reactions to the hostile environment she lives in. Growing up, Jermaine did not receive the care, support, and nurturance that she deserved due to the early death of her mother as well as the racist environment we are all in. I can only imagine what it was like for her to grow up in that neighborhood and work as an exotic dancer. It is remarkable that she is here attending school and wants to finish her studies. She seems to value taking responsibility and often blames herself for what is wrong with her relationships with others.

She reported having panic attacks before, and it is possible that she had one yesterday during the group discussion. I would be very curious about her awareness of possible triggers of her panic attacks and how she has dealt with them. She says she often feels crazy and wants to "feel normal." She is probably really uncomfortable about feeling different and having disagreements with others about certain issues. The cultural environment she is in seems to make her feel that it is her problem and that something is wrong with her. Her wish to fit in or feel normal is encouraging and may motivate her to learn more about how she might have integrated negative social perceptions into her self-perception.

What should I focus on in the next session? I will help her feel safe and feel that she has allies and that I am going to be one for her and for the African American community. I also want her to feel that her reactions, including the panic attacks, to some environmental stressors (e.g., being perceived as a criminal, hearing negative comments about her race, sensing dislike from peers) are "normal" and reflect a clear sense of identity, an effort to control herself, and an ability to think differently than others. Helping her normalize these feelings might help reduce her panic symptoms.

Session 2

Continuing to be mindful of the power differential, Mr. Scott introduced the same seating arrangement as in Session 1, except he made sure that the tissue box was reachable from where Jermaine would sit. He wanted to avoid the action of passing her the box. After initial greetings and checking in, the second session began.

Mr. Scott: I thought about you after our last meeting, Jermaine.

Jermaine: Really? What about?

Mr. Scott: I feel grateful to you for your trust. I learned a lot from the life stories you shared with me.

Jermaine: What?

Mr. Scott: It takes courage to trust a White man who is part of the group in society that hasn't treated you fairly.

Jermaine: (silent, looking at Mr. Scott with curiosity)

Mr. Scott: Your trust shows your generosity, and it is significant to me.

Jermaine: Well, you are different. (a short silence) But in class, I am OK with everyone, you know. Then I feel crazy when they . . . when they see me like that . . . I mean, I should not have said things. I don't know why I can't control myself. Why can't I just be like others? Be normal?

Mr. Scott: You show self-doubt when you feel that others are judging you or saying mean things about you.

Jermaine: Because they do not know me, and they do not know what it is like to live my life. (speaking faster, voice becoming louder) You know, it is easy to say this is good and that is bad, but what do you do when you have no choice? And when you need to take care of yourself and your family? I just feel . . . sometimes I feel I am getting crazy. I want to yell, and I want to curse. Then I regret it. I know I am not a nice person to be around, not nice!

Mr. Scott: It sounds as if you were talking about being nice to others when you do not feel they are nice to you.

Jermaine: You know, it doesn't matter. Whether you're nice or not, they do their things. (becoming quiet and teary eyed)

As the session went on, Jermaine opened up about her experience with abuse from different men when working as an exotic dancer. At the end of the session, she said to Mr. Scott, "I do not know why I talked about all this. I did not want to but am surprised that I am OK about it now."

Share your observations about the following questions:

1. From a multicultural point of view, what cultural dynamics surfaced in this short encounter between Jermaine and Mr. Scott?
2. How do Mr. Scott's words reflect his multicultural skills?
3. Although a minor point, what do you think about Mr. Scott's intention to avoid the action of passing a tissue box to her when needed?

Observations of Mr. Scott's Work With Jermaine

Mr. Scott demonstrated intentional effort in establishing a trusting relationship with Jermaine in several areas, including reducing the power distance between them and focusing on helping Jermaine feel respected, understood, and empowered. Although the techniques (empathy, validation, reflection, etc.) he used may not be unique for diverse clients, they reflected his understanding of the multicultural dynamics between him and Jermaine and recognition of the negative effect of social oppression that Jermaine may have experienced. He avoided pathologizing Jermaine's symptoms and instead focused on validating her experiences and seeing her symptoms as reflections of her coping efforts.

Notably, Mr. Scott tried hard to use himself as a helping instrument in this relationship. By sitting on the floor with Jermaine, he allowed his White identity to strengthen the message to Jermaine that "I am with you." Mr. Scott was careful and tried to make Jermaine feel safe with him through verbal and nonverbal behavior, including the seating in the room. Moreover, he openly disclosed his appreciation for the trust that he felt from Jermaine, which can be empowering for her. In dealing with Jermaine's anxiety symptoms, Mr. Scott did not directly focus on them, which might make Jermaine feel that she had problems or disorders; rather, he gently approached the topic by addressing contextual factors. Jermaine's awareness of the dynamics between her and others made it possible for her to let her guard down and engage in the counseling sessions.

General Discussion

How Can We Be Most Effective in Helping Jermaine?

While discussing the following questions, keep in mind the following items:

- Your developmental status of a multicultural identity, especially racial, sexual, and class identities
- How multicultural counseling is defined (Chapter 6)
- What social justice counseling entails (Chapter 14)

1. How do you conceptualize the major clinical issues Jermaine presented?
2. In what ways might your multicultural identity influence how you view Jermaine?
3. What goals do you want to set for your work with Jermaine?
4. In what ways are your goals reflective of a multicultural counseling perspective?
5. What directions and strategies do you want to use in achieving these goals?
6. How does a social justice counseling paradigm influence your decisions?
7. What possible differences do you see between traditional counseling approaches and your approach as reflected in the answers to the above questions?

16

Helping Darryl and Samar to "Fight Fairly"

Backgrounds

Clients

Darryl and Samar are both in their mid-30s and have been together for 11 years. They got married about 15 months ago, shortly after their state passed a marriage-equality law. Soon after the marriage they started talking about having a baby through a surrogate. They came to counseling because "things have become rough," and they found themselves "starting to doubt" their relationship.

Darryl is a European American male with an MBA degree and owns a small business that offers party-planning services. He is from a large Christian family with parents still living and six adult siblings, but Darryl said, "I am not sure how they are doing," when the counselor asked about his extended family members. He did explain that he has contact with one of his younger sisters, who has had some "issues." Darryl said that his business was "OK" but not as good as he thought it should be.

Samar is an Indian American male who immigrated to the United States when he was 15 years old. He speaks with an Indian accent. He has a master's degree in computer science and has worked for a shoe company as a database manager. Because he has computer skills, he has done most of the computer-related work for Darryl's business, such as managing the website, programming the system for cost estimation for new customers, and so on. Recently, he let Darryl know that some changes need to happen with their current working arrangement (i.e., his working for Darryl)—either he will work for Darryl's company full time, or he will not be able to do any of the work.

Counselor

Dr. Goody is an immigrant from Turkey and received her college and graduate education in the United States. She is in her 40s and has worked in community mental health settings for over 10 years.

Dialogue 1

Dr. Goody: Good afternoon. I am Dr. Goody.

Darryl & Samar: Good afternoon.

Dr. Goody: May I address you by your first names?

Darryl: Sure!

Samar: Yes.

Dr. Goody: Who wants to start telling me how I can be helpful to you?

Samar: Let him start.

Darryl: You see, he is always like this. He won't say what he has on his mind but makes me look like the bad one when I speak.

Dr. Goody: Please elaborate how he makes you look bad.

Darryl: OK, I will just talk about myself. I have not been feeling good about the relationship for a while—since we got married to be accurate. I feel that he does not support me as he used to and that he is even distancing himself from me. I work so hard each day with long hours, and at the end of the day, I have to see a cold, uninterested face. Worse yet, he shows his temper sometimes, although he doesn't say much.

Dr. Goody: That does sound difficult—coming home tired and not feeling supported. Did you let Samar know your feelings about this?

Darryl: He knows. It is not new, but he is not helping. So we came here.

Samar: I am sorry. Yes, we have talked about it.

(silence)

Darryl: Why don't you tell your story? You see, this is what I mean. I feel like a whiner when there is another person present. I do not know why we are here! If only one person is going to talk, only one person needs to come. You know, sometimes we fight, more often now, sadly, but if you did not see us do that, you would think one person is crazy and the other a nice one.

Dr. Goody: This communication pattern apparently bothers you, Darryl. How about you, Samar?

Samar: Yes, it really bothers me, too. That is why we are here.

Dr. Goody: Do you care to say a bit more about the ways this bothers you, Samar?

Samar: I can say more, but I am really afraid that would make things worse.

Dr. Goody: OK, let's put our heads together and figure out how things will get worse if Samar starts saying more.

Darryl: I don't get it. I have always asked for more, but he is not giving it—he is actually giving me less and less. We used to talk a lot. Don't you think our past talks helped both of us? Now you are saying that you can't talk? You are being passive aggressive!

Samar: I am afraid that we are going to drift apart.

Darryl: How? By talking or not talking? We are going to drift apart if you are like this. You wanted to come here, but you are not talking. Now I am actually feeling afraid . . . for the first time.

Dr. Goody: Well, let's talk about your fears.

Share your observations about the following questions:

1. What did Dr. Goody do in the session that you think was effective or ineffective?
2. If you were Dr. Goody, what directions would you take to reflect a "multicultural approach?"
3. At this point, what is your sense of the major issue the couple is facing?

Dr. Goody: Reflection I

Although communication appears to be a key issue for the couple, I suspect that their social experiences or experiences as gay individuals and as a gay couple are an undercurrent. Additionally, Samar's ethnic background and the cross-cultural nature of their relationship add more dimensions to the issues at hand. I have a hunch that marriage is a victory for them in some ways but a new and maybe unrecognized challenge in other ways. It has possibly brought them a whole set of new challenges that result from social discrimination and oppression. I am really curious about their experiences in their work and social settings because I think some of the social and interpersonal dynamics they experience at work may replicate in their relationship.

Dialogue 2

Darryl: I am afraid that it is all a big mistake.

Dr. Goody: What are you referring to by "it?"

Darryl: I don't know. Everything, I guess.

Samar: I am afraid of losing what we had—friendship, companionship, and the dependence on each other. Of course, being the first to get married—I mean, of those like us—and the first divorced would be terrible.

Darryl: You are saying the word, I'm not. Is it what you have been thinking about all along? Why didn't you say it before? It is so unfair that we were probably fighting for different purposes! You always have reasons, but never this one. You see, we can't even fight equally and fairly.

(silence)

Dr. Goody: Could both of you share what you are feeling at this moment?

Darryl: I am angry. I have invested . . . I don't know. I don't know. I am very angry now.

Dr. Goody: How about you, Samar?

Samar: Anger, fear, maybe being unsure.

Dr. Goody: Obviously, your feelings have a lot to do with what is going on between the two of you, but I wonder if these feelings are familiar—do you have similar feelings in other contexts, such as at work or with your folks or friends?

Darryl: Yes and no for me. I can't ever feel angry toward my customers—sometimes I have to force myself to smile, even if I'm mad inside. You know, we used to share those experiences, Samar and I, and then we would laugh them off or block them out of our minds. Not anymore. I do not have anyone to do that with anymore. No one is interested. (a few seconds of silence) The other day I was talking with an African American teenager about her upcoming high school graduation party. Her mom literally pulled her out of my shop as soon as I said something like, "In our gay community . . . ." She let me hear her disgust with her "Lord knows . . . ." as they were walking out the door.

Dr. Goody: I can see you are feeling some emotions, Samar.

Samar: I am not sure. I feel conflicted. Darryl is right. We have not been offering much support to each other. I sometimes do not feel I have enough to offer. Maybe I am too depleted. I am also angry—angry at myself.

Dr. Goody: You both sound as if you have some feelings, including anger and being conflicted or not supported, that the other may or may not know. Perhaps we can spend some time here just to share some of those emotions.

Darryl: We probably should.

Share your observations regarding the following questions:

1. In this part of the session, which aspects did Dr. Goody focus on that were therapeutically effective?
2. What do you think about Dr. Goody's thoughts concerning the "undercurrent" of this couple's issues?
3. Did you feel empathic toward Darryl and Samar? In what ways?
4. If you were Dr. Goody, what directions would you take from this point on?

Dr. Goody: Reflection 2

I see some readiness to face emotions, and I want to use this opportunity to make them aware of how their social and work experiences influence their relationship. It is most likely that diversity and multicultural issues are present in their lives, and bringing them awareness of those may help them to understand their own emotions and appreciate the other's as well. When individuals experience unfair treatment in social contexts, it is countereffective, even harmful, to focus exclusively on internal reasons in explaining their "symptoms." Putting things in social perspective can be stress relieving for this couple.

Dialogue 3

Dr. Goody: I am curious that you said you are angry at yourself, Samar.

Samar: Yeah. Sometimes I know that Darryl probably had a rough day at work because he shows it at home. Then I feel irritated with him. Actually, I can be short fused to start with after a long day at work, and then I get even more irritated. I have to bite my tongue not to say anything. I avoid looking at him. I hate myself for being that way, but I can't do better, especially when he acts bossy. That makes me really nervous.

Darryl: Gosh! You think I am bossy. Your passive aggressiveness really irritates me. If you are not happy with me, say it, and let's fight. I know that if we fight, we can get over it. I hate it that you don't let me know you are not happy, especially when your facial expressions are screaming unhappiness, and you are avoiding eye contact. I can't please you. I don't feel trust or respect.

Dr. Goody: It seems both of you bring emotions home from your day job. How are things for you at work lately?

Darryl: Talk about work. . . . In this economic situation, things have not been great. When Samar said that he wanted his involvement in our business to change, I was just dumbfounded! Are you trying to break us? He knows that we do not have the volume of business to have him go full time, but I need his help with computer stuff. I guess it is his way to . . . somehow ever since we were married, things have been different.

Samar: It feels that *we* are breaking us, not me breaking us. You are right—since we got married, you seem to have changed. Maybe I have changed, too.

Dr. Goody: Let's try to figure out what changes have come with the marriage. You two were together for several years before the marriage. What changed after the ceremony?

Darryl: You know, Samar and I have talked about that before. We seem to have experienced more alienation after marriage than before. I don't think things have changed much in terms of how we live our lives, but others seem to have more difficulty in dealing with the fact that we are married. That really surprised us.

Samar: I was jolted by some of the reactions about our marriage from friends and family. Some of them were supportive and sympathetic to us before, but then . . . I don't think they agree with gay marriage. That really bothers me. Last Thanksgiving we stayed home and had turkey sandwiches.

Darryl: That doesn't bother me, it angers me! They want to support us but can't stand being equal to us or, rather, us being equal to them.

Samar: When I went to the human resources office to add Darryl to my health insurance right after we got married, you should have seen their faces. It was not like they didn't know before that I had a partner. Well, that was not even the worst thing that has happened. Mike, one of my supervisors, has been more critical and pickier than ever about me and my work. Even his manner has changed when he talks to me. Sometimes he is so domineering. I don't know what to do about it. Sometimes I want to quit, but we can't really afford it, especially if we have or adopt a baby.

Dr. Goody: It seems that you both had new experiences after you got married that have caused additional stress for you. In other words, your experience of ill treatment outside the marriage has caused stress, which has entered into your relationship.

Darryl: (appears intrigued along with Samar) I thought I was good at keeping all that shit outside our marriage.

Samar: Maybe. Maybe staying away from hostility is not enough.

Share your observations regarding the following questions:

1. How would you describe what Dr. Goody was trying to achieve?
2. How effective do you think her attempt was?
3. What is the dynamic relationship between Darryl and Samar at this point?
4. How would you proceed if you were Dr. Goody?

Dr. Goody: Reflection 3

I think they are gradually becoming aware that their marital problems are actually rooted, to a certain degree, outside their relationship. The sexual-orientation discrimination they receive causes stress for each of them and contributes to their relationship difficulties indirectly. I would be interested in learning if Samar's ethnic identity also affects his experience at work and their relationship dynamics. From a social justice perspective, I have the responsibility to help them see that sometimes they are not the problem, even if they feel they are. The unfairness and injustice they receive due to social prejudice creates negative problems in their life. Of course, that does not mean that they don't have communication issues that need to be addressed.

I would think, however, those issues can be effectively dealt with only within the larger social context.

Dialogue 4

Dr. Goody: Well, do you want to share your experiences of "that shit" or "hostility" and how you have been dealing with it or managing your life around it?

Darryl: I do the same as we have done for the past 11 years. We used to talk about it till we could forget or laugh them off. But not much lately. You know, in the business I do, I can't afford not trying to please customers or material vendors, regardless of what they say about me or how they make me feel. I am used to it, and that is OK. Samar and I used to say to ourselves that it is not our problem but theirs and joke about it. But it does anger me that some people I considered friends—not close friends, but friends— became weird around me since we got married. Perhaps they see us as their equals now, and that is not OK for them.

Samar: The other day our new administrative assistant asked me if I was married, but I really did not know what I should say because I knew that Jon was in the next cubicle. That was awkward. Even though everyone knows that we are married, it just felt uncomfortable. I was really angry at myself for being a coward.

Darryl: What? What? I can't believe it! I could write, "We are married!" on my face! How do you suppose that makes me feel?

Samar: Darryl, I am not you! I'm sorry. I wish I were like you. You know, you do not have a job to lose, but I do; you do not have to repeat something simple that you say three times when the person keeps saying "pardon," but I do; and you do not have to eat in the lunchroom where you answer questions like, "Which of you two does the laundry and the cooking?" but I do.

Darryl: We have talked about it before.

Samar: But I live it all the time. You can be tired of it, but I don't have that choice.

Darryl: Why don't you talk about it again? I mean, tell me that it still bothers you.

Samar: Because I do not think you understand.

Dr. Goody: OK, let me say something. You both have had experiences outside of your home that you want the other person to know about, to appreciate, and to understand, and both of you feel that you do not have that—I mean, not enough of that. You don't feel sufficiently supported or appreciated by the other.

Darryl: Yes, I just want to be able to talk things over and fight if necessary. I am OK with a fair fight. You will feel better afterwards. Samar, I invite you to do it.

Samar: Thanks, Darryl, but fighting is not particularly appealing to me. I need you to hear me. When you don't, I get frustrated.

Share your observations regarding the following questions:

1. How do you view this part of the therapeutic interaction?
2. Knowing more about how Samar feels now, did you change your assessment of his "unreasonable" request in terms of his role in Darryl's business?
3. In what ways do you think Dr. Goody is effectively addressing the couple's therapeutic needs?
4. What characteristics of Dr. Goody's intervention are consistent with what you think reflects multicultural competency?

Observations of Dr. Goody's Work With Darryl and Samar

Dr. Goody's approach to working with Darryl and Samar reflected cultural sensitivity and social justice context awareness.

First, she put significant focus on the role of external cultural and social factors in the issues that Darryl and Samar presented. Although she did not say it specifically, she encouraged them to recognize how their experience of social discrimination influences how they relate to each other. This is one very important aspect of multicultural counseling—for the counselor to be fully informed in terms of the larger social context of their clients, especially when their clients are members of oppressed cultural groups. Dr. Goody achieved some degree of success in this regard as evidenced by the outcome of the session interaction.

Second, Dr. Goody encouraged emotional expression, even if her major goal was to help the couple to understand that their problems were not completely theirs, but they were rooted in a larger social context. In multicultural counseling, it is critical to create a safe place for clients to share emotions related to the prejudice and discrimination they experience and to feel validated. Using exclusive cognitive interventions may inhibit the clients' sharing of emotions experienced in their social context, which in turn narrows the opportunity for counselors to validate and acknowledge their clients' contextual experiences.

Third, Dr. Goody appeared aware of the cultural differences between Darryl and Samar and her own ethnic minority status. She made an effort to not take sides or empathize more with Samar. She identified an important process phenomenon, which is that both of them feel lack of support. It is important that when working with individuals with diverse cultural identities, the counselor does not selectively show empathy or attention. Respecting and validating their experience holistically is helpful.

There will be challenges in the area of cultural diversity that Dr. Goody may face in working with this couple. For example, at some point Darryl's White privilege may be challenged. Dr. Goody's ethnic identity will come into play in terms of how she navigates the session to help both of them feel validated. Additionally, the cultural issues related to Samar's "passive aggressive" behavior will surface again. How she leads the effort to address it will require high sensitivity in order to maintain a meaningful balance between respecting cultural practice (e.g., Darryl's direct/active communication style vs. Samar's indirect/passive style) and facilitating willingness to accommodate in order to improve the couple's relationship.

General Discussion

How Can You Be Most Effective in Helping Darryl and Samar?

While discussing the following questions, keep in mind the following items:

- Your developmental status of a multicultural identity, especially racial and sexual identities
- How multicultural counseling is defined (Chapter 6)
- What social justice counseling entails (Chapter 14)

1. How do you conceptualize the major clinical issues Darryl and Samar presented?
2. In what ways might your multicultural identity influence how you view Darryl and Samar?
3. What goals do you want to set for your work with Darryl and Samar?
4. In what ways are your goals reflective of a multicultural counseling perspective?
5. What directions and strategies do you want to use in achieving these goals?
6. How does a social justice counseling paradigm influence your decisions?
7. What possible differences do you see between traditional counseling approaches and your approach as reflected in the answers to the above questions?

Epilogue: From the Authors' Chairs

Question: There is certainly an abundance of insightful points found within this text. But if you were asked to identify a single point or theme from all that is presented that you would hope would stand out and stick with the reader, what would that point or theme be?

We really wish that you had asked us to list as many themes and points in this book as we think necessary because we do have a long list. However, we can also tell you that it is not difficult for us to identify a dominant and an overarching one. In order to remain a viable helping profession in the 21st century, the field of counseling must be diligent about preparing counseling professionals to be multiculturally effective. In other words, we believe the sustainability of the counseling profession will require all practitioners to be multiculturally competent and able to integrate social justice issues into their practice. These goals are not attainable without the development of a multicultural identity. Also, it is our position that the development of a multicultural identity is a lifelong journey—a journey that we are proud to travel. We hope our readers will share our passion for and commitment to this lifelong journey, which will require them, like us, to develop and cultivate a multicultural identity, enhance their understanding of how traditional systems of counseling may represent forms of oppression, and recognize the power differentials in their counseling relationships with marginalized and oppressed groups. No one can become multiculturally competent overnight, nor can anyone remain competent without continuous learning, unlearning, and relearning. We hope our readers join us on the journey!

Question: In the text, there is a great deal of research cited and theories presented. Could you share from your own experience how the information presented within the text may actually take form in practice?

Research is a path toward knowledge. Multicultural counseling has been an emerging field of scholarship and practice. We do not think there is any significant doubt about the need for it at the present time, but the answers to the "how to" questions are still evolving. It is through research we enrich our understanding of the phenomena and learn to practice multiculturalism. Research is informed by what is on the ground level of counseling practice. The past decades have witnessed the roles that research has played in advancing the course of multicultural counseling. Our understanding as reflected in this text is shaped accordingly. For instance, our proposed model of multicultural competence development (described in Chapter 6) is informed by the research in racial and cultural identity development, the negative impact of social oppression on health, the role of cultural values and worldviews in human psychology, the acculturation process, the person-environment interaction, cultural variations in communication styles, and many other areas. However, we want to remind our readers that the knowledge we have is not static; newer understanding is destined to emerge, and thinking is a process of continuous renewal. We all should strive to be part of this renewing process and support research by testing and retesting our knowledge in multicultural counseling practice.

Question: As authors of this text, what might this book reveal about your own professional identities?

Our professional identities have no doubt played a role in how we planned and wrote this book. Our brief biographic information is on pp. xxix–xxx. As we articulated in the Preface, we acknowledge that our cultural identities and biases as reflected by our racial and ethnic minority status and our gender-conforming, sexual orientation, and social class majority status will likely come through in the text. We encourage readers to consider our multiple cultural identities as well as their own. We further urge them to attend to how their own cultural identities inform their work with clients. We believe this is an important step in developing one's multicultural identity. When we think about the benefits of being aware of our clients' multiple cultural identities, we realize that this awareness provides a deeper understanding of their presenting issues and concerns. Nonetheless, at the end of the day, it is our profession's code of ethics that mandates our multicultural competence in the provision of services to our culturally diverse consumers. We want our readers to know that multicultural competence is a lifelong commitment, and we welcome the continuous learning.

Question: What final prescription or direction might you offer your readers as they continue in their journey toward becoming professional counselors?

We see our readers as travel companions on the journey toward multicultural competence. Due to our age, which gives us the advantage of having been on the journey longer, we are probably a step ahead of them. Our readers should know that we are thrilled they have chosen to join us on this journey. We also want to alert them to the ups and downs, positives and negatives, and comforts and discomforts along the way. It is important for our readers to know that most learning occurs when we overcome our challenges. Therefore, we hope our writing will provide the encouragement that our readers will need to do this important self-reflection work—we believe doing so will be both freeing and enlightening. As an example, consider the individual who feels defensive in the process of recognizing his or her own social privilege; he or she will likely act out the defensiveness, as it is a habit for most people. Unfortunately, behaving in this way leads to getting off track and increases the unpleasant experience of defensiveness. To the contrary, putting down the defense to hear the unpleasant but factual or beneficial messages may be liberating. Our final prescription is that we all find the courage to be open-minded in developing a new identity—a *multicultural* identity—and a new consciousness—a *multicultural* consciousness.

Index

Abels, A. V., 293, 294
Ability privilege, 169
Ableism, 64, 149–150, 169, 281, 284–285
Abnormality, 10–12
Abramovitz, M., 340
Acculturation, 210–211
ACES (Association for Counselor Education and Supervision), 60
Activities. *See* Class activities
ADA (Americans with Disabilities Act), 279
Adams, G., 64
Adams, M., 64
Adler, P. S., 211
ADRESSING model, 115–117, 116 (table)
Adults, older, 150
Advocacy. *See* Social justice; Social justice advocacy; Social justice counseling
Advocacy Competencies (ACA), 293
Ægisdóttir, S., 47, 63, 117, 119
African Americans
  Black racial identity development, 205–207
  effects of colonization on, 58
  family structures, 198–199
  inadequate service to, 40
  mental health of, 58
  and police brutality, 332–334
  provision of services to, 40
  reflection on being, 60–61 (reflection)
  and refusal to disclose personal information, 17
  and religion, 199
  shared experience of oppression, 38
Ageism, 64, 150
Alas! A Blog (Deutch), 169
Albee, G. W., 371
Alexander, C. M., 9, 38
Ali, A., 84
Ali, S. R., 250, 251, 261, 372
Alleyne, V., 284
Allport, G. W., 173
Ally, becoming, 360–363, 363–364 (table), 365
Altemeyer, B., 151, 308
Altman, N., 9
American Counseling Association (ACA), 6, 47, 58
  Advocacy Competencies, 293
  advocacy competencies model, 373, 373–376 (figure)
  Code of Ethics, 20, 121, 122, 184, 234, 293, 304, 313 (table), 315, 351
  Counselors for Social Justice, 344
  international work, 63
  and training for social justice counseling, 293, 348, 373, 373–376 (figure)
American Personnel and Guidance Association (APGA), 58
American Psychological Association (APA), 12, 47, 63, 258
Americans with Disabilities Act (ADA), 279
Anderson, N. B., 197
Anderson, S. L., 64
Anhalt, K., 227
Ansley, T. N., 307, 308
Anti-isms, 136
ANWC (Association for Non-White Concerns), 59
APA (American Psychological Association), 12, 47, 63, 258
APGA (American Personnel and Guidance Association), 58
Aponte, H. J., 316
Appelman, A. J., 7
Arguello, J., 372
Arkin, R. M., 7
Arnett, J. J., 64
Arredondo, P, 19
Asch, A., 281, 293
ASERVIC (Association for Spiritual, Ethical and Religious Values in Counseling), 312, 313 (table)

Assessment biases, 265–266
Assessments, of religion/spirituality, 316–317
Assimilation, 19
Association for Counselor Education and Supervision (ACES), 60
Association for Non-White Concerns (ANWC), 59
Association for Spiritual, Ethical and Religious Values in Counseling (ASERVIC), 312, 313 (table)
Atkinson, D. R., 59, 207, 281
Autonomy, 6, 8, 11, 21
Awad, G. H., 135

Bailey, J., 281
Baker, R., 339
Balcazar, F. E., 294
Baldwin, M., 8
Banks, M., 281
Barber, S., 377
Barefoot, J. C., 17
Barker, R. L., 162
Baron, A., 36, 105
Bartoli, E., 302
Beauchamp, T. L., 21
Beckles, G. L., 259
Becoming an Ally (Bishop), 360
Behaviors
  explanation for, 7
  and poverty, 258, 268
  and social inequality, 340
Belaire, C., 311
Beliefs, of counselors, 106, 107 (exercise)
Bell, L. A., 343
Beneficence, 21, 36
Bergin, A. E., 305, 306, 307, 319
Berry, J. W., 211
Besnier, N., 227
Biaggio, M., 227
Bickell, N. A., 111
Bidell, M. P., 228
Bilodeau, B. L., 225, 227
Biracial identity, 210
Bisexuality, 44, 231. *See also* LGBTQ persons; Sexual orientation
Bishaw, A., 199, 256
Bishop, Anne, 360
Bisonó, A. M., 305
Black-Gutman, D., 12
Black Men Walking (BMW), 333
Black racial identity development, 205–207
Bluemel, J., 135
Blustein, D. L., 261
Bobo, L., 7
Bowling, B., 9
Boyd, C. J., 11
Brach, C., 111
Bradatan, C., 200
Brammer, R., 69
Brault, M. W., 279
Briones, E., 210
Britain, influence of on U.S., 57–58
Brooks, J. E., 135
Brown, C., 227
Brown, L. S., 226, 227, 228, 229
Brown, Michael, 38, 333, 371
Brown, S. D., 347
Bryant, R. M., 15, 88
Bullis, R., 310
Bullock, H. E., 255, 257
Burger, J. M., 7
Burke, M., 140 (reflection)
Burke, P. J., 135
Burn, D., 21
Bushong, Carl, 225
Butler, Robert Neil, 150

CACREP (Council for Accreditation of Counseling and Related Educational Programs), 1, 77, 93, 121, 122, 127, 189, 327
Callanan, P., 379, 380
Camarota, S. A., 346
Campbell, F., 64, 149
Cancelli, A. A., 88
Careers, and social justice counseling, 346
Carroll, L. C., 225, 228, 234
Carter, R. T., 173, 284
Casas, J. M., 9, 38, 282
Case, K. A., 228
Case illustrations
  context, 39–40 (case illustration), 53–54 (case illustration)
  cultural competence, 380–381 (case illustration)
  demands for multicultural counseling, 28–29 (case illustration)
  developing multicultural identity, 131 (case illustration)
  disability, 280–281 (case illustration)

ethics, 380–381 (case illustration)
LGBTQ clients, 236 (case illustration)
multicultural counseling, 28–29 (case illustration)
multiple cultural identities, 82 (case illustration)
oppression, 160–161 (case illustration)
redefining and renewing counseling, 102 (case illustration)
religion, 304–305 (case illustration), 317–318 (case illustration)
social class, 249 (case illustration)
social justice, 330–331 (case illustration), 345–346 (case illustration), 357–358 (case illustration)
spirituality, 304–305 (case illustration), 317–318 (case illustration)
working with diversity, 193 (case illustration)
Cashwell, C., 311
Cass, K. A., 224
Cawthorne, A., 256
Cecero, J. J., 44
Center for Education Policy Analysis, 339
Century Foundation, 339
Change, client, 14–16
Chen, J., 13
Cheung, F. K., 9
Chiao, H., 47, 93, 117
Children, 150, 258, 332, 339, 341
Childress, J. F., 21
Chinese culture, communication in, 17
Choice, emphasis on, 6
Chope, R., 346
Chow, J. C., 111
Christian privilege, 151, 181
Cisgender, defined, 144
Cisgender identity, 145–146
Cisgenderism, 144, 146, 146 (reflection)
Citizenship
and privilege, 170
second-class citizenship, 284
Civil rights movement, 59–60, 286
Claibom, C. D., 303
Clark, D., 233
Clark, G., 261
Class, social
awareness of, 250–251
case illustration, 249 (case illustration)
class activities on, 250 (activity), 263 (activity), 265 (activity), 269–270 (activity)
and gender, 255–256
and health, 269
and microaggressions, 262
and other dimensions of diversity, 253, 253 (box)
overcoming biases in assessment, 265–266
and privilege, 251–254, 254–255 (table)
and race, 255–256, 256 (figure)
resources for working with, 270–271
social class identity development, 148–149
vs. socioeconomic status, 250
and underuse of mental health services, 105
upward mobility, 261
values and worldview, 264–265
See also Class identity; Poor; Poverty; Socioeconomic status
Class activities
class, 250 (activity), 263 (activity), 265 (activity), 269–270 (activity)
classism, 258 (activity)
class privilege, 252 (activity), 258 (activity)
colonization, 58 (activity)
communication, 204 (activity)
context, 55 (activity), 65 (activity), 215 (activity)
counseling as cultural phenomenon, 6 (activity)
cultural identity, 194–195 (activity), 212 (activity)
cultural strengths, 215 (activity)
disability, 291–292 (activity)
identity development, 215 (activity)
intersection of cultural identities, 114–115 (activity)
meritocracy, 260 (activity)
multicultural identity development, 153–154 (activity)
multiple cultural identities, 83 (activity)
poor, 265 (activity)
poverty, 267–268 (activity), 269–270 (activity)
privilege, 143 (activity), 170 (activity)
racism, 176 (activity)
religion/spirituality, 320 (activity)
social justice, 338 (activity), 347 (activity)
working with diversity, 198 (activity)
Class identity, 148–149, 248, 262–263
Classism, 33, 64, 148, 251, 258 (activity), 259–262, 264

Class privilege, 169–170, 251–254, 252 (activity), 254–255 (table), 258 (activity)
Clinical trials, minorities in, 15–16
Code of Ethics (ACA), 20, 121, 122, 184, 234, 293, 304, 313 (table), 315, 351
Cognitive-behavioral treatment, 13
Cohen, M. C., 310
Cohen, S. H., 227
Cokley, K., 105
Cole, D., 151
Collaboration, 371
Collectivism, 68–69, 183, 199–200, 202
Collins, C., 148
Colonialism, 170
Colonization, 57–58, 58 (activity)
Colonization, psychological, 18
Coloradans for Immigrant Rights, 170
Color blindness, 135
Color of Fear (film), 36–37 (activity), 88
Comas-Díaz, L., 10, 11, 55, 179
Committee on Definition of the Division of Counseling Psychology, 12
Communication
  blockers, 109–110 (table)
  class activity on, 204 (activity)
  complexity of, 200–201
  context-driven, 202–203, 203–204 (table)
  focus on emotion in, 17
  implicit communication, 17
  nonverbal, 201–202
  self-disclosure in, 17, 105
  styles of, 16–17, 201–203, 203–204 (table)
  See also Language
Communities, 198–199
Community services, 371
Competence
  and ethics, 304, 315
  and perception of mental health, 11
Constantine, M., 15, 84, 86, 87, 114, 307
Consultation, 371
Context
  attending to, 89–90, 95
  case illustrations, 39–40 (case illustration), 53–54 (case illustration)
  challenges of integrating into practice, 86–87, 91–92, 95–97
  class activities on, 55 (activity), 65 (activity), 215 (activity)
  considering, 90–91 (box)
  counselors' role in, 66
  exercise on, 54–55 (exercise)
  formation of, 66
  at individual level, 83–87
  at international level, 93–97
  need to consider, 55, 64, 112–113, 179–180, 194–195, 213, 370
  need to understand, 66, 195–204
  relating to, 56 (table)
  and social justice counseling, 367
  at societal level, 87–93
Coon, H. M., 69
Copeland, E. J., 59
Copeland, L., 16
Corbett, M. M., 13
Corey, G., 315, 379, 380
Corey, M., 379, 380
Cornish, J. A. E., 293, 294
Counseling
  development of, 6–7
  goals of, 12–14, 344
  redefining and renewing, 101, 102–103 (questions), 102 (case illustration), 103, 111–113, 119–120, 121. *See also* Training
  sustainability of profession, 404
Counseling the Culturally Different (journal), 60
Counseling theories, 104–105
Counselors for Social Justice, 344
Cox, O. C., 172
Crime, minorities associated with, 339–340
Crosley-Corcoran, Gina, 253 (box)
Cross, W. E., Jr., 205
Cross-cultural competence, 117, 118 (table)
Croteau, J. M., 84
Cultural competence
  case illustration, 380–381 (case illustration)
  and ethics, 379–382
  resources for, 216
  See also Multicultural competence
Cultural context. *See* Context
Cultural encapsulation, 20–21, 59, 96
Cultural homogenization, threat of, 64
Cultural identity
  activity on, 114–115 (activity)
  ADRESSING model, 115–117, 116 (table)
  Black racial identity development, 205–207
  case illustration, 82 (case illustration)
  challenges of integrating into practice, 86–87
  class activities on, 83 (activity), 194 (activity), 212 (activity)

complexity of, 114
counselors' need to examine, 88
development of, 205–211, 212 (activity)
exercise on, 80–81 (exercise)
holistic perspective to understanding, 86, 89
inclusivity in addressing, 114–117
intersectionality of, 84–86, 114
model of development of, 207–208 (table), 207–209
need to recognize, 136, 194–195, 405
reflections on, 92–93 (reflection), 209 (reflection)
self-assessment of pre-existing awareness and knowledge of, 80
at societal level, 87–93
unawareness of, 138
See also Context; Multicultural identity; Multicultural professional identity
Cultural identity development model, 207–208 (table), 207–209
Cultural pluralism. *See* Pluralism
Cultural shock, 211
Cultural values. *See* Values
Culture
European, influence of, 9
failure to see as relevant, 135
reflection on role of, 18 (reflection)
role of in shaping individuals, 367
Currie, J., 339, 340

Daley, Thelma, 60
D'Andrea, M., 7, 19
Dashjian, L. T., 227
D'Augelli, A. R., 225
Davidov, B. J., 47
Davidson, B., 227
Davidson, M., 225
Davis, A. D., 163
Davis, C. S., 16
Davis, K., 342
Day, L., 15
Deafness, 283
DeAngelis, T., 224
Dear, M. J., 111
Decolonization, 58
DeFanti, E., 310
Defensiveness, 406
Delaney, H. D., 305
Dell Orto, A., 281
Democracy, majority tyranny in, 10
Demographic changes, 42–44
Denney, J. T., 258
D'Errico, K. H., 169
DeRubeis, R. J., 13
Desegregation, 196
Deutch, B., 169
Diagnostic and Statistical Manual of Mental Disorders (DSM), 63, 227
Dias, S., 84
Dichotomous thinking, 12, 108
Differences, need to consider, 71
Differential social treatment, 336. *See also* Isms; Oppression
Diller, J. V., 173
Dillon, F. R., 147
Dimock, M., 266
Dinsmore, J. A., 377, 378
Disability, 64
ableism, 64, 149–150, 169, 281, 284–285
adjustment to, 290
attitudes toward, 281–282
case illustration, 280–281 (case illustration)
class activity on, 291–292 (activity)
defined, 279–280
discussion, 289 (discussion)
models of, 285–293, 288 (table), 290–291 (table), 292 (table)
as multicultural issue, 281–283
reflections on, 275–278 (reflection), 279 (reflection), 285 (reflection), 287 (reflection)
resources for working with, 295–296
self-assessment of pre-existing awareness and knowledge of, 274–275
as social construct, 283–284
and terminology, 279
See also Persons with disabilities
Discrimination, 106, 181. *See also* Oppression
Discussion questions
disability, 289 (discussion)
multicultural professional identity, 90 (questions)
oppression, 159 (questions)
redefining and renewing counseling, 102–103 (questions)
sexuality, 223–224 (questions)
Distancing behavior, 269
Diversity
celebrating, 69
complexity of, 64, 70–71, 114

and ethics, 121–123
and need for counseling services, 35–36
need to meet demands of, 30
See also Multiculturalism
Diversity, working with
case illustration, 193 (case illustration)
class activity on, 198 (activity)
self-assessment of pre-existing awareness and knowledge of, 192
understanding cultural contexts, 195–204. *See also* Context
See also Multicultural competence; Multicultural professional identity
Doane, A. W., Jr., 139
Dominant groups
need for identity development, 139
and power, 139
reflection on, 140 (reflection)
White racial identity development, 140–143
See also Social dominance
"Don't Ask, Don't Tell," 135
Dornbusch, S. M., 200
Draper, M., 36, 105
DSM, 63, 227
Duan, C., 13, 136, 199, 363
Duncan, G. J., 259
Duncan, L. E., 6
Dunleavy, D. G., 347
Dunleavy, E. M., 347
Dunston, K., 250, 264
Duran, E., 180
Dynamic sizing, 232

Ebrey, P. B., 14
Economic inequality, 195–196, 335. *See also* Class, social; Poor; Poverty
Education, 196, 259, 339
Edwards, K. E., 363, 365
Einstein, Albert, 378
Elder, K., 347
Emotion, 17, 201–202
Employment, disparities in, 196–197
Empowerment, 369–371
Enns, P., 136
Entitlement, unearned. *See* Privilege
Environment, social. *See* Context
Escobar, J. I., 336
Ethics
aspirational ethics, 379
case illustration, 380–381 (case illustration)
Code of Ethics, 20, 121, 122, 184, 234, 293, 304, 313 (table), 315, 351
and competence, 304, 315
and cultural competence, 379–382
mandatory ethics, 379
and multicultural professional identity, 19–21
and need for multicultural competence, 36, 44, 47–48
and referral, 379
and religion/spirituality, 312, 313–314 (table), 314–316
and reparative therapy, 234
and responsibility in eliminating oppression, 184
and responsibility to work with cultural diversity, 121–123
and working with persons with disabilities, 282, 293–294
Ethnocentric monoculturalism, 18
Ethnocentrism, 8–10, 9, 14–16, 58, 64, 96, 104–105. *See also* Ethnocentric monoculturalism; Monoculturalism
Evans, K. M., 304, 308
Everyone Here Spoke Sign Language (Groce), 283
Evidence-based treatment (EBT), 15
Exercises
becoming an ally, 365–366 (exercise)
context, 54–55 (exercise)
cultural identity, 80–81 (exercise)
curriculum development, 97 (exercise)
developing multicultural identity, 131–132 (exercise), 137 (exercise)
gender identity, 238 (exercise)
isms, 87 (exercise)
LGBTQ clients, 235–236 (exercise)
multiculturalism, 5 (exercise)
oppression, 34–35 (exercise), 160 (exercise), 171 (exercise)
personal beliefs, 107 (exercise)
privilege, 171 (exercise)
on race, 34 (exercise)
religion/spirituality, 319 (exercise), 322 (exercise)
social justice, 349–350 (exercise)
social justice advocacy, 365–366 (exercise)
social reality, 31–32 (exercise)

Existential-humanistic treatment, 13
Expressiveness, 105
External locus of control, 14–15
Eyler, A. E., 226

Faith. *See* Religion; Spirituality
Faith development models, 308–309. *See also* Religion; Spirituality
Faith identity, 151. *See also* Religion; Spirituality
Faiver, C., 307
Familism, 200
Family structure, 198–199
Family therapy, individualism in, 8
Fanon, F., 18
Fassinger, R. E., 230, 233
Fausto-Sterling, A., 225
Feeley, M., 13
Feisthamel, K. P., 9, 38
Feminism, 61–62
Feminist therapy, 62
Feng, Y. Y. J., 214
Ferguson, A. D., 85
Ferguson, Missouri, 38, 333, 371
Fidelity, 21
Fine, M., 293
Firehammer, J., 180
Firestein, B., 228
Fisher, C. B., 48
Flores, M. P., 135
Foley, P. F., 378
Fontenot, K., 199
Ford-Grabowsky, M., 309
Fouad, N. A., 343
Fowers, B. J., 47
Fowler, J., 308
Frame, M. W., 44, 302, 303, 306, 307, 309, 315, 316, 319
Fraser, I., 111
Fredrickson, B. L., 367
Friedman, A. S., 8
Fryberg, S. M., 135
Fukuyama, M. A., 85, 304, 310, 311
Fuller, R. C., 305
Fundamental attribution error, 7, 15, 213

Galgay, C. E., 284
Gallo, L. C., 250
Gany, F., 111
Gao, G., 203
Garrett, M. T., 199, 200
Gay rights movement, 62–63
Gays. *See* Homosexuality; LGBTQ persons; Sexual identity; Sexual orientation
Gedeon, K., 347
Gelf, L. A., 13
Gender
  defined, 144, 225
  nonbinary gender identity, 234–235
  and perception of mental health, 11
  self-assessment of pre-existing awareness and knowledge of, 220
  transgender identity development, 227
  women's movements, 61–62
Gender binary, 221, 223–224 (reflection), 227, 234–235
Gender development, defined, 144
Gender dysphoria, 225, 227, 234
Gender identity
  and considerations in working with clients, 237 (table)
  and counseling issues, 237 (table)
  development of, 145–146
  exercise on, 238 (exercise)
  and hate crimes, 334
  pathologization of, 234
  reflection on, 342 (reflection)
  See also LGBTQ persons; LGBTQQCIAI persons; Transgender persons
Gender identity development, 225–226, 226 (table)
Gender inequality, 61–62, 341
Genderism, 144, 146
Genderqueer, 224
Gerstein, L. H., 47, 63, 93, 119, 343, 348
Gibson, M. A., 211
Gilroy, P. J., 225, 228, 234
Glasser, W., 15
Glassgold, J. M., 226, 227, 228, 229
Glied, Sherry, 259
Globalization, 45, 63. *See also* International competence; Internationalization movement; International work
Global literacy, 113
Glosoff, H. L., 44, 113
Goals
  of counseling, 12–14, 344
  and perception of mental health, 11
Goldfried, M. R., 224, 231
Golston, S. S., 310

Gonsiorek, J. C., 301
Gonzalez, J., 180, 339
Goodman, L. A., 345
Good society, 261
Gorgens, K. A., 293, 294
Gorski, P. C., 260
Gorsuch, R. L., 311
Graebner, R., 347
Graham, M., 169
Granderson, LZ, 333
Greene, B., 10, 179, 228
Greenleaf, A. T., 88
Griffin, P., 169
Griggs, L., 16
Groce, Nora Ellen, 283
Group memberships, 138
Gu, B. L., 16, 17
Guidelines for Psychotherapy with Lesbian, Gay, and Bisexual Clients, 230
Guinier, L., 10
Gunnings, T. S., 122
Gustavsson, N., 378
Gutierrez, F., 198

Haan, M. N., 346
Hackett, G., 281
Hackney, C. H., 306
Hage, S. M., 15, 310, 369
Hall, E., 16, 202
Hall, G., 15
Hall, L. K. B., 181
Hall, N. F., 181
Han Xu, 17
Hardiman, R., 139, 145, 149, 162, 163, 262
Harkinson, J., 333
Harley, D. A., 85, 286
Harm, avoiding, 21, 36, 213
Harmony, 14
Harro, B., 169
Hartmann, H., 257
Hartney, C., 162
Hass, R. G., 281
Hate crimes, 114, 151, 334
Hathaway, Patsy, 334
Haug, I. E., 315
Haveman, Joe, 351
Hayes, P. A., 282
Haynes, R. B., 15, 380
Hays, P. A., 115–117
Head, T., 62
Healing methods, cultural, 214
Health
  and class, 258, 259, 268, 269, 339
  disparities in, 197
  medical model of, 369
  views of, 14
Health insurance, 259
Heath, B., 333
Hegewisch, A., 257
Helms, J. E., 9, 38, 345
Heppner, P. P., 47, 63, 93, 117, 119
Herlihy, B., 20, 21
Heterosexism, 224, 232, 350–351
Heterosexual identity development, 146–148
Heterosexuality, in dichotomous thinking, 12
Heterosexual privilege, 169
Hickson, F., 12
Hierarchical thinking, 12, 108
Higgins, P. C., 283
High-context cultures, 16
Higher Power, 305
Hill, C. E., 13
Hill, P. C., 307
Hipolito-Delgado, C. P., 184
Hispanics
  population growth of, 43
  See also Latinos/Latinas
History, U.S., 8–9
Hodges, Shannon, 119, 120
Hof, D. D., 377, 378
Hofstede, G., 68
Hogg, M. A., 138
Hollingsworth, D. K., 282
Holmes, James Eagan, 333
Homelessness, 258, 340–341
Home ownership, 196
Homophobia, 230–231, 232
Homosexuality
  and development of sexual orientation identity, 146–148
  in dichotomous thinking, 12
  "Don't Ask, Don't Tell," 135
  gay rights movement, 62–63
  increasing openness of, 44
  reflections on, 43 (reflection), 103–104 (reflection)
  removal of from *DSM-II,* 63
  and same-sex marriage laws, 147
  See also LGBTQ persons; Sexual identity; Sexual orientation

Hopps, J., 250, 264
Hopson, A., 310
Hosie, T. W., 282
Howard-Hamilton, M. F., 87
Howe, S. R., 230, 231
Hoyer, M., 333
Hsieh, S., 196
Hu, B., 13
Hudiburg, S. K., 257
Hunsberger, R., 151
Huntington, S. P., 58
Hypothesis-conformity strategies, 213

Ideals, and perception of mental health, 11
Identity
  denial of, 284
  globalization of, 93–94
  See also specific identities
Identity development model, 145, 146, 149–150, 262
Identity theories, 134–135
Immigrants
  identity development, 210–211
  increased presence of, 45–47
  and nativism, 151–152
  occupations of, 346
  and power, 95, 348
  and privilege, 46
  reflection on, 46 (reflection)
Income inequality, 341–342. *See also* Poor; Poverty
Individual, emphasis on, 105
Individualism, 7–8, 12, 13, 15, 42, 68–69, 183, 199–200
Inequality, 33–34, 35
Ingersoll, R., 307, 315
In-group favoritism, 7, 9, 12, 64, 134
Injustice, 32, 72, 88, 171–179. *See also* Isms; Oppression; Social justice; Social justice advocacy; Social justice counseling
In-session counseling interaction worldview, 69–70 (counseling interaction)
Insight-oriented treatment, 12
Internal locus of control, 14–15
International competence, need for, 45, 46–47, 117, 119
Internationalization movement, 47, 63, 93, 117, 119
International work, 93, 95–96, 347–348
Isms, 172
  basis of, 64
  exercise on, 87 (exercise)
  influence of, 336
  and linear thinking, 108
  obligation to combat, 136
  See also Oppression; *individual isms*
Israel, T., 71, 230
Ivey, A. E., 7, 251, 253
Ivey, M. B., 7

Jack, D. C., 84
Jackson, B., 139, 145, 149, 162, 163, 262
Jackson, J., 261
Jackson, Jesse, 343
Jackson, J. S., 197
Jackson, L. M., 151
Jackson, M. L., 59, 60
Jaffee, K., 111
Jaffer, S., 347
James, William, 308
Jefferson, Thomas, 62
Jennings, R. L., 16
Jensen, J. P., 305
Jha, A., 197
Johnson, A., 32
Johnson, K., 333
Joiner, T., 367
Jolivette, K., 85
Jones, S. J., 262
Journal of Non-White Concerns in Personnel and Guidance, 59
Jun, H., 11, 12, 64, 84, 86, 107, 108, 145, 212
Justice, 21. *See also* Injustice; Social justice; Social justice advocacy; Social justice counseling
Just society myth, 172

Kaiser, C. R., 181
Kaplan, G. A., 346
Kaplan, Jay, 351
Kaschak, E., 281
Katz, I., 281
Katz, J. H., 7
Kaufman, J., 340
Kearney, E. M., 105
Kearney, L. K., 36
Keller, R. M., 284
Kelly, E. W., Jr., 306, 317
Kelly, N., 136

Kelman, H., 366
Kemmelmeier, M., 69
Kemp, N., 281, 282
Keys, C. B., 294
Keysar, A., 44
Killermann, Sam, 252
Kim, B. K., 17
Kim, E. K., 258
Kindaichi, M. M., 15
Kinesics, 202
King, E. B., 347
Kinsey, Alfred, 229
Kinsey scale, 229, 230 (table)
Kitayama, S., 183
Kitchener, K. S., 21
Kivel, Paul, 360
Klasik, D., 339
Kocarek, C. E., 228, 233
Koenig, H. G., 307
Kohut, A., 266
Kosmin, B. A., 44
Krueger, P. M., 258
Kurtis, T., 64
Kushner, H. S., 306

LaFromboise, T. D., 17
Laird, J., 234
Lake, B., 12
Landale, N. S., 200
Landau, Alex, 333–334
Language, 105, 111. *See also* Communication
Larson, D. B., 307
Larson, J., 227
Latinos/Latinas
  commitment to family life, 200
  effects of colonization on, 58
  family structure, 199
  mental health of, 58
  population growth of, 43
  reflections on, 43 (reflection), 103–104 (reflection)
  values of, 11
Latta, R. E., 345
Laws, and social inequality, 336–337
Lee, C. C., 20, 184, 371, 382
Lee, Courtland, 113, 370
Lee, R., 227
Lee Mun Wah, 36, 88
Lei, Y., 13
Leininger, M., 8, 18
Leland, J., 44
Lent, R. W., 347
Leong, F. T. L., 47, 93, 96, 117
Lesbians. *See* Homosexuality; LGBTQ persons; Sexual identity; Sexual orientation
Leung, A. S., 119
Leung, S. A., 47, 63, 119
Lewis, J. A., 344, 345, 366
Lewis, Victor, 88
LGB identity development, 224–225
LGBTQ persons
  awareness for working with, 232
  case illustration, 236 (case illustration)
  considerations in working with, 237 (table)
  counseling issues for, 235 (table)
  development of sexual orientation identity, 146–148
  discrimination against, 63
  exercise on, 235–236 (exercise)
  gay rights movement, 62–63
  gender binary, 221, 223–224 (reflection), 227, 234–235
  homelessness among, 340–341
  increasing openness of, 44
  and internalized homophobia, 230–231
  knowledge for working with, 231–232
  laws affecting, 62
  minorities, 231
  reflection on, 221–223 (reflection)
  refusal to counsel, 350–351
  reparative therapy, 234
  resources for working with, 231–232, 239–244
  skepticism of regarding counselors' competence, 233
  skills for working with, 233
  terminology, 224
  violence against, 334
  See also Homosexuality; Sexual identity; Sexual orientation; Transgender persons
LGBTQQCIAI persons
  population of, 224
  working with, 227–235
  See also Homosexuality; LGBTQ persons; Sexual identity; Sexuality; Sexual orientation; Transgender persons
Liang, B., 345
Life span model, 225
Linear thinking, 11–12, 108

Link, B. G., 268, 269
Literacy, global, 113
Liu, W. M., 250, 251, 253, 261, 264, 372
Locus of control, 14–15
Locust, C., 14
Lofquist, D., 44
Lopez-Baez, S. L., 42
Lorde, A., 10
Lott, B., 250, 251, 252, 255, 257, 262
Low-context cultures, 16

Macartney, S., 199
Macaskill, A., 15
MacEachron, A., 378
Mackelprang, R., 286
Magnuson, K., 259
Mahaney, E., 62
Mahmood, A., 372
Major, B., 181
Malebranche, D., 229
Male privilege, 164 (box), 168–169
Mallinckrodt, B., 281, 282
Maloney, H. N., 302
Maltby, J., 15
Maragos, A., 227
Marinelli, R., 281
Markus, H. R., 183
Marriage, right to, 334–335
Martin, C. E., 229
Mason, B., 229
Matthews, K. A., 250
Mays, V. M., 47
McCallum, D., 181
McCollum, V. J. C., 212
McCormick, K., 85
McCoy, S. K., 181
McCroskey, J. C., 9
McDavis, R. J., 19
McDonald, K. E., 294
McDonnell, K. A., 6
McGuire, T. G., 110
McIntosh, P., 32, 66, 142, 163,
    164–168 (box), 169
McLellan, B., 38, 55, 73
McMinn, M. R., 301
McNally, C., 307
McNamee, S. J., 33, 72, 106, 261
McWhirter, B. T., 341
McWhirter, E. H., 261, 370, 371
McWhorter, J., 340
Medical model of disability,
    286, 288 (table), 290 (table)
Medicine Wheel, 14
Men
  applicability of feminist therapies to, 62
  and gender privilege, 145
  male privilege, 164 (box), 168–169
Mental health
  application of dominant theories of, 11
  perceptions of, 10–12
  and Western medical model, 13–14
Mental health services, use of, 35–36, 38,
    105, 110–111
Mental illness, prevalence of, 110–111
Meritocracy, 91–92, 106, 166 (box),
    260 (activity), 261
Microaggressions, 176–177, 177–179 (table),
    262, 284, 347
Microassaults, 176
Microinsults, 176
Microinvalidations, 177
Middleton, R. A., 286
Migration Policy Institute, 45
Mihara, R., 227
Military, 135
Miller, G., 308, 319
Miller, R. K., Jr., 33, 72, 106, 261
Miller, W. R., 305
Millett, G., 229
Minkler, M., 346
Minnich, Elizabeth, 164 (box)
Minorities
  associated with crime and violence, 339–340
  in clinical trials, 15–16
  counseling profession's failure to
      serve, 35–36
  and cultural identity development,
      205, 207–208 (table), 207–209
  and diagnosis of mental disorders, 12
  diagnosis of pathology in, 10
  effects of ethnocentrism on, 9
  and health insurance, 259
  incarceration rates of, 72
  increase in, 42–43
  lack of opportunity for success for, 339
  overdiagnosis of mental disorders in, 38
  recognizing cultural strengths of, 212–213
  and use of mental health services,
      35–36, 38, 105, 110–111
  and White liberal syndrome, 141

Minorities, sexual. *See* Homosexuality; LGBTQ persons; Sexual orientation; Transgender persons
Minority model of disability, 286–287, 288 (table), 290–291 (table)
Minuchin, S., 8
Miranda, J., 110
Mohr, J. J., 139
Mokhtari, R., 196
Monk, G. D., 57, 58, 66, 67, 94, 96, 162, 269
Monoculturalism, 14–16. *See also* Ethnocentric monoculturalism
Monocultural practice, 7, 104–105
Monson, S. P., 293, 294
Montgomery, M. J., 210
Moon, D. G., 251
Moral model of disability, 285–286, 288 (table), 290 (table)
Moral principles, 21
Morgan, J., 136
Morgan, W. B., 347
Morris, J. R., 59
Morris, T. L., 227
Morrissey, M. R., 8
Morten, G., 207
Moser, K., 197
Moulton, P., 380
Mullins, D., 196
Multicultural ability, 134
Multicultural competence
  case examples, 386–403
  case illustration, 41 (case illustration)
  as ethical responsibility, 44
  model for developing, 132–138, 133 (figure)
  need for, 36, 37, 42–44, 45, 103, 113, 404
  and professional training, 108
  reflections on, 112 (reflection), 120–121 (reflection)
  resources on, 124
  See also Cultural competence; Multicultural ability; Multicultural professional identity
Multicultural consciousness, 134, 363, 406
Multicultural counseling
  barriers to, 104–109
  case illustration, 28–29 (case illustration)
  defined, 112–113
  self-assessment of pre-existing awareness and knowledge of, 28
Multicultural ethical competence, 47–48
Multicultural identity
  and ageism, 150
  defined, 137–138
  developing, 130, 131–132 (exercise), 131 (case illustration), 134–154, 137 (exercise), 152–153 (table), 153–154 (activity), 405–406
  dimensions of, 138
  in multicultural competence development model, 134
  and nationality, 151–152
  need to develop, 363
  and religion, 150–151
  resources on, 154–155
  self-assessment of multicultural self, 152–153 (table)
  self-assessment of pre-existing awareness and knowledge of, 130
  See also Cultural identity; Multicultural professional identity
Multiculturalism
  attention to, 20
  complexity of, 70–71
  and ethics, 121–123
  exercise on, 5 (exercise)
  resources on, 23, 49, 73, 98
  use of term, 60
Multicultural movement, 57–64
Multicultural personality, 134
Multicultural professional identity
  defined, 19
  discussion questions, 90 (questions)
  and ethical standards, 19–21
  formulation of, 22–23
  need for, 19, 92
  reflection on developing, 108–109 (reflection)
  See also Multicultural identity
Multiracial identity, development of, 210
Munley, P. H., 6
Murphy, J. A., 230, 231

Nanin, J., 284
National Center on Family Homelessness, 258
Nationality, 151–152, 170, 348
Native Alaskans, 200
Native Americans
  effects of colonization on, 58
  family structures, 199

healing methods, 214
mental health of, 58
values of, 11, 200
view of health, 14
Nativism, 151–152, 170
Naturalism, 181
Neuliep, J. W., 9
Neville, H. A., 33, 135, 172, 173, 174
Nickerson, K. J., 9, 38
Nigrescence theory, 205–207
Noebel, D. A., 180–181
Nonbinary gender identity, 234–235
Nonmaleficence, 21, 36, 213
Normality/norms, 10–12, 227, 284
Norsworthy, K. L., 47, 63, 119

Oakes, P. J., 138
Obama, Barack, 261, 339, 360
Obligations, lack of consideration for, 8
O'Brien, E., 307
O'Brien, L. T., 181
Ohlemacher, S., 196
Olkin, R., 279, 280, 282, 283, 285, 286, 287, 289, 290, 293, 294, 295
Oppenheimer, V. K., 199
Opportunity, lack of, 338–339
Oppression
acknowledging role in, 142
agents of, 163, 163 (table)
case illustration, 160–161 (case illustration)
defined, 162
discussion questions, 159 (questions)
effects of, 35, 37–38, 72, 162, 171–179
exercises on, 34 (exercise), 160 (exercise), 171 (exercise)
failure to account for effects of, 38
forms of, 33
of immigrants, 46
impact of, 179–180
interlocking, 167–168 (box)
at international level, 72
and just society myth, 172
and laws, 336–337
levels of, 71–72
maintenance of, 33, 106
and maladaptive behaviors, 340
and microaggressions, 176–177, 177–179 (table)
and need for counseling services, 35
need to recognize, 179–180
obligation to combat, 136, 184. *See also* Social justice; Social justice advocacy
perpetuation of, 362–363
presence of, 32
recognizing, 164 (box)
reflections on, 159 (reflection), 162 (reflection), 174 (reflection)
resources on, 185
and self-assessment of multicultural self, 152–153 (table)
self-assessment of pre-existing awareness and knowledge of, 158
shared experience of, 38
targets of, 163, 163 (table)
types of, 161–170
See also Isms; Minorities; *individual isms*
Orchard, S., 227
Oropesa, R. S., 200
Osmo, R., 213
Out-groups, 64, 134
Outreach, 371
Oyserman, D., 69

Pachankis, J. E., 224, 231
Pain, endurance of, 13
Paladino, D. A., 344, 345, 366
Palombi, B. J., 280, 286, 293, 294
Pampel, F. C., 258
Pantheism, 181
Paralanguage, 202
Pargament, K. I., 301
Parks, A., 179
Pathology, 10, 11
Patterson, D. G., 229
Patterson, J. B., 282
Paul, K. I., 197
Payne, R. K., 264
Payton, G., 310
Pedersen, P., 20, 57, 60, 96
Pelling, N. J., 228, 233
Penelope, J., 172
Perry, J. C., 261
Personnel and Guidance Journal, 59
Persons with disabilities (PWDs)
ableism, 64, 149–150, 169, 281, 284–285
discrimination against, 284
identity as, 280
microaggressions against, 284
as minority group, 294
need for mental health services, 281, 282

population of, 279
preparation for working with, 282
reactions toward, 281–283
skills for working with, 293
and terminology, 279, 280
See also Disability
Perspectives, respecting, 213
Petrino, K., 227
Pew Research Center, 303
Phelan, J. C., 268, 269
Phillips, C., 9
Physical ability, 274–275. *See also* Disability; Persons with disabilities
Pickett, K. E., 259
Pickett, T., 250, 251, 253, 264
Pinderhughes, E. B., 369
Pledger, C., 283, 293
Pluralism, 88, 158, 180–184, 185
Police brutality, 332–334
Poll, J. B., 309
Pomeroy, W. B., 229
Ponterotto, J. G., 9, 38, 47, 57, 88, 93, 282
Poor
blaming of, 258, 266–267
class activity on, 265 (activity)
psychological characteristics of, 269
social context of, 257–262
stereotypes of, 257, 260–261, 266, 341
See also Class, social; Poverty
Portman, E. A. A., 200
Postmodernism, 181
Poston, W. S. C., 210
Poverty, 255–257
in African American community, 198–199
among Native Americans, 199
and behaviors, 268
children in, 339, 341
class activities on, 267–268 (activity), 269–270 (activity)
and education, 339
effects of, 257–258, 339, 341–342
and gender, 256–257
and health, 259, 268, 339
in Hispanic community, 199
impact of, 335
and mental health needs, 110–111
and psychological characteristics, 269
and race, 198–199, 256 (figure)
rates of, 256
See also Class, social; Poor
Power, 13
characteristics of, 66–67
class activities on, 143 (activity), 153–154 (activity)
counselors' use of, 21
and dominant groups, 139
effects of, 67–68
and immigrants, 95, 348
and international work, 95–96
and sexual identity, 146–147
and social class, 252
white privilege as expression of, 32
Power distance, in worldview, 69
Practicum experiences, 372
Prevention, 368–369
Prilleltensky, I., 179
Princeton Religion Center, 306
Privilege, 13
awareness of, 169, 170, 171
characteristics of, 66–67
and class, 148
class activities on, 143 (activity), 153–154 (activity), 170 (activity)
complexity of, 170–171
effects of, 37, 67–68, 136
exercise on, 171 (exercise)
and immigrants, 46
and international work, 95–96
maintenance of, 67
and nationality, 151–152
recognizing, 67, 164 (box)
and religion, 151, 181
self-assessment of multicultural self, 152–153 (table)
and social class, 251–254, 254–255 (table)
types of, 161–170
and White racial identity development, 140–143
See also Isms; *individual privileges*
Professional advocacy, 377
Project Atlas, 45
Propst, L. R., 315
Proxemics, 201
PWDs (persons with disabilities). *See* Disability; Persons with disabilities

Queer
use of term, 224
See also LGBTQ persons; Transgender persons

Race
and class privilege, 253, 254–255 (table)
and color blindness, 135
and economic inequality, 195–196
and education, 196
exercise on, 34 (exercise)
experiential learning activity on, 36–37 (activity)
and health, 197, 259
and police brutality, 332–334
and poverty, 256–257, 256 (figure)
reflections on, 335 (reflection), 338 (reflection)
and unemployment, 196–197
Race Card Project, The (National Public Radio), 68
Racial identity
biracial identity development, 210
Black racial identity development, 205–207
multiracial identity development, 210
racial/cultural identity development model, 207–208 (table), 207–209
reflections on, 34–35 (reflection)
White racial identity development, 140–143
Racial identity stages, 205–206
Racial profiling, 11–12
Racism
awareness of, 162
class activity on, 176 (activity)
and class privilege, 253, 254–255 (table)
and colonization, 57
color blindness as, 135
and cultural identity development, 205
cultural racism, 173–174
defined, 172
effects of, 33
environmental racism, 174
individual racism, 173, 176
institutional racism, 172–173
and microaggressions, 176–177, 177–179 (table)
presence of, 33
racial profiling, 11–12
recognizing, 168 (activity)
reflections on, 142–143 (reflection), 162 (reflection), 174 (reflection)
resources for working with, 216
types of, 172–174, 175 (table)
See also Oppression
Rampton, M., 61
Ratts, M. J., 344, 345, 366
Rawlings, E. I., 230, 231
Ray, N., 340
Reardon, S. F., 259, 339
Redefinition, of counseling practice, 111–113
Referral, 379
Reflections
on being African American, 60–61 (reflection)
on being a nonbinary transgender individual, 30 (reflection)
on being Latino/Latina, 43 (reflection)
on cisgenderism, 146 (reflection)
on cultural identity, 92–93 (reflection)
on cultural identity development, 209 (reflection)
on disability, 279 (reflection), 285 (reflection), 287 (reflection)
on dominant group identity, 140 (reflection)
on gender binary, 221–223 (reflection)
on gender identity, 342 (reflection)
on homosexuality, 43 (reflection)
on immigrants, 46 (reflection)
on Latino community and homosexuality, 103–104 (reflection)
on multicultural competence, 112 (reflection), 120–121 (reflection)
on multicultural professional identity development, 108–109 (reflection)
on oppression, 159 (reflection), 162 (reflection), 174 (reflection)
on race, 335 (reflection), 338 (reflection)
on racial identity, 34–35 (reflection)
on racism, 142–143 (reflection), 162 (reflection), 174 (reflection)
on religion/spirituality, 299–302 (reflection), 316 (reflection)
on sexual identity development, 148 (reflection)
on social justice, 338 (reflection), 343–344 (reflection)
on social justice advocacy, 362 (reflection)
on White racial identity development, 142–143 (reflection)
Reicher, S. D., 138
Relationship patterns, 198–199
Relationships, interpersonal, 69

Religion
  in African American community, 199
  assessing, 316–317
  avoiding values imposition, 315–316
  case illustrations, 304–305 (case illustration), 317–318 (case illustration)
  clients' desire to discuss, 307–308
  and client welfare, 314–315
  in counseling development, 44
  counselors' orientations to, 305–306
  defined, 302–303
  difficulty of integrating into counseling, 305–306
  and ethics, 312, 313–314 (table), 314–316, 350–351
  exercises on, 319 (exercise), 320 (exercise), 322 (exercise)
  as harmful/pathological, 318–319
  impact of counselors' perspectives on, 309, 310
  increased diversity in, 44
  integrating into counseling, 310–311
  and mental health, 306–307
  need to consider, 89–90
  need to integrate into counseling, 307
  prevalence of, 306
  reflections on, 299–302 (reflection), 316 (reflection)
  and religious prejudice, 150–151
  reluctance to integrate into counseling, 303
  resources for working with, 323
  self-assessment of pre-existing awareness and knowledge of, 299
  vs. spirituality, 305
  and training, 303, 307, 310–312, 320–321 (table)
  and working with LGBTQ clients, 234, 350–351
  and worldview, 181
Religion identity development, 308–310
Remley, T. P., 20, 21
Remy, G. M., 35
Renn, K. A., 210, 225, 227
Reparative therapy, 234
Research, importance of, 404–405
Resnick, S., 13
Respect, 268, 269
Responsibilities, lack of consideration for, 8
Reynolds, A. L., 88
Richards, P., 301, 306, 307, 319
Richardson, W. S., 15
Richie, B. S., 230
Ridley, C. R., 17, 162, 176 (activity)
Robinson, D. T., 59
Robinson, T. L., 87
Robinson-Zañartu, C., 58
Rogers, C. R., 11
Role-play, 233
Rolison, G. L., 251
Rollins, C. W., 286
Romano, J. L., 369
Root, M. P. P., 210
Rose, E. M., 307, 308
Rosen, A., 213
Rosenberg, W., 15
Ross, L., 7, 15, 213
Rothblum, E. D., 63
Rotter, J. B., 14
Roughgarden, J., 225
Rousso, H., 281
Rowles, J., 199
Ryan, J., 225, 228, 234, 281

Sackett, D. L., 15
Salsgiver, R., 286
Salter, P. S., 64
Same-sex marriage laws, 147
Sanders, G. S., 306
Satcher, David, 110, 171, 197
Satir, V., 8
Sauer, E. M., 6
Sausa, L. A., 225
Savage, J. S., 310
Savoy, H. B., 147
Schiff, T., 169
Schneider, M. S., 226, 227, 228, 229
Schulte, D. L., 303
Schwartz, L. M., 111
Schwartz, R. C., 9, 38
Schwartz, S. J., 210
Scientific thinking, 107–108
Scofield, T. R., 377
Scotti, J. R., 227
SCWM (social class worldview model), 264
Seeman, M., 8
Seeman, T. B., 8
Segregation, 196
Self, and collectivist cultures, 13

Self-actualization, 11, 12–13
Self-assessments of pre-existing awareness and knowledge
  class identity, 248
  counseling, 3–4
  cultural identity, 80
  development of multicultural identity, 130
  disability, 274–275
  gender, 215
  multiculturalism, 3–4
  oppression, 158
  physical ability, 274–275
  pluralism, 158
  redefining and renewing counseling, 101
  religion/spirituality, 299
  sexual orientation, 215
  social justice, 329–330
  social justice advocacy, 357
  working with diversity, 192
Self-concept, 183
Self-disclosure, 17, 105
Self-serving biases, 7
Selvidge, M. M. D., 230
Serlin, I. A., 13
Service learning, 372
Sevig, T. D., 304, 310, 311
Sex
  defined, 144, 226
  and privilege, 144–145, 164 (box), 168–169
Sex identity, development of, 144–145
Sexism, 33, 62, 144–145, 341
Sexual identity
  defined, 147
  gay rights movement, 62–63
  pathologization of, 234
  resources for working with, 239–244
Sexual identity development, 147, 148 (reflection)
Sexuality
  binary construction of, 223–224 (reflection)
  discussion questions, 223–224 (questions)
  heterosexual privilege, 169
  and need for discussion of gender, 233
  See also Homosexuality; LGBTQ persons; Sexual orientation
Sexual orientation
  categories, 229, 229 (table)
  complexities of, 229
  and counselor competency, 230–233
  defined, 144
  described, 228–229
  gay rights movement, 62–63
  and hate crimes, 334
  Kinsey scale, 229, 230 (table)
  resources for working with, 239–244
  self-assessment of pre-existing awareness and knowledge of, 220
  See also Homosexuality; LGBTQ persons; LGBTQQCIAI persons
Sexual orientation identity, 146–148
Sexual orientation identity development, 224–225
Seybold, K. S., 307
Shafranske, E. P., 302
Shallcross, L., 113, 372
Sheperis, Charles, 372
Shin, C. E., 173
Siegel, M., 310
Silence, 202
Simek-Morgan, L., 8
Sinclair, S. L., 57, 94, 162, 269
Singh, A. A., 11
Skinner, T. A., 303
Slavery, 57
Smart, D. W., 282, 294
Smart, J. F., 280, 282, 283, 286, 294
Smith, E., 367
Smith, R. C., 172
Smith, S., 136, 363
Smith, T. B., 309
Snowden, L. R., 9, 111
Social change, 62, 136. *See also* Social justice; Social justice advocacy; Social justice counseling
Social class identity development, 148–149. *See also* Class, social
Social class worldview model (SCWM), 264
Social consciousness, development of, 139
Social context. *See* Context
Social dominance, 32, 135, 138. *See also* Dominant groups
Social identity, formation of, 138
Social inequality
  and behavior, 340
  effects of, 338–342
  expression of, 332
  and human rights, 334–335
  types of, 336–337
  See also Class, social; Isms; Oppression; Social justice

Social injustice
  expression of, 332
  impact of, 333–334, 335
  types of, 336–337
  See also Isms; Oppression; Social justice
Socialization, 106
Social justice, 136, 214
  ability to address, 343
  access to, 343
  case illustration, 330–331 (case illustration)
  class activities on, 331 (activity), 338 (activity), 347 (activity)
  competency development, 359–366
  defined, 342–343
  exercise on, 349–350 (exercise)
  and globalization, 120
  goal of, 343
  group activity on, 350–351 (activity)
  integrating into counseling practice, 348–349
  and mental health, 344
  reflections, 338 (reflection), 343–344 (reflection)
  responsibility to promote, 73, 366
  self-assessment of pre-existing awareness and knowledge of, 329–330
  and training, 348
  See also Social justice advocacy; Social justice counseling
Social justice advocacy, 214
  case illustration, 357–358 (case illustration)
  competency in, 379
  exercise on, 365–366 (exercise)
  reflection, 362 (reflection)
  resources for, 352–353
  self-assessment of pre-existing awareness and knowledge of, 357
  training for, 293, 372–373, 373–376 (figure)
  and working with LGBTQ clients, 234
  and working with persons with disabilities, 293
  See also Social justice; Social justice counseling
Social justice advocacy practice, engaging in, 371–372
Social justice counseling, 344–348
  case illustration, 345–346 (case illustration)
  competency in, 379
  resources for, 383
  strategies for, 367–371
Socially responsive practice, 348
Social/minority model of disability, 286–287, 288 (table), 290–291 (table)
Social reality, 31–32 (exercise), 88–89. *See also* Context; Cultural identity
Social Security Administration, 280
Social structure, influence of on development, 136
Socioeconomic status (SES)
  vs. social class, 250
  social class identity development, 148–149
  and unhealthy behaviors, 258
Soleck, G., 250, 264
Solomon, B. B., 370
Soul wounding, 180
Space, personal, 201
Sparks, E., 179, 345
Speight, S. L., 359, 379
Sperry, L., 302
Spikes, P., 229
Spirituality
  in African American community, 199
  assessing, 316–317
  avoiding values imposition, 315–316
  case illustrations, 304–305 (case illustration), 317–318 (case illustration)
  clients' desire to discuss, 307–308
  and client welfare, 314–315
  in counseling development, 44
  of counselors, 305–306
  defined, 302–303
  difficulty of integrating into counseling, 305–306
  and ethics, 312, 313–314 (table), 314–316
  exercises on, 319 (exercise), 320 (exercise), 322 (exercise)
  as harmful/pathological, 318–319
  impact of counselors' perspectives, 309, 310
  integrating into counseling, 310–311
  and mental health, 306–307
  need to consider, 89–90
  need to integrate into counseling, 307
  prevalence of, 306
  reflections on, 299–302 (reflection), 316 (reflection)
  vs. religion, 305
  reluctance to integrate into counseling, 303
  resources for working with, 323
  self-assessment of pre-existing awareness and knowledge of, 299
  and training, 303, 307, 310–312, 320–321 (table)

Spirituality identity development, 308–310
Spiritual values, compared to multicultural values, 312 (table)
Standards
  CACREP, 1, 77, 93, 121, 122, 127, 189, 327
  Standards for the Preparation of Counselors and Other Personnel Services Specialists, 60
  and training with culturally diverse, 122–123
Standards for the Preparation of Counselors and Other Personnel Services Specialists, 60
Steele, C. M., 260
Stephens, J., 173
Stereotypes, 232, 340, 341
Stereotype threat, 260
Stets, J. E., 135
Stewart, B., 228
Stonewall Riots, 62
Storey, K., 149
Stotzer, R., 334
Straus, S. E., 15
Strength-based counseling, 367–368
Stryker, S., 136
Success, lack of opportunity for, 338–339
Sue, D., 7, 8, 9, 10, 11, 15, 16, 19, 20, 55, 89, 91, 111, 140, 141, 201, 207, 234, 294, 312
Sue, D. W., 7, 8, 9, 10, 11, 15, 16, 19, 20, 33, 34, 35, 42, 55, 59–60, 89, 91, 111, 140, 141, 176, 177, 201, 234, 294, 312, 378
Sue, S., 10, 232
Suhr, R., 377
Sumner, W. G., 8
Suzuki, L. A., 9, 38
Syme, S., 346

Taft, R., 211
Takaki, R. T., 106
Talleyrand, R., 347
Tan, S., 311
Tan, S.-Y., 314
Taylor, Shanesha, 258
Tehranifar, P., 268, 269
Terrell, F., 9, 38
Thayne, T. R., 308
Theism, 181
Thinking styles, of counselors, 107–108
Thomas, P. L., 91
Thompson, C. E., 33, 59, 172, 173, 174
Thoresen, C. E., 307
Tice, K., 85
Tillotson, K., 378
Ting-Toomey, S., 203
Tools, inadequate, 105
Toporek, R. L., 343, 344, 345, 346, 366
T.R.A.I.N.E.R. model, 377
Training
  addressing cultural competency in, 119
  based on Western culture, 174
  cross-cultural strategies in, 117, 119
  and developing multicultural competence, 108
  exercise on, 97 (exercise)
  and experience with culturally diverse, 122
  multicultural strategies in, 117, 119
  and religion/spirituality, 303, 307, 310–312, 320–321 (table)
  for social justice, 348, 372–373, 373–376 (figure)
  standards for multicultural coursework, 60
  and working with LGB clients, 227, 228
  for working with persons with disabilities, 282, 294
Transgender identity development, 227
Transgender persons
  considerations in working with, 238 (table)
  counseling issues for, 237 (table)
  inadequate service to, 40
  pathologization of, 227
  and perception of mental health, 11
  provision of services to, 40
  violence against, 334
  See also Gender; Gender identity; LGBTQ persons; Sexual identity; Sexual orientation
Triandis, H. C., 68, 69, 183
Troiden, R. R., 224
Truman, B. I., 259
Turner, J. C., 138

Unemployment, disparities in, 196–197
United Nations, 280, 332
Upward mobility, 261, 262, 263
U.S. citizen privilege, 170
Utada, A., 8
Utsey, S. O., 57, 88

Valenzuela, A., 200
Validation, 268, 269
Values, 181, 182 (table), 183–184
  in development of counseling, 7
  differences in, 198–204
  dimensions for understanding, 68
Values, class, 264–265
Vaughan, G. M., 138
Vega, W. A., 199
Vera, E. M., 359, 379
Vernaglia, E. R., 147
Victim blaming, 266–267, 340, 369
Violence
  against African Americans, 332–334
  against LGBTQ persons, 334
  minorities associated with, 339–340
Vocational counseling, 58–59, 261, 346
Volscho, T., 136
Vontress, C. E., 122
Vuong, L., 162

Walker, D. F., 311
Wallace, B. C., 284
Wampold, B. E., 13–14
Ward, Julea, 350–351
Warmoth, A., 13
Warner, M., 146
Weeber, J. E., 281
Weintraub, S. R., 345
Weir, K., 268
Welch, H. G., 111
Welfel, E. R., 20
Westefeld, J. S., 307, 308
Westman, J. C., 150
Wetherell, M. S., 138
White liberal syndrome, 141
Whiteness, as standard, 9
White privilege, 32–33, 163, 164–168 (box)
White racial identity development, 140–143, 142–143 (reflection), 143 (activity)
Whites
  and diagnosis of mental disorders, 12
  population growth of, 43
Whitman, J. S., 11
Wiggins-Frame, M., 311
Wildman, S. M., 163
Wilkinson, R. G., 259, 341
Willer, W. R., 307
Williams, C., 257
Williams, D. R., 197
Williams, J. M., 88
Williams, M. T., 135
Williams, W. R., 257
Wilson, B., 202
Wilson, C. C., 198
Wilson, V., 197
Wilton, L., 63, 84
Winkleby, M., 346
Winslade, J. M., 57, 94, 162, 269
Witko, C., 136
Wolch, J. R., 111
Woloshin, S., 111
Women
  effects of sexism on, 144–145
  and gender inequality, 341
  and poverty, 256–257
Women's movements, 61–62
Worldview
  awareness of, 19
  definitions of, 68–69, 180–181
  in development of counseling, 7
  European, 9
  in-session counseling interaction, 69–70 (counseling interaction)
  need for awareness of, 70
  respecting, 213
  and social class, 264–265
  See also Ethnocentrism
Worthington, E. L., 306
Worthington, L., 228
Worthington, R. L., 139, 147
Wrenn, C. G., 20, 59
Wright, G. Talib, 37–38
Wright, K., 226
Wyche, K. F., 257

Yeskel, F., 148
Yin and yang, 14
Young, J. S., 311
Yu, D. H., 16, 17

Zaharna, R., 211
Zalaquett, C. P., 378
Zamora-Hernadez, C. E., 229
Zhang, W., 13
Zubrinsky, C. L., 7